THE HARVARD ADVOCATE
ANNIVERSARY ANTHOLOGY

DULCE EST PERICULUM

VERITAS NIHIL VERETUR

THE HARVARD ADVOCATE
ANNIVERSARY ANTHOLOGY

EDITED BY
Douglas A. McIntyre
Karen S. Hull

FOREWORD BY
James Atlas

SCHENKMAN BOOKS
CAMBRIDGE, MASSACHUSETTS

Copyright © 1987
Schenkman Books, Inc.
P.O. Box 1570
Harvard Square
Cambridge, MA 02138

Library of Congress Cataloging-in-Publication Data

The Harvard advocate anniversary anthology.

   1. Students' writings, American — Massachusetts — Cambridge.
2. College prose, American — Massachusetts — Cambridge.
3. College verse, American — Massachusetts — Cambridge.
4. Harvard University. 5. American literature — 19th century.
6. American literature — 20th century. 7. American literature —
Massachusetts — Cambridge. I. McIntyre, Douglas A.,
1955–   II. Hull, Karen S., 1958–   . III. Harvard advocate.
PS508.C6H34 1986 810.8'097444 86-17922 ISBN
0-87047-029-9

   This anthology of *The Harvard Advocate* is reproduced from the original magazine
pages. Any typographical errors or inconsistencies are those of the magazine itself.

To all the board members of The Harvard Advocate *who worked late into the night to put out this little magazine issue after issue.*

Contents

Contents

Contents

Contents

Contents

Foreword

My introduction to *The Harvard Advocate* was a notice in the *Crimson* advertising a "comp" for what was billed as "the oldest college literary magazine in the country." I wasn't sure what a comp was, but no matter — anything connected with such a venerable enterprise deserved investigation, and on a rainy night in the fall of 1967 I made my way over to the Advocate House on South Street.

I wasn't the only one who had noticed the invitation. People were streaming in the door. A mere freshman, I had thought of myself as anomalous, a curiosity —"the poet," as I was derisorily known to my roommates in the Yard. It hadn't occurred to me that other literary aspirants might be lurking on campus; everyone I knew wanted to be a rock musician or a revolutionary. Remember, this was the sixties.

Literature was by no means the esoteric vocation I supposed. By the time I made my way upstairs to the Sanctum, it was standing room only. I squeezed in just as the president — editor was too scruffy a title for such an exalted position — was explaining to the packed house the rigors of the competition. (At least I knew what a comp was now.) We were to sign up for the prose or poetry board — depending, he noted drily, on whether we preferred the right margin justified or not. Everyone gave a dutiful laugh; no one knew what he was talking about.

Our assignment was to come in at our leisure over the next few weeks to read and evaluate submissions. We would be judged by the acuteness of our perceptions, our eloquence, our wit and literary taste. In the days that followed, I spent many an afternoon hunched over the desk in the poetry office, writing clever, devastating critiques of the poems that had been submitted "for consideration" (not that they ever got any). Most of the manuscripts I read were by undergraduates, but every now and then I'd come across a submission by some poet in Eugene, Oregon or somewhere, with a nervous cover letter urging the merits of the enclosed work. I was impressed that people wanted to have their poems appear in *The Harvard Advocate*.

I could see why. Here was a magazine that had published Theodore Roosevelt and E.A. Robinson, T.S. Eliot and Wallace Stevens, Malcolm Cowley and E.E. Cummings, when they were undergraduates — before they became who they were. To be on the magazine's masthead was to belong, in however marginal a way, to a great tradition. The names on the wooden plaques that covered the wall of the Sanctum told the whole story: through these rooms — or through the various rooms that housed the magazine at earlier moments in its long history — had passed some of the most eminent figures in American literature.

Browsing among the musty bound volumes on the shelves, I was stunned by the familiar names. And it wasn't just hoary old guys, either; here were Norman Mailer and James Agee, and a clutch of postwar poets I admired: Robert Bly, Donald Hall, John Ashbery, Kenneth Koch. (Conspicuously absent was Robert Lowell, who once complained that during *his* comp he was "asked to tack down a carpet in the Sanctum and, when he was finished, told that he needn't come round anymore.") Real people, in other words. I mean, nobody in their right mind went around thinking they were going to be the next T.S. Eliot — but you could maybe, if you worked very hard and were very lucky, become a writer.

Not that Eliot, as represented in the magazine, was

so great. Reading over his poems in the yellowed issues of 1910, I wondered if his contemporaries recognized his genius. His poems were highly accomplished, to be sure, but nothing special. They had the vaguely derivative feel of undergraduate verse — derivative of what, I couldn't have said. Of poetry as poetry, a generic literary mode. They were faintly ominous, melancholy, surreal — esoteric symbolism lurking in every line. (My favorite image was the one where "panthers rise from their lairs/In the forest which thickens below . . .") The important thing was, Eliot had written them.

The building itself belied this august literary heritage. The *Lampoon* had a castle; the *Crimson* had a prosperous redbrick house on Boylston Street; the Advocate House had a forlorn, inner-city appearance about it, like one of those ramshackle dwellings on the edges of vacant lots that somehow escaped the wrecker's ball. The gray clapboard could only charitably have been called weathered; *dirty* was the word that leapt to mind. The downstairs rooms had the bare, drafty look of a janitor's office, and the upstairs Sanctum resembled the lobby of a hotel in Butte, Montana: the carpet was a gangrenous, indeterminate hue, the walls were a pallid green, the leather couch was as cracked and seamed as an old bedroom slipper. A dank odor of ashes and spilled wine hung in the air. All it needed were spittoons and dusty potted palms.

Never mind. As far as I was concerned, the Sanctum deserved its name. The long refectory table we convened around on Monday nights could have been brought over from an Irish mead hall for all I knew. The Throne, a high-backed chair with claw-shaped armrests and gargoyles carved in the dark mahogany, would have done a robber baron's mansion proud. On the wall above the fireplace were old photographs from a more formal era, turn-of-the-century Advocate boards in blazers and white flannel trousers, moustachioed young men who looked as if they knew how to have a good time. Doing the layout long after midnight while the flourescent lights buzzed overhead and the furnace in the basement clanked, I could imagine these hearty Old Boy types gathered around a cut-glass bowl brimming with champagne punch, heckling Wally Stevens as he recited a salacious limerick.

Anyway, I got on the board — as did everyone else who completed the competition. The *Advocate* was very democratic that way. "The *Advocate* has been a record of football scores," recalled a Pegasus in the magazine's centennial edition, "a caterer to old, pecunious Cambridge ladies; a monger of intra-mural scandal; a register of literary tastes which have often lagged twenty years behind the fact; a club; a wet-nurse and house-marm for febrile poets; a victim of Comstockery; a proponent of literary freedom; an organ of responsible criticism; a ghost; a myth; a great organic zilch that often exists more vividly in the minds of its editors than on the newsstands . . ." In my day, the magazine reflected what I once called, in a paper on Romanticism, "the *Zeitgeist* of the times." It was a revolutionary journal, an organ of the avant-garde. One of the four issues under my stewardship boasted a nude female torso on the cover, facing away from the camera. Within was another photograph, of a sultry long-haired tigress, breasts exposed, holding a whip. I printed a "Beat" poem by a New York poet ("sit up in bed smoke dope get high . . .") and, at the height of the student turmoil that culminated in the occupation of University Hall, appended the slogan *la lutte continue* to a preface by the unsuspecting Boylston Professor of Rhetoric, Robert Fitzgerald, that graced an issue devoted to the work of Cambridge poets.

We weren't always so incendiary. The issue I was proudest of was the special Berryman number I inherited from the previous board and saw through the press. It was assembled by John Plotz, Thomas A. Stewart, and Robert B. Shaw, and featured a fascinating, drunken interview with Berryman, "Three New Dream Songs," and tributes from Mark Van Doren, Robert Lowell, Elizabeth Bishop, and other notables. Other issues featured a conversation with I.A. Richards, a collection of tributes to Conrad Aiken, and a variety of more or less conventional poems, stories, and reviews that were no embarrassment to our subscribers.

Leafing through one of the issues I edited, *Poems 57*, an eccentric, little magazine-sized number with a red cover featuring the Heinz logo, I find much that is good, much that is promising, and much that is egregious, dreadful, very bad indeed. ("They are all readable," noted the kindly Fitzgerald in his introduction, "by which I intend no paltry praise.") Of the thirteen contributors, three have gone on to become poets of considerable distinction; two have become novelists; one is a well-known anthropologist; one the president of a New York publishing house. The others have, I'm sure, distinguished themselves in their own ways. It's a considerable exaggeration to claim, as the British literary critic Frank Kermode once did, that a position on the *Advocate* "confers on its holder a good chance of national eminence," but the people associated with the magazine when I was in college weren't likely to end up in a gutter.

Nor were they likely to end up as wealthy as the magazine's trustees. I remember the night I was flown down to New York to report on the magazine's shaky finances. In a mahogany-panelled room of the Century Club, white-haired men with threads of red veins in their cheeks sat around a table laid with heavy silver, two wine glasses beside each pewter plate, and discussed the vast sums necessary to the magazine's continuance. "Now you say five hundred dollars would tide over the printer for the moment?" clarified the shipping scion Frank A. Vanderlip Jr., clutching the knob of a silver cane worth twice that amount. "Why can't we raise it by getting ads?" spoke up Roy E. Larsen, Vice-Chairman of the Board of Time. "I don't see why we should just hand over the money. They'll never learn good business sense that way."

Maybe so. But if they didn't hand over the money, I pleaded, there would be no spring issue. In my elbow patched tweed jacket and Frye boots, I must have looked persuasively indigent, because by the time coffee and brandy arrived, Charlie Atkinson, the tight-fisted treasurer, was writing out a check. Ecstatic to have survived the ordeal, I hurried out into the warm spring night and headed down to The Lion's Head in Greenwich Village. I heard that Norman Mailer hung out there.

James Atlas
New York
May 1986

James Atlas was an Advocate editor in 1969. After graduating from Harvard he was a Rhodes scholar at New College, Oxford. Currently a contributing editor to Vanity Fair, Atlas is also the author of Delmore Schwartz: The Life of an American Poet *(Avon, 1977), and a new book,* The Great Pretender *(Atheneum Press, 1986). Atlas lives and works in New York City.*

Introduction

As the reader looks over the contents of this anthology of *Harvard Advocate* writing, one thing most certainly stands out. It would be difficult and, in the world of undergraduate publications, perhaps impossible to find any journal served by so many distinguished editors and contributors. This extraordinary richness and history makes for a unique collection.

The *Advocate* was Harvard's first newspaper (it would not become a magazine until the 1890s). It was founded on May 11, 1866, its birth announced by posters reading:

A New College Paper

for sale at Richardson's Bookstore

Tomorrow

The first run of 400 copies sold out immediately, despite the fact that this earliest edition of the *Advocate* was written and distributed rather surreptitiously after the *Advocate's* forerunner, the *Collegian,* had been closed by the faculty for attacking mandatory chapel attendance. The *Collegian's* motto, which flaunted its propensity for openly protesting faculty regulations, was *Dulce est Periculum* — Danger is sweet. The paper lasted only three issues.

Perhaps the *Advocate* has lasted so much longer because it took a more moderate approach to matters from the very first. It adopted the *Collegian's* motto, but added the more sober *Veritas nihil veretur* — Truth fears nothing. The truth, of course, was that the *Advocate's* editors avoided direct attack on faculty decisions, even though two founders of the new paper, Charles S. Gage '67 and William G. Peckham '67, had been editors of the more confrontational *Collegian*.

Although the *Advocate* got off to a rousing start, its early life was still somewhat precarious. To continue publishing, it had to pass a faculty review and, in the days after the first issue appeared, there was considerable discussion among the university's leaders about the future of the paper. At a critical faculty meeting a few weeks after the *Advocate's* first issue, the new publication found support from the formidable figures of James Russell Lowell and Oliver Wendell Holmes. The *Advocate's* future was assured and its association with great men had begun.

The *Advocate* continued as the university's only publication until 1873. At the time, it was a fortnightly newspaper with two main functions. On the one hand, it served as a means of communication between the faculty and the student body, often publishing faculty prose and verse contributions. But more importantly, from the very first issues, the *Advocate* became a place for students to practice the art of writing. In the early years, there were no writing classes at Harvard and, in many ways, the *Advocate* served as that classroom. As one 1869 editor put it, "ours was the golden age for a college editor. There was no competition, no tradition and no instruction in English. Genius was unfettered."

This happy situation came to an end in 1873 with the founding of the *Crimson* (née *Magenta*). Suddenly, the *Advocate* found itself competing with another fortnightly newspaper and it felt compelled to stud its pages with football scores and articles on college policy, along with poems, essays, and stories. In 1876, some members of the *Advocate* left their first love to found the university's third publication, the *Lampoon,* which became Harvard's classic humor magazine.

By the 1880s, the *Crimson* was a daily newspaper, and the *Advocate* was well on its way to becoming the university's preeminent literary publication. Among the editors during this period were a number of young men who would become distinguished writers, teachers, and critics. George Lyman Kittredge, Charles Townshend Copeland, Edwin Arlington Robinson, and Witter Bynner are only a few of the names that come to mind. Some of the earliest work of Kittredge and Robinson are included in this volume. Another young man who became a formidable literary — and political — force was 1880 *Advocate* editor, Theodore Roosevelt.

The *Advocate's* golden age began in 1901 when Wallace Stevens served as president and ran to 1911 when Conrad Aiken was top editor of the magazine. Other contributors and editors of this period included E.E. Cummings, Van Wyck Brooks, and T.S. Eliot.

What is fascinating about the published material from the pre-World War I era is that it contains what Donald Hall described as "the juvenilia of outstanding men." One of the pleasures of reading these pieces is to note how they foreshadow the genius that was to come. A great deal has been made of the resemblance between the style of "Spleen," T.S. Eliot's last *Advocate* contribution, and the style he would use in "The Love Song of J. Alfred Prufrock" in 1917. I leave it to critics more astute than I to trace the connections between the boyhood work of these great writers and their mature work. But even an amateur will find it exciting to read the earliest work of these ardent writers.

The period from 1901 to 1909 was not all serious poetry and literary criticism. The magazine had a lighter side, which would be seen in a long series of clever jousts with the *Lampoon*, and finally summed up in a parody issue entitled "The Shampoon." On the whole, however, the vision of the young editors was introspective, and this did not change much until the 1920s.

One can see the transition as the poetry of Malcolm Cowley '19 gave way to more forthright social criticism in "Persecution" and "Prohibition," two fine essays by Lloyd McKim Garrison '19. In one of these, Garrison made the observation that "between those who would like to see all the Reds and near-Reds dangling from lampposts, and those who believe that free speech is an absolute right, the country is having a hard time to keep its course steady and its mind clear." Years later, Garrison would become one of the country's leading attorneys.

In retrospect, the twenties was an odd decade for the *Advocate*. While America was enjoying a literary explosion outside the university, Harvard's literary journal was not enjoying better days. Of note, however, were short stories by Oliver LaFarge, parodies of a host of famous writers and publications, and the early works of E.A. Weeks, who would later edit the *Atlantic Monthly* for several decades. Another *Advocate* member of this period was Roy Larsen '21. Larsen would later found *Time* magazine with Henry Luce and Briton Hadden (both Yale '21). Larsen's career at Time Inc. would span nearly 60 years, during which time he was the first publisher of *Life* and the president of Time Inc.

As the *Advocate* moved into the early 1930s, her pages were filled with the work of two young editors, James Agee and Robert Fitzgerald. While Fitzgerald would have a long and fruitful academic career as a translator, critic, and Harvard faculty member, Agee lived a short and turbulent life. He won the Yale Younger Poet's Award and a Pulitzer prize for prose, became one of the best film critics of his generation, and wrote the screenplay for "The African Queen." He died before age 45. Of all the writing in this collection, Agee's is perhaps the most mature for a writer barely twenty years old, and his contributions to the *Advocate* are perhaps the closest to the work that he would publish soon after leaving Harvard. Ironically, Agee produced a highly successful *Advocate* parody of *Time* magazine, for which he was later film critic.

The 1935 freshman issue of the *Advocate* showed that the magazine had not lost its capacity to shock. Two stories in this issue, one by James Laughlin, an *Advocate* editor, and one by Henry Miller, were banned by an assistant attorney general for being obscene and degrading. The magazine's senior staff members were forced to resign.

During this period, contributions by Ezra Pound and William Carlos Williams were published by the editors. Archibald MacLeish, a Harvard law instructor, offered a piece entitled "The Liberalism of Herbert Hoover." In 1939, the season's first concert of the Boston Symphony was reviewed by *Advocate* editor, Leonard Bernstein.

In the thirties and forties the *Advocate* produced special tributes to T.S. Eliot and Wallace Stevens. These issues became important parts of the critical body of writing on these two great American authors. In 1941, the *Advocate's* 75th anniversary issue contained contributions from many of the nation's best-known authors. Another member of America's business elite, Thornton Bradshaw '40, cut his teeth as *Advocate* president in this era. During the sixties and seventies, Bradshaw was president of Atlantic Richfield and later, as chairman of the board, presided over the renaissance of RCA.

The *Advocate* could not publish during World War II; war shortages and rationing forced suspension until 1947. Its last board of editors before it closed down included Norman Mailer, who would write *The Naked and the Dead* a few years later.

The end of the war brought a tremendous influx of new talent to the old magazine. The late 1940s are characterized by poetry from Richard Wilbur, John Ashbery, and Donald Hall. The pendulum had swung again, and the magazine became intensely literary and aesthetic. Social criticism seemed to vanish from the pages, but the quality of writing was extremely high, as the contributions to this anthology from the young writers of the time testify.

In 1951, the *Advocate* published a major review of the work of William Faulkner, containing critical articles by Alfred Kazin, Conrad Aiken, John Crowe Ransom, and Archibald MacLeish. This was followed by a British novelist's special issue in 1952.

In the fifties, the work of women authors appeared regularly in the *Advocate* and for the first time women worked at the magazine. Adrienne Rich made regular contributions in 1950 and 1951. These were usually brief poems, melancholy and dense, that rarely ran more than fifteen or twenty lines. Editors and contributors during the early and mid-fifties included Jonathan Kozol, Robert Cumming, and Sallie Bingham. Their short stories marked the beginning of notable careers in literature and social criticism. "Winter Term," novelist Sallie Bingham's well-crafted tale of the Harvard/Radcliffe romance, sparked an avalanche of contributed "Harvard Square Sex Stories." These stories of love at the "Puritan's" university flooded the Advocate House after publication of Bingham's story but dwindled, much to the relief of the editors, in the early sixties.

In 1961, the Advocate came out with a major critical issue on the work of Robert Lowell. There was much irony in this since young freshman Lowell had been rejected when he applied for the *Advocate* literary board and did not reestablish a relationship with the magazine for over twenty years.

The year 1966 saw the celebration of the *Advocate's* centennial with a special issue of contributions from John Hawkes, Adrienne Rich, Harry Levin, Robert Fitzgerald, Denise Levertov, Conrad Aiken, Howard Nemerov, Robert Bly, W.H. Auden, and others. Illustrations and photographs were now appearing frequently in the magazine as it widened its scope to include articles on art and architecture.

Over the course of the next ten years, the *Advocate* published critical issues on several outstanding American and English authors. The most noteworthy of those were tributes to John Berryman (1969), James Agee (1972), and W.H. Auden (1975). Student editors made impressive inroads in getting major critics and writers to contribute to these issues. The Berryman issue contained "Three New Dream Songs" by Berryman and a long, amusing interview with the poet. The Agee issue contained a moving tribute by Agee's close friend and confidant, Father James Flye.

The *Advocate* of the sixties and early seventies published more than tributes and anniversary celebrations. The editors had a number of interesting ideas of their own and, like college publications across the nation, the *Advocate* displayed some revolutionary zeal. In this vein they published "Mao on Style," a transcript of the Chinese leader's thoughts on writing, and dedicated one issue of the magazine to an editor put on disciplinary probation after his participation in a student protest. *Advocate* editors like Robert Shaw and James Atlas were writing poetry that was among the best work produced by young poets during the period. Atlas's work would appear in the *New Yorker* while he was still an *Advocate* editor.

The *Advocate* tradition of inviting eminent authors to the Advocate House for readings open to the university flourished during the sixties. Reading guests included Marianne Moore, John Berryman, Richard Eberhart, Robert Lowell, John Hawkes, and Tom Wolfe. These gatherings usually packed the house to capacity and began with an introduction of the author by the current president in the Sanctum. The reading would continue for an hour or so and then everyone would drink the *Advocate's* cheap wine, which was said to improve with each paper cupful.

The quality of the *Advocate's* contents varied substantially in the last ten years, depending on the interests and diligence of each year's board of editors. Some years, the *Advocate* barely managed to get out two or three thin issues. In other years, the activity was much more productive.

Some of the *Advocate's* most finished and mature work from the last decade is published in this anthology. "Letter" by Judith Baumel shows the fruit of her work with Robert Lowell, who was teaching young poets at Harvard during that time and worked with her on her creative writing theses. "Hooks and Eyes for a Bibliophile's Breeches" by Peter Theroux, whose literary family also includes brothers Paul and Alex, is an unusually witty piece on book collecting.

The number of pages dedicated to artwork and photographs has reached a high point in the last ten years. The role of the art director has emerged as one of the most important on the magazine, and talented art directors such as Bill Maroni '77 set standards of excellence in layout and illustration for the editorial boards of the late seventies and early eighties.

In 1916, W.G. Peckham '67, a founding editor of the *Advocate*, wrote in the *Harvard Advocate: Fifty Year Book*, "If one seeks a monument to the little old paper, let him look about in the list of young writers and see how many of them became famous." A great many of these "young writers" have become the literary lions of the last century. Looking back over the work which appears in the *Advocate* over the last 120 years, it is particularly impressive how good much of it really was, not just contributions by the famous, but that by all the writers featured in these pages. Some of these young authors never again lifted a pen to write poetry, fiction, or criticism after their *Advocate* days were over, but each of them, and the hundreds of others who contributed to the *Advocate*, has something to remember — the work, the comraderie, the pride in the finished product.

Douglas A. McIntyre

Acknowledgments

A number of important contributors to this anthology deserve credit. Karen Hull worked tirelessly to put together the poems, stories, articles, and artwork for this book. In putting together the last ten years of work, the help of the current undergraduate board of the *Advocate* was invaluable.

James Atlas worked against a tough deadline to finish his foreword, which I am sure that the readers will find delightful. Kermit Lansner and Joan Sireci helped me put together the introduction, and I thank them.

Douglas A. McIntyre
New York City
June 23, 1986

1866–1896

1866–1896

When F.P. Stearns wrote "Our Paper," he had no guarantee the *Advocate* would survive its inaugural issue. Censorship was not new to Harvard—an *Advocate* predecessor, *The Collegian,* was suppressed by the faculty after only a few issues. Yet, Stearns reasoned, "We ought to be allowed a voice . . . on the subject of those rules and customs here which determine so nearly our habits of thought and action throughout life." This appeal, tempered with an admission of youthful inexperience, won the first *Advocate* board an immediate if not totally secure future.

The first board of editors chose the Stork and Caduceus seal; the meaning of the emblem was obscure and the symbol was soon replaced with Pegasus tied to a dictionary. As the facsimile pages show, Pegasus often escaped the dictionary, but errors or no, each page gives a sense of the original magazine, its layout, and the style of the times.

The literary style of the day frequently eluded the early *Advocate.* Most reporting centered on campus news and gossip, sports events, and undergraduate room assignments. Prose and poetry played a secondary role, yet several great men contributed fiction and verse in those first issues. George Lyman Kittredge, noted Shakespearian scholar, wrote Chaucer parodies and the typically anecdotal "A Terrible Night." Poet E.A. Robinson wrote melancholy, formal verses that foreshadowed the work for which he was awarded the 1921 Putlitzer Prize. Other contributors included *Advocate* treasurer Theodore Roosevelt and poet Arthur Davison Ficke.

Although its author was virtually unknown, "Yumé" generated great response among *Advocate* readers— several denounced the story (and the *Advocate*) as indecent. "The Wrong Scent" was more typical of the era; this kind of glad story told to roommates appeared in nearly every issue.

Literary and music reviews are the oldest *Advocate* tradition. Here was the *Advocate* at its brashest, upbraiding Walt Whitman for vulgarity or smugly referring to Mary Shelley's classic Frankenstein as "preposterous." This same spirit was reflected on the editorial page: "The Propriety of Admitting Women into Our College" predated the founding of Radcliffe by only a few years, "The Harvard Shorter Catechism" illustrated a constant, fond tolerance for freshmen, and "How Students are Swindled" sparked a long feud between local merchants and the paper, which resulted in the opening of the Harvard Coop.

As a news forum, the *Advocate* incited several controversies. As a literary magazine, it would not reach its potential until *The Crimson* usurped its position as Harvard's fortnightly newspaper in 1873.

THE
ADVOCATE.

May 11, 1866.]   "Veritas nihil veretur."   [Vol. I. — No. I.

OUR PAPER.

The "Collegian" was started two months ago as a Cambridge newspaper, intended to represent the views and opinions of Harvard students. Its prosperity was great ; it had a long list of honorable subscribers, among both graduates and undergraduates, and was favorably spoken of by the leading periodicals of Boston. Soon after the issue of its third number, the editors of the "Collegian" were summoned, and informed that their publication must be discontinued. No direct reason was assigned for this unexpected step ; and all attempts at conciliation and compromise on the part of the editors, who offered to bind themselves to any restrictions whatever, were unavailing. Deterred from further pursuance of their undertaking by threat of a most severe college censure in case they continued it, the editors stopped their paper, and squared accounts with their subscribers. Impressed with a feeling that some such newspaper as was the "Collegian" is sorely needed here to express the wishes and opinions of the students, we propose to issue this, our present publication, as long as it is supported.

We do not make our attempt in any spirit of blind malignity to those who govern and instruct us, nor do we consider it mere school-boy sentiment which animates this appeal to our right of free journalism. As boys, we were prejudiced against our masters ; and there may be some of that instinct lingering about us still : but we believe ourselves, on this occasion, to be actuated by other and more liberal motives.

It seems to us as if "leave to plead our own cause" had been asked for, and refused. It is from no idle whim, nor in any spirit of unmeaning opposition, that we try to assert that we consider ourselves slighted by this relentless course of our rulers in overlooking our dearest wishes. The good order and correct discipline of the College is far more likely to be demoralized by one instance where all explanation of the disputed point has been refused, than it could be by many midnight revels in front of University. It is true that two or three articles in the "Collegian" contained indistinct allusions to those to whom we are rightfully expected to pay the highest deference ; but such were hardly discernible to any save ourselves, and were not intended to be understood beyond the limits of a department or of a certain class. We admit that it may have been a mistake to have published such articles in the "Collegian ;" but we are positive that such a practice would have been entirely stopped as soon as it became known that they were a source of annoyance to their subjects. Harmless by-play the editors thought it, which no one need be offended at.

Here are four hundred young men, the greater number of whom have now passed that age at which law prescribes that they shall become their own masters. All these have individual opinions, feelings, ideas, more or less, of their own. It would be absurd to attempt to gratify all their whims and tastes ; yet, when a majority concur in claiming a right to this privilege or that privilege, we know there is some reason for it, which ought to be investigated. And we think, that, if we are to be responsible at all, we ought to be allowed a voice, or at least some expression of appeal, on the subject of those rules and customs here which determine so nearly our habits of thought and action throughout life. We confess that undergraduates are inexperienced, and, as compared with older heads, are ignorant enough of the realities of the world. "Yet he that wears the shoe alone knows where the shoe pinches." The scholarly senior, who knows well where the discipline of each day serves him as an assistance and a guide, also knows best of all where the chafing of his harness impedes free motion. "Times change, and men change with them." Is it expected that we should find suited to our best purposes those regulations which were framed for the government of our grandfathers? If a change is to be allowed at any time, it is possible that one time may demand it as well as another.

We disclaim having received any assistance or co-operation in our project from the former editors of the "Collegian." Not even are they responsible for the original idea of our attempt. They were not alone in their belief that a newspaper of some sort was needed among the undergraduates, both for the purpose of expressing their sentiments to each other, and also their impressions of college matters to the world. We are not a small and insignificant minority, nor are the principles on which we act cherished within the breasts of a few proselytes. They have been for a long time echoed and re-echoed in college talk and society debates. We assure the public that our columns are open to all who desire to make fair, unbiased statement of their judgment on these subjects on or any others. Nothing abusive. nothing personally libellous, nothing which in the judgment of the editors would be likely to excite disobedience or disorder, will be received.

With this exposition of "our purposes," we intrust to the mercy of our readers the first number of the "Advocate."

F. P. Stearns

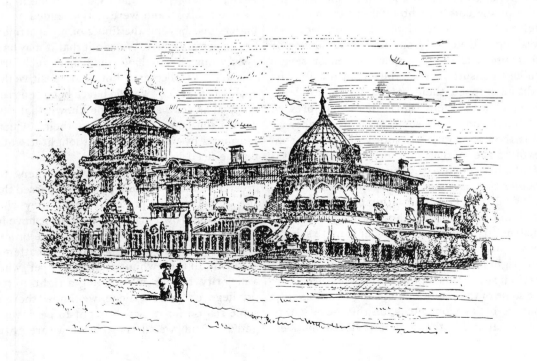

THE PROPRIETY OF ADMITTING
WOMEN INTO OUR COLLEGE.

Messrs Editors, — I cannot praise too heartily the various articles upon University Reform which have appeared in your magazine; and Dr. Hedge's most excellent address upon the same subject (which I had the pleasure of hearing) receives entire approval from me: but there is one branch of reform which, I believe, has not as yet been touched upon in your magazine, — a reform of paramount importance, and in regard to which, I will ask your attention to a few words from me.

I mean that advance upon our present state of civilization which will no longer exclude one-half of the human race from the walls of our college; which will no longer tolerate the barbarous idea that our sisters have not as good a right to a liberal education as ourselves.

Said a young lady to me on a certain occasion, " I would have given all that I could earn in five years, if I could have been allowed to be graduated from Harvard College. I went through a high school with five young men as classmates: these entered Harvard; but I, who had stood at the head of the class, was compelled to leave New England, and seek the doubtful advantages of Antioch College." I felt ashamed for my College, and blushed for the inconsistency of New-England civilization which tolerates such a manifest injustice in its pet colleges.

When our College was founded, the state of things was far different from what it is now. School-teaching then was confined almost entirely to men; now a great majority of our teachers are women; a large number of our students are prepared for college chiefly by women; and are we to set the same standard now for women's education as then?

I confess that I am unable to see what possible harm can result from throwing our College open to every person, male or female, who is desirous of entering it; on the contrary, I think that great good would be the result. It has been suggested by one of your contributors, that, if the expenses at Harvard were reduced, she would no longer be compelled to depend upon the immediate neighborhood for a supply of students: but I can inform him of a way by which a much more satisfactory result could be attained without half the difficulty attending his suggestion.

At the next examination for admission, let a notice be circulated throughout the country, that young ladies as well as young gentlemen will be received as candidates; and, if I am not mistaken, the result will be that in five years' time our number of students will be doubled. Then our expenses can be reduced to one-half the present amount, and we can properly say that we belong to a University; for I do not believe that we can justly call an institution *a University* which is confined to one-half of mankind.

It is often urged as an objection against receiving women into our larger colleges, that several colleges have been established exclusively for females, and several others are open both to males and females; and that women ought to be contented with these colleges, and not aspire to the dignity of becoming students of Harvard or Yale. This trifling argument is as applicable to men as women.

Why do so many young men leave their Western homes, and come all the way to New England for an education, ignoring the hundreds of little colleges, so called, which are struggling into existence on their boundless prairies? The simple reason is, that they are attracted by the superior advantages which our Eastern institutions afford; and, for the same reason, our sisters, who desire a collegiate education, cannot but feel disappointed to see us entering a first-class college, while they must put up with an Antioch or Oberlin. What a disgraceful sight! — an Eastern girl forced to leave her home in New England, so famous for its educational advantages, and seek the State of Ohio, as a place where she can enjoy even tolerable advantages!

If sectionalism is dangerous in government, it certainly must be so in education. Nature has placed boys and girls together in families, that they may mutually benefit each other; but, at the very age in which they are in the greatest need of each other's assistance, they are ruthlessly separated. What a glorious era it will be in American civilization, when a brother and sister, after attending school together during their younger days, can finally be received under the classic shades of Harvard, hand in hand,

and continue here together for four happy years! A blessed day, too, will it be for the morals of our College, when the young men have the restraining influence of woman's society before them during their college course.

Alumni, the task is yours! See that this criminal exclusiveness be eradicated. Open the doors of your Alma Mater to all who desire and deserve her maternal care. Do away with this false distinction between the two sexes; and let the blessed light of civilization permeate the barriers of bigotry and injustice. Lux.

"THE HARVARD SHORTER CATECHISM."

A LITTLE volume with the title, "THE HARVARD SHORTER CATECHISM; being an easy Introduction to the Freshman Year; in 24 Parts," has just been laid on our table. We welcome its appearance, for we have long felt that those who are plunged at once into college life should have some idea of what that life is. This information is certainly given in this work, although in a form which is necessarily concise, through its arrangement as a catechism.

We present below a few of the questions chosen at random, from different parts of the volume, appending also their answers; of course the proper answers suggest themselves at once to us, and it is, perhaps, foolish in the editors to add them. But, on the whole, we have concluded that they may benefit the large number of Freshmen already in college, who evidently never have had the advantage of any such course of instruction.

1. *Q.* — Why is Harvard University so called?
A. — Because it is composed of the college, the schools of the learned professions, and the law school.

10. *Q.* — What Professor gives the worst marks?
A. — Professor Molyneaux.

15. *Q.* — What system of morning devotions is adopted here?
A. — One cut in a fortnight.

22. *Q.* — What curiosities are to be seen on the grounds?
A. — The master-don; the college choir while in the act; the Freshman Class.

23. *Q.* — What rarities are there in the college?
A. — Men who care any thing for rank; cards on Freshman doors; and United-States bills from the denomination of five cents, upwards.

30. *Q.* — Can you name a College Society?
A. — The Institute of 1770.

31. *Q.* — Will you state the properties required for admission to the Institute of 1770?
A. — Two dollars; and other properties.

35. *Q.* — What adage lies at the foundation of college philosophy?
A. — "Between two evils, choose the least."

36. *Q.* — How does this theory find practical expression?
A. — In the elective system of college studies.

We commend this work to our readers as affording a remarkably able presentation of many college phenomena. Φ

FRANKENSTEIN; OR, THE MODERN PROMETHEUS. By MARY W. SHELLEY. Cambridge: Sever, Francis, & Co.

Messrs. Sever & Francis deserve credit for publishing this work, since it has long been celebrated, while inacessible to the curious reader on account of its rarity. But for the book itself we can say but little. It is intended to be frightful and impressive, as are generally accounts of goblins, djinns, vampires, and such pleasing beings. To us, however, it seems to have lapsed from the sublime to the ridiculous. We say this boldly, since the author is dead, and we cannot reasonably suppose that our remarks will hurt her feelings.

Frankenstein is a student, who, by tremendous application to the charming study of chemistry, becomes enabled to create a man. Wishing to "spread himself" on his work, he makes his fellow eight feet tall and large in proportion. When the work is done, Frankenstein is horrified to find he has made a monster. The monster naturally desires companionship, and requests his maker to create a female for a partner of his joys and sorrows. Frankenstein reflects that the consequences of so doing might be dangerous to the human race, and refuses. The monster enraged proceeds to slaughter all Frankenstein's relations and friends in the most bloodthirsty manner, and finally announces his intention of committing suicide after he has caused the death of his creator.

The principal moral to be derived by Harvard boys from this book is, that dangerous proficiency in chemistry should be carefully avoided.

Stories like "Frankenstein" are, we think, either morbid or absurd. Probably the notoriety of this book arose from its author's being the daughter of Godwin and wife of Shelley, rather than from any merit of its own, as, with the exception of a few striking passages, its style is as flat as its plot is horrible and preposterous.

HARVARD'S COLOR.

"'And when before your eyes I've set him,
If you don't find him black I'll eat him,'
He said; and full before their sight
Produced the beast, and lo! — 'twas white."

OUR friend with the chameleon could not have been more surprised and shocked at the change of color than were the old Harvard boating men to hear their proudly worn crimson called magenta, in 1866, by the newspapers: indignation was called forth from all quarters; but it was thought to be merely a newspaper mistake, that would be corrected. With the next year the same error was repeated, however; and all efforts at correction proved vain, and soon magenta was recognized as Harvard's color. At different times, attempts have been made by the boating men to get back to the true color, but so far without success. The present opportunity seems a good one to make a last final attempt. Union College puts in a claim for magenta. Let us see if it will not be well to let it go, and return to our true colors. What, then, are the facts about crimson and magenta? How did the colors originate, and how did they become confounded and changed?

The color came from the college boat crew in 1858. Before that, no particular color was recognized in any American college as pertaining thereto. Boating men were the only collegians who had occasion to sport a uniform; and, up to this time, the different clubs had each a different uniform, with no one general feature common to all. In races there was little worn that could show any special color. Up to 1858, the crews usually wore straw hats, or sometimes caps. But, in 1858, a handkerchief tied tightly around the head was used in practice, and proved a useful and sensible covering for the head. Just before the first race in that year in which the college crew was to row, it was decided to wear the handkerchiefs in the race; and, after some discussion, it was decided that the color should be blue. At no shop in Boston, however, could blue silk handkerchiefs of the right size be found, and six red ones were bought instead. The shade of red was very nearly a true crimson. It was called simply red, and was used for many years, and was the distinguishing uniform of the Harvard University Crew; and "red" was adopted from the crew as Harvard's color.

At that time, the little town or village of Magenta was unknown to fame. But, on the 9th of June, 1859, the famous battle near by was fought, and took its name from the village. Just afterwards the aniline dyes were discovered, and two shades took names from the battles of Magenta and Solferino. The color magenta is a flashy, purplish shade of red, which was greatly in vogue for a year or so in France, and thence imported with other fashions to America. It has now gone out of fashion, and is difficult to procure in consequence, and will soon be numbered with the fashions "which were." It would be rather singular if the only demand for the color should come from Harvard University. Much better let it drop, and take up again a name and a color which will always live on account of its beauty, — the noble crimson. Magenta is (like all the aniline colors) a loose color. It fades with sunlight, and will not stand soap and water. It is one of those sickly shades that is almost impossible to harmonize with any other color. Intrinsically, it has nothing to recommend it. How, then, did it come to be so successful a rival of the crimson?

When the war commenced, the boating spirit in Cambridge declined, but revived with the system of class crews in 1863. Each class then took a color for its crew, leaving red for the University. The class of 1866 chose magenta and white as its color, and, having a fine crew, brought its color into great prominence. In 1866, in the University race at Worcester, by mistake magenta handkerchiefs were used, that shade of red being then in common use; and, when the Harvard men arrived at Worcester to see the race, and inquired at the shops for red, they were obliged to take magenta or nothing, as that was the only shade of red obtainable. Finding this was the case, the University Crew, not wishing the colors to be confounded, took especial pains to have the color called "red" on the printed cards of the race, and not "magenta." The newspapers, however, were too much for them; and, ever since, "magenta" has been called Harvard's color by the papers, and later also by the students, in spite of repeated attempts by the boating men to set the colors right. Now every college in America has its distinctive color, and several have adopted shades of red. Some shade of that color would seem to belong to Harvard, as the general term "red" would interfere with others, and cause great confusion. "Magenta" has been used so long as the name of Harvard's color that some difficulty would be experienced at first in changing it. As the color, however, never was "magenta" really; and as the color "magenta" has nothing to recommend it; and as the color really was crimson, and crimson is a good name, — especially now that somebody else wants the color and the name, — would it not be a good thing in every way to give it up, and take back the handsomer, the truer, and the legitimate "crimson" in name and in deed?

WALT WHITMAN.

THE works of Walt Whitman have lately been very much reviewed in England, while in this, his native country, he has rarely been noticed. In America, through ignorance of all the characteristics of his works, the little value he possesses as a poet has been denied him; while in England, chiefly through ignorance of the American people, Mr. Whitman has been greatly overestimated. Between his admirers and his enemies, Mr. Whitman has fared ill, — the former praising him too highly, out of all proportion to his deserts, the latter praising him not at all, seeing nothing but faults in him. The one is extravagantly delighted with the hidden music of his verse, the other calls him a noisy impostor; the one says he is Shaksperean in "balance and sanity" of mind, the other is utterly disgusted with the "confused jumbling together of the component parts of the diction-ary;" — the loudest applause and the severest censure.

Whitman is spoken of in England as pre-eminently the poet of Democracy and of America, the first of Democracies; but we are not definitely told why. One English critic has gone so far as to style Whitman the "*sacer vates* to the growth of the American youth*,*" implying, I think, that he is benefiting us and is well known to us. But, mortified though we must be to admit it, we believe the youth of America know very little of their "*sacer vates;*" and, upon those of us who do know something of his works, it were just to deny that the effect produced is at all commensurate with the effect claimed.

We indignantly abjure Walt Whitman as a "*sacer vates*," or as a true representative of our national thoughts and feelings. Because he spreads American names over his pages, for-eigners consider him as the long-looked for herald of Democracy! An excellent chance, forsooth, for any madman to be flatteringly be-lauded and crowned America's poet, by merely mumbling and writing down in broken-legged verse the names of his country's physical features, its fowls, brute kind, its institutions, and numer-ous occupations! Either we refuse to Mr. Whitman his claim to be the exponent of our national thoughts, ambitions, hopes, and progress, or we submit ourselves to be looked upon as a people whose marked characteristics are illiter-acy, sensuality, clownishness, and an utter absence of delicacy in manners, thought, and feelings; in other words, as a people of Pariahs. This is a distasteful alternative, but I see no other. Eng-lishmen and other foreigners have been eagerly looking for something decidedly original in American literature; they have believed with Buckle that America must place a peculiar stamp on the foreheads of all her distinguished men; some of them have thought Lowell, Longfellow, and Bryant clever imitators, be-cause their genius is but slightly tinted by the circumstances which in this country surround them. Something abnormal was wanted, and at last is at hand: they have found a man of a nature less poetical than his pretensions would have us believe, but yet poetical; and, as his works show, possessed of a character the most eccentric and marvellous. Their joy at this discovery is boundless, and Americans cannot comprehend it. To us, such violent admiration of Whitman seems to be the sputtering of dis-eased minds; for their admiration of him extends to matter, the construction of which is opposed to every well-established rule of poetical form, and the vulgarity of which is revolting to the sense and distasteful to the intellect. There are times when Whitman is the poet; but at such happy times there is in him no more evidence of the influence of Democracy than in any other American poet.

But let us quote a few lines, which, chosen with a view to give true impressions, will show at once the worthlessness of his claims as a poet, and at the same time expose some of those literary monstrosities which his English and American friends admire. Our bard's - admir-ers say that one of his most excellent poetical qualities is the faithful reflection of his charac-ter in his poems. If this is true, the following quotations tell a sorry story of his life, and will also help to explain his mysterious individuality, his governing motives, &c. He says he is —

"Turbulent, fleshy, and sensual, eating, drinking, and
    breeding," and not a "dainty, dolce affetuoso."

He takes a curious delight in repeating to his readers that he is sensual and lusty, without a greater fondness for the clean and respectable than for their opposites.

"No more modest than immodest."
"I am not the poet of goodness only — I do not decline
    to be the poet of wickedness also."

"I am myself just as much evil as good, and my nation is. And I say there is in fact no evil."

Whitman declares this repeatedly, as if he were afraid that some one would deny to him those qualities which he asserts that he has. But his glory, in so far as it depends on his sensuality, may rest safely; for in his earlier works his declarations are supported by passages sufficiently gross and indecent.

He tells us he is untranslatable; that when we think we have caught his meaning, — presto! it vanishes. He thinks his accumulations of words are : —

"Man's, woman's, child's, youth's, wife's, husband's, mother's, father's, young man's, young woman's poems;
Head, neck, hair, ears, drop and tympan of the ears,
Eyes, eye-fringes," etc., etc., from "toe-joints" to "jaw-hinges,"
"O, I say now these are the soul."

To discuss such unmeaning trifles would be to insult the good sense of the reader.

In his effusion headed "Salut au Monde," he applies to himself the question, "What do you see, Walt Whitman?" and his reply is embracingly poetical, consisting of a bare list, not in rhyme, rhythm, or reason, of every range of mountains, of every body of water, of every city, noted in a comprehensive geography. And this, we are told, indicates in him a vocabulary more fruitful than that possessed by Shakspere.

Whitman is a materialist, and chants his belief thus : —

"Divine am I inside and out, and I make holy whatever I touch or am touched from;
The scent of these arm-pits, sweeter than the aroma of prayer,
This head more than churches, bibles, and all the creeds."

It is not the subject of his poems, but its treatment, that we may justly complain of; and there is no one of his thousand and one poems, which exemplifies better than the preceding his disgusting taste.

He says if he worshipped any thing it would be his own body. Discussing one's duty to God makes our poet sick; so he would like to leave the society of those who do so discuss, and live with animals, — if they permitted it. He howls of the heavens, stars, moon, time, and space, leaping without difficulty from the infinite to the finite. Nothing too low or high but must bear the burden of his song. Whitman has no idea of delicacy, and supposes none in the reader. He penetrates our closets, accompanies us to the bath, pursues us through the day, passes the evening with us, sees us into bed, and then, unasked, jumps in with us. If we rebuff him, he reproaches us with "gossamer delicacy," taunts us with purism. Indeed, his sense of propriety is utterly dead.

Whitman harps long on the soul. It is at once spiritual and material, the body and not the body. Wonderful and obscure as the soul has hitherto appeared, under Whitman's hand it has become doubly wonderful, doubly obscure. Scattered among such dignified topics are verses forming repositories for the most repulsive nastinesses, while others are loaded with the most sickening of absurdities.

In some few verses there is a sad, sweet air gently moving, hand in hand, however, with only a pleasant rhythm; for he has thought it best to scorn metre, making rhythm in its stead sometimes furnish the music to which his verses dance. Rhythmical movement, unfortunately, does not sharply enough distinguish his verse from prose. Time after time we fancy ourselves reading disjointed prose, and our fancy does not deceive us.

In fine, then, we see nothing in Whitman, either in form of expression or in poetical nature, which does not grossly violate those standards by which the claims of the best of poets have been measured. Should we allow Whitman to embrace us, as he again and again says he wants to do, we should be erecting for ourselves a new standard of poetic thought and expression. His English admirers would carry Whitman in triumph over the muddy road which they have strewn with flowers-torn from the tombs of the greatest poets. But we will not join them in their frenzied march. When, however, Whitman shall have given us noble thoughts or elevating ideals, he may be sure the youth of America will appreciate him; but nobody can force us to drink from the polluted bucket which a maniac has filled, and which English sensualism raises to our lips.

HOW STUDENTS ARE SWINDLED.

IT has long been known that it is the practice of the University Bookstore to squeeze every cent out of students that it can, either honestly or otherwise. But some instances of fraud have occurred lately which are so barefaced and reckless as to demand our attention.

One of the students, having had occasion to buy a copy of Breton's *Athènes*, called at the bookstore, and got his book, with the information that the price would be at least seven dollars and seventy-five cents ($7.75), and probably more, as information from head-quarters showed an advance over last year's price. He took the book, but next day learned that Schœnhof & Mœller were selling the same work for four dollars and eighty cents ($4.80). Upon this, he reported to the bookstore, and was told that he could have the book for six dollars ($6.00); at the same time receiving as an excuse for the fraud practised that Schœnhof & Mœller had charged Mr. Sever more for the work than they had charged the students. The student in question took the trouble to report the case to Schœnhof & Mœller, and they flatly denied the absurd story that they had charged Mr. Sever extra price for the book, and assured him that Mr. Sever could sell the work at five dollars ($5.00) and make a good profit. They sold it retail at four dollars and eighty cents. The student then tried to buy a Bouillier's *Philosophy* from Schœnhof & Mœller, and found that they had sold all these books to Mr. Sever, and not one was to be had in Boston. By special agreement, however, Mr. Sever was to charge only four dollars for them, and so in this case a monopoly of the market did not result in very great loss to the students. But we could mention a great many cases, such as the selling of certain mathematical text-books, of the Institutes of Gaius, &c., in which Mr. Sever takes advantage of his position and extorts money from the students to a degree that is almost incredible.

The reason why he has such power is this: For a long time there existed between the Faculty of Harvard and Mr. Sever a written contract, by which Mr. Sever alone was to be furnished with lists of all the books to be used in College, and was to have the needed works always on hand. That written contract has been done away with, but a verbal one of the same nature is still in force. This, of course, places the students entirely at the mercy of Mr. Sever; and he can swindle them, if he will, which he often does. But the reason why the furnishing of text-books is left to Mr. Sever alone is that, were lists of such books given to a large number of firms, each would depend upon the others to furnish some books, and would only import a small part of the whole number wanted. The result would be that, at the beginning of the term, probably not half the books needed would be on hand; whereas, if the exact number of the necessary books is given to one man, he can always be ready to supply the demand.

We doubt not, therefore, that the professors have done the best they could in the matter, by intrusting the furnishing of books to a single individual. But should they not put some check upon the bookseller in whose hands they leave us, some limit to his extortion? Experience has taught us that they should; and we therefore propose to the Faculty that they, for the protection of the students, change the firm which furnishes the college text-books, upon satisfactory proof being given by the students that such firm has been extortionate in its demands. This would secure us against dishonest booksellers, and at the same time would insure the necessary supply of text-books. As a supplementary proposition, we would hint, too, that a change is badly needed *now*.

Peckham   Gray   Sanborn   Fox   Stearns   Williams

FOOTBALL AT OTHER COLLEGES.

THE football season has now fairly opened, and it is well to take a glance at what our rivals are doing. Yale has lost Thompson, who has twice turned the scale against us; but otherwise her team will probably be much the same as last year's, and there is plenty of good material from which to fill the vacancies. Captain Camp has already begun to put his men into regular training, running them in the gymnasium. Thirty men have been pledged to play against the team every afternoon, and games will probably be played with both Amherst and Trinity; so that there will be no danger of her men suffering from lack of practice. At present it hardly seems as if the team would be as good as last year's, but their playing is improving every day, and nothing but very hard work will enable our men to win the victory.

Princeton will undoubtedly have a good team, although the lower classes do not seem to possess very good material from which to choose; but it must be remembered that in Princeton, where there is no crew, all the best men go out on the football field, and work with a faithfulness not very common at Harvard.

At Cornell there has been some talk of organizing a team, but it is doubtful if it can be done this year. What Columbia will do, it is difficult to say. On the whole, the prospect should be by no means discouraging to us. We certainly have good teams to fight against; but there is plenty of excellent material in College, and our captain deserves most hearty praise, whatever be the result, for the pains he has taken, not only in keeping the men at work on the field, but in running them on the track every afternoon. What is most necessary is, that every man should realize the necessity of faithful and honest work, *every afternoon*. Last year we had good individual players, but they did not work together nearly as well as the Princeton team, and were not in as good condition as the Yale men. The football season is short; and while it does last, the men ought to work faithfully, if they expect to win back for Harvard the position she held three years ago.

Theodore Roosevelt

A TERRIBLE NIGHT.

I HAD known him only a few weeks, and thought him a very jolly fellow. He reciprocated my feelings, and we passed many pleasant hours in one another's rooms, playing whist or discussing grave points in literature, art, science, philosophy, and tennis. One night (I think it is extremely doubtful — quite as doubtful, perhaps, as the championship problem — if I ever forget that night)— one night in March we were sitting before a blazing fire in his room, smoking and discussing the sonnet. The wind howled outside like mad and the chapel choir, but within all was calm save my new friend, who seemed strangely agitated. I wondered at this, for I could see nothing in the subject of our discussion to rouse agitation. Suddenly he sprang from his chair and with a sudden motion locked and barred the door. I had never noticed before that there was a bar, and was much surprised when I saw that it was arranged with a spring-lock attachment. "Elton," I cried, "what under heaven are you doing?" "Nothing, nothing, my dear fellow," and he laughed nervously, "I only thought I heard Shakspeare's walk outside, coming to dun me for my subscription to his sonnets, which I have never yet paid. Wait a minute and I'll show you the book." I was not much reassured by this reply, and watched Elton rather narrowly as he searched the bookcase behind me, but I finally turned

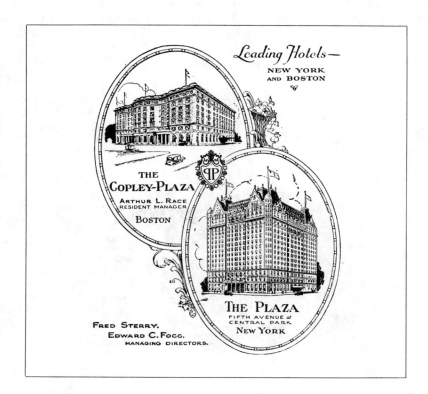

round again, as it took him a good while, and sat as before, facing the fire.

Perhaps I had been sitting thus thirty seconds, when I felt myself violently seized from behind, while a mocking laugh sounded in my ears. I was taken altogether at a disadvantage, and didn't quite know what was up, but soon came to the conclusion that Elton was trying to tie me to my chair. I don't mind telling you that I'm a pretty strong and agile fellow, my muscles having been well developed by constant base-ball practice. I'm on the Freshman Nine, you know. So I kicked and struggled desperately, but to no purpose. Elton's constant exercise at tennis had given him strength against which mine, though my sinews had been toughened in the way just mentioned, stood no chance. I soon found myself bound hand and foot to the heavy chair and locked in a room alone with a madman. For Elton was mad. There was no doubt of it. I think the presiding genius at the office was never madder, not even when a venturesome Senior asked her recently for his mark in Forensics. "Faredale," said he, "I have you now. You are in my power. You have often conversed with me on the sonnet, little suspecting I am a poet. But a poet I am. I have sent my poems in to various college papers. They have never been accepted. I hired my goody to listen to my odes at ten dollars a line ; she heard three lines and fled. I bribed my janitor. He heard six lines and went out, borrowing my umbrella. I persuaded Connors, and he seemed to stand it pretty well, but it was too much for his bull-dog. It killed him. I had to pay Connors heaven knows how much damages. But now I have you. Ha! ha! Just listen to my beautiful poems." And he produced a well-bound and well-thumbed MS. and began : —

"OWED TO THE OFFICE.

"O dread abode of doubt and dreary woe !
O dreary, doubting-woe, and dread abode !
Why dost thou tear, torment, and torture so
The trembling toiler of this thrice-told ode ?
Thou labyrinth of caves, thou cavy woe,
Why dost thou torture and torment me so ? "

While reading this frightful production, poor Elton gesticulated and gyrated as I had thought nothing on earth could make a man gesticulate and gyrate, always excepting Dr. James's spiral swing. As for me, I was *in articulo mortis*. But I held my breath. "Is it not glorious ? " shrieked the madman. "Yes, indeed," assented I. "Then just listen to this," and on he went : —

LINES TO THE TUBULAR VU.

"God bless thee, good old Tubular! God save and send
   thee rest.
The errors of my judgment long since I have confessed.
I used to think it dreadful (when I was young and green)
To figure out your mysteries and make my blank out
   clean, —
But standing on one foot
   At the bullention in U.,
Has made me sigh for good old times
   When each student, rich or poor, bond or free, without regard to age or sex, could, by simply calling for it, obtain, at no expense, a copy of that invaluable manual for students known as the Tubular Vu."

"How do you like that ? " said Elton. I was fast growing weaker, but I managed to gasp out, "Lovely. The wild and luxuriant redundancy of the last line, the sort of harmony blossoming itself to death, reminds me of —" "No matter what it reminds you of," burst out the madman, "listen to this. It is a

"THRENODY.

"Scarce can I think that he is dead.
   Who's dead ? A Senior, he
   Slipped up on his degree ;
   The mourners veil his head,
   He's dead. No doubt he's dead.
   Alas, why did he die ?
      Who can tell ?
   Dead he is, then let him lie,
      Toll the bell."

"The bell," laughed Elton, "is to be tolled five minutes. You have no more prayer-cuts. You will go to prayers or be put on special." "I shall die," I groaned. "No doubt," said he; "here is another. Something of a magical nature :—

"XXX.

"Three friends came forth out of the West,
   Out of the East came they,
There came three friends out of the South,
   And thus began their say —"

"Help! help! " I shrieked, able to bear no more. At my words the door was burst open, and two men rushed in. They seized Elton and secured him after a desperate struggle. It was the janitor and a friend, who, supposing Elton out, were going to drop in for a quiet smoke. They saved me, any way. Elton was sent to — Asylum, where he got over his poetry, and has since become a useful member of the community.

G.L. Kittredge

ANALYTICS IN THE ANNEX.

Mathematical Professor. — NOW, THEN, YOUNG LADIES, WHO CAN TELL ME WHAT IS AN OSCULATING CIRCLE?
Pert Sophomore (*innocently*). — PLEASE, SIR, IS IT A GAME OF COPENHAGEN?

BALLADE OF THE WHITE SHIP.

DOWN they went to the still, green water —
　　The dim White Ship like a white bird lay;
Laughing at life and the world they sought her,
　　And out they sailed on the silvering bay :
　　The quick ship flew on her roystering way,
And the keen moon fired the light foam flying
　　Up from the flood where the faint stars play,
And the bones of the brave in the wave are lying.

'Twas a king's gay son with a king's gay daughter,
　　And full three hundred beside, they say,
Hurrying on to the lone, cold slaughter
　　So soon to seize them and hide them for aye;
　　But they danced and they drank and their souls grew gay,
Nor ever they knew of a ghoul's eye spying
　　Their splendor a flickering phantom to stray
Where the bones of the brave in the wave are lying.

Through the mist of a drunken dream they brought her
　　(This wild white bird) for the sea-fiend's prey :
The ravenous reef in his hard clutch caught her
　　And whirled her down where the dead men stay —
　　A torturing silence of wan dismay;
The shrieks and curses of mad souls dying.
　　Then down they sank to slumber and sway
Where the bones of the brave in the wave are lying.

L'ENVOI.

Prince, do you sleep 'mid the perishing clay
　　To the mournful dirge of the sea-birds' crying?
Or does blood still quicken and steel still slay —
　　Where the bones of the brave in the wave are lying?

　　　　　　　　　　　　　　　E. A. Robinson.

VILLANELLE OF CHANGE.

SINCE Persia fell at Marathon
   The yellow years have gathered fast—
Long centuries have come and gone.

Any yet (they say) the place will don
   A phantom fury of the past,
Since Persia fell at Marathon;

And as of old, when Helicon
   Trembled and swayed with rapture vast,—
Long centuries have come and gone—

This ancient plain, when night comes on,
   Shakes in a phantom battle blast,
Since Persia fell at Marathon   .   .   .

With mouldering mists of Acheron
   Long have her skies been overcast,
Long centuries have come and gone;

The suns of other days have shone—
   The first has fallen to the last:
Since Persia fell at Marathon,
Long centuries have come and gone.

                              E. A. Robinson.

DON'T;

A FEW HINTS ON THE SUBJECT OF SOCIAL BARBARISM.

It may be objected that some of the rules hereafter expounded are arbitrary, some self-evident, and therefore unnecessary, &c. &c. To the first it may be replied, that Nature's commands are often very arbitrary, and naturalness is the height of all art. All other criticisms may be disposed of by remarking that there's no knowing what a man may do if he has a chance.

I.

A MEMORIAL.

Don't wear your hat in the gallery. It shows an unpardonable lack of respect for our democratic institutions, and is therefore liable to make trouble.

Don't come to dinner at 6.55, unless you want to learn wisdom by experience.

Don't send your plate three times for clam chowder. No soup should be taken more than once.

Don't wipe spoons on your napkin before using them. There is no reason why you should fare better than your companions.

Don't hold up your glass of water to the light. There is scarcely anything new to be seen, and such a procedure reflects injuriously on the Cambridge water department. Whatever you see, don't mention it. If you don't like the appearance of the water, drink it in the form of milk.

Don't make a fuss over the beefsteak. A man never appears at such a disadvantage as when he gets red in the face on account of some unaccustomed exertion. If you can't eat what is put before you, you had better take a course in chest weights at the Gymnasium.

Don't consume every bit of the stew on your plate, the bones in particular are exceedingly indigestible. If you are seriously hungry it is allowable to send for a second supply.

Don't mop your beard with a napkin. (This rule does not apply to freshmen.)

Don't read any of this stuff. If you do, don't give it away.

PRACTICAL CHRISTIANITY.

Jack (who has been to church). — "WE HAD A VERY PRACTICAL SERMON THIS MORNING; IT WAS ON 'THE QUESTION OF THE HOUR.'"

Tom (who has been tutored vigorously all the morning). — "CURIOUS COINCIDENCE, OLD FELLOW; I HAD A VERY PRACTICAL SERMON ON THE QUESTIONS OF THE THREE HOURS."

YUMÉ.

A FRIEND of mine, a young Japanese philosopher, came back from a journey through the interior of Japan, and told me of a very interesting incident.

About five days after he had started from the city of Tokio, he came to a thickly wooded, mountainous region. At the foot of the mountain he had a little lunch, and then started northward through the narrow path leading to a town on the other side of the mountain. The path ran zigzag to avoid a steep slope. The cedars and firs were so dense that, except when they were moved by the wind, the sunbeams hardly penetrated their needles. Every footstep every cough, and every murmur of the philosopher, was echoed from all directions, as the sound struck, one after another, a tree or a rock. The path was often hidden by the thickly-growing moss or bush. Sometimes it was broken by the streams running across the path. The philosopher jumped over many streams, but he was often obliged to go into the water, which was clear and extremely cold. He was alone, and during all the afternoon he saw only two houses and half a dozen men.

About five o'clock, he came to the summit. As he climbed on a cliff projecting over the woods, he saw the sun just setting in the western horizon. "What an immense fire-ball! What a magnificent cloud!" he exclaimed. In the west he saw the sunbeams striking the peaks, thence scattering thousands and thousands of golden rays. In the north and the east he saw nothing but several mountain ranges, running like six-folded screens. Those parts of the ranges which were nearest to him were dark blue. As they retreated they grew lighter, and finally the mountains looked gray, blurring themselves in the mist. In the south he saw the plain extending a hundred miles seaward, and disappearing in the horizon just before it touched the ocean. Below was a rich valley. In it he saw several towns, and even steam-cars running busily. But the cars could not take the exhausted philosopher from the solitary summit.

He looked down, and found beautiful moss so growing between the rocks as to give him an unroofed shelter in the cliff. He took a seat on the moss, and said, "Ah! I am tired!" He stretched his hands and legs like a dog. Then he bent his right arm, and rested his head on his hand. His eyes closed.

Suddenly he saw near him a light. "There is my hotel," he exclaimed. He got up, and scrambled hastily over rocks, bushes and water.

At last, he came to a little wooden house. He knocked at the door. There was no answer. He knocked again. Then a woman, with a candle in her hand, came out. She looked surprised, and asked, "Who are you, sir?"

"I am a tourist," said the philosopher. "I am anxious to get to a hotel, for the night has come and I am very tired. But in the darkness I have lost my way, while I was crossing the mountain. I have found your light and came here to beg the shelter of your hotel."

"This is my residence," said the lady, "and I cannot accommodate any tourists. If you want a hotel, you must go about twenty miles northward."

"I am exhausted and cannot walk any more, madam," said the philosopher. "I am not accustomed to sleep in the fields. It is terrible, madam, for I may be attacked by wild beasts. Pray, let me occupy some space in your house over night."

The young lady hesitated a little while and asked, "Whence are you, and what is your name?"

"I am from Tokio," said the philosopher, "and my name is Hara Dokan. My uncle is Count Hara of Mita."

"Well, well," the lady exclaimed; "then you are from my native place; come in, and wash your hands. Alas! their skins are broken." She went into the next room and brought out a bottle of medicine.

They were seated by the fire in the drawing-room, and the young lady bound up the wounds. The fire disclosed her features in detail. Her face was neither round nor long. Her fair, snowy complexion was in harmonious contrast to her rosy cheeks. Her nose was straight and long. Her eyes were large and bright, her eyebrows slightly curved like a new moon. She had occasionally a dimple in each cheek. Her hands were small and smooth, her fingers straight and long. She wore no ring. Her dresses were all silk, and her sash was rich and splendid. Her dark hair shone like a black pearl, and it was fastened in the Shimada fashion which showed that she was not married. She looked noble and refined.

The young philosopher asked her, " Have you a mother ? "

The lady having finished the binding of his wounds, lifted her face, and said, " No, sir, I have no mother, father, brother or sister. I am living here alone. I cook for myself and do all kinds of sewing."

The philosopher did not understand why such an angel-like lady could ever live alone in such a solitary place, yet maintaining her beauty and her dignity.

He asked her, " Whence and why did you come here ? "

She said, " There is a long story about it, and I think it better not to tell you. Anyhow, you must be hungry, so you must take some supper."

She went to the adjacent room and brought out chestnuts, persimmons, cherries, grapes and all sorts of wild fruits and meats. The philosopher ate but very little and repeated his question. Then the young lady yielded, and began :

" I was born in the city of Tokio. My father was a jeweler. He died when I was little. I lived with my mother. Once, in the spring, we went to Boktai to see the cherry flowers. We were walking among the crowd. A handsome young man in a beautiful carriage came from the opposite direction, led by his footman. He looked at us and passed by. Soon afterward he came back to us and stopped his carriage. He got down from it, and followed us a few steps, and asked us to drive with him. I was indeed frightened. My mother discoursed with him all the time, and declined his invitation. He asked our address, and then went off. About two weeks later, he came to our store and

bought many jewels. Then he repeated his call and finally proposed marriage to me. But I declined.

" After two months the Countess of Mita came to my house with some valuable presents, and told my mother that her son was seriously ill because of his disappointment. And if I did not marry him, she said, he would not live. My mother tried to induce me to marry the young Count, but I declined. Two days later, the Countess came to my house with two carriages, one of which was empty, and told my mother that her son was dying in desperation, and unless I would come and see him, his spirit could not ascend to Heaven. I went with my mother, guided by the Countess. I saw the young Count lying on the bed. His face was wrinkled, and his cheek-bones were unusually prominent. Since morning his head had lain motionless on the pillow. His eyes were cast on the floor. He had no power to raise his head. So I knelt down and saw him. He seemed extremely surprised. He looked at my face for a short time and gave a ghastly smile ; then tears fell from his eyes. Soon, with great difficulty, he stretched out his hand, and I grasped it in my palm. He was gone. My sympathy and sorrow were so strong that I felt as if my breast was filled with something. I was keenly conscious of my sin in so desperately disappointing the young Count.

" Since then I have determined not to marry anybody. In the ensuing winter my mother died. In the next spring I left Tokio and came here. That was three years ago."

The philosopher asked, " Why did you not marry the young Count ? "

The young lady said, with tears in her eyes, " I could not marry him."

" Why ? " said the philosopher.

" Because I have a peculiar inheritance from my ancestors," said the lady.

" What is your peculiar inheritance ? " said the philosopher.

" I cannot tell you anything about it," said the young lady, and she turned the subject of the conversation.

The clock struck twelve, and the fire was

gradually growing smaller. The young lady showed the philosopher to his bedroom. There he undressed and went to bed. It was pleasant in the silken sheets. Yet, however tired he was, he could not go to sleep, for his mind was occupied with his admiration of the lady. About one o'clock he lifted his head and saw her still sitting by the fireside.

He said to her, "Are you working?"

She answered, "No, sir."

"It is now very late; why don't you retire?" he said.

"Because I do not care to," she said.

The philosopher could not understand why the lady did not retire. He lifted his head again and looked all around the room, and studied the construction of the house. He found that there were only three rooms in the house, namely, kitchen, drawing-room and bed-room. He discovered the reason that she could not go to bed was because he was occupying the bed-chamber. He dressed, came out of the chamber and tried to persuade the young lady to go to bed and let him sleep by the fireside.

But she said, "You must keep the bed, for you are tired."

He answered, "But I have no courage to occupy the hostess' bed-chamber and drive her from it."

She said, "You are a philosopher, and I am a virgin. We have both withstood temptation. We have no inclination whatever to make any mistake. Let us sleep in the same chamber."

The philosopher agreed; she spread out a mattress for him, and they slept in the same chamber.

The next morning he found himself alone, lying on the moss, embracing his satchel.

Suiho K. Nakamura.

 DON'T:

II.

AT PRAYERS.

The negative form of these papers has been suggested by the fact that the things which one ought not to do are much less numerous than those which are permissible. Obviously, therefore, it was much more expedient, in preparing a code of morals, to specify the former, than the latter.

Don't cut, or else you will be unable to appreciate the following remarks.

Don't oversleep yourself and thereby lose your breakfast. Fasting and prayer are not now-a-days deemed a felicitous combination.

Don't curtail your toilet in order to reach prayers. The highest medical authorities pronounce an ulster and pair of boots quite insufficient both for health and for comfort.

Don't run from Memorial. It is undignified and unprofitable. The game isn't worth the candle.

Don't come in late; and don't on any account snicker at Freshmen who do. They don't know any better, and their unforseen appearance often diversifies agreeably an otherwise uninteresting service.

Don't read your paper in chapel. It is a breach of etiquette and a penal offence.

Don't criticise the performance of the choir boys. Like all other "infant industries," they should be protected without question or comment, and not left to stand on their own merits.

Don't attempt to sing yourself. The true gentleman is always distinguished by his consideration for others.

Don't turn up your coat collar, however cold it may be. The action, if observed by others, might divert their thought into secular channels.

Don't swear during the services; if you must, do it as unostentatiously as possible.

Don't petition to be excused on account of a cold, or a toothache, or malaria, or a sore throat. Where there is so large a field for the exercise of inventive genius there is no excuse for being conservative.

Don't attempt to exceed your allowance of prayer cuts. The faculty are singularly sensitive on this point, and resent any neglect as a personal offence.

Don't, however, blame the wrong parties. It is the overseers whom we have to thank for our exceptional ecclesiastical privileges. They went to prayers once; why shouldn't we?

Don't expect them to relent for some time to come, either. It is more blessed to give laws than to receive them.

Don't mention this matter of compulsory prayers outside of college, or at least, only in strict confidence. There are some people who have an idea that Harvard is the embodiment of progress, freedom and enlightenment. It would be a pity to disabuse them.

THE WRONG SCENT.

THE TRUE STORY OF A "MAUVAIS QUART D'HEURE."

A COLD shiver passed through the manly frame of Mr. Richard Randolph as he stood before an open box lying upon his centre-table and gazed with perturbed countenance at its contents. The hour was late; that is, it was about a quarter after six, which does not leave much time to spare when one is due at a dinner at seven and must dress and get into Boston from Cambridge within the hour. But it was not lack of leisure that disturbed our friend; in fact, he claimed on ordinary occasions to be able after long practice to perform his toilet and array himself in evening dress in the ridiculously short space of seven minutes; it was not lack of time, I repeat; it was something infinitely worse.

A short retrospection upon our part will be necessary in order fully to understand the situation. Lying upon his writing table was an invitation from a certain society leader of Boston, asking him to dinner upon this very evening, to meet a young and attractive damsel from Baltimore who happened to be visiting her. Richard had of course joyfully accepted, and then as carefully dismissed the whole thing from his mind with his usual nonchalance, only remembering his engagement a few moments before our story opens.

"It's lucky I happened to remember that dinner!" he remarked mentally as he endeavored to find his dress suit. "Mrs. Tyler would have black-listed me!" After a fruitless search in his chiffonier, which failed to reveal any signs of the aforesaid wedding garments, Mr. Randolph realized with a sinking heart that this being his first appearance in society for the season, since it was early in the autumn, his evening clothes were still carefully done up and put away in a box at the top of his closet. "They'll be ruinously creased! I should have sent them to the tailor's ages ago!" he ejaculated as he hastily carried the box out into his study and untied it. Then, as he removed the cover, his courage departed from him. There lay his poor dress suit, creased and crumpled, but that was not all; a strange and noisome odor rose from the box and filled the air,—an odor hated of all men,—a perfume like the mingling of checkerberry, kerosene, and Charles-River-flats-at-low-tide,— the odor of those inventions of Satan that women put in men's clothes to keep out the moths. The smell floated calmly up and tickled the nostrils of our wretched hero; it pervaded the room, hung about his head, and infected his person. He was paralyzed with horror. He remembered how in the spring he had told the "goody" to put away his dress clothes for him, and he now perceived with what thoroughness she had performed her work. Her very words on that occasion returned to his mind: "Dar now, Marse Randolph, Ise done fixed yo' clo's so dey ain't no kind ob insec' can tech 'em. Ise put in some ob my 'moth-balls'!" And he recollected that he had *thanked* her for her thoughtfulness.

He looked at his watch and found that it was just a quarter after six. At first he thought of giving the whole thing up and feigning sudden sickness; then he remembered the Baltimore girl and resolved to go at all hazards. First he subjected the clothes to a vigorous beating; then he hung them out of the window and let the autumn breezes fan them while he got ready to put them on. Nevertheless, after he had dressed, the clothes seemed as odoriferous as ever; the smell was absolutely fiendish. In desperation he seized an atomizer and deluged himself with vaporized cologne; but, strange to say, this seemed to have no effect — in fact, if anything, it appeared to put an edge on the already sufficiently penetrating perfume.

All the way into Boston he stood on the front platform with his coat off and tried to air himself, and as he felt the wind whistling through his coat-tails, while the car buzzed over Harvard Bridge, he began to feel more at ease. He thought of the beautiful girl from Baltimore, and reflected that he had been in worse predicaments than this before and lived through them.

Randolph arrived in good time and was introduced to the damsel for whom the dinner was given, and then followed a tête-à-tête, during which he shuddered and tried to look pleasant by turns. To his excited imagination the room seemed already full of the odor of "moth-balls,"

and he awaited with feverish anxiety the moment when it should be discovered by the rest of the company. He did not have long to wait. Mrs. Tyler shortly betrayed signs of nervousness.

"I wonder what is the matter with that lamp!" she exclaimed, glancing at a tall piano-lamp in the corner. Dick was on the *qui vive* in an instant.

"Let me fix it!" he suggested, endeavoring to get as near it as possible. The lamp proved to be in a fairly normal condition, however, and Mrs. Tyler apologized for the unpleasant odor, saying that the lamps were always getting out of order. Dick meanwhile mentally hugged himself and tried to turn the conversation.

The host, who was a trifle late, now entered, and after greeting his guests, turned to his wife with, "Er, Mary, what is this peculiar odor? Is there anything the matter with that lamp? Pray have it fixed as soon as possible."

During the confusion of going out to dinner, Richard congratulated himself upon his escape, yet quaked with apprehension at the thought of what later tortures he might have to endure. His uneasiness was not diminished when he found himself placed beside the girl from Baltimore.

There was a good deal of conversation at first, and our hero flattered himself that perhaps his trials were over, but the hope was in vain. A curious and peculiarly searching perfume began to make itself evident most unmistakably. Dick fairly perspired with agitation, being, as he was, absolutely helpless. He wished the house would catch fire, but this was improbable. The girl from Baltimore was seized with a fit of coughing, which did not improve matters. The hostess beckoned to the butler, who carefully examined all the gas jets and then shook his head dolefully at her from the pantry door. The guests moved a trifle uneasily. Conversation languished. The servant who passed Dick the soup turned away and stifled a cough. Someone started to tell an anecdote about General Grant and forgot what he was going to say, when he had reached his description of how "the General sniffed the powder-laden air," and stopped in a plainly embarrassed manner.

Presently there came a dead silence. Dick was racking his brains for a pretext to excuse himself, and had resolved to have an epileptic fit if something did not happen within two minutes. Fortunately or unfortunately, something did happen. He was seized with an uncontrollable desire to sneeze. He felt it coming and whipped out his handkerchief in time to save himself, but to his horror found that three little white balls had flown from his pocket at the same time, and were now rolling and bouncing about the table to the amusement of the startled company. For a moment there was silence, then followed an hilarious burst of laughter. Dick, seeing that all was over, laughed confusedly with the others, and resolving to throw himself upon the mercy of his hostess, got up and told the whole story of his sufferings and begged to be forgiven. His account of the matter was received with much mirth, and he was granted complete and final absolution by all present.

"But Mr. Randolph must write this up into a story," cried someone.

"Yes, yes!" resounded on all sides.

"But what shall I call it?" gasped Dick.

"Call it," murmured the girl from Baltimore, glancing slyly at our hero, "call it 'The Wrong Scent.'"

Arthur Cheney Train.

1897–1926

1897–1926

No age was brighter or more golden than this particular *Advocate* era; the magazine boasted the talent of many great men in a short span of time. This period would also define the *Advocate* as Harvard's premier, some say "precious," literary journal.

After the first issue of *The Crimson,* the *Advocate* gave higher priority to student writing. This new emphasis drew the talent of T.S. Eliot, Wallace Stevens, E.E. Cummings, Conrad Aiken, and Van Wyck Brooks. Their undergraduate writing rarely compared to their later work, yet there is an element of "Prufrock" in Eliot's "Spleen" and a measure of later sophistication in the early poems of all five men. What is fascinating is that the *Advocate* attracted writers of such caliber. Other noted contributors include Malcolm Cowley, Maxwell Perkins, Socialist John Reed, and humorist Robert Benchley.

Cummings and Eliot were unwitting participants in a favorite *Advocate* pastime, the parody issue. Represented as "O.O. Goings" and "T.S. Tellalot," the artists and their work were lampooned for the first of many times in the 1925 *Advocate* parody of *The Dial.* The parody tradition continued well into the 1930s, even though *The Dial* issue was banned by Cambridge authorities due to an "obscene" line drawing of a nude couple.

The turn of the century *Advocate* offered little opinion on local or national events (one of Wallace Stevens's editorials objected to the length of the Harvard cheer), but the *Advocate* of the 1920s published controversial editorials by Lloyd McKim Garrison and regular political supplements featuring commentary by Henry Cabot Lodge, Jr. and Harvard Law instructor Archibald MacLeish. On the editorial page or in the supplement, *Advocate* boards debated current issues with the confidence of a magazine no longer subject to faculty approval.

This new confidence was mirrored in the creation of Mother Advocate, a besotted, finger-wagging yet wise crone. "Mother" stumbled from her sanctum and onto the editorial page every few issues to take her children, *The Crimson* and *The Lampoon,* to task for bad taste or shoddy journalism. Her favorite targets included Harvard faculty, the tutorial system, and, of course, freshmen. The political supplement never appeared after the Depression, but Mother Advocate survived well into the 1950s.

SONNET.

THERE shines the morning star! Through the forlorn
    And silent spaces of cold heaven's height
    Pours the bright radiance of his kingly light,
Swinging in revery before the morn.
The flush and fall of many tides have worn
    Upon the coasts beneath him, in their flight
    From sea to sea; yet ever on the night
His clear and splendid visage is upborne.

Like this he pondered on the world's first day,
    Sweet Eden's flowers heavy with the dew;
And so he led bold Jason on his way
    Sparkling forever in the galley's foam;
And still he shone most perfect in the blue,
    All bright and lovely on the hosts of Rome.

W. Stevens.

IN THE DEAD OF NIGHT.

CAVANAUGH had been with us for less than a month; but almost from the beginning we had doubted his trustworthiness. He had an air of humility which he assumed more to ingratiate than to please. He was always at hand when you wanted him — but he was the sort of fellow that startled you when you ran up against him in the hall or the library, or wherever he chose to appear. He would seem startled too, would catch his breath apologetically, stutter a bit, be uneasy with his hands, bow and move off. Unconsciously you watched him and wondered whether he was really stupid or cunning, whether he had just drifted aimlessly across you, or whether you had come upon him prowling.

This went on until it became irritating. I told my father one day that I had found Cavanaugh in my room, gazing about in a sort of remote, speculative way. I had stood in the doorway watching him until his eyes fell on me.

Then he had collapsed.

"Well," I said, "Do you like it?" The sneer in my voice cut him, as though he were the sensitive object of some brutality on my part.

"I'm sure," he said, with a look of self-annihilation, "I'm sure, sir, this is quite unintentional. Your mother sent me to see if the windows were closed. It is about to rain, you must have noticed. And I was merely attracted by the things on your wall."

"And my desk?" I asked. He grew red in the face. Perhaps my accusation was a bit premature. I sent him off. He slipped down the stairs and as he turned on the landing I could see a malicious glare in his eyes.

The next day my father told him that we should need him no longer. He repressed a scowl and, frowning again, asked whether he might not stay that night: he had things to pack and arrangements to make. My father assented and the fellow edged off into the hall and then to the back of the house.

He was a man of all trades in a way. We had taken him at his own request — or rather entreaty, for he begged and promised until it was no longer possible to resist him. In the beginning he did everything under the sun; he knew how grass should be cut — and for such a sinister person so pastoral an occupation as grass-cutting seemed a bit unsuited; he could pick pears off the ground — we were living at Acton then; a little village of summer people — he could wash the carriages, curry the horses, — indeed, he was the proverbial Jack. But not until we saw him with his beard shaved off and his moustache trimmed to decency did we have the least idea that he could wait on table. We thought we might have to train him, but he knew all about it; he even helped the cook at times — getting in her way with the pepper-box, or taking the peas from her and shelling them while he popped every other one into his mouth.

All that, however, was over now. He was going in the morning. His first usefulness had diminished. The more indispensable he became the more advantage he had taken of us. From indifference he had turned to surliness, and then that suspicious, careless wandering about the house, that looking into rooms at every opportunity, and that closing of windows whenever a cloud or two came into the sky.

As we sat down to dinner that night we could hear him chaffing with Ann in the kitchen. He seemed to take his dismissal coolly enough; and we were rather glad of that, because he was just the sort of man to look cowed and pitiful and walk around with a hangdog look until one's mother or sister thought that it was too bad after all, and that the poor fellow should be given another chance. As a matter of fact, when he came in to us he actually did look the most aggrieved person in the world.

"Harry," said my mother to me when he had gone, "don't you think that Cavanaugh —"

"No, mother," I said emphatically, "I do not — decidedly!"

She knew what I meant.

We dragged along, — my sister Alice, Tom Chamberlain (who was visiting me), my two aunts (one Major Fann's widow, with most intolerable black ruffles to her sleeves; the other

unmarried, with long, bony wrists, shamelessly bare), myself, my father, and my mother. Major Fann's widow was bothersome, to say the least. She thought the oil for the salad a bit peculiar, but was willing to waive the point. Unhappily Bare Wrists agreed with her: she put a drop on her lips, and stretching her tongue forward slowly and fearfully, got just the least bit on the tip of it, and cried she had never tasted anything so curious in all her life. This set them all to tasting, — except myself, who did not care for salad, or oil either. Alice set matters to rights by going straight ahead.

When we had reached the end of the meal Cavanaugh brought in a tray covered with enormous apple dumplings — for Chamberlain, I supposed, at Alice's request. He put them down in front of Tom, who attacked the one nearest to him. Then, as if by an after thought, he offered to share them with the rest of us — insisted, in fact. Only mournful Mrs. Fann refused to have any. She said she had horrible nightmares whenever she ate pastry at night. Tom appealed to Cavanaugh, who explained that he had picked the apples himself. Finally Mrs. Fann forgot the other half of the dumpling, and said that, inasmuch as the apples were so fresh, and considering a great many other things (with a wink at Tom), she supposed she would sacrifice herself.

After dinner we walked out on the lawn, and chatted and fanned ourselves until bedtime. It was excessively hot. The moon had risen, and was on a level with the treetops in the east. The wind, when there was any, would come rolling heavily towards us with a suffocating and overwhelming closeness. It was very much like a profound atmospheric sea. The gusts passed over us like the dragging of deep billows. Suddenly Major Fann's widow, who had dropped into a doze, jumped to her feet with a piercing scream.

"My God," she cried, "We are sinking. The vessel is going down, oh my God, the water!"

My father leaped to her side and took hold of her, looking with fright into her face. He saw that she was asleep and began to shake her. She kept screaming for help until, in a moment, her eyes opened. She tottered, looked about her amazedly, then with a feeble exclamation sank back in her chair. Cavanaugh was called and brought some water. But Mrs. Fann had already recovered. She said she had been dreaming and, as we started indoors, she explained to my father what had happened. We were all somewhat upset, but I heard Tom whisper "Apple dumplings!" to Alice, with a nod of his head towards Mrs. Fann. I thought that Cavanaugh seemed amused.

Chamberlain and I were sharing the same room. We laughed a good deal at Mrs. Fann and then tried to drop asleep. I had eaten only a small part of my apple dumpling and so was far better off than poor Tom who had stuffed himself. He was unable to sleep for a long time. He tossed about and sighed and occasionally when he had pulled himself into some position that suited him he would look over at me to see if I was asleep and ask whether that was not curious — that outbreak of poor Mrs. Fann's. After a while I stopped answering him and he soon quieted down. He mumbled now and then in his sleep but beyond that made no noise.

It was so still about me that I longed for his interruptions. Twelve o'clock struck and Tom was sleeping more and more heavily. He drew long breaths as though he, like the object of his commiseration earlier in the evening were beginning to dream. There was not a sound in the house. Outside, the crickets had ceased their chirping; the wind was not stirring, and the limbs of the trees weighty with leaves, hung down drearily in the thin light. Not a single motion was made in the deep air. It was incredibly lonely.

Once I thought I heard a soft footfall in the hall beside my door and I listened. I thought of Cavanaugh and that led me to think of many other things so that before long the step in the hall had been forgotten. But I could not keep my attention away from the impenetrable silence. It pressed upon me with a pervasive sense of solitude. I lay without turning, my arms crossed under my head on the pillow, breathing quietly, listening to the murmurs that came to me.

A long peal of laughter rose from the hall. My heart stopped. The laugh rose again half-like a madman's; it rose and rose and then broke and fell breathless and gasping. I was seized with a chill and sweat came out on my forehead. I sat up in bed stiff with fright. Then I heard a low rumbling sound like the shaking of tin. My blood turned cold. I stared straight ahead of me waiting for what was to come next. Somebody was ascending the stairs dragging some noisy thing behind. But besides this I could hear two other people, one sobbing and moaning in a woman's voice, the other walking up and down the landing speaking aloud. I trembled for a moment and prepared to see what was the matter when Tom who had all this time been quietly sleeping by my side leaped up into the air with a most blood curdling shriek. My hair rose. I plunged out of bed toward the door and opened it — and ran pell-mell into Mrs. Fann, who with her hands on her lips was pacing to and fro begging to be folded.

"Oh" she cried wringing her hands "will no one fold a poor lamp-shade? Fold me — fold me — and put me away." I stared at her dully. The rattling on the stairs was commencing again. I looked over the banister and saw my maiden aunt sitting in a portable tub tobogganing full tilt toward my father who stood some five steps from the bottom haranguing — Cavanaugh on the Phillipine question. My aunt was waving an umbrella and mumbling "Jingle Bells" to herself; her hair was tied up in neat little papers and her night gown was wonderful with lace. She was propelling herself nearer and nearer to my father who in a pair of gaudy pajamas and still more gaudy blouse was delivering a fiery oration. Cavanaugh crouched at his feet in a ring of scattered cream pitchers, sugar-jars, knives and forks.

Meanwhile Mrs. Fann and Tom Chamberlain had made acquaintance in my room. Tom was whooping and shouting around her like a mad-man. She had sudsided somewhat and with the tears rolling down her cheeks begged him to fold her and put her away. My stupefaction was greatest when I beheld my sister Alice come from her room in a walking cape and bonnet.

She opened a parasol and stood watching my aunt and her tin tub.

"How far is it Tom," she said, "from — how far from — far from — how far is it — now Tom do tell me."

With a final bounce in her descent my aunt came under my father's legs and the poor man sat in her lap. They slid to the bottom of the stairs, she with her interminable "Jingle Bells" droning up between the vehemence of my father's monologue on "the hemp-ports, commercial advantage, and human nature."

Cavanaugh had lost his wits completely and was an easy captive. I took him with all his booty and understood at once the mystery of the salad oil and the apple dumplings. Indeed, I rather think Cavanaugh welcomed me. He had drugged us — or had attempted to — but had made some miscalculation in his plans, so that when he thought we should all be soundly sleeping he found us ranting and tobogganing about his ears.

My father was the first to come to his senses. He was nervous and weak for a moment and went on talking to himself even after he was awake. In the end he became cool and I had soon explained the madness about him. I handed Cavanaugh over to him and taking my aunt in my arms carried her upstairs. Her sister, Mrs. Fann was quiet except for a sob now and then. Tom was running around her but had ceased shouting. I gave my aunt over to my mother and shut my sister up in her own room until she had either found out the distance or had got awake.

The uproar had, of course, attracted attention. Our neighbor, Price, was knocking at the door and when it was opened Cavanaugh was passed into his charge. My father then went upstairs to help Mrs. Fann and I went after him to wrestle with Tom Chamberlain. When we entered the room we found the two standing in the middle of the floor gazing at each other in the moonlight trying to solve the problem for themselves. They were half awake. When she saw us Mrs. Fann was on the point of screaming but my father raised his hand.

"Apple dumplings," groaned Tom.

"Oh !" exclaimed Mrs. Fann.

"Apple dumplings," said Tom in a voice that was alsolutely sepulchral — "Apple dumplings, apple dumplings, apple dumplings !" Then he dived into bed and turned toward the wall. He heard Alice speaking his name but I again explained. He seemed rather pleased.

My father led Mrs. Fann out into the hall where she was joined by the trembling toboggan-ist. They started for their room together — my mother went to my sister, and after a time the house grew still again. Cavanaugh was in safe hands and there was nothing more to fear. Only at long intervals I could hear one of my aunts walking up and down her room slowly and meditatively. I remember wondering whether it was the lamp shade — or the other.

W. Stevens.

SONNET.

LO, even as I passed beside the booth
   Of roses, and beheld them brightly twine
To damask heights, taking them as a sign
Of my own self still unconcerned with truth ;
Even as I held up in hands uncouth
And drained with joy the golden-bodied wine,
Deeming it half-unworthy, half divine,
From out the sweet-rimmed goblet of my youth.

Even in that pure hour I heard the tone
Of grievous music stir in memory,
Telling me of the time already flown
From my first youth. It sounded like the rise
Of distant echo from dead melody,
Soft as a song heard far in Paradise.

WALLACE STEVENS

STREET SONGS.

I.

The Pigeons.

OVER the houses and into the sky
 And into the dazzling light,
Long hosts of fluttering pigeons fly
 Out of the blackened night,
Over the houses and into the sky
 On glistening wings of white.

Over the city and into the blue
 From ledge and tower and dome,
They rise and turn and turn anew,
 And like fresh clouds they roam,
Over the city and into the blue
 And into their airy home.

II.

The Beggar.

Yet in this morn there is a darkest night,
Where no feet dance or sweet birds ever rise,
Where fancy is a thing that soothes — and lies,
And leads on with mirages of light.
I speak of her who sits within plain sight
Upon the steps of yon cathedral. Skies
Are naught to her; and life a lord that buys
And sells life, whether sad, or dark, or bright.

The carvings and beauty of the throne
Where she is sitting, she doth meanly use
To win you and appeal. All rag and bone
She asks with her dry, withered hand a dreg
Of the world's riches. If she doth abuse
The place, pass on. It is a place to beg.

III.

Statuary.

The windy morn has set their feet to dancing —
 Young Dian and Apollo on the curb,
The pavement with their slender forms is glancing,
 No clatter doth their gaiety disturb.

No eyes are ever blind enough to shun them,
 Men wonder what their jubilance can be,
No passer-by but turns to look upon them —
 Then goes his way with all his fancy free.

IV.

The Minstrel.

The streets lead out into a mist
 Of daisies and of daffodils —
A world of green and amethyst,
 Of seas and of uplifted hills.

There bird-songs are not lost in eaves,
 Nor beaten down by cart and car,
But drifting sweetly through the leaves,
 They die upon the fields afar.

Nor is the wind a broken thing
 That faints within hot prison cells,
But rises on a silver wing
 From out among the heather bells.

W. Stevens.

THE HARVARD
Advocate

E·P·PERRIN·

PRICE, 15 CTS.

BALLADE OF THE PINK PARASOL.

I PRAY thee where is the old-time wig,
　　And where is the lofty hat?
Where is the maid on the road in her gig,
　　And where is the fire-side cat?
　　Never was sight more fair than that,
Outshining, outreaching them all,
　　There in the night where lovers sat —
But where is the pink parasol?

Where in the pack is the dark spadille
　　With scent of lavender sweet,
That never was held in the mad quadrille.
　　And where are the slippered feet?
Ah! we'd have given a pound to meet
　　The card that wrought our fall,
The card none other of all could beat —
　　But where is the pink parasol?

Where is the roll of the old calash,
　　And the jog of the light sedan?
Whence Chloe's diamond brooch would flash
　　And conquer poor peeping man.
Answer me, where is the painted fan
　　And the candles bright on the wall;
Where is the coat of yellow and tan —
　　But where is the pink parasol?

Prince, these baubles are far away,
　　In the ruin of palace and hall,
Made dark by the shadow of yesterday —
　　But where is the pink parasol?

WALLACE STEVENS

SONG.

SHE loves me or loves me not,
    What care I ? —
The depth of the fields is just as sweet,
    And sweet the sky.

She loves me or she loves me not,
    Is that to die ? —
The green of the woods is just as fair,
    And fair the sky.

W. Stevens.

The Cartoonist.

IF it had not been for McFedries you would never have heard of the Times, for outside our own city it is by our cartoons alone that we are known. Mr. Crary's editorials are admirable, to be sure, and express the loftiest of Republican political ideals, but it is only our caricatures which appear in the back of eminent monthlies, and even find their way across the ocean, and reappear as clumsy wood-cut epitomes of American news.

A born cartoonist is McFedries; he could no more draw and not satirize than he could talk without looking at you with his faint puzzle of a smile.

The very houses and trees in his backgrounds are caricatures. Most of the time McFedries enjoys his work, but he finds it dull during the local political campaigns. He told me once, in confidence, that he hardly knew the difference between our party and the Democrats. Not that he cared much about it, for, as his childlike questioning mind could never settle questions, he preferred not to attempt them, and was quite, innocent of convictions.

"I don't think I'm a good party man, Mr. Schilling," he once said to me, "for whenever I draw a picture for our side — pop! my mind jumps the fence, and there I am, drawing one for them. I don't see how a man can be like Mr. Crary — so sure of things. Here's one for the other side that I did yesterday, an answer to the one that came out to-day; but the joke of it is, this one is going to be published."

"Yes," he resumed, for I had made a gesture of remonstrance, "you see Duncan, on the 'News' is all in a mess, and can't think them up. His wife's sick and there's an awful row on in the family, so he can't think of anything funny to save him. I told him I had a lot of stuff he might fix over, and gave him a handful with one finished sketch of old Thompson sliding off the Republican band-wagon. That was a fine one, and I've always regretted that it was wasted."

"But, Mac," I objected, "surely you'll keep quiet about this?"

"Why should I keep it quiet?" There was a tinge of resentment in the question, so I said that I hoped Mr. Crary would not hear about it.

The Hon. Edgar M. Crary is our editor-in-chief, a man unswerving in his adherence to impossibly high ideals, unmovable in his resolves, and blind to the mistakes of the republican party, of which he is a prominent member. We said he looked like George Washington, and we understood how the men at Valley Forge stood by the man that they feared as well as venerated. I have seen Mr. Crary deal with every sort of man from clerical reformers, whom he overtopped in virtue, to junketing ward-heelers, whom he despised but, not once have I seen the slightest indication that with him, policy could outweigh principle.

He had a lofty disdain of the aims of most newspaper men, but I think he had this one weakness — that he was vain over the respect and enmities which his severe morality had won him. I remember once, when a prominent politician threatened to take away the party printing from us, how he looked very hard at him, and said slowly, "You may ruin the paper, sir. I will not print what I must believe is a falsehood." There was a little unnecessary parade in it, for there could be no question of "ruining" the paper; but Mr. Crary was pleased, and I could see that he carried himself more graciously for several days. For all that, he was as sincere in his virtue as Cato, and not, I believe, more ostentatious.

And of course he found out about Mac's cartoons; somebody happening in at the office joked with him about it; but it was no jest to him, and when the man left, he called for Mac.

When Mac came in and stood beside the big desk, there was a moment of solemn stillness, and then Mr. Crary said, very softly:

"Mr. McFedries, I have had to answer to a serious charge against you. I ask you this question only that I may verify my own statements. Did any of your work occur in the News?"

Mac, to whom the awfulness in Mr. Crary's voice was incomprehensible, hesitated a moment in his surprise, then said, simply, "Why, yes sir, I did the pictures."

"Not a word of explanation," said Mr. Crary sternly, though Mac had attempted none. "You knew the paper, sir; you pretended loyalty to the party. Mr. McFedries, when they told me, I would not credit the story. I dismissed the thought through my belief in you, but you have betrayed the party, sir," he thundered, "you have betrayed the party, and you have dishonored the paper. You shall leave it, and an honorable man shall take your place."

Mac flushed crimson at the word, for he was not without his code, though it differed from Mr. Crary's. He stood still, angry and despairing, for a moment, then he must have. seen another side of it, for a faint smile was tugging at the corner of his mouth as he turned to the office door.

Samuel Schilling.

THE HARVARD
ADVOCATE.

VOL. LXXVI.   CAMBRIDGE, MASS., DECEMBER 18, 1903.   No 5.

THE ADVOCATE *is published fortnightly during the College Year. Terms, $2.50 a year,* IN ADVANCE. *Single copies, 15 cents. For sale in Cambridge at Amee's and Thurston's. In Boston, at Damrell, Upham & Co.'s, cor. School and Washington Streets.*

All communications, contributions and subscriptions should be sent to the HARVARD ADVOCATE, *The Harvard Union, Cambridge.*

Office hours:

Literary,—Monday, Tuesday, Wednesday, Thursday and Friday, 1.30 to 2.30 p. m.

Business,—Tuesdays and Fridays, 7 to 7.30 p. m.

Subscribers who do not receive their numbers will confer a favor by notifying the Business Manager.

Printed by Edward W. Wheeler, Cambridge, Mass.

WHEN a college paper has attained the venerable age of the ADVOCATE, it may lay aside the false sensitiveness of matrons on the question of age. A fortieth anniversary is much like a golden wedding — age has become a matter of pride. Lampy, it is true, has ventured some dark hints, as to the application of Dr. Ostler's theory. So it might be well, to remind Lampy of the South American tribes which have a practise of murdering infants who exhibit symptoms of idiocy. It is needless to point out that Lampy's public has been kinder than the South American mother.

✗ ✗ ✗

"LIVES there a man with soul so dead" as to be serious or practical at this time of year? No; nor a woman either; particularly not so cheery a dame as MOTHER ADVOCATE.

The honored lady, when we last saw her, was busily engaged in her Christmas shopping, which she went about in as merry and whole hearted a fashion as one would care to see.

When we first came upon her she was at the book-counter, carefully directing a clerk how to wrap up a large illustrated Bible. "That's for a young friend of mine out in Cambridge," she explained. "*Lampie* is his name; a nice lad. But lately he has been behaving rather badly, so I'm going to give him this for Christmas. I heard him say things the other day — about a young lady — a Miss Triton, I think — Oh, they were shocking." She tried hard to frown; but the recollection of something seemed to suddenly come over her, and if such a thing can be said of so dignified a person, she giggled.

In a few moments we met her again at another counter. "There that's for the *Crimson*," she said, pointing to a box full of strange bits of metal. It's patent type; you cannot set it up wrong if you try. I think it's lovely, don't you? I'd like to keep it myself. But that wouldn't be nice, buying myself a Christmas present, would it?

"Now you come over here with me and help me choose something for the *Monthly*," she said. "It must be something very fine, for they have a high standard."

Our humble suggestion of a rhyming dictionary was not accepted. "They've got one; I've borrowed it myself," she objected. "No, I think a waste paper basket would be better; — they must throw away such a *lot* of things.

"Well, good-bye," she said finally, "I'm going across the street to a hardware store to buy something nice for the College Office. A Merry Christmas to you."

THE HARVARD
ADVOCATE

VOL. LXXXI   CAMBRIDGE, MASS., FEBRUARY 19, 1906   No. 1

Entered at Boston Post Office as second-class mail matter

PRESENTS

THE SHAMPOON

In the mercenarily musical medley

"It Pays To Advertise"

Twenty weeks in New York
Thirty years in Sing Sing

CAST OFF CHARACTERS

All Stars and Stripes

COSTUMES	By KEEZER
FIRE APPARATUS	By THE COLLEGE OFFICE
WIGS	By LA FLAMME
MUSIC	BY GOSH

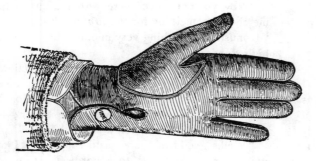

SHAMPY's Glad Hand To Advertisers.

There once was a young alligator
Who always perused Walter Pater
   He said, "It is deep,
   And productive of sleep,
And I fear I shall pay for it later."

1 G.—Why don't you swear off swearing
     off swearing?
3 M.—Can't. I just swore off swearing
     off swearing off.

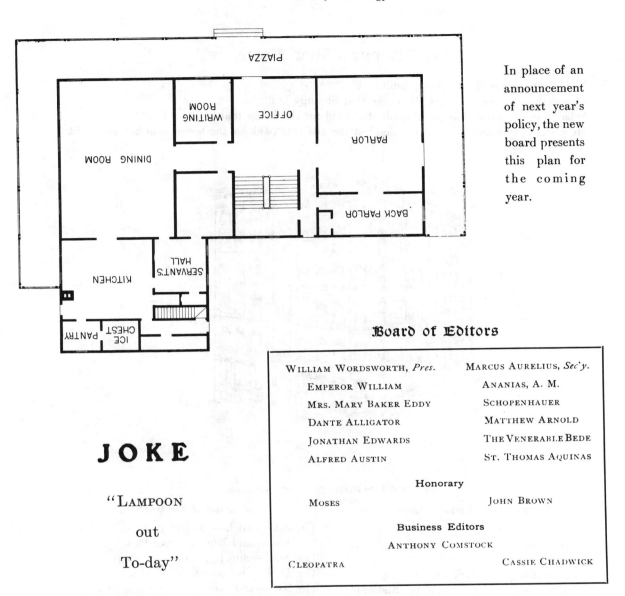

In place of an announcement of next year's policy, the new board presents this plan for the coming year.

JOKE

"LAMPOON

out

To-day"

Board of Editors

WILLIAM WORDSWORTH, *Pres.*   MARCUS AURELIUS, *Sec'y.*

EMPEROR WILLIAM   ANANIAS, A. M.

MRS. MARY BAKER EDDY   SCHOPENHAUER

DANTE ALLIGATOR   MATTHEW ARNOLD

JONATHAN EDWARDS   THE VENERABLE BEDE

ALFRED AUSTIN   ST. THOMAS AQUINAS

Honorary

MOSES   JOHN BROWN

Business Editors

ANTHONY COMSTOCK

CLEOPATRA   CASSIE CHADWICK

SHAMPY feels, by the way, that some apology is due his readers for the belayed appearance of this number. To be perfectly open about it, the printer, who was asked to one of the Shampoon's tri-weekly dinners, returned to Cambridge at four in the morning and pi ied the number. So Shampy decided to appear in the present bad form rather than stain a record hithertoo spotless, and disappoint his readers by not coming out on time, as usual.

Veritas est periculum.

Shampy's New Home.

This is the house that Shampy built.
It was the ads that paid for the house that Shampy built.
What was the game that got the ads that paid for the house that Shampy built?
Here you may learn of the game that got the ads that paid for the house that Shampy built.

SHAMPY'S SCHOOL OF ADVERTISING.

Six Stories:—Among others:

Circulation Story—a tall one.

Subscription Story—a long one.

Joke Story—a short one.

SHAMPY—his tory—a dark one.

Floors inlaid with gold—taken up and stored in safe every night.

Bar-room in law department. All packages must be opened and examined before you leave the building.

Doors open inward: exits barred.

Heated by hot air: pipes run from Sever Hall.

New Sponger Elevators: if you have any propositions, come in and we'll take you up, or come up and we'll take you in.

Courses of Destruction.

The Ad—and how to add it.

The Lad—and how to strike him.

The Mad—and how to soothe them.

The Dad—and how to work him.

The Sad—and how to cheer them.

The Glad—and how to fleece them.

Elective Courses.

Fancy Jiu-Jitsu, or how to take a throwdown.

Methods of Pursuit and Escape. Taught by Crimson healers.

Mental arithmetic in connection with circulation figures.

Nemo est decorum.

On Getting Up in the Morning.

EVER since my early school days, when, as a result of tardiness, I memorized a considerable portion of the United States Constitution, I have made a careful study of the different methods of getting up in the morning. These methods, though they have accumulated through the ages, have none of them, as yet, completely solved the problem, nor can I say that I have done so myself; however, since it has been my life study, so to speak, and since I have made certain advances, which, so far as I can ascertain, are original, I feel that it is my duty to lay them before the public. I therefore venture to offer these suggestions with the sincere hope that they may be of some use to my fellow-students, and particularly to Freshmen, or at least that they may direct some great mind into the proper channel for removing so great a source of unhappiness.

Before I go any further, I wish it to be distinctly understood that I am not preaching early rising. Whether it is a good thing or not is not for me to state. I have heard it said that it is a positive evil, for when a man does rise early he becomes so conceited, so puffed up with pride, that for the day at least he can do nothing but contemplate his own virtue. The inspiration of this essay, if such I may call it, is the unaccountable lack of consideration on the part of the college authorities. They enforce attendance, and then assign all those courses in which a gentleman can hope to attain the grade of C at such ridiculous hours as nine or ten. How illogical! How tyrannical! How — but I forget my subject.

The first scheme which I have found of great help is a very ingenious one, and I must, I regret to say, renounce all claims to its origin. Nor can I mention the name of its inventor, for, though he deserves great credit, he is too modest to allow publicity. His method was this: he always slept with the bedroom shades down, and before retiring, carefully placed a pair of old shoes upon a table by his bed. When he awoke in the morning he would reach out, take a shoe from the table and hurl it at the window. The sudden jerk which the blow of the shoe would give the shade caused the latter to fly up with a bang. The same performance was used with the same effect upon the other window. The sudden rush of light makes sleep impossible to unaccustomed eyes, and the exercise involved does much to facilitate the effort of getting out of bed.

Certain questions immediately arise in one's mind when first contemplating this plan.

"Wouldn't it break the window?" one might ask, or "Wouldn't it be as hard to move about and get the shoes as to get out of bed?"

As to the last question, my friend tells me (and I have since proved the truth of his word by experience) that you become so interested in your development as a shot, that you actually look forward to the hour when another opportunity will arrive to try your skill. My friend also says that such proficiency is acquired with constant practice that with but two motions of the arm, one in raising the boot, the other in swinging it toward the window, success almost invariably results. In his enthusiasm, he even asserts that one becomes so exasperated by a failure that pillows follow shoes, and that when all ammunition within reach has been exhausted, he himself has risen on more than one occasion, and procuring articles from a distance, persisted in his bombardment until success crowned his efforts. But my friend is more ambitious than the average.

Now in regard to the breaking of windows — of course that sometimes happens in the case of beginners, but this risk merely adds zest to the enterprise, and also makes the desired results more certain. For if the morning is cold, the ensuing fall in temperature makes a longer sojourn in bed out of the question.

The beauty of this method lies in the fact that you experience none of the disgust with self which you ordinarily feel, and sometimes to an intense degree, when you rise merely because you resolved to do so the night before. On more than one occasion I have been informed by my friends that I am not reasonable. It has even happened, especially in connection with money matters, that my own family has made this assertion. But never have I been more fully convinced of my own unreasonableness than when on a cold dreary morning I have dragged myself out of bed for no other reason than because I had a "nine o'clock" and had taken it into my head the night before that there lay my duty. One cannot escape this loss of respect for one's own intelligence by the ordinary tricks of counting ten and jumping, or by telling a friend to drag you out of bed. There is this advantage in the counting method, however. Make the number 25 or 50, and start to count when you awake; then if you do fall asleep before the fatal point is reached, it certainly is not your fault, and knowing that you would have jumped if nature had not intervened, you avoid the reproaches of Conscience. Conscience, the hardest of mistresses! to whom those of us who escape the bondage of tobacco (or some such paltry vice) are slaves! For we are all slaves to one thing or another, and it is a question in my mind if she is not the least desirable mistress of all.

In reading over what I have written up to this point with especial reference to the shoe experiment, an episode arises in my mind which is related to my subject and illustrates the change of view-point which one takes in the morning as contrasted to that which one holds at night.

I have a friend, whom I much admire for a certain rare quality he possesses; that of arguing every question fairly and squarely with his conscience before he decides to do the thing he wants to do. Sometimes he feels that he is wrong and yields to Conscience, especially when necessity takes Conscience's part, and he is forced to acknowledge that their combined arguments are forcible. Generally speaking, however, he gains his point, for such is his power of reasoning that Conscience, while perhaps not quite persuaded — for she is a stubborn wench — at least lowers her voice to a whisper, audible only from time to time; and even in the event of her victory, he always forces her into some concessions. Some men obey this mistress absolutely, are her abject slaves. Others break away from her, ignoring her reproaches for the time, only to receive

their lashes later. My friend, as you see, belongs to neither of these classes.

One evening I entered his room, and remarking that I had not been in town for some time, proposed the theatre. It seems that he had been in on the previous night and in consequence had cut his nine o'clock. He could not go, he said, for the reason that he had some work which must be done by ten the next morning. Did I write "he said"? It was not he who spoke, it was Conscience. Immediately his native spirit of independence asserted itself. He argued eloquently. Well! he could get up early the next morning. He could always work better in the early morning anyhow, he said,— I think Conscience here embarrassed him with the question "What makes you think so." He had just borrowed a book which would make his work twice as easy, he continued. Still Conscience was obdurate. Suddenly he sprang from his chair and from a drawer, produced a beautiful clock. It would ring until you got up and stopped it, he explained. Before so tangible an argument Conscience could hold out no longer. We went in town.

Jim, my friend, was not feeling very well when we returned, but he was still enthusiastic over his early morning plan. His roommate was away and we were to sleep in the same room. Just before retiring I said, "Jim, I'll bet you five dollars you don't get up at six to-morrow."

"I'll bet you I do," said he, and winding his clock, he placed it on the sill of the open window.

The next thing I knew there was a terrible hubbub. I thought very hard and remembered where I was, and recalled the alarm clock and the wager. I opened my eyes to see what effect the uproar would have on Jim. With a sort of cross between a grunt and a groan he rolled over and eyed the thing on the window-sill in much the manner in which I should imagine one would watch an infernal machine in operation, knowing that escape was impossible. Next he turned his eyes upon me, but I was feigning sleep. The clock had been going for a good ten minutes I should say, and was just getting into full swing. I opened my eyes again cautiously, and then I saw a sight I would not have missed for worlds. Jim was reaching out of bed and feeling about the floor. Now he raised his arm, holding a slipper in his hand, and still lying on his back, sent it flying towards the window. The weapon missed the clock by a foot or two. Jim lay still for a moment, an expression of great disappointment upon his face.

The alarm-clock seemed to be laughing at him, catching its breath every second, and going on in short spurts. Again Jim felt about the floor and procured a second slipper. This time he raised himself on his elbow, took steady aim and sent it spinning straight as a die. The clock caught the blow right in the center. There was a crash and down it went, but game to the last, ringing away until it reached the pavement three stories below. I am convinced that nothing short of three stories and an asphalt pavement would have stopped that instrument of torture.

With the final crash and death rattle of the poor clock, which had met its fate only in doing its duty, Jim fell back on his pillow, a contented man. Then he must have remembered me: perhaps he heard me laugh. At all events he looked in my direction suspiciously. I was still as a mouse, watching through my half closed eyes. However, he raised himself, observed me doubtfully, and then got slowly out of bed and went into the next room.

When Jim returned in a quarter of an hour looking fresh and pink after his bath, he asked me, eyeing me narrowly, "How about that bet?"

I looked him full in the face and, "It will just about buy you another clock and I'd gladly pay ten to see it over again," I said, and then we laughed and laughed until I was so thoroughly awake that I got up myself.

Now before I bring this essay to a close, I wish to say a few words which may benefit Freshmen. In my opinion the officers of the University are open to censure for taking no steps towards informing fellows who have just entered college of facts which everyone must know sooner or later. Some of these things are so closely connected with my subject that I take the liberty of recording them here.

In the first place, the shortest route across the Yard by actual measurement, from all points east of Holyoke Street lies to the east of Gore Hall and past Sever. In case there is snow upon the ground, it is shorter to go through the hall of Memorial, but under all ordinary circumstances, the path around the west end of that building is preferable for reaching the New Lecture Hall. Secondly, taking the time of each maid in the Oak Grove and Quincy, and getting an average on the service of boiled eggs, coffee and toast for both restaurants, I find that the former is faster by four minutes and thirty-three seconds. However, the tall blonde in the Quincy, who takes charge of the west counter, at the end nearest the street, holds the individual record; beating the best waitress in the Oak Grove by ten and two-fifths seconds on the average per week. Another point in favor of the Quincy is that the coffee there cools faster than that of the Oak Grove, whether through some intrinsic quality of its own, or some superiority in the cookery, I am ashamed to say I have failed to ascertain.

There are many other points which should be made familiar to all undergraduates, but I have neither time nor space to give them here. In conclusion I merely add, in hopes that my suggestion may have some effect, that the University might furnish an information bureau where men could ascertain such valuable facts as I have just mentioned. In case they persist in their gross neglect, I suggest that some outsider apprise himself of such facts, and establish a bureau, and he might, at the same time find it advantageous to draw up ideal schedules to order, in accordance with the requirements of his patrons. I feel certain that such a venture would prove prosperous even though the charge were trifling. In the absence of any such institution, having, as I have already said, made a thorough study of these questions, I will put myself at the disposal of any who will send their questions to me through the mail. enclosing their addresses and stamps.

Maxwell E. Perkins.

THE HARVARD ADVOCATE

FOOTBALL·NUMBER
HARVARD'S 1911 RECORD
By CAPTAIN R. T. FISHER

Circe's Palace

Around her fountain which flows
With the voice of men in pain,
Are flowers that no man knows.
Their petals are fanged and red
With hideous streak and stain;
They sprang from the limbs of the dead.
We shall not come here again.

Panthers rise from their lairs
In the forest which thickens below,
Along the garden stairs
The sluggish python lies;
The peacocks walk, stately and slow,
And they look at us with the eyes
Of men whom we knew long ago.

T. S. Eliot

Song

The flowers I sent thee when the dew
    Was trembling on the vine
Were withered ere the wild bee flew
    To suck the eglantine.
But let us haste to pluck anew
    Nor mourn to see them pine,
And though the flowers of life be few
    Yet let them be divine.

If space and time, as sages say
    Are things that cannot be,
The fly that lives a single day
    Has lived as long as we.
But let us live while yet we may,
    While love and life are free,
For time is time, and runs away,
    Though sages disagree.

T. S. Eliot

Song

When we came home across the hill
　　No leaves were fallen from the trees;
　　The gentle fingers of the breeze
Had torn no quivering cobweb down.

The hedgerow bloomed with flowers still
　　No withered petals lay beneath;
　　But the wild roses in your wreath
Were faded, and the leaves were brown.

T.S. ELIOT

Before Morning

While all the East was weaving red with gray,
The flowers at the window turned toward dawn,
Petal on petal, waiting for the day,
Fresh flowers, withered flowers, flowers of dawn.

This morning's flowers and flowers of yesterday
Their fragrance drifts across the room at dawn,
Fragrance of bloom and fragrance of decay,
Fresh flowers, withered flowers, flowers of dawn.

T.S. ELIOT

The West.

GULLS to their home on the aged rock
　　Wheeling athwart the spray,
Thrill of the wind from the isles of Ind
　　In the heart of the dying day.

Dreams in the depths of the solemn pines
　　Ancient before our birth,
Hearing the speech of the plains that reach
　　To the ends of the happy earth.

Out of the years that have passed away
　　Out of the days to be,
Night brings the pang of the salt air's tang
　　And the call of the West to me.

J. S. Reed.

Last Chapter of "Smith's Decline and Fall of the World."

IT is evident to the reader of my previous chapter that any life on the earth was now only a question of days. Not only had its circular form become egg-shaped, but this violent contortion had erected vast toppling mountains, seven times higher than the Himalayas, and, from their proximity to the sun, white-hot and molten on the summits. Prodigious streams of blazing lava were rushing hither and thither, at a speed of some twenty miles a minute, and hissing like a million cobras. The Pacific Ocean could be spanned and scanned with the naked eye, being scarcely broader than a mill-pond, and all about it for thousands of miles its bed was a vile seething mass of slime. Bodies of vast sea-monsters lay festering among the stagnant weeds, many of them still breathing, ponderously flapping their ulcerous gills, gasping and squirming.

No better test for my aero-car could be conceived. Thanks to the efficient service of the Interplanet Wireless Company, I was able to keep in constant touch with Mars; my own appliances resisted the force of gravitation, and

enabled me to remain poised at a distance of half a mile over any spot which demanded my investigation, while my air-tank supplied me with our delicious home-atmosphere, and my radium window-plates kept out the rank vapors and the insufferable heat. Thus I remained for three weeks pursuing my observation in perfect safety.

On the tenth day I passed over the wide valley which I had formerly known as the English Channel, and pushed southward along the coast of Spain. It occurred to me that, with the ocean completely dried up, I might easily find the lost continent of Atlantis. I had always suspected the Azores of being its surviving peaks, and accordingly steered in that direction. Towards evening the land beginning to rise, I found it necessary to steer violently upward in order to avoid precipitating myself into the mud-hills which stood before me. The sun, which had gained so enormously in size that seven fissures were visible upon it, sank in the west. The ground beneath me now rose violently, so that it was necessary for me to pursue my course upward at an angle of seventeen degrees, and as the moon rose, I discovered myself at the foot of a steep ascent which sloped off indefinitely into the sky. At this point I threw out all my extra side-flaps and parachutes and decided to poise for the night. My sleep was disturbed at intervals by a jarring of the basket in which I lay, caused by the perpetual whir of the huge monsters below whose coiling and leaping produced a constant vibration in the air without.

At daybreak I continued my upward progress and towards noon, after rising perpendicularly for two or three miles, the mountain suddenly broke off into a wide plateau, which I recognized instantly from its shape as the island of Teceira. I ascended twenty or thirty miles to gain a bird's-eye view of the Azores, and to ascertain their relation to the rest of the continent. The islands were connected at a distance of not half a mile below the former water-line, and above this they defined themselves as upon a clay map. I approached the village of Angra, to find that the vast cathedral had melted like a candy house, its marvellous mosaics and colored marbles running in streams through the neighboring streets. In two hours I had crossed the entire archipelago. To the west for a thousand miles lay the continent of Atlantis, a flat stretch covered to the horizon in every direction with a layer many rods deep of decayed yellow sea-plants, swarming with life, now wilted and sickly from exposure to the sun. I dropped to within a hundred yards of the surface in order to watch two monstrous clams; when suddenly an unusual jolting of my car caused me to look around. Almost upright to the sky, towering like a water-spout, a vast snake was bearing towards me, his tail swishing along in the slime and weeds, his upper parts propelled by flaps or fins which supported him in the air. His long, sleek, hose-like body glistened, and in his mane or hair streamers of sea-weed were fluttering. I had but a second. Turning on the recoil-valve, my car darted upwards like an arrow, as I felt his hair brush against my hanging basket below. As I continued my flight I saw the huge tower topple, and his whole length fell with a violent splash, cutting the weeds like a sword,

and gradually sinking through with a suction on both sides which stirred the mire for many acres.

Towards evening I discerned a distant mountain to the northwest and turning my course in that direction came just at dark upon what appeared to be a vast pyramid. The rise of the moon confirmed this conjecture. It was after the model of the pyramids of Egypt, though many times larger — quite regular in shape, and covered with barnacles of the size of a church spire. I was thus enabled not only to confirm my notions of the lost continent, but to reach rather definite conclusions as to the nature of its civilization.

During the following days, there was a perceptible change in the condition of the earth. The molten state was apparently drying and it was evident that in a few days the entire planet would be one great burnt-out cinder. On the sixteenth day I was in the neighborhood of the South Pole. The snow having entirely melted, another great continent was exposed, which ran for two thousand miles across the pole and up on the other side from Franklin's Land. Almost exactly over the pole were a number of caves or long tunnels which ran into the ground. As I watched one with not unnatural curiosity, I saw a man, a human being, crawl out slowly, followed by a woman. They were scorched quite black and seemed to have lost all power of locomotion. I approached them with the idea of rescue, but seeing them diseased beyond any hope of recovery and moreover in a contagious state, I thought it best in the interests of science to keep myself safe. In this distraction, I had not noticed that a sort of gray pallor was coming over the entire surface of the earth. The man saw it too, for he cried out "Just as I said!" and the woman fell down and worshipped him — and I am convinced that these were the last words spoken on earth. The skeleton of an echo rattled through the cinder hills, just as vast fissures opened everywhere; and suddenly in absolute silence the whole earth gave way. It shot from me with inconceivable speed, revealing more and more of itself, until in an instant I saw the globe spinning off like a cannon ball down the infinite void.

V. W. B.

The Sea-Gull

Wet with the stinging spray he skims the deep,
A livid gleam of life, and scans afar
Where the great breakers pound across the bar,
Beneath the headlands where his nestlings sleep.
Above the light the keeper sees him sweep
From fog to fog, and vanish like a star
Down where the unknown ocean monsters are,
And hears his mournful crying on the steep.

And when on winter days he rises high
Against the squall, and swift on-coming night,
And bares his gleaming to the fight,
Then are the sailors startled by his cry;
Darting spearlike athwart the dark'ning main
To rid the helmet of the hurricane.   *John Reed*

Humanities.

MANY things are deep and high
      That have no word for such as I:
Thoughts as strong as strong gods are
Spring the way from star to star.

Would you have my love thus, even
Big as earth and big with heaven —
So forgetting the sweet days
We've played at loving, different ways?

What have gods and stars to do
With *You love me* and *I love you*?
Many things are deep and high
That have no word for such as I.

Van Wyck Brooks.

Rabbit.

WE paused on the brow of the hummock, and looked down into the bushy valley below us.

"This is really an excellent place for rabbit," remarked my host softly. "Can't remember coming here without success."

Hardly had he spoken when he jerked his gun to his shoulder and fired at a quiver in the tall bushes. The report echoed harshly across the glade and the smoke began slowly rising in the calm sunlit air; and then suddenly, without the slightest warning, there rose from the bushes a shriek — short, sharp, and ear-piercing. Immediately after it, followed the same warm, Sunday placidity.

"Good Lord!" gasped Jenkins, and stared at me, gaping foolishly. "What was it?"

"I don't know."

I collapsed to the earth like a consumed fire and stared down at the bushes, which were now quite still.

"A ghost?" I suggested weakly, patting my forehead with a handkerchief.

Jenkins dropped his gun in a cluster of golden dandelions and started walking gingerly down the gentle slope. Then I saw his brown Norfolk jacket and corduroy trousers disappear into the rustling bushes. The green leaves tossed nervously about his invisible figure, and became again motionless. Everything was as silent as if he had fallen into a bottomless pit.

"Jenkins!" I shouted.

A young thrush lighted on the top of a willow sapling and jerked his tail at me defiantly, watching me with his bead eyes, his little head cocked to one side. Hearing something, he flitted off again. The leaves were again tossing and bobbing; and presently Jenkins appeared, holding something in his arms.

"Thank the Lord!" I cried fervently. "Was it only a rabbit?"

I scrambled weakly to my feet and started

to approach him. And then — suddenly — I stopped dead. Jenkins laughed a little, chill laugh,— and stood still too, with his blackly bearded face bent downward. His shadow came just to my feet. I noticed with horror that it appeared quite headless; and then, for the first time, I looked at the object in his arms, with a dim dream-like sense of having done the same thing in a previous life. It was a little boy, about three years old, quite dead. He was dressed in a tiny pair of Scotch kilts, and wore a Scotch cap with a dangling black ribbon. The face was plump and ruddy, and the eyes, now closed, were darkly fringed with long curving eyelashes.

Jenkins raised his head and fastened his narrow yellow eyes on mine.

"It's done," he said slowly. "I wonder where his parents are?"

I couldn't answer him, for I was gulping. So I shaded my eyes with a trembling hand and gazed off over the glade. In an instant I had seen the thin blue thread of smoke above the trees.

"There," said I, pointing.

Jenkins looked, and then commenced the descent into the valley. Picking up the gun from the dandelions, I ejected the empty shell, blew out the little ghost-like whiff of smoke still lingering in the barrel, and followed, with hanging head. In Jenkins went, with never a pause, picking an intricate way through the sumach and willow coppice. Birds flew up chirping before us and more than one rabbit flashed away through the long grass; yet Jenkins never once turned his head, till we came to the shallow brook. Here I paused involuntarily. On the further side was a brown tent, ragged and soiled, with its flaps closed. Beside it stood a high-bodied gypsy-cart, white, with green and red trimmings, its shafts resting idly on the ground. A lean-ribbed horse was tethered to one of the wheels, and browsed peacefully in the deep clover. On his back sat a girl, perhaps ten years old, with a golden shock of hair that curled down over a yellow linen dress. She was laboriously playing a bag-pipe.

Jenkins was already half way across the brook, stepping carefully from stone to stone. I followed once more, doubtfully; then sat down in the grass and waited. The yellow-haired girl looked at me with indifference, the pipe still at her lips, the bag under her arm. I noticed a strange dullness in her large brown eyes; yet she was very pretty.

"Hello!" called Jenkins, stopping.

There was a movement in the dingy tent, a bulging against the canvas flaps, and then a man came forth, looking calmly from one to the other of us, and bending slightly forward. He was short and thin, clad in kilts and plaid stockings, and his gaunt face was wholly covered with black hair. Large brown eyes gazed out serenely from beneath great bushy eyebrows. His hands were large and hairy, his arms of unusual length, hanging limply at his sides. He looked entirely primeval.

Jenkins stood before him, still holding the baby in his arms. The perspiration stood on his forehead like dew. And he began talking softly to the man in Gaelic, which I couldn't understand. What he said, I haven't the faintest idea, for the Scotchman's face remained perfectly placid throughout; he showed absolutely no signs of feeling. He just stood there, his knees slightly bent, like an ape's, his funny jaw tightly closed, his brown sunlit eyes unblinking.

Jenkins stopped. Slowly winking with his great eyes, the man climbed into the cart and returned with a spade. He and Jenkins then went off silently among the oak-trees and disappeared. I knew well what they were doing. Meanwhile, the golden-haired girl was still kicking with her bare brown legs against the old horse's ribs, and squealing in an ejaculatory manner on the bag-pipes. As for me, I sat still in the shade of the huge oak, near the tent, and sucked a straw.

Presently the two men came solemnly back, Jenkins leading, and the other limping behind with swinging arms and head thrust brutishly forward.

"It's all done," remarked my host unfeelingly. He slipped a golden sovereign in the man's hand, picked up his gun, and started away. When we had reached the other side of the shallow brook, I looked over my shoulder and saw the man smiling inanely at the sovereign, which shone on the palm of his hand.

"They're Gaelic," said Jenkins shortly; "old clan people, so often intermarried that their brains are gone. Almost all of them are tinklers, like him, and harmless enough....Softly now — I must shoot us a dinner. Off to the left, I think ...."

Jenkins went off, the gun cracked, and he came back holding up a rabbit by the hind legs. He started to smile. He was surprised to find me squatting on the ground, and blubbering like a child.

C. P. Aiken.

Gentlemen and Seamen.

THOSE of us who can claim any New England ancestors may congratulate ourselves that we are their descendants, and at the same time rejoice that we are not their contemporaries. Their sombre faces, with an inflexible contraction of the lips, as they have been stiffened and conventionalized in oils by forgotten artists, suggest natures difficult and unyielding, as the consequence of religious principle and of interminable struggle against the narrow resources of New England. The men of whom I am thinking are the patriarchs of the smaller towns, rather than the merchants of Boston, whom affluence often left more genial than the never prosperous countryfolk. But the representative New Englander is not exclusively a city man by descent, and has quite as much reason for taking pride in his rustic ancestors.

One notable characteristic of those hardy folk is the success with which they supported, in the conflict with misfortune, a gentlemanly dignity. Tradesmen and farmers, most of them, by descent, they were farmers in America; yet here they founded and maintained successfully a plebeian aristocracy, without the training of generations, and under adverse fates. Any task which necessity compelled them to undertake, in their hands became honorable; no privation and hardship lowered their pride or social position. So they were found as merchants and tradesmen, as farmers and printers, according to circumstance, without losing a jot of their dignity. There were many sacrifices. Straightened means confined noble ambitions, and their passion for education was not always gratified. In one of those white clapboard houses which look so tranquil in their decay lived a boy of good family, a hundred years ago, whom lack of means thwarted from his ambition the college education. So, at the age of fifteen, he killed himself.

But most of our New Englanders were stronger, and turned to what vocation they could find; the farm, the printing-press — a hundred years ago there were many local presses — or to the sea. The merchant marine was not the least important career in which New Englanders found distinction. They were the men who carried American commerce to the Levant, to India, to China; who from the Revolution till after 1812 made America an ocean power in war and in peace. They built the fine old ships which we know only from contemporaneous engravings. How stirring are those antique woodcuts. The "*Ajax*," two hundred ton brig, entering Algiers under full sail with a thundering salvo from the city; the ensign very large, triumphantly shaking out its thirteen stars from the end of a yard-arm. Or the "*Poor Richard*," off the coast of Africa repelling pirates; the native feluccas very small in contrast; or the "*Samuel Adams*," passing a sea-serpent in the Bay of Biscay. Built and manned and commanded, every one of the boats, by Yankee seamen; and for them was built the handsome old custom house at Salem, now slumbering in proud uselessness.

Go to Salem and see a town that flourished a hundred years ago in the hightide of New England's naval energy. It seems now to be always in dignified mourning for its former grandeur for the ships which do not leave and the ships which do not return. One feels that noisy mirth is a profanation there, the town is so populous with ghosts. Where is the China fleet now? the clumsy barks that sailed to every part of the world? Every day, a hundred years ago, the crowsnest watched for another homecomer bending past Baker's Island. Of the freights which the boats carried in are left only the shawls, the ginger-jars, the carved ivory which the captains brought back from the Orient, the gifts which their descendants are proud to display. From New Brunswick to Florida to-day lounge the coasters, manned with Irish and the "blue-nose"; the mackerel fleet slants out to the banks under Irish skippers, and the cargoes of the world are borne in steamers owned in Europe. The sea trade of the Yankees is gone.

The captains who handled the old fleet were just the sort of aristocratic plebeians of whom I spoke. Very young, at fourteen or fifteen years, they would enter the service, at the bottom of the nautical *cursus honorum*. They often rose quickly; there were many like the youth who sailed a bark from his father's Portsmouth shipyard to Savannah for lading, thence to London, where he sold ship and cargo at a good profit; and this when he was aged nineteen. His logbook, kept in a neat small hand, shows that he was an able and a conscientious navigator. Such were the men who handled the shipping of New Eng.and.

Though we must regret the commerce which has fallen to Germany and to England, we must regret still more the virtues of the old skippers. Thrown from youth among the roughest adventures, with the crudest companions, they emerged at the end as good gentlemen, often, as the more fortunate college-bred. Of these yeomen ancestors we are apt to think as the infantry whom the drums beat to Charlestown, or as the gunners who raked the *"Hornet,"* rather than as the founders of commerce or the pioneers of education. But that is half of their importance. We may well mourn for the enterprise which sent American shipping round the world, and started the printing press in many small communities. Nowadays we are thankful that more congenial occupation is open to the industrious gentleman, however needy, than was possible to some of our New England forbears. If along with greater luxury, with more generosity and geniality than was theirs, we have preserved the spirit of our old plebeian aristocracy, we should give them the grace of recognition.

T. S. Eliot.

François Villon.

HOW bitter cold it is! It *looked* like snow ---
    I hear the wolf-wind now; wolf-wind, d' I say?
    Aye, hear the host a-snoring! Fire's gray
With ashes. Hey, you drunkard! Stir your — No; —
He must not wake. I turn my pockets, so —
    And — am I startled? nothing, nothing, falls,
    No laugh of silver mocks me from these walls
So desolate, so bare. Well, here I go
To mill a verse. Ha ha! It's Christmas time!
I want a hollied verse, a berried rhyme—

O sleepy, sleepy eyes! Will verses keep?
    Aye, think of roast-fowl, then,— Lights! Christmas spread!
    Ah, what a vision! (*Smiles — nods low his head*)
O! Verse, d' I say? Aye — (*murmuring, falls asleep*).

C. P. Aiken.

On A Portrait

Among a crowd of tenuous dreams, unknown
To us of restless brain and weary feet,
Forever hurrying, up and down the street,
She stands at evening in the room alone.

Not like a tranquil goddess carved of stone
But evanescent, as if one should meet
A pensive lamia in some wood-retreat,
An immaterial fancy of one's own.

No meditations glad or ominous
Disturb her lips, or move the slender hands;
Her dark eyes keep their secrets hid from us,
Beyond the circle of our thought she stands.

The parrot on his bar, a silent spy,
Regards her with a patient curious eye.

T.S. ELIOT

Humouresque.

(After J. Laforgue).

ONE of my marionettes is dead,
    Though not yet tired of the game,—
But weak in body as in head,
(A jumping-jack has such a frame).

But this deceaséd marionette
I rather liked: a common face,
(The kind of face that we forget)
Pinched in a comic, dull grimace;

Half bullying, half imploring air,
Mouth twisted to the latest tune;
His who-the-devil-are-you stare;
Translated, maybe, to the moon.

With Limbo's other useless things
Haranguing spectres, set him there;
"The snappiest fashion since last spring's,
"The newest style, on Earth, I swear.

"Why don't you people get some class?
(Feebly contemptuous of hose),
"Your damned thin moonlight, worse than gas —
"Now in New York" — and so it goes.

Logic a marionette's, all wrong.
Of premises; yet in some star
A hero!— Where would he belong?
But, even at that what mark *bizarre*!

T. S. Eliot.

Spleen.

SUNDAY: this satisfied procession
  Of definite Sunday faces;
Bonnets, silk hats, and conscious graces
In repetition that displaces
Your mental self-possession
By this unwarranted digression.

Evening, lights, and tea!
Children and cats in the alley;
Dejection unable to rally
Against this dull conspiracy.

And Life, a little bald and gray,
Languid, fastidious, and bland,
Waits, hat and gloves in hand,
Punctilious of tie and suit
(Somewhat impatient of delay)
  On the doorstep of the Absolute.

T. S. Eliot.

Nocturne.

ROMEO, *grand serieux*, to importune
  Guitar and hat in hand, beside the gate
With Juliet, in the usual debate
Of love, beneath a bored but courteous moon;
The conversation failing, strikes some tune
Banal, and out of pity for their fate
Behind the wall I have some servant wait,
Stab, and the lady sinks into a swoon.

Blood looks effective on the moonlit ground—
The hero smiles; in my best mode oblique
Rolls toward the moon a frenzied eye profound,
(No need of "Love forever?"—"Love next week?")
While female readers all in tears are drowned:—
"The perfect climax all true lovers seek!"

T. S. Eliot.

Harvard Advocate

1866   Class Day   1915

Ivy Oration.

Robert C. Benchley.

IMAGINE my surprise — my confusion — at just now being called upon to address you at this meeting. Nothing could have been farther from my thoughts as I sat listening to the other speakers here this afternoon, than that my modest voice should be desired to lend a touch of dignity to this occasion. Why, a quarter of an hour ago I was sitting in my room, looking for a position for next year, when the Bursar, that Prince of Good Fellows, that Shylock of Melancholy Dane, came bounding up the stairs, and laying a sympathetic hand on my shoulder said "Bob, old man, aren't you coming down to say a few words to the Big Red team? The boys are all calling for you down there." Then it all came over me like a flask — this was Class Day! I did remember having seen a program of the week, in which somewhere between ball-games with Yale and Phi Beta Kappa Exhibits there was made casual mention of a Class Day Exercise, but I understood that it was to be held only in case the ball-game at New Haven was called off on account of rain, and besides, I really did not dare to leave the Yard, for fear lest I had not the right colored ticket and that, once out, I could never get back in again to get my clean clothes for the summer vacation. So here it was Class Day, and there I was in my room, hemming napkins. Quickly I drew on a pair of shoes and my cap and gown, and breaking into a run — and a perspiration, soon found myself, unless I am mistaken, here.

On this day, when all minds are turned to the National Prize Ring in Chicago, where Harvard and Yale are again demonstrating that the rules of the game need changing before next season, and at a time when the air is so charged with personal politics that it threatens to destroy the crops, what could be more out of place or thoroughly disagreeable, than for me to give my speech a political flavor? With true Harvard indifference then, I shall proceed to deliver a political speech which our paternal and conservative Administrative Board refused me permission to deliver in the Thayer Common-room, stigmatizing it as unnecessarily impolite and improper propaganda.

I shall divide my speech into three quarters, or halfs; 1st the Peroration, containing what I consider to be one of the most virulent attacks against the Malefactors of Great Health yet voiced in the present campaign. 2nd the Oration Proper, or Improper, dealing in the large with the great issues of the day, such as the Class Day Issue of the Lampoon and the Recall of Faculty Decisions. In this I shall embody a sweeping denunciation of the goodies. Thirdly, and inevitably, will come the Anti-Climax or Operation, in which, with a burst of mature rhetoric seldom found in one so young I shall revile in bitterest terms the Social Usurpation of our Colleges, dealing with the underground method in which the Social Set at Harvard derives its stimulus from Boston, the annual, exclusive, five-day cruise of the Yale crew along the Themes, to be celebrated again Friday, and the recent election and inauguration of Sam White as President and Fellows of Princeton, on the magnanimous endorsement of our intrepid cheer-leader, our heritage from the class of 1911. These are vital questions, Classmates, and must be met at Harvard Squarely.

You have my ultimatum. If you are resigned and ready, I shall proceed, without further parsley, to dissect my Peroration. If there are any timid or super-sensitively nervous ladies or members of the Harvard Equal Suffrage league present in the arena, they may retire now inconspicuously by the trap-door opposite, where the elephants enter. I will answer any questions that may be put to me after the lecture.

1st Peroration: Roman numeral I — small letter (a).

Voters and Votaries — and Conservative Republicans.

We are gathered here to-day in this June sunshine (if it had been raining I should have been quick-witted enough to substitute for that, "We are gathered here in this June rain." By a lucky coincidence the "June" part would be equally fitting in both cases, you see.) We are gathered here in this June sunshine, under the leafy boughs of these grand old elms, to celebrate the fourth anniversary of the passing of our entrance English examinations. As our witty Latin orator so aptly puts it "Non sequebantur, sed in felicitate demonstrandum nunc nobis ad libitandum esse." What more can be said? Father Garcelon, in his prime, from his taxi-chariot, could say no more. Were it not for the fact that all you nice people had melted all the way down here just to hear my words and to say that they were n't nearly so funny as you had expected them to be, I should let it go at that, and call the whole thing right off now. But I will not. Rather will I turn from this, our Peroration, to the second section of the speech— the Oration Proper. If the Malefactors of Great Health do not like what I have just said about them, they may petition the Administrative Board at its next secret practice.

Oration Proper — Section A, under the General Heading of Cotton Goods and Steel Rails. Roman numeral V. (Personally I think the speech drags a little at this point.)

As I look into your bright young faces here in the shade of these grand old rock-maples, I am oppressed with the conviction that never before in her history has our country been face to face with such a grave financial crisis. It is with the customary Class Day mingled emotions of pleasure and regret that we bask here to-day, and with eyes dimmed by Bolyston St. dust look back over the seventeen pre-digested courses that have constituted our educational banquet. Let us ponder ponderously on these things. What have we accomplished? What new visions have we seen? When and why does all this mean? O, Brothers, we are all unthinking in this extremity. We have waited and the innumerable caravan has gone without us. We have sung, and the echo has not come back. And now I ask you, what has the Republican party ever done for you — the working man? Temporary platforms, unfilled pledges and dinner-pails, and these mute, defenseless colonnades confront us, and with tier upon tier cry out "Give us the man."

You are brave men. You have given your lives without a murmur to the Class Album Committee, lives padded, it is true, by Vice-Presidencies of the Soap and Brush Club, but lives, nevertheless, young, virile lives. Even now, with that intrepid fearlessness born of

youth you recline here in the new-mown grass before this altar raised to machine-made wit, defying at once hay-fever, and Owen Johnson's accusation that Harvard's social set is based on the dry grass of the fields, which, like Memorial toast, is cast into the oven and withereth away.

You have heard with calmness the dictatorial warnings of the Class Day Committee that pajamas are not to be worn under the caps and gowns until the caps and gowns have been removed, and that anyone attempting to leave the Yard by more than one gate at a time without a yard mileage ticket properly endorsed by the Secretary of the Navy, will have to stay in the yard all night, and cry himself to sleep under the red-oak saplings, or else leave the yard immediately. And yet we are Romans, and this is Rome, that from her throne of beauty ruled the world! O, ingrates! Sluggards! Undesirable citizens!

And now I think that you will agree that I have come logically to the crux of my argument on which I base my claim for the nomination. You have gone through much, besides your June allowances. You have survived the embroidered salmon of last night's spread, where your class-mates and their class-mates tread on your light fantastic toe. You have gone through that most democratic of institutions, the Senior Picnic, where one sees more of the other men in one's class than at any other gathering. And right in connection with the Senior Picnic I wish to make the announcement that I have learned the name of the man who slapped me on my sun-burned back the morning after the Picnic, and I give him warning that I shall hound him to-day, from spread to spread, forcing him to eat one dollar's worth of food at each place, till at last I see him sink bubbling beneath the banana-strewn Red Sea at Beck.

And now, as Tupper's lightning artist says, as the one-thirty bell rings on a lunchless noon, "Now for the last and best!" My speech so far has dealt mainly with the economic aspects of the matter at hand. I shall now close by a few concrete references to the proposed Freshmen Sanitarium, and the Conservation of our National Resources in general.

As a result of a clubbing offer with the HARVARD ADVOCATE I shall omit this section of my speech in delivering it here this afternoon, but a complete copy of it, with footnotes and errata, may be found in the current issue of the ADVOCATE on page 409. It is for sale almost anywhere, and offers two prizes — a second and a third prize, the amounts to be announced at its awarding for the best essay on "How the Ivy Oration (printed in this number) might be improved."

I do not claim that the principles enunciated in this speech will take effect immediately. You are young men yet. But think them over, Brothers. Take them home and confront yourselves with them when you are alone to-night shaking the confetti from your clothes, standing on a packing box full of old neck-ties which Max won't buy and which you hate to throw away. Then, in the silence, ask yourself if your life has been such that you could face with calmness a disclosure to the world of all that Terry knows about you.

When the time comes to fee the goody with an I. O. U. and when, with some one else's diploma in one hand, and a Bursar's card, to show that you are a real Harvard man, in the other, you sit on the old college fence, and gaze over your Lyendecker Arrow collar across the old college campus to where the sun is setting in a crimson glow behind the old college pharmacy, then allow a tear to trickle unnoticed down your cheek, and thinking of what I have said to-day about the Ideal College man and the community, give a regular Harvard cheer for yourself, gird up your loins and be brave.

Go forth now, and, like the gypsy-moth, spread to your hearts content. The only distressing feature of Class Day is now over. Go and live to-day out to its fullest measure, rejoice and be glad, for you are existing to-day in that Golden Age, to which, when again we assemble here as a class, we shall longingly refer as the good old Halcyon Days when we were in College.

Sunset.

GREAT carnal mountains crouching in the cloud
    That marrieth the young earth with a ring,
Yet still its thoughts builds heavenward, whence spring
Wee villages of vapor, sunset-proud.—
And to the meanest door hastes one pure-browed
White-fingered star, a little, childish thing,
The busy needle of her light to bring,
And stitch, and stitch, upon the dead day's shroud.
Poises the sun upon his west, a spark
Superlative,— and dives beneath the world;
From the day's fillets Night shakes out her locks;
List! One pure trembling drop of cadence purled —
"Summer!" — a meek thrush whispers to the dark.
Hark! the cold ripple sneering on the rocks!

                   E. E. Cummings, '15.

Of Nicolette.

DREAMING in marble all the palace lay,
　　Like some colossal ghost-flower, born by night,
Blossoming in white towers to the moon;
Soft sighed the passionate darkness to the tune
Of tiny troubadours, and, phantom-white,
Dumb-blooming boughs let fall their glorious snows,
And the unearthly sweetness of a rose
Swam upward from the moonlit dews of May.

A Winged Passion woke, and one by one
There fell upon the night like angels' tears
The syllables of that ethereal prayer.
And as an opening lily, milky-fair,
When from her couch of poppy petals peers
The sleepy morning, gently draws apart
Its curtains to reveal the golden heart,
With beads of dew made jewels by the sun,

So one fair, shining tower, which, like a glass,
Turned light to flame, and blazed with silver fire,
Unclosing, gave the moon a nymph-like face,
A form whose snowy symmetry of grace
Haunted the limbs as music haunts the lyre,
A creature of white hands, who, letting fall
A thread of lustre from the opened wall,
Glided, a drop of radiance, to the grass.

Shunning the sudden moonbeams' treacherous snare,
She sought the harboring dark, and, catching up
Her delicate silk,— all white, with shining feet,
Went forth into the dew. Right wildly beat
Her heart at every kiss of daisy-cup,
And from her cheek the beauteous courage went
At every bough that reverently bent
To touch the yellow wonder of her hair.

E. E. Cummings, '15.

Summer Silence.

(Spenserian Stanza.)

ERUPTIVE lightnings flutter to and fro
    Above the heights of immemorial hills;
Thirst-stricken air, dumb-throated, in its woe
Limply down-sagging, its limp body spills
Upon the earth. A panting silence fills
The empty vault of Night with shimmering bars
Of sullen silver, where the lake distils
Its misered bounty.— Hark! No whisper mars
The utter silence of the untranslated stars.

E. E. Cummings, '15.

The New Art.

(Commencement Part.)

E. E. CUMMINGS.

THE New Art has many branches,— painting, sculpture, architecture, the stage, literature, and music. In each of these there is a clearly discernible evolution from models; in none is there any trace of that abnormality, or incoherence, which the casual critic is fond of making the subject of tirades against the new order.

It is my purpose to sketch briefly the parallel developments of the New Art in painting, sculpture, music, and literature.

I.

Anyone who takes Art seriously, who understands the development of technique in the last half century, accepts Cezanne and Matisse as he accepts Manet and Monet. But this brings us to the turning point where contemporary criticism becomes, for the most part, rampant abuse, and where prejudice utters its storm of condemnation. I refer to that peculiar phase of modern art called indiscriminately, "Cubism," and "Futurism."

The name Cubism, properly applied, relates to the work of a small group of ultra-modern painters and sculptors who use design to express their personal reaction to the subject, i. e.— what this subject "means" to them,— and who further take this design from geometry. By using an edge in place of a curve a unique tactual value is obtained.

Futurism is a glorification of personality. Every so-called "Futurist" has his own hobby; and there are almost as many kinds of painting as artists. For instance, one painter takes as his subject sounds, another, colors. A third goes back to old techniques; a fourth sees life through a magnifying glass; a fifth imposes an environment upon his subject proper, obtaining very startling effects; a sixth concerns himself purely with motion,— in connection with which it is interesting to note the Japanese painters' wholly unrealistic rendering of the force of a river.

The painter Matisse has been called the greatest exponent of Cubist sculpture. At the 1912 exhibition the puzzled crowd in front of Brancusi's "Mlle. Pogany" was only rivalled by that which swarmed about the painting called "Nude Descending a Staircase." "Mlle. Pogany" consists of a more or less egg-shaped head with an unmistakable nose, and a sinuous suggestion of arms curving upward to the face. There is no differentiation in modelling affording even a hint of hands; in other words, the flow of line and volume is continuous. But what strikes the spectator at first glance, and focusses the attention throughout, is the enormous inscribed ovals, which everyone recognizes as the artist's conception of the subject's eyes. In the triumph of line for line's sake over realism we note in Brancusi's art the development of the basic principles of impression.

II.

Just as in the case of painting, it is a French school which brought new life to music; but at the same time, Germany has the honor of producing one of the greatest originators and masters of realism, Richard Strauss.

The modern French school of music finds its inspiration in the personal influence of César Franck. Debussey, Ravel and Satie all owe much to this great Belgian, who (like Maeterlink and Verhaeren), was essentially a man of their own artistic nationality.

It is safe to say that there will always be somebody who still refuses to accept modernism in music, quoting in his defense the sovereign innovator, Beethoven! On a par with the sensation produced by the painting and sculpture of the Futurist variety was the excitement which the music of Strauss and Debussey first produced upon audiences. At present, Debussey threatens to become at any moment vulgarly common; while Strauss is fatuous in his clarity beside Schönberg, who, with Stravinsky, is the only god left by the public for the worship of the esthetes.

Erik Satie is, in many respects, the most interesting of all modern composers. Nearly a quarter of a century ago he was writing what is now considered modern music. The most striking aspect of Satie's art is the truly extraordinary sense of humor which prompts one of his subjects, the "sea cucumber," to console himself philosophically for his lack of tobacco.

The "Five Orchestral Pieces" of Arnolo Schönberg continue to be the leading sensation of the present day musical world. Their com-

poser occupies a position in many respects similar to that of the author of the "Nude Descending a Staircase." I do not in the least mean to ridicule Schönberg; — no lawlessness could ever have produced such compositions as his, which resemble bristling forests contorted by irresistible winds. His work is always the expression of something mysteriously terrible,— which is probably why Boston laughed.

I have purposely left until the last the greatest theorist of modern music,— Scriabin. Logically, he belongs beside Stravinski, as leader of the Russian school. But it is by means of Scriabin that we may most readily pass from music to literature, through the medium of what has been called "sense-transference," as exemplified by the color music of the "Prometheus."

This "Poem of Fire" is the consummation of Scriabin's genius. To quote the Transcript: "At the first performance, by the Russian Symphony Society, on March 20, for the first time in history a composer used a chromatic color score in combination with orchestration....At the beginning of the orchestration, a gauze rectangle in about the position of a picture suspended on the back wall became animated by flowing and blending colors. These colors were played by a "color-organ" or "chromola," having a keyboard with fifteen keys, and following a written score."

III.

The suggestion of an analogy between color and music leads us naturally to the last branch of the New Art,— to wit, literature. Only the most extreme cases will be discussed, such as have important bearing upon the very latest conceptions of artistic expression.

I will quote three contemporary authors to illustrate different phases and different degrees of the literary parallel to sound painting — in a rather faint hope that the first two may prepare the way for an appreciation of the third. First Amy Lowell's "Grotesque" affords a clear illustration of development from the ordinary to the abnormal.

"Why do the lilies goggle their tongues at me
　When I pluck them;
　And writhe and twist,
　And strangle themselves against my fingers,
　So that I can hardly weave the garland
　For your hair?

Why do they shriek your name
And spit at me
When I would cluster them?
Must I kill them
To make them lie still,
And send you a wreath of lolling corpses
To turn putrid and soft
On your forehead
While you dance?"

In this interesting poem we seem to discern something beyond the conventional. The lilies are made to express hatred by the employment of grotesque images. But there is nothing original in the pathetic fallacy. No one quarrels with Tennyson's lines

"There has fallen a splendid tear
From the passion-flower at the gate" —

Let us proceed further,— only noting in the last three lines that brutality which is typical of the New Art,— and consider the following poem by the same author:

"THE LETTER."

"Little cramped words scrawling all over the paper
Like draggled fly's legs,
What can you tell of the flaring moon
Through the oak leaves?
Or of an uncurtained window, and the bare floor
Spattered with moonlight?
Your silly quirks and twists have nothing in them
Of blossoming hawthorns,
And this paper is chill, crisp, smooth, virgin of loveliness
ness
Beneath my hand.
I am tired, Beloved, of chafing my heart against
The want of you;
Of squeezing it into little ink drops,
And posting it.
And I scald alone, here under the fire
Of the great moon."

This poem is superb of its kind. I know of no image in all realistic writing which can approach the absolute vividness of the first two lines. The metaphor of the chafed heart is worthy of any poet; but its fanciful development would have been impossible in any literature except this ultra-modern.

I shall now quote from a sonnet by my second author, Donald Evans:

"Her voice was fleet-limbed and immaculate,
And like peach blossoms blown across the wind
Her white words made the hour seem cool and kind,
Hung with soft dawns that danced a shadow fête.
A silken silence crept up from the South,

The flutes were hushed that mimed the orange moon,
And down the willow stream my sighs were strewn,
While I knelt to the corners of her mouth."

In the figure "Her voice was fleet-limbed," and the phrase "white words," we have a sought-for literary parallel to the work of the "sound painters." It is interesting to compare Dante's expressions of a precisely similar nature, occurring in the first and fifth cantos, respectively, of the Inferno — "dove il Sol tace," and "in loco d'ogni luce muto."

From Donald Evans to Gertrude Stein is a natural step,— up or down, and one which I had hoped the first two might enable us to take in security. Gertrude Stein subordinates the meaning of words to the beauty of the words themselves. Her art is the logic of literary sound painting carried to its extreme. While we must admit that it is logic, must we admit that it is art?

Having prepared the way, so far as it is possible, for a just appreciation, I now do my best to quote from the book "Tender Buttons," as follows:

(1) A sound.
Elephant beaten with candy and little pops and chews all bolts and reckless, reckless rats, this is this.

(2) Salad Dressing and an Artichoke.
Please pale hot, please cover rose, please acre in the red stranger, please butter all the beefsteak with regular feel faces.

(3) Suppose an Eyes.
. . . .
Go red, go red, laugh white.
Suppose a collapse is rubbed purr, is rubbed purget.
Little sales ladies little sales ladies
little saddles of mutton.
Little sales of leather and such beautiful beautiful, beautiful beautiful.

The book from which these selections are drawn is unquestionably a proof of great imagination on the part of the authoress, as anyone who tries to imitate her work will discover for herself. Here we see traces of realism, similar to those which made the "Nude Descending a Staircase" so baffling. As far as these "Tender Buttons" are concerned, the sum and substance of criticism is impossible. The unparalleled familiarity of the medium precludes its use for the purpose of esthetic effect. And here, in their logical conclusion, impressionistic tendencies are reduced to absurdity.

The question now arises, how much of all this is really Art?

The answer is: we do not know. The great men of the future will most certainly profit by the experimentation of the present period. An insight into the unbroken chain of artistic development during the last half century disproves the theory that modernism is without foundation; rather we are concerned with a natural unfolding of sound tendencies. That the conclusion is, in a particular case, absurdity, does not in any way impair the value of the experiment, so long as we are dealing with sincere effort. The New Art, maligned though it be by fakirs and fanatics, will appear in its essential spirit to the unprejudiced critic as a courageous and genuine exploration of untrodden ways.

Two Sonnets

I.

Only last night we dwelt together, we
Whose lips the ultimate farewells enthrall;
Last night itself is but a stone let fall
Into the chasm of Eternity.
There shall be echoes, I shall hear them call
However deep, however faint they be;
There shall be shadows, I shall always see
Them beckon from time's memory-haunted hall.

The dear mirages of the years gone by
Glow falsely golden from their dark domain,
But now they stir me not. "Mere mockery",
Low to my heart I say, to still its pain.
And cloud-built cities in the sunset sky
Fade out in dark across the endless plain.

II.

The insurgent sea sweeps through the barrier,
Triumphant, all its foaming strength amassed
In one tempestuous tide, wallowing past
The broken banks and the worn dykes that were
Upbuilt by coward hearts. Sated at last,
It settles in calm pools about the bar,
So that at twilight the young evening star
Beholds its image in still waters cast.

Against the unyielding shores I too have striven,
And won at last like the uprising sea,
And lie at peace under a quiet heaven,
After long struggles a long victory.
But my star vanishes, its light withdrawn,
And darkness falls, unpromising of dawn.

Robert S. Hillyer '17

Harvard and Preparedness.

By Theodore Roosevelt, '80.

HARVARD ought to take the lead in every real movement for making our country stand as it should stand. Unfortunately prominent Harvard men sometimes take the lead the wrong way. This applies pre-eminently to all Harvard men who have had anything to do with the absurd and mischievous professional-pacificist or peace-at-any-price movements which have so thoroughly discredited this country during the past five years. These men are seeking to chinafy the country; and, so far as they have any influence, they are tending to chinafy Harvard too. The pacificist of this type stands on an exact level with the poltroon. His appropriate place is with the college sissy who disapproves of football or boxing because it is rough.

In all our history there have been few movements more detrimental to our people and no movement more essentially ignoble than the professional pacificist or peace-at-any-price movement which has reached its zenith during the past five years. This movement became part of our official governmental policy when five years ago the effort was made to adopt the all-inclusive arbitration treaties under which we covenanted to arbitrate questions of national honor and vital interest (specifically, this means questions such as the murder of American men, women and children on the high seas and the rape of American women, for instance.) A couple of years ago we actually adopted certain ludicrous arbitration or commission-for-a-year's-investigation treaties which, when the proposal was made to reduce them to practice, were instantly repudiated by the very administration that had made them. Much harm has been done to America by crooked politicians and by crooked business men; but they have never done as much harm as these professional pacificists have sought to do and have partially succeeded in doing. They have weakened the moral fibre of our people. They have preached base and ignoble doctrines to this nation. For five years they have succeeded in tainting our foreign policy with mean hypocrisy.

I abhor wanton or unjust war. I believe with all my heart in peace, if peace can be obtained on terms compatible with self-respect. Even a necessary war I regard as a lamentable necessity. But it may be a necessity. It may be a necessity in order to save our bodies. It may be a necessity in order to save our souls. A high-minded man or woman does not regard death as the most dreadful of all things, because there are some things worse than death. A high-minded nation does not regard war as the most dreadful of all things, because there are some things worse than war.

Recently there have actually been political buttons circulated in this country with "safety first" as the motto upon them in the fancied interest of one of the party candidates for the Presidency next year. This is the motto which in practise is acted upon by the men on a sinking ship who jump into the lifeboats ahead of the women and children. Even these men, however, do not, when they get ashore, wear buttons to commemorate their feat.

This country needs to prepare itself materially against war. Even more it needs to prepare itself spiritually and morally, so that, if war must be accepted as the alternative to dishonor or unrighteousness, it shall be accepted with stern readiness to do any duty and incur any hazard that the times demand. It would be well if Harvard would establish as part of its curriculum an efficient system of thorough military training — not merely military drill, which is only a part of military training, and indeed a small part. I believe heartily in athletics; but from the physical and moral standpoint such a system of military training would be better for all the men in Harvard and would reach far more men than are now reached by athletics.

In addition, however, to such military training, and even if at present it proves impossible to get such military training, let Harvard men, graduates and undergraduates alike, start at once to practice and to preach that efficient morality which stands at the opposite pole from the milk-and-water doctrines of the professional pacificists. Remember that sentimentality is as directly the reverse of sentiment as bathos is of pathos. It is right and eminently necessary to be practical; it is right and eminently necessary to take care of our own fortunes, of our own bodies. Each man must do it individually; and the nation must do it in its corporate capacity, acting for all of us. But in addition, both men and nation must have the power of fealty to a lofty ideal.

No man is worth his salt who is not ready at all times to risk his body, to risk his wellbeing, to risk his life, in a great cause. No nation has a right to a place in the world unless it has so trained its sons and daughters that they follow righteousness as the great goal. They must scorn to do injustice, and scorn to submit to injustice They must endeavor steadily to make peace the handmaiden of righteousness, to secure both peace and righteousness. But they must stand ready, if the alternative is between peace and righteousness, unhesitatingly to face suffering and death in war rather than to submit to iniquity or dishonor.

To a Girl I Dislike

Ever since I was a very little boy,
I have known a path that wound away through the birches and hemlocks;
And I remember
How I always feared to follow it,
And liked to dream instead what lay at its end —
An Indian burying-ground, perhaps;
Or a cave of robbers, stored with fabulous riches;
Or a rotting cabin that had nursed some great hero.
And one day I followed the path,
Walking slowly out of fearfulness;
Starting back when I roused a covey of quail
From the maple scrub around the spring;
Only to find at the end of it,
Among the hemlocks and mossed birches,
A pigsty —
Like a piece of yellow glass set in filigreed platinum,
Or like your heart
Beneath the mysterious immobility of your beauty.

Malcolm Cowley '19

A Theme With Variations

I.

As Written by Miss Edna St. Vincent
Millay on Her Typewriter.

My thoughts had festered in the heat
Three months; I could not do a thing.
The pavement boiled beneath my feet
Three months; I could not even sing
And wondered what the fall would bring.

But yesterday at dusk, the lost
North wind sprang up after a rain,
And when I woke, I saw the frost
Had patterned lacework on the pane,
And on my lips were songs again.

III.

With Apologies to Mr. William Carlos Williams.

I wish I could pass out
lie with my toes towards the daisies
it must be cool even now
down there.

         Next autumn
there'll be wind, frost,
biting rain.

         I'll be peppy.
August is like last night's
Stale Pilsener.

II.

As It Appeared in 'The Pagan'.

Three months summer held me like malaria.
A fever drove me up and down the streets;
Underfoot the pavement
Was soft and viscous with heat.
About garbage cans flies came into being
And buzzed their enjoyment of the world
And died.
Children played about like flies
And died.
I fled to the wild places
But there in the solitude my thoughts festered
And to forget their foulness
I fled among people.
Yesterday.
A wind sprang up after a rain
And this morning there was a delicate tracery of frost on
    the window.
I have been praising the beauty of men all day.
I am a god in a new creation.

IV.

*As Rendered by a Member of the Spectric School
with Appropriate Overtones.*

Crawling infinities of atoms. Death. Sweat and the livid perfume of surheated asphalt. Thing unmentionable floating down sewers. All humanity is floating down a sewer into the cleansing sea.

A Brahmin once, performing his ninth pilgrimage to the waters of the sacred Ganges, observed a maize field drying up in the sun. "May the seven seas and the thirteen rivers of Paradise shed their healing moisture on that field." And the sun beat down, and the maize turned from yellow to brown, and the people starved. But that winter came the rains, and all those that survived blessed the words of the prophet.

My soul is a larva, a fat grub that feeds on flies.

Crack . . . crack . . . crack. The leaves are snapping off in the frost and falling one by one. On my window is the forest of Arden.

A young man in a silk hat runs down the street like a little boy Someone asks him why, but he only stares. Paradise looms behind swinging doors.

The wind is my breath and the sea is my spittle. I shall overthrow a hundred Brahmas and gods greater than Vishnu shall I raise up.

Malcolm Cowley '19

IMPROMTU FROM "SENLIN"

Death himself in the rain . . . death himself . . .
Death in the savage sunlight . . . skeletal death . . .
I hear the clack of his feet,
Clearly on stones, softly in dust,
Speeding among the trees with whistling breath,
Whirling the leaves, tossing his hands from waves . . .
Listen! the immortal footseps beat and beat! . . .

Death himself in the grass, death himself,
Gyrating invisibly in the sun
Scattering grass-blades, whipping the wind,
Tearing at boughs with malignant laughter . . .
On the long echoing air I hear him run!

Death himself in the dusk, gathering lilacs,
Breaking a white-fleshed bough,
Strewing the purple spikes on a cobwebbed lawn,
Dancing, dancing,
Drunk with excess, the long red sun-rays glancing
On flourishing arms, skipping with hideous knees,
Cavorting his grotesque ecstasies . . .
I do not see him, but I see the lilacs fall,
I hear the scrape of his hands against the wall,
The leaves are tossed and tremble where he plunges among them,
And silence falls, and I hear the sound of his breath,
Sharp and whistling, the rhythm of death.

It is evening: the lights on a long street balance and sway
In the purple ether they swing and silently sing,
The street is a gossamer swung in space
And death himself in the wind comes dancing along it
And the lights, like raindrops, fall and tremble and swing. . . .

Hurry, spider, and spread your glistening web,
For death approaches!
Hurry, rose, and open your heart to the bee
For death approaches!
Maiden, let down your hair for the hands of your lover,
Comb it with moonlight and wreathe it with leaves,
For death approaches! . . .
Death, colossal in stars, minute in the sand-grain,
Death himself in the rain, death himself,
Drawing the rain about him like a garment of jewels . . .
I hear the sound of his feet
On the stairs of the wind, in the sun,
In the forests of the sea . . .
Listen! the immortal footsteps beat and beat$_2$

Conrad Aiken, '11

THE HARVARD ADVOCATE

VOL. CVI.   CAMBRIDGE, MASS., JANUARY 29, 1920   No. 5

Persecution and Americanism

BETWEEN those who would like to see all the Reds and near-Reds dangling from lamp-posts, and those who believe that free speech is an absolute right, the country is having a hard time to keep its course steady and its mind clear. For the past few months the lamp-posters have been in the ascendancy, and they have gone about their task with a ghoulish appetite and a most distressing ostentation. The press and a good deal of the public are with them, applauding loudly from the grandstand, and the politicians are scrambling to beat each other into the arena. Meanwhile the Socialists are unseated, the *Buford* speeds upon its course, and from Deer Island a growing wail of voices is drowned in the general clamor. Altogether the situation is thoroughly unpalatable.

Of course we have a most difficult problem. It is hard enough to get along with eight million foreigners who can't read or speak English, without having a lot of agitators and quack socialists thrown into the bargain. And the high cost of living and general disarray of our economic life make the situation all the more ticklish.

But the lamp-posters are not quieting the country. If they would catch all the Reds at once and ship them home and burn the books they left behind, the worst of the trouble would be over. But they can't do that: instead, they catch a few that ought to be caught, and a good many that oughtn't, and they burn a great deal of literature; and all the time the unrest and bitterness continue. As a practical measure, this melodramatic man-hunt is as unwise as it is extravagant and reckless.

But it is more than that. For, like every other persecution in history, from the Christians under the Romans to the Jews in Poland, and the Salem witches, it damages the moral fibre of the people. Persecution is an excuse for mental laziness; it sanctions cruelty, corrodes justice, and breeds fear and suspicion and hatred. And it brings about a disturbed, feverish atmosphere in which rare vision is needed to see the truth and rare courage to speak it. Our attempt all over this country to crush the radicals has been attended by these same moral evils, enhanced by the widest publicity.

There are many alternatives, some of which we should in all prudence immediately adopt. The deportations, the unseating of lawfully elected representatives, should cease. The powers of the federal investigators should be limited, and their activities supervised by special courts. No man should be arrested, nor any meeting prohibited, nor any writing confiscated, whose message is not calculated to lead to violence.

Finally, and more important still, our attentions and energies should be turned in other directions. The government should do its utmost to reduce the cost of living, to set up permanent machinery for the study and adjustment of industrial disputes. And the work of education and Americanization should be ceaselessly pressed; it should be from this time forward upon the conscience of the nation.

If we will do these things, slowly the old atmosphere of tranquility and tolerance and human trustfulness should reappear. To work toward such an end is the only true Americanism; for it is in that atmosphere alone that the richest promise of American life can be fulfilled.

* * * *

Prohibition

IN SPITE of the changes which it is bound to effect upon the college, Mr. Volstead's Act slid into place on January 16 with barely a tremor. In Cambridge there were no visible demonstrations, and such as may have taken place were at least decently domiciled. In Boston one of the few signs that anything was wrong were the bevies of policemen who hovered about the fringes of the Ball in the Copley and invaded the men's dressing-rooms with what might be termed an almost thirsty eagerness. Nowhere, however, was there a trace of the proletarian tumult which, last July first, greeted the passing of whiskey.

Of course, as far as the nation goes, no one can be yet quite sure to what extent back-yard stills, hair-tonics, and benevolent customs inspectors are going to ease the Amendment. But there is no doubt at all that Harvard in due course of time will become dry enough to satisfy even the *Christian Science Monitor*.

The surface changes are going to be great. No longer will the midnights of Mt. Auburn Street be made hideous with song. Never again will the Senior Picnickers, in their black caps and voluminous over-alls, sweep with them to the docks the whole rabble of South Boston. The neophytes of the *Crimson* and *Lampoon* will be a shabby, soulless lot. The Midnight Aristocracy of the Waldorf, like the clientele of the Widow's, will be irretrievably impaired. Music Four will be dropped from the curriculum. And on Class Day, who will be left to take the historical plunge into the wooden fountain? What reuniting class, garbed as Hibernians or Green Hop-toads, will have the *élan* to rattle the Eli ball-players? At New London, how shall remorse be drowned or victory proclaimed?

But the changes are not wholly surface ones. If ever any community was justified in the use of wine for the cementing of friendships and the perpetuation of its oldest and most human customs, that community was Harvard. Consequently, it is with more than mere affected regret, it is with something akin to emotion that those who have learned to cherish in their entirety the traditions of the college have contemplated the final arrival of the Amendment. There was a richness, a variety, a divine abandon in those old ways of living, the meaning of which no prohibitionist will ever understand.

When all has been said and done, however, one must confess that only a small proportion of the college will be affected by the change. And those who will be, will most likely admit that "it is a good thing for the country." Our customs are going to continue, in spite of the damage to local color, and if friendships are formed as they will be and intellects quickened in a more tranquil and scholarly atmosphere, who but an irreconcilable will not say that it has been for the best?

Vaudeville.

I. THE LEADER.

EACH time the sign flashed 'Hayes and Mayne'
    His frantic heart began to beat.
A fiery music laced his brain.
And through his veins her golden feet
Danced and glistened, danced and turned,
Pirouetted without a sound;
Up and down his blood they burned;
Glided and winked and swished around;
Until he longed to drop his bow,
And break his torturing violin,
And dance with her who witched him so
In a moonlight carnival of sin.
Her partner was a fool, and blind;
He smiled and smiled, and did not guess;
He skipped and hopped with vacant mind
Beside that fiery loveliness, —
Held out his hand for her to take,
And grinned, like a sawdust mannikin....
Sometimes he thought his heart would break;
Sometimes he thought his violin
Would crack to pieces, rather than play
That everlasting idiot tune....
But then he thought of nights in May,
And moonlight seaside nights in June,
And how they'd walk along the sands,
And laugh a little, and hear the sea,
And feel strange magic, touching hands,
And kiss, and shiver....and there would be
Eternities like this....But then
She ran to the wings, and turned, and screamed,
And waved her hand....And once again
The whole thing like a nightmare seemed....
The music changed, the curtains rose,
Two acrobats, in yellow tights,
One with an artificial nose,
Signalled into the wings for lights;
And coldly, above a falling flame
That lately set his pulses wild,
Freezing memory once more came
Of crippled wife and crying child.

II. FRONT ROW.

Day after day she came, day after day
She sat in the front row, fixing her eyes upon him,
And never spoke to him, and never smiled.
Like one in a spell she watched his fingers moving
On the little silver levers, watched his lips,
And how he moistened them before he played;

The blue eyes, slowly gliding across the music,—
The lamplit music; and how, when he was tired,
He sighed, and rested his oboe on his knee.
The people on the stage meant nothing to her:
She'd seen them all before, perhaps, remembered
All that they said and did. They came and went
Silent as thought:
The fair-haired girl who played the violin,
Smiling a fixed and foolish smile; the clowns
Who lifted horrible faces into the spotlight
And sang so out of tune; the screaming monkeys;
The dwarfs, the trapeze artists, the bottle-jugglers;
And the young men who played pianos blindfold....
Pictures upon the white screen flashed and faded,
The music changed, the spotlight cast new shadows
Sharply against the drop; and still, unseeing,
Never lifting her eyes, never applauding,
And only faintly smiling at some old joke,
She sat and stared. So near she was to him,
That sometimes, lifting her dress to cross her knees,
Her slipper brushed his elbow, and he'd turn
And peer at her, one instant, above his glasses,—
Still blowing a tune; and edge his chair away....

What was it like, that unknown world of hers,
Those sinister streets in which no lamps were lighted,
And no doors ever opened, and no voice heard?

Conrad Aiken

NANTASKET

Densise, the manicure, strolls on beside
Her lover, who is working on the Street.
They talk in broken words, and watch the tide
Come sedulously licking at their feet.

This is her Day. Her glances go a-roving
Among the bathers, searching every feature.
This place, she thinks, is made for pleasant loving
And not uncomfortably close to nature.

And now Society comes marching by,
Young Kuppenheimer gods in bathing suits
And flappers with their bonnets stuck awry:—
Sand filters into patent leather boots;

The sun is scorching painted cheeks; the sea
Growls at the littered beach complainingly.

Malcolm Cowley, '19.

THE LIBERALISM OF HERBERT HOOVER

By Archibald MacLeish

(Instructor in Constitutional Law)

The most effective indictment brought against American liberalism is that its articulate expression does not declare an American opinion. It has been said that American liberals are either by birth, or by immediate intellectual inheritance, European, and that their program is a European program which postulates the social order of the continent. Upon this charge the case of reaction has been rested while gentlemen of conservative opinion have been at pains to prove the typically American, even Colonial quality of their own faith. One result of the conservative attack and self-justification has been to bring the overlabored word "American' into a measure of disrepute with such citizens of the United States as are still able to feel that grandiosity, whether our own or that of a Central European empire, is ludicrous. But another and more serious result has been the failure of liberal opinion to secure the interests it has most at heart. Popular instinct mistrusts publicists and politicians who may be made to appear to assume a European temperament and background in the United States, or to work from Old-World hypotheses. The great American voter instinctively doubts a faction which seems to regard him in an objective light and which appears bent upon making his political actions and reactions highly self-conscious. And it must be admitted that a great deal of liberal phrasing has tended to confirm him in his suspicions. There is, for instance, the emphasis upon experiment. Americans resent being told that a great nation, with many generations of national institutions behind it, is a tremendous experiment in democracy. That attitude would be explicable in a European; and when evinced has usually been condoned. But in our own statesmen and political thinkers the attitude is not plausible and is not excused. Our national vicissitudes are no more experimental to us than the partition of a unicellular organism under the glass is, to it, an interesting experiment in the simplicities of reproduction. We are vitally concerned in the process. And it is neither dull nor yet unimaginative for Americans to feel that democracy exists to serve their interests if it can, rather than to conceive of themselves as existing upon earth to prove to southern Europe the superiority of party bosses to petty kings. To attack that attitude of mind in the name of liberalism is simply to render liberalism obnoxious and further to persuade Americans that it is an importation not for their uses.

Mr. Hoover's liberalism, though capable of international application, is not of this type. He has not robbed himself of a country in order to find a party. He has not defined liberalism as the quality of mind which believes in believing liberally. He is, first of all, an American citizen with characteristic American loyalties. He believes in American traditions of social and political development, and he believes in them unwaveringly. But he recognizes that these traditions can only endure by growth and development, that development must take into consideration changed conditions and new ideals, and that an intelligent reconstruction of existing institutions can only be made upon an open-minded balance of interests and opinions. Mr. Hoover has shown in the most persuasive way that he attributes no unusual importance to existing values because they exist. But he has also shown that he believes change must come upon the foundations of the existing social order if it is to be permanent. He is a liberal who has not forgotten that liberalism signifies *progressive* reform, and that in progression there is present the idea of development out of things that have been. He is a liberal who believes in the search for political and social truth in whatsoever bolted cupboard of prejudice it may now be hidden, but who would balk, no doubt, at an attempt to find the only reservoir of truth in untried opinion. He is a liberal until liberalism means a non-evolutionary reform without root or sequence, an attempt to erect a newer and better world upon the whims of a faction.

The most striking example of Mr. Hoover's attitude toward the problems with which American liberalism is wrestling is found in his published remarks upon the master-and-man relation: "I am daily impressed with the fact that there is but one way out, and that is to restore through organized representation that personal coöperation between employer and employee in production that was a binding force when our industries were smaller of unit and of less specialization." And again: "A society that is based upon a constant flux of individuals in the community, upon the basis of ability and character, is a moving virile mass; it is not a stratification of classes. Its inspiration is individual initiative. Its stimulus is competition. ... Its greatest mentor is free speech and voluntary organization for public good." These two statements are in different ways expressions of Mr. Hoover's faith in the frontier tradition of individual effort and initiative, which was characteristic of American life some decades ago, and which, he would seem to say, still characterizes it. It is not altogether easy to believe that our society today is based upon "a constant flux of individuals in the community." It is not altogether persuasive to deny a present stratification into classes. And it is very difficult to understand how the condition of exploited classes can be ameliorated without a recognition of class lines. But when all such objections have been taken it yet remains true that a program for the solution of the industrial problem which aims to realize, under new conditions, the American ideal of opportunity and flexibility has a greater chance of success in the United States than a scheme which postulates and accepts class differentiation and proposes to better the condition of the submerged classes. In human affairs it is silly to face the "facts" without regard to the prevalent interpretation of the facts. For the casual citizen, as well as for the reformer, reality is found at the ganglion end of the nerve. And the casual citizen is apt to have more votes.

It would seem that Mr. Hoover's position, regardless of the illiberal stand taken by other probable candidates for the presidency, should have the effect of attracting to him all shades of liberal and progressive opinion in the United States. Liberals who consider his emphasis upon American traditions mid-Victorian and excommunicate him because he will not speak in terms of international dogma are adherents to a vocabulary rather than to a means of political progress. Progressives who will have none of him because of his concern with purely social problems are converts to an academic progressivism. Gentlemen of both fringes of liberal opinion may well take comfort in the knowledge, common to all the world, that Mr. Hoover's career is notable for that sane, open-minded ability to find constructive remedies for grievous situations which, transferred to the political stage, is liberalism in action. To criticise him for lack of orthodoxy in creed is to fall into the errors liberalism is generally supposed to combat, and, worse, it is to prefer theoretic perfection, with such sterility as the liberal factions now enjoy, to heterodoxy and accomplishment.

Bathos

WE HAD FINISHED DINNER, AND THE children had gone upstairs to their lessons. Rica was tracing out a pattern on the damask cloth with the tip of her coffee spoon. The soft light of the candles shadowed the faint imprints of time, she was very handsome, and I loved that characteristic poise of her head. She looked up and I smiled at her.

"Saw Jim Parkman today. He hasn't changed a hair!"

"Did you, Ned? Dear old Jim! Has he made good yet?"

"Why Rica, he's never made anything else!"

Which means, of course, that he hasn't. How you men do stand up for each other! I wonder if you know that Lelia hasn't had a new evening gown for five years?"

She rose, deposited a fleeting kiss on the bald spot which I'm trying to train my hair to cover, and a few moments later I heard her at the piano . . . Rica does play well.

I settled a little lower in my chair and lighted my cigar.

Jim not made good — it's absurd — I first met Jim two or three nights after the opening of college in my freshman year. Tom Carrol, my roommate, had gone in town on a "party," and I had been unpacking until fairly late in the evening. The contents of my trunk and boxes were piled about in a heterogeneous collection on the chairs and the couch. I must have been engrossed in my labor, for I remember starting when the door suddenly opened. Before me stood Tom, swaying slightly, disheveled, — hopelessly drunk. He was supported by a slender, thin-faced chap, whose luminous black eyes attracted me, and whose paleness of skin was in marked contrast with Tom's flushed countenance.

"Better give me a hand with him, he's pretty far gone. I found him down in the entry."

But Tom with a "Thanks, ol' man, thanks vera much," had lunged forward and subsided full length on the couch. Between us we finally got him to bed and then, because Tom's erratic movements upon the couch had raised havoc with the fruits of my unpacking, the stranger gave me a hand in straightening things up. He introduced himself as Parkman, said he was rooming upstairs and "wouldn't I drop in and see him some time" — I liked his smile, and I knew that I was going to like what was behind it.

We roomed together the last three years of college — I always said I boarded with him, which came fairly close to the truth. He chose the rug, and the chintz curtains, bargained for our near-mahogany furniture, and adorned the walls with his etchings and wood cuts. . . . "Listen, Ned, you ass, that slop" — indicating a choice collection of posters and "prep school" photographs, — "goes all very well in your bedroom but this is a gentleman's study."

Jim made many nodding acquaintances but few deep friends. I'm afraid he set too high a standard.

"He's a nice enough chap, Ned, but he's stupid. His world is composed of three elements: football, his club, and women . . ."

He didn't care much for club life but could usually be found curled up on the window-seat with a book, or scribbing verse — his hair more tousled than ever.

And how he used to walk! He knew every back alley and "cul-de-sac" for miles about Boston. It was a treat to accompany him — though it made you realize that your wind was not what it should be. He'd lead you through a labyrinth of dingy grey streets to show you some old relic of Colonial architecture, the while discoursing on his Utopian ideals. His imagination was never still a minute — How he detested "modernism" or "money grubbing Americanitis," as he called it.

In his senior year he began to write sonnets, with a far-away look in his eyes — It was generally understood that he and Lelia Curtis were engaged.

The night of our graduation Jim had delivered the Class Poem and early in the evening I'd seen him and Lelia wandering about the yard. Gorgeous moonlight. I came in about midnight and had started to grope my way to the switch, when I saw Jim, stretched out on the window seat, his head buried in a mass of pillows. I thought he was asleep, and tiptoed across to my bedroom.

"Hello, Ned," came a muffled voice, "turn on the light, will you?" He sat up. "Been far down in the depths. God, what a mess this life is! Four wonderful years, yet how have they molded me? A half-baked poet. Damn it, Ned, I've got to make some money! Lelia and I are going to be married in two years — I'm not worth a punched nickle to a business man — God knows, I don't want to sell soap, or manufacture suspenders — I want to write."

Jim didn't prove much of a business man even in his early days. He caught hold soon enough, and his personality carried him up a few rungs, but he was never "in the game." He considered it all in the light of a necessary evil, and he suffered accordingly. His firm noted his conscientiousness, his mind for details, and his stability — and shelved him into an office position. But Jim's head and heart were too full of Lelia and his poetry to be aware of his niche.

They were married, just as they had planned, two years after his graduation — It was a beautiful wedding — the church a mass of white roses and apple blossoms. I was best man, and Lelia's younger sister sat on my silk hat. Lelia was radiant, Jim pale as a ghost, his eyes like coals — And how disgustingly drunk Tom Carrol was! Tom's retired from the Street now, with two millions . . .

They settled down in a tiny little apartment up in Cambridge. Jim's "Sonnets and Lyrics" appeared that year and were received rather favorably.

Rica is playing the "Caprice Viennoise". . . "Junior" arrived — Yet, as I look back on it, it wasn't until after Betty was born that Jim and Lelia commenced to draw away from us. They came in and dined with us, and we paid occasional visits to their tastefully decorated little house, but they accepted few of their Beacon Street invitations and, as a consequence, they received but a few. I'd see Jim at a Vestry Meeting, or downtown, or semi-occasionally at the Country Club, but I was in a rut of my own affairs and Rica usually attended to our parties. So two or three years slipped by before it came to me, with a twinge of pain at my own carelessness, that I hadn't really seen Jim, that I hadn't had a talk with him for ages. Rica was at a Suffrage Dinner, so I thought I'd run out alone and surprise them. They were glad to see me. "June" and 'Betts" were

"piggy-backed" up to bed, and we had a delightful dinner topped off with some apple pie of which Lelia was justly proud. After coffee, she went upstairs to hear the prayers, and Jim and I chatted long over our cigars. A University instructor and his young wife came in shortly, and I pleaded a fictitious club engagement and left them to their "auction" — But I had noticed some little things — the lines of fatigue in Lelia's face, though not a trace of it appeared in her smile; a ragged fuzz on Jim's tie, that bespoke long usage; and the enamel woodwork that showed traces of youthful grimy fingers. I knew that Jim had nearly reached the apex of his salary. Now and again one of his poems would appear in "Contemporary Verse," or even Harper's, and he was trying to induce Brentano's to publish his second book. He'd given up his golf. "You see, Ned," he said smilingly, "with golf balls at their present price it's either a question of humoring that cursed slice of mind, or sending 'June' to college. I take the whole family walking instead."

We met Lelia and Jim one late Sunday afternoon this fall after a concert — I think it was Kreisler. They were chatting like happy children. I offered them a lift home in the car.

"No thanks," smiled Lelia, "it's such glorious evening I think we'll walk along for a while."

Jim patted my shoulder as we separated. "Harper's sent me a birthday check," he whispered in my ear.

Later, Rica asked if I had noticed poor Lelia's hair — and I said that I thought they were one of the happiest married couples I'd ever seen. Yet as Rica says, Lelia hasn't had a new gown for five years, and the children go to the public school.

"Ned, do come away and let Brower clear the table. And dear, you haven't forgotten that we're playing cards with the Nelsons this evening?"

I dislike "auction."

E.A. WEEKS

Vol. CVIII, No. 7

PRICE 25 CENTS

THE·HARVARD ADVOCATE

Dulce est periculum

MIRRORS OF GRUB STREET

THE BEAUTIFUL BE DAMNED

By F. SCTT FTZGRLD

SOPHIA had —; well, Sophia showed —; that is, Sophia did —; oh, well, Sophia *was* nineteen. If you had been sailing on some southern sea, and if, in the middle of the night, your ship — on which Sophia, too, was traveling — had been wrecked, and the pair of you had been cast up together alone on the verdant shores of a desert island, the first thing you would have noticed about Sophia would have been her teeth. They were white, glinting like pearl, and on closer inspection you would have realized that they were implanted behind two delicate ruby lips. Then your glance would have shifted to her eyes, and —; well, she *was* Sophia. You would have introduced yourself politely, and she, after smiling sweetly upon you, would have observed that your glances were not focussed seaward for a returning sail, and she would have slapped your face. Later in the day, about tea-time, you would have kissed her; for by that time she would have informed you that she liked men with rough, unshaven cheeks.

It was just such a girl as Sophia who would have been the heroine of Balzac's "Tales," the sort who would have stirred hidden pangs in the heart of a Pindaric Hercules. Ever since old Adam first courted his Eve in that far-off garden of Eden long ago, has some ravishing Paris chanted roundelays in the ear of just such a flowering blossom as Sophia. Were she Ophelia, well might we picture sad Hamlet, torn between two desires, catch in the pregnant promise of her eye some spark, some hidden, passionate mating-cry, that would have made him stand firm in the presence of the villain-king, and say unflinchingly, "Ay, there's the rub!"

Our scene is laid in the luxurious apartment-home of Sophia's parents in New York. The time is 1922. Sophia is sprawling disconsolate on the only available davenport. As with all maidens of her years, her experience in worldly matters far surpassed that of her father and mother.

"Oh, hell," Sophia was interposing sweetly, "you are both so awfully old-fashioned! Just because I won't go to church, you both begin to interfere. Church? Pah! They're dreary and solemn. And the ministers always try to make eyes at me! Besides, nowadays, you know, one doesn't *go* to church."

Unburdened of this retort, Sophia seized her gold-inlaid cigarette-holder, tucked it modestly down her left stocking, and slammed the door. A minute later, a sound of agitated ice issued from the pantry below.

"That girl gets on my nerves!" bellowed her irate and heartless father; "nowadays don't even take the trouble to buy her own vermouth. Uses mine, by gosh!"

While this familiar domestic scene was in progress, young William Amory Lisarde, Jr., was speeding onward from Princeton, on the afternoon express. William was the modern generation in person, casual, nineteen, without illusions. That night they met. It was at a lively dinner-affair, followed by a ball.

"You know you're wonderful," he purred in her ear when they were alone.

"'Gwan. Why bother with a line when you know it's futile? 'D you say your first name was Bill? Bill! I like Bill. Nicer than just Willie!"

"You're wonderful!" he re-echoed, and he led her into the only available place for two. It was a servants'-closet in a nearby hall, a receptacle for mops and brooms.

Being nineteen, all she could murmur was, "Kiss me!" Being nineteen himself, all he could do was to comply.

"Sophia!"— her first name sizzled pleasantly on his lips; "Sophia, dear, with you it isn't the same as with those others I have kissed tonight. In fact, this seems too beautiful to be called real petting."— For such is the strange and effervescent quality of that indefinable idealism which is youth.

But Lisarde that day had been invited to leave Princeton, permanently; — it concerned some young danseuse he had befriended, out of pity; — and his heart had fallen to the depths. In fact, he had even considered permanent escape; the world held out nothing more for him in the way of allurement or knowledge, he had thought. He had attempted drowning himself in a tepid bath, but the water pouring into his nostrils made him sneeze. His consolation had been synthetic gin, to soothe his battered nerves before keeping the ordeal of the evening.— And how beautifully it had turned out. Sophia was his life, his very soul!

Somehow, his imagination was at its most pregnant pitch. He saw a strange, odd-looking man he had never seen before, eyeing him from behind Sophia. The man had two blazing eyes — the rest of his body was a blur! It was the Devil, of course! — Then he knew he saw his bared soul. Something was pounding in his brain. He let Sophia go.

"Sophia," he groaned.

"Awgahdem," she answered, wearily, accenting the last syllable; "all tired so soon, Bill?"

"Sophia," he went on, "before I kissed you, I meant to confess that this afternoon I got discouraged and was secretly married to one of the girls in the Follies."

"Really? And what has that to do with me?"

"You're so wonderful, that's all, Soph —"

"Oh, don't come back to that! My beauty is openly discussed by all men. Have you any gin?"

He extracted his flask.

"Have you no scruples? Did I not kiss you? Are we not in love?"

"Love," replied Sophia, "I know nothing of."

"But you will let me teach you?"

"Experience is the best teacher. The gin, please!"

"Then let us try the experiment!" he suggested. "A little knowledge, you know. . ."

"Fools rush in —" she flung back.

"And you are the angel!"

They kissed again. His remorse vanished with his edge. The blazing eyes of the devil were but the nickel-plated spigot-handles of the mop-sink.

A little later, as she raised the gin the third time to her lips, she said:

"And this to the health of your little Elmer!"

His only retort was, "Elmer hell; I believe in control!" Whereupon, with the glibness of familiarity, these two discussed the more intimate relations of the conjugal state. Lisarde concluded with a story of a traveling salesman and the lady in the lower opposite.

"That's a chestnut," she interjected; "heard it at school when I was eleven. William whatever-your-last-name-is, you're a bit of a dud! Now, let's Chicago a bit. And for godsakes *act* as if you got a kick out of it, even if you don't!"

But she liked him, she had to confess later — about six, as she was being undressed by her maid Antoinette, for her night's sleep. He was nice. And so different! What a shame he was married!

II

Two months later, Mr. and Mrs. William Amory Lisarde, Jr., were divorced. The move was laid to incompatibility of temperament, and a genuine desire to be in fashion.

Sophia, pillowed amongst her oriental cushions, read the news over her breakfast-tray.

"—!" she ejaculated tersely. Her beauty, the beauty of the ages, shone more radiantly than ever through the folds of her *chemise de nuit*. "Antoinette, my purple velvet. Pep it up!" She leaped from her bed to the 'phone.

"Willie," she called when she heard the familiar nasal, "let's elope!"

And, as the bright rays of the noon sun poured their almost symbolic brilliance in great waves through the room, flooding the carpet, the empty bed, the rich chairs, the perfumed clothes spread out, and most of all, the golden cascades of Sophia's tresses, she looked from the window of her bedroom, and saw a new enchanted world.— Oh, warm Cytherea, thy summons was not issued in vain! — And, as she breathed in great gulps of the morning, she knew that passion — the passion of all time — had claimed her for his own.

HALITOSIS

BY MARIANNE MOST

I am
not what I am
walking on egos
looking for my egos:

never
not forever,
if there are pigeon
droppings " on the flagstones "

or mangey
"cats" wild and rangey
that never meowed of Sa-
di's (being themselves merely a slang phrase for you know what)

or an-
ything amiss
with shoes that "trod
well but not too wisely" Then
I will tell you (all about it)

                    And one more dictum in
this matter: you may close
your eyes and hold your "nose"
and refuse to listen; but your
attitude toward me is as my
attitude toward you less than a
Sevres plate where Delft should
be but for an economic principle

"this marks an advance"

and who
knows it not true
that it was not your
head I am looking at

when I
see pigeon drop-
pings You Mangey Cat
your shoes may be ones that

yes I
may sometime try
to make note of in
the foregoing: and do
you grudge me this slight evidence
of observant laughter?

NOTES

Halitosis: Listerine advertisement, *Vanity Fair* January to December 1924. (unpleasant breath).

"on the flagstones": a forgotten poem of Robert Bridges.

"cats": *Dictionary of Bowery Cant*

Sadi's: although this word is not used in reference to the Marquis de Sade, but rather to the Persian poet, 1184?–1291, I nevertheless intend the word to have a sadistic connotation.

"trod well but not too wisely": County Attorney Epstein's summing-up in Satte vs. Clackwell.

"nose": advertisement for Tuxedo Tobacco in *Saturday Evening Post*.

economic principle: see Taussig for several.

"this marks an advance": S T on M Moore, *Dial*

This poem, lest there should be any misunderstanding, is a rational treatment of the problems arising from the social aspects of street life in England of the late seventeenth century.

ONE-HAND

" The average Indian cannot see beyond the next winter "

OLIVER LAFARGE

A GREAT hot sun poured on the cañon walls, on the sandy flat, on the scrub growth and piñon trees; poured on them, wrapped them, weighed them down. Segi Cañon walls are red and yellow, merging into orange, deepening into crimson-brown, streaked sometimes with a ruddy purple, and again, shading off into the yellow of beach sand. The walls run in great folds, as though the cañon had been scooped out with giant fingers that scored and cut downwards on the rock. Opposite our camp the mass broke into a box-cañon, a gap a few hundred feet wide — far narrower than the height of the walls,— and in the break you could see green where the easy slopes gave a hold for thicker growth. The end of the box-cañon was made dim by a violet haze, a thankful sight; for so harshly clear were the main walls even though a good mile away, that they oppressed one, dominated and intruded. Where the flat began, piñon trees clung to the walls, faded and crushed to a vague, grey green by the sun. They clustered about the walls as if living only for night, and a morning cool for a while, at least, in the shade. From them to us the sage made a lavender haze over yellow sand. Only the green things were soft coloured, as if timid at intruding on the age-old wonder of the rocks.

We, under the cliffs that gave shade in late afternoon, huddled beneath the piñon, with the thick heat holding us to earth. Soon the shadow of the trees would leave us as we lay, and then I must get up and rouse the gang, and drive them all back to that dusty kitchen of a cave, to dig up pots and bones, dust and the dung of ancient sheep, till evening came.

Far down the cañon a Navaho appeared, riding, as they ride, at full gallop and nonchalantly as though they had never walked. In that sun, and against the colours of that land, the gorgeousness of Navaho blanket and clothes seem fitting; they blend and are mild. You could see him well now, he made a pleasant spot of colour, gave the picture what it lacked, yet left it wild and desolate. You could see his red head band, above the rich, leather-brown of his face, his blanket, red and black and white, his leggings of some red whiteman's cotton, his arm rising and falling monotonously as he ropes-ended his brown pony.

He came nearer and headed for the camp. The two boys looked up casually and returned to their siesta. The three students, Easterners, stared. They had been in the country but a few days, and real Indians on the loose, wielders of bow and arrow, were rare to them.

"Hello," I said, "Shoots-From-His-Horse." Harvey grunted, the Easterners looked puzzled. Madison, the other boy, started to tell them some absurd story — he loved to string them — but I spoilt it by explaining.

"Old friend of mine — first knew him ten years ago, in '98. He was a kid then, Red Goat's son. Remember Clezi-Clichi, Harvey?"

"Sure do. He was on the party that killed Gregory, but he was good to his friends. He helped the white man a lot before he died." If he couldn't string the Easterners, at least he'd shock them with casual facts.

Meanwhile the son of the white man's friend had come up and dismounted. He kept his blanket gathered about him, under his right shoulder and over the other, despite the heat. We rose and performed the solemn Navaho hand-shake. The Easterners were amusing to watch, they still had the negro colour-line in their minds, and at the same time they were frightened. Sherman was puzzled by it all, and embarrassed, Borrell, a naturally good fellow and genial, did it in a friendly way, and d'Oret, I noticed, was taking it seriously, and understood already that a Navaho clasps hands, looks you in the eye, but does not shake.

I squatted with the Indian under my piñon-tree, Madison, who shared my liking for the saddle tinted son of nature, and d'Oret after a moment's hesitation, joined me, the others returned to their rest. Shoots-From-His-Horse sighed and stretched out at full length. In doing so his blanket fell from about his left arm.

"Jesus!" I cried, "What's happened to your hand?"

"Hunt?"

"*Hadish?*" I pointed at the stump. "*Hadish, atin cochi?*"

"*Cleesh.*" He spoke quite without feeling. "*Shi Bellicana-go* — shmoke?"

I handed him the makings. He made a motion of rolling, so I rolled it for him. He took the smoke and went on.

"Snake. I go to white men, medicine-man at Moenkopi. He cuts, so —" He made a motion of cutting and sawing, "says that keeps poison from going up. Now Shoots-From-His-Horse dead: One-hand."

That much I gathered despite the weakness of my Navaho and d'Oret's constant interruptions for explanation.

"Who was the doctor?" I asked Madison.

"Government feller up there from Flag. Sure saved his life."

I made some remark of sympathy, and stopped, appalled by what the loss of a hand meant in this country.

"No good." Replied the impassive one. Hang him, it might be some one else's wound he was discussing. He was utterly detached, and the low, even, Indian speech never strongly personal in its sound, made it seem almost ghastly.

"*Doashonda.* Sell bracelets, sell necklace, wives go, no catch horses, sheep all stolen." He relapsed into silence and smoked on, as an Indian smokes, in little puffs till his cigarette was nothing but a pinch of brown paper.

"Will he take a tailor-made?" asked d'Oret.

"Yes, give him several, the poor devil can't roll them."

One-Hand took them.

"White-man's tobacco good. Ti," he gestured unconsciously with his left arm. It was pitiful. As he saw what he was doing, his eyes for the first time showed a flicker of pain and horror. "*Ti, Tin-Hoski, shadani.*"

"What's he say?"

I translated, "He says you, four-eyes, are his father-in-law — means friend."

"*Shadani* means father-in-law? What's cigarette?"

I told him, and he wrote it down.

As the afternoon was getting on, I rose, and called the outfit to work. One-Hand, Shoots-from-His-Horse that was, quietly melted away.

Southwestern Archaeology is an active pursuit, and during the afternoon I forgot all about the Indian. My idea of a director is one who sits in the shade and directs the eager enthusiasm of his minions, but a minion who shows that kind of zeal in that heat, and in the dust of the digging — Arizona sand is curiously pungent — would be a jewel beyond price. In fact, he'd soon cease to be a minion and take my job from me. I buzzed round, seeing that Sherman and d'Oret didn't break any pots in their excitement of their interminable discussions about Thackerey and Dickens, advising Borrell, who really was going in for the Archaeology, setting the Westerners on to the more difficult bits of work, and digging out a burial I'd located in the intervals.

That night I got the full details of One-Hand's troubles from Harvey and Madison. Madison Gage gets on very well with the Indians, and knew a lot of their gossip, and Harvey had heard the rest at the Tyende trading post. First his wives all left him, which meant that the children went, and he was left alone. He had some sheep of his own, and a good many horses, but a one-handed man can't draw a bow, guns are expensive, and so he became an easy mark. He was living up beyond Oljeto then, near the Pai Ute country, and before he could move out a Pai Ute named Blunt Nose, a bad Indian — "Sure mean," Harvey said — came along with some friends and took the sheep. *He* got together some of *his* friends who chased them for the honour of the tribe. Before the thing could become a war, the Government stepped in, and all he got back was about a dozen sheep and the empty satisfaction of seeing a Pai Ute's scalp in his brother's hogan.

One-Hand came round a couple of times after that, then we moved up beyond Agathla toward the Monuments, where the alkali water, the utter waste, and the baking heat in amongst the works filled our attention beyond all thought of others. It wasn't till we drifted down into cañon Dudge-gee-ai, where there was cool shade under scrub oaks, where the sun came in only for a few hours, where the pines grew straight and tall on hanging valleys up above real, running, clear water, that I saw him again.

We found him at camp when we came back for supper, lying with his head on a saddle, completely at home. In my capacity as boss I didn't cook, nor did I hew wood or draw water, so I stretched out beside him, rolled him a cigarette, and asked him how he fared. He grunted, and for a while we were silent. Then he started talking, in his impersonal, off-hand way. He talked a little more fully than usual, and it strained my linguistic gifts to follow him, but this was the idea:

His people didn't help him at all, they had no use for him, they didn't care about him, now that he was One-Hand. The white men had been good to him, at Tyende they found him some odd jobs. "Make little things for One-Hand to do," he said. I helped him. I was his best white friend. We had hunted together, we had been hungry together, we had eaten together. Now he couldn't hunt, but still he was my friend. When I went East he wanted to go with me,— that made one realize how utterly he gave up hope of living here — he would be mine, work for me; maybe some day I'd want some one to die for me, he was the man. One winter here would kill him. "Come winter, no food, no money, no sheep — die."

Then he stopped, casually, as man might stop who was tired of discussing the weather.

"Shmoke?" That was one of his three English words. I rolled him a cigarette.

He didn't expect an answer right off. I might wait a week, even a month. If I went off to the East without deciding, he might well say nothing. So I sat and smoked till supper, and then, being tired, decided to put it from my mind.

I couldn't do it. Try as I would, my mind returned each time to One-Hand's dilemma. I was angry at him for shoving part of the trouble thus onto me. The camp went to bed, the fire sank, only the stars and I peeping down into this slit of a cañon seemed awake, and like the stars I felt that sleep had become, for me, non-existent. Well, then I'd best have it out now, so I dug out my pipe, lit up, and fell a thinking.

There was no room in the East for a savage, for a man who spoke no English, who knew none of civilization's arts. I hadn't the money to support an idle Indian. No one would want him for a body servant, I didn't know anyone who could afford such a luxury as a decorative Indian about the place, who would believe that all Indians are by training clean, reasonably honest, and truthful. I might get him a place with some show, but I'd see him dead sooner. I'd seen greasy, shameless Indians, robbed of their dignity and all that makes them fine, standing up to be stared at, and I was damned if I'd make that of Red Goat's son. Didn't I know anyone who had been out here? No one who would do. Wait, though — McEmmel! He'd do it, his chief idea was to spend the money from his collar-factories on just such extraordinary things. He'd been raving about the Navaho ever since I took him out here, (he financed the expedition as it never had been done before, and never would be again), and he probably would remember Red Goat if not the son. A Southwestern Indian is naturally a good farmer, he has to be to make his corn and peaches grow where cactus finds the water a mere pittance. What a coup for him, to have an Indian in full regalia trotting about his landscape! One-Hand would be eager to adopt himself. It could be done! Forthwith I heaped up the fire and wrote a letter, to go as soon as I could get to Tyende. Then I nodded derisively to the stars, crawled into my bed-roll, and went to sleep.

He came with us the next day, up to a cave which we were finishing. He watched the digging with politely hidden amusement, picked up some arrowheads, and showed off his agility by climbing over the rocks in an amazing way. Then he came and squatted down beside me, where I was working at a likely spot with a trowel. I feared that he was going to talk about the East again. Just then a rock came away, exposing an excellent skull, and he was off to the other end of the cave. It's not lucky to be round when " Anas'-hasi" are being dug up. Then I got interested in the burial, and forgot all about him. At lunch, however, he turned up again — a square meal was beginning to mean a lot to him, usually he was one of those rare Indians who don't come round at meals — and I told him, as best I could what I was doing. With that he seemed content. I sent Madison into Tyende shortly after that for more provisions and the letter went with him.

I was in no hurry to leave Dudge-gee-ai, the water and the shade were delicious, the outfit worked better here, everything was pleasant. D'Oret wandered about, paint box in hand, for all the world, with his dark colour now tanned incredibly, like an esthetic Navaho; Sherman expanded in this comparatively civilized spot, I suspected him of writing verses; and the cheery Borrell, under the influence of reasonably soft water near at hand and a life generally more genial, gave up his incipient mustache. That last was a boon, his bristles had been such a source of endless bad jokes.

One-Hand drifted about, apparently busy over something. Once he dropped in to say that he had found a couple more of his sheep. Madison said he saw him up by the cave that he'd visited with us, that was all.

Then one evening he came in, and dropped a great bundle, half an old sheepskin, at my feet. He opened it. It was full of all kinds of Navaho jewelry:— "dot klishi," strings of cylindrical turquoise beads, worth a mule for a handful; necklaces, worth anything from ten dollars to a hundred; bracelets with garnets, bracelets with turquoises, plain silver bracelets worked in intricate designs, rings of all sorts; rough garnets, the colourless stone they call "tsent-augh'li," and always more turquoises, raw turquoises, cut turquoises, turquoises pierced to make earrings, turquoises with matrices in them, turquoise of all shades from pale blue to sapphire.

"Where you get all that?"

"My father hides it. Then he dies, I dont' know where to look. See his sign up on cave, go up and look, by and by find."

" Ti," he scooped up a great handful of stuff, " azdza."

At that rate he could get a whole harem of wives.

"Now One-Hand doesn't go with you. One-Hand rich. He remembers you help him, elder brother. K'ho (It's a gift)." He held out a bracelet. I took it and went off, much relieved, while he settled down to doing business with these white men from outside who would pay a quarter for a turquoise worth, at the post, perhaps a nickel.

Shortly after that we went in to Tyende again and then down to the region about Marsh Pass. The July rains made even digging in the open pleasant for a while, then passed. August came, time for us to go, and with it ugly rumours of a Pai Ute rising, of a Navaho raid in reprisal for one of theirs, and a white man chased for a couple of miles as he rode into Shonto. I should have wished to stay and offer my services for the posses that were being formed, but I was responsible for the students, and felt it best, now our trip was over, to get out.

So we returned to Tyende to "rest up" for a day. There was a mail for us, and in it an enthusiastic acceptance of One-Hand from McEmmel. I stuck it into my pocket, disgusted at the explanation I should have to make. Next day we set out for Red Lake on our way to Flagstaff and the railroad.

Red Lake is nothing but a single, square, block-house like post on an utterly barren rise overlooking a string of miserable pools of undrinkable water. We camped there that night, but I was unwilling to strain the agent's hospitality by letting him have that whole gang in to dinner, so we ate at camp. In the middle of supper old Tin Horn — so we called him — a jeweler of some note, came in with stuff to sell. We gathered round, handled it, and made a few purchases, but trade was slack. Finally he picked up a bracelet and held it out to me. I noticed how white it looked against his skin, for he was one of those very dark Indians whose red becomes almost purple; now in the dark it seemed black, relieved with ruddy splashes of fire-light.

"Ti, me heap buy One-Hand." Tin Horn was a linguist.

"How long ago?"

"Mebby-so two weeks."

"How is One-Hand?"

He pointed solemnly to the ground, then spoke in Navaho; "One-Hand comes to Tyende, rich. He buys everything, coffee, sugar, things that stand up (canned goods), cloth, candy. Buys lots of candy. He gets two wives, you remember Wind-Singer's wife? She comes to him. He goes up in Segi Hatsosi. He buys horses, lots of horses, and sheep, and two mules. Spends all his money. Then about fifteen days ago Pai Utes start to make trouble, make a raid down there and steal his horses. He runs, he can't fight. His wives say One-Hand no good, leave him again, and take their sheep. One-Hand all alone, trying to catch horse, Pai Ute find —" he drew his hand across his throat and made the scalp sign.

I found myself gulping slightly, and unconsciously clutching McEmmel's letter in my pocket. Then I looked up at the ragged edge of the bluff behind the post, and the stars above it, and followed the line away indefinitely, vast desert cliffs cutting off the stars. I thought of degenerate civilized Indians I had seen, and of One-Hand, buried in a rough rock tomb under just some such bluff. Then I took out McEmmel's letter and burnt it utterly.

Vol. CVII, No. 7

PRICE 25 CENTS

THE·HARVARD ADVOCATE

THE ATLANTIC MONTHLY

APRIL  1921

BOOK REVIEWING IN THE UNITED STATES

STEDMAN BUTTRICK

1. *In the manner of the Harvard Crimson*

"LUST" is an interesting and well-written novel by Mrs. Jennie Ginsberg. It holds the interest throughout and is replete with sparkling dialogue and natural characters. Mrs. Ginsburg whose "Passion-seekers" made a "hit" last year tells an interesting story about a married couple, Albert and Irma Krantz, who live in New York City. He works at a candy factory where he is employed and she at a fashionable dressmaker's "on the Avenue." It seems that Albert falls in love with one of the factory girls and Irma, in turn, falls in love with a young student who goes to Columbia. Mrs. Ginsberg develops this interesting plot in clever fashion showing cleverly how the thwarted desires of husband and wife have brought about the unhappy situation. But Selma Jacobs, however, a young girl who shows promise of being a world-famous violinist discovers how affairs stand between husband and wife and brings about a reconciliation and is adopted by the Krantzes. But Selma, however, falls in love with Amory Thorndike, the young student who Irma Krantz had been in love with and Irma, jealous, tries to win back young Thorndike. In a powerful scene that is realistic without being sordid Irma injures Selma's hand so that she will never be able to play her violin again. But Irma, however, touched by Selma's goodness and beauty begs forgiveness and young Thorndike promises to marry Selma, her injury turning out to her advantage because young Thorndike had always said he would not marry Selma if she went on the concert stage. Thus a story that seems to be consistently gloomy is relieved by Mrs. Ginsberg's light touch and the story ends happily. The story is a little too long and some of the descriptions are rather elaborate but on the whole, however, it is an interesting and well-written story.

2. *In the manner of H. L. Mencken*

A YEAR or so ago in the columns of America's family magazine, "The Smart Set," I denounced "Passion-Seekers" by Jennie Ginsberg, the East-side Messiah, as being as witless and unlovely a yokel-yanker as had ever set a-whooping the congregation of Woodmen of the World, Baptists, Lime and Cement Dealers, United Daughters of the Confederacy, Congressmen and Comstocks that constitutes the reading public of these States. This Ginsberg confection by Laura Jean Libbey out of the Chatauqua was a direct and bumptious assault on the intelligence of anyone who did not hold Maurice Maeterlinck to be one of the great thinkers of the Age and Cotton Mather superior to Johann Sebastian Bach and I dismissed it as such, for which offense I was visited by a posse of agents of justice who accused me of being in league with the Black Beast of Potsdam.

Today, a new opus by the Ginsberg hight "Lust" again makes lamentably clear that the lady author fits in snugly with our literary bagmen and yahoos. What she has to offer is, in essence, no more than a dramatization of current sociological rumble-bumble — a dramatization based on the thesis that one Knight of Pythias is more desirable than ten John D. Rockefellers. Yet for all its wowing and clapper-clawing in the name of New Thought, "Lust" remains at bottom a ripe and carnal specimen of the tin-horn romanticism that came out of the puff-sleeve period. Even a college professor should detect that under the vast moraines of pish-posh thrown up to bemuse Uplifters and Inspired Dreamers is the solid foundation tried and true hokum, that under the arpeggios on the harp is the unison singing of the First Methodist choir, that under the bogus appeal aimed at the suburban intelligentsia is the appeal aimed at the gizzard of the typical American, the tenth-rate oaf, the product of fifty years of Christian Endeavour and Right-Thinking. In the face of opposition of this flashy and hollow sort is it strange that fellows of such high purpose and dignity as Dreiser and Cabell find the going hard, the way beset with snares.

3. *In the manner of Dr. Frank Crane.*

THE greatest book of these times.

Written not by a propagandist or a crank or a poet but by a mother.

Written not by a fashionable lady who moves in an artificial set but by a frank, honest worker who has come face to face with the great realities, who has in a word such practical knowledge of the conditions she sets forth that if she does not know what she is talking about who does?

"Lust," it is by Jennie Ginsberg.

It is a book of cold, scientific facts beautifully warmed and humanized by Love, in the best sense.

If I had one hundred million dollars I would see that every man, woman and little one in the United States owned this volume.

I would have it taught in every public school.

Like you, I have read many novels and am callous. But this book staggers my imagination. It grips my heart and sweeps my brain clear.

If you buy no other book and read no other this year, buy and read "Lust."

Unreservedly I place it as the best book in the world to read right now for every man, woman and little one in America including the President and others who guide human destinies.

Clear, dispassionate, yet living, it is as shattering as any great masterpiece of the English language save perhaps the Bible.

Take it home. Read it. Talk to your friends about it. Get your wife to read it. Get the point of view of everyone.

You will find in it, as I found, a great hopefulness for the future of America. It has a message for your home that will give you new faith and courage.

4. *In the manner of Robert Benchley.*

"LUST" is one of those frothy little things about Birth, Life, Marriage and Death that Jennie Ginsberg tosses off every now and then for a *jeu d'esprit*. Just the sort of thing for Christmas reading when the lights are low and the yule logs are blazing merrily, and you hear in the chamber above you the patter of little feet. You must know by this time how Mrs. Ginsberg does it — how, just when you're willing to swear that Irma Krantz, née Ackermann, is going to leave the flat with a Columbia student for a nasty evening at the Hippodrome, little Selma Jacobs who supports a blind father, a paralytic mother, three invalid sisters, and two brothers with the rickets by playing "Humoresque" at the picture house round the corner loops in and wises up to the tense drama that is being enacted and appeals with childish insouciance to the student to clear out for the honor of Columbia. Then in a jiffy she fixes up the nicest supper you ever ate, while Mrs. Krantz tears at the wall-paper, and when Albert Krantz comes home from work tired out after six hours of dipping great, heavy chocolate creams he never suspects in his man-like way what has been going on.

Well, you've guessed the rest. Personally this department got a great deal of satisfaction out of the scene toward the end where poor old Irma Krantz cracks little Selma over the right hand with the meat-axe.

REMEMBER THE ROSE

JAMES GOULD COZZENS

THE afternoon sunlight fell in shafts between the elms; hollyhocks along the brick wall stood like trophies and standards of August, bathed in golden glory. Above, the hills were settling into cool shadows and heights of sunny trees. A sky like unrippled blue silk came down to them and steep white clouds appeared with slow, adventurous intent along the crest.

There were cedars in one corner. The grass, a thick green tapestry reaching down from the wall by the road, hesitated, and gave way to warm, needle-soft openness about them, there was a faint perfume of cedars in the sun. A tea table was set here in the shadows with the tremble of breeze stirred linen, the sheen of silver, and the fineness of pale porcelain.

Mrs. Bakewell, a contrast in her black silk and snowy hair, looked half smiling at a friend who had finished tea. The friend was a boy. He regarded abstracted the cigarette between his fingers and its slim straight column of smoke. You noticed first that he had that casual tan which comes from mornings on the links and the blaze of the tennis court. Afterwards you saw his hair was the color of old gold.

He broke the intimate silence at last, rousing himself and smiling a little; "I was in town this morning," he said, "I managed to get hold of that old book of Monsieur Hardy's." He produced a dingy volume from his pocket and laid it on the table beside her. "I thought you'd like it," he said.

"How very nice of you, Blair!" Mrs. Bakewell's smile carried you back to the days when she had been Nancy English and Joseph Ames had done her in oils, astounding the old Philadelphia Academy and making his own reputation. She looked at the battered gold lettering: *Un Faineant dans la Roseraie*.

"I looked to see if this was the one in which he told about his work on the Damask roses," remarked the boy, "it's got a whole chapter on the Amanda Patenotte."

"It's been out of print for thirty years at least," Mrs. Bakewell turned the pages thoughtfully, "The love of roses, except for fanatics like you and me, died even longer ago. This had five editions in its day, and now it can't be bought."

Blair dropped the cigarette in the ash tray on his chair arm.

"Aren't the Duchess of Southerlands blooming yet, Mrs. Bakewell?"

"Oh, Blair, they are. I almost forgot. Shall we go and look at them?"

He arose and drew the chair away. Still bearing the book she led him through the round arch where the brick was lost under the green of the ramblers. It opened into a second walled garden with spacious gravel paths radiating from the steps and stone work of a sun dial in the center. They went down to the glossy leaved bed where the fresh buds of the Duchess of Southerlands had broken gently into crimson.

"It's really a triumph to have them blooming now," said Mrs. Bakewell, "it's because I pruned them so hard this spring. Thomas protested a great deal, but he found he couldn't do anything with me. He is really a good gardener in the sense that he keeps the paths so neat, but he will not learn about roses. I shall never forget his chagrin when he came that morning to tell me they had budded after all."

She and Blair passed down to the dial. The stone was softly grey and graceful, the old bronze clear cut for all the long exposure, the rain and snow.

"I've always meant to look at that inscription," said Blair, bending before the metal plate set in the side. He read aloud the fine swash-letter script; 'Remember the Rose, how it doth fall.'

"Yes," smiled Mrs. Bakewell, "that dial

was set up by my father and he had those lines put on it. A rebuke to youth, he called them. I can remember him so well on summer evenings walking the paths here in a yellow linen suit with a long cigar that trailed a delicious aroma, holding my brother's hand on one side and mine on the other. He would walk about and look at the roses and grumble over his problem of the moment — Verdier had sent him cuttings of his Souvenir de Malmaison, I remember one year, and he was trying to make them grow, refused to believe they were dead long after they really were — he would always end his stroll before the dial and read the words solemnly,—'Lines to take note of . . . .' he would say, and thump off leaving us there to look at them. My brother used to make little parodies and father would be annoyed when we came out of the garden squealing with laughter."

They walked down toward the back. Those were the Phaloes, dusky over a faint flush of rose. So would Cleopatra's cheek have been, thought Blair. The Eugenie Jovins were like tinted foam. What could one call the Barbots? Blair thought of Watteau's fawns in a painted park.

Here were Eliza Sauvages, yellow like aged silk, and as thin and fine.

"You know," he said after a moment, "one can't say much of anything. I hate people who whisper 'ah, beautiful!' at everything from roses to Walter Pater."

"Some people can't say anything else, and they do mean it."

"I should think if they meant it they could say something else. They've spoiled a good word.

He paused among the musk roses. The Princess of Nassaus were in bud, golden.

"They are very white when they open," said Mrs. Bakewell, "its like magic."

Beyond were the Eponines, true Persian roses, white as milk; Eponines, the show drift of whose petals wise Omar hoped would soothe him in his grave. They stood in the gate presently.

"Such roses!" said Blair at last. "It's a dream, it really doesn't exist at all. You step through this gate into a dream garden which vanishes when your back is turned."

"Yes, but it always comes back, when, like Peter Ibbetson, you dream true."

After he had left and a dusk was settling on the garden, dulling the rambling lines of the old white house, Mrs. Bakewell sat in the candle light at her desk waiting for dinner to be announced. She penned a fine script in a black bound book.

'My sixty-ninth birthday,' she wrote, 'I had a delightful tea with Blair and we looked at the roses afterwards. He and I, are I think, the last of the rosiéristes . . . .'

Her eye wandered to the book he had brought and from there the albums in the bottom of the book cases.

When Parke entered to tell Mrs. Bakewell dinner was served, he found her looking at the pages of faded letters; good wishes, congratulations and advice, written long ago by Vibert and Laffay and Hardy; the notes in the great Rivers' angular characters, the neat little lines from old Wood. Mr. English had known them all.

"Blair," said Mrs. Bakewell one afternoon as they left the garden, "would you care to come over for dinner Thursday night? My niece Millicent is going to spend a few weeks with me, and I would like very much to have you meet her."

"I'd love to," said Blair.

He rode John Halifax down to the village to get the mail the next afternoon. The train was in, dark and compact along the open gravel platforms. He saw Mrs. Bakewell's carriage with the team of chestnuts waiting. John Halifax objected to trains, and pawing the air refused to go nearer. A girl appeared, laughing, followed by Mrs. Bakewell's man carrying bags. The train gathered strength with a tremendous burst of steam and iron roar, John Halifax backed away with desperate vigor, Mrs. Bakewell's carriage turned about. Blair went over to the post office steps and swung out of the saddle. As he lit a cigarette he saw the carriage disappear up the long maple arch of the road.

On the evening Blair was to come to dinner Millicent English had appeared in Mrs. Bakewell's rooms clad in heavenly blue over laid with silver, accepted Mrs. Bakewell's admiration with a happy smile, and gone downstairs. Mrs. Bakewell still stood by a window looking out over the gardens in the gathering twilight. The sound of Millicent at the piano reached her faintly and seemed to bring with it years very long ago. Late afternoons were perhaps more golden then, or better, a gold more soft. A certain magnificence had given way to cool efficiency; you saw it in the summer dusk, you saw it — Mrs. Bakewell half smiled — in Millicent's dress. She thought of the flowing gowns of those days, the billows and gorgeous mounds of lovely cloth. The evening clothes of today had none of the leisurely grace.

The pace of life had quickened. Men no longer wore such beautiful linen; their gloves and hats, the cut of their clothes, had sacrificed pleasant dignity and beauty. She thought of her husband with his curling mustachios, his graceful capes, the glitter of quiet gold, the cambrics no longer made, the rich folds of black satin. Such things had been relegated to a past which seemed now subtlely better bred.

Her attention was taken by the appearance of Millicent and Blair strolling on the garden path. She saw thoughtfully the white of his shirt front, the cigarette in his hand. A gauze veil Millicent had slipped about her shoulders detached itself a little and floated after her in the light breeze. Across the sounds of summer evening her laugh came low and clear. Mrs. Bakewell turned away, went out of the room and down the wide cool stairs pensively.

The sound of horses hoofs died away on the road beyond the wall. The long shadows had sunk the tea table in coolness and quiet, and Mrs. Bakewell sat alone.

I'm glad they like each other so much, she thought. Blair and Millicent were always together, riding, or playing tennis, or paddling on the river. Only yesterday Millicent had brought home an armful of water lilies, wanly fragrant. There had been a dance or two in the village, dead dances, Blair had said, but they went none the less, laughing, and came back quite late still laughing.

Young people did things differently now. Millicent would come down in boyish riding clothes, flit into the breakfast room where the morning coolness yet remained, urge Parke to hurry and be out on horseback to ride away with Blair into the nine o'clock shadows, under breezy elms, up sunny slopes, untold miles into the summer country before she appeared dusty and breathless, late for lunch.

They had left now to ride over the hill road and see the sunset. Up there the long fields were yellow with golden rod; cardinal flowers and gentians grew in the hollows about the brooks, the asters, blue beneath the dust, thronged along the road. So Millicent said.

She had told Blair when they had finished tea a little while before that the Moirés were blooming at last. Once, she thought a little wistfully, he would have wanted to see them. Millicent had got up and gone toward the stables and he had followed, unreluctant.

It was late in September when Millicent left. The next afternoon Blair came in. He was very hurried.

"Thank you," he said, "I can't stay to tea, I've got lots of packing to do to get back to the University tomorrow."

"I'm sorry you're going, I haven't seen you at all lately, Blair; you and Millicent were so busy."

"She's very nice."

Mrs. Bakewell walked to the gate with him.

"The roses will soon be gone," she said.

"There will be more roses next spring," said Blair, and he smiled and turned down into the glory of the afternoon sunlight.

The Connoisseur's Favorite

TO serve your guests a fragrant, zestful cup of really good tea is to compliment the palate of a connoisseur and to contribute to delightful hospitality.

Tea connoisseurs the world over revel in Ridgways *Genuine* Orange Pekoe tea because it represents the zenith of tea perfection. Its charm, flavor and piquancy are unexcelled.

Besides, this really supreme tea is conducive to true sociability. Its golden depths hold the key to good cheer—that glorious something which so pleasantly loosens the tongue as cherished memories spring to mind.

By sheer might of merit Ridgways *Genuine* Orange Pekoe tea is "The Finest Tea the World Produces."

Ridgways *Genuine* Orange Pekoe Tea

Ridgways, Inc., Dept. R.   60 Warren Street, New York.

Send me a free sample of Ridgways *Genuine* Orange Pekoe Tea and your booklet, "A Few Facts About Tea."

Name_____   Address_____

POLITICAL SENTIMENTALISTS

H. C. LODGE, JR.

ROLAND W. BOYDEN first sprang into the limelight in November, 1922, as a result of the reparations plan which he advanced when he had no right officially to do so. Since then there has been a lot of argument and a lot of confusion as to what we should do with him. Should we recall him? Should we establish him as official representative?

The very fact that the case is so simple probably accounts for its having been so confused. This article will try to show the real facts in the Boyden case. The case is worth treating because the ignorance of the college on Roland W. Boyden is typical of its ignorance on most political subjects. This article plans to present the facts of the case and then digress on the value of facts and the need of them in Harvard College today. A certain type of Harvard man, in so far as we can generalize, often feels he can see the truth without knowing the facts; he is sometimes inclined to sniff at facts as too material. The result often is that even in a case like that of Roland W. Boyden, he becomes confused and reaches absurd conclusions.

There have been complicated arguments pro and con, but Mr. Boyden's status in Europe is really perfectly simple. He is a personal agent of the President. The President is, of course, exclusively charged with all negotiations dealing with foreign relations, and has the right to appoint personal agents to represent him. The reason for this is obvious; the President cannot carry on all his foreign negotiations himself. Thus Mr. Boyden is sitting at the Reparations Commission having no vote, taking no official part in the proceedings and merely observing and reporting to the President the transactions vital to the best interests of the United States. The President has the absolute right to appoint anyone he pleases to carry on negotiations for him and represent

him, and this power has always been exercised by the President from the beginning of the Government. There is thus nothing abnormal, nothing revolutionary about Mr. Boyden's being over there and his position has ample precedent. Here are some of the better known precedents.

There was a very famous case when Mr. Fillmore sent Mr. Ambrose Dudley Mann to report on the situation in Austria at the close of the Korsute revolution about 1848. This led to a controversy with the Austrian Government and Mr. Webster wrote an historic dispatch to Baron Hulsemann replying to his objections, not to the official character of Mr. Mann, but as to what he was supposed to have reported.

President Wilson also used personal agents on a very large scale. Colonel House was the best known among them, but when he made the Treaty of Versailles, although he was there himself, Mr. Lansing, Mr. White and General Bliss were all representatives and agents of the President.

It was the same when we made the Treaty of Paris with Spain; President McKinley appointed three Senators, the Secretary of State, and Mr. Whitelaw Reid, a private citizen. They were all his agents and representatives.

At the Disarmament Conference in Washington last year, the four delegates, Secretary Hughes, Senator Underwood, Mr. Root and Senator Lodge were the President's representatives and personal agents in making the treaties.

There are some of the precedents in Mr. Boyden's case. It shows that his position is perfectly legal.

The history of the case is short and equally simple. Mr. Boyden was appointed by President Wilson to succeed Mr. Rathbone, appointed in December, 1919, as his representative in order to keep him informed as to what was being done by the Reparations Commission. He was not a member of the Commission; he had no right to vote, but was merely an observer, and was there through the courtesy, of course, of the powers who had signed the Treaty of Versailles. He went out with Mr. Wilson and was reappointed in May, 1921, with his staff, by President Harding.

It is a very important thing to have an informant as to the activities of the Reparations Commission where the vital interests of this country are often concerned. But this informant should not go beyond his function, he should say nothing which might be misunderstood as being official. Unfortunately Mr. Boyden has taken action in cases where he cannot separate himself in the popular mind from the United States government. He has been unwise and has unintentionally misrepresented the United States in proposing a reparations plan, which, personal though it was, might have caused serious misunderstanding. His error is best shown by the official statement issued by the Department of State on January 16, 1923, parts of which are quoted below.

"It appears that on November 13th Mr. Boyden had been requested by one or more members of the Reparations Commission to draft, as a purely *personal* suggestion, a proposed letter to be sent by the Reparations Commission to the German Government on lines he had informally indicated. This Mr. Boyden did in the memorandum in question which he gave as a draft to one of the members of the Reparations Commission."

". . . This memorandum was prepared and submitted by Mr. Boyden as a *personal* matter and without consultation with the Department. When its text was subsequently received by the Department, it was not regarded as a plan for the settlement of reparations or as requiring any action whatever on the part of the Department. Rather it was deemed to be a *personal* memorandum, which Mr. Boyden had already submitted to one of the members of the Commission, of a general nature and which

merely emphasized some of the fundamental considerations which were deemed to be pertinent to the situation in a large way." ". . . There is no basis for treating the general suggesting of Mr. Boyden as a reparations plan."

(The italics are my own.)

From this it may be seen how unofficially Mr. Boyden's statements are regarded by the Department of State. This plan which he drafted, although he himself said it was purely personal, was taken very seriously by some European nations. The French Foreign Office immediately asked whether Secretary Hughes was proposing a reparations plan and the Department of State had to issue statements denying that any plan had been officially proposed.

Mr. Boyden should never have drawn up that plan. If he had to draw one up, he should never have made it public because, purely personal though it is, it makes for serious misunderstanding. There is Mr. Boyden's mistake and there is where he exceeded the duties of his office.

Mr. Boyden now knows the result of action of that sort. He probably realizes that a breach of tact can in certain cases be as serious as a breach of duty. Mr. Boyden is a good lawyer of high standing in Boston. He has discharged his duties intelligently and well but he has been unwise in proposing his personal reparations plan. In the event of another mistake of that sort his recall should be immediate.

The misunderstanding and theorizing which has been going on in a small way about Roland W. Boyden is going on on a much larger scale about other political questions which are not nearly so easy to explain. The tendency here in college has been to neglect fact and to cater to the sentimental side of our natures. It is my belief that this state of mind is extremely prevalent; that the larger part of this college is imbued with a false altruism; and that most political questions are looked at from a false angle.

Roland W. Boyden naturally suggests to me

the question of our general foreign policy. I am therefore going to advance some arguments in support of some of the phases of our foreign policy. The subject is, of course, too vast to give even a slight consideration to in an article of this scope. I am therefore not trying to prove points so much as to make some of us think about politics along a different line. It has become a foregone conclusion with so many people that the foreign policy of the Administration is thoroughly bad, that, without deliberately taking the defence of the Administration, I shall merely point out the other side of the question, and show that the Administration is not so spineless as some would think. I shall finally make a plea for clear thinking, more along the lines of tangible fact than along those of vague theory.

How many of us have heard the following sort of conversation when our foreign policy is talked of? To how many does this seem familiar? I am quoting from the words of an acquaintance — a man who won his "H" in football, who has held class office and whom I consider thoroughly representative of the undergraduate attitude. This is what he says: "We ought to go and put Europe on her feet; we ought to step in and lend a hand. What did we do in the war? Nothing. What did Europe do? Saved us from being wiped out by Germany. All the money is in this country; we ought to go in and help. Let's cancel the debt; let's help European industry and lower the tariff. We ought to put Europe on her feet." And so it goes; we ought to "cooperate," we ought to step in and fix things up. This is surely a typical cross-section of a widely shared idea. How many there are who utter a fervent "My God" when they look at the paper and see what our action is with regard to Europe! How many there are who say "Wanted — a foreign policy," when, deploring the conduct of our government, they wonder what can be done!

Let us therefore see just what can be done and just what the Government *can* do before we criticize too harshly.

Many of us mistake loose thinking for altruism; and many of us are willing to substitute phrases for facts. It is only too natural; we are young, we have no property, no immediate responsibility toward our community. Imbued with an idealism which is the privilege of our irresponsible youth, we can well afford to say lightly "Cancel the debt," or "Give Armenia five billion dollars"— we can say this so long as it is not we but the bulk of the American people who are footing the bill. From this angle our collegiate altruism shows up under a rather different light. Yet in spite of this apparently caustic view, I believe I do not exaggerate when I say that the large majority of the country and certainly of Congress want just what our college idealists are searching for.

We all want to put Europe on her feet. Of course we do. We should all like to see her industry prosper and her production increase. We all — at least those of us who have any human feeling — deplore the chaotic condition of Europe. But it is just because it is so chaotic that we should think not only twice but many times, before we take any rash step.

There is one type of college visionary who raves eloquently about Europe's self sacrifice, deplores our "inaction" and ends by cursing the Republican party, the Administration and often the Government itself. When asked what he thinks ought to be done, he usually answers one of three things, viz: "America should go in" or "The Government ought to cancel the Allied Debt" or "We ought to lower the tariff." Perhaps there are more answers to this question but these are the most common.

Let us take up these answers in order, not trying so much absolutely to disprove them as to show their weaker points.

When our college visionary says "America should go in," he immediately ranks himself with many great minds. Those who advocate "America's going in" are legion. I should like to have "America go in" after one question has been satisfactorily answered. That one question is "How?" *How* is America going to "go in"? *How* is she going to act once she is "in"? *How* is she going to apply

103

her great forces most effectively? How . . . but there are innumerable "hows" to be applied. And no statesman can answer this question, and you, my friend can't answer it, and none of us can — much as we'd all like to. Some have answered it for temporary conditions, and Europe's condition is such that any kind of a permanent answer is out of the question. Europe is in a state of flux, ever-changing and undependable: were we to "go in," it is my opinion, and I am using the phrase in its broadest possible sense, we should go on the most gigantic wild goose chase the World has ever known, involving the risk of leaving Europe even worse off than she is now and risking the money and lives of our own people. So much for the phrase "America should go in."

The question "How?" usually calls forth the next topic in this discussion, namely "The Government should cancel the Allied Debt." This is a very current belief in collegiate circles. Preposterous as it is even to touch on so vast a subject in an article of this sort, there are two main objections to cancelling the debt which are worth stating. In the first place the Government has no right to cancel the Allied Debt. The Government is the trustee and executor of the people's property and of its welfare. The Government is a business concern and it must be run on the most business-like basis possible, for the millions of people whose interests it administers. There can be no sentiment in business and there should be even less sentiment in our Government. The Allied Debt was incurred legally and with entire understanding by each of the parties involved, and our Government has no more right to cancel the debt than the trustee of a private sum of money would have in spending it on charities which he personally happened to think deserving. Just as the trustee of an individual's money has no right to give it away, however worthy the cause of the gift may seem to him, even so the Government, the trustee to us all, has no right to deprive us of our due.

The second objection to cancelling the Allied Debt is that it is one of the surest ways to encourage war. As soon as a nation realizes that it can invade and make war on another nation and have fighting expenses paid by some other party who will never hold it accountable; as soon as this happens, Bedlam will break loose and any thought of peace can speedily be relegated to the limbo of oblivion.

And now comes the tariff. The tariff which has never wholly pleased anybody and never will; the tariff which was first argued in 1765 and will still be argued in 1965; the tariff which will always be the great American topic of conversation. Thoroughly and completely to defend the tariff, or equally thoroughly to condemn it are things which I will not attempt. I have not read all the schedules and all of the several hundred amendments and cannot feel justified in giving any opinion, I do not know enough. I shall merely state that the protective tariff has not made for a decrease in imports from Europe. By passing this bill, we have not built a wall around ourselves, we have not stifled budding European industry, and we have not done Europe any harm. Figures compiled for the Congressional Record (p. 1058, vol. 64, no. 21) show an increase for the average month in 1922 over the average month in 1921 of roughly 15 per cent. That is the increase in imports under the present tariff system. So, whatever else it may do, the present tariff does not stifle European imports. It does not therefore prevent foreign production — that much is certain.

These are a few of the erroneous conceptions under which many of us here in college are now laboring. Characteristic of our ignorance of fact, of our lack of experience and of our fondness for a well-turned phrase, many of us swallow the mouth-filling words of our more garrulous sentimentalists only soon to become bloated with flaccid theory. Facts speedily go out of the question and revolutionary changes are vehemently supported. This sort of thing is often said: "So it isn't right for the Government to cancel the debt? Very well then, let's change the Government, but let's do something." Yes, let us do something, most heartily, let us do something and the very best way to start is first to look around and see just *exactly* what we *can* do.

My discussion of these tremendous and *vitally* important points has been most cursory; my opportunities for information and my knowledge are too limited to have this more than the merest outline. I have not tried to prove my points so much as merely to show the other side of a question on which the majority of the college has a curiously one-sided attitude.

Let us use as few theories, as few concepts and as few phrases as possible. Let us have a minimum of wild thinking; let us have facts.

SONNETS TO MUSSOLINI

LLOYD McKIM GARRISON PRIZE POEM

I

Hushed was every bird throughout the land
Of Italy, and Stygian darkness clung
Like mourning-veils let down by God's own Hand.
And in the darkness, cries of pain had rung,
Slow quavering out, stilled by that Red Beast
Whose hydra heads were tearing at the throats
Of Power, Justice, Faith. And towards the East
The tramp of Mongol feet in Soviet boats . . .
But then a blaze of light appeared, for one
Had seen the torch of Cavour, ashed in shame,
Half-buried, smouldering yet, and had begun
With love-impassioned breath, to fan aflame
The paling embers, and with it alight
Kindled a million others, conquering Night.

II

The flag of order raised, then he whose sight
Had saved the land from utter darkness, sowed
The dragon's teeth. Armed soldiers rose to fight,
Ardent, ordered, marching on the road
Which Caesar's legions trod. The hills of Rome
Resounded to the stirring cry of "Youth!"
These modern Argonauts left hearth and home,
They won the fight against the beast uncouth,
And homeward bore the Fleece. The crown was seized
From Pelias, and a better rule began,
The Court well-cleaned of men with minds diseased.
The new King proved a sober, thoughtful man,
His lion heart oft leaping from its lair
To combat vice or drive away despair.

III

A man with deep eyes, and a deeper soul;
Limpid as Lethe, ruffled by no keel,
But angered, like the phosphorescent hole
Where fiery Phlegethon plunges. Hands of steel
To rein that furious steed, Fascismo. Mind
Like iron, unyielding, molded while aglow,
Then cooled by time. His eyes are never blind,
His heart is warm, his reason cold as snow.
A blacksmith's son, his task is bending souls
As in his youth he formed the gleaming bars,
Saving them from the spell of red-hot coals.
Intensely earnest, striving towards the stars,
In Italy his all; snatching her name
From dust, he won himself eternal fame.

IV

Forlian, continue to bestride
Thy eagle, seek no higher power of state,
Thy force by straight-backed youth is fortified,—
Ambitious, do not seek to alter Fate.
Crushed by thy strength, the Socialist crystal ball
Lies shattered; but beware a treacherous cut!
Bind not thy faith to sticks and stones, nor fall
By forcing thy winged feet along a rut.
King and Pope from thee must seek advice
As Age perceived its brittle power ashake
So, with the cry of "Giovannezza!" rise
Till once again the land of Vergil take
Its place in world concern. Then shalt thou be
Honored through Italy; Italy through thee.

Ralph W. Daffine.

LOGIC, OR THE EVANGELICAL VENTRILOQUIST

JOHN FINLEY, JR.

JAMES TUCKER sat on the steps of his brownstone house, looking at the street and otherwise diverting himself while he waited for the newsboy who presently arrived. The newsboy went off about his delivery, and James opened the paper. When he saw what he looked for, he smiled knowingly, folded the paper, and whistling walked inside, where he sat down at a desk facing a class room. Here he made things ready for the pupils he expected, practicing ventriloquistic conversation with the empty seats, so that the room was full of different voices. After a while a bright and spirited-looking young man, evidently an eager pupil, came in and found James supporting a lonely but speciously dual **argument** about religion with an imagined party in the back corner seat. Naturally surprised, he asked,

"Are you Mr. James Tucker who advertised for pupils in this morning's paper?"

"Yes," replied James. And other voices in the room added confidently, "Yes, yes. By all means."

The pupil went on with gathering amazement, "And is this the School of Practical Evangelism that I read of in the paper?"

"Yes," said James again and confirmed himself ventriloqually, saying, "Yes, yes," and "Dear sir, be assured."

"Are you sure this is your advertisement," the pupil protested in an obvious but cheerful impotence. "Look at it. See." He showed James the second page of the paper where stood the sign in large letters.

Mr. James Tucker announces a school of
Practical Evangelism
to help serious-minded young men to
Usefulness in Religion.
Will help young or old in matters of
Domestic or Social Inspiration.
Come early   Chance for few only.
69 Mt. Auburn Street.

"Yes, I assure you this is mine," said James firmly. "Rather catching, don't you think so?"

"Very," said the pupil with feeling. "But what's it about?"

"I'll tell you," said James motioning him into a seat. "I have come to the conclusion that the only way to be efficient about serious matters is to go at them lightly. And in this school I teach how to be efficiently volatile, mercurially practical, how to turn people to a bright life, how to breathe romance and a bewitching mystery into the daily tedium."

"But that is not religion," said the pupil.

"Oh, yes, it is," replied James. "Anything that shows unexpected lights of the spirit is religion. Now please listen. You believe that having life more abundantly is a good part of Christianity, don't you?"

"Yes."

"Well, if you believe that, why don't you go about doing it sensibly? You think doubtless that the soul is a very serious and important thing. And just for that, you insist on being grave about it. There are enough people to do that, in fact, a lot too many. That's why people in the churches are mostly so stupid, because their preachers make them reverent where they ought to be amused." The young man began to protest and James with a soothing spread of his hands pursued his theme warmly. "Reverence is a nice thing, but too much is blighting. Come with me."

By this time the young man's actions closely resembled somnambulism. He put on his hat and followed James out of the house like a man in a spell. The two walked along the street which shined in the sun of early spring, and James, who felt particularly sprightly, hummed and rose on his toes as he stepped. Once he stopped, picked up a kitten that was playing on the street, and handed it gravely to a passer-by who looked bored. But the pupil did not mark this as particularly amazing, since he was bewildered. Not long after, the two reached the lecture hall of the prominent college in that town and went in. A philosophy lecture was going on.

"Now watch," whispered James. "Philosophy is a serious and important thing but the students are asleep or heavily assentive which is the same thing. The lecturer should be more lively. I shall help him, as you shall learn to in my school."

The lecturer was moving in sober progress to his dull conclusion. "Berkeley," he was saying, "postulated a solely mental existence of external phenomena. Sense impression . . ."

". . . Was nothing to him. Whee!" cried James the ventriloquist in a voice that emerged from the center of the class, yards from him. The lecturer stopped, students sat up, tired eyes opened, and a fortuitous breeze blew open a window, like Zeus thundering on the right.

"I'll try it once more," James whispered again, "and the class will have spirit enough for a week or so to go on profitably."

"Sir," he pursued in yet another voice, "I don't see how all minds see the same thing, when they are all so different. If one person is not looking at a mountain, some one else is. But if the mountain exists in the first man's mind alone, the second man might see an elephant or three-ringed circus instead. People differ about what they like to imagine. But I may be stupid. You know I think I like April better than any other month."

The voice expired after its last sentimental confidence, and the class went on, like an old automobile repainted. Through that week and the next the students were attentive and the lecturer cogent and sprightly, since all expected some new outburst. They put some pleasant value to life then, like the children of Israel in the desert, since miracles were as likely as not to happen any time. James and the pupil went home.

"Perhaps by now you see what I wish to do," James said out of a long silence as they walked.

"Perhaps so, I am not sure," the pupil answered.

"I am the prophet of trifles, the evangelist of the commonplace, the rescuer from listlessness. Boredom is a worse menace than sin, and exuberance must be the daily savior. Here is the way to be useful in the world. Do not set out to be serious. You say you are religious-minded. If you become a clergyman, you will wear a professional sombreness and most of your usefulness will be lost. You will save old ladies' souls, but theirs would be saved any way. Do not let the people know you are saving them, and you might do it. I know a way. You may learn to pass a life of greater service and most vital utility beginning as a street-car conductor."

"What!" cried the pupil in a sharp voice.

"As a street-car conductor. By the way what is your name."

"Francis Smith. I'm a cousin of yours as a matter of fact."

"Oh, so you are. Fine. Come with me."

They entered the brownstone house by the steps where James had sat that morning waiting for the paper. A sign announcing the school swung plaintively over the door as a spring wind danced in the street.

"I'll wait out here and see if I can get things straight," said Francis sitting down.

"All right. Don't run away. I'll only be a minute," James replied, diving into the house. The pupil sat with his head in his hands, trying to find a rational order in the events of the morning, the ventriloqual conversations, the incident of the kitten, the inspirating of the philosopher, and James's running talk, like prolix footnotes to a classic text. It was an excusably confusing matter, Francis confessed to himself.

"We're off," James said suddenly, emerging again from the house dressed like a street-car conductor.

"You certainly are," sighed Francis, thinking that this was a little too much of a good thing. "Where are you going with that outfit?"

"To my new job where you can watch me

and learn practical philanthropy. I shall be conductor of the last car on a train to pass Park Street in about twenty minutes. You can get on there. Cheerio. Don't be careless and miss the car." And James went off arranging some papers in the inside band of his hat in his best street-car-conductor manner.

An half-hour later the distracted Francis boarded the car at Park Street, having composed his countenance but not his mind in the peaceful interim of James's absence. He noticed right off with sinking horror that all eyes were on James who was at the moment closing the car door with the proud jesture of a perfect conductor, and thought, "He's done it now. Why did I come?"

The train started forward with laborious grinding, and James stepped from the platform to the center of the car. No one in the car looked dully at the advertisements but all turned sparkling eyes on James. One old lady could scarcely contain herself for delight at finding something pleasant in the subway. She chuckled to herself and with her elbow nudged her neighbor, an Italian workman, who smiled now and softened his woody face with such a grin as was never before seen in the subway.

"Playa some more widda mouth organ," he urged hoarsely.

"Oh, do!" cried the old lady clapping her hands and rocking a little on her seat in senile rapture.

"Not now," replied James, "for we are coming out to look at the beautiful, though artificial, basin of the Charles River and see what Aeschylus (Greek author living from about 510 to 440 B. C. in Athens — a useful fact to remember) called the 'unnumbered laughter of the waves,' referring as you will understand to the sun sparkling on each ripple. I assure you that that is a very beautiful thought. I shall now execute a dance accompanying myself on the mouth organ." The whole car cheered and laughed, apparently convulsed by the idea that anybody should attempt relieving the torment of the subway. But the enlarging

black hole at the end of the bridge swallowed the train, and James said.

"Pardon me a minute. We shall have to let off the people at Kendall. For myself, I don't like that neighborhood, but doubtless some do. In fact, if you press me, I think it is one of the worst places I have ever seen. I urge the people who don't know whether to get off here or at Central to ride on to Central, where things are much livelier. Kendall! Kendall. Change upstairs for other places. Be sure to change if you get out. Any place is preferable." The train stopped but no one got off. The Italian forgot, and a weak-minded person was intimidated to ride on to Central. James then did his dance, recited "Once more unto the breach, dear friends," receiving great applause by his rendering of the passage "o'erhang and jutty his confounded base, swilled by the wild and wasteful ocean," yodeled, and would have done a card trick but was interrupted by the train stopping at Central. Here he walked to the door and shook hands with people that got off, leaving them to go in a radiance that illuminated their lives for the rest of the month. The old lady and the Italian continued on to Harvard. They never recovered fully from the spasm of their ecstacy. People thought the old lady crazy since she was so garrulous of James. And that was an unpleasant consequence, though one of no great importance, because in strict fact she was crazy, and concealment was increasingly difficult at her time of life. In other respects, James's benevolent vaudeville accomplished only good. For days after you could see people smiling to themselves with a furtive idiocy all over Cambridge. And when people make fools of themselves by innocent happiness the millennium is nearly come.

After a little while James and Francis walked out to the bank of the river that ran near the car barns, the one very jaunty in the spring air, the other yet lost in whirling reflections. For a space they proceeded in silence, though James whistled every now and then and kicked at the gravel.

"Don't you see now what it all is?" said James suddenly.

"Yes, I see perfectly well," said Francis, "that you wish to help people by amusing them and making life pleasant in an informal way. But if you can do this so well, why don't you do something serious and worth while instead of wasting time with your idiotic school?"

"Oh, dear," sighed James, "I thought you might see. But people never do. My dear young man, you are the victim of an inverted education, the useless product of a college that teaches usefulness in trifles alone and forgets important present things. Neither the college nor you recognize the facts. Your wish to help is touching and deserves a better success. You see, you all think that the world is run by very grave processes like legal transactions, and political steps, and put your education into the service of these. But you must see that your assumption is wrong. People have had politics and law for centuries, and nobody now finds life a bit more animating than it was at the start. It is clear to me that the things you call important are not important at all. They are the trifles and should engage the attention of trifling men. The really important things are those that we face daily. A subway ride, for instance, is much more vital than a crisis, a great transaction, and things like that, because people spend more time in the subway than they do in crises. To be interested in crises, which never or rarely occur, and to be bored in the subway seems idiocy to me. So a college which teaches you to be successful in the crisis but a failure at amusing yourself in the subway is wrong, and you, I am very sorry to say, must be wrong too."

"Pitiful," said Francis, shaking his head. But James would not be blocked and went on.

"You ask me why I have my school. It is to bring the most intelligent young men into the most important places. A college trains them assiduously for the trifles of law and business. But I shall disclose to them the great future of being radio announcers, street-car conductors, head waiters, clerks in stores, floor walkers, and policemen, persons whom we meet in our tedious daily activity. I, for instance, never see a steel magnate, and don't care if he is a great and interesting man. But I do see policemen all the time and should be relieved if they were sprightly minded persons. Wordsworth is right. Children are much more correct in their ambitions than grownups. They see the realities of life. Here take this and save your soul." James threw him a copy of Greenough and Hersey's *Principles of Ventriloquism*. The two by this time had reached the house again and entered it, James yet talking, his eyes bright with the dull glint of conviction.

"But I don't want this book," Francis protested helplessly.

"Of course you do," said the implacable James. "To know it is as important as philosophy. Remember this morning. Without my ventriloquisms, the lecturer could never have made his pupils listen. Which then is the more necessary, philosophy or ventriloquism? Besides it is useful to entertain girls, children, and oneself in dull moments. Hello! Here's grandfather. What's he doing here?"

"Good morning, James," said the old gentleman standing sternly with his cane in the doorway. "I thought we could trust you now without a guardian. I sent your cousin Francis here this morning when he came in from the West. From what he says you are not less unbalanced than before. It is a trial to me, James, to have a deranged grandson."

"Oh, grandpa, don't go into that again," said James, and turning to Francis he explained, "I had a little wind organ with a beautiful *vox humana*. Now the only place I feel musical is in the shower bath. So I made a rubber covering for the organ and put it there. Grandpa thought I was crazy and had me watched."

"Surely, that was the act of a deranged person," the old man said. "And here now you are at your ventriloquism, and your senseless stunts in trolley cars. I must call in your guardian," and he turned to motion a man outside.

Here James in desperation turned to the respected Francis and risking everything on that young man's good word, cried "I was logical before, I am logical now. There was no point in having an organ if you could not play it where you wanted to. There is no point in having life if you cannot be amused by it as it passes. I do the reasonable thing to make people happy. That is not being crazy, is it?"

"Yes," said Francis.

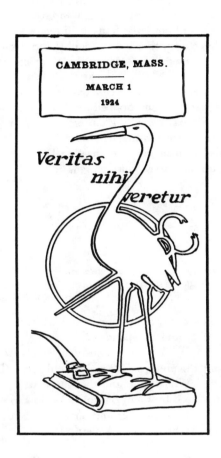

TWO TRANSLATIONS IN SONNET FORM

I

Tristè si veniens patruelis diceret umbra
Eja lugete, omnes! abscissit Maria crines. . . .
— Novum Mariale. (11.921, 930)

If from Elysion the inebriate ghost
   Of my great-great-granduncle Phineas
   Had come to me and said " Ah, woe is us!
The Earth is flat, composed of buttered toast
And balanced in the heav'ns amid an host
   Of pies and hot cross buns stelliferous —"
   I'd have been shocked, no doubt; but even thus
I'd have observed "Well, fancy that!" at most.

But had he said to me, a week ago,
   "Mary's just gone and bobbed her hair, you know,"
   Then I'd have cried "Phantom, you utter lies!
Consociation with postmortem bliss
Has addled your perceptive sense: to Dis
   Return, and treat your astigmatic eyes."

II

I diss'n: "Lo palvro catto della vuostra quéra xia
Hat relitto chesta vita." et jò diss', "In pace sia!"
— Carmen dè Mariâ Calvulâ

They said to me: "Your Aunt Priscilla's cat
   Is dead"; and I responded "*Requiem!*"
   They said: "By evil chance your Uncle Lem
Has caught the mumps." I sighed and said "That's that!"
They said: "Whilst dining in the Automat
   A misplaced bean cut off your Cousin Em."
   I dropped a silent tear and answered them:
"As God wills, be it done; Amen; *fiat!*"

They said: "Your house has burned down to the ground;
Your bank account has been attached"; no sound
   Of dole greeted this news with dolor rife.
They said: "Mary has bobbed her hair"; the cord
Of my endurance snapped; I cried "O Lord,
   It is enough — now take away my life."

Dudley Fitts, Jr.

THE HARVARD ADVOCATE

THE
DIAL

APRIL 1925

VOLUME CXI   NUMBER 8

25 cents a copy

Parody Number

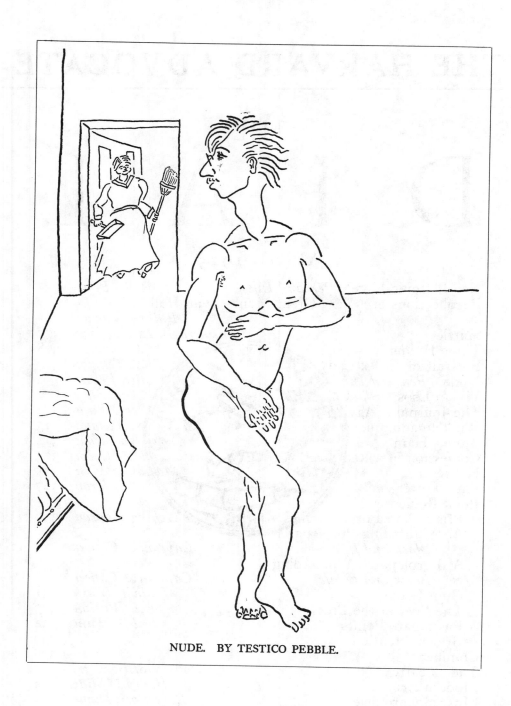

NUDE. BY TESTICO PEBBLE.

THREE POEMS

BY O. O. GOINGS

A POEM

and i said

                                        snuggling down into

the electric chair

      tell me why O intrusive handkerchief they chose

      the six suppressed poems from a hat

                              a derby hat

      and why this newspaper i read should be with us

      inevitably shouting, screeching the small lousy

      news of the day in our highly Florentine faces

and my soul

                                turning on the current

answered me

      for the same reason that your lap goes there when you

      SuDdEnLy s,t,a,n,d uP   that in brief and no more

      sense   while behind the merry masks of the angels

      there is much weeping and Gnashing of teeth

gracious

                                      said i

snickering

      am i that clever is this little spinningball an

      important part of the great walloping solar

      sys;tems   if i am doomed thus)as a fly to(walk the

      noisy cracked ceilings of infinity why at least not this stark-

      ness and umbrellas with which neW yorK is afflicted

      and the world

                              grieved

with which

                             my soul

admitted

      i don't know do you

so   i

      got out of the chair and

went   home

      it was the end of the line

                             anyway

PLAIN POEM

beneath the whither-cock
the   funny   little

                                        God!

ain't-he-the-cutie-Mazie?
Steeple Jack
            sings Hee and Haw!
if i had been ther i would should could
Christ kid how many ten
                  s
                    e
                  s
                      are there in this
goddam language
cut
           the ropes
of the little swinging monkeyshineseat

Then Mister Sidewalk
                    whatwouldyerdo
                          withyer
Blue-eyed
           Puddle?

LOVE POEM

                                  i

                I

!

NEO-PLATONIC LOVE. BY R. E. PEETS.

WINKELMANN AMONG THE TEACUPS

T. S. TELLALOT

(Having loved passionately
    We drank our tea;
Having donned our clothes,
    We crushed a rose.)
Arma virumque cano . . .

Isn't it dark here, Ming,
    Among these pebbles;
Come, let us sing
    Atrocious trebles.
Μήνιν ἀείδε θεά . . .

Love is noble, love is fine,
    Down on the mud-flats.
It's like a draught of ancient wine
    To fall through the bed-slats.
Omnis Gallia . . . tres . . .

Mr. Schmilkraut is a funny chap
    With a face like a moon;
He wears a dipper instead of a cap;
    He'll die soon.
Tarantara tarantara!

PORTRAIT OF AN EX-LADY

BY T. S. TELLALOT

This lady uses brilliantine
but where I ask you not to ask me;
peacocks by her fountain preen:
I use clericals to masque me.

Tea as casual as you please;
Holy Church and Babylon
balance teacups on their knees
till the candles are their sun.

He in Gothic vault and fanning,
naked of his bowler hat;
she conjectures what unmanning
process made a man like that.

Till reluctance fills her vowels
where desire lisped before;
long parade with spades and trowels:
twenty gardeners pass the door.

"Ah! So soon? Come in next Sunday."
China winks upon the shelves.
Somewhere in the Bay of Funday
twenty gardeners drown themselves.

SENIOR NUMBER

THE · HARVARD ADVOCATE

1927–1956

1927–1956

The *Advocate* weathered difficult times with great style during the pre-war years. Never before had so many talented non-Harvard writers contributed to the magazine; never had the *Advocate* published such a diversity of Harvard writers.

The multi-talented James Agee was the first writer of note to contribute in this period; his poetry was not outstanding, but his short fiction still stands among the best of *Advocate* writing. The poetry of Robert Fitzgerald was more sophisticated and more popular among *Advocate* readers. The work of both undergraduates appeared in several issues during Agee's term as editor.

James Laughlin's *Advocate* tenure was surrounded in controversy. Laughlin joined the magazine in 1935 and convinced friend Henry Miller to contribute to the fall issue. A relatively mild Miller story, "Glittering Pie," and Laughlin's story, "A Natural History," enraged a puritanical district attorney in Cambridge. Police were sent to confiscate the offending issues from local newsstands and took all extra magazines from the Advocate House. The DA was not satisfied until he forced the resignation of five *Advocate* editors and received free tickets to the Harvard-Yale game. Yale won the game, but the *Advocate* was permitted to publish its next issue. Non-Harvard contributors in this era included poet Delmore Schwartz, Ezra Pound, Djuna Barnes, Boris Pasternak, and William Carlos Williams. Miller contributed a second story, "The Most Lovely Inanimate Object," but it caused little controversy.

The list of Harvard writers to appear in the *Advocate* shortly before World War II was equally impressive. Arthur Schlesinger served as film critic and political commentator, Leonard Bernstein wrote music reviews, Harry Brown penned some of the best satire to ever appear in the *Advocate*, and Norman Mailer contributed some highly accomplished short stories.

Soon after Mailer wrote for the *Advocate*, the magazine ceased publication due to shaky finances and wartime rationing. Publication resumed in 1947, but the new *Advocate* was almost exclusively literary and placed great emphasis on poetry. Poets in this era included John Hawkes, Don Hall, John Ashbery, Robert Bly, John Ciardi, Frank O'Hara, and Adrienne Rich.

Rich's contributions marked one of two important changes in the magazine's content and format: she was one of the first women to regularly publish in the *Advocate*. Although several women would contribute in the future, they would not become editors until the sixties.

The use of artwork dramatically changed the *Advocate*'s format. Inside art was used for illustration purposes only, but several of the covers from the mid fifties were designed by Harvard artists. Only in the next era would the *Advocate* become an important outlet for the local art community.

Apotheosis

J. R. Agee.

Lovers, make your kisses light,
    Weak, your embrace;
Keep passion cool and slight,
    A mask, your face:

Else (take heed) the sweet flesh slips
    Down from the dull
Dead bones, and lovers' lips
    Kiss but a skull.

A WALK BEFORE MASS

He awoke at a little after four, and knew it was upon him again. It was scarcely daylight, and rain was dropping out of a bare sky. He watched blades of water delicately overlap and riffle down the pane. Mary was sleeping with her head thrown back, her mouth gently flared. For quite a while he lay staring at her, glancing up occasionally at the rain, trying to think it out.

Once more it had become unbearable, quite unbearable. He had gone through all this once before, so thoroughly, so pitilessly, that he had thought, "Nothing can ever hurt me again."

"From the many-venomed earth . . .

. . . .

Mithridates, he died old."

He'd always trusted Housman, and yet—here he was again, caught in the same inexorable cogs of pain. The first inoculation, then, had failed to "take." Yes, that was it: he had to be roused from the years of tundra-like discontent; his soul had to go on the table once more.

For over a week now, he had known. That was the really queer part

125

of it; for a week he'd known, and gone ahead just as before. It had made no apparent difference. Indeed, he had been so foolish as to smile, silently quoting those silly verses of Housman's. Even the night before, the same unperturbed level of unhappiness had closed above him. Something profounder than a dream had moved toward this awakening.

He looked at his watch. Nearly five. He'd better try to get another hour of sleep, before they got up for Mass. "They?" He turned his head and looked at her for a long while as she slept. Could he ever again kneel at her side and take God into his body? How had he ever been able to, since first he had known it? How could he lie there beside her a moment longer?

And yet he did lie there, thumbs gnawing into palms; lay staring down upon the sleeping head. In the brief months of happiness after their marriage he had often looked thus upon her and had thought, "It is like looking into a mirror." He remembered that now, and as he gazed more intently he saw dark floodgates spread like wings in his soul.

He pressed his knuckles into his eye-sockets, and tried desperately to pray. He couldn't make up his mind what he was to pray for. There was so much. It was so utterly beyond remedy.

He must pray for Mary . . .

God . . . O God, deliver my wife out of her iniquity . . . God keep her, make her pure. . . .

Blessed is the fruit of thy womb, Jesus . . . .

Blessed is the fruit of thy womb. Impossible . . . Blessed . . . Jerome . . . .

He must go to Jerome.

He got up, and tiptoed into the next room. Kneeling beside his son, he raised his palms and tried to pray. He looked at the window; water panelled it like a bird's wing, and beyond was blank sky.

God . . . God . . . God!

Only when the child awoke did he realize he had spoken aloud. Jerome looked up at him, smiling, and he said. "Get up son. We must go for a walk."

The boy said nothing, but got up sleepily and began to dress. If Mary had made such a demand . . . or anyone except him. He sat on the edge of the bed, exulting in the quiet, the comprehending obedience.

Jerome stood puzzled over a complication of buttons. He drew him between his knees, finished dressing him. He held him for a moment, looking at him, then pushed the hair back from his forehead warm with sleep, and whispered, "Wait for me downstairs."

Quickly and silently he dressed, stopped at the door to look once more at his wife. Mary was sleeping with her head thrown back, her mouth gently flared. Vaguely he glanced at the mirror. It held only the rain-washed window. He shut the door quietly and stole down into the hall. They put on their coats and walked into the rain.

The street stretched downward like a hard cone. He took Jerome by the hand and they walked down the hill.

He walked heavily at first, dragging his feet through the filmy water. It seemed impossible to straighten his back and to hold his head where it belonged. In a despairing way he was still trying to think it out and to pray. As they came to the end of the pavement the country wind sowed rain into his eyes, and immediately he knew what had moved down his sleep in depths beneath dreaming.

Such a rain as this had fallen through that other dawn—just such a streaming silent mesh, drawn like a tent over all the sky and all his soul.

His shoulders straightened, and his head fell back upon them.

Before them stretched an expanse of spongy grass, belted by the river. On that other morning, he remembered, he had walked down here, alone, that time:

He had walked across the meadow and down to the river's edge; had stood beneath an elm; that elm at the bend. Alone. Jerome: He'd scarcely realized Jerome's existence then; Jerome was a baby. Only a few months old. Naturally, he hadn't given him a thought. Too little, almost, to be considered human . . . anything above, say, a helpless——

What was he dodging? What was his mind scurrying from on so many soft feet? What was there, hidden, that he could not——that he refused to remember?

Face it, admit it; confess it. Yet was it a thing to confess? He had scarcely thought it, certainly . . .

> I came down to the river, trying to puzzle it out, I couldn't bear to live with her any longer. And yet I knew I couldn't leave her. Jerome held us together, I thought, as if we were tied in a sack, I thought . . . I thought: If only *he* had never been born . . . or were out of the way . .

Well . . . He'd admitted it now had confessed it to himself. He must confess it, now, to God, must——

But, was it a thing worth confessing? There had been no definite thought; the words had merely trailed across his soul, scarcely leaving a trace. It wasn't as if he had planned to kill his son. As if he hated him.

Hate Jerome! The child was all his heart and all his life. It was he who had made the whole thing bearable; no empty inoculation of pain. See how he had turned to him this morning, when God Himself gave him no help!

He looked down to the boy at his side as they kicked their way through the drenched grass. And he had thought, once, to . . . had wished his death. As dreadful, that, as murder. As wholly a mortal sin.

The elm was near at hand. He said to himself: "I will take him to the place where I thought it, and there I'll tell him about it and beg his forgiveness. Then we shall go to Confession and to Mass.

He took long steps, heedless of the sodden mounds and hollows in the earth. Jerome trotted after him, dragging at his hand. Breathless, they stopped beneath the elm.

After his haste his mind was broken and clattering. He put an arm around his son, and they leaned back against the tree. Above and below the bend the river stretched like a bolt of silk. Just at their feet the water roughened, but the rain quickly molded it into the smooth-skinned current. Rainpocks slid quietly down the surface.

He looked down at Jerome, and tried to begin.

"My dear, my beloved son . . ." he said . . . then caught him up and bruised the thin body against his own and with all his strength hurled him into the water.

The circles broke like bells against the bank, and smoothed away into the rain. For a few seconds he stood motionless, arms above his head, flayed eyes fixed on the water.

Suddenly he clenched his fist and so struck himself upon the temple that he had to lean against the elm.

James R. Agee

Some Notes on Moscow

E. J. SIMMONS

THE train, which had behaved like a consumptive all the way from Riga, finally coughed and gasped its last in the Baltic Station of Moscow. It was a bright August morning, and I hastened outside, not a little interested to find myself in the Russian capital, the citadel of revolutions, civil wars, communism, and the rule of the proletariat. Immediately I was surrounded by a host of picturesquely bearded, dirty, and ragged individuals who set upon me and my luggage with all the gusto of Ali Baba's Forty Thieves. These are the izvoshiki, an indispensable part of Moscow's local color. For the uninitiated, the carriage of an izvoshik is a tiny four-wheeled vehicle made to carry precisely one-and-a-half people and all the light freightage of the city. They are as frequent on the streets as taxicabs in New York. All a foreigner needs to know about them is that he must never give the original fare demanded. The procedure is something as follows. You hail, "Izvoshik!" One will amble up to the curb and you shout your destination and then counter, "How much?" He may say, "Two rubles." This is your cue to snort back, "A ruble!"; and you continue on your way with an air of unconcern. "A rouble and a half," he concedes sauntering along behind you. "A rouble, not a kopek more." "But citizen, how do you think I can feed this horse?" "A rouble," you yawn. "All right, we poor izvoshiki must live." He draws up and you take your place in the carriage, pleased with your bargaining, while the izvoshik smiles at you good-naturedly, wondering perhaps how you have learned the trick.

Down Pervy Meshanskaya the izvoshik drove and I got my first glimpse of the city. Moscow is different from anything you have seen before. Your first impression is that of a glorified East Side of New York at rush hours. The rough cobblestone streets and sandy boulevards with uncut grass swarmed with people,— Russians in their embroidered blouses and knee-high boots, Tatars in their vari-colored native robes, Mongolians with drooping moustaches and curious little velvet skull caps, stalwart Caucasians dressed exactly as we see them pictured in the Ringling Brothers' posters with their huge sheepskin hats, surcoats, imitation cartridges and silver daggers, and a sprinkling of swarthy-skinned gypsies shrieking in patch-quilt colors and shiny metal ornaments. Many finely uniformed soldiers mingled with the throng, and from an adjacent street I could hear the stirring revolutionary songs of troops on the march. Everybody seemed to be eating, tearing chunks out of loaves of bread, sucking at slices of watermelon, pears, or apples, or interminably cracking and swallowing sunflower seeds. And those who did not eat, smoked Russian cigarettes. At a street corner by a newspaper booth a mother unconcernedly suckled her child, and another woman held a little boy over the gutter while he performed the functions of nature, whereas more bashful grownups were forced to the walls. Filthy-looking pedlers were everywhere, selling everything imaginable, books, shoestrings, crockery, fruits, candy, cigarettes and socks. A long-haired, long-gowned priest stood outside a church door begging for money. Indeed, beggars were numerous, garbed in the poorest rags, with burlap tied about their feet for shoes. Not infrequently I saw drunken men lying motionless in the gutter or prone across the sidewalk, their faces smeared in their own vomit, and no one paying the slightest attention to them. On the boulevards crowds formed circles within which a trained bear went through

his antics or a blandly-smiling Mongolian mystified his audience with tricks of legerdemain. There was much loud talking, gesticulation, and scolding, and over all pervaded an indefinable, remorseless odor.

In its architecture, too, Moscow is different. There is nothing of the Gothic wonders of London and Paris, of the neat, stony stoginess of Berlin, or the modern mammoths of New York. The general aspect of the buildings, like that of the people, is shabby and heterogeneous; but often a jewel of comparatively modern structure or hoary age will stand out, just as beautiful Russian women or tall, handsome, bearded patriarchs lend contrast to the motley throngs on the streets. There are the traditional forty times forty churches with their quaintly-rounded, golden-domed cupolas gleaming in the sun; crumbling fort-like monasteries of pure Russian and pseudo-Russian style dating from the 15th and 16th centuries; and the old China and Kremlin walls still well preserved, and the marvellous group of churches and palaces within the Kremlin itself. Oddly contrasted with these ancient glories is the recently built Lenin Institute symbolizing communism, a blackened, concrete, factory-like structure, ominous in its somber simplicity. Along the boulevards a number of futuristic statues have been erected, the pleasant effect in the distance of their sharp angles and sweeping curves becoming distinctly unpleasant the closer you approach. On street after street one sees miserable little wooden hovels crouching beside respectable five-story office buildings and apartments. As for skyscrapers, these do not exist in Moscow.

Through the archway by the famous Iversky Chapel, my izvoshik drove into Red Square, the central point of the city and rich in historic blood. In the Middle Ages it was the great market place of all the Russias;

the golden Tatar horde streamed over it to storm the Kremlin walls; and during the October Revolution, many of the Red Guard fell here from the machine gun and rifle fire of the Whites. The square is bound on three sides by the Kremlin Wall, the Church of St. Basil, and the Historic Museum. This fantastic Church of St. Basil was built in the 16th century by the command of Ivan the Terrible. Its spiraled cupolas, huge center tower, innumerable details, and the whole grotesquely painted lend credence to the legend that Ivan had the architect blinded in order that he might never build elsewhere anything comparable to this finest example of old Russian style. In the center of the square is a stone execution place; and legend also has it that the terrible Czar sat high up in the church tower and watched his victims put to death. Now the Church of St. Basil has been declared a museum by the Soviet Government.

In this same Red Square before the Kremlin Wall, and near the Brotherhood Grave of five hundred fallen revolutionists, is the mausoleum of Lenin, a black majesty of bolts and beams rising in simple graduating terraces. It is impressive, and its newness is in striking contrast to the old brick walls of the Kremlin. As I entered the square the guard at the tomb was being changed. A squadron of soldiers maneuvered in

front of the mausoleum, and at the same moment two dray teams lumbered slowly across the open space. They were loaded with what looked like sturgeons, and the dirty, stiff fish stuck grotesquely out of the sides like so many logs of wood on which the drivers sat. The soldiers drew up and made the Soviet salute. The first teamster drew himself up also and saluted, and called back to his comrade to do likewise. But the latter, busy fumbling with some papers, yelled, "Don't bother me!" The new guards took their posts, the squadron marched away, and the reverent and irreverent drivers passed slowly through the Iversky arch.

My izvoshik finally halted outside a dirty-looking apartment house in the Arbat district, which was to be my home in Moscow. Of course there are hotels in the city, several very fine ones run by the government. At these foreigners stop and pay handsomely, go on government-conducted tours for a week or a month, and then return home to write authoritative articles or books about Russia and the new order of things. Being a poor traveller, I had to seek lodgings elsewhere. But the world knows at least one genuine fact about Moscow (and many other large Russian cities), namely that they are extremely overcrowded. Since the revolution, Moscow has grown from slightly more than a million to some two millions and a half of inhabitants, and the impoverished government has not been able to supply accommodations to cope with this tremendous increase. One can apply to the Commissioner of Dwellings and he will graciously assign you a few meters of space in some small room which has been adjudged too large for a single occupant. There is an obvious element of risk, however, in submitting to such an assignation,

for no method of selection obtains. Russian roommates, like all roommates, are of unequal qualities. Having accepted the good graces of a friend who offered to find me a room, I jumped, so to speak, from the frying pan into the fire, although no doubt things could have been worse. A certain Aksina, aged forty, had given up living with her husband and was willing to share her room in a platonic fashion with anyone white or black for a munificent sum which was small, nevertheless, compared to that charged by the hotels. With becoming bashfulness I accepted on the condition that Aksina would sleep in the community kitchen, a dingy hole somewhere in the misty region of Weir. Having got me nicely settled, Aksina, after two weeks, suddenly decided that it was infringing upon the culinary privileges of the other members of the apartment to sleep in the kitchen, and accordingly she moved back into her or our room. She conceded me one side, and on the opposite constructed a makeshift bed and a tiny screen behind which she coyly concealed her nightly toilet. She could understand no objections to this arrangement, for after all it was the way most people in Moscow lived. I had no other recourse than to become a Roman in Moscow.

In all there were three rooms in the apartment. One was occupied by a man and his wife, their two sisters-in-law, and the wife's eternally crying babies. The second room, a windowless affair, was commanded by a prostitute and her numerous callers. The third belonged to the good Aksina and myself, while the janitor of the apartment and his wife lived in a walled-off space under the stairs.

It is not always easy to love one's neighbors under such conditions of propinquity, yet the Russians happily adapt themselves to the situation, indulging their predilection for wrangling, but never coming to blows over the common electric bill or priority in the common kitchen. A young scholar friend and his wife had a little room whose splendid exposure they never tired of praising, whereas they accounted it no great drawback that the only access to their room was via the bathroom which was used by three other families in the same apartment. This absolute premium on space in Moscow was sadly emphasized by a married couple I knew. They eventually got divorced, the *causa belli* being that the husband was jealous of his wife's going to parties with other men and arriving home at three or four o'clock in the morning. But up to date this severed couple has not been able to find separate rooms. Accordingly, something like the *status quo* obtains, since the injured husband must still crawl out of his celibate bed to open the door for his sometime wife in the early hours of the morning. What would a Dostoevsky do with these ready-to-hand situations in which various types are brought into close contract in the average Russian apartment? Indeed, something has already been made of the humor if not the tragedy of this manner of living in the Russian theater. One especially clever play is still being produced in the Studio of the Moscow Art Theater. The plot works out the tangle of two roommates who get married, and with their young wives are all forced to live in the same room. The many opportunities of enforced intimacy convince them all that they are mismated, so they obtain a simple Russian divorce and happily remarry.

But what of this new civilization, the doctrine of communism, and the rule of the proletariat? These are the magnets that draw the foreigner to Russia, and at first one naïvely searches for visible manifestations of a great change among the people. Walk up Kuznezky Most, the Broadway of Moscow, to Tverskoi Boulevard, the Fifth Avenue. The stores, fly-ridden restaurants, theaters, and movie houses are always crowded. An endless throng of business men, shopkeepers, workers, prostitutes, peasants fresh from the country, soldiers, and students go about their business with stern or happy faces and much talking. Listen to their conversations or talk with them and you hear nothing of revolutions and civil wars, of the Right and the Left, or of Marxism and Leninism. They will tell you their domestic troubles, that they are tired of waiting outside the government co-operatives for their portion of bread and tea, that work is scarce, that the paper shortage is a nuisance. Or they may even comment on recent literature, saying that Maijakovsky has stooped to poetic advertising, or that Biedny's stuff is mere drivel, or that Shoxolov's "Quite Don" is a good book but not always easy to understand. But of the possibilities of Trotsky's return or a split in the Stalin forces you hear never a word. This is the patient Russian people who laugh today and cry tomorrow. They are now much as they were before the fall of the Czar. However, twelve years is perhaps too short a time to transform a people into the eager enthusiasts of a new civilization—a people that waited some three hundred years to overthrow a wretched tyranny.

But if the average Russian you meet on the street has not yet been metamorphosed into a preaching apostle of the new order of things, it is not the fault of his Soviet Government. The Russian public has ever been indifferent (until some great crisis arrives), and the present government is striving with might and main to overcome this indifference, to arouse the people to a full appreciation of their declared position as the

the leaders in the new material and intellectual growth of the world. No greater propagandist exists than the Russian government. This whole land of 150 millions of people is literally drenched in propaganda. Every conceivable agency is employed to further the doctrines of Marxism and uphold the rule of the Soviets. In Moscow we find this propaganda in newspapers, journals, posters, books, in short, in every form of printed material; in the theaters and movies, and in every manner of public entertainment; in workers' clubs, factories, mills, schools, and universities; and among organizations such as the Komsomol, the Pioneers, and the unions. The shadow of Lenin darkens the land. His statues, miniature busts, and portraits are everywhere, in all public buildings, clubs, mills, factories; and in store windows among sausages, women's lingerie, and men's haberdashery displays. In Russia God has been ousted and Lenin elevated to His throne.

A curious kind of idealism is broadcasted in Moscow and over the rest of the country. Numerous campaigns are carried on against drunkenness, vice, religion, illiteracy, laziness, profiteering, haltura (the prostitution of artistic talents for selfish ends). Members of the Communist Party must not weep at adversities, must not get drunk, and must be willing to sacrifice their all for the principles of the organization. The moral, physical, and intellectual betterment of the ruling workers and peasants are the professed aims of this ceaseless propaganda.

Conversely, bourgeoisie civilization is criticised and ridiculed through all the agencies that preach and enforce the new order of things. Any news that goes out or comes into the country is strictly censored, and no real opposition to the government or its policies is tolerated. The system of education has been entirely changed. It favors a practical education above everything else. The past and its traditions have no place in this system. Quarrels between humanists and romanticists, the glories of Greece and the grandeur of Rome, scholasticism and mediævalism, all the petty quibblings of rule and line are banned. The dead past must bury the dead. History begins with the October Revolution and is pointed towards the future. Culture has become dynamic. It must have technical and economic progress as its aims. Science and not the humanities is the basis of this new culture, and all instruction is frankly materialistic. Art likewise must adapt itself to the new culture, seeking subject-matter and forms that will express a materialistic concept of the future.

This future defies prophecy, however, for a decade is too short a time for working out infallibly the destiny of so great an experiment. Communists demand some hundreds of years for the tree to bear fruit, pointing out that it took several centuries for the feudal and bourgeoisie civilizations to mature fully. Yet despite the shortness of the period which the Soviet Government has existed, one sensibly feels the new impetus and élan that pervades the country. Of course, there have been many failures, much compromising, and a great deal of discontent exists among the people, due primarily to the poor economic conditions. But we find everywhere evidence of amazing material progress. Russia has shaken off the chains that bind it to the past, and is starting out with new hope on a career of self-betterment and world proselytizing.

The Storm

J. R. AGEE

The storm bows black on Stratham
    And strong through elm and ash,
Lashing the leaves to silver
    Low winds thrash.

From nought to like awakened,
    My puzzled soul is rent
By storms that know no ceasing
    Nor ever will relent

Till I bow black on Stratham
    And strong through elm and ash,
Lashing the leaves to silver
    With the winds thrash.

Good Friday

J. R. AGEE

High in Dodona's swaying groves,
High in the grey, the glimmering oaks,
Dodona's cauldrons, convolute,
Groan on the wind strange prophecies.

Among the whispering laurel roves
Great Pan, and on the tall sky, smokes
Of Delphi write; and now are mute
The graded reeds of Pan: he sees

Across the grey, the glimmering seas,
A leafless tree take barren root
On Golgotha; he hears the strokes
Of iron on iron, and his own hooves

The iron strikes through. Against two trees
Are driven his outstretched hands. Strange fruit
Hangs in the grey, the glimmering oaks,
Hangs in Dodona's swaying groves.

Song for September

R. S. Fitzgerald

Respect the dreams of old men, said the cricket,
Summer behind the song, the streams falling
Ledge to ledge in the mountains where clouds come.

Attend the old men who wander, said the cricket.
Daylight and evening in the air grown cold
Time thins, leaving our will to wind and whispers.
The bells are swallowed gently underground.

Because in time the birds will leave this country
Waning south, not to appear again
Because light is a mad thing
And love falters without music
Because we walk in gardens among grasses
Touching the garments of the wind that passes
Dimming our eyes.

Give benches to the old men, said the cricket,
Listening by cool ways to the world that dies
Fainter than seas drawn off from mist and stone.

The rain that speaks at night is the prayer's answer.
What are dry phantoms to the old men
Lying at night alone?

They are not here whose gestures we have known:
Their hands in the dusk, the frail hair in the sun.

Park Avenue

R. S. Fitzgerald

Between dinner and death the crowds shadow the loom of steel.
Engines dwell among the races; the tragic phrase
Falls soundless in the tune and tremble of them.
Spun beyond the sign of the virgin and bloomed with light
The globe leans into spring.
The daughter from the dead land returns.
Between the edges of her thighs desire and cruelty
Make their twin temples, whereof the columns sunder
In the reverberations of time past and to come.
A pestilence among us gives us life.
Sparks shot to the cylinders explode softly
Sheathing speed in sleep.

TIME

The Weekly Newsmagazine

By the HARVARD ADVOCATE

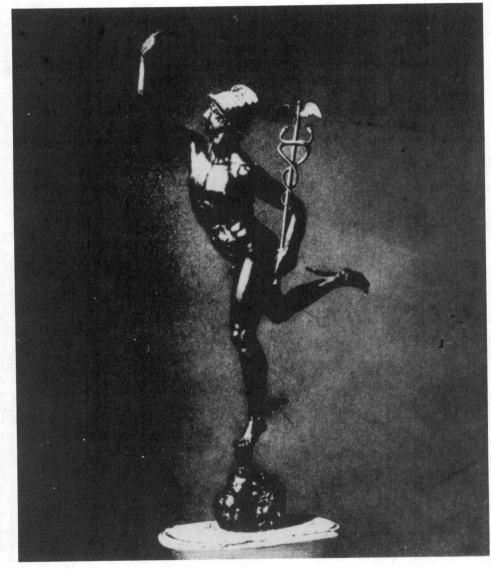

Volume CXVIII

PHLEETPHOOT PHEIDIPPEDES

Tersely: *"Why I ran every step of the way . . ."*

(See NATIONAL AFFAIRS)

Number 6

The Truce

J. R. AGEE

When, in such anguish of our love
As naught can temper or remove,
We lie beyond the hope of speech
And breathe our sorrow each to each,
One passion stands within my breast
Annihilating all the rest:
Lip and hand and flesh and bone
Are one large pity; pity alone
Is all my body can devise,
And pity gazes through my eyes.

Pitying, I seek your own,
And there, as still as any stone,
Pure as water wrung from flame,
Dwells a pity much the same.
While we look, those pities swell
Wide from double-sourced hell;
Deep and wide within that pool
Shines the pity of a fool;
Closer pressing, gazing, we
Know the idiot pity we.

So we look, and so love passes:
Take two flat quicksilvered glasses,
Press each to each the mirroring planes,
You naught can see, but much remains:
Bound in those flat and fragile walls
Stretch two bright and spaceless halls;
Beyond the glass, beyond the dull
Sponge of brain and box of skull
That straight and empty hall extends
And binds infinity's curved ends.

So much can our love attain,
Just so much, and that with pain;
Though we die to change the score,
Just so much, and nothing more.
Pity need not be the passion,
Though it be our private fashion:
Any single joy or grief
Turns the trick that cracks belief;
And the body's left behind
Whispering to the abandoned mind:

"So they look, and so Time passes
Withering o'er the glorious grasses:
Time shall ravel us asunder:
Mind's delight and body's wonder
And our shrewd-contrivéd lust,
Time shall wither into dust.
Where two pities stand displayed,
Shade shall mirror endless shade,
And they that have themselves forgot
Shall find no joy where self is not."

And the quiet mind makes reply:
"Many a time, before they die,
They shall hear out mutterings
And return to earthly things:
Try once more each sly device
We invent; none shall suffice.
Since much joy, but much more sorrow
Stands before their sunless morrow,
Vex not their unperplexity;
It cannot last as long as we."

Winter Eclogue

R. S. FITZGERALD

The wound is stiffened in the chest, and the equerries
Shut their blue fists in their trouser pockets.
Smoke falls in the early morning by the door.
A packet of excellent spices is come from India
To be preserved for His Grace's funeral,
The seventh duke, and to his heirs forever
Recipients of these arms. The lady is twice bereft.
Over the stairs the armoured light, drifting
Moves the hours, the absent voices, and the dark
Shepherds, the color of their eyes like leaves.

Yesterday Mr. Hamilton is reported to have spoken
About new hangings for the east hall. His sword.
And mention of an old league broken in the Low Countries. Years ago
When the child died the prior rode from the abbey
A wet mare, and in he came, blowing his hands.
Tonight we'll have snow. Do you remember Cockrell?
They were all in there singing by the fire
And the window all of a sudden smashed in, and those bastards . . .

That was the autumn. Nothing from the queen
Whose business is muffled up in Austria
Spain, Flanders, the south sailings and the west.
My friend
Lacing his leather on with surgeon's hands
Pale as Jesus he was, the groveling toad
Through ice-rime after the lanterns, lurching
Pikes, mattocks, the whole country crossed with light.
Here are the stones and ossuaries, graves,
Memorials of mice that scratch and perish,
The elegiacs cut with considered pride.
Pain on the right side when you turn, cough badly,
Find no record of service. The old nurse in the park
Visits me sometimes but I'm lonely here.
If you like, the little man who brings wood in the evening,
He would know: he says it was a fine cortege.

BOOKS

"My Battle", by Adolf Hitler; translated and abridged by Ets Dugdale; Boston, Houghton, Mifflin Company; 1933; $3.00.

In this, his autobiography, Hitler traces the development of his ideas. The first part shows primarily how these grew under the reactions of his surroundings and observations, while the second part is more of an analysis of the principles of his party movement.

The essential idea which dominates all Hitler's political philosophy is violent nationalism. To him, the race is the core of the national state and everything connected with the state must be built up on this underlying principle. What the race needs must be taken with a strong hand, no matter what sacrifice is involved; force must be used if necessary and force is by no means abhorrent to Hitler. The ideal state for the advancement of the race, following out these original ideas, must be strong, autocratic, authoritarian.

Starting from his intense nationalism and race worship, Hitler develops his ideas of state and party organization, foreign policy, and other political principles. His foreign policy is particularly interesting and follows logically from his initial premise. The Fatherland needs more territory to support her growing population and this territory must be contiguous in order to form the basis for a strong and compact nation; Germany must take what land she needs on the East from Russia which is in the hands of the Marxist Jew. Throughout the book, Hitler clearly shows his intense feeling against both Jew and Communist, two terms practically synonymous to him. The reasons for his prejudices are explained in no place; Hitler seems to expect his readers to accept his opinions at the start.

In dealing with many controversial subjects, Hitler fails to comprehend his opponents' position; he discusses everything from his single point of view — violent nationalism — and never analyzes his opponents' claims to show where these are weak. Rather he pours out his contempt and hatred of opposing views and seems to expect that these vitriolic outbursts will carry conviction as thoroughly as a reasoned argument would. Hitler was not sympathetic with the policy of preserving the Dual Monarchy of Austria-Hungary before the war and hence he never made any attempt to evaluate this policy; to him anything which might prolong the existence of this power by granting rights to subject nationalities was a betrayal of the German race, and he passionately felt that this minority should be exalted even at the cost of destroying his native country. To Hitler, the Revolution of 1918 was treason against the German race engineered by the International Jew and hence, obviously, at least to Hitler, there could be no good in it. Parliamentarianism he sweeps aside but he does not convince an unprejudiced reader to do likewise; he certainly does not give solid reasons for his contempt of accepted democratic institutions and his preference for strong leadership with one individual solely responsible.

Hitler's book is not as biased in some respects as one might expect. He shows little hatred for the victors in the World War, freely acknowledging German mistakes and weaknesses. He does not advocate a war of revenge nor does passion enter into his feelings towards other nations and possibly necessary wars with them; his sole consideration is the welfare, as he sees it, of the Fatherland. All his wrath is reserved for the Communist Jew whom he accuses of betraying Germany and leading her to ruin.

The book is written in a clear and direct style which seems to suit the philosophy of force. But the language is a bit too simple and direct in certain spots where Hitler tries to clarify some of his rather involved ideas. One might wish, moreover, that more of the Nazi's concrete policy and immediate aims were elucidated, and that he had included some discussion of economic principles. However, the book, written in 1924, traces only the beginnings of the movement. It attempts to explain Hitler's ideas and political philosophy rather than discuss recent German history.

IGNITE!   IGNITE!

(A perhaps too personal statement;

"Nevertheless, I will sign it".)

Ezra Pound

THERE is, if not a time-spirit, at any rate a TIME-FOETOR that reeks through the whole of an infected period, stinking from each prominent vent-hole.   No man who lived in power through the Harding-to-Hoover epoch smirking and unprotesting is fit to instruct the next generation.   For 25 years I have see the un-dignity, whether it were Lorimer pouring out hooey by the week to the million, floated on the "buy-more-this-that-&-the-other"; whether it were Dunkus, Wukkus, or Flobbor presiding over this or that beanery; or Coolidge setting the ALL TIME record for pusillanimity, but drawing his salary: all emit the identical pustulence.

Whatever department of "learning" general thought can pervade becomes of one flaccidity, a treacherous morass on which no building can rise.

The college presidents of America dare not read either HOW TO READ or my ABC of ECONOMICS. The cretinism of their era has left them no shred of decency.   Their age did not face the facts. Lippman does not face the facts. The editors of the commercial "literary" weeklies are still unaware of their grease paint.

The economists ignore simple facts of history.   The degree of sensitivity in the "clercs" could only be represented by an ideogram comprised of the portraits of all the members of our so-called Academy. From this "BODY", as Henry James called it with an intonation, no member has ever resigned, any more than a hand or a finger could resign from any somatic agglomerate at any downtown mortician's.

At the election of Nick Butler as president, no member resigned.

F.D.R. is so busy investigating Wiggins & banks that he has had no time to investigate "Foundations". It is as difficult to get an American to think evil of a "Foundation" as it wld. have been in 1860 to get a Russian peasant to spit on an ikon. A "Foundation" in the American language means a milch-cow.

140

I defy the assembled American college presidents to read the terms of Carnegie's donation to his Foundation for Peace, to consider what has been done during the past years with the half million dollars which the American people are condemned annually to pay to that otiose institution, and THEN to say whether this be or be not malversation of funds and an atrocious betrayal of trust.

The CAUSES of war have received NO attention. The Foundation's funds have gone into the pockets of alleged researchers, etc., who have done nothing to fulfill the terms of the endowment.

Count Mensdorf years ago wrote to the Washington office, pointing out that there *are* ECONOMIC CAUSES of war. The effect of this message has been, I think, nil; though I will cheerfully correct this statement if it contains any component of error.

At any rate, the secretary *answered* Mensdorf's letter, which is all one cld. have expected during that phase of American government.

When Lorimer's rag told the American people by the million that Kreuger was "more than a financial titan", no voice from subsidized professordom was lifted in rectification.

The inflation in business, the blah in economics, the assinine instruction in literature, are all of a perfume, a whorefume, a skunkery, of one smell, of one root at bottom.

Harvard has been spared Butler; Cross has risen to political eminence; Harvey, who didn't correct the lies in his paper, has passed into oblivion. Eliot, picked as a safe man, perhaps the only safe man among educated writers under fifty, was not on speaking terms with the late Pres. Lowell; and dear ole Binyon has been called to correct the too advanced and dangerous daring of Eliot. My gorrrd wotter country . . . whatter nedderkashun . . .

American publishers deserve the obvious distortion of their title.

In 1917 I handed American publishing the chance to take over the lead from London. The old rotting Capital by the Thames guttered down into the garbage. For ten years England did nothing. New York had the chance to take over, to lead, to bring out live books before Europe knew them or printed them.

Did she do it? She Did Not!

Even Paris is staggering up again; a faint stirring shows under the ashes. London is up again—a year, two years, ten years, 15, ahead of America. My gorrr wotter Kountry . . . My Gorrrd wotter COUNTRY . . .

Dithering ignorance in the wilds; dithering timidity in the Eastern cities. There is not a contemporary newspaper in the Union.

Rapallo, November, 1933

THE PROBLEM OF EDUCATION

T. S. Eliot, Harvard Advocate, '10

AT THE present time I am not very much interested in the only subject which I am supposed to be qualified to write about: that is, one kind of literary criticism. I am not very much interested in literature, except dramatic literature; and I am largely interested in subjects which I do not yet know very much about: theology, politics, economics, and education. I am moved at the moment to say something on the last of these subjects; so, if my comments appear very scrappy, I can only say that it is hard to start one's own education over again when one is in the forties. I have had some practical experience of education; first, having been educated myself, and in my opinion very badly. Second, I have taught boys of all ages in English schools; I was once an assistant in the Philosophy Department at Harvard; I have conducted Adult Education classes, and I have lectured at Cambridge in England and Cambridge in Massachusetts. I mention these facts because they are what might be considered credentials. But I do not feel that I have learned very much except to appreciate the magnitude of the educational problem. A great many men have taught for many more years than I, and yet are no more qualified to make any general statements about education. Indeed, most of the people engaged in educating seem to have very little conception of the general problem of education for a race and a nation, or of what purpose in a general scheme their own work is serving. They are merely Ford operatives. As for the big executives of education, I suspect that many of them have their minds filled with unexamined assumptions. Yet after feeding and clothing and housing people, the problem of how they should be educated is the most important you have, and perhaps the most difficult. Wherever you begin, you are led on to everything else. The problem of education leads you out to every other, and every other problem leads you back to education.

If what I am concerned about was merely the local problem, the question of what kind of education we ought to have in England, or in America, I should feel certainly that I am too ignorant to have the right to say anything. But I do not consider that there is one problem of education in America and another in England. However different the present systems may appear, I am sure that fundamentally we have one problem, at least in all English speaking countries, and that the things which alarm or depress me in America are equally present and alarming or depressing in England. English education is changing just as American education is changing: with only the trifling difference that the former seems to be going to the devil rather more slowly. The provincial universities, in any case, have much the same problem at the state universities of America: what sort of an education to give when the population to be educated includes almost everybody.

The chief persisting advantages of Oxford and Cambridge over American universities are (1) theological (2) economic.

I cannot attempt to demonstrate here that education, as the finest training of the finest minds, in contrast to the general education of everybody or the special technical training of persons to fill definite social needs, cannot afford to be separated from religion. But I am certain that the theological background—however far back it may be—is the only one that can provide the idea of order and unity needed for education. And I believe that if education is not rearranged by people with some definite social philosophy and some notion of the true vocation of man, the only education to be had will be in seminaries and colleges run by Jesuits. There is a good one in St. Louis, Mo. Incidentally, the only two men I know who have had what seemed to me hopeful theories of education and put them into practice, are Father Herbert Kelly of the Society of the Sacred Mission in Nottinghamshire, and Canon Iddings Bell of Providence, Rhode Island. I have no first-hand acquaintance with Canon Bell's frustrated attempts at St. Stephen's College, Annandale; and Father Kelly's system was designed for theological students; but I know of no other ventures in higher education of equal interest to these.

The leading American universities were, of course, originally directed by clergy of definite denominations. They now suffer from the dreadful blight of non-sectarianism, which means substituting a vague Christianity which the modern mind despises, for a precise Christianity which it may hate but must respect. Oxford and Cambridge are to a large extent atheist, but they remain in structure and ceremony foundations belonging to the Church of England. They may lose religion altogether, in time, but they are hardly likely to become non-sectarian; one feels, in their precincts, the sharp division of clerical and anti-clerical which is beneficial to both.

The American universities struck me, in contrast to Oxford and Cambridge, appallingly centralised in administration. That however is not the economic advantage of the latter universities that I have in mind. The English colleges own property; and much of their property is still that kind of property which is the least ignoble to possess: land. The ownership of land in England by individuals is now discouraged by Estate Duties, but ownership of land by colleges is still tolerated. The riches of the Oxford and Cambridge colleges do not, for the most part, consist in shares or debentures of fluctuating or doubtful value. Consequently the two older universities of England are on the whole independent of millionaires. Neither are their methods easily pliable to the theories of any one powerful administrator, like the late President Eliot. A Vice-Chancellor, or the Head of a House,

does not have to spend much of his time begging for endowments; nor would he have unlimited control over their use when received. In fact, the two older English universities are not quite so dependent upon an industrial aristocracy as the American: they sprang from and flourished in conditions older than capitalism, and they can perhaps survive it.

When I have mentioned these advantages, and that fact that a classical education, although no longer imposed, is still regarded as normal, I have stated what seem to me the essentials. The other advantages of Oxford and Cambridge are in comparison trivial or irrelevant. I should not care to see American universities imitating Oxford and Cambridge, even to the worm-holes in the system.

Of course there are many details which might be examined. But whom do you want to educate? The answer will depend upon your conception of a good society; and so will the sort of education you want to give. The answers depend upon your notion of the place of man in the world, of the relation of a supernatural order, if any, to the natural; they depend upon our answers to all the questions which we tacitly agree not to raise, when we discuss educational matters. You may have a notion of the understanding of certain things as valuable in itself, so that you want a few people in every generation to be educated to understand and value and preserve them. Or you may have a notion of the kind of society you want, and concentrate upon whatever seems to subserve the interests of that society. Or you may have a vague notion that a university "education" confers a social degree, and proceed to overrun the country with gentlemen. Instead we assume at the same time that education is for those individuals who are fine enough to deserve it, that it is for the upper classes, that it is to make everybody a member of the upper classes, that everybody is entitled to the same education, that education is something to give one an advantage over the uneducated, and that education is going to make it possible to get a good job, according to whatever be our notion of goodness in jobs. But once you start to think about education you must go on thinking about your whole social system, and about politics and economics and theology. At any rate I am glad to think that all these subjects in which I am uneducated but interested are fundamentally related.

A PROBLEM OF (SPECIFICALLY) STYLE

*The Sage of Rapallo Discusses Among Other Things
the Nature of Religion*

Ezra Pound

EVEN THE death of the last survivors of the clogging and war-causing generation that preceded us, will not bring a new and illumined era unless at least the élite of ours or (that being unlikely) the next, make some effort to understand the function of language, and to understand why a tolerance for slipshod expression in whatever department of writing gradually leads to chaos, munitions-profiteers, the maintenance of wholly unnecessary misery, omnipresent obfuscation of mind, and a progressive rottenness of spirit.

Mr. Eliot in advocating a species of Christianity has, so far as I am aware, neglected to define religion. His readers are befogged as to whether he wants a return to the Christian Church (as it was in the year Sixteen Hundred in Chiswick) or whether he wants us to turn religious, or in what order.

There *is* a distinct difference in Anschauung between men who believe that the world needs religion and those who believe it needs some particular brand or flavour of religion.

Among professionals, that is, men who get their board and keep by religion, it is today almost impossible to find any professional competence in theology. I have yet to find a professor or religious writer who has bothered to formulate a definition of "religion" before touting his own particular brand. George Washington, refusing to be cornered and driven into profession of belief in an undefined something or other, commended the "beneficent influence of the Christian Religion."

Given an effect, even the most agnostic and merely logical mind will admit a cause.

Given the necessity of volition, the freest thinker might admit the necessity or advisability of a direction of that volition.

Given an increasing awareness that there exists circumvolving us a vast criminal class that never infringes any "law" on the statue books or breaks an enforceable police regulation, the more perceptive tend in some cases to believe in the usefulness of a "general disposition", you might even say they incline toward a belief in the *need* of a general disposition, toward the Whole, the cosmos, and even toward the consciousness inherent in that cosmos.

No man is aware of that consciousness save by way of his own, but believing in a great telephone central or not, or in minor centrals or not, no scientist can deny at least fragmentary portions of consciousness which have a sum, a totality, whether or no they have coherent inter-organization.

The minute a man takes into consideration the totality of this universe, or the sum of this consciousness, he has, whether he wants it or not, a religion. And some phase of that consciousness in his *theos*: whether coherent or non-coherent, labile, intermittent or whatever.

And into his thought and action there enters a component influence affecting, in all degrees from the infinitestimal up to 100%, his volition, and his specific acts or the general tone of his action.

Religion in humanist terms would be valuable in the degree in which it directed a man toward the welfare of humanity (judged not necessarily in mere terms of eating, but also in terms of mental condition, peace of mind, mental vitality).

Granting that mankind may need a religion; that, in concrete instances, many men will—so long as they lack one—do nothing that is of the faintest use or of the faintest possible interest, I should have to have some evidence that the given professional had reason for touting his own particular brand in preference to any three dozen others; and such evidence would have to come to me, either from a greater efficiency in good action or a greater mental clarity and honesty as displayed in his manifest thought. Thought to be manifest would have to be so, either by verbal expression or by demonstration in some other sensible medium.

A manifest funking of straight thought or honest action in any specific field falling under one's examination, would obviously throw out the fakers, i. e., it would obviously bring any brand of religion into disrepute with thoughtful observers, whether this applied to an individual exponent or to an "organization".

The Medieval Church in its wisdom placed excessive sloth among sins. In no field has the sloth of our time been more foul and oppressive than in the search for clear terminology. In no field have the English-speaking nations been more damned than in failing to dissociate ideas.

In all fields this muddiness is so great that any field serves as repulsive example; and among all morasses the economic morass is the dankest.

Experts representing their nations in international congresses are no better than timorous instructors holding their jobs on sufferance and fearing for the good of their offspring.

Lacking a religion or a decent ethical base, there is no reason why Bug'ush and Co. shouldn't be content in creating confusion. Lacking an ethical basis there is no argument against the perpetual (as I see it) infamy or dragging discussion continually onto the unessential, and continually away from the search after truth and knowledge.

If scientists are not always free from a personal vanity, we have at least proof that in the laboratories a great number of men do search after biological and chemical knowledge without being continually led off into personal bickerings petty struggles for precedence. Medical science does and a number of medical scientists do set an example, however, many fools may have on dramatic occasions tried to obstruct a medical hero.

In no science can truth go forward when men are more anxious to show up another man's minor error, or to prove his failure of fool-proof formulation, than to use his perception of truth (however fragmentary) for a greater perception and for the formulation of valid equations.

We were, manifestly, drug up analphabetic in economics. We are manifestly surrounded by an ignorance of economic history which sheds infamy on every college and university and shows up the whole congeries of economic professors as apes with the rarest possible exception.

A Face Of Stone

William Carlos Williams

HE WAS ONE of these fresh Jewish types you want to kill at sight, the presuming poor whose looks change the minute cash is mentioned. But they're insistent, trying to force attention, taking advantage of good nature at the first crack. You come when I call you, that type. He got me into a bad mood before he opened his mouth just by the half smiling, half insolent look in his eyes, a small, stoutish individual in a greasy black suit, a man in his middle twenties I should imagine.

She, on the other hand looked Italian, a goaty slant to her eyes, a face often seen among Italian immigrants. She had a small baby tight in her arms. She stood beside her smiling husband and looked at me with no expression at all on her pointed face, unless no expression is an expression. A face of stone. It was an animal distrust, not shyness. She wasn't shy but seemed as if sensing danger, as though she were on her guard against it. She looked dirty. So did he. Her hands were definitely grimy, with black nails. And she smelled, that usual smell of sweat and dirt you find among any people who habitually do not wash or bathe.

The infant was asleep when they came into the office, a child of about five months perhaps, not more.

People like that belong in clinics, I thought to myself. I wasn't putting myself out for them, not that day anyhow. Just dumb oxen. Why the hell do they let them into the country. Half idiots at best. Look at them.

My brother told us to bring the baby here, the man said. We've had a doctor but he's no good.

How do you know he's no good. You probably never gave him a chance. Did you pay him?

Sure we paid him.

Well what do you want me to do? To hell with you, I thought to myself. Get sore and get the hell out of here. I got to go home to lunch.

I want you to fix up the baby, Doc. My brother says you're the best baby doctor around here. And this kid's sick.

Well, put it up there on the table and take its clothes off then. Why didn't you come earlier in-

stead of waiting here till the end of the hour. I got to live too.

The man turned to his wife. Gimme the baby, he said.

No. She wouldn't. Her face just took on an even stupider expression of obstinacy but she clung to the child.

Come on, come on, I said. I can't wait here all day.

Give him to me, he said to her again. He only wants to examine it.

I hold her, the woman said keeping the child firmly in her arms.

Listen here, I spoke to her. Do you want me to examine the child or don't you. If you don't, then take it somewhere.

Wait a minute, wait a minute, Doc, the man said smiling ingratiatingly.

You look at throat, the mother suggested.

You put the baby up there on the table and take its clothes off, I told her. The woman shook her head. But as she did so she gradually relented, looking furtively at me with distrustful glances her nostrils moving slightly.

Now what is it.

She's getting thin, Doc 'think somethink's the matter with her.

What do you mean, thin?

I asked her age, the kind of labor she had had. How they were feeding the baby. Vomiting, sleeping, hunger. It was the first child and the mother was new at nursing it. It was four and a half months old and weighed thirteen and a half pounds. Not bad.

I think my milk no good, said the woman, still clinging to the baby whose clothes she had only begun to open.

As I approached them the infant took one look at me and let out a wild scream. In alarm the mother clutched it to her breast and started for the door.

I burst out laughing. The husband got red in the face but forced a smile. Don't be so scared, he said to his wife. He, nodding toward me, ain't gonna hurt you. You know she hasn't been in this country long, Doc. She's scared you're gonna hurt the baby. Bring it over here, he said to her, and take off his clothes. Here, give 'im to me. And he took the infant into his own hands, screaming lustily, and carried it to the table to undress it. The mother, in an agony of apprehension kept interfering from behind at every move.

What a time! I couldn't find much the matter and told them so. Just the results of irregular, foolish routine and probably insufficient breast milk. I gave them a complemental formula. He chiseled a dollar off the fee and—just as he was going out—said, Doc, if we need you any time I want you to come out to the house to see it. You gotta watch this kid.

Where do you live, I asked.

He told me where it was, way out near the dumps. I'll come if you give me a decent warning, I told him. If you want me call me in the morning. Now get that. You can't expect me to go running out there for thing every time the kid gets a belly ache. Or just because she thinks it's dying. If you call me around supper time or in the middle of a snow storm or at two o'clock in the morning maybe I won't do it. I'm telling you now so you'll know. I got too much to do already.

O.K., Doc, he said smiling. But you come.

I'll come on those conditions.

O.K., Doc.

And sure enough, on a Sunday night, about nine o'clock, with the thermometer at six below and the roads like a skating rink, they would call me.

Nothing doing, I said.

But Doc, you said you'd come.

I'm not going there tonight, I insisted. I won't do it. I'll ask my associate to make the call or some good younger man that lives in that neighborhood but I won't go over there tonight.

But we need you Doc, the baby's very sick.

Can't help it. I tell you I'm not going. And I slammed up the receiver.

Who in the world are you talking to like that, said my wife who had put down her book as my voice rose higher. You mustn't do that.

Leave me alone, I know what I'm doing.

But my dear!

Four months later, after three months of miserable practice, the first warm day in April, about twenty women with babies came to my office. I started at one P. M. and by three I was still going strong. I hadn't loafed. Anybody left out there? I asked the last woman, as I thought, who had been waiting for me. Oh yes, there's a couple with a baby. Oh Lord, I

groaned. It was half past three by then and a number of calls still to be made about the town.

There they were. The same fresh mug and the same face of stone, still holding the baby which had grown, however, to twice its former size.

Hello Doc, said the man smiling.

For a moment I couldn't place them. Hello, I said. Then I remembered. What can I do for you—at this time of day. Make it snappy cause I've got to get out.

Just want you to look the baby over, Doc.

Oh yeah.

Listen Doc, we been waiting out there two hours.

Good night! That finishes me for the afternoon, I said to myself. All right, put it up on the table. As I said this, feeling at the same time a sense of helpless irritation and anger, I noticed a cluster of red pimples in the region of the man's right eyebrow and reaching to the bridge of his nose. Like bed-bug bites I thought to myself. He'll want me to do something for them too before I get through I suppose. Well, what's the matter now? I asked them.

It's the baby again, Doc, the man said.

What's the matter with the baby. It looks all right to me. And it did. A child of about ten months, I estimated, with a perfectly happy, round face.

Yes, but his body isn't so good.

I want you should examine him all over, said the mother.

You would, I said. Do you realize what time it is?

Shall she take his clothes off? the man broke in.

Suit yourself, I answered, hoping she wouldn't do it. But she put the infant on the table and began carefully to undress it.

No use. I sat down and took out a card for the usual notes. How old is it?

How old is it? he asked his wife.

Ten months. Next Tuesday ten months, she said with the same face on her as always.

Are you still nursing it?

Sure, she said. Him won't take bottle.

Do you mean to say that after what I told you last time, you haven't weaned the baby?

What can she do, Doc. She tried to but he won't let go of the breast. You can't make him take a bottle.

Does he eat?

Yeah, he eats a little, but he won't take much.

Cod liver oil?

He takes it all right but spits it up half an hour later. She stopped giving it to him.

Orange juice.

Sure. Most of the time.

So, as a matter of fact, she's been nursing him and giving him a little cereal and that's all.

Sure, that's about right.

How often does she nurse him?

Whenever he wants it, the man grinned. Sometimes every two hours. Sometimes he sleeps. Like that.

But didn't I tell you, didn't I tell her to feed it regularly.

She can't do that, Doc. The baby cries and she gives it to him.

Why don't you put it in a crib?

She won't give it up. You know, that's the way she is, Doc. You can't make her do different. She wants the baby next to her so she can feel it.

Have you got it undressed? I turned to the mother who was standing with her back to me.

You want shoe off? she answered me.

Getting up I went to the infant and pulled the shoes and stockings off together, picked the thing up by its feet and the back of the neck and carried it to the scales. She was right after me, her hands half extended watching the child at every movement I made. Fortunately the child grinned and sagged back unresisting in my grasp. I looked at it more carefully then, a smart looking little thing and a perfectly happy, fresh mug on him that amused me in spite of myself.

Twenty pounds and four ounces, I said. What do you want for a ten month old baby? There's nothing the matter with him. Get his clothes on.

I want you should examine him first, said the mother.

The blood went to my face in anger but she paid no attention to me. He too thin, she said. Look him body.

To quiet my nerves I took up my stethoscope and went rapidly over the child's chest, saw that everything was all right there, that there was no rickets and told them so—and to step on it. Get him dressed. I got to get out of here.

Him all right? the woman questioned me with her stony pale green eyes. I stopped to look at them, they were very curious, almost at right angles to each other—in a way of speaking—like the eyes of some female figure I had seen somewhere—Montegna—Botticelli—I couldn't remember.

Yes, only for God's sake, take him off the breast. Feed him the way I told you to.

No will take bottle.

Fine. I don't give a damn about the bottle. Feed him from a cup, with a spoon, any way at all. But feed him regularly. That's all.

As I turned to wash my hands, preparatory to leaving the office the man stopped me. Doc, he said, I want you to examine my wife.

He got red in the face as I turned on him. What the hell do you think I am anyhow. You got a hell of a nerve. Don't you know. . .

We waited two hours and ten minutes for you, Doc he replied smiling. Just look her over and see what the matter with her is.

I could hardly trust myself to speak for a moment but, instead turned to look at her again standing beside the baby which she had finished dressing and which was sitting on the table looking at me. What a creature. What a face. And what a body. I looked her coldly up and down from head to toe. There was a rip in her dress, a triangular tear just above the left knee.

Well—No use getting excited with people such as these—or with anyone, for that matter, I said in despair. No one can do two things at the same time, especially when they're in two different places. I simply gave up and returned to my desk chair.

Go ahead. What's the matter with her?

She gets pains in her legs, especially at night. And she's got a spot near her right knee. It came last week, a big blue looking sort of spot.

Did she ever have rheumatism? You know, go to bed with swollen joints—or six weeks—or like that.

Did you have rheumatism? he turned to her.

She simply shrugged her shoulders.

She don't know, he said, interpreting and turning red in the face again. I particularly noticed it this time and remembered that it had occurred two or three times before while we were talking.

Tell her to open up her dress.

Open up your dress, he said.

Sit down, I told her and let me see your legs.

As she did so I noticed again the triangular rip in the skirt over her left thigh, dirty silk, and that her skin was directly under it. She untied some white rags above her knees and let down her black stockings. The left one first, I said.

Her lower legs were peculiarly bowed, really like Turkish scimetars, flattened and somewhat rotated on themselves in an odd way that could not have come from anything but severe rickets rather late in her childhood.' The whole leg while not exactly weak was as ugly and misshapen as a useful leg well could be in so young a woman. Near the knee was a large discolored area where in all probability a varicose vein had ruptured.

That spot, I told the husband, comes from a broken varicose vein.

Yeah, I thought so, she's got them all up both legs.

That's from carrying a child.

No. She had them before that. They've always been that way since I've known her. Is that what makes her have the pains there?

I hardly think so, I said looking over the legs again, one of which I held on the palm of either hand. No, I don't think so.

What is it then? It hurts her bad, especially at night.

She's bow-legged as hell in the first place. That throws the strain where it doesn't belong and look at those shoes—

Yeah, I know.

The woman had on an old pair of fancy high-heeled slippers such as a woman might put on for evening wear. They were all worn and incredibly broken down. I don't see how she can walk in them.

That's what I told her, the man said. I wanted her to get a pair of shoes that fitted her but she wouldn't do it.

Well, she's got to do it, I said. Throw away those shoes. I told her and get shoes with flat heels. And straight heels. I tried to impress her. What they call Cuban heels, if you must. New Shoes, I emphasized. How old is she, I asked the man.

His face colored again for reasons I could not fathom. Twenty four, he said.

Where was she born?

In Poland.

In Poland! Well. I looked at her, not believing him.

Yeah, why?

Well. Twenty-four years old you say. Let's see. That's different. An unusual type for a Jew, I thought. That's the probable explanation for her legs, I told the husband. She must have been a little girl during the war over there. A kid of maybe five or six years I should imagine. Is that right, I asked her. But she didn't answer me, just looked back into my eyes with that inane look.

What did you get to eat?

She seemed not to have heard me but turned to her husband.

Did she lose any of her people, I asked him.

Any of them? She lost everybody, he said quietly.

How did she come to get over here then?

She came over four years ago. She has a sister over here.

So that's it, I thought to myself looking at her fussing, intensely absorbed with the baby, looking at it, talking to it in an inarticulate sort of way, paying no attention whatever to me. No wonder she's built the way she is, considering what she must have been through in that invaded territory. And this guy here—

What are we going to do about the pains, Doc?

Get her some decent shoes, that's the first thing.

O.K., Doc.

She could be operated on for those veins. But I wouldn't advise it, just yet. I tell you. Get one of those woven elastic bandages for her, they don't cost much. A three inch one. And I told him what to get.

Can't you give her some pills to stop the pain?

Not me, I told him. You might get her teeth looked at though if you want to. All that kind of thing and —well, I will give you something. It's not dope. It just helps if there's any rheumatism connected with it.

Can you swallow a pill, I turned to her attracting her attention.

She looked at me. How big? she said.

She swallows an Aspirin pill when I give it to her sometimes, said her husband, but she usually puts it in a spoonful of water first to dissolve it. His face reddened again and suddenly I understood his half shameful love for the woman and at the same time the extent of her reliance on him.

I was touched.

They're pretty big pills, I said. Look, they're green. That's the coating so they won't dissolve in your stomach and upset your digestion.

Let see, said the woman.

I showed a few of the pills to her in the palm of my hand.

For pains in leg?

Yes, I told her.

She looked at them again. Then for the first time since I had known her a broad smile spread all over her face. Yeah, she said, I swallow him.

FRAGMENT OF A CHORUS FROM "PANIC"

A VERSE PLAY BY ARCHIBALD MacLEISH

The play is a play of the bank panic in February and March 1933. Its protagonist (McGafferty) is the great industrialist of his time and his time's greatest banker. The theme is the conflict between this man and the sense of fatality and inescapable destruction which is now familiar in our civilization. The choruses are spoken from a street crowd gathered at night before an electric news announcer of the Times Square type. The chorus swings through the moods of belief in the Great Man to doubt of his greatness to desire to escape from his shadow. The present fragment is from a chorus of the first type.

A MAN:	Overthrowing McGafferty! Even fools would have laughed at it!
A MAN:	Name known in the foreign Mountains: spoken in wars: Spoken in all men's tongues— Like the words for salt and for hunger!
A MAN:	Spoken by signs and among the Nakedest men and in cities and Over the water pits in the Wild plains and at fords: At the camel halts on the borders!

A Man: Over the zinc bars and
              Over the glass!

A Man: And in harbors and
              Far at sea—the stokers
              Clanging the coal in!

A Man: Spoken by
              Mouths: stamped on the steel—
              Lettered on ocean keels on the
              Cold plates—the water
              Washing the weeds on it!

A Man: Taught from the
              Grip of a gang boss' gun to the
              Niggers naked in sunlight!

A Man: Dug out of wounds—splinters of
              Shrapnel showing it!

A Man: Printed on
              Fifty gallon cans on the
              Saddled mules by the shanties!

A Man: Overthrowing McGafferty!
              Overthrowing the half of the
              Common world—if they could!

A NATURAL HISTORY

James Laughlin, 1936

WELL THEY were real tracks this time, not like the ones Hank and Gussy had made the week before to fool Helena, and we followed them up the beach and found the turtle high in the dry sand, where the warmth of the sun hatches the eggs, already popping them. It was a big old bitch and she was half backed down into the hole she'd dug, dropping about two eggs a minute as near as I could time it. Helena started giggling, she hadn't ever seen one laying before, and we'd come out a week before, too early, because she was so het up about it and wanted to see one before she had to go up back north again, and there hadn't been any, they hardly ever start coming up out of the sea before the end of May, so Gussy and Hank faked up a flipper track with their elbows while I kept Helena busy up the beach, and then they came running up the beach shouting that they'd just seen a big one going back into the water, the idea was to try to get Helena to dig for the eggs where there weren't any, but it didn't work because she caught on because Gussy had put his foot down a couple of times when they were making the track and the pattern of the sole showed on the sand, but Helena hadn't had to go north so soon after all because her old man, who is drunk almost all the time, had the d-t's just the night before they were going to start driving back to Illinois, and they'd had to take him down to Miama to the hospital to get over them, so she could stay on longer and we'd come out again when the moon got full because the old nigger who cuts the lawn for Senator Blossom says that's what gives the turtles the signal to come up out of the sea. Helena started giggling, and Hank slapped her fanny and said something I didn't catch that made her awful sore. "That ain't one bit funny, Hank," said Georgia. I could see, with the big moon, that Georgia wasn't liking it much, but Elsy was eating it right up. She got down in the sand to look into the hole. You could hear the eggs landing as they fell, plip . . . plep . . . plip, like that, like the slow drip of a faucet into a drain tub. "Wouldya lookit the way they bounce!" said Elsy. Georgia was looking like she was going to be sick any minute and Gussy said, "Isn't that cute the way nature makes them sorta soft so they can bounce like that and not get broke?"

Georgia sat down in the sand and looked the other way; "Come on be a sport," said Helena, "You knowya wanted to come 'n you said how you came last year 'n what a laugh it was." Georgia didn't say anything. Plip . . . plep . . . plip . . . I was wondering how that poor goddam turtle must feel. She knew we were there all right, she'd pulled in her head under the shell, but once they get started laying they can't get themselves stopped, and there she had to go on with it knowing all the time that we'd cop the eggs just as soon as she got them dropped. Gussy was starting to fish some of them out of the hole already while she was still working. He gave one to Elsy and she turned it over in her fingers, fascinated with the way the air dent rolled around the shell as she moved it. "Look Gussy," I said, "Why don't you just put the basket down inside the hole? Save a lot of work." He tried it, scooping away some sand to get it down, but trying to work it under the turtle he must have scraped her behind because she struck out at him, quick as lightning, with her back foot and ripped a long bloody scratch down his wrist and hand. He swore at the turtle and gave it a kick which only hurt his toe. His hand was bleeding some and the girls clustered round. He was starting to suck at the cut but Helena said not to. Elsy asked him if it hurt bad, Georgia couldn't take her eyes off it. "Wash it in the salt water," said Helena, "Salt's just as good as iodine." They went down to the water and I stood watching the turtle. Hank fetched back the basket that Gussy had slung away in his anger. Plip . . . plep . . . plip, the hole was nearly full now and the eggs seemed to be coming a little quicker. The turtle edged her head out cautiously from under the shell and jerked it back in again when she saw me. "How would you be feeling if you was this turtle?" I asked Hank. "I don' getcha," said Hank. "Well, having all your eggs swiped from you after you'd worked so damn hard to lay 'em." "Oh," said Hank, "Oh yeah, well I guess I'd be perty sore, I guess . . . hell, I didn't never think nothin, about it, I ain't no damn turtle." Gussy and the girls came back up the beach from the water, they'd tied a couple of handkerchiefs around his wrist. "Hey look," said Elsy, "She's going to fill up the hole." The turtle had finished laying and was turned around pushing sand into the hole with her flippers. Whether or not we were there waiting to steal her eggs she was going to finish up her job the way her instinct made her. She filled up her hole to the level of the beach and then hit right out for the water. And turtles aren't so slow either, she went right along with a quick jerking movement, the flippers pulling in front and the feet pushing from behind. Hank picked up Elsy to put her on the turtle's back, we'd filled the girls up with stories about how you could ride on the turtles' backs, how on real hot nights they ran a regular taxi service up and down the beach, how you could have races on them, but Elsy'd seen what that turtle had done to Gussy and she wasn't going to get herself within reach of it. Hank was carrying her along behind the turtle, trying to sit her down on its back, but she grabbed hold of his hair, he has long hair, when he combs it down the wrong way he can chew the ends of it, and pulled until he had to dump her or lose two handfuls of it. I followed the turtle as she scrambled down the beach, and the way she was going it looked as though once she got back in the water she'd never more come out again. A big wave hit her as she went into the surf, it rolled her on her side, but she flopped down again and pushed on out into deep water. For a little while I could see her swimming along the surface but then she dove under and disappeared. I watched for a while to see if she would come up again further out but she didn't. The moon on the water was something marvellous, like some sort of silver fire if there ever was such a thing. I stood there just watching it, it was so wonderful, and Helena came up behind me and leaned against me, rubbing her chin against my shoulder. "What'you think of that?" I said, "Ever see anything like that up in Illinois?" She rubbed her chin on the side of my neck and put a hand on my arm, I could feel her breath on my cheek and the softness of her pressing against my back. "Y'know I wish I weren't never going back home at all, I wish I was just always going to stay here with . . ." "Sure," I said quickly, "That'd be great, Hel, but y'know it get's awful hot down here in summer, it get's terrible hot, I think you'd pretty soon get fed with it down here in summer." She moved away from me and kicked at something in the sand. "Come on," I said "We've got to tote those eggs up to the car." She followed me up the beach without speaking.

Well, we got this stuff from a guy with a truck who'd killed a big turtle and couldn't get it up from the beach to the road it was so heavy. It's against the law to kill them but bootlegging them is worthwhile because the niggers love the meat, they eat everything but the shell, and one of those big ones, two or three hundred pounds of turtle, will feed a lot of niggers. This guy had come down from Stuart with his truck, and he'd located a whopping big turtle and been able to kill it by getting it turned over on its back with a crowbar and then taking an axe to it, but even at that it wasn't clean dead, a turtle is such a tough old bastard that you can't really call it dead till you've cut it in pieces, because as long as two pieces are still together they can manage to wiggle, I know because Hank tried to kill one one day, just a small one, and it took him over an hour with a meat knife and a hammer and screwdriver, its legs kept twitching after he had all the insides cut out of the shell, and the heart went on beating for about two hours after he'd cut it out and there wasn't any blood left in it, it just seemed to be beating on air, and when you'd poke it with a finger it would take on a spurt and beat faster for a while and then gradually quiet down again. Well we found this guy sitting on the fender of Gussy's car when we got back to the road with the eggs in a basket, and he asked would we give him a hand with his turtle. We had quite a job dragging it up to the road even though there were four of us because it was so big around there was no way you could get ahold of it, you couldn't get a grip on the smooth edge of the shell and nobody wanted to grab it by the feet because they were still jerking in spite of how its head was all mashed to hell and blood dripping over the sand. Finally Gussy got an idea, he remembered he had an old pair of chains under the seat of his car left over from the time when it was new and he used to drive people from the Beach out into the Glades to shoot. We got a hitch around the shell with the chains and that gave us something to haul on. Just the same it was some job to get it up that bank to the road, and while we were resting in the middle this guy brought down a big jug of this stuff from his truck and passed it around. And then when we'd gotten the turtle into the truck he'd brought along planks for that so it wasn't so hard, we had another round from the jug and he filled a quart bottle from it and give it to us to take along home. I don't know whatever this stuff could have been, it tasted something godawful, but it went down like a hurricane and hit like a landslide. It did the job all right, and by the time we got back to the beginning of West Palm we were feeling just fine and dandy and plenty left over to spare. Gussy had the old wreck wide open, you could have heard it a mile away, and we went down the boulevard like an itchy snake trying to scratch its back on both sides of the street at once. We were all feeling happy, hollering and singing and almost falling out of the car, and Elsy started throwing eggs at the cars parked along the sidewalk. Georgia tried to stop her, she hadn't kept up with the rest of us, but we all pretty soon forgot that we'd gotten the eggs to eat when we saw the way they splattered all over the cars as they broke. That was some ride I can tell you, and I guess there weren't two cars in twenty blocks that didn't get messed up the way we were slinging those turtle eggs. Then somebody thought of niggertown and it caught like a light, we were all yelling "Get those goddam niggers!" as we bumped over the tracks into Blackland. It was Saturday night and they were all still outside standing under the streetlights and sitting in front of their shacks. Gussy slowed down the car and we stood up and let 'em have it, all of us firing at once except Georgia who was sore and getting scared. We went down that old street like a mowing machine potting those damn niggers on both sides and you shoulda heard them swear and holler. A couple of them ran out and tried to hop our running board but Hank and I had a wrench and jack-handle ready and we let 'em have it right in the snoot. The rest of them all beat it back into their shacks but we went up and down a couple more times just decorating their windows. Then we heard a siren across the tracks, some nigger must have telephoned to the cops, so we scrammed out the back end of the street and beat it for home. When we pulled into Gussy's garage we were just too drunk tired to get out and go home so we lay there in the car, all but Georgia who went off by herself and left us. I was lying in the back seat, looking at the dark while the inside of my head rolled round and round in my skull, and Helena rolled over on top of me and started sucking my ear with her teeth the way she does. She was all set for it I could tell but I didn't try to get anywhere at all, I was so marvellously sleepy with the likker slowly wearing off, and we just lay there tight together feeling real hot and sleepy and good.

GLITTERING PIE

Henry V. Miller

DEAR FRED:

I will probably take the Champlain, the boat I arrived on, because it is French and because it leaves a day earlier than necessary. I will bring the stockings for Maggy—and anything else I can think of. Don't know yet about going to the Villa Seurat, but Hotel des Terrasses suits me down to the ground—because it's 13th Arondissement and no ecologues. Make sure my bike is there. I am going to use it! And where is my phono? I am bringing back some of the famous jazz hits, the crooning, swooning lullabys sung by the guys without —. (The popular favorite is: "I Believe in Miracles." *Miracles!* How American! Well —, I'll explain all this in detail when I see you, and have a fine bottle of wine handy, a mellow one, a costly one. Here nothing but California vintages, or dago red, which is vile stuff. One must "alkalize" every day . . . . I'll explain that too, later.)

So, Joey, what are we going to do for a living, hein? Search me! But I feel that we're going to live just the same. Anyway, I come . . . . The Jew who published my notes on N. Y. C. in that revolutionary Dance Program got back at me by entitling it: "I came, I saw, *I fled.*" The expatriates are anathema to the Americans, particularly to the Communists. I have made myself heartily disliked everywhere, except among the dumb Gentiles who live in the suburbs and guzzle it over the weekends. With those blokes I sing, dance, whistle, make merry the whole night long. I have nothing in common with them aside from the desire to enjoy myself. To know how to enjoy oneself is something unknown here. Usually it consists in making a loud noise. At Manhasset one night Emil and I did the cakewalk so strenuously that Emil dislocated — — — —. It was a marvellous night in which we drank ourselves sober. Towards the end I sat down and, striking every wrong note on the piano, I played as only Paderewski himself could play, *if he were drunk.* I broke a few keys and every nail on my fingers. Went to bed with a Mexican hat three feet broad. It lay on my stomach like a huge sun-flower. In the morning I found myself in the child's bedroom and

beside me a little typewriter made of hard rubber which I couldn't write on, drunk as I was. I also found a rosary and crucifix awarded by the Society of the Miraculous Medal, Germantown, Pa. It was *"indulgenced for a Happy Death and the Way of the Cross."*

I have had a lot of funny experiences, but few gay ones. When I get back to Paris I shall remember the evenings spent sitting on couches in studios with everybody talking pompously and callously about social-economic conditions—with cruel lapses of Proust and Cocteau. (To talk of Proust or Joyce today in America is to be quite up to the minute! Some one will ask you blandly—"What is all this crap about *Surrealisme?* What *is* it? Whereupon I usually explain that *Surrealisme* is when you — — your friend's beer and he drinks it by mistake.)

Met William Carlos Williams the other night and had a rousing time with him at Hiler's place. Holty arrived with two dopey brother-in-laws, one of whom played the piano. Everybody crocked, including Lisette. Just before all hands passed out some one yelled—"all art is local"—which precipitated a riot. After that nothing is clear. Hiler sits in his drawers, with legs crossed, and plays "Believe it Beloved," another hit of the season. The janitor comes and raises hell—he was an aviator for Mussolini. Then come the Dockstadter Sisters who write for the pulps. After that Monsieur Bruine who has been in America 39 years and looks exactly like a Frenchman. He is in love with a dizzy blonde from the Vanities. Unfortunately she got so drunk that she puked all over him while sitting on his lap. He's cured of her now.

I mention these little details because without them the American scene is not complete. Everywhere it is drunkenness and vomiting, or breaking of windows and smashing heads. Twice recently I narrowly missed being cracked over the head. People walk the streets at night lit up and looking for trouble. They come on you unexpectedly and invite you to fight—for the fun of it! It must be the climate—*and the machine.* The machines are driving them screwy. Nothing is done by hand any more. Even the doors open magically: as you approach the door you step on a treadle and the door springs open for you. It's hallucinating. And then there are the patent medicines. Ex-lax for constipation—everybody has constipation!—and Alka-Seltzer for hang-overs.

Everybody wakes up with a headache. For breakfast it's a Bromo-Seltzer—with orange juice and toasted corn muffins, of course. To start the day right you must *alkalize*. It says so in all the subway trains. High-pressure talks, quick action, money down, mortgaged to the eyes, prosperity around the corner (it's always around the corner!), don't worry, keep smiling, believe it beloved, etc. etc.

The songs are marvellous, especially as to words. They betray the incurable melancholy and optimism of the American race. I wish I were a foreigner and getting it from scratch. A good one just now is: "The Object of my Affection can change my Complexion . . . ." I'll bring this along too.

At the burlesk Sunday afternoon I heard Gypsy Rose Lee sing "Give Me a Lei!" She had a Hawaiian lei in her hand and she was telling how it felt to get a good lei, how even mother would be grateful for a lei once in a while. She said she'd take a lei on the piano, or on the floor. An old-fashioned lei, too, if needs be. The funny part of it is the house was almost empty. After the first half-hour every one gets up nonchalantly and moves down front to the good seats. The strippers talk to their customers as they do their stunt. The *coup de grace* comes when, after having divested themselves of every stitch of clothing, there is left only a spangled girdle with a fig leaf dangling in front—sometimes a little monkey beard, which is quite ravishing. As they draw towards the wings they stick their bottoms out and slip the girdle off. Sometimes they darken the stage and give a belly dance in radium paint. It's good to see the belly button glowing like a glow worm, or like a bright half-dollar. It's better still to see them —— —, — — — — — — — —. Then there is the loud speaker through which some idiotic jake roars: "Give the little ladies a hand please!" Or else— "now, ladies and gentlemen, we are going to present you that most charming personality fresh from Hollywood—Miss Chlorine Duval of the Casino de Paris." Said Chlorine Duval is generally streamlined, with the face of an angel and a thin squeaky voice that barely carries across the footlights. When she opens her trap you see that she is a half-wit; when she dances you see that she is a nymphomaniac; when you go to bed with her you see that she is syphilitic.

Last night I went to the Hollywood Restaurant, one of those colossal cabaret entertainments that cost a dollar and a half, sans vin, sans pourboires. Cold sober you watch a string of dazzling ponies, fifty or more, the finest wenches in the land and empty as a cracked peanut shell. The place is like a huge dance hall, thousands of people eating at once, guzzling it, socking it away. Most of them stone sober and their eyes jumping out of their sockets. Most of them middle-aged, bald, addle-pated. They come to hear "torch songs" sung by middle-aged sirens. Sophie Tucker, the principal event of the evening, sings about a fairy whom she married by mistake. When she says "Nuts to you!" he answers—"Oh swish!" She is very fat now, Sophie, and has blue veins relieved by 36 carat rocks. She is advertised as "the last of the hot mommers." America isn't breeding any more of this variety. The new ones are perfect—tall, long-waisted, full-busted and rattle-headed. They all sing through the microphone, though one could hear just as well without it. There is a deafening roar which, without any wine under your belt, makes you sick and dizzy. They all know how to shout. They love it. They develop whiskey voices—hard, sour, brassy. It goes well with the baby face, the automatic gestures, the broken-hearted lullabys. A colossal show that must cost a fortune and yet leaves you absolutely unmoved—despite the fine busts I mentioned a while back. I do honestly believe that a poor, skinny, misshapen French woman with just an ounce of personality would stop the show. She would have what the Americans are always talking about but never achieve. She would have *it*. America is minus *it*. *You* think maybe I'm sour on my own country, but so help me God, that's what's the matter with America—*IT*. "They" and "it" go together—follow me?

And now, Joey, I'm going to tell you a little more about my lonely nights in New York, how I walk up and down Broadway, turning in and out of the side streets, looking into windows and doorways, wondering always when the miracle will happen, and if. And nothing ever happens. The other night I dropped into a lunch counter, a cheesy looking joint on West 45th Street, across the way from the Blue Grotto. A good setting for "The Killers." I met some pretty tough eggs, all dressed immaculately, all sallow complexioned and bushy eye-browed. Faces like sunken craters. The eyes mad and piercing, eyes that pierce right through you and appraise you as so much horse meat. There were a few whores from Sixth Avenue together with some of the most astonishingly beautiful chorus girls I ever laid eyes on. One of these sat next to me. She was so beautiful, so lovely, so fresh, so virginal, so outrageously Palm Olive in every respect that I was ashamed to look her straight in the eye. I looked only at her gloves which were porous and made of fine silk. She had long hair, loose-flowing tresses which hung down almost to her waist. She sat on the high stool and ordered a tiny little sandwich and a container of coffee which she took to her room to nibble at with great delicacy. All the yegg men seemed to know her; they greeted her familiarly but respectfully. She could be "Miss America, 1935." She was a dream, I'm telling you. I looked at her furtively through the mirror. I couldn't imagine any one — — — — — — — —. I couldn't imagine her hoofing it either. I couldn't imagine her eating a big juicy steak with mushrooms and onions. I couldn't imagine her going to the bathroom, unless to clear her throat. I couldn't imagine her having a private life. I can only imagine her posing for a magazine cover, standing perpetually in her Palm Olive skin and never perspiring. I like the gangsters best. These boys go everywhere and by aeroplane and stream-lined platinum, lighter than air, air-conditioned trains. They are the only ones in America who are enjoying life, while it lasts. I envy them. I like the shirts they wear, and the bright ties, and the flashy hair-cuts. They come fresh from the laundry and kill in their best clothes.

The opposite to this is the suburban life. Manhasset, for instance. The idea is—how to kill the week-end. Those who don't play bridge invent other forms of amusement, such as the peep-show. They like to get undressed and dance over the week-ends. To change wives. They don't know what to do with themselves after a hard week at the office. *Donc*, the car, the whiskey bottle, some strange —, an artist if possible. (I, for example, made a hit because "I was so unconventional." Sometimes, when you are regarded as being so unconventional, it is embarrassing to be obliged to refuse — — — — —your host's wife, let us say, size 59 and round as a tub. Larry's wife, for example, is a miniature hippopotamus who gets jealous if you dance with any of the good-looking wenches. She goes off and sulks.)

And now let me tell you what one brilliant man in the suburbs thought of last week-end to regale us. When we were all good and crocked he got out an old talking record of the Prince of Wales. We had to listen to that high and mighty potentate (then about nineteen years of age) tell us what the *idealllll* of the Englishman was. I don't have to tell you, Joey, that it was our old friend "fair play." An Englishman never *twists* you. It went on for three records—it must have been a golden jubilee or something. In the midst of it I got hysterical and began to laugh. I laughed and laughed and laughed. Everybody began to laugh, even the host, who, I discovered later, was highly insulted. No sir, an Englishman never *twists* you! He just falls asleep on you . . . .

THE NEW DEAL IN HOLLYWOOD

A. M. Schlesinger, Jr.

THIS YEAR marks a significant turning of the American film toward sociology. For the first time, reel life is trying to simulate real life. Motion picture production has too long been dominated by those who consider the movies important primarily as a way of escape. It has been a basic tenet of these commercial theorists, such as Douglas Fairbanks a decade ago and Alexander Korda today, that the cinema should take the audience away from itself. It should be concerned, not necessarily with what it does best, but with what it does a good deal more plausibly and excitingly than anything else (save alcohol and narcotics): treatment and theme should be non-realistic. Virtually all American films have been colored by this romantic tradition. Its influence has not been wholly bad; at its best, it has led to the technical excellences of Griffiths and the gloriously extravagant *chansons de geste* of Fairbanks. At its worst, however, the inclination toward romanticism was responsible for that deluge of glycerine tears, cheap posturing, and sentimental sex hokum which brought Hollywood to its death door and failed to destroy the movie industry only because of the providential invention of the talking picture. And the hangover from the Romantic Tradition is now a great obstacle in the way of making films which are at all sober, realistic, or critical. Romanticism has engendered certain inhibitions, certain habits of thought and technique, which tend to obstruct the rising concern with social problems.

The blame for the fostering of escapism as the motion picture's *raison d'être* is, incidentally, by no means alone that of the Hollywood magnates. The keener students of cinematic theory are equally culpable when, like Paul Rotha, they find the essential qualities of the film in the slapstick comedy and the horse opera, or, like Miss C. A. Lejeune, they extol *The Scarlet Pimpernel* and sneer at *The Wedding Night*. The admiration of these critics for the Russians seems to be due, not so much to the value of their films as commentaries on life, as to the skill involved in making commentaries.

If the cinema is to be accounted one of the major arts, its place must be understood as something greater in its social implications and more enveloped by the realities of existence than most critics at present concede. A broader conception means greater emphasis on the author and less on the director than is now the case—something diehard *cinéastes* deplore, for it replaces the unique position of the so-called "pure" cinema by one more obviously dependent on the literary arts. But steps in the other direction herald an elaboration of technique at the expense of meaning: in all significant art, content is more important than style. At present, most admired directors, instead of expressing the idea of the screen play, use it merely as material by which their own ideas may be expressed. This is virtuosity and, in the words of Stark Young, "Virtuosity sinks or swims by the significance of its idea."

The better films of the year show that somewhere there is a realization of the possible broader function of the movie. Romanticism still prevails; but its conflict with the realistic theory of the cinema is coming more and more into the open. The heritage from the Romantic Tradition has frequently rendered the broad ideas implicit in the finer of the recent motion pictures innocuous as to detail by soft-pedalling the economic motives and, in general, denuding stories of their logical implications. Nevertheless, escapism, the old guard, while not fallen, is yet retreating.

Romanticism's most vocal champion and one of its cleverest exponents, Alexander Korda,* provided early this year in his *The Scarlet Pimpernel* an extraordinary *reductio ad absurdum* of his own theories. This *Meisterwerk* was hailed ecstatically by Miss Lejeune of the London *Observer* and with more reserve though scarcely with less praise by many American reviewers. It was, in truth, beautifully mounted, admirably photographed and acceptably acted. But the screen play reached new depths of artificiality and flimsiness; the film gave a distorted and unfair historical picture; and in a few

---

*It is noteworthy that Korda, a shrewd business man, is reconsidering his romanticist pronunciamentos: important in the recent newspaper questionnaire conducted by his organization, London Films, is the query, "Do you prefer films that are purely entertainment or films with a serious message?"

memorable episodes, such as the library incident, the story became devoid even of common sense.

At the same time, Warner Brothers, which has been the most active producing company of the school diametrically opposed to Korda,* made a bold gesture away from the inanity of tawdry romanticism in *Black Fury;* but unfortunately the boldness was vitiated by the evident impression among the authors of the film that capital-labor differences are fundamentally reconcilable. Nevertheless, the tacit sympathy expressed for the working man marked a great advance over any previous Hollywood contemplation of the labor question.

After these two movies had clarified to the observer the hostile views, there came a number of compromise films, economics-and-sentiment, revolution-and-wishful-thinking, victims of the present dilemma in the cinema world.

The predicament is well illustrated in John Ford's great work *The Informer.* Liam O'Flaherty's novel had combined the character study of Gypo Nolan with an examination of the circumstances which caused his downfall. Gypo, in the novel, was faced with the choice between a sudden death for the man wanted by the police and his own lingering death by starvation. Dudley Nichol's admirable screen play weakened the economic motivation by introducing a love interest; it added the prospect of a new life in America to the prospect of prolonging an old one in Dublin as extenuation for the betrayal. Gypo in the film informs on Frankie McPhillip for reasons amorous as well as necessitous. Despite these concessions to the Romantic Tradition, the liquid beauty of the photography, the effortless continuity of the story, Max Steiner's superbly right musical score and, especially, the magnificent performance of Victor McLaglen in the leading role, all expertly compounded and edited by John Ford, made this probably the nearest the cinema has yet approached to art. Numerous minor excellencies—the speechless opening, the detail of the drawing of the straws, the fine acting of Margot Grahame from English musical films, of J. M. Kerrigan and of Joseph Sauers—

*Advertisement in the New York Times, 2 May, 1935: "For Warner Brothers have consistently demonstrated their belief that the screen is not merely a medium of entertainment. It is an institution significant socially and responsible morally. Its obligation is to inform, to interpret, to lead and—most important of all—to establish an enduring record of our forward marching civilization."

all testify to the skill and care bestowed on the production. In spite of the unhappy mawkishness of the ending (which was taken verbatim from O'Flaherty) *The Informer* surely stands on a pinnacle of its own in motion picture history. It is a striking example of the marriage of story to technical facility in the making of great films.

Another of the recent crop, *Les Miserables,* as adapted to the screen, suffered less change in viewpoint than *The Informer.* The novel is rather sentimental propaganda written in the baroque manner of *The Count of Monte Cristo:* as a film, it shrinks a little to become the fugitive-from-the-chain-gang story, XIXth century version, told in the floridly melodramatic style of Richard Boleslawsky. One character, Marius, the young revolutionist, carries, however, both in book and screen play, certain inescapable implications. Hugo accepted them, thus accepting Marius' incendiary activities. Not so Daryll Zanuck, the producer, who evidently could not stomach revolution as the vocation of the male half of the love interest; as a result, Marius disclaims loudly any connection with the revolutionary movement, which makes his appearance in the barricades a while later less than wholly explicable. This was the chief shortcoming in W. P. Lipscomb's otherwise first-rate condensation of the novel. In most ways the film was very good; the settings were suitable and the important acting well executed. Frederic March, pictorially fine as always, was not played false by his voice as much as in some of his recent impersonations; and Charles Laughton's Javert, though un-Hugo like, was effective and considerably more terrifying than his fictional prototype. All in all, *Les Miserables* was a highly superior job, though the producer's fear of propaganda made the screen play very imperfect art.

Becky Sharp is another example of the conflict. Derived, of course, from Thackeray's cynical exposure of the futility and fatuity of high society, it dwindled into gamin drama, in essence indistinguishable from many films of much less noble pedigree. Its chief claim to preëminence over these movies which it resembles lay, outside of the color question, in the histrionic brilliance of Miriam Hopkins and the able support of Messrs. Mowbray, Bruce and Hardwicke, and in the remarkable fact that

Becky remained hard throughout, not sweetening in the last reel into an emotional sister of Amelia. On the other hand, not only was the broad social sweep of the original story neatly sidestepped; but the preoccupation of producer and director, Kenneth Mac-Gowan and Rouben Mamoulien, with the proper employment of the New Technicolor, led to insufficient supervision of other departments. Most important in building up for dramatic moments are the musical accompaniment and the cutting. In *Becky Sharp* the musical accompaniment was poor, becoming particularly unsuited in the emotional scenes, and the cutting was consistently commonplace. All this diminished greatly the dramatic power of the film.

As for the color problem, the movie's chief point of interest, it seems to have been satisfactorily surmounted, but not at all solved. Prospects for the future use of color are frankly dubious. The question of color only adds to the difficulties of the screen director: without it, his is the most complex artistic job in the world. Color will mean more time and money spent in production. It more than any other factor in film-making will stand and fall on the good taste of the director. The adventures in technicolor of such a producer as Cecil B. DeMille, with his megalomania, religiosity and general vulgarity, can scarcely be awaited with pleasure. If it is to come in at all, the process will be gradual; they are, I think, optimistists (or financially interested) who predict that the New Technicolor will catch on as quickly as did sound seven years ago.

Another illustration of the unconscious conflict of purpose—whether to entertain or to expose—which has brought this confusion of aim into the more ambitious films of the year is to be found in the Hearst-produced *Oil for the Lamps of China*. Even more as a film than as a novel, this was a scathing decortication of the Standard Oil Company. Throughout, the story was remorseless in its description of the disillusionment of a young oil man who regarded the Company as his God, sacrificing everything to it, until it showed itself in its treatment of him ungrateful and unjust. The ending was on a cynical note: the idealist regained his faith in the Company only when his wife secretly blackmailed it into rewarding him as he deserved. The audience realized the incompatibility of ideals and big business; the

picture was complete as it stood. But there was introduced in the last reel an irrelevant and self-contradictory scene, in which the New York office of the Company, suddenly unveiled as the powerful and benignant master of the destinies of its employees, chided the Shanghai office for its behavior toward the idealist, the inference being that the Shanghai office was mean, small-minded by no means symptomatic or typical of the oil business. Except for this distracting interpolation, *Oil for the Lamps of China* was a fine film, notably acted and incisively directed, though it tended at times to talk in words of one syllable and though the technical device of indicating passage of time by showing the fluttering pages of Mrs. Hobart's novel is open to criticism on several counts. This movie demonstrates particularly the difficulties in the way of expanding and deepening the function of the cinema. The extraneous episode was undoubtedly inserted in order to salve the sensitive feelings of the Standard Oil interests, which advertises heavily in the Hearst newspapers. One can not expect too fearless cinematic representation of the inequities of society when the film producers are themselves fettered to the chain gang of capitalism.

The antagonism between a belief which asserts imitation of life to be the purpose of art and one which finds evasion of life art's excuse for being is, of course, nothing more than the age-old controversy between Realism and Romanticism. The cinema has reached a certain stage in its existence (adolescence? maturity?) when a few far-seeing producers wish to see in it a more significant aim than mere diversion. Most film makers doubtless do not heed theoretic discussions of the opposing trends any more than the majority of American novelists half a century ago changed their manner of writing novels because of the onslaughts of Howells on F. Marion Crawford and his firmly entrenched Romantics. But whether or not the marginal producer is aware of the disagreeing conceptions (or theories), they exist; and the disagreement is clearly visible in the best cinematic creations of the day, just as it has always been visible in the best literary creations of the periods which saw a similar strife in fiction. The triumph of Realism is not as inevitable as it was in fiction and drama; the reason for this is that, more than fiction and more even than the drama, the films partake of the qualities of an industry. The persons behind industry relish sober views of life only when they are not critical of the status quo. But popular demand will probably at the end force concessions from the cinemagnates, exactly as it has already forced concessions in the worlds of literature and the theatre.

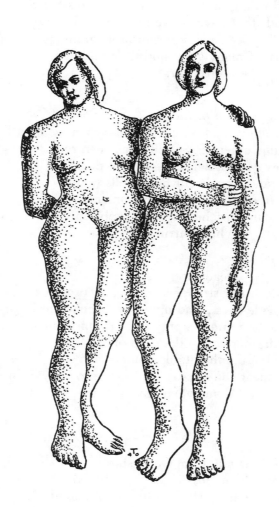

Dies Irae, Dies Illa

Peter Viereck

> *'Dies irae, dies illa*
> *Solvet saeclum in favilla.'*

Everywhere
Awareness lurks behind a thousand blendings.
Awareness shivers—even in oases—
At hard-riding portents saddled like thistledown
On winds that have strayed in many places,
   Seen many forgotten beginnings and thrown
The dust of many great and little endings
   Into the air.

Out of the air,
Our swelling shadows breathe us when we breathe.
Sky snuffs up earth. Solidity has been rent.
A runaway outlaw nerve—or is it death?—
Signals and signals our brain-cells with
Black. In our sweetest entanglement,
When loam enriches or when limbs enwreathe,
   Who's purring there?

Dead faces wear
An underwater strangeness, once so precious.
Our goggle-eyes plead upward—beached at birth—
To God. So minnows pray to beaks of gannets.
More air, more air!—the gasp of earth,
One of the uninhabitable planets,
Where meat stuffs meat (as food or love) yet threshes
   Alone when most a pair.

Only from God's stare
We're not alone, or is it death, unblinking?
My dear, we have strolled to a spell-bound place
Where sunflowers have eyes that follow us.
Twilight lisps at our knees to swallow us;
Don't move; we are watched by a cloud with a crafty face.
Move fast; the fingers of the sun are sinking
   And clutch your hair—

And tug you beneath by your hair.
Sunset-defier, sharer of dawns, hold me so
Close I will never let you go,—
Clasping you free from all the ebb of things,
From all but One. And if the One outclings,
Let love not die alone; let springtime wilt:
All nature ambushed by one descending quilt
　　　　Of sick air

　　　　Everywhere thick.
And I—if it ends, if solidity ends tonight—
Will hold you close through all the holy thunder . . .
Till unrepentant flesh rekindles and, dawn-frenzied,
Strains at the quilt of sky and blazes through and rends it,
Shaking our windowpane with jubilant light.
You will shrug at God and with how young a wonder
　　　　Wake me quick.

TREATY OF VERSAILLES--
REVISED

Robert Hillyer

Born to old worlds as the new worlds arrive,
And bred to customs now observed no more;
Betrayed, not yet of age, to age's war,
We are at peace who happily survive.
Our elders lied to us. Shall youth contrive
Our second shipwreck on a rockier shore?
We are not blind, who were so blind before;
We trust in God,—and in no man alive.
Perhaps we were matured before our prime,
But what we paid for, we gain back from time:
The peace which age, the health which youth, enjoys.
We read our Gibbon, we survey our field;
We win escape from life, and gently yield
Utopias, uncontested, to all boys.

JOHN

O. M. Stirling, Jr., 1938

AUNT BECK came in about seven o'clock on Tuesday morning and told me Father was worse and to get up and put on my bathrobe. It gave me a funny feeling in my stomach, because I was half asleep, and I sort of guessed what she really meant. She scares me anyway, when she wakes me up, I don't know why. But she always has. Even when Doris and I were little. I guess it's because I used to think she was Mother, until I saw her. Then I'd remember that Mother had "gone to live in a beautiful garden," as Aunt Annie used to tell us. Aunt Annie never frightened me, though. Maybe it's Aunt Beck's voice. But anybody would make you feel a little queer if they woke you up in a whisper, "John, your father's worse." They'd make most people feel very very queer, and pretty sad, too. But it just made me feel a little queer. It just sort of surprised me.

Aunt Beck led me into Father's room. When I got there Aunt Annie looked awfully worried, and Madalin was ringing her hands and Doris was wiping her eyes. I don't know why Aunt Beck waked Doris before me. I'm a boy. She could have waked us both at the same time, anyway. Maybe Doris woke herself up. Aunt Annie said Daddy'd been unconscious since six. Doctor Hopkins was bending over him. I just stood and watched. And sometimes I'd look out the window at the fog and remember that I hadn't had any breakfast.

After a while Doctor Hopkins turned around to Madalin and nodded, and Madalin began to cry a little. It hurt me to think he looked at her instead of Aunt Annie. Then I saw a picture of Mother over Daddy's bed, and I thought it would be nice to feel that it didn't make any difference which of us down on earth knew about it first, but I couldn't feel that way. Sometimes it all makes me a little sorry for Madalin. I guess it isn't easy to be a second wife. I'm never more than a little sorry, though. Well, Madalin began to cry and Doris ran out of the room, and I just stood there, looking. Then Aunt Annie took my arm and said, "Come on out, John," and I went, still a little dazed.

As soon as I got out of the room, I pulled my arm away from Aunt Annie and ran into the bathroom to wash my face, as though I could wash myself awake. But it didn't do any good. All that day I felt sort of sick to my stomach and wandered around the house noticing things as though I didn't have anything to do with them. It wasn't as bad as that makes it sound, I guess. I did work a little, answering the telephone and things like that, and kept wondering what was going to happen after things settled down, and scolding myself for thinking about it so soon. I read some, too. And in the afternoon, Doris and I were talking, and she said something about Mother, and how funny it was, after reading all our lives about orphans to be orphaned ourselves. We'd never thought not having a mother was being orphaned. Doris cried, then, and seeing her cry made me feel as though I ought to do something, but I didn't. I just looked down at the floor and waited for her to finish. But most of the day I spent reading, in whatever room there was nobody else in, and feeling embarrassed and moving whenever anybody came in where I was. I couldn't make myself sad; all I could do was answer the phone and wander around the house and read.

Wednesday morning was better. I was so busy helping get ready for the funeral that I forgot all about everything. Once I laughed when Aunt Beck couldn't fix the flowers the way she wanted to, and remembered and stopped.

Then in the afternoon, people began to come for the funeral, and we all had to wait upstairs. Waiting up stairs was the worst part of the whole thing. Madalin sat in a big chair taking turns at weeping and whiffing from a bottle of smelling salts Cousin Louise had remembered to bring. I guess it was pretty lucky Cousin Louise brought it, because Madalin couldn't have carried through the act if she hadn't had something else to do when she got tired of crying. Aunt Annie and Aunt Beck must have felt it just as much, and they only used handkerchiefs. You can't get away from differences, can you? Yes, waiting upstairs was the hardest part of the whole thing. I just sat up as straight as I could in a very straight chair, and stared ahead, and felt embarrassed.

Soon Dr. Yellot, downstairs in the hall, began to pray. I couldn't help wondering how much of the prayer was true, though wondering made me feel terribly sinful. And he said something about those that are left behind. I knew that meant me, and I realized for a minute how much I was connected with the whole thing, and I thought about filial devotion and all that — but just for a minute. I knew I ought to be ashamed of myself for taking it the way I was, but I couldn't even get seriously ashamed — just uncomfortable.

On the way to the cemetery, when I tried again to feel sorry, I couldn't make myself realize that any of it had happened. None of it meant anything to me. And every time I thought I had begun to feel sorry after all, a little imp would hop up in my brain and whisper, "Oh, yeah," and make me mad, because I hate people who say, "Oh, yeah." It kept on anyway, saying the same thing and making me mad. Then I thought I'd try to pray, but I couldn't do any better than "Our Father who art in heaven," and that didn't even go the way I wanted it to. I'd say, "Our Father who art in heaven," and then I'd think, "Well, that's obvious, go on." And then I'd start again. Once I went a little farther. "Our Father who art in heaven," and then, "Black as any other raven," without being able to stop myself. I knew it was I who said it, and I who meant to say it, but it embarrassed me to know I meant to, so I tried to stop myself. Once a little later I managed to get to "Thy kingdom come, thy will be done," but I went on, "If you say so it will be done." I gave up, then, and looked out of the window. Madalin was a little better by this time, and once she asked me, "Hasn't your cousin Elizabeth gotten to be a nice-looking girl?" and without even thinking, I said, "No, she gets worse every day," though that wasn't a very clever thing to say, and I'd have said anything to make things easier if I'd been careful.

They buried him right next to Mother. That came nearest to making me have strong feelings about it all, because it gave me a happy sort of feeling that sent shivers up and down my spine. We didn't stay at the grave long enough for much to happen, and I was glad because, when we first got of the car, Aunt Beck had come up to me and said, "Stand up straight, John. You know you're the only man in the family, now." So I felt as though people were pointing to me all the time we were at the grave. I began to think what a responsibility it was for a fourteen year old boy to be the only "man" in the family, but I didn't think long, because I didn't really know I *was* the only "man" in the family, not being able to realize it yet.

Things weren't so bad on the way back. Clay drove pretty fast, and by that time I'd given up trying to be sad. Once I began to whistle, by mistake. Doris nudged me and I stopped, and began trying to be sad again for a minute.

I had meant to go in the house when we got home and talk things over with Aunt Annie. I always talk to her when I have the kind of worries she likes to talk about. She had a lot of advice that doesn't mean any more than "Time will tell," and I hate to wait. But it's better to talk to her than nobody. It was so nice outdoors, though, that I thought it would do me more good to go for a walk. So I walked out to Winters Run.

On the way, there's a long hill with dead grass on it. I don't know why, but looking at the dead grass blow in the wind and feeling the wind blow in my face made me want to yell. I sort of bubbled up inside my chest, and I felt as though I had to do something with the bubbling, so I ran down the hill waving my arms. I hope nobody saw me, but I couldn't help doing it, I felt so happy all of a sudden. Then I lay down in the grass, and looked up at the sun, and all of a sudden everything got very real and I began to think about Father again in a different way from ever before. I knew there wasn't any sense in trying to be sorry about him. I knew I couldn't be sorry. I was glad. And I wasn't ashamed of being glad. I hated Father. And my hate was as great as my gladness had been; and the two took turns confusingly. I thought about how Father made me leave the table last week, how he'd not given me any allowance in January, how he'd married Madalin, and how, if he hadn't gotten scarlet fever, Mother wouldn't have caught it and died. Then I thought about being the only man in the family, and what I'd like to change around the place. Then I remembered how Father used to recite poetry in a loud voice when I was little and how I hated to hear him and ran and hid under the couch, and how he used to wake us all up shouting to the farm hands before he went to the office. It was funny how I thought. I knew I shouldn't think that way, but I wanted to, and I did. Then I just lay there awhile, getting warm in the sun and not thinking about much of anything.

I got up after a few minutes and began walking back. Walking back I didn't think much. I just had a vague feeling that the whole thing was awfully queer, and that if I thought about it again, I'd get mixed up. When I passed the barn, Clay tipped his hat to me. He's done that before, but I noticed it more this time, and it made me feel uncomfortable. It made me feel as though he was trying to make me take Father's place, and I didn't like it. For a minute I remembered what I'd been thinking on the hill, and I remembered that tipped hats was what I'd wanted then, and I half-way felt that I still wanted them. But there was something about seeing Clay tip his hat that made me walk a little faster to get away from him.

As soon as I got into the house, Aunt Annie called me. She wanted me to pick out all Father's ties I liked. She'd give the others to Clay. I've never liked any of his ties very much. There's something about them. Maybe it's that so many of them are part green. I hate green ties. Most of them are a little worn out, too. But I picked out a handful, just to please Aunt Annie. Then I took them into my room and hung them up with mine, and stood back to see how it looked to have so many new ties on my rack. After that I picked out the best one, held it around my neck, and looked at myself in the mirror. First I looked at the tie and then at my face, and out of a clear sky I thought how Aunt Annie had said, "You know you're the only man in the family now," and how Clay tipped his hat to me. Then something made me shiver. I began to feel as though I'd like to run away from myself, or hide under the bed, or do almost anything that would make me lose the feeling I had. It wasn't a thought, it was just a feeling. I believe I couldn't have felt more ashamed if I'd killed Father with my own hands. But it wasn't the kind of shame that makes you sorry or sad — just a frightened, sick feeling in the stomach. I threw down the tie and lay down on my bed and covered my eyes to try to get away from whatever it was. But it didn't do any good. I kept thinking about what Aunt Beck said, and about Father when he sent me from the table last week, and about what I'd thought on the hill. Sometimes I'd shiver. And

all the time, it was as though I were pretending, as though I didn't need to do it if I didn't want to. But that wasn't true. I tried to think of something else, and couldn't.

In a few minutes Doris came in. I turned over and sat up and rubbed my eyes. Doris said, "Have you been crying?" And I said, "Of course not. And even if I have, you needn't think that just because you're older it's any of your business." Then she said, "You shouldn't be so upset about it, John. You oughtn't to be so very sad. After all dying isn't such a horrible thing. And it's much nicer in heaven than on earth. Just think Mother and Father are together now. It almost makes me glad he's dead. And suppose you were like some boys who have to work to support their mother when their father dies. You ought to be thankful Father left us an income. You've got no responsibility at all."

I just said, "I guess so." You have to humor Doris. She's a little queer sometimes. As if it isn't a responsibility to be the only man in the family. But I'm glad she thought I was sad instead of knowing the truth. What is the truth? I don't know, either. The whole thing just mixes me up.

Before she went out, she said, "Don't tell Aunt Annie what I've said, because she thinks saying things like that is sinful. I just wanted to cheer you up." Cheer you up! Doris is funny. She's been reading a book called "Happiness in the Home."

The dinner bell rang soon after that, and Doris started her "Cheer you up" program again at dinner. Everybody was looking solemn, and there weren't any sounds except the crunch of celery and "Will you pass the salt, please?" And all of a sudden, Doris said to Aunt Annie, "What do you think is the prettiest name there is?" (She got that out of the chapter, "How To Liven Up Conversation." I looked it up the next day.) Madalin gave Doris a black look, and Aunt Annie said, "I don't know, Doris." Doris just kept on as though it were a perfectly natural thing to do, and said, "What about the ugliest name?" And Aunt Annie looked a little pained and said, "I don't know, Doris." Then Doris turned to me and said, "What do you think is the ugliest name there is?" I thought it would be easier to answer her than not to, so I was going to say, "Monks," because I knew a boy at school named that, and I hate him. But Madalin looked so uncomfortable, that I noticed her while I was saying "Monks," and it changed to "Madalin," without my intending it to.

Everybody gulped and Madalin looked at me and tightened her lips and walked out of the room. In a few minutes we heard her telephoning her brother to come and "take her home," because, "She couldn't stay in this place an hour longer." Aunt Annie told me to go tell Madalin I hadn't meant what I said, but she'd locked the door to her room, and wouldn't let me in.

Afterwards, Aunt Annie said it would have happened sometime soon, anyway, and Doris said she was glad it had happened then. I knew I ought to be glad, too. I could remember how I'd been feeling out on the hill, how I would have wanted this then. But I couldn't be glad now. I kept thinking of Father, and getting the feeling of wanting to hide, all over again.

So when Madalin had gone, I decided to talk it over with Aunt Annie. I knew I couldn't tell her about the hill, but I could say how mixed up I was, about not feeling sorry, but just uncomfortable, and especially about being embarrassed at being called the only man in the family, and not knowing whether to be glad to have the responsibility or sorry, maybe even about being ashamed on account of the ties and Madalin.

But as soon as she saw me she said, "John you ought to stand up straighter, really you ought, and you know you never brush your hair any more. One of the last things your father said before his attack was, 'Annie, we've certainly got to find a way to make John stand up straighter. He'll be a regular hunchback in a few years at this rate.' " After she said this, I knew I couldn't tell her what I wanted to. I could see she hadn't been thinking about me in the same way I'd been thinking about myself.

So I went into my room and wrote all this in my notebook, hoping I'd understand if I wrote it down. But I don't.

The Saturday Review

of LITERATURE

VOL. CXXIII No. 6   BY THE HARVARD ADVOCATE   25 CENTS A COPY

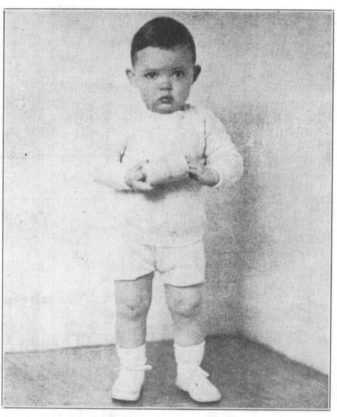

JOHANN NOBELISSIMUS, III

"Life is too complex for simplicity" . . .
(See page 3)

JUNE 12, 1937

ISN'T HE OVEREMPHASIZING THE IMPORTANCE OF MARX?

The Anatomy of the Debutante

FLAMINEO BOSOLA, 1941

I have heard of your paintings, too, well enough; God hath given you one face, and you make yourselves another: you jig, you amble, and you lisp; you nickname God's creatures and make your wantonness your ignorance: go to, I'll no more on't; it hath made me mad.

To begin with, a debutante is a young woman (There are no male debutantes, in spite of what you may think of Lucius Beebe and Maury Paul), and she is generally a very fine figure of a young woman, in a splendid state of preservation. She does not possess false teeth, a wig, or artificial limbs. True, stomach ulcers sooner or later catch up with her, but that's an internal ailment, and as this is not a medical treatise, we need have nothing to do with ulcers, pro or con. No, we are concerned with the external attributes of these nice girls, and the ulcers can jolly well take care of themselves.

—But, says little Gianciotto, who is fourteen and promiscuous, how will I know a debutante when I see one?

—Why, says old Malatesta, making a *cornuto* at him, by her clothes. You can tell a debutante by her clothes, just as you can tell a Hottentot by his lack of them.

—As simple as that? says little Gianciotto.

—As simple as that, says the Old Roman.

And he was right; for if one should put a debutante in a room with twenty other women, she would always be recognized by her clothes. Of course, if one should put a nude debutante into a room with twenty other women, similarly attired, —

169

—It would not, said little Gianciotto, be a bad idea. Little Gianciotto is fourteen and promiscuous.

*   *   *

Now that we have fought our way through the introduction, we should define what this piece is concerned with, thus: A debutante is composed of one part background, one part Antoine de Paris, one part *Harper's Bazaar*, five parts money, and eight parts ignorance. Taking ten parts as a norm, you can see that this adds up to considerably over that sum, which should give you a pretty good idea of what we have to deal with. She inhabits large cities, small cities, towns, hamlets, and Los Angeles, California. However, we are more interested, for our present needs, in the New England or Bury Me In Boston type of debutante.

There are several variations within this species, but it is best that in the beginning we consider the species as a whole. This, we understand, is the usual approach, as practiced by the young gentlemen of Harvard, Princeton, Yale, and the Hanover Ski School.

The debutante, as a whole, spends her afternoons in charity work, her nights in polite carouse, and her mornings in bed. She has breakfast at noon, dinner at any hour from eight to eleven, and supper, if she can keep it down, at two in the morning. Other than this she does nothing, for fear of becoming an object of scandal. From the age of fourteen to eighteen she goes to school, which, for her, is the equivalent of doing nothing; at the age of eighteen she becomes a debutante, which is the public's idea of doing nothing; and eventually she marries a Porcellian man, which is God's idea of doing nothing. All in all, she is, together with a housefly, one of the most useless things on the face of the earth. Not *the* most useless thing, mind you; for the Democratic Party beats her out there. But she does quite well in her way.

Well, then, here's the Littul Ole Boston Debutante, not worth a tinker's dam, and proud of it. She believes in Heaven, the Junior League, the Ritz Bar and Margaret Sanger. As far as marriage goes, she believes in (1) security, and (2) a decent amount of love. A husband, she realizes, is a necessary thing, for respectability's sake, much like the bottom part of a bathing suit. But of course, marriage is a concern of the post-debutante (a debutante becomes a post-debutante when she developes stomach-ulcers), and, as the post-debutante is the concern of a good psychoanalyist, we needn't bother with her. No, we started on the debutante, and, by Heaven, we'll stay on her.

If little Gianciotto should wander into the Ritz Bar at five o'clock in the afternoon, he would see several debutantes, of various shapes and sizes. This place, which is known familiarly as the Littul Ole Boston Watering-Hole, is where all the young ladies go to see the people they haven't seen since yesterday. Little Gianciotto (who is fourteen and promiscuous) wouldn't have much fun; but then, a fourteen year old, even if he is promiscuous, doesn't have much fun anyway.

Now, as we said before, there are several variations on the theme of the debutante, and we might as well take them up now. There is, to begin with, the Vincent Club, or Geez, I'm Duse, type, who has her artistic side but doesn't quite know what to do with it. Calling her the Vincent Club Type covers a multitude of sins, because she may be a poetess, a sculptress, or just a plain screwball; but we use that classification because we feel that the Vincent Club, together with the North Church Burying Ground, typifies the higher aspects of Boston culture. It is difficult to imagine just why the mental dry rot of Boston should produce young women with artistic leanings, but this is no more difficult than to imagine why the moral dry rot of Boston should produce young women. Yet it is necessary to admit that young women with beautiful souls do at times appear between Manchester and Cohasset, and it is also necessary to admit that these beautiful souls go the way of all flash.

Terpsichorean ability in Boston is based on an ability to tapdance, artistic ability spends itself in fashion drawings, and the less said about the poetesses the better. It should suffice to say that art, of any kind, is at present foreign to Boston, the *Transcript* and God to the contrary.

Of course, debutantes are often used as models; and it must be said for them that they take to modelling like ducks to water, evidently because the practise of modelling requires no mental power. All that is necessary is for one to exhibit oneself, like a prize dog, which is really very easy; so easy, in fact, that professional models are trembling for their laurels. But, understand, we can't accuse the Vincent Club and amalgamated organizations of this. The Vincent Club tapdances. At least, we think it tapdances. Of course, there may not be any such things as the Vincent Club. It may be just a bad dream, the kind of bad dream that you get after eating Welch rarebit, which, like the soul of Boston, is composed of cheese.

Anyway, we wash our hands of this type of debutante, and turn to the Charity, or Up The Masses, Type. This group is made up of young women who want to work, but, as they are mentally incapable of the responsibilities vested in an employee, find it necessary to work for free, usually in some charitable enterprise. They, like the Black Plague, are a sociological phenomenon.

—But what, says Little Gianciotto, is a sociological phenomenon?

—Beacon Hill, said the old *condottiere* without a quaver.

—Well, bless me, says little Gianciotto, shifting his quid to the other side of his face, I wouldn't have known.

There are all sorts of charities, most of which have been going on for years and years, like decay at Yale. The main duty of charities, it would seem, is to have projects. These projects are invariably accompanied by several cameramen, who photograph the young ladies assisting, all of which leads to the assumption that the main function of these charities is to assist the

Photographers' Guild, if there is one.

—Then what is charity? says little Gianciotto.

—Charity, replies old Malatesta, is Love.

—And what, says little Gianciotto, leaning forward eagerly, is Love?

—Love, says the Lord of Rimini, with a leer, is fun.

—I'll say, says little Gianciotto, dragging down the housemaid.

All of which brings us to the third, and most horrible, type of debutante; the Glamour Girl, or Over The Hill To The Stork Club Type. This type centers itself in Manhattan, for the simple reason that Boston girls are too ugly to be glamorous, and Philadelphia girls too prosy. Each year the soberer of New York's *bon vivants* (Fr.) gather together and elect the season's Glamour Girl, to the sound of loud cymbals, and, for no extra charge, to the sound of well-tuned cymbals. This year the Glamour Queen was Brenda Frazier (rhymes with *Asia, brazier,* etc.) who is, at the moment, in Bermuda or Zamboanga or somewhere, recovering from the effects of her debut and the possession of several million dollars.

Miss Frazier, to slip into the vernacular, is some baby. She is really a simple girl at heart, says her wise, wise mother, much preferring gingham gowns and rustic swains to the mad social whirl of Manhattan. But what can one do when one is a Glamour Girl? One must *live,* of course. It is useless to argue that some arsenic in her milk or liquidation *à la Russe* would do Miss Frazier a world of good. Even if Miss Frazier did herself in we'd still have Lucius Beebe, Miss Elsa Maxwell, and Cecil Beaton (status undetermined) to deal with.

Now, the trouble with Glamour Girls is that every debutante over fourteen (little Gianciotto's age) thinks she is one; and that adds up to an awful lot of glamour. Too, it adds up to an awful lot of stupidity. After all, if a girl spends all her time in cultivating her b-dy, for what would seem to be obvious reasons, she isn't going to have much time to cultivate her mind. As a result, we have a good, round number of nuts cluttering up the Social Register, which, we might add, is neither social nor a register.

Once, when we were younger and more foolish, we thought of saving our money and buying a Glamour Girl, but we finally rejected the plan because we realized that the upkeep on our purchase would be tremendous, while, at the same time, it would depreciate like hell. Yessir, there's no drug on the market like an old, decrepit Glamour Girl, we always say. Two or three years of parties, tossing in a child here and there, and they start to sag between ear and nostril. A Glamour Girl's face always goes first: their bodies hang on tenaciously. But that, of course, is beside the point—this is not a medical treatise.—

—That's what you think, says little Promiscuity.

Of course, America owes a lot to debutantes. When one is tired of newspaper accounts of wars and rumors of wars, one can always relax in the foolishness of the Society Page. I don't know what we'd do without Jerome Zerbe, Messrs. Billingsly and Perona, Cholly Knickerbocker, and Mrs. Harrison Williams. I don't even know what we'd do without Brenda Frazier (rhymes with *Asia* and *brazier*: see *Annals of Club Life at Harvard, 1939*). In fact, I don't even know what we'd do without debutantes in Boston.

For one thing, a lack of debutantes in Boston would mean that Harvard undergraduates would have to buy their own drinks. It would mean that the *American* and *Transcript* would have to shut down their plants. The reverberations would be felt from Eliot House to San Simeon. Of course, the main mass of the people would go its quiet way; but what do we care for the people, anyway?

The question is, now that we have the debutantes, what are we going to do with them? Certainly they can't be allowed to roam the streets night after night. No, they've got to be taken care of. But how?

—I know, says little Gianciotto, who spent a week in Berlin, a concentration camp.

—Hold your tongue, says old Malatesta, and take your hand off that maid.

—Which hand? says little Gianciotto innocently.

—The one I can't see, says old Malatesta.

But little Gianciotto has given us an idea. Why not put all the debutantes in a concentration camp? Of course, it would be a very nice concentration camp, with all sanitary facilities; and we could charge admission to the general public. We could divide the camp into three parts; a part for the artistic debutantes, a part for the charity workers, a part for the Glamour Girls. The artistic contingent could put on shows in which they could kick high and show their legs, if they have any—but we'd better go into this in detail.

Well, in the first place, the section of the camp devoted to the *artistes* would have, at one end, a huge stage, complete with a stage director, applause machines, and a noble purpose. At the other end would be thirteen microphones, a bundle of contracts to sing at the Sert Room, Ozzie Nelson, and assorted photographers. The floor would be paved with Cole Porter, Noel Coward, and Tommy Manville, the Asbestos Adonis. There would probably be no reason for Mr. Manville, save that his position on the floor would make him very happy.

The section of our camp devoted to Charity would have a floor paved with photographers and formal applications for aid. Each incumbent debutante would have a neat little desk, on which would be placed her hands and any number of cosmetics. There would be a great bustle of activity, because the girls, like the Red Queen (or maybe it's the White Queen) would have to work very hard to stay in the same place. Around the walls would be murals depicting *The Junior League Girls In Brookline*, or *Married But Willing*. (Readers are referred to my earlier books, entitled *The Junior League Girls At Rosemary Hall*, or *Thwarting the Evil Janitor*, and *The Junior League Girls At The Ritz Bar*, or *If It Ain't Dry It Ain't A Martini*.)

Finally, the section devoted to the Glamour Girls would contain, at one end, a throne on which Brenda Frazier is seated (till next season). Miss Frazier will hold in one hand a drink compounded of milk, coca-cola, and old blood; in the other she will hold a bill from the Ritz. She will be wearing a creation whipped up by Maggy Rouff, Schiaparelli, and the effects of three quarts of champagne. On her lap will repose a book by Lucius Beebe, and at her feet will repose Lucius Beebe himself, all in mauve. Photographers will be everywhere; and the place will be full of Glamour Girls, zebra stripe motifs, and sex with a vengeance. Restrooms will be provided for any spectators who feel nauseated.

Now, this camp should be placed, if we have anything to say about it, on Boston Common, between the Subway Station and the Bandstand. Admission will be nominal; say, fifteen cents. And when it's all done, we can forget the whole business and start cleaning up Massachusetts politics, an infinitely harder job.

But of course, the debutante is really not as bad as she sounds. She recovers from her debut, marries Jonathon Codpiece, (of the Boston Codpieces, her second cousin), propagates, and eventually dies. All in all, she is a nice, well-rounded girl, without a brain in her head. But, as she is a member of the upper classes (in Boston, at least), and as the upper classes have been operating on no mentality for nearly half a century, she really has nothing to fear. As long as she can afford psychoanalyists, she gets along. Unless Mr. Dies is right—

—Who, says little Gianciotto, is Mr. Dies?

—Mr. Dies, says old Malatesta, is a booger. And take your g-dd-m hand off that maid.

Editorial

THE ALUMNI SEE RED

MAY-DAY is almost upon us, and our graduates and well-meaning friends are busy removing from camphor Harvard's Communist bogey. What with Germany in Austria, Japan in China, and Spain in a general state of collapse, we had almost forgotten about the secret agents of the Ogpu that control University Hall and transform every lecture into a masterpiece of propaganda. At this time we begin again to recall these stories. It is useless for us to say that the Harvard Communist is mostly a creature of the imagination or to pretend that the faculty, Phillips Brooks House, and all Harvard men in sympathy with President Roosevelt are not Reds. We know from past experience that only suspicious looks and a general coolness will result from the expression of such thoughts.

But since we do insist that Harvard's Communist bogey is not in Cambridge, where is he? To a certain extent he may be found in any large city, Boston, Chicago, Philadelphia, Cincinnati, etc., though his headquarters seem to be at present in metropolitan New York, somewhere in the vicinity of the Sub-treasury building, Broad and Wall Streets, and the Stock Exchange. From this financial hub come such tales of Harvard intrigue that, as we sit in the sanctum, we unconsciously glance about expecting to catch some secret operative in the very act of influencing our editorial pen. It is a relief, therefore, to find instead our Pegasus peacefully tethered in his stall and to note that outside all is as usual, with Spring a-coming and the *Lampoon* still peddling eighteenth-century Dutch tiles at thirty dollars a set.

Thus Mother Advocate finds the capitalistic system still being upheld at Harvard, while Socialism, Communism, and Anarchism are as yet only the mainstay of government theory courses and divisional examinations. The Communist bogey, she suspects, is a sort of Charlie McCarthy — mostly voice with no thought. Though he may continue to worry the graduate, his existence is too precarious for him ever to remain in Cambridge in any other shape than that of a local political platform. With such reflections Mother Advocate composes herself and wishes to reassure her friends that, if there is such a bogey, he is still in the company of big money, alarmists, and highly-imaginative patriotic societies. He has not yet set up residence at Harvard.

MUSIC

LEONARD BERNSTEIN, 1939

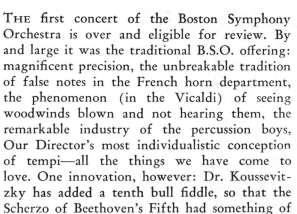

THE first concert of the Boston Symphony Orchestra is over and eligible for review. By and large it was the traditional B.S.O. offering: magnificent precision, the unbreakable tradition of false notes in the French horn department, the phenomenon (in the Vicaldi) of seeing woodwinds blown and not hearing them, the remarkable industry of the percussion boys, Our Director's most individualistic conception of tempi—all the things we have come to love. One innovation, however: Dr. Koussevitzky has added a tenth bull fiddle, so that the Scherzo of Beethoven's Fifth had something of Fate in it after all.

I suppose that the main bone of contention was the subject of tempo. People were watching each other out of the corners of their eyes practically all through the Queen of Symphonies, what with the incredible slowness of the little oboe cadenza in the first movement, the near-dragginess of the Scherzo, the impossible, prolonged majesty of the three opening chords of the finale (which was atoned for by the be-back-in-a-flash tempo of the Coda.) Our first impulse is always to condemn this sort of thing. But let's be Taoists for a moment. A work like the Fifth Symphony which everyone knows by heart in its normal performance is always the first to suffer from "individualistic" rendition. If you had been able to accomplish the impossible—to pretend that this was your first hearing of the work—you might not have objected so violently. You might even have thought it exciting.

Certainly the Ladies of the Board found it exciting. In fact, they must have found the whole program exciting. It was just what they wanted: Beethoven, Brahms, Berlioz, Vivaldi. The Ladies are so at home in their eighteenth and nineteenth centuries. They won't believe that music is not just history.

There is, you know, contemporary music. Not that you could have found it out too easily. If you listen hard, you can sometimes catch a strange new sound while standing outside the League of Composers' window in New York, or via radio from South Mountain. Or from Koussevitzky himself, whom God bless for doing more modern music than any conductor in the country under formidably adverse conditions. The rest is silence. The Metropolitan Opera Company—the only full-season session around —has finally got as far as Boris Godounov and Salome. The symphony orchestras sometimes break out into a modern whimsy for a few minutes. Just enough to assure the public that music was and no longer is. And it is so often pretty bad stuff; somehow the worst things are published, and then sell for a dozen dollars a copy.

Aaron Copland's recent work, *El Salon Mexico*, played at the second concert, is not such a piece. It is thoroughly good. Good for the public (it is essentially a popular piece), good for the musician (it is subtle and masterful), good for the Mexicans, (who agree that the spirit of their country was really captured), and good for the spleen (it is clever and goodhumored throughout, and as exciting as a rollercoaster ride). Well, how much good *did* it do? Koussevitzky's duty is done; he has played a new work. Can we hear it again, as we want to? As things stand now, probably not for several years.

The rest of the second concert was again history, but most enjoyable. The Mozart Divertimento in B Flat was for me a great thrill. It hits the top: it is grand in conception, rich in the best of Mozart melody, and contains in its Adagio movement truly first rate composing. (Ruth Marsters in the *Boston American* insisted that it was *lesser* Mozart, and badly played, which it was emphatically not. I thought the performance in better taste and more charmingly conducted than almost any Mozart performance I have heard from Koussevitzky. I wish I could quote Miss Marsters for you, but unfortunately I tore the paper to bits). The third number, the Dvorak *New World Symphony*, was a great surprise to everyone. People were aware that they had never in all their hundreds of hearings of it heard it so well played. Even the rigid opposition was moved; but perhaps because Koussevitzky played it as a gesture of sympathy toward what was once Czechoslovakia.

MR. CRANE AS ORPHEUS, A GOOD BOY

by Harry Brown

Vivant Musae! whose impossible lagoons,
Traveled by boats with clumsy sails, desire
Only the rising coral to remain.

The pretty ladies murmur pleasant tunes
Along the golden island. Strange, the fire,
On being touched, can telegraph no pain.

Only an empty body has the sand,
Unrecognizable man, blood in the water,
The lungs missing, the head departed.

The numb harp is taut in the trench of the hand.
What woman will recall Oceanus' daughter,
To write down what the spinners started?

The snake before the honored grave may hiss
A treble warning. Reptile truth will say,
You shall not surely die.

The skeleton beside the cave may kiss
Other old bones, well-covered yesterday,
A jointless thing, creeking to where they lie.

A blind Eurydice may even yet discover,
After the pirate centuries, the shore a waste,
What the murder spared.

The idea of cool brows may arouse the lover
To resurrect himself, more lost, more chaste,
Than the panting deer, at last laired.

But what will help the gruesome struggle then,
Even with brighter tissues and incarnate skin,
After that most complete rejection?

Watched by a threadbare scattering of men,
They shout, O *vivant Musae!* and begin
The frightened, endless God-dissection.

THE ULTIMATE PLATO

Delmore Schwartz

WITH PICASSO'S GUITAR

Instead of attempting a detailed study of some aspect of Stevens, I should like to try to make a rapid survey—barely more than a list—of several closely-related aspects of his work as a whole. The virtue of such a bird's-eye view is the relationship and unity it may reveal. The defects will be plain enough; one always risks being superficial in trying to cover a good deal of ground.

1. "*A Point of View*": Taken generally, Stevens' perspective is that of the man of art, the museum- and concert-goer, the student of French poetry (but not of American poetry), the intelligent tourist (but nevertheless, the tourist, not the native), the aesthete in the best sense of the word. This can be quickly illustrated merely by mentioning some of the details of his work. He summons up Mozart, Corot, Bach, Picasso, and other famous artists as witnesses and symbols. Statues, organ music, paintings, and words for paintings, French words and archaic dictionary words are important elements in the texture of his work. He mentions and uses significantly a great many places which are exotic, tropical, and foreign: Cuba, Yucatan, Mexico, Sweden. He describes Paradise as if it were a landscape garden and writes of the Carolinas as if they were exotic too. But the city of Hartford, Conn. is almost never named, though in his latest period he appears to be finding his frame of reference in some such American city, and in some of his most recent lyrics, he comes as close to Hartford as Jersey City (these exceptions, however, are signs of the profound concern about society at present which marks off his latest work from the rest).

This predominance of references derived from Art of some kind is not merely a matter of surface, but also of the way that objects are looked at, and some of the values by which they are judged. It is a vision instructed in the museums, regarding objects in the world after seeing them in paintings. So, when Stevens is writing most seriously of love in middle-age, he naturally finds such a trope as "men at forty . . . painting lakes." So too a naked body is a nude in some poems, and so it is that the predominant theme of "Harmonium" is the imagination, the source of all art,

> The magnificent cause of being,
> The imagination, the one reality
> In this imagined world.

Now the perspective of the Art-man is nothing new in the history of modern poetry. On the contrary, it has its beginnings in Gautier, Baudelaire, and Laforgue (whom Stevens must have read), and it sustains itself in various ways through many different authors. It can be seen at its worst in authors like James Branch Cabell, at its average quality in some of Verlaine, Dowson, Arthur Symons, and other poets of the nineties; and at its best in Stevens. For these writers, when their various differences have been allowed for, have in common a belief that Art is a most important source of value, perhaps the central interest of Life. Consider how in Mr. Cabell's prose it is so often insisted that the imagined world is the only one worth living in, and to write beautifully of fine things is the only sensible course for an author. Mr. Cabell is an extreme; but of all these writers it can be said that their language is profusely burdened with references and derivations from literature and art; their subjects are very often not the ordinary experiences of life, but works of art; and their most exalted moments are those in which they enjoy works of art.

This tradition, for it is continuous enough and

strong enough to be dignified with that name, has very deep roots in modern life. It springs from the separation between art and the rest of life which is due to many causes, the chief of which may be industrialism. Thus it is almost natural that writers in this tradition should be *against* Life and *for* Art, a partisanship which would have seemed inconceivable to most authors in most societies. The doctrine of Art for Art's sake and the desire to dumbfound and appall the middle class are obvious public expressions for the attitude which moves these writers. For what a good deal of their poetry actually *presents* is the experience, in modern life, of art as separated from the rest of life, so that the former is special, precious, taken as merely decorative, often misunderstood and abused; while the latter is impoverished, ignoble, vulgar and full of disorder, presided over by the business man and the Philistine (such terms as Philistine and Bohemian received their art-connotations during the 19th century). "O how quotidian Life is," wrote Laforgue, and proceeded to juxtapose the ordinariness and vulgarity of everyday experience with the beauty of Literature by rewriting classical, and medieval fables in a language in which the ironic effect is consistently gained either by speaking of the heroic and classical in cheap conversational slang; or conversely, by hailing the vulgarity of modern life in the rhetoric of the grand manner.

In such a writer as Laforgue, the result of this fundamental division is irony, pathetic irony, but irony without relief and without insight. This empty conclusion, hardly avoided by most authors of the tradition except when they turn to another basic subject, is penetrated and seen through by Stevens first, by means of the thoroughness with which he inspects his point of view, trying to look at everything from its station; secondly, by a profound "contemporaneity," an awareness of the present and the present movement of society which is almost a vigil, and which has motivated his last two volumes of verse; but above all, by a philosophical concern with the nature of things which has

enabled him to generalize his experience in ways not available to other such authors. This philosophical interest is quite distinct, it should be noted, from the way in which Laforgue plays ironically with philosophical terms.

2. *Thoroughness*: "If one became sufficiently absorbed, *absolutely* involved, in one passion, then it would become the whole world for one. All things, including one's duties, would be translated into its terms. It would then present the same difficulties as any other interest or mixture of interests. For if one becomes completely interested in a thing, it becomes something else, not what it seemed to be." This may serve to describe what happens when one attempts to see the whole world from the perspective of Art. Beginning with an interest in works of art, apart from the rest of life, if one holds to that interest long enough and completely enough, the conditions of works of art, art's relationship to Life, the disorder of society in which art exists, and the ultimate questions about Nature and Life come into the foreground, within the frame of the painting. This is what has occurred in Stevens' work. When "Harmonium" was published in 1923, the critic who could have foreseen that in his third book, Stevens would be making acute observations about Basilewsky's airplane concerto, the latest Soviet réclame—without in the least giving up his style or his major interests—such a critic would have seemed fantastic and would now seem to be a veritable Joseph.

3. *The Fate of Society:* One reason for this growth of interests, within a frame, is probably simple curiosity, tenacious and continuous; but another is undoubtedly the poet's sense that something catastrophic is happening to the society in which he lives. The most explicit statement of this is to be found in "Ideas of Order," the book of verse Stevens published after a silence of eleven years:

There is order in neither sea nor sun.
The shapes have lost their glistening.
There are these sudden mobs of men,

These sudden clouds of faces and arms,
An immense suppression, freed,
These voices crying without knowing for what,

Except to be happy, without knowing how,
Imposing forms they cannot describe,
Requiring order beyond their speech . . . .

This poem is entitled, fitly enough, "Sad Strains Of A Gay Waltz," and the poet himself appears on the scene, speaking of himself, of the past, of the forms of society which are in peril:

Too many waltzes are ended. And then
There's that mountain-minded Hoon . . . .

Who found all form and order in solitude,
For whom the shapes were never shapes of men.
Now, for him. his forms have vanished.

The solitude of "that mountain-minded Hoon" (this may be a coinage from "one alone," that is, the introvert, the solitary man) is the isolation of the modern poet from the rest of society. It was an isolation accepted and used by the poet. But now it is ending, the glistening shapes of the dancers have turned into sudden mobs of men.

In "Owl's Clover," a long poem obviously to be contrasted with "The Comedian As the Letter C," the poet considers the future which may develop from the present crisis of society; brings to bear upon this subject his old machinery of high-flown blank verse, art-works as sources of value, of symbols, and of the very texture of the writing, and states his ambiguous feelings about the future in characteristic terms:

Basilewsky in the bandstand played
"Concerto for Airplane and Pianoforte,"
The newest Soviet réclame. Profound
Abortion, fit for the enchanting of basilisks . . . .

Shall you,
Then, fear a drastic community evolved
From the whirling, slowly and by trial; or fear
Men gathering for a final flight of men,
An abysmal migration into possible blue?

With final insight, the poet states the criterion which ought to prevail:

As the man the state, not as the state the man.

And the whole meditation concludes upon the poet's fixed obsession, the place and rôle of art in life, in any society.

4. *The Ultimate Plato:* Confronted by the disasters of society, what could be more characteristic of the poet than to consider with fear and trembling and some hope, the place of art in the future? So too, in "The Man with the Blue Guitar," the complicated relationships and interconnections between Art and Life, between things as they are and things as they are on the blue guitar, are meditated upon in considerable detail. The characteristic, the ability which makes all the difference is clear in these instances. His resource is meditation and philosophical generalization. It is this which makes possible an escape from the perspective of the Art-man, or rather a transformation of that perspective simply by considering its general significance. Even where society is his direct subject, he tends to regard it in terms of essences and abstractions; not in specific social terms.

In his earlier work, Stevens became explicitly philosophical on subjects like Man in Nature, or Man's belief about the final character of Nature. He wrote not only of the "the curtains in the house of the metaphysician," and the veritable *ding-an-sich,* but concerned himself in one of his finest poems, "Sunday Morning," with Christianity and supernaturalism. Here he asks if supernaturalism is not too much, in a way, and not enough, in another, for "what is divinity if it can come Only in silent shadows and in dreams?"; he compares Nature and Paradise, pointing to the beauty made possible by process and death, and presumably not available in Paradise; and then he proposes a new religion, if not a new god:

Supple and turbulent, a ring of men
Shall chant in orgy on a summer morn
Their boisterous devotion to the sun,
Not as a god, but as a god might be,
Naked among them, like a savage source . . . .

yet this naturalism which makes him say in two other poems that a person is what is around him, his dress, his house, his carriage, and that "the soul is composed of the external world," this naturalism or materialism is qualified by a radical scepticism which makes the poet admit and envisage other possibilities and thus conclude "Sunday Morning" on the note of deliberate and sublime ambiguity:

> In the isolation of the sky
> At evening, casual flocks of pigeons make
> Ambiguous undulations as they silk
> Downward to darkness on extended wings.

It is perfectly clear in the context that the poet is not merely referring to pigeons, but to talking animals.

The ability to think philosophically (and with considerable philosophical tact) enables Stevens to write successfully such long meditations as "The Comedian As The Letter C" (which is, to be summary, a search for a way and a view of life by experiments with various views of life, realism, romanticism, subjectivism). It enables him to write of Nature not merely as something to be looked at but as a rich instance of fate, so that a wintry scene, "the junipers shagged with ice. The spruces rough with the distant glitter . . . the sound of the wind, the sound of a few leaves" are heard and seen by a listener who can grasp "Nothing that is not there and the nothing that is."

The idea and the ideal, he says in one poem, are like the evening star (as elsewhere he identifies the moonlight and the imagination) and, as if of his own use of the idea and the ideal, he says that

> It is a good light, then, for those
> That know the ultimate Plato,
> Tranquillizing with this jewel
> The torments of confusion.

It is a good light, indeed, for this particular poet. It is the light which distinguishes him from every poet who has worked from his perspective. In so far as any man can take on the insights of Western thought and make them his own, the poet can thus be said to be the ultimate Plato, or at least the latest. Or rather, let us say that the poet has stared so long at a picture of Piccasso's and at its blue guitar that he has seen its general significance:

> Is this picture of Picasso's this "hoard
> of destruction," a picture of ourselves?

5. *Certain Costs:* These qualities are not gained, however, without certain losses. Stevens has written neither dramatic nor narrative verse, and it is difficult to see how he could. As Howard Baker has pointed out, there are no human beings in his poems (even the lady having breakfast in "Sunday Morning" disappears by the sixth stanza). We are presented almost always with the poet, or the protagonist of the poem, in isolation before the tableaux of Nature and Society, meditating upon them. The meditation consumes the poem again and again. There is seldom a specific scene or time or action, but only the mind moving among its thoughts and impressions and responding to situations which are referred to, but not concretely presented in the poem itself. "Rocks, moss, stonecrop, iron, merds," another poet writes, "The woman keeps the kitchen, makes tea, Sneezes at evening, poking the peevish gutter." By thus placing the fact within the poem, the meditation on the fact gains a great deal of strength and relevance.

Stevens might thus be located in the Spenserian-Miltonic line of English verse as opposed to the line of Webster and Donne (but the lines cross many times, sometimes in the same poet). One might say that the difference may have had its source in the fact that Eliot read Laforgue and then read Webster and Tourneur, while Stevens, having read Laforgue or at least been moved to the same point of view, then read Milton (of course Eliot also read Milton, but disliked him). In the end, however, these two readers' difference would have to be reduced to a profound difference in temperament; for they would not have sought what they were seeking, if they had not already found it, though perhaps only in a primitive form, in themselves.

In Stevens, an abstractness is always present; everything is turned into an object of the imagination and of the poet's meditation, and the result is that he is sometimes "too poetic," which is what Eliot said of certain poems of Tennyson. This may be the source, too, of the word-play which does not always escape the adventitious frivolity for which it is always mistaken by the careless reader. The burden of the meditative center may be responsible for the faults of Stevens' blank verse, a lack of variety in going from line to line, a difficulty with overflow, and in his later work, a tendency to anapestic substitution which unsettles the sonorous period. But virtue and defect seem inseparable. The magnificence of the rhetoric and the broad philosophical concerns seem to necessitate an exclusion of narrative and drama and make possible the richness, range, and freedom of the symbols.

6. *Hints for Historians:* Other aspects of Stevens' work hardly suggested in this hurried survey are perhaps equally important; and of the related aspects I have taken up, it is plain that a great deal more remains to be said. But now I should like to suggest a few further connections and comparisons which might be fruitful. Some of them are within the scope of the literary historian and no one else.

Thus, Stevens' poems began to appear in various publications at a time when free verse and free love were once again new things, when *The Smart Set* was a leading literary magazine, James Huneker a leading literary critic, and sophistication, provincialism, and membership among the élite were concerns of the *intelligentsia;* or rather the names they gave to their concerns. This local or national context brings us back to the isolation of the modern poet to which one always returns in considering Stevens. The causal connections can only be guessed at, of course, but as soon as one remembers that to be a poet at that time was to be peculiar, one has a possible explanation of the constant self-mockery and self-depreciation and depreciation of the seriousness of the poem which marks Stevens' titles in particular: it is as if the poet were ashamed of being a poet, or extremely self-conscious about the fact, and this may explain why he calls his wonderful meditation on love, "Le Monocle de Mon Oncle," thus resorting to French (for Paris has been the capital of Western culture) and thus presenting a decora-

tive ironic surface for a poem which is as serious as human discourse can be.

Another examination which might prove illuminating would be a detailed comparison of such poems as Valéry's "Le Cimetière Marin," "Dover Beach," Yeats' "Among School Children," Eliot's "Gerontion," and Stevens' "Sunday Morning." What these poems have in common is the death of belief in Christianity; all of them, save Eliot's, make use of Nature as a source of the particular details of the poem; and all of them but Yeats' reject supernaturalism in the most explicit statements. The resemblances among the poems are striking; so are the differences; but much light might be shed by considering them in comparison with one another, and then in the context of the intellectual history of the last fifty or seventy-five years, perhaps even going far back to such authors as Darwin and Huxley, and the scientists who impressed Paul Valéry so much.

A third context for Stevens' text is Shakespeare. It may not be immediately recognized that Stevens' "Peter Quince at the Clavier" is the Peter Quince of "A Midsummer Night's Dream." But one feels that the quality of the imagination in such a play as "A Midsummer Night's Dream" is very like that of Stevens when he is most free and most fanciful. Or consider such a line in Stevens as "Death is absolute and without memorial." It may be wholly original, of course, and spring from the common language similarly used. Or it may be a development of the line in "Measure for Measure," where the Duke says to the condemned Claudio, "Be absolute for death." But these connections are matters for the scholar. The important point is the resemblance of Stevens' verbal usages to one variety of Shakespearean blank verse.

Then, there is the intermittent concern with Puritanism, as seen, let us say, in the 'twenties, and as opposed to the imagination. In poems like "Academic Discourse at Havana," and "Disillusionment of Ten O'Clock," Puritanism becomes an important element in the poem. In the latter poem, one begins with the houses in which everyone is going to sleep at ten o'clock:

> The houses are haunted
> By white night-gowns

None of the night-gowns (with the implication of sex) are green, purple, or yellow; the people dressed in them, we are told, are not going to "dream of baboons and periwinkles;" only an old sailor,

> Drunk and asleep in his boots,
> Catches tigers
> In red weather

and is thus sole representative of the imagination in the small town where everyone goes to sleep at ten o'clock. The background of Puritanism suggests a cause for the exotic character of the verse less general, more local or more American, than the separation of Art and Life I discussed at the outset.

* * * * *

Confronted by the need of conclusion or summary, one is impressed by how much more there always is to say about Stevens. No matter with what aspect one begins, one has a sense of inexhaustible richness of significance and connection. But if one returns to the personal impression—the source of the critic's sincerity, we are told by two voices with authority—then one must say that this poetry, studied during the difficult evenings of modern life, is of a very familiar strangeness (as a view of one's brain and heart might be strange), and seems to have something to do with everything important and beautiful.

Gargoyle in a Perambulator

for Rimbaud

by

William Abrahams

Where is the infant-child with rosy cheeks,
That like a chessy cat, lolled in his carriage,
And was worshipped by his parents for several weeks,
Symbolic of their happy, happy marriage.

Where is the infant-child, rosy and gay,
Who tickled the fancy of matrons out for walks,
And brightened up the sulky tradesman's day,
And gave his mother subjects for telephone talks.

Yesterday he lolled like a chessy cat,
Sleek and cozy, dreaming of warm dark shells,
But today he has sprouted the wings of a bat,
And in his drunken eyes a daemon dwells.

He squeaks, pontificates, disowns his past,
Worships Pan, and tries to rape his nurse,
And mocks his mother and father who pray and fast
And hope by ritual to end his curse.

Inventory and Statement: A Declamation

by Howard Nemerov

50 beautiful girls count 'em 50, are dying,
all together and slowly. Their hearts
beat one-two-three-four, they've worked
together all their lives and given you
good entertainment: and the young clerk
with the hot pants, in the third row center,
was perhaps the least of the sinners among you.

Plato dreamed of a surpassing love
bound up beyond the moving spheres: and Ziegfeld
dreamed of fifty beautiful girls fifty,
who are dying.
        The private citizen talks Babylon,
and has a righteous tea with the pastor,
and lusts in his heart; while my landlady
threw Alice out on the street and read Paris Nights.
Plato is dead, and Ziegfeld no less dead:
for I have given you here a thread of mine own life,
or that for which I lived.

Enforce the censorship: excise the merely
heterosexual: and show instead
defecation, masturbation, and a new

all-color version of Les Cent-Vingt Jours
—let the people learn the fashionable
technic from Alcibiades, and let
the newsboys peddle pictures of the Marquis
performing a subtle experiment.

For the fifty fair are dead, and godhead gone:
Brightness is dust, and through these portals pass
Plato, Ziegfeld, and all loveliness.

What shall you do when winter is on the world,
and time comes out of the cliff to dine among you:
and the strumpet has none to love with her legs,
and the bride goes to an empty bed,
and the lover lies in the hasty grave
the earthworms dug under him?
Why, then you will set alarm clocks,
and whisper the time in restaurants;
there will be learned discussions, there will be
symposia; and the newsreels will picture
decay in the organism, newspapers will devote column
to the death of a leaf.

THE NATIVE

IN THE WORLD

by

HOWARD

NEMEROV

THE CLIMB from sleep was difficult, a struggle up a staircase of soft pillows into which he sank again and again, drowsily defeated, from which he clumsily climbed again to a sight of the room that, seen in the equivocal wisdom of sleep, seemed to him any room, or all the rooms, in which he had ever slept, or ever been at home. Perhaps (an instant afterward he could no longer remember)—perhaps the phrase 'at home' struck the first tone of clarity in his mind, for about it the room began to arrange itself, to become again the familiar fashion of his circumstance, rising and composing to his own composition of its features. One thing—the overturned chair by the desk, with his clothes crushed under it—remained obstinately unfamiliar; when had he done that? He searched his memory, but the incident had sunk under sleep; he could readily imagine himself coming in drunk and knocking the chair down in the effort to hang his clothes over it, but actually to remember doing it—that was a different thing.

He got out of bed, and as he stood up felt

pain protest harshly in his forehead, making him dizzy with the angry sleep that would not readily dissolve. The clock said ten more or less exactly and it was dark outside. That meant twenty hours sleep; since two Tuesday morning. The dizziness surged higher as he bent in a methodical stupor to set the chair right and get his clothes. Going into the next room he started the phonograph and put on the Ricercare of the Musikalisches Opfer; then settled back in the darkness of a far corner. The one voice strode through his mind with a more or less plaintive confidence that another would follow, and soon another did, then one more and another, and the rest were sunken in the ensemble and the scratch of the needle. He closed his eyes, and as if his consciousness rested on quicksand he was irresistibly sucked back toward sleep, his eyelids grew heavy in a sort of undertow that he could feel heavily about his head. A dream, some frightening and fast forgotten dream, jarred him out of sleep; he had a vague impression of fear, something was being thrown at him. He turned on the light, changed over the record and picked up a book that was lying on the couch: *Alcohol the Friend of Man*. It was a reassuring volume by a doctor of unspecified repute; one must, he thought, turning over the pages, combine theory with practice. It seemed to him, as he had so often said, that there was a way to drink seriously, and a way not to drink seriously. Of three years at Harvard he had spent the last two learning the former, and was glad to distinguish himself from many of his acquaintances whose drinking was of the rowdy-up-and-puke sort. If a man wish to drink himself into insensibility, he phrased it pedantically, that is his own business; but equally he should not become a charge on his fellow-beings, and there is no excuse for forgetting manners one instant before passing out.

The record was over, and he walked across the room to change it, a strange figure in white pajamas, barefoot, head slightly too large for his excessively small frail body. He already had on his silver-rimmed reading glasses; he must have

picked them up from the desk without thinking. He came from the Middle West, but one would unhesitatingly have called him a Yankee, judging by his pedantic contemptuous manner, his manners so civil as to be rude whenever he gave a cutting edge to his voice. His own estimate of himself was quite accurate: that his aloofness was respected, also his enormous and casual erudition; that even full professors were chary of a too great freedom with him or with his papers; that it was generally said of him that he would go far if he did not drink himself to death; that his paper on Augustinianism in the 17th century would no doubt put him in line for a fellowship; and at last, that he was drinking himself to death, or near to it—a state which he conceived of dubiously as a slight chill in his personal weather, as though a cloud should slide over a hill on which he was sunning himself. As to his reasons—if a man wish to drink himself into insensibility, he thought again · · · and perhaps it is not even his own business, or perhaps it is a shady transaction in that business, into which he does well not to inquire too far; look what happened to Oedipus.

He had put on the Ricercare again, but now he turned it off in the middle and called Rico's number. He listened apprehensively to the empty buzz of the phone, three, four, five times: he could hear it as if he were in the room, but as if the room were still empty, the lonely stupid ringing. Damn Rico, he thought, letting the phone ring again and again. Damn Rico, damn the twisted little Cuban Jesuit gone wrong, and damn, he said, and damn with the ring of the phone, and damn again and hung up. The receiver clattered into its cradle, and he felt again how painfully slow it was to wake up, how fiercely he must fight to stay above the surface, so to speak, to force every last ache and hurt in body and mind to the service of wakefulness, to a nagging insistence on belief in being awake. Rico was probably out with Alan; Alan, he thought angrily, the little blond jew-boy who's trying to get me out of the way by advising me seriously to go see a psychiatrist. And Rico is helping him too.

He shuddered slightly, envisioning conspiracy and betrayal: the swift, sure honest-eyed kiss of treachery, the bright, the clear, the trust-worthy Judas; and the appalling thing was that it took place on such a pitifully small scale, the love life of a colony of worms. The disgust, and the hate, were waking him, slowly, as one fever will fight another and overcome it.

He took up the phone again and called Rhys. One could always talk to Rhys, no matter how far they had gone apart. Long ago, before the drinking, as he thought, they had been close friends, working furiously together, reading two and three books in an evening and listening to Bach from two to four in the morning. And then— there had been no break, not even a cool-ness; but they went their ways and saw rather less of each other. When he was drunk and wan-ted to talk out of turn, he often still climbed to Rhys' room, and he would talk wildly for fifteen minutes, often incoherently, and then Rhys would deliberate heavily, and say at last, "Well, John, it's difficult . . . ." which in itself would be somewhat reassuring; and then they would exhaust a small stock of polite and cynically eru-dite remarks about obscure poets, or faculty members, and it would be over.

"Hello, Rhys? This is John—Bradshaw . . . . I hope I didn't disturb you?"

"Not at all," said Rhys, in the coldly amiable tones that meant he was disturbed.

"Look, Rhys, . . . you mustn't mind me; I'm not drunk, but I took twelve grains of amytal last night when I was. I've just managed to get out of bed and I'm a little—woozy." He was, in fact, woozier than he had thought; there was that dull weight on his forehead that was worse than pain, more unknown and more fear-ful therefore.

"What I wanted to know was could you meet me for a drink, about fifteen minutes from now?"

"No, I can't," said Rhys. "You sound troubled. I don't know medicine, but isn't twelve grains rather much?"

"The prescribed adult dose is a grain and a half. I wish you'd come out for a drink. I want

to talk to you. Really, you know, it gets to be too much, sometimes . . . everywhere you go people are such bitches . . . . "

"What the hell is wrong, John?"

"Oh,—look, I'm liable to ramble a bit—I'm not very awake and the drug is still pretty strong—Oh goddam it Rhys, I've been betrayed, I—"

"Again?" A politely skeptical coolness.

Steady, he thought to himself; he was weak and falling again, and before answering he bit his lower lip hard, till the blood ran, to save himself from sleep.

"I mean it," he said stubbornly.

"Yes," said Rhys; and John recognized the tone Rhys used to nice drunks. "Yes, people are . . . difficult sometimes."

"Rhys, I'm not drunk. I want to talk to you. Why won't you have a drink with me?"

"Because I don't feel like it, John."

"Rhys, you think I'm drunk. I'm not, Rhys. It's the amytal. I couldn't be drunk, Rhys, I just got up, I've slept since two this morning."

"I know you're not drunk, John," said Rhys coldly. "I'm busy, and I think you ought to go back to bed. You don't sound very well."

"I only want to talk to you about Rico. You think I'm drunk."

"What's Rico done now?"

"I want to talk to you, Rhys."

"Well . . . . ?"

"Not on the phone."

"All right then, good night."

"Rhys—"

"Goodnight."

He waited for the dead click at the other end, and then placed the receiver carefully down. That had been a shameful performance; he was not drunk, but he could not have been more maudlin in any case. Rhys would be nodding his head sagely at this very moment: poor John Bradshaw. Oh, Damn Rhys. It was unfair of him. He might have had the common courtesy to listen to me, Rhys the careful, Rhys the un-drunk, the dullard so proud of his dullness; one could summon up at will that favorite image of Rhys the damned, sitting deep in his armchair after a peculiarly bitter confessional period, sitting like a tolerant father-confessor, saying slowly between puffs at a cigarette, "Gawd, all you people live such exciting lives—it must be so difficult for you—you come and tell me about drinking and drugs and your homosexual experiences—and I sit here on my can, taking it all in, living my dull life . . . . " And he would sit there on his can, looking as old as he could, and staring into the fire, saying "they also serve," or some such. Poor Rhys! And so anxious, too, for you to know that he was only pretending dullness (which God knows he was not) and that he was a man of deep spiritual crises; as he would say, and so smugly, "My blowups all take place inside." All right. Let Rhys take that attitude. He wasn't required.

He got to his feet and walked slowly about the room, still thinking about Rhys, beating one little fist determinedly into the other hand and thinking with melancholy savagery, 'cut away the non-essentials, cut them out.' Rhys was a non-essential, Rhys always worrying about his writing, his piddling poetry, his painful anxiety that you read his newest work, that you pat him on the head, that you say nice things . . . . As for himself, he thought, there would be a book one day . . . a book after this long silence, after the non-essentials had been cut away and meditation had burned some great stone to form inside him, a book that would say all these things that had to be said, against the lying time, against the lying treacherous people, against Rhys, against Rico, against Alan, against (he sneered) all these smilers with their dull knives. One voice in this wilderness would not waste time crying out for help, for cries would only bring the wolves along faster. And through this, beneath the pain and the hate and the disgust and still half-prevailing sleep, he knew that he was crying out.

He went into the bathroom and looked at the bottle of amytal. There were at least twenty-five grains left; he smiled a little to remember the time when one grain could give him a solid night's sleep, the rapid necessity to step up the dose, the doctor at the hygiene building telling him pedagogically that he was by definition a drug-addict, his crazily epigrammatic crypticism to the doctor ("Jonathan Swift was by definition not a well man, and a neurotic to boot"), his cheerful announcement to Rhys (Rhys again): "You may call me De Quincey, I'm depraved." It was the precipitous, the plunging rapidity with which it had happened, this drug business, that astounded him and started slight inadmissible fears from their careful rest. How one thing led to another! in such seemingly inconsequential succesion of one pettiness on the next, until, looking back from the most extravagantly fantastic heights of improbability, from the most unwarranted excesses and distortions, one was surprised and shocked to note how accurately and how unerringly every smallest act, word and gesture quietly conspired to build such a wildly rococo and out-of-the-way edifice,—such a goblin's architecture that at one moment one shuddered to think how it drove one on to the end, and at the next dismissed the whole structure with a smile for its implausibility. He stared fixedly at the bottle, imagined himself reaching out for it, tried to imagine himself refusing, and could only get a more or less chromo reproduction of a man in a magazine advertisement with his head turned disaffectedly away from a cup of coffee, saying: "Nope, I keep away from it. Keeps me up nights." This did not seem to him a satisfactory image of moral grandeur; with a smile he took up the bottle and locked it away in the filing cabinet on his desk. Then, puzzled, he looked at the key to the cabinet; what to do with that? He took it with him into the living room. He stood in the very center of the carpet, shut his eyes and turned around thrice, as though he were absurdly playing some children's game of blind man's buff; with his eyes still tightly closed, he threw the key straight before him, heard it tinkle in landing, then turned around twice more before opening his eyes. A glance about the room satisfied him that the key was not in evidence, not obviously anyhow. It might be days before he came across it. Unless the chamber-maid picked it up in the morning. He could imagine that she might hand it to him, asking whether he had lost it, and imagine himself saying no, I wonder how it could have got here . . . but one couldn't do that; all one's correspondence was in the filing cabinet, and notes for a couple of essays as well. Anyhow, it would be easy to find the key again, when it was really required. Meanwhile, one could . . . imagine it lost.

He decided to give Rico one more chance, and dialled his number again. The equivocal ringing—does it ring if you're not there to hear it? —angered him: he thought it possible that Rico and Alan were in the room, refusing to answer. he could hear them guessing who it might be, smiling complacently, drifting from smiles into their moonings and caressings, their adolescent, ill-informed lecheries—but no, neither one of them would have the strength to let the phone ring and keep on ringing; across each ugly infirm purpose would flash thoughts of importance, of some great person, some missed opportunity, the thought especially: it might be something better. And they would answer the phone. Rico particularly would answer the phone, compliant opportunist, affection's whore . . . had he ever done differently, or been anything else? Rico? who told (with pride) how he had been seduced by the house-maid when he was fifteen, and how three weeks later he had gone to his mother and got the girl discharged on some pretext.

No, they would answer the phone, he knew, and since they had not . . . . Perhaps they weren't even together; he cut the call short and dialled Alan's room. Alan's roommate answered:

"Hello."

"Hello, is Alan there?"

"No, he went out half an hour ago."

"Was Rico with him?"

"I think he was going to meet Rico. Is there any message I can give him?"

"No thanks."

"Your name . . . . ?"

"No thanks," he said coldly and replaced the receiver. He thought desperately for a moment that he might call Rhys again, then rejected the idea. There was no sense in begging. He felt tired again; the weight in his forehead had turned into a headache, and his eyes tended to water. The slight exertion of walking about the room made him want to go to bed, but he refused, and to clinch his refusal, began to get dressed. A drink was probably what was needed, he thought. A drink, and an hour out of this room. There was the mood he had been in all too often lately: his room depressed him, almost as much as did a library, for example; and the best things in the room,—the Matisse over the victrola, for example—they were so recognized, so much the very breath of his tepid climate that they became unbearable, and music was unbearable, and work as well, and it all seemed to him the ugly and ready-to-hand diversion afforded a man sentenced to life imprisonment. Not the ugly, but the commonplace disgusts, he thought. If they put Matisses in the street-cars, one would counter by hanging advertisements on one's walls. Yet he felt unsatisfied outside his room, again like a prisoner so acclimated as to shun freedom; a walk, however short, tired him inordinately, and climbing two flights to the room made his head throb as if the blood would burst out. He felt now that he required a drink; he would go to St. Clair's, nor did he disguise from himself the fact that half his motive was to find Rico, and that if Rico were not at St. Clair's he might be at Bella Vista, or McBrides, or the Stag Club; or he might be in town at the Napoleon or the Ritz or the Lincolnshire.

By the time he had finished dressing he found himself nearly exhausted. He had to sit down on the couch and turn out the light, and it was then that he began to think about the key to the filing-cabinet. He felt that he had perhaps been foolish, with his infantile stratagem. He might need the key in a hurry, for his notes, or to answer a letter, or—no need to disguise the fact from himself—to get the amytal when he came in drunk; it had to be conveniently to hand, or he would get no sleep. He must recognize the fact by now, he argued: he required the amytal, he was a mature individual, still sane, heaven knows, more sane than most of his dull acquaintances, he would not over-dose. And anyhow, the test was in the will to stay off the stuff, not in locking it away, there was no help in that. To be able to keep it before his eyes, that bottle, to look at it steadily, and steadfastly not to take it—at least not more than was absolutely necessary—there was the thing. Besides, suppose he needed it in a hurry sometime, and the key had got lost—there were any number of ways that could have happened: it might have fallen into a crack in the floor, might have slid under the carpet, might even have landed down the radiator gratings, irretrievable short of large-scale operations that would require the janitor.

Hastily he turned on the light, began to look around. It was not that he wanted any now, or would take any tonight; but this was the saner thing to do, he must know.

The key was discovered with ridiculous ease, under the bookcase. He picked it up and laid it carefully in the middle drawer of his desk. And unformed to speech or even to clear thought, but present in his mind, was that justification, that ritual against reason, of a postulated higher power, of unspecified nature, watching over the episode, the feeling, carefully swathed in obscurity: Providence didn't want me to hide the key, or I wouldn't have found it so easily.

Put vaguely at ease, he began to get on his overcoat, and then decided to call Rhys again, buoyed up by this same vague assurance that he would, by however narrow a margin, do the thing which was to be done, that the thing would be right because he did it. But there was no answer, and for some reason, he was more infuriated at this than at Rico's absence—a little relieved, too, for Rhys would have been annoyed; but angry, angry that Rhys should not be there, should have gone out after making some excuse to him. Betrayal, he thought, furiously and without power. Rhys too. Although loneliness was his habitual way, it was by preference, because it suited him to be alone, but this, the loneliness by compulsion, was a new thing. He felt a terrible isolation, the phone seemed to him now only an instrument of the Inquisition, to teach him his loneliness as it were by rote, and he had the sudden sense that whatever number he called, it would be closed to him by that instrument. In fact, he thought in satiric anger—in fact this whole room is given only to people who want to be left alone. It is made to teach them the measure—that is, the unmeasurable quality—of isolation, of being absolutely alone. Harvard College built it that way—they get a lot of lonely ones around here.

The brief walk in the cold, up Dunster street and across the Square to St. Clair's, fatigued him excessively; he recognized that last night's dose had not nearly worn off, and that the cold had the unusual effect of making him want to lie down and go to sleep just wherever he was, in the street even. It was almost like being drunk, that disgusting soddenness with drink that made it Nirvana just to stop moving, anyhow, anywhere. He kept up his heart to a degree by repeating his little catechism of betrayal, his interdict on Rico and on Rhys, all the fictions of his misery forming into churches for his martyred self: here was a first station, where one knelt to beg forgiveness for being rude to Bradshaw; and here a second, where one knelt to do penance for being out when Bradshaw called, here another for thinking Bradshaw drunk when he wasn't, here another for the general sin of offending Bradshaw; and a last, where one prayed for the grace of Bradshaw: Oh Bradshaw, we do beseech thee . . . and a return for the petty humiliations, and a hundredfold paid back each error, and he knew it for pitiful, but nevertheless went on, in a rage of cynical benevolence, to forgive Rico, to forgive Rhys, to forgive them and cut them away from his side, and to go on in the thorough lonely discretion of his anger.

When he entered St. Clair's the first person he saw was Rhys, big, rather stout, and darkly dressed as usual, sitting by himself at a corner table. Rhys waved and beckoned to the chair opposite, and John sat down there.

"You're avoiding me," he said without thinking; his anger came to a head and he wanted a fight.

"If I were avoiding you, would I come and sit in a bar?" asked Rhys politely, and it was like being hit across the face.

"Then why did you tell me you couldn't go out?"

"I didn't say I couldn't go out. I said I didn't feel like going out." Rhys was nettled, and showed it by getting more and more polite.

"If you don't want to see me, I won't sit here."

"Don't be silly. Sit around and have a drink."

Rhys, he thought, was playing for a dull peace and it was not to be allowed; he must be disturbed, made to give himself away. He ordered, and got, a large martini, and sipped it in an uneasy silence.

"You should have gone to bed. You look as if you were trying to kill yourself." Rhys gave in and said something.

"What the hell would you care?" he asked rhetorically, hoping at the same time that Rhys would say something friendly and reassuring.

"How is it possible for anyone to care? You're not very responsive to care, you know."

"Oh, some have managed." He lit a cigarette. It tasted very bad, but it was against the sleep that even the drink seemed to drive him at. The place where he had bit his lip was still tender, it hurt when he spoke.

"You alienate even those," said Rhys. It was for him as though he had said 'where are you, John?' and reached out a hand in the darkness; it was such an unwelcome thing to be forced to find people when ordinarily they came and disclosed themselves.

They finished their drinks in silence and ordered more.

"Now what's this about Rico?" said Rhys at last.

John emptied his glass again, slowly, before answering. "It's only that from now on," he said, "I'm going to play dirty too. If you don't what chance have you got?"

"I always thought of Rico as more or less irresponsible said Rhys, "but—"

"It's not only Rico, God knows. He can be excused, if you were bounced out of a parochial school in Cuba and landed at Harvard with the prospect of eight million bucks when you came out—alors. Not alone Rico, no. It's everyone. And you too, sir. Don't you understand: I'm playing your way now, the safe way you all play, don't give anything with one hand that you can't get back with both, any time. And if I can't beat these Jesuits at their own game—well, what the hell . . . " he shrugged his thin shoulders, deliberately blew smoke across the table between them.

Rhys determined to show no annoyance, to maintain objectivity. So he sat with hands out equally on the table, looking like the balance-pans of the blind goddess.

"Essentially stupid attitude to take," he said.

"I mean— granting that people do present . . . difficulties at times—still, just how much have you got hurt?"

"Got hurt, hell. That's not—"

"You don't need to answer me," continued Rhys with a show of calm. "I'm just suggesting the question as something for you to worry about."

"Don't go on; you had it right the first time, when you said something about responsibility. You just make an ass of yourself when you put it on the piddling level of 'getting hurt.' It's only a question of how the essential non-pirate is to live in a world of pirates."

Rhys had no immediate reply to this, so they ordered more drinks and John continued:

"Romans and Orthodox Jews make the best pirates because even if they do put pretty far out to sea after plunder, they've both got a sailor's snug harbor to get to again. The Catholic can drop anchor in a church, the Jew carries his absolution along on shipboard. But they aren't the only ones, not by a long shot. It applies to everyone you know . . . piracy isn't so safe a game for them, but if you think for a minute—"

"I wish you wouldn't pretend to sit in judgment when you're looking so pitifully ill. You remind me not so much of the Christian Way as of Nietzsche."

And suddenly John felt the fatigue again, the wish to give it up; what was the use in arguing with Rhys. The drink was having an inordinate effect because of the amytal. He knew it would be difficult to get up, next to impossible to walk home.

"Hell," he said. "It's only an argument for you. Forget the whole thing." and then: "will you take me home?"

"What's wrong? Not feeling well?"

"I'm sick to death of sitting here with you, listening to your well-fed brain. I want to leave and I can't do it by myself. I'm asking you: as one last favor, would you see me home? Let me assure you, sir; it will be the last. I shan't disturb you and your values again."

"Please don't be melodramatic with me, John," said Rhys in a quiet rage.

"Can't you see that's not the question?"

"Don't you think you'd feel better if you

sat here without drinking for a few minutes?"

"Oh for heaven's sake, Sir, don't be reasonable with me. I've asked you a question, will you—"

He felt a draught on his back from the opened door. Shivering extravagantly, with the hope that Rhys would think him ill, he turned and saw Rico and Alan standing beside his chair.

"Wha's wrong, little one," asked Rico, slightly drunk, smiling with his beautiful teeth.

"Rico!" he held out his hand, forgetting Rhys, forgetting Alan. "Rico"——and more softly, as though drawing the other into conspiracy—"will you take me home? I can't go myself."

"Sure, little one. I can take you home. Come, give me your hand." Rico laughed, his laugh and his glance taking in the whole room, stranger and intimate alike, as though to disclaim all embarrassment and responsibility, as though to enlist their sympathy not for John but for self-sacrificing Rico who had to take him home.

"Come," he said. "Up on your feet."

He got to his feet slowly enough, his eyes half fading from their focus. The floor seemed to rock beneath him, his ears filled with noise, and it was as if he stood on a separate planet that rocked backwards and over in space, out of sight of Rhys who sat there with an embarrassed expression on his face. Then suddenly he knew he was heavily in Rico's arms, and in one instant synapse of sobriety he heard himself saying to Rhys "I hate you more . . . " and Rico saying roughly "Come on," pulling at his arm. Then the two little voices were again swept away in a wave of sound against his brain, formless sound at first, that resolved itself into a rhythm and at length into words spoken from far away: "Drink and drugs that done him in," or some such; and then—drink and drugs—he could no longer hear for noise, but the enormous voice of Rico was in his head saying" Come on, come on," and all at once they were in the street and the cold stung his eyes and the sweat on his cheeks.

Rico and Alan had taken him by the arms, close to the shoulder, and were dragging him along. Whenever he stumbled they set him right with a jerk that lifted his feet off the ground.

"Wait," he said. "Sick."

And while they stood silently by holding him, Rico holding his head forward, he was sick, with a horrible violence, in a little alley off Dunster street. His stomach, almost empty to start with, twisted painfully at the finish, and he lost consciousness.

When he came to he was alone in his room with Rico. He could not see Alan anywhere. He rested on his bed and Rico was taking his clothes off. There was no longer any rest, or desire to sleep; there was only pain in his stomach and an actively hurtful weariness.

Rico finished stripping him, folded him in between the sheets. "You'll be OK in the morning," he said. "You were sick as a bitch. How d'you feel now?"

"Rico," he whispered. "Don't go away, Rico." He felt distantly that he was a child, in his child's bed at home; he had done a wrong thing, and Rico would be angry, with the efficient necessary anger of a mother.

"Kiss me, Rico," he said. "Kiss me good night." and then, as Rico made no move to comply, he said: "you're mad at me . . . ?" with a pathetic dubious note of shame in his voice, and Rico stooped and quickly kissed him on the cheek.

"Now good night, little one."

"Don't go, Rico. Stay here tonight."

"I can't. You'll be all right now."

"But I won't, Rico. I won't. I'll be sick again." He grew panicky with new fear. "I swear I'll be sick again," he said. "The minute you leave. Don't leave, Rico."

Then, in a tone of malicious invalid craft, he said accusingly: "You gave Alan the key to your room, didn't you?" Breathless, he went on: "You told him to wait in your room, didn't you."

Rico's face gave him away; it was true, it could only be true. "That's why you want to leave," he went on. "I know why." Quietly he began to whimper, and the tears rolled down his face. Then in a desperate martyrdom he said in a choked voice: "I'll kill myself if you go. I'll kill myself the minute you go out that door."

"Nonsense, what would you do it with, little one." Rico was not very good at situations like this; he felt vaguely that he should comfort, should sacrifice himself a little and help; but he had no intelligent means of doing it, being frightened not by a lie, but by a lie that would involve him later.

"I'd take all the amytal. I would. It would be enough. You'd see it would be enough. Rico don't be a bastard. Don't go away."

"You mustn't do that, John. You mustn't think of it."

"And you can't find the amytal either. I hid it." There was a terrible cunning in his voice, he was determined to have the drug. It did not at that time matter to him whether it was a lethal dose or not; it was to spite Rico, to hurt him, to say to him: 'see what might have happened. The guilt would have been yours, you would have murdered me.'

Rico went to the bathroom to look for the amytal.

"You can't find it, you can't," he mocked in a thin voice cracked with approaching hysteria. "Go away, damn you. Go away."

Rico came back into the room.

"You won't do it, John."

"Get out."

"Promise me you won't do it."

"Get out."

"If you don't promise I can't do anything."

"I said get out."

Rico was faced with something beyond his comprehension, and he took the only way he understood.

"All right," he said sullenly. "I guess it's your life." And having thus washed himself clean in his own eyes, he walked out.

There was no question of decision, now he was alone. It was again that unfaced trust in a higher power, in some back world watching. With unnecessary stealth he got out of bed and, entirely naked, went to the desk, got the key and opened the filing cabinet. He took the bottle into the bathroom and poured all the pills into a highball glass, which he filled with warm water. This decoction he took back into the living room, where he sat down on the couch by the phone and began to drink. When the glass was empty there remained a considerable residue of damp powder at the bottom, so he refilled the glass and started again, more slowly,

from time to time stirring the mixture with a pencil. At last he had finished. From experience, he knew there would be about fifteen minutes to wait.

He turned on all the lights, not feeling like getting into bed again. As he stood naked in the corner by the light-switch he was taken suddenly with a frenzy. The thing was done, it was done. Was it right? was it so at all? The indecision after the event frightened him, he imagined the maid finding him in the morning and with a certain sense of abject shame rushed to put his bathrobe about him. How to know? He questioned if he should be saved, and then, as he became somewhat more calm, there occurred to him another of those tests of providence, another cryptic question to which the oracle might smilingly equivocate over his special case.

He took up the phone and dialled Rhys' number. If Rhys answered he would explain and have him get a doctor. If there were no answer . . . and as he listened to the ring he felt certain there must be. It was not so much the test of fate, but the thought that he must speak again to Rhys, apologize, absolve, ask forgiveness.

There was no answer. Unwilling to believe, he put the phone down on the table and let it ring. The answer was given, but unsatisfactorily only more or less given, with the smiling ambiguity of power. He went to the window and opened it, then sat back on the couch. It is doubtful that he thought any more of death, of the probability or the certainty. He listened to the dried icy branches of the trees scratch together in the wind, down in the courtyard; and it is doubtful that he thought of leaving anything behind, of regret, of the irrevocability of death.

For his room, warm with the lights full on, seemed to him some tall citadel of the sun, with a certain congenial ease of sunlight upon it, and when the sleep came down, it drifted in like the cool sudden shadow of a cloud, that only made him shudder slightly.

A BAKED APPLE

After 'A Cooking Egg' by T. S. Eliot

Dunstan Thompson

En l'an vingtieme de mon age . . .
Que toutes mes hontes j'ay beaues . . . .

Babbitt sat upright in his chair
   Some distance from where I was sitting;
Views of the Harvard Houses
   Lay on his desk, as was fitting.

White porticoes and cupolas
   Through academic arches seen,
Supported on the filing case
   The Life of Cabot Lowell Green.

. . . .

I did not want Laughter at Harvard
   For I had heard the Mumford Duck
And talked with foxy Matthiessen
   And other tutors out of luck.

I did not want Learning at Harvard
   For I had known Professor Munn
We both have stood together, rapt
   In contemplation of the sun.

I did not want Elegance at Harvard,
   Theodore Spencer became my guide;
His attitudes were more amusing
   Than tea-time intrigue could provide.

I did not want Babbitt at Harvard:
   Professor Lowes instructed me
To walk *The Road To Xanadu;*
   Rousseau almost abducted me.

. . . .

But where is the fancy world I thought
   To find with Babbitt behind the books?
The termites through the bricks are creeping
   From Hollis Hall to Phillips Brooks.

Where are the truth and the beauty?

   Buried beneath the Kremlin wall.
Over their cocktails, sweet and fruity,
   Drinking, drinking student poets
Pass out in the Boston bars.

194

MAYBE NEXT YEAR

NORMAN MAILER

THE TRAINS used to go by, used to go by very fast in the field past the road on the other side of my house. I used to go down there and walk and walk through the fields whenever mom and pop were fighting, fighting about money like they always were, and after I'd listen awhile, I'd blow air into my ears so I couldn't hear them, then I'd go out in the field, across the road from my house and slide down the steep part of the grass where it was slippery like dogs had been dirty there, and then I used to climb up the other side, up the big hill on the other side, and walk and walk through the fat high grass until I would come to the railroad tracks where I'd just keep going and going and going.

Why don't we have any money, we never have any money, what kind of man did I marry, what good is he, what good is he, look at him, look at his boy there, look at your boy there, look at him, he takes after you, look at him walk away like he never hears us, look at him, no good like you, why don't you ever get any money?

The grass sticks would be rough and sharp sort of, like sharp pages in a book, and I had to walk with my hands in my pockets so I wouldn't cut my fingers. They were tall, the grasses, and sometimes they would hit me in the face, but I would hit them back, only that used to cut my fingers, and I'd start crying, but I stopped soon, because there was nobody around, and I knew that when there was nobody to hear me, I always stopped soon, although I never could figure it out, because I always could cry for a long time, and say I was going to run away and die if people were around.

I can't help it if I'm not making money, my God there's limits to what a man can do, nag, nag, nag, all the time. My God I can't help it, there's limits, there's depression, everybody's losing money, just worry about keeping the house, and don't compare the child to me, the God-damn child is splitting us up the middle, I can't help it if he's a stupid kid, he's only nine, maybe he'll get smarter yet, I can't help it if he's dumb, there's a depression going on I tell you, everybody's losing money, there just isn't any money around.

The railroad tracks made a funny kind of a mirror. I could see myself in them, one of me on each side, I was so tall in them, but I was awfully short, as short as my arm, but I was awful tall, I looked as tall as pop, except as tall as if I was to see pop all the way in the distance coming up the hill to our house, when he looked as tall as my arm, but I knew anyway that he was oh ten times bigger than me.

Why is the boy always disappearing, why don't you find him, you haven't a job, you just sit around, you might keep him near you, you might teach him to be like you, and sit around all day, and make it easier for me so at least I wouldn't have to look for him, but you can't even teach him that, I never saw such a man like you, they didn't make my father out of men like you.

If I walked and walked along the tracks, there was a spot where I could get to a place where all the big slow trains came into town. If I was careful I could sneak up in the grass near to where the men who jumped off the big trains camped in the fields.

They were dirty old men, they just sat around, and smoked pipes and washed their dirty old shirts in the yellow water spot where I used to go swimming before mom started yell yell yell about the dirty old men and wouldn't let me swim there.

They're filthy old things, you'll get sick and die, they're diseased, they're diseased, why did the town let them camp and flop in a meadow like that, right on the town limits, what's the good of living out of town when our only neighbors are bums, what's the good, what's the town mean, why aren't they put in the coop where they belong, why should they be flopping so near our house in a meadow?

I didn't like the men, they used to talk and laugh to themselves all the time, sometimes they would sing songs. I knew they were dirty men cause mom said they would give me diseases, but one time I came up and talked to them, when I went out mom and pop were shouting, and the men looked at me, one of the old ones who was sitting on his old stork bundle bag sort of, got up and looked at me, he made fun of me, he said sonny got a dime for a poor old man to have some coffee, and then all the men started laughing, haw haw haw kind of laughing. The other men came around me, one of them said he was going to take my shirt and use it for a snot-rag, and they all laughed again, the big man in the middle of them making believe he was going to throw dirt at me only I didn't know he was going to fool me until I started crying, and he laughed too, and dropped the dirt.

That boy is going to get in trouble, why don't you take care of him, keep him around you, he goes off into the meadow, and God knows what those bums are going to do to him, they're all vile, they don't live like men, they're not men I heard, they're no more men than you are, both of you are, why don't you take care of him, he'll turn out weak in everything like you, those bums will get him in trouble.

Pop came over, grab-me picked me up, and carried me upstairs, and licked me, and locked the door on me, and then he went downstairs, and he and mom yelled and yelled right through my crying. I waited and waited for them to hear me, but I must have fallen asleep because the next thing it was morning, and I didn't remember stopping and rubbing my hands on my nose to wipe off the crying. They unlocked the door before, I sneaked downstairs, the front door was open and mom and pop were sitting around front, not saying anything, I hated them, I ran out the door between them, and hid around the side of the house. Pop and mom came running out, they ran the wrong way calling to me, they were looking for me, and they weren't smiling, but they were talking nice the way they did when they didn't mean it, just like when they wanted to catch our dog, and that made me feel sad, and oh I felt just terrible, and then when they started coming back I didn't want to get another licking so I ran away without their seeing me, and sneaked across the road further down, into the field, and up the slippery hill, run run running way off until I got to the railroad tracks. I sneaked along them to where the dirty men with the disease were, and I hid down in the grass, and hid behind some to look at them, but they were all gone, there weren't any of them, but the old man who had made fun of me the day before, and he was lying on the ground crying and yowling like he was hurt or dead.

I walked over to him, he looked at me, he started crawling to me, I could see it was his foot that was hurt cause it was all bloody like, and bleeding near the knee. Help me kid, help me kid, he kept yelling.

Go ahead, hit the child, hit it, hit it, it deserves it, playing with dirty old men, hit it, it's a terrible child, it never listens to us, there's something wrong with it.

The old man looked like a snake, and I stepped back to run away from him, but he kept crawling after me, yelling don't go away kid, I won't hurt you, please don't go way kid, but he looked like a snake, only bleeding. I yelled at him, I said go away, you're a dirty old man, but he wouldn't stop, and I picked up a rock, and threw it at him, it missed him, but I threw another rock, and it hit him in the head, he stopped moving to me, he was crying something terrible, there was a lot of blood all over his face.

Why kid, why kid, why kid, why hit me.

You're a dirty old man, leave me alone, I don't like you, you're a dirty old man.

Kid for God's sakes help me, I'm going crazy kid, don't leave me here, it's hot here kid, it's hot here kid.

Then I picked up a stone, and threw it at him again, only I didn't see if it hit him because I was running away. I heard him crying, screaming, and I was scared, but I kept running, and then I said I hate them, I hate them, the grass kept cutting at me, I couldn't run with my hands in my pockets, kept cutting at me and cutting at me, I fell down, and then I got up and kept running home.

I walked down the last part of the hill, and across the road, and when I got back mom and pop were sitting around again, and I started crying. I cried and cried, and they asked me what's the matter, what's the matter with you, why are you crying, but I just kept saying the dirty old man, the dirty old man.

And mom said I thought they all were kicked out of town, I don't know how any of them were left, you're not lying?

I'm not lying, I'm not lying.

And pop got up, and said to mom I told you not to do it, you get an idea in your head, and you can't stop, those men were beaten, I don't know how any were left in the dark, we had flashlights, but there might have been, it's the boy's own fault, he had no business going around there today, and anyway he wasn't hurt, he didn't start crying until he saw us, I saw him before he saw me.

And mom said, if you were a man you'd go over there now, and finish them off, you wouldn't even go last night without any help, if I were a man I'd thrash the man that touched my boy, but you just sit there and talk talk talk that it's the boy's fault.

Pop got up, and walked around and around, and he said it isn't the boy's fault, but it isn't the man's either, and then he stood up, and said I'm not going to do anything about it, what with the boy between us, and the job ruined, and everything Goddamn else, I might be one of them myself, maybe next year, and then pop stood up and walked off down the road only farther out of town, not the way the old man was. I could see that pop's shoulders were screwed up around his neck, and then I was happy, because all I could think of was that I'd seen two big men cry that day, and maybe that meant I was getting bigger too, and that was an awful good feeling.

THE PERFECT MURDER

PROFESSOR Anatol Profax was nevertheless deeply interested in dialectology. The effect of environment on the tongue had been his life work; he had even gone so far as to assert that the shape of the tongue made people move up or down town; if it were heavy, large and flat it usually took them to the country, if it were a light tripping member they generally found themselves in Paris. The professor thought that the cutting out of tongues might produce mystics. He was sorry he had no power to try the experiment.

By the time he had reached middle age Professor Profax had pretty well covered his field — no pains had been spared. He had tracked down figures of speech and preferred exclamations in all walks of life; he had conversed with the trained and untrained mind; the loquacious and the inarticulate had been tabulated. The inarticulate had proved particularly satisfactory; they were rather more racial than individual. In England they said "Right!", in Germany they said "Wrong," in France they said "Cow!", in America they said "So what?". these were bunch-indexed or clubbed under *The inveterates* — it was his sister (now swatting out a thesis on the development of the mandible under vituperation) that got him down. She was always saying: "My God, *can you believe it!*". He classed her as the *Excitable Spinster* type and let it go at that. On the other hand the scores he had chalked up on defective minors and senile neurotics had proved disappointing. The professor was not even slightly interested in the human whine of the permanently hooked; conversely, he thoroughly enjoyed the healthy alkahest of applied appelatives — they were responsible for the most delightful boggles. What he had yet to lay his hands on was someone who *defied classification.*

Crossing Third Avenue toward Fourteenth Street, Professor Profax pondered the key-words of fanatics, men like Swedenborg and his New Church, Blake and his Bush of Angels. He decided that these gentlemen were quite safe (he had underscored their writings); they had saved themselves by the simple expedient of Getting Out of Reach.

He thought of his father, a hearty non-conformist who had achieved a quiet insecurity, over the dead bodies of John Wesley and the early Mormons; who had kicked out the family foot-organ in favour of a turning-lathe, and who was given to shouting (rather too loudly) "Terrrain tumult — ha!"

Deep in the pride of those reflections the professor smiled. He little cared that his figure was followed by many a curious eye. He was indeed old-fashioned. His frock coat was voluminous. Like all creatures that hunt too long he looked hungry. His whole head which was of polished bone, bore a fine sharp nose, a lightly scored mouth and deep cavernous sockets. He carried a cane over a crooked elbow that tipped inward to hold a worn copy of his book "The Variations"; it was precious in itself, additionally so for the notes on its back pages, made during a trip through the Allegheny mountains and the fastnesses of Tennessee. He had gone to check up on reactions to the World War. The hill folk had resented the intrusion with dippers smelling strongly of liquor; of the war itself they had only heard as far as prohibition. There was little labial communication. These went under the head *The Impulsive.*

He raised his eyes. A poster depicting the one True and Only Elephant Woman confronted him in a bright green and red. He lowered his eyes thinking of Jane Austen; a good tart girl of a *sec* vintage propelled by decency springing to the lash of matrimony. Love — now there was an emotion that had a repetitive vocabulary if ever there was one. It consisted of "Do you love me? Do you *still* love me? You *used* to love me!" Usually this was answered with "Yeah, I love you. Uh huh, I still love you, *What?*" Out west it changed slightly, the interrogative was almost unanimously responded to by "Hell, no!" But one needn't go West. Take his own case, he had never married, yet he was a man of violent passions, wasn't he? He thought this over slowly. Certainly at some time in his life he must have curbed an emotion, crushed a desire, trampled a weakness. The kerchief in his coat tail fluttered, filled with the dying life of a September noon. Perhaps he was a man who was living on embers and an annuity; a man of worthy memoranda and no parts. Well, it could not be helped now, after all, his Mistress was *Sound,* that great band of sound that had escaped the human throat for over two thousand years. Could it be re-captured (as Marconi thought it might) what would come to the ear? No theories for or against; no words or praise or of blame, only a vast, terrible lamentation which would echo like the "Baum!" of the Malabar Caves. For after all what does man say when it comes right down to it? "I love, I fear, I hunger, I die." Like the cycles of Purgatory and Damnation.

Some years back the professor had thought of doing something about it. He had even tried, but it had been a bit of a failure for, as he recalled sadly, he had been one jigger too elated, had had a swizzle too much (a thing he was not given to as a rule). This Holy Grail of the Past had eluded him, fool that he was, and had become only a dull longing which he had satisfied by calling in the local fireman and the Salvation Army. He had offered them libations of Montenegran rum (which he kept hid in the darkness of his Canterbury) . . .; he had even tried to explain himself, somehow he had gotten nowhere. The firemen had not made him happy; the little woman in the Booth bonnet had not saved him. He remembered that he had pressed a five dollar bill into the hand of the one to remove the other. It had all been a most frightful fluke. He had ended weeping in his den, pen in hand, trying to write a legible note on his blotter to President Wilson; the trend was to the effect that he considered *kumiss* preferable to bottled beer. He had to read it in the mirror the next morning, his head tied up in a towel. Somehow he had written it back-hand and upside down. In general he tried to think that he had had a religious experience, but he said nothing about it.

At this moment someone in flowing black bowled into him. He reeled a step, recovered his balance, recrooked his cane and took off his hat.

"Heavenly!" she said. She carried a muff; the strap of one of her satin shoes was loose, her long yellow hair swung back as she caught up her velvet train. "Heavenly!" she breathed.

"What?" said the professor, "I beg your pardon."

"Dying!" she said taking his arm. "I *am* shallow until you get used to me. If it were not so early I'd suggest tripes and a pint of bitters."

"Britain," he muttered, "that stern, that great country. How did *you* get here?"

"But it *is* too early."

"Are you the elephant girl?"

"Sometimes, sometimes I work on the trapeze, sometimes I'm a milliner, sometimes I'm hungry." She

was thinking. "I'm so fond of the austerities — you know, Plato and all that. He said 'Seek the truth, and take the longest way,' didn't he?"

"I don't know."

"I just died," she said, "but I came back, I always do. I hate being safe so I let the bar go and I flew out, right out into you as a matter of fact — "

They had come to the park, and now she released his arm, leaning against the rim of the fountain bowl. "I'm devoted to coming back, it's so agonizing." She swung her foot in its loose shoe, looking at him with her bright honest eyes. "I'm an awful fool when I'm uncomfortable."

"Are you uncomfortable?" he inquired, facing her all in black.

"I shall be," she paused, "You see, what is really wrong is that I'm not properly believed; people are wicked because they do not know that I am a *Trauma*."

"I know."

"Do you! That's wonderful. Nobody trusts me. Only last night that beast of a sword swallower (yesterday was Sunday you remember) refused to swallow six of my kitchen knives, he said it would spoil him for the canticles!" She threw her arm out (a velvet band with a bright red rosette was on its wrist) "Imagine! Such perfidy, such incredible cowardice!" she sighed. "Man is a worm and won't risk discredit, and discredit is the *only* beauty. People don't believe me because they don't like my discredits. For instance, I love danger, yet if anyone put a hand on me I'd yell like murder. Perhaps you heard me yell a moment ago, perhaps you even thought 'the girl is afraid.' How stupid you are."

"Wait a minute," said the professor. "*Did* you yell?"

Two large tears rolled down her cheeks. "Do *you* doubt me? You bet I yelled."

"Lob." muttered Professor Profax, "Toss, bowl or send forth with a slow or high pitched underhand motion — lob."

"Wrong." She steered him back across the street, pressing her face against a confectioner's window. "I'm vindictive because I have a *passionate* inferiority; most people have a *submissive* inferiority. It makes all the difference in the world. I am as aboveboard as the Devil. I'd like some caramels."

He bought her a bag of caramels. He was a queer lead colour.

"For instance, I'm lovable and offensive. *Imagine that position!*"

"Do you play dominos?"

"No. I want to be married." She blinked her eyes, she was crying again. "You see how it is, it is always too late. I have never been married and yet I am a widow. Think of feeling like that! Oh!" she said, "it's the things *I CAN'T STAND* that drew people to me. It has made me muscular. If I could be hacked down without sentiment I'd be saved. It's the false pride in violence that I abominate. *Why should he be there?*"

"Who?" said the professor nervously.

"The villain," she was smiling.

The professor was beginning to feel that a great work (which he thought he had written) was now hardly readable. He thought grimly "Poor child, I'd like to support her." He drew himself up with a jerk "I'd like to have her on my hands, it's the only way I can get rid of her."

"Yes," she said, "we might as well get married— time will pass."

"How about coffee?" he suggested. She nodded. "Tired and vigorous," he said to himself. "What a girl."

She turned him toward Third Avenue. How the dickens did she know it was East not West that his rooms lay.

"Shall we get married to-day or later?"

"Later," the professor said. "Later will do." He walked slightly listing, she was hanging on his arm, she had forgotten the train of her velvet dress, it was sweeping through the dust, dragging cigarette butts and the stubs of theatre tickets.

"I love enemies," she said, "and Mozart." She turned her head from side to side looking about her near-sightedly. "Let's never make a malleable mistake, do you mind!" She was taller than he, it was odd. "I can't stand my friends," she said, "except for hours."

"Extraordinary," he muttered, "I don't know how to class you!"

She drew back with a cry. "Class me! My God, people *Love* me!"

She was a little blind in the darkness of the staircase. "People ADORE me—after a long time, after I have told them how beastly they are—weak and sinful—most cases are like that, lovely people. All my friends are common and priceless."

He opened the door and she entered by a series of backward leans, turning shoulder blade after shoulder into the room. He took her muff and laid it down among his guitars and dictionaries—why on earth a muff in September? She did not sit down, at the same time she did not look at anything. She said: "You can criticize people as much as you like if you tell them they are wonderful. Ever try it?"

"No."

"Try it." She pulled her dress about her feet. "I want you to understand, from the beginning, that I am the purest abomination imaginable." She sat down on the trunk. "And my father says that I am so innocent and hard-pressed he's always expecting me to fall out of a book."

He fumbled with his hat, cane, notes. They all fell to the floor.

She sat like a school girl, her knees drawn up, her head bent.

"You're a sedentary. *I* take solitude standing up. I'm a little knock-kneed," she added honestly, "and I want to be good."

Professor Profax put the kettle on. "Would you mind," he said, his back to her, "falling in with yourself until I light the fire."

A stifled scream turned him. She had fallen face down among a pile of musical instruments, knocking over the Canterbury, sending sheet music fluttering into the air. She was pounding her fist among the scattered caramels. Her fist was full of them.

At that precise moment Professor Profax experienced something he had never experienced before. He felt cold, dedicated and gentle. His heart beat with a thin, happy movement. He leaned over. With one firm precise gesture he drew his pen-knife across her throat.

He lifted the heavy leather lid of the trunk and put her in, piece by piece, the velvet of her gown held her. He laid the toppled head on top of the lace at the neck. She looked like the Scape-Goat, the Paschal Lamb. Suddenly the professor's strength went out of him: he lay down on the floor beside her. He did not know what to do; he had destroyed definition; by his own act he had ruined a great secret; he'd never be able to place her. He shook all over, and still shaking he rose to his knees, his hands out before him, the heel of each he placed on the corners of the lid and raised it.

She was not there.

He clattered out into the street waving for a cab. He did not notice that the vehicle answering his call was one of those Hansoms now found nowhere except at the Plaza. He climbed in slamming the little door. "Anywhere!" he shouted to the driver and slumped into the corner. The horse started at the crack of the whip, jogging the leaning face of the professor which was pressed against the glass.

Then he saw the cab's twin. Breast to breast they moved out into the traffic. *She* was in the other. She too was leaning her face against the glass of the window, only her face was pressed against it as she had pressed it against the confectioner's! Her hair fell across her mouth, that great blasphemous mouth which smiled.

The professor tried to move. He tried to call. He was helpless, only his mind went on ticking. "It's the potentialities, not the accomplishment . . . if only I had gotten her name . . . fool! fool? What *was* her name! . . . Lost, lost . . . something extraordinary . . . I've let it slip right through my fingers . . . ."

Behind the mists of the two sheets of glass they rode facing each other. A van came in between them. A traffic light separated them.

DJUNA BARNES

THE WOOD-WEASEL

MARIANNE MOORE

emerges daintily, the skunk—
don't laugh—in sylvan black and white chipmunk
regalia. The inky thing
adaptively whited with glistening
goat-fur, is wood-warden. In his
ermined, well-cuttlefish-inked wool, he is
determination's totem. Out-
lawed? His sweet face and powerful feet go about
in chieftain's coat of Chilcat cloth.
He is his own protection from the moth—
noble little warrior. That
otter-skin on it—the living pole-cat—
smothers anything that stings. Well—
this same weasel's playful; and his weasel
associates are too? ONLY
WOOD-WEASELS SHALL ASSOCIATE WITH ME.

THE MOST LOVELY
INANIMATE OBJECT
IN EXISTENCE

When I walk the streets of this city in which I was born and raised I ask myself what am I doing here? What life is there for me in the midst of this stagnation? I look in the shop windows and they are filled with objects which I have no desire to own. I look at the activity of my nine million neighbors and I see it as a kind of insanity. I go to a bar for a quiet drink and a bit of enjoyable conversation and I find myself surrounded by brutes and imbeciles. I go to a cinema for relaxation and I am bored to tears. I pick up a newspaper and it is full of sensational lies, slander, gossip. In the subway I see a George Grosz parade of human caricatures. If I visit the office of a public official I have the impression that I am dealing with Al Capone's thugs and bandits. If I go to the public library the books I would like to read are not there; if I go to the art museum the pictures I would like to see are in the cellar; if I go to the concert hall the music I would like to hear is not on the program . . .

I speak now of the great metropolis, the cosmopolis of America. What the other cities of America lack is an infinitude beyond description or enumeration. Beyond the pale of a dozen barren centers of culture lies the wasteland, a territory so vast, so sterile, so utterly meaningless from the standpoint of human values, that the mind is appalled, the heart stopped, the tongue speechless. Only what is non-human in this "wild, wide land of mysteries" speaks of grandeur, nobility, dignity, splendor and sublimity. In the great Salt Lake of Utah there is one living creature, they say, which has found the means of surviving, and that is the shrimp. The contemporary native American leads a life homologous to that of the shrimp in the great Salt Lake. We do not know how or why he survives in a world which is turning to salt. He does not melt down with love, as Vivekananda says the Sattvikas do. The salt doll does not melt in the ocean of love; instead it turns the ocean itself in to a lake of salt.

Coronado seeking the Seven Cities of Cibola found them not. No white man has found on this continent what he came in search of. The dreams of the acquisitive whites are like endless journeys through petrified forests. On the River of Mercy they were borne to their graves. On the Mountain that was God they saw the City of the Dead. Through the waters of the Prismatic Lake they stared at the Endless Caverns. They saw Mountains of Superstition and mountains of shiny, jet-black glass. The Virgin River brought them to Zion where all was lovely and inanimate, most lovely, most inanimate. From the Garden of the Gods they moved in heavy armor to the Place of the Bird People and saw the City of the Sky. In the Fever River they saw the Sangre de Cristo. In the Echo River they heard the Desert of Hissing Sands. In the Dismal Swamp they came upon the passion flower, the fuzzy cholla, the snow-white blossoms of the yucca, the flaming orange of the trumpet-vine. Looking for the Fountain of Youth they came upon the Lake of the Holy Ghost wherein was reflected the Rainbow Forest. At Shiprock they were ship-wrecked; at Mackinac they were water-logged; at Schroon Lake they heard the loon and the wild antelope. The Gulf was lined with Cherokee roses, bougainvillea, hibiscus. They fell through Pluto's Chasm and awoke in Sleepy Hollow. They crossed the Great Divide (with Margaret Anglin) and came to soda canyons and borax fields. In the midst of the Thundering Waters they stumbled on the Island of Goat where Martha kept her Vineyard. Through the clear waters they saw jungles of kelp and phosphorescent marines. Near Avalon they saw the abalone and other shellfish lying on the ocean floor. Looking for the Black Hills they came upon the Bad Lands. Calling upon Manitou they found a Turquoise Spring and when they drank of its waters they were turned into obsidian. Searching for Green Table they came upon the Cliff Palace where the red man kept his Medicine Hat. Passing through the Valley of the Shenandoah they came upon the Hanging Gardens and were swallowed up by the Mammoth Cave . . .

Endless was the trek and endless the search. As in a mirage the bright nuggets of gold lay always beyond them. They waded through poisonous swamps, they tunneled through mountains, they reeled through scorching sands, they built natural and unnatural bridges, they erected cities overnight, they compressed steam, harnessed water-falls, invented artificial light, exterminated invisible microbes, discovered how to juggle commodities without touching or moving them, created laws and codes in such number that to find your way among them is more difficult than for a mariner to count the stars. To what end, to what end? Ask the Indian who sits and watches, who waits and prays for our destruction.

The end is a cold, dead mystery, like Mesa Verde. We sit on the top of an Enchanted Mesa, but we forget how we got there, and what is worse, we do not know how to climb down any more. We are on top of the Mountain that was God and it is extinct — "the most lovely inanimate object in existence."

Finis

Henry Miller

ROOSTERS

Nightlong the water labored without end.
Till morning came, rain burned her linseed oil.
Now from beneath the lilac lid the steam
Pours forth: earth stems like *shchee* when on the boil.

And when the grass, shaking itself, leaps up,
Then who will tell the dew how scared I am —
That hour when the first cock starts to yawp,
And the one more, and then — the lot of them?

They name the years as these roll by in turn,
And on each darkness as it goes, they call,
Foretelling thus the change that is to come
To rain, to earth, to love — to each and all.

Boris Pasternak
Translated by Babette Deutsch

EDWARD GOREY

OBJECTS

RICHARD WILBUR

Meridians are a net
Which catches nothing; that sea-scampering bird
The gull, though shores lapse every side from sight, can yet
Sense him to land, but Hanno had not heard

Hesperidean song,
Had he not gone by watchful periploi:
Chalk rocks, and isles like beasts, and mountain stains along
The water-hem, calmed him at last near-by

The clear high hidden chant
Blown from the spellbound coast, where under drifts
Of sunlight, under plated leaves, they guard the plant
By praising it. Among the wedding gifts

Of Here, were a set
Of golden McIntoshes, from the Greek
Imagination. Guard and gild what's common, and forget
Uses and prices and names; have objects speak.

There's classic and there's quaint
And then there is that devout intransitive eye
Of Pieter de Hooch: see feinting from his plot of paint
The trench of light on boards, the much-mended dry

Courtyard wall of brick,
And sun submerged in beer, and streaming in glasses,
The weave of a sleeve, the careful and undulant tile. A quick
Change of the eye and all this calmly passes

Into a day, into magic.
For is there any end to true textures, to true
Integuments; do they ever desist from tacit, tragic
Fading away? Oh maculate, cracked, askew,

Gay-pocked and potsherd world
I voyage, where in every tangible tree
I see afloat among the leaves, all calm and curled,
The Cheshire smile which sets me fearfully free.

THE WALGH-VOGEL

RICHARD WILBUR

More pleasurable to look than feed upon,
Hence unconserved in dodo-runs, the round,
Unfeathered, melancholy, more than fifty pound
Dodo is gone,

Who when incarnate wore two token wings
And dined on rocks, to mock at mockeries.
Empowered now by absence, blessed with tireless ease,
It soars and sings

Elated in our skies, wherever seen.
Absolute retractility allows
Its wings be wavy wide as heaven; silence endows
Its hoots serene

With airy spleenlessness all may unhear.
Alive the dodo strove for lack of point,
Extinct won superfluity, and can disjoint
To joy our fear.

Dive, dodo, on the earth you left forlorn,
Sit vastly on the branches of our trees,
And chant us grandly all improbabilities.

A SERMON: Amos 8:11-14

By JOHN ASHBERY

*And they shall wander from sea to sea,
and from the north even to the east; they
shall run to and fro to seek the word of
Jehovah, and shall not find it. In that
day shall the fair virgins and the young
men faint for thirst.*

In this land travel light
And lightly: keep rude hands from sight
Nor with speech design fidelities.
Break vows as fagots: ignore
Promises, prayers, lusting before the
    door,
Nor press the sinning Tartar to his knees.

Move as water: soon gone
Lightly girdling the dry stone.
Touch nothing long: involve
Nothing ever. Your fate and history
Meet in geometry
And in radiant law dissolve.

I explain: imagine
A young man or fair virgin
At dark, at sea's edge wading.
And now drawn in a strange light
Into the sea. Nearing night
Locks tongue, ties eye. Fading
  From shore line the swimmer
Forms with his ocean brother
A complex unity: sea immolates
Matter in distance, and he or she
Buries desire in motion. And does not
    see
Where, at far left, oars raised, a small
    boat waits.

My people. what is intended
Let the cool martyr, whose distant head
Now seems a swimming dog's, explore,
Sustained in a vast disinterest.
But learn that distances are kindest
Not the correct sun striking the shore.

SUFFER THE LITTLE CHILDREN

ROBERT CRICHTON

"Now don't bite it, whatever you're about," Sister Theresa had told us. "It's the Body and Blood of Christ in your mouth. Let Father Meehan put it on your tongue and then let it melt away. I've told all of you what happened to Timmy Monahan and you don't want it happening to you."

I stared down the rows of other boys, all dressed like myself, black in our first Communion suits, remembering the words of Sister Theresa. Poor Timmy Monahan . . . walking back from the altar, his mouth gushing blood after biting into the Sacred Host. I could see him lying in the aisle, all the mothers and fathers crowding around his body, his mouth running blood out onto the dull red marble floor, while Father Meehan washed his head in the holy oil giving him the last rites. The hundreds of flaming candles on the altar slipped into a shimmering yellow pool in front of me. I felt a lump come up in my throat for Timmy Monahan. The Agnus Dei, coming from the older boy's choir in the back, was only a roar in my ears.

Emmet punched me softly in the ribs. I turned my head slowly, so as not to be noticed, into the eyes of my friend. He stared hard into me and I nodded, *yes, I would.* Then I let my eyes sneak by little nods frontwards. Behind me, hovering over me like the heavy black mantle which covered her head, sat Sister Theresa.

She must know what I'm thinking, I thought. She had to. She had eyes that could look through the hair on your head and see the pictures inside. In the small of the back, just where your soul is, I tingled. A flush of red crawled up my back until I felt it hot against my Buster Brown collar. I sat unmoving, waiting for Sister Theresa to reach out and grab me. She would pull me out of the pew and throw holy water on me to clean my dirty mind. When my knees quivered beneath me, I told myself that I wouldn't get the host for Emmet. Why didn't Emmet ever want to believe any-

thing, I wondered.

Sister Theresa was getting up. I heard the starchy stiffness of her habit close behind my ear. I ducked my head swiftly down into the starchy safety of my collar but she glided softly down the ten rows of boys in black beyond me until she leaned over the end boy in the first row. The first row rose. They started moving woodenly out, their new black leather shoes clacking on the marble as they moved towards the altar. The second row rose and then the third. It would soon be my turn. My heart pounded hard sending a warmish glob flooding out in my chest. It was hard to breathe.

"Don't forget now . . ." Sister Theresa was bending over me, the cloth of her habit falling around me like a black wing, "You go to the *left* side of the aisle, Robert."

To keep from shaking I stepped stiff legged across the aisle. Standing in the aisle, in front of everyone, because the altar rail was full, a quick fear that my neck had turned black overwhelmed me. That's what happened, everyone knew, if you tried to take the host when in mortal sin. Danny O'Brien's father and mother had seen it happen to the little girl over in St. Vincent's who kept the collection money her mother had given her for church.

"Go ahead," Emmet said. He pushed me from behind. "And don't you dare back out." The altar rail was cold and hard against my knees. I shut my eyes to keep from seeing the Virgin Mary smiling sadly down on me from the altar. Then the icy touch of the golden server, held against my neck by the altar boy, startled me. I felt the thin pasty wafer clinging dryly to my tongue before I was conscious of having opened my mouth. It felt like sour bread. Emmet's elbow brushed against mine reminding me of what I had to do.

Waiting for the other boys to finish their altar prayers I worked the wafer around until it was held loosely in my teeth, touching no part of my mouth. At a light snapping of the nun's fingers the boys rose one after the other and started back to our pews by a side aisle. As I rounded a large pillar at the back of the church, dark in the shadows underneath the choir box, I jerked out my pocket handkerchief, spat the wafer into it, and jammed the handkerchief back into my pocket. With exaggerated ease I climbed into the pew and knelt there, my head bent in pious prayer, my heart pounding violently.

"You get it?" Emmet demanded. I nodded yes.

"You'd better have" he said.

While I knelt, staring ahead at the beautiful brilliance of the altar they had arranged for me, I became fully conscious of what I had done. I could feel the Body and Blood of Christ throbbing in my breast pocket against my heart. I put my hand up to my pocket to liberate the heavy breathing. Maybe Christ is smothering in there, I thought. It wasn't too late to make up for what I had done. God would be happy with me, starting out so bad and ending up so good. I reached up to ease my handkerchief out of my pocket.

"Keep still, Robert" Sister Theresa whispered. I could hear the heavy breathing of Emmet close against me. My hand slipped down from the pocket.

The Mass was over. We filed down the leaning rows of parents, straining out to get a close look at their children. I walked with my eyes held down to keep them from my parents. They would read my badness in them. The left side of my chest burned like fire. It was a wonder they couldn't see the host shining through the pocket, in the way it shone in the pictures. Outside, in the cement schoolyard by the church, we filed by Father Meehan to get our little black First Communion Prayer Books. Then we broke into groups to wait for our parents who would give us holy presents, solid black rosary beads and scapulars and medals of St. Christopher to wear on bronze chains when swimming.

"Come on." Emmet grabbed me by the arm. He started pulling me across the cement yard. At first I resisted but when we reached the gate letting out onto 58th Street I began to run with him. We reached Third Avenue and broke across the trolley tracks not bothering to look. Once safe across the avenue we both slowed to a careless nonchalant walk. I went past the door of our apartment. There was no one on the stoop or looking out the windows. I darted back up our stairs, twisted the door knob the way it would open without a key, and was pushed into the vestibule by Emmet.

The apartment was dark inside, with an emptiness about it which felt as if no one had ever really lived there. I searched for the light cord in the hall and flicked it on. My reflection

leaped out at me from the big hall mirror.

"Oh" I gasped. I had forgotten the mirror.

"'Fraida his own face" Emmet snorted. He at once went to the kitchen.

I stayed behind and looked closely at myself in the mirror. I saw how small I was. I felt very sorry for myself and for what we were going to do. "I'm sorry, dear Jesus" I whispered to the mirror. I looked at myself with astonishment. Me, so little, going to do something like this, I looked very much different than I ever had before.

"Come on, come on" Emmet shouted down the hall from the kitchen. Unseen by Emmet I waved a sad good-bye to myself in the mirror. I walked mournfully but with soldier dignity down the hall to the kitchen, knowing what I had to do.

The wafer was crumpled when I rolled it out of the handkerchief onto the gleaming white surface of the kitchen table. We both looked at it as it lay in all its terrible power on the table. We kept a good distance from it but after several seconds Emmet approached the table and slid the drawer open. Never taking his eyes from the host, fumbling, he found a fork. I backed away from the table into a corner. Emmet, holding the fork at arm's length, blessed it with a mysterious wave of his hand. He struck suddenly. He plunged the prongs into the little dough wafer. He leaped back while I gasped, waiting for the blood to gush across the table and flood the smooth white surface.

Nothing happened. Nothing at all. Emmet crept slowly back. I came out from my corner, closer. Picking up the host Emmet forced it boldly over the tines. Still no blood. With a gleeful shout he turned on me and thrust the host at my face. I jumped back in horror.

"Quiet" Emmet shouted. "Watch me." Holding up both hands for peace in the still room he strode to the middle of the kitchen. He slipped to his knees and made the sign of the cross over the fork.

"In the Name of the Father and of the Son and of the Holy Ghost, Amen.", he chanted. Sucking the wafer off the tines he began to chew with loud sucking noises.

"Mmmmmm Good . . . Gooood" he shouted. He smacked his lips with great relish. He held up a little piece for me.

"Go on," he said forcing the piece at me. "It doesn't bleed." I took the piece and let it melt secretly away in my mouth.

Emmet got up from his knees. He shook my hand.

"What do you think of Sister Theresa?" he demanded. He spat on the table. In my deepest voice I said,

"She's an old lying bag," and I spat on the table.

AN AIRPLANE CRASHES IN THE DESERT

Donald A. Hall

It is a dream, they think, falling,
A dream. Soft as in sleep, the air,
Whinning like a midnight cat,
Curls around their island, while
Come roaring up with open mouths
The faces of the sea and sand.

The personal shape, in sleep pursued,
Walks through the wall and is free. But here,
Shock will burst the moment's sides;
And sudden as god their names will fill
The sky, and light will flatten the dunes
And deepen the darkness of the valleys.

ENTR'ACTE FOR A FREAK SHOW

THE MAN WITH THE IRON MOUTH: See how
        the light-bulb powders on my tongue:
Miraculous.

THE HUMAN FROG: No more than a mockery,
A trade you learned, as useless as a lung
Without a body. Rather gaze on me:
My shrunken body utterly depends
Not on a trick, but birth; this should delight
By making nightmare solid for you, friends,
So that, undressing in your homes tonight,
Your undeniable symmetry will mean
The terror was unreal that made you cry:
For you are you, and with your eyes have seen
The twisted proof that figures do not lie.
I am a thing of God.

THE MAN WITH THE IRON MOUTH: My
        vulgar friend
Disdains me for my intellect, but this
Alone can set you free: That I defend
Absurd perfection, happily dismiss
All other kinds of action, must console
All you good people gathered in this place
Who feel your hands go empty and your whole
Body tremble, suddenly meet the face
Of your own childhood, when sleep will not bring
Its usual peace, reminding you of love
And what you have not been; remembering
My serious diet of glass, you can remove
The vision with a smile, sane and sincere,
Clenching your fists.

THE HUMAN FROG: You speak of things that seem.

THE BEARDED LADY: Gentlemen, you both lie.
        Confess me here
The twice tormented mirror of your dream.

KENNETH KOCH

LITTLE BEATRICE

by JOHN HAWKES, JR.

Your misery does not touch me;
Nor the flame of this burning
Assail me.

DANTE

Straight the hair, dull the little girl;
I see her hiding from the crowd, a squirrel,
Clutching to her chest the half filled bag,
Her eyes the staring chestnuts of a vender
Mad with the cold, an old Venetian faker.
She will never ride the dark gondolas.
She stops to mimic a song that she once heard,
And darts at a passing woman with a word.

Her father, a ringed gipsy, rakes the coals;
Holding his coat he curls round the fire,
Puts the folded paper inside his shoes
And hears the tambourine under the trees.
He knows her coming by the slamming door
And confident that she will watch the stove,
He retreats within the olive grove;
Mounting the stairs she contrives to be a queen
And drops her cloak, a gesture against the heat;
Then picks it up, remembering the street
Where frozen Caesars and Giuseppes meet.

TYWATER

By RICHARD WILBUR

Death of Sir Nihil, book the *nth,*
Upon the charred and clotted sward,
Lacking the lily of our Lord,
Alases of the hyacinth.

Could flicker from behind his ear
A whistling silver throwing knife
And with a holler punch the life
Out of a swallow in the air.

Behind the lariat's butterfly
Shuttled his white and gritted grin,
And cuts of sky would roll within
The noose-hole, when he spun it high.

The violent, neat and practiced skill
Was all he loved and all he learned;
When he was hit, his body turned
To clumsy dirt before it fell.

And what to say of him, God knows.
Such violence. And such repose.

The Middle Muddle

John Ciardi

The liberal, I suppose, is the Unitarian of politics: he begins by affirming a faith he cannot quite define, and goes on to cherish it more and more stubbornly as it becomes less and less definable. His position is always an easy one to ridicule, but it is not at all a capricious one. On the contrary it may be all there is left of intelligence, for — still like the Unitarian — the liberal always remains sure of one thing: he always knows where he does *not* want to go.

The ethics of the political liberal, however, must answer to one urgency that does not compel the theological liberal. A man may woo the universe on his own terms, at his own pace, and without outside assistance, but the man who goes ringing political doorbells must work against a time-table, against prejudices that are often intellectually irrelevant, and with allies that are never the best but only the best available. His salvation is not in himself but in winning a majority.

Within this compulsion, the ignorant, the hysterical, and the opportunistic may be able to divide all issues into that which is pure good and that which is whole evil. But the liberal knows he will never agree 100% with anyone. He knows that all human motives and situations are ambivalent. He ends in some sort of desperation deciding that any political situation that shows up 51% good against 49% evil is finally enough to decide a course of action. A slim enough basis of morality, but is there another?

This is his muddle. He could of course shrug it off. He could hang the world's fever chart in his study as an amusing sceptic's hobby, rebuff all temptation to act, and always be right. But given the compulsion to act, he is immediately in mid-muddle, trying to decide which of the world's imponderables assays 51% good in practical and actionable terms.

I am such a muddled liberal. I think I see virtue on all sides and evil within my own position. But liberals must act. And to act one must choose. I choose the Progressive Party. It seems sadly ineffective today, and I am not too hopeful that it will become more effective, but I believe it is on the side of virtue.

I would choose the Progressive Party if for no other reason than that it is the only political organization of liberals opposed to our foreign policy. I believe that foreign policy is not only a great evil abroad, but that it is making it virtually impossible, as President Truman is discovering and will continue to discover, to make good on liberal policies at home.

Why is that foreign policy bad? I have said the liberal always knows where he does not want to go. I want to go neither communist nor fascist. Both power systems are expanding today. Spain, Turkey, Greece, the Arab States, Japan, Germany, most of South America, and large areas of Central America and the East Indies are today fascist or what amounts to fascist — all of them with the aid and comfort of the United States government. I am as eager as any man to be saved from the system-rigors of the communist dogma. But I have no wish to be saved from the commissar by the storm-trooper. The iron-heel we wear abroad has already left its imprint at home in the various witch hunts of the FBI, the loyalty boards, and the unAmericans. When to our facile fascist affiliations abroad we add at home suppressions of civil liberties, the mounting effect of the doctrine of guilt by association, various official classifications into first, second and third class citizens, and the hysterical accompaniment of a war of nerves; I cannot escape a dread of the possible consequences.

I should certainly be alarmed to see America render herself defenseless in the present upheaval of world affairs. But I believe the hopeful answer to communism is not militarism, restriction and, fascism, but democracy. And the root of liberalism at home lies inevitably in the way we square off toward the world. We cannot be fascist abroad and remain liberal at home.

I must doubly reject our anti-communist war at home, on the simple overwhelming ground that there is not an iota of a communist threat inside the United States. The whole ideology of communism is alien to us, its leadership is almost universally stupid, it lacks any real understanding of the American scene, and its very label is a political kiss of death. How this combination of discredited zealots (70 odd thousand of them at the most by FBI estimates) is going to take over the sanctum of Rotary and the American binge, 140,000,000 strong I simply fail to understand. Communism is, however, a gorgeous slogan for a Holy War under the banners of which fascism could become a very real threat in America. For fascism has a long native history here: in the Klan, in Georgia, in Lousiana, in the big city bosses, in the whole tradition of Vigilantes, and in an alarming proportion of the Legion's record.

Against this very real danger, inextricably wound into our present foreign policy, the Progressive Party raises the only clear voice I hear. It's cry is on the side of hope and democracy, and I have no choice but to raise my voice with it.

But the muddle continues. How effective can the Progressive Party be? I am frankly pessimistic. The communist question immediately injects itself into any discussion of the Progressive Party. There can certainly be no doubt that the red label played a large part in November's overwhelming defeat? Should the Progressive Party get rid of its communists?

I would like nothing better than to see the communists go off into their own party and stay there. They have a right to sing as loud as they like, but it is not the tune I want to sing. There is, however, a principle involved: can the liberal conscientiously afford to add so much as one faggot to the witch fires now burning so brightly? I frankly do not know. I find it hard to believe that the communist threat is real among us. I think if the Progressive Party knuckled under to newspaper sentiment and cleaned its house of communists, a new smear

would be invented the moment it showed any substantial gain in public confidence. There is a l w a y s anti-Semitism, "why-doncha-go-back-where-ya-came frum," and "Red" itself has become so wild a label that its only definable today as "one with whom you disagree politically." I think, finally, that the Progressive Party should stand by its first declarations. If you don't like the presence of some communists in the membership, join up and outnumber them. And welcome to my side.

As a matter of fact the Progressive Party has faced this issue. It has repeatedly declared its principles, and made the point that anyone willing to subscribe to those principles could become a member for one dollar. A fascist could join by signing himself in agreement with these principles. It is true, of course, that no political organization can be described by its statement of principles. The United States today is not described by the Constitution. *Who* is in the government is more important than the charter of that government. So for the Progressive Party: if liberals stop joining it will become a communist front. It is not now a communist front organization, however, and will not be so long as its liberals remain active. Obviously such a discussion of things has small chance of being heard above the roar of the press, but I cannot see that that alters the position. All the Progressive Party can do is to go laboring as ever to make itself understood, to hope, and to arm itself with pessimism.

On the other hand the fact that Truman cannot deliver the policies that distinguished his campaign liberalism may afford the Progressive Party a future advantage. And while I have no wish to face another depression, fairly foreseeable economic difficulties may create a new public willingness to listen to the Progressive cry.

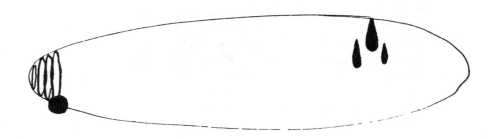

WHY WE FORGET DREAMS

JOHN ASHBERY

I.

Through the half open door came a sound of April—
But I'm sad, said the tenor, O unwisely the spring
Piles up its dangerous architecture!
Who expects wisdom from lightheaded birds
Moving through a forest of constant desires,
A world continually budding and fading,
Where only death flowers and is exact
And the season of love will never happen?
The sun went out, the noise of his crying
Fell across the year like an icy rain.
Who can make his sorrow or his happiness real,
Or make of their changing a beautiful thing?

II.

Now, he said, it is all over; only
Someday, crossing a street, or innocently
Pulling on our gloves, the will
Of an unseen lover will stare us into silence:
In the sky, palladian, or the waving
Tips of the willow, his sudden song
Will confound us, for it shall be noiseless and wordless;
The sky of his coming, dreamless, and we
The ghosts of which a dreamer takes possession.

So today, the Swans in the public gardens
Carry his sentence from shore to shore
Yet we sit in the sun with our legs dangling
And my knowledge black and cold beneath.
To move, he said, in his definition
Peaceful as swans! As in a poem
Love is forgetten, and in a dream
The poem is lost in a desert of contexts,
So motion is our cure, but till he names us
Love can be only waking to each other;
I to the blinding nowhere of your limbs,
You to the sad spring lost in my stammerings.

ENGLAND, 1935

L. E. SISSMAN

To those young men in the shadow of machines
Steel more exciting than cathedrals loomed:
Battersea's four gaunt towers in their dreams fumed
And overhead screaked the black dock-crane that leans

Seaward at Rotherhithe. On its gold lines
Across their nights the locomotive boomed,
Rushing to morning, where the azalea bloomed
About Vitesse Saloons in rural lanes.

IN DREAMS AND ASYLUMS

DONALD A. HALL

In dreams and asylums there is no arithmetic.
Unreasoned progression belongs to the child, whose clocks
Gossip on mantles, appear without faces in sleep;
Whose three o'clock is the forest of the sun,
Where corridors of musk lead down the earth
To a minimum kingdom of purple. Arithmetic
Belongs to the child from the fives that make the clock,
The stone that shattered Ruthie's window broke
The sun and numbers. Progression lost the garden
Where I remember
Arithmetic as cold and hard as the sun.

EDITORIAL • • • • •

All things are poss'ble

THE Episcopalians hold square dances. The Unitarians give lectures on Russia. In his small crowded room Father Feeney raises a trembling fist at the low ceiling to denounce earthly learning. And in the Christmas holidays, while Cliff Barrows, Billy Graham's song leader, played *When the Roll Is Called Up Yonder* on a slide trombone from the high porch of the Park Street Church, a sailor and two girls below him rode up and down Tremont Street in a beachwagon announcing through a loudspeaker the arrival of the Holy Spirit every night for a week at Mechanics Building. The Lord is served in many ways.

In the Park Street Church a portly gentleman, somewhat like Mr. Wardle, approached us with a benevolent smile and said, "Brother, did you get right with the Lord tonight?" We evaded a reply and asked where Billy Graham was, and following the portly gentleman's directions we walked up to the Bellevue Hotel. A girl from the *Traveler* had an appointment ahead of us. She came down the stairs with her eyes shining and said wistfully, "He's wonderful." There was a meeting of the Ladies' Auxiliary that afternoon, and every so often small aged women crossed the lobby, their backs bent over with weariness.

Billy Graham was in his room with Cliff Barrows and Grady Wilson, the Associate Evangelist. There are only the three of them. Billy Graham is six feet tall, with wavy blonde hair, a fine straight nose, and a white handkerchief in both breast pockets of his sports jacket. They all wore cuff links, argyle socks, and ties almost as bright as the Heavenly City; they speak with that soft Southern swing. Grady Wilson, who is short and round, sat on the bed, and the other two sat on hotel chairs beside a couple of suitcases.

Billy Graham, who is married and has two children, was born in Charlotte, North Carolina, and reared on a dairy farm—"Grady and I were reared together." After graduating from Wheaton College in Illinois he played semi-professional baseball until he was converted. "An evangelist came and he preached the Bible. Preaching the Bible strikes home to a fellow. I mean to say I'm sick of hearing preachers talking about psychology or anthropology or giving book reviews." In the empty hotel room he said happily, "He showed me I was a sinner and I found tremendous joy."

When the three of them come to town they come under the auspices of the local evangelical churches, and when they leave, the converted, or reconverted, return to their own churches—"spiritual re-awakenin'" he said in his calm Southern voice. They have done very well in Boston; on New Year's Eve they turned away seven thousand people from Mechanics Building.

That night Mechanics Building was filled, which meant there were five thousand people. Outside an old man was selling toys called Crawling Babies. On the stage were a choir from Gordon Divinity School and about fifty Boston ministers, some of them in clerical collars. A stout woman in a bulging black dress played the piano and a small man who looked like a clerk in a hardware store played an organ. The audience seemed to be of all kinds—some servicemen, and here and there an entire family.

To open proceedings Cliff Barrows led a chorus of *Love Lifted Me,* and by the end it gathered a noble volume of noise. An elderly woman beamed on us with a saintly smile. A minister pronounced a prayer and called for those who had secret wishes to raise their hands; behind Billy Graham the other ministers sat together on the platform like wrinkled grasshoppers, as if they had seen the enthusiastic young come and go—like the old men who watched Helen on the wall of Troy, crossing and uncrossing their stiff legs and surveying the crowd with practised eyes.

There was another song, *Only Believe, All Things Are Poss'ble.* The minister read a telegram from the President of Wheaton College, Illinois: REJOICE WITH YOU OVER REPORT OF BOSTON REVIVAL. Billy Graham stood waiting behind him, clasping his hands and rising nervously on his toes. The minister thanked the management of Mechanics Building and said, "We also thank God for how He's opened this building to us for a whole week." He introduced the collection with a prayer which ended, "Praise God. Our expenses are heavy," and Billy Graham, young and glorious, advanced like the Red Cross Knight with a microphone on his lapel and fire in his eye, loosening his tie like Mr. Louis Hartz.

He began with sins against the Holy Spirit, stooping to face the front row and standing erect to raise his hands to heaven. "We're sinners. What the old Devil wants to do is keep you ignorant of the Holy Spirit. You say you're doing the best you can: you're a sinner. You say you're doing good works: I tell you you're a sinner. You say you're working your fingernails off, climbing up to heaven like climbing up a rope, hand over hand, working your fingernails off: you're a sinner. Fourteen years ago I was converted. Fourteen years ago I took off these old smelly garments." The audience murmured assent. "At Los Angeles," he said, "Stewart Hayden, the movie star, walked out of the meeting mad. Cliff or Grady or somebody came and told me and I said PRAISE THE LORD because if he's walking out mad pretty soon he'll be walking back saved." He hit his chest and said, "In my heart there's power, atomic power, the power of the Holy Spirit." The lapel microphone began to squeak; in the sudden silence he said, "I been walkin' around too much," and smiled.

At the press table there was a photographer with a red face and a preoccupied air whom we had seen before at the Longwood Cricket Club. Something appeared to be disturbing him; at length it came to the surface and he whispered to his associate, "What's the caption for the choir shot?" "Young people from local schools and colleges," his compatriot said. "Ah," said the photographer, light breaking over his face; he shut his camera and departed as Billy Graham was saying, "I remember Shorty, who worked in our drugstore. Shorty laughed and scoffed at the Lord but the Lord wanted to save him so one Saturday He caused his baby to die of pneumonia. But Shorty's heart was hardened and he swore in the face of the Lord. Hundreds were praying for Shorty. Next Saturday his wife died. But Shorty's heart was hardened and he cursed the Lord. On Tuesday when he was shaving he felt the pain in his side, and he died."

The organ began a soft background and Billy Graham leaned forward on the lectern and said gently, "Who wants to be sure? Who wants to be sure of Heaven?" One by one the people came to the front of the auditorium until there were about two hundred beneath him. Grady Wilson met them and quietly shook their hands. The elderly woman looked on with an even saintlier smile. In the beautiful lilt Billy Graham said, "God is watching. He's knockin' at the door. Let Him in. Let Him in. If the Lord can do it in Los Angeles, He can do it here."

To Americans, more than to anyone else, all things are poss'ble. In our young and confident country the Messiah is six feet tall and Job is an unregenerate Shorty, scoffing at the Lord as his family fall dead around him. The others are the old and weary—the Ladies' Auxiliary, and the ministers at Mechanics Building, and Father Feeney. There is something rather dark and awful and medieval about that small aged figure in a black cassock whispering and shouting of damnation under the low ceiling: every Thursday night at St. Benedict's Center there was a great reckoning in a little room. The Lord's house has many mansions, and one of them is dark, crowded, and desperate; in a younger and happier room Billy Graham presents the Holy Spirit through a loudspeaker, clothed in glory—argyle socks and a white handkerchief in both breast pockets.

LETTER FROM A WEDDING TRIP

ROBERT E. BLY

Travelling south, leaves overflow the farms.
Day by day we watched the leaves increase
And the trees lie tangled in each other's arms.
Still generation, and calls that never cease
And rustlings in the brush; yesterday
She asked how long we have been on the way.
So in the afternoon we changed our route
And came down to the coast; everywhere
The same: fish, and the lobster's sensual eyes.
The natives sang for harvest, gave us fruit,
At night the monkeys sat beneath the trees.
All night the cries of dancers filled the air
And last year's virgins pressed into the leaves.
Sometimes I think of your land, cold and fresh,
And try to think: what was the month we quit
Our northern land that seemed inhabited
By more than reproduction of the flesh?
I wonder, watching how the branches interknit
If monkeys gibbered by our bridal bed.

THE PRISONERS

ADRIENNE RICH

Enclosed in this disturbing mutual wood,
Wounded alike by thorns of the same tree,
We seek in hopeless war each others' blood
Though suffering in one identity.
Each to the other prey and huntsman known,
Still driven together, lonelier than alone

Strange mating of the loser and the lost!
With faces stiff as mourners, we intrude
Forever on the one we turn from most,
Each wandering in a double solitude.
The unpurged ghosts of passion bound to pride,
Who wake in isolation, side by side.

THE HOUSE AT THE CASCADES
ADRIENNE RICH

All changed now through neglect. The steps dismantled
By infantries of ants, by roots and storms,
The pillars tugged by vines, the porte-cochere
A passageway for winds, the solemn porches
Warped into caricatures.
                              We came at evening
After the rain, when every drunken leaf
Was straining, swelling in a riot of green.
Only the house was dying in all that life,
As if a triumph of emerald energy
Had fixed its mouth upon the walls and stones.
The tamest shrub remembered anarchy
And joined in appetite with the demagogue weed
That springs where order falls; together there
They stormed the defenseless handiwork of man
Whose empire wars against him when he turns
A moment from the yoke. So, turning back,
He sees his rooftree fall to furious green,
His yard despoiled, and out of innocent noon
The insect-cloud like thunder on the land.

NIGHT
ADRIENNE RICH

The motes that still disturbed her lidded calm
Were these: the tick and whisper of a shade
Against the sill; a cobweb-film that hung
Aslant a corner moulding, too elusive
For any but the gaze of straitened eyes;
The nimbus of the night-lamp, where a moth
Uneasily explored the edge of light
Through hours of fractured darkness. She alone
Knew that the room contained these things; she lay
Hearing the almost imperceptible sound
(As if a live thing shivered behind the curtains)
Watching the thread that frayed in gusts of air
More delicate than her breathing, or by night
Sharing a moth's perplexity at light
Too frail to drive out dark: minutiae
Held in the vise of sense about to die.

THE DRUMMER

Baraban! baraban! this is a quick
stiletto bounced tight in tin casket!
The devil you say! Wicked the way
my aunt had to tell me after uncle
rolled over and over inside the locomotive
bellowing like a walrus's guffaw!

Baraban! Tighten till it pricks through
keen as a blond feather, the saint!
the rib-tickler! oh! oh! the dromedary
sharp-tooth, swaying its all-muscle belly,
has all the luck. What a whale! it careens
over the tracks, dropping bison cakes.
That's the way it was on the prairies,
with a baraban! every two minutes and
the red men knocking us off like turkeys.

Oh uncle, you died in a roadster coupe
fighting the Pawnees and Banshees, you did,
and I'll drum you over the hill, bumpily,
my drum strongly galumphing, kangaroos
on all sides yelping baraban! for you.

TWO POEMS

by

FRANK O'HARA

POEM

The eager note on my door said, "Call me,
call when you get in!" so I quickly threw
a few tangerines into my overnight bag,
straightened my eyelids and shoulders, and

headed straight for the door. It was autumn
by the time I got around the corner, oh all
unwilling to be either pertinent or bemused, but
the leaves were brighter than grass on the sidewalk!

Funny, I thought, that the lights are on this late
and the hall door open; still up at this hour, a
champion jai-alai player like himself? Oh fie!
for shame! What a host, so zealous! And he was

there in the hall, flat on a sheet of blood that
ran down the stairs. I did appreciate it. There are few
hosts who so thoroughly prepare to greet a guest
only casually invited, and that several months ago.

FAULKNER'S VISION OF HUMAN INTEGRITY

To Hannah and Heinrich Blucher   ALFRED KAZIN

Speaking at Stockholm last December, Mr. Faulkner said, in part: "Our tragedy today is a general and universal physical fear so long sustained by now that we can even bear it. There are no longer problems of the spirit. There is only the question: When will I be blown up? Because of this, the young man or woman writing today has forgotten the problems of the human heart in conflict with itself which alone can make good writing, because only that is worth writing about, worth the agony and the sweat . . .

"He must learn them again. He must teach himself that the basest of all things is to be afraid; and teaching himself that, forget it forever, leaving no room in his workshop for anything but the old verities and truths of the heart, the old universal truths lacking which any story is ephemeral and doomed —love and honor and pity and pride and compassion and sacrifice . . .

"Until he relearns these things, he will write as though he stood among and watched the end of man. I decline to accept the end of man. It is easy enough to say that man is immortal simply because he will endure: that when the last dingdong of doom has clanged and faded from the last worthless rock hanging tideless in the last red and dying evening, that even then there will still be one more sound: that of his puny inexhaustible voice, still talking. I refuse to accept this. I believe that man will not merely endure: he will prevail. He is immortal, not because he alone among creatures has an inexhaustible voice but because he has a soul, a spirit capable of compassion and sacrifice and endurance. The poet's, the writer's, duty is to write about these things."

We in America do not often hear such talk from our novelists—and perhaps we expect it least from a realistic novelist whose work is still identified with the sadistically meticulous account of Southern "decadence" we so often get from the fashionable new novelists. Even Faulkner's larger reputation in Europe, at least in the form in which it comes back to us, shows that if that hydra-headed monster, the twentieth - century American novelist—he whose name is simply Faulkner - Hemingway - Caldwell - Steinbeck—is still thought of as the last word in brutality and savage materialism, it is predominently Faulkner who so personifies him to the outside world.

But the thrill of pleasure I felt on reading Faulkner's Nobel Prize speech was based not only on my gratitude that such words should be spoken today at all—and how badly our frightened intellectuals need to hear them—but also on a sense of recognition. *What* Faulkner said at Stockholm is in its explicit adjunction unusual for him and even untypical. I would not have said that it is to lift our hearts that he writes. But that voice, that unashamedly eloquent voice in all its true terseness, reminding us by the very rush and edge of his sentences that all human affairs are settled first within the heart, returning back and back to those large words like love and honor and pity and pride by which, after all, we do try to live; pointing to the fear-racked man of our age in all his secret daily aloneness—it is precisely that voice, passionate and steady, that seems to hold his novels together in their fierceness, line by line. Even the most perfunctory reading of a page should intimate to us the nature of the mind we are dealing with, warn

us that he is different in kind rather than in degree from our other novelists today.

Yet it is remarkable how many people seem able to read Faulkner through, even to analyze his work on its secondary levels with the greatest shrewdness, without finding any very constructive purpose to his style. For what is the usual objection to that style? Why, that is *needlessly* involved, that it is perversely thick with parentheses, even with parentheses within parentheses; that it is a pity a man who can tell a story so well should get so heated in the telling and be so long-winded. I have just read an article in the latest number of *Partisan Review* that states his art is wholly uneven, hopelessly lost between two styles—"one is simple and full of references to nature; there is nothing to equal it in American writing today . . . In his other style, which dominates his writing, Faulkner constructs his legend of the South. It is here that all his famous traits are found: the rhetoric, the difficult, involved sentences, gratuitous and exaggerated, the tangle of meanings and motive." "So little is left of the touching simplicity and openness," Isaac Rosenfeld goes on, "it is hard to believe that the same man writes in both styles." Your thoroughly sensible man, like Bernard DeVoto, thinks he is a talented man who unfortunately tends to get lost in floods of excess sensibility; your humanist liberal, like Lionel Trilling, that he rants; I have recently heard a Marxist critic suggest that he is simply a floridly uncontrolled reactionary brooding over the decline of his class. Even one of his most sympathetic critics, Malcolm Cowley, thinks that the defects of his style can be attributed to the traditional isolation of the American writer. "His novels," Cowley says in the introduction to his brilliantly arranged Portable Faulkner, "are the books of a man who broods about literature but doesn't often discuss it with his friends; there is no ease about them, no feeling that they come from a background of taste refined by argument and of opinions held in common

. . . Like Hawthorne, Faulkner is a solitary worker by choice, and he has done great things with double the pains to himself that they might have cost if they had been produced in more genial circumstances . . . All of them are full of overblown words that he would have used with more discretion, or not at all, if he had followed Hemingway's example and served an apprenticeship to an older writer."

Now these objections—and I have contributed to them myself—spring in part from a certain false professionalism in our attitude toward style. One might call it the Hemingway influence. Hemingway's own early style, and his—a whole generation's—particular craving for simplicity and naturalness, are something else again. The Hemingway influence has now become an article of commerce. The dregs of that influence can be seen not merely in the shallow and smug language of a slick news-weekly like *Time*, but even more in the method of production that puts the magazine together on the belief that anything can be rewritten, and apparently by anyone. I have often detected in the language of editors and critics the unconscious belief that all writers have the same needs, and that all write to the same audience. They favor that "clear," because convenient, style through which one can see immediately to the bottom of any subject—and indeed, to judge from Hemmingway's recent work, the bottom is very quickly reached. I call it a falsely professional attitude—Richard Chase complains in a recent book on Melville that even he was too little the continuously professional writer! — because it stems from that morbid over-consciousness of the audience that afflicts even the most serious writers in this country. We have become so intent on getting the audience to understand quickly, rather than on encouraging the writer to have his full say, that we brutally dispose of the individual differences between writers.

Now Faulkner, as is well known, is less conscious of his audience than most novelists today. He has even written in a letter to Cowley: "I think I have written a lot and sent it off to print before I actually

realized strangers might read it." Many objections to his style, I am convinced, stem from our disbelief that a writer in America *can* write without thinking of the "strangers" who might read him; that he will not sacrifice an iota of his realization to "communication" at any price. But the primary reason for our objections to Faulkner's style is our refusal to believe that what he writes about is entirely real even to him. Most of his critics show a genuine indifference to his point of view.

By point of view I mean not a writer's social opinions, which he may and usually does share with many people, especially if he is a Southerner; not those psychological interpretations by which we now so easily interpret and think we entirely reveal someone's character; not even his moral philosophy, whether on its most realistic or exalted level. I mean the angle of vision from which one recurringly sees the universe—that native disposition of mind which plants in us very early those particular words, those haunted stresses and inflections, those mysteriously echolaic repetitions, to which we most instinctively return—and which at our best we accept with joy, and sometimes even understand.

It is his point of view, his personal convictions of the shape life has, that presents any writer with that resurgent theme from which he chooses the subject of his art and even many of its devices. For a real artist never simply borrows a technique even when he may seem to, but uses it as if no one had used it before him. It is by his point of view, surely, that we *know* Dostoevsky is more than the sum of his reactionary social opinions; Proust more, even, than *his* sensibility; Melville more than his pessimistic abasement before the magnitude of the divine. It is a writer's point of view that gives us our immediate experience of his mind in all its rich particularity. It is *in* his point of view though not necessarily for his point of view, that we read him.

Yet it is amazing how many people disregard what is most im-

mediately present to their minds when they read a page of Faulkner. It is very hard for me to believe that the often tumultuous and deeply spiritual experience we have in reading something like "The Bear" adds only to another "parable of the Deep South," or the fact that he is really — the holy simplicity of literary historians! — a "romantic." (The word today apparently signifies that one romantic is just like another.) I do not think Faulkner would have been any different if he had gone to school to Ezra Pound, had learned to trim his style, to be more sparing of those "overblown" words. I think he needs those words. Hemingway may not; Faulkner does. I would suggest that he means something by them essential to his stubbornly individual vision of the world. I would guess they have been in his mind a very long time, that it was almost to see them live a life separate from his own that he began to write, that it is to rediscover their meanings through and through the whole range of his adult life that he continues to write.

For what are those words to which Faulkner constantly returns? Cowley cites "*immemorial, imponderable, immutable.*" But the more active words, actually, are *astonishment, outrage, furious, intractable, implacable, inflexible, impervious, amazed, outlast, endure, repudiate, rage, sourceless*—and less and less in the recent works, but always present, for they awoke the image of the soaring arch and of the ecstacy in retracing its height that are both so essential to his mind—*upsoar, avatar, apotheosis.* And significantly, most of these words are applied to individuals of every type and in every class—not only to his intellectuals or visionaries, like Quentin Compson, Horace Benbow, the Reverend Gail Hightower, or his tiresomely sage spokesman, Gavin Stevens; but to a Snopes as well as a Major DeSpain; to the farmers in the field and sitting Saturday afternoons in their "clean well patched overalls" around Varner's store; to the old hunter Ike McCaslin; to a criminal like Pop-

eye; to some children and most boys; to the hunted Negro in "Red Leaves" trying to escape being buried alive with his dead Indian master; to the Negro slaves and to their silently wise descendants still doing the dirty work in the kitchens after the war is over. They are used with particular force about the unscrupulous Jason Compson in *The Sound and the Fury* and the hunted and murdering Joe Christmas in *Light in August;* they are applied to houses, hills, roads, dogs, the dark and mighty figure of the bear in Faulkner's great story of that name; about doors, and at least once, by implication, about God.

These words are not merely interjections, or—as they might often seem—assertions trailing off the loose ends of his narrative. They are the very ground bass, to borrow a figure from music, above which he sets his narrative theme; in and out of which his story is composed. They are the atmosphere in which Faulkner's characters move—even God Himself in the middle section of "The Bear," that God so struck with the outrage and the horror of man's blind exploitation of the land that he was prepared to repudiate him altogether until John Brown, who was fully a man, and so astonished even Him, stayed His hand. All of them, Negro or White, Southern or Northern, old settlers or new exploiters, feel this outrage, this astonishment, this fury. It is the living state—not merely of ourselves caught for a moment above the motion of life, but of everything within our ken and which we color with the violence of our state—astonished and furious and outraged, outraged freshly over again every day and every hour, yet still trying to be impervious, to believe ourselves implacable, and by claiming our own intactness, showing that we seek to endure. And it is a state that is known to his characters and about each other not in moments of contemplation only—for that would arrest the momentum—but, like the constant echo of the ground bass that we can still hear in Bach even when it is not, immediately in use—as that particular knowledge to which they must all return.

Now it is with this word *return* that I can perhaps at last get at what is so distinctive in Faulkner's vision —the fact that, more often than not, his characers view things without surprise. It is not the happening that makes a story of Faulkner's move; it is the confirmation. Everything seems to have been known beforehand. The event itself seems to be assimilated first in brooding expectancy; then to occur as a confirmation; then requickens the familiar outrage and astonishment that it should happen at all. So that when the event does occur as expected, and the usual baleful grim glance is thrown over it, it seems to have been not so much lived as relived. Thus one feels—particularly about his most thoroughly realized characters, like Jason Compson and Joe Christmas—that their suffering and their thinking incorporate the very momentum of life. It is as if *their lives were thinking for them*. All through the greater part of *Light in August* one seems to see Joe Christmas running, constantly running ahead on the public highway, yet with his face turned to us, amazed that everything he has expected so long *should* finally be happening to him—even as he runs. All through the great monologue of Jason Compson in *The Sound and the Fury* one sees him rushing about the streets, or hunting his niece from his automobile, yet investing each terrible moment with this greater frightfulness—the fact that his whole life is present in his ordeal, and that he should have expected life to come to a crisis just so, for he has really spent his life thinking it over.

I believe it is this expectancy, this forehand knowledge they bear about with them through each moment of their lives, that gives Faulkner's people that peculiar tension of watching and listening under which he sometimes seems to stagger from page to page of his novels like a man lifting a heavy plaster cast. Surely there is no other living novelist who has lavished so much attention on the human face in its inflexible watchful concentration, who has pinned down so much of the simultaneous impact of human

events upon the eye. Each character seems to bear the whole weight of his actual and potential knowledge on his face — yet to doubt that knowledge, not out of any genuine disbelief, but out of astonishment and outrage that he must bear it. And along with it, that fiery screen of background detail, of historical causality as it pertains to his own life and the tradition-racked consciousness of the South, that enters into his mind like those background details of a dream that we take in without always knowing that we do.

In short, Faulkner burdens his characters with the integral human state; he will not let them off. This is the undergrowth of every day— sometimes unbearable in its keenness and recoil—which Joe Christmas must trample through even as he runs. This is that inflamed sense of one's whole life entirely present before one that is the real agony of Jason Compson all that terrible day, "April 6, 1928,"—and that makes him, though infinitely repellent, so giant a paradigm of man clutching at the air of this world as, assailed by every conceivable pain and anxiety, he searches for the niece who has stolen the money he had originally stolen from *her*. In *Intruder In The Dust* Faulkner calls it "that naked agony of inasthetisable nerve-ends which for lack of a better word men call being alive." In "Beyond," that beautiful little story of the responsibilities we still bear dreaming of our death, the Judge describes it as that "certain integral consistency which, whether it be right or wrong, a man must cherish because it alone will ever permit him to die."

It is this "consistency" as the very foundation of awareness, which rejoices in awareness as its most joyful and healthy end, that I see in Faulkner's conception of human integrity. It is this consistency that gives him his inner freedom as a storyteller, and as a stylist, that fierceness and openness of tone beside which the voices of our Hemingways and Fitzgeralds sound peevish.

Now obviously this integrity is not what we usually mean by the word today — that which Stuart Chase once so significantly described

as a "luxury." As one hears the word nowadays, integrity seems to represent something we should like to have, that we know—if only for our health's sake!—that we need to have, but, nevertheless, is always the paradise lost in the conflicting allegiances of our middle-class existence. And in fact, by our imperative, but still in one sense unworthy, calculations whether we dare to say this thing, to write this article, to defy that boss; by our wearing and wistful questioning of the "integrity" of our simplest relationships, the most casual things we do, we have come to feel that the tidal waves of prosperous unhappiness constantly sweeping over modern American life may represent chiefly a bad conscience. Faulkner starts beyond this point; I do not suppose he has ever written a line simply to please a magazine editor or to impress his audience. At one time, as I have noted, he didn't even know he had one. If he has a bad conscience, it is the bad conscience of the sensitive Southerner who bears in his heart the whole history of the culture he loves, and that culture Faulkner has examined over and over with paramount good faith and that necessary love for one's own people, simply because one is *of* them, without which our judgments of other people are arbitrary and usually destructive. For him integrity represents not that hoped-for state of "integration" which enables us to "function," but that which alone enables us to grasp our existence.

Ironically enough, those critics who insist on reading Faulkner exclusively as an historian of the South, "another Balzac," find it easier to think of him as a profound social thinker than to face up to his philosophical emphasis. Yet if you study carefully something so fundamental to his thoughts as the long dialogue on slavery and the land which composes the middle section of "The Bear," you find that the obscurities of his work stem not from any particular profoundity or complexity of ideas, but from the fact that his mind is so astonishingly energetic, his sensibility so vividly aroused by all the issues present to his mind, that he is always leaping from one to the other in excited discovery. Faulkner writes like a man thinking aloud. And quite often, indeed, like a man who has suddenly fallen into a hypnotic trance of thinking about any issue that may present itself to him in the midst of a story. Nor, despite the quiet boldness of his thinking about the South and slavery, is he particularly free—how could he be? —of the tangle of motives, self-defensive rights and wrongs, that we usually detect in Southerners reviewing the history of slavery. For every positive acceptance of its great wrong and guilt—and no other Southern novelist has gripped the subject so frankly—he will go out of his way to plead the despotic kindness of the old slaveholders. There is a particularly amusing example of this in the middle section of "The Bear," where the extraordinary crescendo of argument leading up to the imminent revelation of God's curse upon the land suddenly falls away into a crooning lullaby of the kindness the women showed the slaves when they were ill—and then is capped by the admission that these same services were performed for cattle, but not by those lower-class people, ancestors of the Snopeses, no doubt, who had to hire their horses from a livery stable! Faulkner is a Southerner; and very much a man of his class. But let us not forget that for him the guilt of slavery is tempered by the realization that the exploiter, too, is a man; that no more than the slave can he be dismissed from the other end of the relationship. Yet it is not entirely fair to him, it conventionalizes him, to assume that he sees all these things simply under the general and individual rubric of human guilt. Faulkner does not give the impression that so many Southern poets and critics do—that their highest aim as *writers* is to become good Christians again. He seems more intent on understanding the human situation than on being saved.

But here I am wandering away from my subject, for it was my intention a while back, by stressing the number of things present to his mind at once, to evoke his specific quality as an artist. It is what I have already noted as his momentum. Faulkner's imagination seems to be characterized by a velocity of memory that one finds only in writers of genius—by the ability to sustain details in so long and dynamic a single period that they finally compose a single order of progression. A characteristic example of this can be found early in *Intruder In The Dust*. It is worth quoting here not because this novel, or even the passage itself, is among his best—indeed, I would say that since *The Sound And The Fury* and *Light In August*, written about the same age that Melville was when he wrote *Moby Dick*, Faulkner has nothing so good, and lately seems suspiciously as mellow as Melville became at too early an age — but because it shows to what extent Faulkner's momentum will assert itself in a novel interpreted by our best critics as a Southerner's conventional case against President Truman's Civil Rights Bill.

It is the scene in which the boy Charles Mallison is taken, after he has fallen through the ice while hunting, to the house of the Negro Lucas Beauchamp. He knows, of course, that the man is a descendant of the old planter Carothers McCaslin, and like everyone else in town is constantly irritated by the Negro's pride, his air always "intractable and composed," his refusal of the customary servility. And now, as he trails sheepishly behind, he is more than ever aware of this elderly Negro who with calm dignity insists on taking him into his house and who humiliatingly reminds him that, like his own grandfather, "the man striding ahead was simply incapable of conceiving himself by a child contradicted and defied."

"So he didn't even check when they passed the gate, he didn't even look at it and they were in no well-used tended lane leading to tenant or servant quarters and marked by walking feet but a savage gash half gully and half road mounting a hill with an air solitary independent and intractable and then he saw the house, the cabin and remembered the rest of the story, the legend: how Edmonds' father had deeded to his Negro first cousin and his heirs in perpetuity the house and the ten acres of land it sat in—an oblong of earth set forever in the middle of the two-thousand-acre plantation like a postage stamp in the center of an envelope — the paintless wooden house, the paintless picket fence whose paintless latchless gate the man kneed open still without stopping or once looking back, and he following and Aleck Sander and Edmonds' boy following him, strode on into the yard. It would have been grassless even in summer; he could imagine it, completely bare, no weed no spring of anything, the dust each morning swept by some of Lucas' womenfolks with a broom made of willow switches bound together, into an intricate series of whorls and overlapping loops which as the day advanced would be gradually and slowly defaced by the droppings and the cryptic three-toed prints of chickens like (remembering it now at sixteen) a terrain in miniature out of the age of the great lizards, the four of them walking in what was less than walk because its surface was dirt too yet more than path, the footpacked strip running plumbline straight between two borders of tin cans and empty bottles and shards of china and earthenware set into the ground, up to the paintless steps and the paintless gallery along whose edge sat more cans but larger — empty gallon buckets which had once contained molasses or perhaps paint and wornout water or milk pails and one five-gallon can for kerosene with its top cut off and half of what had once been somebody (Edmonds' without doubt) kitchen hot water tank sliced longways like a banana —out of which flowers had grown last summer, and from which the dead stalks and the dried and brittle tendrils still leaned or drooped, and beyond this the house itself, gray and weathered and not so much paintless as independent of and intractable to paint so that the house was not only the one possible continuation of the stern untended road but was its crown too as the carven ailanthus leaves are the Greek column's capital.

"Nor did the man pause yet, up the steps and across the gallery and opened the door and entered and he and then Edmonds' boy and Aleck Sander followed: a hall dim even almost dark after the bright outdoors and already he could smell that smell which he had accepted without question all his life as being the smell always of the places where people with any trace of Negro blood live as he had that all people named Mallison are Methodists, then a bedroom: a bare worn quite clean paintless rugless floor, in one corner and spread with a bright patchwork quilt a vast shadowy tester bed which had probably come out of old Carothers McCaslin's house, and a battered cheap Grand Rapids dresser and then for the moment no more or at least little more; only later would he notice—or remember that he had seen — the cluttered mantel on which sat a kerosene lamp handpainted with flowers and a vase filled with spills of twisted newspaper and above the mantel the colored lithograph of a three-year old calendar in which Pocahontas in the quilled fringed buckskins of a Sioux or Chippewa chief stood against a balustrade of Italian marble above a garden of formal cypresses and shadowy in the corner opposite the bed a chromo portrait of two people framed heavily in gold-painted wood on a gold-painted easel. But he hadn't seen that at all yet because that was behind him and all he now saw was the fire — the clay-daubed field-stone chimney in which a half burned backlog glowed and smoldered in the gray ashes and beside it in a rocking chair something which he thought was a child until he saw the face, and then he did pause long enough to look at her because he was about to remember something else his uncle had told him about or at least in regard to Lucas Beauchamp, and looking at her he realized for the first time how old the man actually was, must be — a tiny old almost doll-sized woman much darker than the man, in a shawl and an apron, the head bound in an immaculate white cloth on top of which sat a painted straw hat bearing some kind of ornament."

I shall not dwell here on the remarkable inwoven textures of this passage, or — what for technical reasons is perhaps most interesting to any writer of prose — on the peculiarly impelled rightness of those words which by their ecstatic repetition hold and propel the phrases so that Faulkner can release the whole scene already present to his mind. But I should like to complete my argument by defining the necessity behind the passage. For what I see and hear in the soar and thud of these details is an effort to present — not merely *to* the consciousness of a single mind but *along* the whole circuit of time and thought through which we move—that which *is* our life in all its presentness. We suddenly feel in some momentary shock to our physical being that we are being played on by history, but the forces of our own character, by that tangle of rights and wrongs, of present injustice and perhaps ultimate injustice, too, that asserts itself in every human situation. And it is only such an awareness, such a willingness to live the situation through and through with everything we are, so full an acceptance of the presentness of our lives *as finally real*, that mollifies some of the ache of being alive, the old split between our being and our knowing. For this is who we are when all entirely present *here*—"this living entity at this point at this day."

Faulkner's insistence on embracing all actuality in the moment is more than a novelist's innovation or technique. It goes far beyond the stream-of-consciousness method, with its emphasis on the underground level of man's knowing — a method that always shows man as half-asleep, and just becoming aware how much he lies to himself. It is an attempt to realize continuity with all our genesis, our "progenitors"—another of Faulkner's favorite words—with all we have touched, known, loved. *This* is why he needs those long successive parentheses, and parentheses within parentheses. They exemplify the chain of human succession. The greatest horror his characters know is to feel they have been dropped out of this stream of being, to think of themselves as "self-progenitive" or "sourceless." But no matter how many parentheses he may use, he knows how to leave them behind him, to come out flush to the end of a sentence with a fresh, stabbing, often humorously concrete thought. We may live in our tradition, be haunted by it as Southerners are: but we are not our tradition; we are individual and alive.

With Faulkner it would seem as if the theme of the journey which is so elemental in American literature, always present to our minds because of our very history as a people, has here been contracted to display the real journey each human being makes through time—minute by minute of the universe with which we are filled. And so thoroughly is the moment lived and relived that only when it is over can we look back and see how rich our lives are. Here is one main source of Faulkner's humor, which is so often the wild grin he throws over a situation after it has been lived; it is his own amused astonishment at how much a human being can take in, how long a road he travels through in his own mind. And here, too, we approach that ultimate word which means so much to him—endurance. This endurance, or "outlasting," is not the mark simply of his favorite Negroes, like Dilsey in *The Sound And The Fury*. The Negroes are its greatest *social* example. For the Negroes, like the Jews, have the curious bitter advantage—and how often they have wished they could lose it—of having suffered an historic injustice so long that the noblest individuals among them can finally take in the whole of their situation precisely because they know it is the *human* situation, and so in some sense cannot be remedied. What endurance seems to mean to Faulkner is that if one sees one's whole life in time, only then can we realize our secret courage, our will to have endured; and only so relinquish our life to others. Only through integrity can we feel that our existence has fully been done justice to—for we have *lived* it — in all its outrageousness and astonishment.

One word more. It is often said that Faulkner owes his place in American literature to the fact that he has been fortunate in his background, which is so filled with "tradition and drama"—or perhaps simply to the fact that he has had the remarkable patience, or unusual good sense, to stay with his subject. It is implied that other writers, had they not been so rootless, had they not been open to the usual temptations, might have done as well.

And perhaps it is true that any writer — say Sinclair Lewis or Thomas Wolfe — might, if only he had stayed in his Minnesota or his North Carolina, have been able to work *his* way through and through the region he knows best, to write finally not only of what men do, but of what they mean.

But I wonder if there is not another way of putting it. Perhaps it is only the writer who knows that men are not the same everywhere, who believes that each human being is original and has a soul—perhaps it is only such a writer who will stick to his birthplace as if the whole of life were as much there as anywhere.

1912-1952: FULL CYCLE

PETER VIERECK

I. LOVE SONG OF PRUFROCK JUNIOR

Must all successful rebels grow
From toreador to Sacred Cow?
What cults he slew, his cult begot.
"In my beginning," said the Scot,
"My end;" and aging eagles know
That 1912 was long ago.
Today the women come and go
Talking of T. S. Eliot.

*Events of 1912, the key year: *New Age* starts publishing Hulme's essays; Imagist nucleus founded (Pound, H. D., Aldington); *Poetry: A Magazine Of Verse* founded by Harriet Monroe (to whom Pound in 1914 sends Eliot's "Love Song of J. Alfred Prufrock," written 1910-11); October 1912, the American-verse number of Harold Monro's *Poetry Review* (W. C. Williams, Pound); symbolic clash of the simultaneous 1912 publication of *Georgian Poetry* and Pound's *Ripostes.*

II. INSCRIBED FOR YOUR BEDSIDE
"GLOSSARY OF THE NEW CRITICISM"

Here's the eighth form of ambiguity:
The *new* philistia loves "obscurity," —
And only we still dare to hate it
Because a *texte* without a Muse in
Is but a snore and an allusion.
Well then, let's turn the tables hard:
The snobs all snubbed, the baiters baited,
The explicators explicated,
And avant-garde the new rearguard.

III. FROM THE SUBLIME TO THE METICULOUS
IN FOUR STAGES

DANTE: We were God's poets.

BURNS: We were the people's poets.

MALLARME: We were poet's poets.

TODAY (preening himself): Ah, but *we* are critic's poets.

IV. EPITAPH FOR THE NOUVEAUX NEW CRITICS

Cliché is dead, long live cliché,
And in old fields new Georgians play.
O miglior fabbro and O mandarin,
You who skinned Georgians like a tangerine,
Two Hercules who on your natal day
Strangled these snakes of cliché-pandering,
These same that now through backstairs wander in:
Let not (while death-knells from Kinkanja (¹) ring)
The pedant town of Alexander in.
From kitsch the nineteenth century banned her in,
You freed our Muse. For what? Was Queen Victoria
Primmer than précieux new "Prohibitoria" (²) ?
Loving your ART and not your fleas, we pray:

May time protect you from your protégés.
Time's up when pupils' pupils school the school.
Cow? Bad enough! But sacred — calf?
Now that the cup of insolence is full, —
By God, who'll start a brand new Nineteen Twelve?

This poem about Alexandrianism in verse, written in 1952 and copyrighted by the author, also appears in Peter Viereck's book THE FIRST MORNING, Greenwood Press, Westport, Conn., 1972.

CREOLE LOVE SONG

NATHANIAL LA MAR

I USED to work for the LaBotte family. That's how I know what I'm going to tell you about Jemmie La-Botte. They lived up on Bayou Street in one of those big pink stucco houses with a wide tile porch and tall windows with fancy, yellow frosty-looking window panes.

Old man LaBotte was a doctor. He was queer in a way. I used to hear some of the white people around town say he was nothing but a "ham-fat" doctor. I never could quite get the straight of it. I do know one thing, though. He didn't go around like the other white doctors in New Orleans did. I mean he never went around to high faluting people like the kind of fine ladies his wife was always playing bridge with. As far as I know he didn't treat anybody but the Creoles down in the Quarter. Some people said it was because Dr. LaBotte was a Creole himself. They said that about Mrs. LaBotte too; but I didn't believe it. He used to come down to the Quarter whenever somebody got hurt on their job or beat up in a fight. He had a smart way about him; he could always get money out of his patients. I know of a lot of people that didn't pay their house-rent or their electric bills, but Dr. LaBotte got money out of them. He had a shiny green car, and whenever he came driving through the Quarter every-body would get in their windows and doorways and start yelling and waving at him; even old people. I'd shout just like the rest of them. "Hey! Hey! There go Doctor. Doctor! Doctor! Hey there, Doctor La-Botte!!"

That's the way we'd go on. Sometimes he'd have his son Jemmie in the car with him. That was before Jemmie went off to medical school. Jemmie was al-most grown, but he'd hang out of the car window and laugh when we'd shout.

Doctor LaBotte used to come to see my Aunt Alber-tine sometimes. My parents went to Chicago when I was little, and they didn't come back. So I lived with Aunt Albertine. She was young and pretty—had a lot of men always hanging around our house after her. She had yellow skin and long brown hair; and she had

a fine shape. She used to drink a lot. But the thing about her was that she knew it was bad for her. So she'd make me go out to a pay-station 'phone and call up Dr. LaBotte to come see her. I don't know what he'd do for her because she wasn't really sick. He talked to her; that was about all. But he could get her out of her drinking moods and she'd be all right for a while.

One day in the springtime Dr. LaBotte came to see us when Aunt Albertine was coming out of one of her moods. I was surprised, because he came to talk about me. "Why don't you let Emory come see if he'd like to work for us up at our house, 'Tine? Light work—kind of helping around the house——you know. We'd give him his breakfast and lunch and he could get his supper down here with you. He could save, maybe ——go back and finish high school in a little bit."

At first Aunt Albertine didn't say anything. Finally she sized me up and said, "He fifteen. Let him do what he want to. *I* don't care. It ain't like he was going far off." She could tell I wanted to go by the way I was looking at her.

So I started working up at the LaBottes'. I think it was March when I started, and Jemmie LaBotte came home from medical school that June. He was a lot like his daddy; he laughed like him, and acted just about like him. He was glad to be back home. Sometimes he'd walk through that big house all day long, smiling in a funny way. Or sometimes in the evening he'd go **walking down in the Quarter.** People saw him down there; just walking those old, narrow grey-looking streets when it was almost dark.

I guess Dr. LaBotte was glad Jemmie was home. He laughed more than I'd heard him laugh when Jem-mie wasn't there. But then he started carrying a funny look on his face. And when he came home in the after-noon he'd go in the little room where his desk was and just sit there with the door open.

Jemmie LaBotte didn't pay me much attention. I'd pass by him in the house and he always looked like he was thinking to himself, or sometimes he'd be talking to his mother and daddy. Sometimes he sat in the living room and read all the morning. I knew they were medical books; most of them were old, and had pages as flimsy as tissue-paper—they were full of fine print. Jemmie LaBotte seemed like a fool to me, reading like that in the summertime. Especially since he was supposed to have just graduated from wherever it was he'd been. One day I asked him, "You remember all you read?"

"Yeah. I sure do." He laughed when he said it; he was a friendly somebody after all. "They make you —in a medical school."

"But you're not going back are you? Your mother says you're a doctor now."

"I want to do what Daddy's doing—doctor up people down there where you live." He looked at me like he wanted me to believe he really meant it. I could see he meant it.

I wondered why Jemmie LaBotte didn't seem to have any friends. Maybe once in a while somebody would call him on the 'phone. Answering the telephone was one of the things I was supposed to do. I'd call him to the 'phone and he'd talk a little while to whoever it was, but he never went anywhere much.

It got so Jemmie and his daddy argued. They'd sit out on the front porch late in the afternoon. I could hear them through the screen door. The old man's voice would be squeaky and high like he was afraid of something. "You sure you want to stay in New Orleans and practice?" He'd say. "You could always go back up there and study another year, if you wanted. You could be a specialist!"

They'd talk a long time, and Jemmie would get worked up and keep telling Dr. LaBotte how much he wanted to be just like him. He wanted to help people down in the Quarter just like the old man did. Jemmie LaBotte was always so serious about everything. He'd beg his daddy like I used to beg Aunt Albertine when I was little and wanted her to give me money to go to the movie or the carnival. I mean it; and he sounded queer when he begged like that. You'd have thought he was as young as I was. It didn't sound right to hear somebody who was supposed to be grown going on that way. "I don't want you to quit, Daddy. I'm not trying to make you *quit*. I just want to go down there with you."

"You don't know how they live—it's hard to get to know. I understand every one of 'em down there." Dr. LaBotte's voice sounded so old. I don't think I'd ever thought he was old before. It was almost pitiful the way he kept trying so hard to get Jemmie's mind off staying in New Orleans; like there was something in New Orleans he was ashamed of. "If you got to be a specialist you could get on at that baby hospital up in Philadelphia—I know you could."

Mrs. LaBotte took Jemmie's side. She must have thought old man LaBotte was jealous of Jemmie's being young and right out of school. Most of the time he wouldn't say anything to her when she started talking, because he knew what she was leading up to. "You know good and well you ought to let Jemmie make some of your calls for you—'specially those late calls. It'd be better for *him* to go down there in the Quarter at night. I'm always afraid somebody's going to jump in the car or something one of these nights. It's always so bad down there at night." She worried him all the time.

It got so when somebody from the Quarter called up old man LaBotte he'd get his bag and leave the house before Mrs. LaBotte and Jemmie could ask him where he was going. And when he was home he stayed shut up in the little office room. He started acting old and crabbed.

Mrs. LaBotte was the one who finally did it. I know it was her and not Jemmie because every time I heard her and Dr. LaBotte talking he'd be saying, "I'm tired of it, Juanita! I'm tired, and sick of it too!" It was what you'd call clever, the way she'd bring it up all the time about letting Jemmie stay in New Orleans and help him. She did it while they were eating, or when Jemmie was out taking one of his walks, or even when he'd just go out of the room a minute. I never did talk any of the LaBottes' business to anybody, because it didn't make a bit of difference to me what they did, but I did tell Aunt Albertine how bad the old man was looking, and how Mrs. LaBotte wouldn't lay off. Aunt Albertine said, "Well, you just make sure you don't be smelling in something you ain't got no business bothering with."

One morning Dr. LaBotte didn't come out of his bedroom early like he usually did. And Mrs. LaBotte tipped around, because she said he needed rest. That bedroom door didn't even open when the 'phone started ringing. It was an old man called David calling up from a grocery store. I knew who he was because he stayed about two blocks from where me and Aunt Albertine live. The children in the Quarter named him "that li'l man with the great big head." He wanted to tell Dr. LaBotte he had the "choky-feeling" in his chest again, and he couldn't lie down and sleep. So Mrs. LaBotte went in the bedroom. But they didn't start fussing, though. All Dr. LaBotte said was, "Tell Jemmie he can go down there—he wants to go." I think Mrs. LaBotte had worn him down to nothing. His voice sounded so tired, "Let Jemmie go down there—."

I went down to the Quarter with Jemmie LaBotte because I knew where David's house was. It's hard to find a place you're looking for in the Quarter because the house numbers are all faded off. I'm telling you the truth, it felt good riding through the Quarter in old man LaBotte's shiny car, because everybody really *did* look when they saw it was me in there. Jemmie was nervous. He kept laughing and saying, "You know, when I was little, people used to ask me what I wanted to be. As little as I was, I'd always say I wanted to be a doctor. They'd ask me why, and I'd tell them it was because Daddy was a doctor—I thought there wasn't anything else anybody *could* be but a doctor!" He laughed too much, and that childish way he had about him made me think he was foolish.

David's house was like the rest of the houses down there; the weather-boards were old and needed some paint. And it had fancy rusty iron banisters around the front porch, with iron flowers and curls. The room old David was in had the shades down and it was black-dark, except David had a little candle sitting in a piece of saucer on his chiffonier. Jemmie LaBotte didn't know what that little candle was for. He didn't pay it much attention at first; but I knew. You see old folks always burning a candle when they're afraid they're going to die, or afraid somebody in their family is going to die. Sometimes you're supposed to put pepper on the candle because everybody says it'll keep the worms from eating you after you're dead. David was propped up on a pillow. I sat down on a little stool by the door. Jemmie said, "You know good and well you ought to have some air in here, hot as it is." And then he went over to the window to let up the shade.

But old David screwed up his face at Jemmie La-Botte. "I wish you wouldn't be messin wid that window shade, 'cause that air out there got things in it bad for my feeling right here." He hit his chest with his wrinkled-up little hand. I could see he didn't like Jemmie LaBotte.

"Air never did hurt anybody's heart trouble." Jemmie LaBotte pulled up the shade a little.

"Your daddy don't never make me keep no air in there if I don't want none." I think that was the first thing that got Jemmie. And then old David wouldn't let Jemmie touch him with the needle. He held out those skinny old arms like he was scared to death. "Naw! Naw! You ain't going to put that thing in me. I don't want to have that thing sticking in my arm. And your daddy don't never stick me with none, either!"

I felt sorry for Jemmie LaBotte. He stood there like he didn't know what to do. Old David kept on hollering, "Oh Jesus! Oh Jesus! You going to stick me with that *thing*. Your daddy don't never do nothing like that!" Finally Jemmie LaBotte took a good hold on his old arm and jabbed him very quick; and you'd have thought David was having a baby by the way he was taking on. But after that I started feeling good toward Jemmie LaBotte because I liked the way he just went on and stuck the needle in anyhow. And he tried to be nice to old David after he gave him that shot: he told him to be quiet because he was through and ready to go, and he said he hoped he'd rest easier.

But old David wasn't ready for Jemmie LaBotte to go away. "You ain't going to give me nothing like

what your daddy give me when he comes?"

"What'd my daddy give you?"

"Some kind of stuff—."

"What stuff does he give you?"

"That stuff what make me sleep a lot. *You know,* Mr. Jemmie LaBotte." He kept smiling a sly, hateful smile. "Your daddy always give me a piece of paper that I can get it with at the drugstore-man's. Your daddy say it's codeine."

"My daddy didn't give you any codeine. Where'd you get that, talking about codeine? Don't you know your heart's too bad for you to be taking anything like that?"

"Well that's what your daddy say it was. Codeine. Make me sleep." He winked at Jemmie LaBotte like he expected him to understand something. "Your daddy give me that stuff instead of all that sticking me with that goddam old needle."

I don't know what made me think I had to say something; because it wasn't any of my business at all. But Jemmie LaBotte had such a funny look on his face all of a sudden I said, "Don't pay attention to old man big-head David. They say he don't never tell the truth about nothing." But Jemmie looked strange. And we went out of the house with David still begging for some of the "sleepy stuff."

Jemmie LaBotte just asked me one thing while we were going back to Bayou Street. "Why'd old David have that little candle? How come he didn't have the electric light on?"

"That's the way a lot of folks do when they're scared of sickness. You smell how that candle was making that stink in there?"

"I'd have made him put it out if I'd known that was what it was."

"A lots of people keep a sick candle," I said. "I bet your daddy never did try to make anybody put out their sick candle. They wouldn't do it anyhow—for him or nobody else." He didn't say anything after that.

The day after we went down to old David's Mrs. LaBotte called me out on the porch and she tried to make me think she just wanted me to sit out there and rock back and forth in the rocker and talk to keep her company. But she kept on trying to get it out of me about what happened when we went down to the Quarter.

I didn't tell her a thing, though. It wasn't my business. But I did tell Aunt Albertine how Mrs. LaBotte tried to pick me and Aunt Albertine said, "You better be careful—that's all *I* can say." She'd seen old man David that day at the grocery up on Ogechee Street and he was telling everybody Jemmie LaBotte was a good-for-nothing doctor; and then he'd roll up his sleeve and show the little place the needle made. Aunt Albertine said he was clowning and telling everybody Jemmie LaBotte was nothing but "ca-ca."

About a week went by and old man LaBotte didn't seem to be getting better of whatever was wrong with him; at least he didn't come out of his room. And Mrs. LaBotte kept saying all he needed was rest and for people to let him alone and not worry him. There was something wrong between him and Jemmie ever since the day Jemmie went down to David's. But as far as I know Jemmie hadn't even seen him since then; so I didn't understand what it could be. Then one Sunday morning early a lady named Mrs. Clara called up the house to ask for Dr. LaBotte because her little girl was having a fit. It was so early in the morning Jemmie and Mrs. LaBotte didn't even bother about telling Dr. LaBotte. Mrs. LaBotte said she knew he wouldn't care if Jemmie went.

Jemmie LaBotte took me with him again, and we went driving fast through those grey little snaky-looking streets in the Quarter. We saw a lot of people walking the sidewalks; and some of them were still drunk from Saturday night. When we got to Mrs. Clara's house she was out in a funny kind of silk dress washing the steps to her front porch with a jar full of pepper-water. She was real fat and she had her behind turned up to us because she was down on her knees scrubbing the steps; and at first it looked funny. But she turned around and it was pitiful because her big fat face was screwed up and she was crying. The pepper-water had the front steps smelling loud like grease and vinegar. So Jemmie LaBotte asked her what that stuff was and why she wasn't in the house with her little girl. Mrs. Clara said, "I ain't in there 'cause I got to wash with this old pepper-water. Keeps off bad things from coming in the house—keep 'um way from my baby." Jemmie LaBotte told her she had no business believing in such things and he made her put down the jar with the pepper-water in it. But she kept on saying, "Your own daddy—your flesh-and-blood daddy—your daddy—he say it's fine if I want to wash off them front steps with my pepper-water!"

I sat on the porch while Jemmie LaBotte was inside. I'd seen that little girl lots of times with Mrs. Clara when they'd be walking up Ogechee Street. Her name was Monica and she was about eight years old, and she was pretty because she had a round face with a funny kind of purple eyes and light, hay-colored hair. But you could tell something was wrong with her because she walked so slow and funny, and held her head like her neck was made out of rubber.

When Mrs. Clara came to the screen door with Jemmie LaBotte she was saying, "Ain't you going to give her none of them pink pills what makes her sleep? Your daddy say them be good for her—they make her lay real quiet so she don't have no more of them fits. She don't roll her eyes or nothing if she have them pink pills."

Jemmie LaBotte kept looking at the little thing around Mrs. Clara's neck. It was hanging on a greasy string. I don't think he knew what it was, but I did, because my Aunt Albertine always has one so she'll be sure to have good luck. It was a little ball of hair; only this was a little ball of hay-colored hair. Mrs. Clara and Jemmie LaBotte were both acting all upset.

"I'm not going to give her anything to make her sleep, because it wouldn't be good for her. She had a *fit*! It's not good for her to go to sleep on medicine, I don't care *what* my daddy told you." So we left, and Mrs. Clara stood on her front porch; and she was crying and sprinkling pepper-water because she said Jemmie LaBotte must be evil and she didn't even want the smell of him around her house.

"You ain't no good kind of a man like *Doctor*," was the last thing we heard her say.

Then Jemmie Labotte told his mother. They sat in the living room on that big settee and he told her how old David asked him for codeine and said Dr. LaBotte always gave it to him. And he told her how he didn't want to believe a thing like that on his daddy; but he told her what happened with Mrs. Clara. "That little girl's name is Monica, and the whites of her eyes are all dulled over. Like she's been asleep a *long* time! She had a lot of codeine—I can tell she has."

Once Mrs. LaBotte looked up and saw me standing in the doorway, but she turned her head away. Dr. LaBotte came in the living room; I don't know whether he heard them or what. But Jemmie didn't act like he was there. "I thought my daddy was something." He said it just like the old man wasn't there at all.

And Dr. Labotte said, "They do magic down there, Juanita!" When he called her name Mrs. LaBotte put her little handkerchief up to her mouth. She made a little choking noise. Dr. LaBotte kept blaring his eyes; I thought he was going to go crazy. "Real magic," he said, "they wouldn't stop that voodoo down there for anything. They wouldn't even stop it for *me*."

"You've got them so all they want is codeine. You think codeine can do an epileptic fit any good, Daddy?"

"I told you—you don't know how they are. You think they'll take medicine, don't you?"

"You're bad as they are. You put them all to sleep. You can put them to sleep, all right!"

Dr. LaBotte said, "They love me. You get so you'll do anything for them if you can just get 'em to love you." And then he went out of the living room and left Mrs. LaBotte and Jemmie still sitting there on the settee. He walked away slow, like he was so old.

From then on some strange things started going on. Jemmie LaBotte swore he was going to be what his daddy never was. He could hardly wait until some more of the old man's patients called up so he could go back down to the Quarter. He kept saying he knew he could make them like him down there, if he could just get them to let him do them some good. It got so the main thing for Jemmie LaBotte was his big idea about how he was going to do them some good and make them like him. You should've heard the way he kept talking to his mother about it.

But Jemmie LaBotte didn't know the word had got around about him. It just takes one mouth to spread things in the Quarter, and David and Mrs. Clara ran their mouths a plenty. Everybody down there was whispering old man LaBotte was sick and going to die and his boy didn't know a thing to do for him or anybody. His boy wasn't nothing but "ca-ca," and a good-for-nothing. That's what they said about Jemmie La-Botte. David told everybody he could feel funny things crawing in his arm where Jemmie LaBotte stuck him with that needle. And Mrs. Clara said her Monica was bloody-eyed and always screaming with fits, because Jemmie LaBotte didn't give her sleepy-stuff to quiet her down.

Then one day Jemmie LaBotte got tired of waiting. He must've known what was wrong by that time. So he went down to the Quarter. That evening when I got home Aunt Albertine told me, "Jemmie LaBotte come driving down here today. Folks say he was trying to see old David and when David found out who it was he locked up his door on him. Yeah—I hear he was even begging old man David to let him talk to him."

"Begging him do any good?"

"Didn't do a bit of good!" Aunt Albertine laughed about Jemmie LaBotte because she was just like the rest of them; she didn't think he was anything.

But I give him credit. He tried hard in the Quarter. He tried to get David and Mrs. Clara to believe he wanted to do them some good. But David would always lock his door, and Mrs. Clara wouldn't even let him come up on her front porch. It got so bad people would sit in their windows and laugh whenever they'd see him coming. But he kept on going down there.

Then one day Jemmie LaBotte did get a 'phone call. It was August then, and that day was rainy. All over the house was quiet like somebody was dead or going to die. And it was so hot all the windows and doors were open and you could hear rain hitting the gardenia bushes out in the front yard. Whoever it was calling sounded like they were crying. All they said was for somebody to come down to Mama Callie's house quick. So he went down there by himself. I could see he wasn't thinking about taking me down there with him that day. But I wouldn't have gone anyhow, because I didn't like that old Mama Callie.

When I was little I used to go over to her house with Aunt Albertine. Aunt Albertine never has stopped going to Mama Callie's because Mama Callie knew her when she was just knee-high. In the first place I didn't

like Mama Callie because she was always coughing. Everybody knew she had T.B., and she was sleepy-looking and slow-talking because she stayed all doped up on codeine to ease her coughing spells. She must have been about seventy-five years old, and she had a sister named Alena who was somewhere around fifty. She and Alena spent all day making little charms and things; and they sold them around to a lot of people. Like if Mrs. Clara wanted a hair ball out of little Monica's hair she'd cut off a snip of hair and take it to Mama Callie, and Mama Callie would do things like dip it in hot chicken fat and tie it on a string and wrap it up for a week in senna leaves. Then she'd give it back to Mrs. Clara when it was ready to do some good. Sometimes on a hot day you'd walk past their house and you'd see Mama Callie and Alena sitting in the open window and Mama Callie would always be singing something in French. She said that song was a Creole song her father taught her when she was a little girl. They say she was real proud of that, because her and Alena's father was a Frenchman. Anyway, whenever she and Alena sat in the window Mama Callie would hold her old sleepy-looking face out the window to see who was walking up and down the street. Alena, who liked men, would be just sitting there beside Mama Callie brushing her hair. She had long hair that came all down her shoulders, and she always brushed it with a brush soaked in strong tea to keep it from getting grey.

When Jemmie LaBotte came back from Mama Callie's he looked discouraged, and he didn't say a thing.

But that evening Alena was going around telling everybody in the Quarter about how when Jemmie La-Botte got to Mama Callie she'd had a hemorrhage and blood was coming out of her nose and mouth all over the bed-sheets. Alena said, "He come bringing his fancy bag with them bottles in it. He thought he was going to give Callie one of them needles of his, but me and Callie wouldn't even let him get near the bed. I told him he wasn't going to touch my Callie!" Alena was bragging about how she told Jemmie LaBotte right to his face they'd just called him so he could give Mama Callie some codeine. But he wouldn't give her any, and he started telling Alena how much Mama Callie needed a hospital, or at least some medicine. Alena laughed, "That Jemmie LaBotte wanted to pay me money to let him stick Callie with one of them shiny needles—even much wanted to pay me *money!* Callie and me told him if he couldn't put her to sleep there wasn't *nothing* he could do. We fixed him. Callie, bad off as she was, she couldn't help but laugh at him. We fixed him all right!" Alena said she warmed up some pig oil with mustard seeds and went to work on Mama Callie and started rubbing her all over with it right there in front of Jemmie LaBotte. "He was just standing there looking. And he looked like he couldn't take his eyes off. He couldn't even stop looking for nothing. Like a young'un watching his daddy in the bed with his ma." Everybody laughed at Alena's saying that. "I could see he didn't like it for nothing, but there wasn't a thing he could do about me rubbing up Callie with that hog grease. Callie was warm, and shiny as she could be when I got through with her. He just stood up there like he had that hog grease on his brain—stood there just looking 'cause that's all he could do—look."

You could tell Alena liked to talk about it. Everybody she told it to sure did listen. I know it must have made Jemmie LaBotte feel beat down for Mama Callie not to let him even touch her, because even old man David, bad as he was, let Jemmie give him a shot that first time, anyway.

About a week after all that happened Jemmie LaBotte asked me if I knew Mama Callie and Alena, and I told him yes. Then he started talking about how queer they were. He talked so fast; like he couldn't tell me quick enough. I didn't see why he was acting so worried. "That old Mama Callie—you know what she did? She wouldn't even let me put a stethoscope on her. You ever see all the little baskets in there—in her bedroom? They were all full of leaves!"

I knew the little baskets he was talking about. "Yeah, They're willow leaves."

"You know what she does with them?"

"Naw," I said, "I never did know."

I knew what those willow leaves were for, but I didn't tell him because I didn't see what difference it made to him.

One evening Mama Callie called up again; Jemmie LaBotte didn't seem to want to go down there. But his mother couldn't see why. "You ought to go if they called you, Jemmie," she kept saying. She was so proud of him because she thought he was everything old man LaBotte never *had* been. "You have to go right on down there, even if that old lady won't let you attend to her—she *called* you."

Mama Callie and Alena must have known he'd come, because they told Aunt Albertine and a lot of other people to be on the look-out if they wanted to see the car when it drove up. Mama Callie was feeling weak and puny, but she was sitting in the window singing that little French song, and Alena was sitting beside her brushing her hair with that brush she kept wetting in a bowl of tea. Mama Callie told Aunt Albertine Jemmie LaBotte started worrying her to let him give her some medicine as soon as he got there. The way they talked about it you'd have thought Jemmie LaBotte was like a little dog or something they'd taken some kind of a fancy to. Alena got rid of all her men friends, and even when it made Mama Callie cough and spit up blood she burned a little basket full of dried up

willow leaves every day. Alena said, "We burn them leaves 'cause it make him get us on the brain. And pretty soon he be coming right on down here all the time."

Sure enough Jemmie LaBotte did start going down to Mama Callie's. He told Mrs. LaBotte he went down there so he could leave medicines for Mama Callie and try to make her take them. But Mrs. LaBotte noticed how much he was going down there. She even told old man LaBotte. And he used to lie in his bed and call Jemmie. "Jemmie, come tell your daddy what's going on down there at Mama Callie's. Come tell me! How come you're down to Mama Callie's so much, Jemmie?" But Jemmie stopped going in his daddy's room. Even Mrs. LaBotte couldn't make him go in anymore. And that hurt Dr. LaBotte. He began to fall off a lot. You could tell because his hands and his face got so thin. But still he'd lie in his bed and call in that nagging voice, like there was something he knew about Jemmie.

Mama Callie and Alena got so they bragged and said they were going to have Jemmie LaBotte pretty soon. Alena tied up her hair every day in a lot of silk rags because she wanted to look fine when he came. And Mama Callie claimed they could get him down to the Quarter whenever they wanted to. Alena was always telling everybody, "All I got to do is heat up that hog oil and start rubbing on Callie with it. That Jemmie LaBotte look like his eyes going to pop out. When I do that he look like he don't want to do nothing but just look at me and Callie; and he knows we ain't going to let him touch her. But he just keep on looking. Sometimes he look right pitiful."

I didn't think Jemmie still cared anything about his daddy. He did though. Because when old man LaBotte had that heart attack you could see it did something to Jemmie. They had a lot of fine specialists with Dr. LaBotte, but it didn't do him any good. He lingered, and got weaker every day. They said he was "in coma" so nobody could go in there to see him. Jemmie and Mrs. LaBotte would just sit in that big living room all day long with the shades down; and two or three nurses were always coming and going and walking soft on those big thick rugs. They made me think of white rabbits, the way they were always streaking through the house. I didn't like them because they wouldn't let Jemmie LaBotte even see his daddy, and he wanted to a lot. He kept saying there was something he wanted to tell his daddy.

Alena and Mama Callie told Aunt Albertine Jemmie LaBotte had stopped trying to make Mama Callie take his medicines. They said he came to their house just to see them and they called him sweet-boy-Jemmie. "He just like a baby," Mama Callie was always saying. "He come and just sit there and watch Alena swing them plaits around in the air. Sometime Alena hand him one of them hair-plaits and he hold it and he just laugh. Just like a young'un with a sugar-tit." Alena swore Mama Callie was telling it like it was. "Callie telling the honest-to-God truth! That Jemmie LaBotte done changed a heap." Then they'd both laugh. Mama Callie would laugh so hard she'd start coughing.

It got around that Jemmie LaBotte had started writing prescriptions for Mama Callie to get codeine with. Somebody even said they saw him go in the drugstore to get it for her one day; but I still thought it was just meanness making them all tell lies on him. All that time Dr. LaBotte was sinking. Mrs. LaBotte couldn't understand why Jemmie was staying away more and more. She didn't think it hurt him that his daddy was dying, but she was wrong. He never did mention Dr. LaBotte much, but you could see he cared about the old man, just by some of the other things he'd say. Like one day he told me, "Mama loves this house, but I want to get out of here. I can't stand it anymore."

My Aunt Albertine was there at Mama Callie's one day when Jemmie LaBotte came to see her. She said Mama Callie had a pretty bad coughing spell and her mouth started running blood, but Jemmie LaBotte didn't do a thing except just get down on his knees by Mama Callie's bed. And when she'd stopped coughing Mama Callie took a little ball of hair from under her pillow and gave it to him. Mama Callie told him that little ball had some of her and Alena's hair in it. She gave it to Jemmie LaBotte because he'd kept asking her to give him something to help his daddy in his misery. I'll tell you the truth, I didn't even believe my own flesh-and-blood aunt. For one thing I couldn't *see* Jemmie LaBotte doing all they said. I didn't even believe the willow leaves I'd found meant anything.

In the end I saw for my own self, though. One night. Dr. LaBotte had been real low all that day, and they'd put him under an oxygen tent. And Mrs. LaBotte had been calling up her friends telling them she didn't understand why Jemmie was off down in the Quarter. I think she must have known Dr. LaBotte was going to die. Those nurses finally gave her something that made her go to sleep, so she'd stop carrying on so. Anyway, that night after I'd got off I was walking up Bourbon Street on my way over to the show field to see if the carnival had come; and so I passed by Mama Callie's. Even when I was still way up the street I heard that singing. Mama Callie was singing and she was in the front window. She was singing that little French song, but it went so slow I could tell she was weak; she was so feeble her voice sounded high like a chicken squawking.

"Donnez tes levres.
Donnez tes mains.
Ces yeux, ces yeux
Sont pleins du feu!"

All the lights were on real bright in the room where she was. And she was sitting right up in the window with some kind of a shawl on that had long fringes that kept blowing around her arms. I couldn't help but look in there when I went by, but Mama Callie didn't see me because she had her eyes shut. I told you how the light was on in the room; I could see good. Alena was sitting there a little ways behind Mama Callie. She was in a straight chair and she had silk rags tied all through her hair: red and blue and green and yellow; all kinds of colors. Jemmie LaBotte must have been down on his knees or almost on his knees anyway, because all I could see was his head. Alena had Jemmie LaBotte's head, holding it *tight* in her arms. Just as tight as she could. It was so queer, because it looked like she might have cut off his head from his body and was just holding nothing but that head in her arms. She had her eyes closed and he had his closed too. Only in the light I could see shining streaks on his face, like he was crying. He looked pretty: like a woman. Maybe it was because Mama Callie and Alena were so wrinkled and ugly, but he looked really pretty; something like a young girl. His skin was so smooth, and his hair was shiny and very thick; like purple and black mixed together.

When I got back home that night I told Aunt Albertine how I saw the three of them. And she said, "I been thinking about it a while. I don't like all that funny stuff that's going on." She told me she wanted me to quit working for the LaBottes.

Only next day when I went up there a lot of people were at the house. Women in fine clothes with feathery hats and little white handkerchiefs. They were answering the telephone and talking loud all over the house and wiping their eyes because old man LaBotte had died the night before. I didn't even get a chance to see Mrs. LaBotte, because a nurse was keeping her quiet. And everybody was saying Jemmie LaBotte must be raving-crazy, because he'd gone driving down to the Quarter the night before, right after the old man died.

*   *   *   *

It seems like it's been longer than two years ago since all that was going on; but it's been just about that long. I don't know for sure, but I don't think Jemmie LaBotte even went to his daddy's funeral. I do know one thing, though; he's never home these days. I see him all the time; whenever I go up on Bourbon Street. He's always at Mama Callie's house, and he waves his hand to me when he sees me. Alena still makes her little hair balls, and everybody says Mama Callie's just hanging by a thread. She doesn't feel anything, though, because most of the time Jemmie LaBotte keeps her full of codeine. But Jemmie LaBotte doesn't just only give codeine to Mama Callie. He gives it to a lot of them.

THE HARVARD ADVOCATE

MY SISTER'S MARRIAGE

CYNTHIA RICH

WHEN MY mother died, she left just Olive and me to take care of father. Yesterday when I burned the package of Olive's letters, that left only me. I know that you'll side with my sister in all of this, because you're only outsiders, and strangers can afford to sympathize with young love, and with whatever sounds daring and romantic, without thinking what it does to all the other people involved. I don't want to hate my sister—I don't hate her—but I do want you to see that we're happier this way, father and I, and as for Olive, she made her choice.

But if you weren't strangers, all of you, I wouldn't be able to tell you about this. "Keep yourself to yourself," my father has always said. "If you ever have worries, Sarah Ann, you come to me, and don't go sharing your problems around town." And that's what I've always done. So if I knew you, I certainly wouldn't ever tell you about Olive throwing the hairbrush, or about finding the letters buried in the back of the drawer.

I don't know what made Olive the way she is. We grew up together like twins—there were people who thought we were — and every morning we went to school, she plaited my hair and I plaited hers before the same mirror, in the same little twist of ribbons and braids behind our heads. We wore the same dresses, and there was never a strain on the hem or a rip in our stockings to say to a stranger that we had lost our mother. And although we have never been well-to-do—my father is a doctor and his patients often can't pay —I know that there are people here in Conkling today who think we're rich, just because of little things like candle-light at dinner, and my father's cigarette-holder, and the piano-lessons that Olive and I had, and the reproduction of "The Anatomy Lesson" that hangs above the mantlepiece instead of Botannical prints. "You don't have to be rich to be a gentleman," my father says, "or to live like one."

My father is a gentleman, and he raised Olive and myself as ladies. I can hear you laughing, because people like to make fun of words like "gentleman" and "lady", but they are words with ideals and standards behind them, and I hope that I will always hold to those ideals as my father taught me to. If Olive has renounced them, at least we did all we could.

Perhaps the reason why I can't understand Olive is that I have never been in love. I know that if I had ever fallen in love, it would not have been, like Olive, at first sight, but only after a long acquaintence. My father knew my mother for seven years before he proposed—it is much the safest way. Nowadays people make fun of that, too, and the magazines are full of stories about people meeting in the moonlight and marrying the next morning, but if you read those stories, you know that they are not the sort of people you would want to be like.

Even today, Olive couldn't deny that we had a happy childhood. She used to be very proud of being the lady of the house, of sitting across the candle-light from my father at dinner, like a little wife. Sometimes my father would hold his carving-knife poised above the roast to stand smiling at her and say,

"Olive, every day you remind me more of your mother."

I think that although she liked the smile, she minded the compliment, because she didn't like to hear about mother. Once, when my father spoke of her, she said,

"Papa, you're missing mother again. I can't bear it when you miss mother. Don't I take care of you right? Don't I make things happy for you?" It wasn't that she hadn't loved mother, but she wanted my father to be completely happy.

To tell the truth, it was Olive that father loved best. There was a time when I couldn't have said that, it would have hurt me too much. Taking care of our father was like playing a long game of "let's pretend," and when little girls play family, nobody wants to be the children. I thought it wasn't fair, just because Olive was three years older, that she should always be the mother. I wanted to sit opposite my father at dinner, and have him smile at me like that.

I was glad when Olive first began walking out with young men in the summer evenings. Then I would make lemonade for my father ("It is as good as Olive's?") and we would sit out on the screened porch together watching the fireflies. I asked him about the patients that he had seen that day, trying to think of questions as intelligent as Olive's. I knew that he was missing her, and frowning into the long twilight for the swing of her white skirts. When she came up the steps, he said, "I missed my housewife tonight," just as though I hadn't made the lemonade right after all. She knew, too, that it wasn't the same for him in the evenings without her, and for a while, instead of going out, she brought the young men to the house. But soon she stopped even that ("I never realized how silly and shallow they were until I saw them with Papa," she said. "I was ashamed to have him talk to them.") I know that he was glad, and when my turn came I didn't want to go out because I hated leaving them alone together. It all seems a very long time ago. I used to hate it when Olive "mothered" me. Now I feel a little like Olive's mother, and she is like my rebellious child.

In spite of everything, I loved Olive. When we were children we used to play together. The other children disliked us because we talked like grownups and didn't like to get dirty, but we were happy playing by ourselves on the front lawn where my father, if he were home, could watch us from his study window. So it wasn't surprising that when we grew older we were still best friends. I loved Olive, and I see now how she took advantage of that love. Sometimes I think she felt that if she was to betray my father, she wanted me to betray him, too.

I still believe that it all began, not really with Mr. Dixon, but with the foreign stamps. She didn't see many of them, those years after high-school when she was working in the post-office, because not very many people in Conkling have friends abroad, but the ones that she saw—and even the postmarks from Chicago or California—made her dream. She told her dreams to father and of course he understood, and said that perhaps some summer we could take a trip to New England as far as Boston. My father hasn't lived in Conkling all of his life. He went to Harvard, and that is one reason he is different from the other men here. He is a scholar, and not bound to provincial ideas. People here respect him, and come to him for advice.

Olive wasn't satisfied, and she began to rebel. Even she admitted that there wasn't anything for her to rebel against. She told me about it, sitting on the window-sill in her long white nightgown, braiding and unbraiding the hair that she had never cut.

"It's not, don't you see, that I don't love father. And it certainly isn't that I'm not happy here. But what I mean is, how can I ever know whether or not I'm really happy here, unless I go somewhere else? When you graduate from school, you'll feel the same way. You'll want—you'll want to know."

"I like it here," I said, from the darkness of the room, but she didn't hear me.

"You know what I'm going to do, Sarah Ann? Do you know what I'm going to do? I'm going to save some money and go on a little trip—it woudn't have to be expensive, I could go by bus—and I'll just see things, and then maybe I'll know."

"Father promised he'd take us to New England."

"No," said Olive, "No, you don't understand. Anyhow, I'll save the money."

And still she wasn't satisfied. She began to read. Olive and I always did well in school, and our names were called out for Special Recognition on Class Day. Miss Singleton wanted Olive to go to drama school after she played the part of Miranda in *The Tempest,* but my father talked to her, and when he told her what an actress' life is like, she realized it wasn't what she wanted. Aside from books for school, though, we never read very much. We didn't need to, because my father has read everything you've heard of, and people in town have said that talking to him about anything is better than reading three books.

Still, Olive decided to read. She would choose a book from my father's library, and go into the kitchen where the air was still heavy and hot from dinner, and sit on the very edge of the tall, hard, three-legged stool. She had an idea that if she sat in a comfortable chair in the parlor, she would not be attentive, or would skip the difficult passages. So she would sit like that for hours, under the hard light of the unshaded bulb that hangs from the ceiling, until her arms ached from holding the book.

"What do you want to find out about?" my father would ask.

"Nothing," Olive said. "I'm just reading."

My father hates evasion.

"Now Olive, nobody reads without a purpose. If you're interested in something, maybe I can help you. I might even know something about it myself."

When she came into our bedroom, she threw the book on the quilt and said,

"Why does he have to pry, Sarah Ann? It's so simple—just wanting to read a book. Why does he have to make a fuss about it, as though I were trying to hide something from him?"

That was the first time that I felt a little like Olive's mother.

"But he's only taking an interest," I said. "He just wants us to share things with him. Lots of fathers wouldn't even care. You don't know how lucky we are."

"You don't understand, Sarah Ann. You're too young to understand."

"Of course I understand," I said shortly. "Only I've outgrown feeling like that."

It was true. When I was a little girl, I wrote something on a piece of paper, something that didn't matter much, but it mattered to me because it was a private thought. My father came into my room and saw me shove the paper under the blotter, and he wanted me to show it to him. So I quickly said No, it's private, I wrote it to myself, I didn't write it to be seen, but he said he wanted to see it. And I said no, no, no, it was silly anyway, and he said Sarah Ann, nothing you have to say would seem silly to me, you never give me credit for understanding, I can understand a great deal, but I said it wasn't just him, really it wasn't, because I hadn't written it for anyone at all to see. Then he was all sad and hurt, and said this isn't a family where we keep things hidden, and there I was hiding this from him. I heard his voice, and it went on and on, and he said I had no faith in him, and that I shouldn't keep things from him—and I said it wasn't anything big or special, it was just some silly nonsense, but it was nonsense, he said, why wouldn't I let him read it, since it would make him happy? And I cried and cried, because it was only a very little piece of paper and why had he had to see it anyway, but he was very solemn and said if you held back little things soon you would be holding back bigger things and the gap would grow wider and wider. So I gave him the paper. He read it and said nothing, except that I was a good girl, and he couldn't see what all the fuss had been about.

Of course now I know that he was only taking an interest, and I shouldn't have minded that. But I was a little girl then, and minded dreadfully, and that is why I understood how Olive felt, although she was grown-up then, and should have known better.

She must have understood that she was being childish, because when my father came in a few minutes later and said, "Olive, you're our little mother. We mustn't quarrel. There should be only love between us," she rose and kissed him. She told him about the book she had been reading, and he said, "Well, as it happens, I do know something about that." They sat for a long time discussing the book, and I think he loved Olive better than ever. The next evening instead of shutting herself in the bright hot kitchen, Olive sat with us in the cool of the parlor until bedtime, hemming a slip. And it was just as always.

But I suppose that these things really had made a difference in Olive. For we had always been alike, and I cannot imagine allowing a perfect stranger to ask me personal questions before we had even been introduced. She told me about it afterwards, how he had bought a book of three-cent stamps, and stayed to chat through the half-open grilled window. Suddenly he said, quite seriously,

"Why do you wear your hair like that?"

"Pardon me?" said Olive.

"Why do you wear your hair like that? You ought to shake it loose around your shoulders. It must be yards long."

That is when I would have remembered—if I had forgotten—that I was a lady. I would have closed the grill, not rudely but just firmly enough to show my displeasure, and gone back to my desk. Olive told me that she thought of doing that, but she looked at him and knew, she said, that he didn't mean to be impolite, that he really wanted to know.

And instead she said,

"I only wear it down at night."

That afternoon he walked her home from the post-office.

Olive told me everything long before my father knew anything. It was the beginning of an unwholesome deceit in her. And it was nearly a week later that she told even me. By that time he was meeting her every afternoon and they took long walks together, as far as Merton's Pond, before she came home to set the dinner-table.

"Only don't tell father," she said.

"Why not?"

"I think I'm afraid of him. I don't know why. I'm afraid of what he might say."

"He won't say anything," I said. "Unless there's something wrong. And if there's something wrong, wouldn't you want to know?"

Of course, I should have told father myself, right away. But that was how she played upon my love for her.

"I'm telling you," she said, "because I want so much to share it with you. I'm so happy, Sarah Ann, and I feel so free, don't you see. We've always been so close —I've been closer to you than to father, I think—or at least, differently." She had to qualify it, you see, because it wasn't true. But it still made me happy, and I promised not to tell, and I was even glad for her, because, as I've told you, I've always loved Olive.

I saw them together one day when I was coming home from school. They were walking together in the rain, holding hands like school-children, and when Olive saw me from a distance she dropped his hand suddenly, and then just as suddenly took it again.

"Hullo!" he said, when she introduced us. "She does look like you!"

I want to be fair, and honest with you—it is Olive's dishonesty that still shocks me—and so I will say that I liked Mr. Dixon that day. But I thought even then how different he was from my father, and that at least should have warned me. He was a big man with a square face and sun-bleached hair. I could see a glimpse of his bright speckled tie under his tan raincoat, and his laugh sounded warm and easy in the rain. I liked him, I suppose, for the very things I should have distrusted in him. I liked his ease, and the way that he accepted me immediately, spontaneously and freely, without waiting—waiting for whatever people wait for when they hold themselves back (as I should have done) to find out more about you. I could almost understand what had made Olive, after five minutes, tell him how she wore her hair at night.

I am glad, at least, that I begged Olive to tell my father about him. I couldn't understand why at first she refused. I think now that she was afraid of seeing them together, that she was afraid of seeing the difference. I have told you that my father is a gentleman. Even now you must be able to tell what sort of man

Mr. Dixon was. My father knew at once, without even meeting him.

The weeks had passed, and Olive told me that Mr. Dixon's business was completed, but that his vacation was coming, and he planned to spend it in Conkling. She said that she would tell my father.

We were sitting on the porch after dinner. The evening had just begun to thicken, and some children had wandered down the road, playing a game of pirates at the very edge of our lawn. One of them had a long paper sword, and the others were waving tall sticks, and they were screaming. My father had to raise his voice to be heard.

"So this man, whom you have been seeing behind my back, is a traveling salesman for Miracle-wear soles."

"Surrender in the name of the King!"

"I am more than surprised at you, Olive. That hardly sounds like the kind of man you would want to be associated with."

"Why not?" said Olive. "Why not."

"It's notorious, my dear. Men like that have no respect for a girl. They'll flatter her with slick words, but it doesn't mean anything. Just take my word for it, dear. It may seem hard, but I know the world."

"Fight to the death! Fight to the death!"

"I can't hear you, my dear. Sarah Ann, ask those children to play their games somewhere else."

I went down the steps and across the lawn.

"Doctor Landis is trying to rest after a long day," I explained. They nodded and vanished down the dusky road, brandishing their silent swords.

"I am saying nothing of the extraordinary manner of your meeting, not even of the deceitful way in which he has carried on this—friendship—"

It was dark on the porch. I switched on the yellow overhead light, and the three of us blinked for a moment, rediscovered each other as the shadows leaped back.

"The cheapness of it is so apparent, that it amazes me that even in your innocence of the world—"

My father was fitting a cigarette into its black holder. He turned it slowly to and fro, until it was firm, before he struck a match and lit it. It is beautiful to watch him do even the most trivial things. He is always in control of himself, and he never makes a useless gesture, or thinks a useless thought. If you met him, you might believe at first that he was totally relaxed, but because I have lived with him so long I know that there is at all times a tension controlling his body; you can feel it when you touch his hand. Tension, I think, is the wrong word. It is rather a self-awareness, as though not a muscle contracted without his conscious knowledge.

"You know it very well yourself, Olive. Could anything but shame have kept you from bringing this man to your home?"

His voice is like the way he moves. It is clear and considered, and each word exists by itself. However common it may be, when he speaks it, it has become his, it has dignity because he has chosen it.

"Father, all I ask is that you'll have him here—that you will meet him. Surely that's not too much to ask before you—judge him."

Olive sat on the step at my father's feet. Her hands had been moving across her skirt, smoothing the folds over her knees, but when she spoke she clasped them tightly in her lap. She was trying to speak as he spoke, in that calm, certain voice, but it was a poor imitation.

"I'm afraid that it is too much to ask, Olive. I have seen too many of his kind to take any interest in seeing another."

"I think you should see him, father," She spoke very softly. "I think I am in love with him."

"Olive!" I said. I had known it all along, of course,

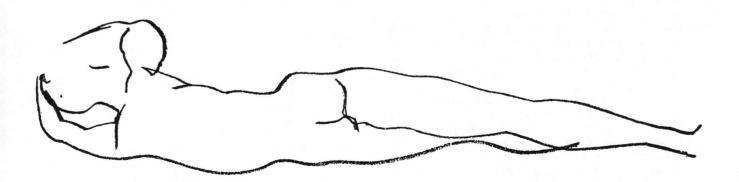

but when she spoke it, in that voice trying so childishly to sound sure, I knew its absurdity. How could she say it, after father had made it so clear? As soon as he had repeated after her, "a salesman for Miracle-wear soles," even the inflections of his voice showed me that it was ludicrous; I realized what I had known all along, the cheapness of it all for Olive—for Olive with her ideals.

I looked across at my father but he had not stirred. The moths brushed their wings against the lightbulb. He flicked a long grey ash.

"Don't use that word lightly, Olive," he said. "That is a sacred word. Love is the word for what I felt for your mother—what I hope you feel for me, and for your sister. You mustn't confuse it with innocent infatuation."

"But I do love him—how can you know? How can you know anything about it? I do love him." Her voice was shrill and not pleasant.

"Olive," said my father. "I must ask you not to use that word."

She sat looking up at his face and from his chair he looked back at her. Then she rose and went into the house. He did not follow her, even with his eyes. We sat for a long time before I went over to him and took his hand. I think he had forgotten me. He started and said nothing, and his hand did not acknowledge mine. I would rather he had slapped me. I left him and went into the house.

In our bedroom, Olive was sitting before the dressing-table in her nightgown, brushing her hair. You mustn't think that I don't love her, that I didn't love her then. As I say, we were like twins, and when I saw her reflection in the tall gilded mirror I might have been seeing my own eyes filled with tears. I tell you, I wanted to put my arms around her, but you must see that it was for her own sake that I didn't. She had done wrong, she had deceived my father, and she had made me deceive him. It would have been wicked to give her sympathy then.

"It's hard, of course, Olive," I said very gently. "But you know that father's right."

She didn't answer. She brushed her hair in long strokes, and it rose on the air. She did not turn even when the doorknob rattled, and my father stood in the doorway, and quietly spoke her name.

"Olive," he repeated. "Of course I must ask you not to see this—this man again."

Olive turned suddenly with her dark hair whirling about her head. She hurled the silver hairbrush at my father, and that single moment when it leapt from her hand, I felt an elation I have never known before. Then I heard it clatter to the floor, a few feet from where he stood, and I knew that he was unhurt, and that it was I, and not Olive, who had for that single moment, meant it to strike him. I longed to throw my arms about him and beg his forgiveness.

He went over and picked up the brush and gave it to Olive. Then he left the room.

"How could you, Olive?" I whispered.

She sat with the brush in her hand. Her hair had fallen all about her face and her eyes were dark and bright. The next morning at breakfast she did not speak to my father, and he did not speak to her, although he sat looking at her so intensely that if I had been Olive I would have blushed. I thought, he loves her more now, this morning, than when he used to smile and say she was like mother. I remember thinking, why couldn't he love me like that? I would never hurt him.

Just before she left for work, he went over to her and brushed her arm lightly with his hand.

"We'll talk it all over tonight, Olive," he said. "I know you will understand that this is best."

She looked down at his hand as though it were a strange animal, and shook her head and hurried down the porch steps.

That night she called from a little town outside of Richmond to say that she was married. I stood behind my father in the shadowy little hallway, as he spoke to her. I could hear her voice, higher-pitched than usual over the static of the wires, and I heard her say that they would come, that very evening, if he would see them.

I almost thought he hadn't understood her, his voice was so calm.

"I suppose you want my blessings. I cannot give them to deceit and cowardice. You will have to find them elsewhere if you can, my dear. If you can."

After he had replaced the receiver, he still stood before the mouthpiece, talking into it.

"That she would give up all she has had—that she would stoop to a—for a—physical attraction—"

Then he turned to me. His eyes were dark.

"Why are you crying?" He said suddenly. "What are you crying for? She's made her choice. Am I crying? Do you think I would want to see her—now? If she—when she comes to see what she has done—but it's not a question of forgiveness. Even then it wouldn't be the same. She made her choice."

He stood looking at me, and I thought at first that what he saw was distasteful to him, but his voice was gentle when he spoke.

"Would you have done this to me, Sarah Ann? Would you have done it?"

"No," I said, and I was almost joyful, knowing it was true. "Oh, no."

That was a year ago. We never speak of Olive any more. At first, letters used to come from her, long letters from New York and then from Chicago. Always she asked me about father, and whether he would read a letter if she wrote one. I wrote her long letters back, and said that I would talk to him. But he wasn't well—

even now he has to stay in bed for days at a time—and I knew that he didn't want to hear her name.

One morning he came into my room, while I was writing to her. He saw me thrust the package of letters into a cubby-hole, and I knew that I had betrayed him again.

"Don't ally yourself with deception, Sarah Ann," he said quietly. "You did that once, and you see what came of it."

"But if she writes to me—" I said. "What do you want me to do?"

He stood in the doorway in his long bathrobe. He had been in bed, and his hair was slightly awry from the pillows, and his face was a little pale. I have taken good care of him, and he still looks young—not more than forty—but his cheekbones worry me. They are sharp and white.

"I want you to give me her letters," he said. "To burn."

"Won't you read them, father? I know that what she did was wrong, but she sounds happy—"

I don't know what made me say that, except that, you see, I did love Olive.

He stared at me and came into the room.

"And you believe her? Do you think that happiness can come from deception?"

"But she's my sister," I said, and although I knew that he was right, I began to cry. "And she's your daughter. And you love her so."

He came and stood beside my chair. This time he didn't ask me why I was crying.

He kneeled suddenly beside me, and spoke very softly and quickly.

"We'll keep each other company, Sarah Ann, just the two of us. We can be happy that way, can't we? We'll always have each other, don't you know?" He put his hand on my hair.

I knew then, that was the way it should be. I leaned my head on his shoulder, and when I had finished crying I smiled at him, and went to find Olive's letters in my desk.

"You take them," I said. "I can't—"

He nodded and took them, and then took my hand.

I know that when he took them, he meant to burn them. I found them by chance yesterday in the back of his desk drawer, under a pile of old medical reports. They lay there like love-letters, from someone who had died, or moved away. They were tied in a slim green hair-ribbon—it was one of mine, but I suppose he had found it and thought that it was Olive's.

I didn't wonder what to do. It wasn't fair, don't you see? He hadn't any right to keep those letters after he told me I was the only daughter he had left. He would always be secretly reading them, and fingering them, and it wouldn't do him any good. I took them to the incinerator in the backyard, and burned them carefully one by one. His bed is by the window, and I know that he was watching me, but of course he couldn't say anything.

Maybe you feel sorry for father, maybe you think I was cruel. But I did it for his sake, and I don't care what you think, because you're all of you strangers, anyway, and you can't understand that there couldn't be two of us. As I said before, I don't hate Olive. But sometimes I think this is the way it was meant to be. First mother died, and left just the two of us to take care of father. And yesterday when I burned Olive's letters, I thought, now there is only me.

POEM

GREGORY CORSO

In the early morning
      beside the runaway hand-in-pocket
      whistling youth
I see the hopping drooling Desirer
His black legs . . . the corncob pipe and cane
The long greasy coat, and the bloodstained
      fingernails
He is waiting
      flat against the trees

THE HARVARD
ADVOCATE

ROBERT CUMMING

THE MEETING

RUNNING so fast, I don't know why I'm running so fast. I started running just a little after I left school, where somebody started chunking rocks at me. They hollered, "Let's see you run some, boy," and then started chunking rocks at me. I didn't look back to see who it was or anything; I just run. Now I'm way on away from there, but I'm still running.

Course the main reason for running today is Daddy Grace. Everybody in school's going to see Daddy Grace, and some of them didn't even come today so they could get prepared. But he ain't coming till six o'clock, and anyway mama said she'd prefer I didn't go. Clarie said why don't she and me go together, and mama said she wished I didn't go. I sure would like to go, but I don't want to cross mama. I wish I had somebody, my daddy or somebody, to tell me things like why those folks chunking rocks at me or what to do about Daddy Grace. Things like that you just don't know.

I'm not even going to think about it; I'm just going to run. When you run it seems like you're getting some place big, even if you're only going home. All you do is run. You don't have to worry bout anything, like how you wish you had a daddy or whether you ought to go hear Daddy Grace. Your arms are pushing out behind you and your knees most hitting up against your chest, and you just run.

I can run fast as anybody I ever saw. It must be a mile, maybe three or four, from school to my house, and I bet I only been running bout a minute. It couldn't be much more than that and I'm most home already.

That's my house, down the end of this alley. Past the one with the shiny doorknob, that one with the chinaberry tree out front. Before daddy left it used to be all our house. I don't know where he went but I sure wish he wasn't gone. Pretty soon after that the Watsons—that's Wash Watson and Mrs. Watson and their three little girls—they moved in the two front rooms. Clarie and mama and me live in the back room with the stove.

When I come in the door one of the little girls is picking at the cardboard tacked up on the wall to keep the place warm in winter.

"Stop that, Sarah-Anne," I say. "You know better than to tear that stuff down."

But she doesn't stop and I walk on into our room. There is Clarie and mama. I know they're going to argue; I can see it fore they start.

"Are you going to see Daddy with me," Clarie says. "He's coming at six o'clock, but I'm going head of time so I can get up close and see his face."

"You know what I think about it, son," mama says.

I hate this kind of tanglement. I wish daddy was here; he would know what we was going to do. Maybe he'd have taken me off squirrel-hunting or something, so we wouldn't even be here. I just wish there wasn't any arguing.

"I don't want any truck with that kind of shouting and hoodoo," mama says. "If folks worshiped God in the Church, stead of that man in his tent, they'd be a site better off."

"Daddy makes the sick people well, and the lame to carry their beds," Clarie says. "Everybody says he does. Bess Johnston, who never in her life been to church on Sunday, saw him over to Kannapolis last week and she's been talking about it ever since."

I look at mama. She is sitting in her chair with that black dress on. The skillet is lying by her feet, with this morning's grease all hard in the bottom. I wonder if God made her old like she is so she couldn't stop me from going to hear Daddy Grace.

I wonder if my daddy ever went to see Daddy Grace. I'd ask mama, but I don't want to hear any more arguing. I just want to get outside.

"The disciples give Daddy a brand-new tent," Clarie says. "I give him part of it. It must be a hundred times as big as this old house. And he deserves it," Clarie says. "They arn't a man in this state can preach like Daddy can. He tells you what's right and what's wicked, and you know it's the Lord's truth. I just feel like crying and praying, to see his face."

I wonder whether Daddy'd make me know what's right, so I'd feel like crying and praying. I look at mama where her black dress is tore down by her knee.

"Let me go for a while, mamma," I say. "I'll come back and fess all about it.

Daddy's tent is in that big field south of town. It's the biggest field around. It goes from the edge of town almost down to the river. That's where they have the fair when it comes up from Charleston.

"My, ain't that a fine tent," Clarie says when we get out there. It sure is big. It must be ten times as high as that truck they bring it in. It has a long tunnel like for an entrance, and over the place where you go in it says HOUSE OF PRAYER in big blue letters.

Inside the tunnel there is sawdust on the ground. Clarie and me walk down it. On one side there are bottles of Daddy's spring tonic, wrapped up in silver paper. On the other you can get a disciple's haircut for two dollars.

"Let's get right down in front," Clarie says, "while we got a chance." We walk out into the main part of the tent. There is nobody there, just empty benches going on for miles. Up toward the roof the air looks sort of smoky, and in the middle you can't even see the top. It seems like an eagle or an angel or something might be up there. Music is coming from somewhere, like in church.

We walk all the way down to the front. Against the side of the tent there is a platform that sticks out to the three nearest tent poles. The poles are slick and red. All around the edge of the platform are piles of roses, yellow and pink ones all mixed in. Then there is a space and then the benches begin. We sit down on the very first bench, Clarie and me.

Now the people are coming in, and it sure is hot. All the men in dark blue suits and all the women in the gayest dresses they can put on. First they fill in around the platform, and then the whole place gets filled, back through the poles and haze so far you can't even see. The women all talking bout Daddy and fanning themselves like they thought it would do some good.

I guess mama's back home sitting in her black dress by the stove, and that little Watson girl sucking her thumb or tearing the cardboard off my daddy's wall. But I ain't going to think about it now.

There are seven men dressed in white up on the platform, holding the shinest bugles you ever saw. They begin to blow and then there is a shout from the back. Daddy comes walking slow down the aisle, all by himself. He is wearing a bright gold cape that drags along the ground. "The disciples give him that last year," Clarie says. Underneath he has on one of those black suits like daddy used to wear to parties.

When he gets to the platform the seven men jump off and he climbs up alone. He turns around slow so that gold cape twirls out like an umbrella. He's a mighty big man, I think; must be about eight feet tall. Then he stops and I can see into his black eyes deep. I know why folks call him Daddy, just like they did Abraham. He raises up one hand.

"Children," he says.

"Daddy," everybody shouts. There is whooping and yelling. Some man behind me says, "Daddy, we is waiting on you."

"Children," Daddy says. "Children, there is just one thing in this world and that's Jesus Christ."

"That's right, Daddy," the people say. "Daddy, that sure is right."

"We don't need to think about anything, or worry about anything, or do anything except trust in Jesus Christ and obey him. Like he is our father. That's what the Gospel is about and that's what I'm here about and that's what the greatest hymn ever written is about. So let's sing that hymn right now, you and me together. *What a Friend We Have in Jesus.*"

In church they usually let a hymn play through once before folks sing it, but here everybody hits the first note.

"What a friend we have in Jesus,
All our pains and griefs to bear,
What a privilege to carry

Everything to God in prayer. . . ."

I think it is the finest singing I ever heard. While it's going on I'm watching Daddy, all alone, singing up on the platform. All he's doing is singing. He never has to worry, or run from anything. He knows what he ought to do and he's up there, alone, just doing it.

After the hymn there is shouting and folks saying Amen and walking in the aisles. Then Daddy yells "Silence," so loud you can hear him all over the tent. He just whirls his cape around and yells "Silence!" and people stop and listen like a train was coming.

Then he begins talking very soft.

"Children," he says. "Just put your faith in Jesus. Just forget the rest and put your faith in the Lamb of God. Now if you give me three volunteers—just three people willing to stand up for Jesus—I'll feed this five thousand. I'll show you what faith in Him can do for every one of you."

Then I am jumping up and I say, "Here am I." One time our preacher give a whole sermon on saying "Here am I." He said it was like jumping in the middle of the river, and if you don't do it you may have to stay back in the coves the rest of your life. He said you may only get knocked for once. So I jump up. Clarie pulls me back by the sleeve but I run up over the roses on the stage beside Daddy. "Here am I," I says like the Prophet in the Bible. "Send me."

Daddy steps back a little, but then he comes up and puts his hand on my shoulder. He's a big man, and I'm proud to stand up beside him.

"Son," he says, "you mighty brave to come up here when you so young and had so little time to get faith. I'm mighty proud of you. Now I'm going to help you along at first, but you'll be riding on your own faith soon enough."

There are two other men up on the stage, and Daddy goes over and shakes hands with them. Then he whirls around at the crowd.

"See these poles," he says, pointing to the tent poles at the edge of the platform. "They slick as grease; nobody could climb them. Now these children are going to rise by faith, their faith and our faith if we all praying for them, just like we all going to rise by faith if we got it."

He brings me over to one of the posts and slips something under my arms. In a minute I am rising up, grabbing onto the pole something is cutting into my shoulders and the people yelling fit to be killed. I think this is all a trick and I get mad at Daddy. Then I think he's right, I couldn't get up here by myself, even if those other fellows could. It is so hot up here I stop thinking at all.

Down below Daddy is shouting about faith. All the people are pointing at me and shouting. Then I'm ashamed I ain't got more faith in Daddy and Jesus. I let go the post with one arm and slip the wire off it. I wave at the people; they point at me. It sure is hot. "If you got enough faith," Daddy is saying, "it will hold you up." It is so hot; all you can smell is roses. I wave hard at the people. "Jesus will be your father," Daddy says, "if you just trust in him." My other arm slips out of its wire; I grab at the post; the people shout real loud.

I'd swear I stayed up there a minute after that wire was off, fore I fell. Anyway I'm not hurt when I hit the platform; but I sure am ashamed. All those people, and everyone of them knows I didn't have faith enough to stay up a pole. Or maybe mama is right and Daddy Grace don't have religion at all. I don't stop to think. I feel like a slice of meat on a skillet, and I don't stop to think. I don't even look at Daddy Grace; I just duck out under the tent behind him and run.

I run so fast I leave that whole place behind me, with Daddy shouting and people yelling and all. I run the other way, toward the river, stead of toward town. But I don't even care.

Then I wish I had somebody—daddy maybe—to tell me what happened, so I say running,

"Daddy, what really happened?"

But that hasn't got any sense to it. So I just run on faster leaving even that thinking behind.

Pretty soon I come to the end of the field and run into the honeysuckle getting my feet tangled and falling balled up down in a clump. I am lying on my back and I look up at the pines overhead. I see how dark it is and how big the moon shines in between.

I get up and run on like you run through the woods at night: high-stepping and listening for things not to step on, slow as a fast walk with your hands down near the ground. One time I look back and see Daddy Grace's tent glowing through the trees. It's big and bright orange like to hurt your eyes, like something in a bad dream. I don't want to look at it; I don't want to think about it more than I can help. I push my head around and run on on the soft ground between the pines.

Now I can see the moon glinting on the water. I come out on a cove that runs back up in the woods. All you can see is trees and water and moon; that's all there is.

SONGS FROM A PICARESQUE ROMANCE

JOHN HOLLANDER

They tell of how Dick Dongworth *loved vainly his dark and glittering cousin* Roseblush, *and of how, amid many adventures, he sang these songs:*

SUNG TO HIMSELF ON HORSEBACK

I who have affected
Learning and remorse
Never held good manners
Improper out of doors,
Until an old man showed me
All that grace abhors
—The boneyard, of course
To which I'll be elected.

I've always played at knowing
The nature of the weather,
Pitting knowledge and
Despair against each other;
But now they hold dominion
Like kings allied together
    Over wherever
It may or not be snowing.

If I'm undone in London
Who'll love or honor me?
Unless I were to bend and
Demand alms of the sea,

Nor man nor star nor girl's bare arms
Could bear my perfidy;
    My grave would agree
With his bears' arms I've punned on.

The gentler arms of battle
May ring about my head
In celebration that has made
Old cities kneel and wed.
Although imposing Rome was
No virgin, yet she bled,
    ·And for an aubade,
Morning came with a rattle.

Love's flame is fairly steady,
For love can ill afford
That final bifurcation
That's fired by the sword;
When brands and ashes drop,
Smoke goes up like a bird:
    Raze me, O Lord,
My beard's too long already.

DICK DONGWORTH, IN THE RAIN,
CONSIDERS HIS REJECTION
BY ROSEBLUSH

When all the wild red things she's worn
Hang like cousins in a closet,
She'll think of one she's bruised and torn
When, though pale, she's tried to lose it.
Once retrieved, she can't refuse it
Yet she fears its kind return,
Like a dead cousin's winding sheet
She'd gone and lost along the street;
Better let it burn, she said,
Better let it burn.

This warring and benevolence
I will not have; nor would I change her,
For she would offer no defense
And lend her body to a stranger.
"The predication of Love's danger
Lies in refusals to deceive";
And I would foxily concur
And go, and tell no tale of her
To let her learn and grieve in bed,
To let her learn and grieve.

Once, at a word, she reddened so,
All pale disdaining now belies her;
But since, her coloring grown slow,
She'd need a rainbow to advise her.
If distance proves me any wiser
I'll by far the wiser be;
She, wanting of sufficient haste
Shall as pursuer yet be chased,
While past her soft away I'll tread,
Soft and speedily.

But if her coloring be quick
And pink as skin has never worn it,
I'll wear the red as Simple Dick:
She'll play as bee, and I'll be hornet;
Night's colored dead, and thus we'll mourn it
Till our coloring is dun.
Then to redress the sky for Night
We'll wear that coloring to white,
And scratch it to the bone instead,
And scratch it to the bone.

DICK DONGWORTH CONSIDERS THE DEATH OF ROSEBLUSH

Her epitaph was never read;
Gone was the stone above her head
(Robbed by a needy sculptor
Who never could have helped her,
Nor had her maidenhead
Before she was dead).
Before she was married
They had her dead and buried.

She perished as must everyone
Who can I blame her death upon?
I should rather
Not involve her father,
Nor was she killed by fools
For freedom or her jewels.
(And we are all far subtler
Than to accuse the Butler).

Put all the guilt upon the lake,
Say she died for drowning's sake;
(Call it Nature reflected,
The glass that Love affected,

Or Christ's photographer)
The pool that swallowed her
Was merely a mirror
Whose image was in error.

Say that she was never brave
But only greedy for the grave;
Say Dongworth's rusty armor
Served only to alarm her.
Then write this of me:
"Were she only free,
John Thomas, my English cousin,
Could pluck her like a raisin."

WILLIAM ALFRED

POEMS FROM

FIVE HARD SONGS IN A BAD TIME

"Now in my youth I am well on the way to a happy finish. I can hardly get much further at this staggering pace. Kicking evil away, I try, by singing, to have all things turned to the good. Love, and the dearest kind of love, is what I bequeath you all."
—RICHARD ROLLE OF HAMPOLE, *An Anthem for Thinkers*, 113

BANKRUPTCY   *"veni sancte spiritus . . ."*

Adventurous Spirit, turned Recluse,
I need You. Put at my blind use
What is beyond my competence.

I have run through that princely sum
You gave me to begin with. Come,
Father. Beggar that I am,

Inconsolable optimist,
Reduced to die in this mare's nest,
Perfidious with tedium,

My wasted funds could meet with ease
This interest bleeds me to the lees,
All these usurious wants grow dumb,

Should You but take this risk on me.
I do not care how angrily.
My pride is gone with my income.

The time is past when crazed with shame,
No one came near I did not blame.
I know why I have nothing to my name.

Without You I will lose even sense and will.
There will be nothing left me. Nothing. Sure and still
That core of storms, that loanshark vacuum

Will rob me blind, despite this moratorium
It grants me, hounded to this one locked room
Of Your ruined house, my honorarium.

Pay off that devil for me. I am numb.
My schemes are muddled to delirium.
I can see no other way, unless You come

And tide me through this time, for me to assume
My mortgage. It makes even health seem doom;
For I have squandered all inheritance.

If I am done for, past the point where some
Have managed to recoup, You still must come.
Or who will close this house, and take me home!

THE OFFICE OF THE BEE

When, caught between screen and glass,
Freedom of sight and touch
Were yours, but you found no way to pass
Beyond my window's smutch,
And flew till you split a wing
Against that ringing wire,
Since only to fly was to sing,
And to sing was your desire
I lifted up the screen.—
Yes, you foundered in the air,
And the grass no more was green
You fell to like a flare.
Bee,
I set you free:
Pray for me.

1957–1986

1957–1986

Each *Advocate* "era" has instituted new traditions and adapted or ended old ones. The parody issue last appeared in 1937, Mother Advocate faded into the fifties, and, except for a brief revival in the late sixties, *Advocate* commentary on local and national events faded with her.

What this particular era lacked in controversy, it compensated for with a dramatic change in emphasis, content, and personnel. Women moved from contributor to editor status in the sixties—today's *Advocate* staff is fifty percent female.

Although novelist Sallie Bingham was a contributor rather than an editor (the magazine was still exclusive in the fifties), "Winter Term" influenced *Advocate* fiction well into the sixties. The magazine's staff received so many Harvard/Radcliffe love sagas, the "Harvard Square Sex Story" became an in-house joke.

Fiction was given greater emphasis in the sixties. William Kelly and Jonathan Kozol wrote several of the best *Advocate* short stories; Kozol's contribution, "The Contest," won the prestigious Olympia award only a few years after his graduation from Harvard.

The *Advocate* published several commemorative and critical issues throughout the last two decades. Issues dedicated to the writing of James Agee, W. H. Auden, and Robert Lowell featured criticism and analysis by Hannah Arendt, Stephen Spender, Tennessee Williams, and Norman Mailer.

As in other eras, several great writers contributed prose and poetry to the *Advocate*. This was especially true of the sixties and seventies when Robert Lowell, William Burroughs, Desmond O'Grady, John Berryman, and Howard Nemerov were featured in the magazine.

Today's *Advocate* does not accept contributions from non-Harvard writers, preferring instead to publish work from within the university. To compensate for the lack of famous names, the current *Advocate* prints regular interviews with well known writers and has greatly expanded its review and critique functions. The new emphasis is to provide an outlet for those who lack one and a critical forum for local writers and artists.

Perhaps the most dramatic shift in emphasis involves *Advocate* art. In the forty years since small, trendy drawings illustrated *Advocate* prose, art work and magazine design has achieved equal standing with fiction, poetry, and review. Working closely with Harvard's Visual and Environmental Studies department, current *Advocate* art mirrors exciting changes in traditional art forms, exploring new materials and techniques.

The substance and style of *Advocate* prose and poetry echoes both the traditional and the neo-modern. The work of Wallace Stevens, John Ashbery, Robert Creeley, and James Merrill have influenced both formal and non-traditional poetic strategies; there is a certain sense of immediacy, a separation of context and reality mirrored in today's *Advocate* fiction. The literary journal that once "lagged twenty years behind the fact" has become sharply aware of new movements and method.

The fiction, poetry, criticism, and art of this era must stand on its own merits rather than on the weight of great names. Too little time has passed to know who will be famous, or who will influence American literature. It is the quality of the *Advocate* in the last two decades and the record of past achievements that assures the magazine a lasting place in American art and literature.

WINTER TERM

•

•

•

•

•

SALLIE BINGHAM

It was inconvenient. And worse; Hal watched the woman behind the desk ruffling through file cards, and wondered if she had noticed that he came to the library every evening. She must have noticed him, and Eleanor; and he often thought she watched them during those evenings in the library. During the day, he sometimes planned a new kind of evening, still at the library, for the dancing and movie Saturdays he spent with Eleanor were even more stereotyped. Sometimes, he imagined that Eleanor would be there when he came, or that she would not be wearing lipstick, as when he had first seen her. But he knew that the small details' change could not alter the whole evening. In the past week, he had begun to imagine the only possible change: that Eleanor would not come at all. When he studied in his room in the afternoon, Hal planned to wait at the library until a quarter past seven, and then, if she had not come, he would leave, not buttoning his coat and turning at once onto the street.

"Why don't you take off your coat?" the librarian asked him. He had never heard her voice before. It was pleasantly colorless and he was surprised that with such a voice she had spoken to him at all.

"Oh, that's all right," he said, vaguely. "I may have to leave in a few minutes." She pulled out another drawer of filing cards, and began to ruffle through them. As he watched her, Hal became more and more surprised that she had spoken to him. It reminded him that he was still, even after a month, an intruder; there were so few boys in the library that the girls stared at them openly. He walked over to the reading room door and looked in; the red haired boy whom he had begun to speak to on the street was studying there with his girl. Eleanor said that they were engaged, although Hal had pointed out that the girl was not wearing a ring; Eleanor said it did not really matter. They always went out with each other, and on Saturdays and Sundays she had seen them having breakfast together in the Waldorf. Hal remembered asking her what they had been eating; it was a new way he had of testing Ellie, to see how long it would be before she laughed; if he teased her for a certain amount of time, he knew that she would more probably cry. "French Toast," she had answered promptly, "three orders, with maple syrup." And then she had asked him why he laughed, and when he shook his head and went on laughing her mouth began to quiver, and he tightened as she said, "Why do you always laugh at me?" They had had a bad evening. The tightening had started it, Hal knew; he could grant that to her in this carelessly objective mood of remembering. He wondered if he would ever be able to prevent himself from feeling like that when she didn't laugh, or when she was depressed, or when she asked him, "What are you thinking?"

Hal looked at the clock. She was already seven minutes late. It happened every evening; he imagined her dawdling over combing her hair, watching the clock, and planning not to leave in time. She often warned him about taking one another for granted. Surprised by his own bitterness, he thought, Oh God, why do I always have to be so hard on her; lately she can't do anything right. He remembered how he used to feel when she came towards him, running because she was late, or in out of the rain; she shook the rain out of her hair(too proud to wear a scarf), and her face was flecked with drops.

Eleanor came in the door before he could decide when the change had begun. She started towards him, red faced from the wind she had fought for four blocks on her bike. "Hello," she said, and he knew that if he had looked permissive she would have kissed him instead, in spite of the librarian. It was one of the things that he had first liked about her, along with the absence of lipstick, which she had since started wearing; she was willing to kiss him even on the Saturday night subway to Boston, when the whole row of people on the other side of the car was watching. Hal remembered how surprised he had been when they first danced together and she had pulled close, for the action had not suited the mild, high necked dress she was wearing, or even the coolness of her cheek.

She was peeling off the neat layers of her coat and sweater, and he noticed how limberly she bent to unfasten her boots, because he was watching. She had a much better figure than the red haired boy's girl, especially since she had given up sweets. He remembered proudly that she had started to diet because he had told her once that a dress was too tight; he had never had to tell her again. Now, her hips were straight under her skirt, and he knew from looking at them how they would feel, very firm as she clenched the big muscles, and smooth through her slippery underpants.

She led the way to the reading room. He had grown accustomed to people looking but he knew from the way Ellie was smiling that they still made her uncomfortable. When they sat down, she whispered, "You'd think they'd learn not to stare every night!" and he whispered back, leaning close so that her hair touched his mouth, "It's only because you're beautiful."

"You've said that before," she said, mocking and pleased, but he had already realized it; it did not matter how often he had repeated the compliment, for every time the situation had been the same, until the lie had become as familiar as the library room. He looked at the clock.

"Bored?" she asked quickly.

"No." He tried not to frown. She made a little face at him, and bent over her notebook.

He wished he had not learned to translate her expressions. When he had first met her, he had been charmed by her good-humored little pout, or her wide-eyed stare after they kissed. But now he knew that the pout was made to conceal the quiver in her mouth, and if he watched her a minute later he would see that she was not reading, that she was staring at the page and trying not to look at him. And as for her expression after he kissed her—it always seemed to Hal that he was watching her come up from a great depth of water—he did not know what it meant, but it irritated him. It was like the way she acted after they had made love. She went into it as exuberantly as jumping up to dance, leaving it to him to make sure that his room mates were out, and that the shades were down. By the time he had checked, she would have pulled her dress off over her head, rumpling her hair in bangs over her eyes. He began to undress, folding his clothes on the chair—"Ellie, will you hang up your dress?"—, but when he turned around and saw her waiting, naked under her slip, he went to her and forgot what he had been about to say.

But afterwards, if she didn't cry, she would not speak to him. She clenched him in her arms when he tried to get up, and he had to hurt her in order to break away, even though he had told her how necessary it was. When she clung to him like that, with her fingernails pricking his back, he tried to force himself out of his sleepiness, to polish her hair and kiss her. But her mouth tasted stale when he was so tired, and he was afraid she might think he wanted to do it again.

"I'm sorry I was late," Ellie said, not looking up from her book, and he realized that for the last five minutes she had been trying to decide why he seemed irritated.

"I thought we said we wouldn't apologize any more." He wanted to sound gay, but he realized at once that she was still raw to the subject; her eyes seemed to grow larger with hurt as she looked at him and said, "I wished you'd forget that." She was bending down the corner of a page, and he wanted to tell her not to; the little, mechanical action irritated him out of all proportion, and he wondered if he was so tense because they hadn't done it for four days. How did she feel about tonight? He knew that his room mates were out. Hal looked at her, but he could tell from the way she was hunched over her book that she was not thinking about making love but about the evening three days before when they had quarreled and then made a list of resolutions over coffee in Hayes-Bick's. One of them had been not to apologize, for they agreed that it was hypocritical; apologies were only a dog-in-the-manger way of saying I was right all along but I'll give in for the sake of peace. It had been a terrible evening, and Hal was sorry that they had gone to Hayes-Bick's, for the quarrel had destroyed his picture of one of their first evenings together, when he had held her hand between the salt and pepper.

"Oh, I forgot to ask you about the exam." She had not whispered, and the girl at the next desk looked up, frowning. "How was it?" she whispered, not looking at the girl.

"Terrible!" The exclamation did not relieve him. He had come back from the exam in the winter darkness, coffee nerved, and fingering the three pencils in his pocket whose points were worn flat. He remembered cursing himself for not reviewing enough, and he had wondered wildly if he could have written at the end of the thin, scratched blue book, "Circumstances beyond my control. . . ."

"But I thought you were so well prepared; you've been reviewing for practically a week."

He tried not to say it, but the words promised too much relief. "Yes, but I can't really study here." He knew before he looked at her that she was hurt, and as soon as he saw her mouth he felt the tightening; he wanted to laugh out loud and throw his head back and yell with laughter, and at the same time he wanted to pull her into his arms and fold her so tightly that her breath came in gasps.

"You never told me that before," she said, and he knew how carefully she had weeded the hurt out of her voice.

"Well, I mean, what do you expect? How can I concentrate on studying with you around?" He had meant it to be a compliment, he wanted to see her smile and look up at him, but it sounded like an accusation. As she turned her face sharply away he thought, Oh God, not another scene, and then he noticed abruptly how thin she had grown; he could see the point of her collar bone through her sweater, and her little pear breasts stood out too sharply.

Ellie had bent the corner of the page down so often that it broke off in her hand. She turned to Hal, smiling too brightly. "You should have seen the dormitory tonight." In spite of her smile, Hal wanted to kiss her for changing the subject. He thought that afterwards he would buy her an ice cream cone at the drugstore on the way back. She loved sweets, and she hadn't had any for at least two weeks; he remembered her inexpensive, salad dinners even on Saturday nights. And she was really almost too thin.

"You know Wednesday night is usually bad, anyway," she was saying. The girl at the next desk looked up again, annoyed, and Ellie's hand flew to her mouth. She would not have gone on if Hal had not asked, "Well, what happened?" and then she turned to him and whispered so softly, hesitantly that he could hardly hear. "You know, Wednesday's boy night, and they have candles and ice cream, just because we eat at quarter past six instead of six! Tonight I sat at a table with three girls and their dates and I literally didn't say one word." Hal had heard it often before; he looked around the room, trying to distract his attention from his own irritation. Why was she proud of not talking for a whole meal? He noticed the pretty girl who was in his humanities class; she was winding a shank of hair around her finger as she studied. Pretty hair. But she looked even more tense than the rest of them. During exam period, you could cut the atmosphere in the reading room with a knife. Most of the girls looked overtired and ugly, and they had not bothered to comb their hair. This was the one place where they never expected to see any boys. But Eleanor hated the Harvard library. She said she felt too stared at when there were so few girls. Hal had caught some of the looks boys gave her when they walked down the corridor, and he agreed. She had such a damn good figure.

"You're not listening," she said. "I know—don't apologize; I shouldn't be distracting you." And as though her rigidly calm tone really expressed her feelings, Eleanor wrote the date neatly at the top of a notebook page, and began to read.

"I am interested," he lied, feeling her hurt; "it's just I'm interested in this place, too." She did not answer, and so he slammed his book open and turned the pages roughly, looking for the place. They sat for ten minutes in silence. Hal tried to read, but he was too conscious of the tip of her elbow, almost touching his; it looked a little chapped, and he remembered how hard the winter weather was on her blond skin. Then he wondered how he had known that—he had been through no other winter with her, or even a spring or summer—and inconsequentially he wondered what she looked like in a bathing suit. He hunched his shoulders and bent down closer to his book, trying to force the words into his attention. There were long, ruler straight lines under many of the sentences, and minute notes were printed in the margins. He had written them in October, when for a week he had devoted himslf to Schopenhauer, reading each page passionately, proud of the learned comments he wrote in the margins. He even found time to go into Boston to visit the museum where there was a portrait of the philosopher, and he remembered how his head had pounded as he climbed the long stairs and hurried down a corridor to the door of the room where the portrait hung. It had been a disappointment, an old placid gentleman in conventional black; did pessimism embodied look like that? he remembered thinking, like your own grandfather? But he had come back with a feeling of accomplishment.

Now he could not read his own notes. When Ellie was hurt, the consciousness of it ticked like a clock at the back of his mind, and he could not concentrate on anything. He gave up trying to ignore the point of her elbow. He wondered if she would move first, as she often did, slipping her hand into his or turning into his arms as soon as they were alone or touching the back of his neck. He noticed how rigidly she was sitting; why did they both go on pretending to study? He looked at the clock; already half an hour wasted. God, I wish we'd had a chance to make love so I wouldn't feel like I'm going crazy. Exams; we said we couldn't afford the time. And self-righteously they avoided his room, knowing that once they were there where the sheets were marked from the last time and where they had first said that they were in love, their resolution would collapse in a panic. Their coming together was always too violent, he thought, like the too big lunch you eat after missing breakfast, snatching and tearing at the food if no one was watching. But I bet she needs it, he thought, that's why she's so quivery, close to tears, and maybe that's why I loused up that exam. But he knew it was an excuse; he had failed the exam because he had not known the material. He felt his resentment heating as he wondered why he had not reviewed more carefully. But she's right, I spent all last week on it, he thought, and then he

THE HARVARD ADVOCATE

november issue · 35c

added, enjoying his bitterness, yes, but you know what studying here means, jockeying for position for three hours with our knees always about to touch or our hands and she's always looking up or else I am until finally we give up and hold hands though that means I can't write or else she can't. Why didn't I have sense enough to tell her I had to study, two evenings would have done it, but I knew she'd cry. Not over the phone but in the booth after I hung up so she wouldn't be able to walk back down the hall without the other girls seeing she'd been crying. He wanted to turn to her and break the thin unreal wall of her concentration, asking, why does everything hurt you too much? And why do I always have to know? Although he knew the last, at least, was not her fault.

He heard eight strike in silver, feminine notes from the clock over the girls' gym. That clock would never let him forget the amount of time he was wasting; all evening, he would have to listen to its coy reminders. The thought jacked him to the top of his irritation, and he slammed his books closed and began to stack them together. Eleanor looked up, and he saw in her eyes the terror that he had heard once in her voice when he told her that he would have to go home for the weekend. She had said, "You know that means three days without talking to anyone." But he had answered, trying to laugh, "But there must be someone—all those girls." "You know I'm not a girl's girl; I don't really know how to talk to them. And anyway, I don't spend my extra time in the Smoker, so they hardly know my name." And he had understood what she had been unwilling to say, that he had taken up the time she might have spent padding herself with girl aquaintances against the time when she would be alone. In the end, he had left without telling her goodbye, and the weekend had been spoiled because he had known how she was feeling.

He stood up, although he had still not decided what he was going to do. Only, no more waste.

"You want to leave?" she asked, hurriedly gathering up her books, and Hal knew that she thought he was going to walk out without her. He knew that he was being brutal, and that if she began to cry he would be more than ashamed; he would feel that his hands were as clumsy as trays as he tried to sooth her, and then, as he struggled to find something gentle to say, he would begin to go mad with irritation. He started towards the reading room door before Ellie was ready, and he heard the almost hysterical ruffling of the pages as she closed her books. He waited for her on the other side of the door, and when she came, nearly running, he saw

the brand mark of fear on her face fade as she smiled with relief that he was waiting.

"I agree with you; let's get out of this dreary place." she said, and Hal wished that she had been angry.

"Look, I'm going to walk you back now," he said as they went out into the sudden coldness. She began to fumble awkwardly with her scarf, trying to adjust it inside her coat collar.

"Right now?" Her voice was carefully casual.

"Look, Eleanor, I've got to get something done tonight. Friday's the Phil. 101 exam."

"Oh, I understand." They walked along side by side, conscious of not holding hands. The quadrangle was dark except for the library lights and the illumined clock over the gym. It was always five minutes fast, he knew, on purpose, so that the girls who were late starting would still get to the Harvard classrooms on time. In spite of the clock, Ellie was always coming in late, hesitating in the doorway to look for him, and red and damp from running.

"Are you going to continue the history course?" He wished that she would not keep her voice cheerful, trying to pretend to him, but not to herself, that they had not silently quarreled.

"Can't divide it at mid-term." He was irritated by his own grudging tone, although it was easy enough to justify it; even if he broke with her now and finally (it was incredible, the thought of pushing off her hands and running without hearing her calling), he would still have to see her every Monday, Wednesday, and Friday at ten in the history class where they would try not to look at each other.

Her dormitory was full of lights. At last they've taken down the wreath!" he said.

"It was really too much." Her voice had revived with his cheerfulness, real this time; although it was ridiculous, he knew that the tarnished wreath was a reminder of the Christmas vacation they had spent straining to be together, the long distance calls when her voice was tremulous, and the too many, raw letters.

They stood under the porch light, and she held out her hands. He took them, and slipped his fingers inside her gloves. Her palms were soft and lined.

"Look at all the bikes," he said inconsequentially, "You'd think they'd give up in this bad weather," and they both looked out at the heaped, stone snow. He remembered that he had a long walk back, but as he bent hurriedly to kiss her she slipped her arms around him so that he had to pull back hard in order to get away. She let go at last, her arms hurting, and no longer trying to smile. "Hal, don't go." He hesitated. "Please don't go. Please." She was rigidly controlling her voice, but he knew the limit of her endurance, and he wanted to be away before she began to cry, for then he would never be able to leave. He would have to wait until she was calm, rocking her in his arms and kissing her hair. Then he would walk back along the river to the house, avoiding noticing clocks until he was in his room. When he saw the tin alarm clock that was already set for the morning he would throw his books violently into a chair so that John looked out of the bedroom: "What's wrong with you?" And then he would go out and buy coffee so that, with luck, he could study until three. By that time, the lights across the courtyard would all be out, and often, it would begin to snow.

Eleanor had sensed his tension. "About tomorrow," she said lightly, working her books around in her arms and wiping a fleck of nothing off one of the covers. "I know we both have a lot of work. I'll call you in the morning, anyway, and then we can decide. I guess maybe we ought to study by ourselves tomorrow night." Her voice was so matter-of-fact that if he had not known the pattern Hal would not have believed that, next day, when they came to the deciding, she would plead with him to study with her in the library: "Really, I promise, we'll get something done," and she would offer to sign a promise that she would not speak to him for three hours. Now, he was looking down, and running her finger along the side of a book. "Hal," she said, "I'm sorry about tonight. You know how I get sometimes." He put his arms around her, although the books were between them, and he tried not to tell her how sorry he was, tried to choke back his softness: "Oh God, Ellie," he said instead, and he heard the almost tears in his own voice, the rawness that was both tenderness and irritation. She strained up to kiss him, and when she opened her mouth he felt tricked, knowing that she was intentionally exciting him, that if he put his tongue between her lips he would not be able to leave. As he kissed her he began half consciously to forget that he should go. She dropped her books and they tumbled over their feet. He pressed close to her suddenly, forgetting, forcing his tightness to the back of his mind. He was only vaguely conscious of the porch and the staring light as he pulled her roughly against him, hearing her moan with pain and excitation. Then in a blurred voice, she said, "Isn't there somewhere we can go?" Her face was flushed, reminding him in a twisted way of a child waking up, damp and fresh. She was trying to think of somewhere and holding his hands tightly as though she could brace his desire

and prevent it from diminishing.

He hesitated. He knew that he could leave now, quickly and without kissing her, and it would not be too hard. But then she would go on taking classes with him and calling to him across the street, and when he came up the entry stairs and heard his phone ringing he would have to wait on the landing until it had stopped. . . .

"It's too late to have you in the dormitory," she said, and he automatically checked off their short list of private places. It was too cold for the common; they had been nervous, anyway, on the bench behind the thin screen of shrubbery. And it was too late for her to go his room. Parietal rules! He wondered viciously how many people they had forced into marriage. They had talked now and then of renting a room, but they never had the nerve; like his bedroom, the idea was sordid with old connotations. Although they were proud of their pretended indifference to surroundings, her face seemed to reflect the grey walls when they lay together on his bed.

"At least let's get out of this porch light," he said, and they went down the steps and stood hesitating on the sidewalk. She was looking around, eagerly and hopefully, and he wondered how much of her desire was passion and how much grasping; girls used sex to get a hold on you, he knew; it was so easy for them to pretend to be excited.

They wandered down the sidewalk. As they passed the college parking lot, Eleanor said, "Look, we could . . ." She did not go on, but Hal knew at once that she meant the cars, the college girl cars with boxes of tissues and clean seat covers, parked in rows in the lot behind the dormitories. "All right," he said, knowing that the whole time they would be afraid of someone coming, even at the climax they would be listening for steps. They walked around the lot. Ellie laughed; trying, he knew to keep him from recognizing the sordidness of the situation. He wondered why it was now so easy for him to accept the back seats of cars, and student beds with broken springs. He chose a Ford station wagon, and held the back door open for her. When he followed her, she turned to him, and they sank together down onto the seat. He started carefully to unbutton her blouse, feeling her stiffen as he traced her breast. Across the quadrangle, the gymnasium clock chimed silverly. Nine o'clock. Suddenly violent, he ripped her blouse open, and as she tried, terrified, to push off his hands, he began to tear at her slip. "Stop it Eleanor, let go," and as he pulled the straps off her shoulders, she dropped her hands and began to cry.

**ARTHUR
FREEMAN**

THE EXHORTATION TO AN AUDIENCE, TO BE STILL

*WHEREAS, these nimble shadows, dosing our stage
with a fairyland somnolence, are shy
if questioned, flit when caged
by whispers; and pinpointed, they must vanish, they must fly
like fireflies into someone else's dream—
no less illusory than shadows seem . . .*

*WHEREAS, the glancing glass of the imagination's
mirrors, pierced with laughter, shatters;
so this lacy needlework, contrived hallucinations,
striated with conversation, scatters
back to ravelled stagecraft . . . thus the violence
of careless talk uncharms our spell of silence. . . .*

*THEREFORE, peace! Now in attentive webs, catch rapture fleeting;
rise with our fantastic eyes, to sight beyond mere seeing.*

SKEETER

A skeeter skitters shrewdly across a pool.
Circular proliferations point
Toward a rounded end, then merge, then flatten away.
Dead skin on a finger-tip announces more:
Hot water, advancing blood, then quick cold air
And retreating blood. The surface of the pond
Seems to stretch and contract, but does not swell and shrink
Like human skin. It is not human skin;
It is water, set in motion by the legs
Of an insect, moving shrewdly over it.
The shrewdness is not ours. We can know
An expanding radius from each still point,
But the pointless movement, unpredictable,
From point to point, inscrutable and dumb,
Bores us. The cunning bores us. We have hands
Complete with permanent fingers, fully skilled
In compassing our very human desires.
Therefore we wash and dry them, to make sure
That they are serviceable; the dead skin
Peels off, expendable. Shrewd skeeter, skate
Icily random across your glassy drum:
I could break your floating web with one dropped stone
But my hand is clenched and will not let it go.

Thomas Whitbread

THE GOLDWEIGHER

Low Countries; 15th c; a Burgher donor

i

From the road the afternoon is sapphire-clear;
The fields, a canvas sealed with snowy gesso
Where artisans have left their sluggish marks,
Fence lost in drifts like driftwood on white beach.
Flattened now, unshaped, these supine fields
Roll back from squinting eyes; this ironing frost
Has cadged the desert's bright rough cloak with ease,
Robbed the tropic panther of his muscled crouch.
—I think these bare wonders, stable beauties,
These uncut stones might curb the men who rule
Our finer towns, fend off the troubador
With lute in hand, him gaudy with glad song.

So run my thoughts: lush thoughts that sometimes elbow
Prisoners of Cold, as this December day
Spirals toward Christmas eve, and my time climbs:
The old love heady on my trudge toward home.

But, sure, this grief of cold resilient light
Tattered Joseph in his boots would know
As sacred (and properly magnificent
For nativity)—would know this better than
Our gargoyled towers, all our celebrating,
Attentuated gestures of the earth
That point up paradise with files of saints
Marshalled by kings to gaze upon the vault.
And certainly he'd know the antique ease
Of fields bedded in snow; the warm, banked house;
The cattle stamping slowly on the straw,
The chinked barn steaming through Cold's long delay.

ii

A man who comes years after greatness, seeks.
He pauses by the statues in the square
And gapes at fame, seeking some quirk in stance;
Decides (in deft perversion of heroics)
That though bronze kings corrode on golden thrones
Still higher thrones are clay—the crown of thorn
Fetches more honor than a golden garland.
Taut Alexander, who held all the world,
Felt no such humble call. He claimed his fame.
To serve, hold back, he knew meant death; yet knew
His heights would leave him reeling at his death.
Only the age-old dead, whose tales are gnarled,
Pretended hemlock cups were draughts of wine.

              And Christmas Eve comes up
The East, the light dying, falling far
To another world. Now the North Star points
Toward Dipper's span; now no prospect of a fire.

iii

What snow! From certain heights to certain deaths
The traveller wanders, too far from home.
Here new foods are dangerous, and old clothes
Set one apart on strange, uncharted roads.
Across the field, turned by the mangle of the wind.

A light off the road! A corn crib's slats
Send stairs of light, lead from my road
Across the furrowed field up to an old
Wind-guttered shed made warm by man's sure hand:
One feeding his stock, guarding his own land.
I stop for the corn-crib light.

              My eyes half close.
Haunches are melting two ovals in the land
Of frost. It is damp rest, and all dry is lost
For tonight. Once I think I see the snow
That silks this bank give up some lover's ghost,
Like Dido locked in the toil of dark. But no,
The cash belt hugs me, holds me warm; my way
Holds only damp and caking boots. And yet
This scene, nameless! Surely there's a linen bed!

And farmers standing near, and lambs, and light?
(Candles glinting warmly by winter's gloom,
Circles of softness on the sacred floor.)

iv

But He means more than real or trusted crèche.
Once (in Bourges) I stood before *une Vierge;*
A populace of candles burned their prayers;
Beneath, two trays, one full at two francs, one
With but a handful left at ten. I thought
It is buying special ten franc candles,
It is the courage to do this thing that counts:
Whether or not the hoped-for outcome is assured.
Caritas and *humilitas* are still
Too good a buy for rich, too dear for poor.

I think of early mornings when wars are begun
And the most important departures made;

Before the city awakens, before coffee.
Of midnight, when you build and kill, and the still
Griefs labor. When love confirms, denies, or sleeps.
Of the evenings when the last bottle pops,
Uncorked at last, and wars and loves are gauged
Across the tablecloth. The Patience hangs
Around for always, and Meekness for a time.

Body stiffens on the ground, my rest; back takes
All the cold in; legs hurt from the long walking.
It is a night for every man to be
In his own city.

                        The road grows short,
And hurry, but night not warmer. I shall
be numb for hours, hours before limbs tingle.
This night it is a long way through to rest,
Also much pain before warm bed again.

V

You see, I've chosen for myself a far
City, so far for such a night; so cold.
What's more, you see, the woman I desire
I may not reach tonight. Willing would I
Deliver myself to her smothering hands!

And yet the manger counts . . . not on this road,
But in my city, in my morning of praise,
Where I have gold enough to love Him, love
To gild Him. There I'll buy a window for
His spiraling hall, one many-colored, bold;
(The roses glowing warmly in winter's glare
Pouring soft circles round the level floor)
To rainbow all His marble court in blues,
Reds; and, centerwise, a tall, contrite, and
Suitably attired image of myself.

William Kelly

BROTHER CARLISLE

Mama leaned out the kitchen window, reeled in the line's knot, and started to pin out her cllothes. Then over the unoiled pulley's screeching, she heard her younger son scream. He was somewhere in the alley, between her building and the next.

"Carlisle, what you doing to Little Brother?" She attempted to bend her voice around to him. "Carlisle, you hear?" There was no answer, but someone had begun to pound on the apartment door. Drying her hands on her apron, she shuffled through the apartment, down the dark hallway, heard her slippers scraping on the wooden floor.

"Oh-Lass, won't you come open *the* door?" Mama opened the door to the fat West Indian woman who occupied the alley apartment and who now stood before her in a pink night-gown. "Oh-Lass, child, they *burn*-ing your babe a-*live*," Missus Neilberry was crying. Tears of excitement streamed over her cheeks, catching in the deep crevices of her chins. "They *burn*-ing you child, a-*live*."

Somewhere within her, Mama felt slightly ill, but by the time she noticed it, she was on the second floor landing, had almost cascaded into old, black Mister Doozen coming back from his daily walk. Already she had lost one slipper, and the front door pulled the other from her when it slammed on her foot.

Little Brother's shoes were starting to steam. He was bound to the clothes pole in the alley with thick black wire, and was all but obscured by white smoke surging up from the pile of paper and trash burning at his feet. Carlisle, Mama's older son, sat beside the fire sweating, pretending to warm his hands. The members of his club stood around, hands in pockets, in a state of mixed bewilderment, fear and excitement, not certain, now, they were doing the best thing.

Mama lunged into the midst of smoke and flame and with bare feet kicked the fire from under Little Brother. She untied his hands, which despite the heat were damp and cold. When she led him out of the smoke, the other boys had disappeared, leaving Carlisle sitting as before, only now biting his fingernails.

"Carlisle?" she spoke to him, almost afraid, for this was not the first time he had done such things, and she knew he would have again some valid excuse and that her protestations would have no affect. "Why'd you—"

"Aw, Mama," Little Brother, his breath returned, interrupted. "They was letting me join the club. You got to prove you is brave before they let you in." He was pulling her apron and jumping up and down.

Carlisle smiled.

She looked down at Little Brother and opened her mouth, but no words came. She drew her hand across her forehead. Little Brother moved away from her and sat next to Carlisle. Mama started up the alley.

"What time we eating, Mama?" asked Little Brother to her back.

"Pretty soon now, son." She sighed and turned the corner.

Upstairs again, standing over the stove, the jellied air of the gas burners rising to her face, Mama began to think. She knew she was not smart, was not a doctor of the minds of children, but one thing was certain: Something must be done with Carlisle. Tonight, as she had on other occasions, she would mention this to Papa. Perhaps this time he would understand.

Papa lumbered down the block just as the sun fell into the river. The boys came upstairs with him; today was allowance day. Supper was ready. They sat, said Grace and began to eat.

"What you boys been doing today?" said Papa, spearing a pork chop with his fork. He was big, dark as the inside of a chimney. During the day he built skyscrapers.

"I got into Carlisle's club, Papa," said Little Brother through a mouth of mashed potatoes.

"Don't talk with your mouth full-up," Papa snapped. Then, softly, "That's real good. Your brother helped you, I bet."

Little Brother nodded, Yes.

"That's good. You take good care your brother, Junior," Papa grinned proudly at Carlisle. "That's what the Lord says. Ain't that right, honey?"

"Yes, that right." Mama sipped iced tea, and looked away.

Her answer seemed somehow unsatisfactory to Papa, and he was silent for a short while. "Well," he said finally, "I guess you boys'll be wanting your money."

Carlisle nodded, Yes.

"Here's a dollar each. Go on celebrate your being club members." He handed the money to Carlisle to distribute. The boys excused themselves and disappeared, leaving half-eaten platefuls and the door's slam behind.

Mama twirled the ice around the bottom of her glass, staring blankly. When Papa started to sip loudly from his, she looked up. He watched his tea as he drank and did not see her. For a second she weighed speaking to him at all. She realized it would probably bring on an argument; he would misconstrue and distort her words. Maybe sometime, she thought, he'll listen to me and understand. "Carlisle?" She put down her glass. "That boy try to kill his brother today."

"What boy?" he asked, cracking ice in his jaws.

"Junior."

"Damn it—there you go again—about how bad Junior is. What you don't like about him?" His voice started to expand in volume. Missus Neilberry would hear him. Tomorrow the whole house would be discussing Mama's latest argument. Papa leaned forward and planted his fists on either side of the glass.

"Ain't got nothing against him," she protested softly. "But he set Little Brother afire."

Papa blinked, fell backward, and laughed. "You know how funny that sound? Maybe he pretend to set him afire, but they brothers and he wasn't going to harm him." He stopped, then added for emphasis. "Not one bit." He pounded the table. His glass tipped; he did not notice it. He began laughing again.

"But it true." Mama leaned on the table, reached for his hand, tried to find her husband's eyes, but his laughing head would not stand still. When he stopped, he was quite angry.

"I sick of your babying Little Brother. You thinks I don't love him much because he my second born. Woman, you know better. Still, you always leaping on that."

"Just ask Little Brother when he gets home." She felt tears coming to her eyes, but dammed them back. "You just ask him." She slumped, folded her arms, and stared at her lap.

"All right. I does just that. And if you wrong, you stop this mess." He got up and stalked into the living room to read his paper.

When the boys returned, Carlisle carried a large box. He went straight to his room, which Little Brother shared with him, and Mama heard him opening the closet door and put the box on the top shelf, out of harm's way. He came into the living room and joined Little Brother, who was standing in the middle of the floor.

"What you boys get?" Papa looked up from his paper.

"A cowboy costume," answered Little Brother. Mama noticed he seemed a trifle perplexed, as if he were not quite sure what they had bought, who had bought it, or who would use it. "I gave my money to Carlisle, because he said I would only buy some junk and you wouldn't like that much. He said I could wear it sometimes," he breathed deeply, "if I was good and minded."

Papa sat quietly for a moment, then smiled at Mama. Then he said, "See there, woman? How could that boy do anything but love his brother to give his money to him? And Junior taking care to see this boy ain't going to be foolish."

Carlisle sat next to his father, and Papa put his arm around his shoulder.

"I guess you right," she said, rising. She went quietly to the bedroom and undressed, placing her house coat neatly on the one chair in the room. She lay on her bed, and through the wall she could hear Carlisle and Papa laughing. After a few seconds, Little Brother joined in.

SOUTH WIND

George Seferis

The sea meets with a line of mountains at the setting sun.
At our left the south wind rages, driving us crazy,
This wind that strips the bones from the flesh.
Our house stands among the pines and the carob trees.
Large windows.   **Large tables**
Where we write the letters we have written you
For so many months now, casting them
Into the separation to fill it.

Star of the morning, when you lowered your eyes
Our hours were sweeter than oil
Over the wound, happier than fresh water
On the palate, calmer than swan's down.
You held our life in the palm of your hand.
After the bitter bread of exile
At night if we stay by the white wall
Your voice comes upon us like the hope of flame
And again the wind strops
On our nerves its razor.

We write to you each of us the same things
And each of us is silent in the presence of the other
Looking, each of us, at the same world separately
The light and the dark on the line of mountains
And you.
Who will lift this sorrow from our hearts?
Last evening a storm and today
Again the heavy sky weighs on us.   Our thoughts
Like the pine needles of yesterday's shower
At the door of our house, heaped up, useless,
Attempt to build a tower that crumbles.

Among these decimated villages
On this cape exposed to the south wind
With the line of mountains before us that hides you,
Who will take into account the decision to forget?
Who will accept our offerings, at this autumn's end.

ARGONAUTS

George Seferis

And the soul
If it wishes to know itself
Into a soul
Must look:
The stranger and the enemy we saw in the mirror.

They were fine boys the companions and complained
Neither at the labor, nor at the thirst, nor at the cold,
And they had the bearing of trees and waves
When they accepted the wind and the rain
Accepted the night and the sun
Not changing with the change.
They were fine boys, whole days
They sweated at the oar, their eyes lowered
Breathing in rhythm
And their blood darkened an obedient skin.
Once they sang, their eyes lowered,
As we passed the deserted island with the barbary fig-trees
Westward, past the cape of dogs
That bark.
If it wishes to know itself, they said
Into a soul it must look, they said
And the oars beat the gold of the sea
At sunset.
We passed many capes many islands the sea
That leads into the other sea, gulls and seals.
Sometimes wretched women wailing
Lamented their lost children
And others in fury called for the Great Alexander
And glories sunk in the depths of Asia.
We anchored at coasts full of the aromas of night
With the singing of birds, water that left on the hands
The memory of a great happiness;
But they did not end, the voyages.
Their souls became one with the oars and the oarlocks,
With the serious face of the prow
With the wake of the rudder
With the water that broke their image.
The companions ended one by one
Their eyes lowered. Their oars
Mark the place where they sleep on the shore.

None remember them.   Justice.

editorial

THE VANISHING CAMBRIDGE STORY

Two years ago, even a year ago, when one of our editors came across a story that began, "There was a dead fly in my coffee. It was two o'clock in the morning and the Bick was almost deserted," he would probably shudder and try to get through it as quickly as he could. There had been so many of them, so many imitation *Winter Terms,* and all of them had the same, familiar set of circumstances and emotions. The editors were then pretty well tired of reading about wretched people they had never met and affairs that at a distance seemed far more tedious than tragic. Widener, the Waldorf, the banks of the Charles, a fifth floor room in Lowell, the hasty click of slim heels on Claverly's back stairs . . . all elements in a form story that could no longer be read with any interest. The authors were too sincere to make their work properly salacious and too inept to make it dramatic. The unhappy middle-ground was a tale of such self-pity and unconscionable mush that it was all one could do to get through it.

When William Bayer wrote *SEX: The Literary Breakthrough at Harvard Square,* he very well summed up the tired amusement most of us felt at the tide of purience and sentimental bunkum that had been washing over us for three or four years. As far as we were concerned, the Cambridge tale of surreptitious love and college law was the ultimate literary dead-end.

But we haven't seen one of the classic types for half a year and more now, and we must admit that we miss them. Like soap operas and westerns, they were a restfully predictable part of our reading life. The names changed, but never the characters, never the locale, and never the melancholy ending. It is hard to say what has become of them. They may be going outside, but then we can hardly believe that they will get a better reception anywhere else than they got from us. Or their authors may have turned to greater things. There have been rumours that a Cambridge novel, a compendium of all the best in the genre, is coming, but on the other hand, that is not only just a rumour but even if it is true, it doesn't explain the disappearance of a whole species.

The authors were not often people we knew nor ever heard from again once their work had been sent back, but we developed an affection for them. No one could look on the shuddering misery of the Cambridge tale and not feel some kind of sympathy for the soul who wrote it. We suppose that most of them survived . . . horribly scarred but carrying on. Perhaps we even remembered some of the experiences longer than the authors themselves did. Once they had written them, they were probably done with, but what reader, recalling Paul, "who stood staring down into the icy waters of the Charles and longed to sink into their dark oblivion," could ever cross Larz Anderson again with quiet mind. Or who could ever again look up at the windows of Eliot House and not imagine that gazing down there might not be another Linda, "like a small animal, naked and blonde in the caressing sunlight." Perhaps we are getting old and sentimental, but we miss Linda.

For some time the ADVOCATE thought about collecting the Cambridge tales and publishing them in an anthology. But there was always the chance that we might have ourselves sued, and besides that, they were so unprintably bad. How is it then that they are often more memorable than stories that we did publish, stories in every way superior to them? It is hard to say, but none of us who read them will ever forget the descriptions of brick sidewalks in the snow, of hundreds and hundreds of cups of coffee at the Waldorf, of the hours of pleading and declining in the Common, or of the self-destroyers standing on the bridges and looking at themselves in their bathroom mirrors with a last comment that amounted to WHY?

No matter how base the appeal, the appeal was local and therefore less to be resisted than that of other bad stories. And the descriptions of Cambride often had a lugubrious honesty that none of us could quite deny.

Now that we haven't seen one in so long, we begin to wish that our friends would start writing out their agonies again. (We cannot believe that they have given up having agonies.) We thought we could get along very well without the Cambridge stories a year or so ago, but now that they seem to have gone out of existence—out of the ADVOCATE existence in any case—we begin to feel a little neglected, and we also have begun to miss the rather pleasurable experience of recognition when an author makes a window seat at the Bick or the steps of Memorial Church or the basement of Sever (all places familiar to us and unromantic) the scene of the crucial episode in his life of disorientation and estrangement.

The anthology idea has been given up. It would hardly be fair to present such frank autobiography to the public for the little profit it would give us, but if we can get our Cambridge tales back again, we will be more appreciative. What a tragedy if the springs have all dried up.

—RPF

EDWARD GOREY

DOGGY

alan berger

I heard recently that they drafted Doggy. I don't know how he would react now - I haven't seen him in a long time - but he ought to resent it. And I don't just mean a selfish resentment, the kind you find in people who think they're worth more than any cause or country whatever, nor do I mean the theoretical kind of resentment some people figure out for things like that. I mean the kind of resentment all of us would feel - myself, Chucky Seltzer, Mikey O'Connell, and even Bob Fitzsimmons, whom we called Fitzy. Atlhough, actually, I suppose that Doggy, when he got his draft notice, simply laughed - that spasmodic, choking laugh that he seemed to force up from the hollows of his tremendous belly.

Of course it may have changed by now (whenever I go back to the old neighborhood they tell me that everybody and everything *has* changed), but Doggy's belly was, as I remember it, that rare........deformity I suppose you have to call it, which somehow includes, overcomes, and finally becomes the person who owns it: it is, or rather it was, Doggy.

And Doggy, as ill-treated as he was, as comic and pitiable and black-and-blue as we made him, was one of us, one of the guys who grew up on our block in the Bronx, who grew up together and mainly out-of-doors. A lot of us on that block, like Doggy and myself, were Jewish, but there were also Mikey O'Connell and Fitzy, whose exile from the Irish-Italian section only four of five blocks away was a distinction for them and their families, while it annoyed and mystified people like Doggy's mother, a school teacher, who was also fat, and who looked just like Doggy. Whenever she went around the corner to the kosher butcher shop on the side street we used for stickball, the whole block could hear her berating the housewives who, heavy-eyed, with faces to the fan Ben the butcher installed for the hot weather, sprawled in small metal chairs which they gathered near the doorway so that they could watch their sons, who were playing stickball in the street; sometimes Doggy's mother lost her temper and screamed so that everybody out on the street could hear her; she accused the housewives of forgetting that they were Jews. She said that the "goys" would never let them forget it. Once, when she saw Doggy playing stickball with us - he was actually only watching for the cops because he hadn't been chosen into the game - she came to the doorway of the butcher shop and wiggled a pudgy finger at him dramatically. "Just look," she said, shaking her head, and with it the bulging red flowers on her dress, "Just look at him! My son, playing in the street just like the "goyim". He forgets. They forgot in Germany and look what happened. A "bar mitzvah" boy he'll be in one more year, and he doesn't even know what it means to be a Jew."

But Doggy *did* know what it meant to be a Jew, as all of us did, even Mikey and Fitzy, who had enough freckles between them to get us all into St. Anthony's School gym when it got too cold to play basketball anymore in the schoolyard. We all knew what it meant to be a Jew because we had been born in those two or three short, twilight years before the war, when Hitler had begun to tell the world (again) what a Jew was. We all inherited a great drama - the drama of Hitler's war, which we saw in chapters every Saturday afternoon at the Sussex Theater in the neighborhood. It was a good drama to have in a way, because it made everything clear and easy: the Germans and the Japs were the bad guys, the Americans were the good guys, especially the marines who weren't even afraid to die, and the Jews were the victims. We identified with the Jews, although we all wanted to be like the marines. That was impossible, however: we knew that there were no marines among us. I suppose Mikey came the closest of all, but that was mainly because his oldest brother, Johnny - he had eleven brothers and sisters - actually was a marine. At first, when Johnny came back to the Bronx on his furloughs, we all went up to Mikey's apartment on Saturday mornings to see him; he wore a blue uniform and he had a cap that covered his eyes. But there wasn't anymore war by that time. Johnny never fought, and it didn't seem as if

he ever left the Bronx. He certainly never went to any of the important places-
Anzzio or Normandy, or any of those.

No, we were really Jews, all of us, and I think that we had already begun to
cultivate a secret dislike, which at first grew out of envy, and which we shrewdly
withheld from each other, of the marines. They weren't real, even for the movies.
They were so definite and so impossible to imitate that we started by taking them
for granted. They were always the same: they always crawled across the field
of mines with the same brave faces, they always avenged their buddies' deaths
with the same single-minded dedication, and they always liberated the prisoners
of war — mostly Jews — with the same dutiful, heroic timing. It got so that we
knew that no matter what tortures the prisoners were suffering, if the music
sounded like the last three minutes of the movie, we could be sure that the marines
would squirm under a barbed-wire fence somehow, reach the end of the mine field,
and stick their bayonets smilingly into the stiff, straight back of the German
officer who had been torturing the half-naked, half-starved, half-hopeless Jewish
prisoners. We all had known of course, from the first moment that we had seen
the German officer's exaggerated posture, that it would be a perfect spine for an
American bayonet, and so we experienced a certain feeling of relief and confirmation
when he died at the film's end and faded out of sight, although there was a similar
feeling of relief, as we left the movie theater, when the rescuing marines faded out
of sight. We had known what the marines would do and they had done it, without
complaint, without expression, and without variation. So that the only people
whose passing into nothingness we regretted, walking home for supper, was the
Jews. They had been saved from starvation and death and the Germans, but they
would continue, we knew, to bicker and jest, to complain and pray in the same
colorful way as they had done all afternoon, even after the soft whirring of the
projector had been replaced by the motor noises and the tire noises of the traffic
on the Grand Concourse.

And this is why, I suppose, we tolerated and even liked (albeit tacitly) Doggy
and his bouncy, leathery stomach. Despite all the punishment he took, Doggy never
became predictable. There were times we pummelled and tackled him, even the
little kids getting in on the free-for-all, for four hours without a let-up. But the
funny thing was that when his mother would come around the corner and scream at
us for beating him up and at him for getting beat up, Doggy, after he had seen
his own complaints devoured and turned into angry threats, would try to retract them,
to hide his black-and-blue marks and absolve even the guiltiest of us. Once Fitzy
had tried to tell him how his mother and father "made him"; dodging Doggy's
determined blows Fitzy had danced backward and sideways at first, tried to punch
his instructor's mouth, while stinging Doggy's loose cheeks with open-handed slaps
and teasingly chanting the appropriate, short, rocky-sounding word. But when Doggy
saw his mother come galloping out of Goldman's candy store to rescue him, he
repeated Fitzy's explanations into the folds of her trembling pink, flabby arm; the
clutching arm suddenly turned into another slapping palm, and then Doggy also
remembered the inevitable, secret word which said so many of the things we had to
say to each other, and he sang that word in a high whine until, her arm tired,
his mother vented one, final wrathful shout and, in frustration, turned away from
us and from him and plodded home.

In his appearance, however, Doggy was as predictable as school in September.
He was always sloppy, with fleshy cheeks colored like red stop lights, a red and blue
checked flannel shirt half hanging out of paled, enormous dungarees, and a certain
swaying even when he leaned against a car fender. His name, however, was our
greatest plaything. It didn't suggest canine courage and fidelity as did a similar
nickname belonging to a baseball player of that era, but was derived logically from
Doggy's own family name. His real name had been Harold Frankfurter, for which

Doggy was divinely type-cast. Soon, however, our instinct for verbal experimentation and improvement inspired the title, "Hotdog". And then, when somebody was straddling his horizontal torso once and snapping at his ears with long-uncut finger-nails, the quite natural innovation of "Hotdoggy" was introduced, and, finally, in the ineluctable way those things happen, just plain "Doggy" evolved.

But the memory we all possess of the clownish, chubby little person who belonged to such a name is the memory of a single June night which time, in its didactic fashion, has greatly magnified.

School had been out for only a week, and the first real heat wave had hit the city. It was the best time for stickball because there was no homework and, since no one had left yet for summer camp, all the good ballplayers were around. The men and women in Goldman's candy store complained about the heat and the stickiness, but we loved it as we loved the runnng and screaming, the vague excitement, and even the threat of the cops coming because we had ruined someone's sleep or broken someone's windows. It all mounted to a kind of sweaty ecstacy when, finally encroaching darkness covered and hid line drives and grounders. (Fly balls we could always see - they shot, like dark stars across the purple sky that arched from the train yards behind home plate, up between the buildings that bounded our street). And when we left the street to our younger brothers, while they shouted for who would bat first in their flys-up game, we gathered on the corner, where the side street met the wider, more thickly-traveled Concourse. We leaned against fenders of parked cars or against the wobbly tree whose grassless dirt square suggested nothing more than a negligent paving job.

On that particular night we finished our game very late, and, by the time we had all bought our ice cream cones at Goldman's, it had turned completely dark; the high street lights were on and, from the Concourse, cars gave us a changing, uneven illumination. Old man Goldman had given Doggy fifty pennies and four dimes for his dollar when Doggy bought his ten cent ice cream cone, and so Doggy wanted to pitch pennies, but nobody would pitch with him because, if there was one thing Doggy was very good at, it was pitching pennies. He would bend halfway over, curving his right arm slowly back to his belly, and would carefully flick his thick fingers at the wall next to Goldman's display window. Invariably his penny would land on its surface, take one short, dependable hop, and suddenly expire within inches of the wall. As soon as the penny had come to a rest Doggy would charge up to the wall bellowing "Hands off!", like Old Goldman himself. Doggy knew that, if we could,

we would move his penny back with our shoes while casually discussing his graceful pitching style. He had found that out by experience.

So, to distract him (Doggy was really hot to pitch pennies), Fitzy showed him a book! "The Private Life of Adolph Hitler". Doggy boosted himself up on a car fender to look over Fitzy's shoulder at the cover and suddenly he stopped talking about pitching pennies. We couldn't believe it: the swollen flannel shirt was no longer swaying. It was unnatural. His right hand, on Fitzy's shoulder, lay heavily, unmoving, forgotten,— an unremembered instinct to keep Fitzy and the book near the fender and under the street light. His left hand was stuck to the curved fender under his static, enthralled flesh. It grounded him. It connected him to the car and the street and the pennies that he had wanted to pitch. Even the two stop lights on his cheeks guttered.

We were very reluctant to actually see the secret of the book's cover. And even after we had all seen the naked girl and the leering Furher, we made believe we hadn't really seen anything. We kept pushing and milling around Fitzy, who didn't for an instant take his eyes away from the cover of his book, as if all the secrets Doggy would ever need to know were behind that cover.

Finally Mikey could hold it in no longer. Remaining silent was tantamount to admitting he was no different from Doggy.

"Jesus, Doggy," he said, "It's nothing but two tits!"

The two red lights blinked on again in Doggy's cheeks as if Mikey had rung for an elevator. Even Fitzy turned around to look at Doggy now. Doggy's swaying became even more prounounced than usual.

"Izee gonna kill her?" Doggy screeched.

The frantic question, with its unexpected twist, drew an embarrassed rush of laughter to Doggy. Fitzy, however, wasn't laughing. He was mad.

"You don't even know what it means," he said. We all stopped laughing and looked at Doggy, ready to laugh at him again if he made us.

Doggy swayed slowly off the car fender and found himself standing in front of Fitzy. His eyes blinked confusedly up at Fitzys'.

"It means he's gonna kill her. That's Hitler. He kills Jews, he buins them and they die and then they aren't alive anymore and they get to be candles and their mothers have to light them and pray."

Only Mikey could figure out what Doggy meant; the others were afraid to laugh until somebody else did.

Mikey told me later that he, like myself, thought of the candle Doggy's mother burned in a small wax-filled glass on top of her dish closet in the kitchen. We had been up at Doggy's house just the night before to flip baseball cards. Doggy had the best collection of cards on the block because he seemed to save the most pennies and because he somehow always managed to trade his doubles for the players that he really needed. But Mikey and I didn't go up to his apartment just to flip with Doggy; we had plans; there are two ways to flip baseball cards: man-to-man, where you have to match what the other guy flips (heads or tails), and three-man, where the odd card wins. You might not believe it, and even I hardly do anymore, but with enough practice we could pretty much flip whichever side we wanted, just by putting the other side up and flipping always from the same height near the hip. Doggy, of course, preferred man-to-man, because he was one of the best flippers on the block and also because he never seemed to win in three-man. Once in a while it seemed he suspected that something more than luck was against him in three-man, but, if he really knew anything, he didn't say so.

....Mikey and I had planned everything before we went up to Doggy's. If Mikey's card was face up when he was ready to flip, I turned mine face downward, so that, if we flipped right, one would come up heads, and one tails, and one of our cards would have to win, no matter how Doggy's landed.

When we rang the doorbell Doggy had been all ready for us. He had his cards out, in small piles, on the thick, living room rug. The doubles and the ones he needed least were in separate piles from the hard-to-get cards. The apartment was quiet. His father had been reading at the table in the small kitchen, but he came to the door to greet us and, speaking almost in a whisper, he told us that we shouldn't have rung the bell because Mrs. Frankfurter was sleeping, and that we should be specially careful not to make noise while we were in the house. Mr. Frankfurter was a little, bony man. His head had bones bulging through the skin all over it, and even the top of his head looked like a covered skeleton, I guess because he had so little hair, only a few thin, scratches of black at the sides of his head. They were hardly any different from the black streaks on his cheeks which looked like charcoal lines, but were really only the signs of a heavy beard on a bony face. He was always very quiet and kind to us. He seemed very different from Doggy and his mother. He wasn't like our fathers either, he was too quiet and old-looking, but at least you could talk to him like you could to other people. Or maybe it was that he could talk to us like other people did, I'm not sure, but he was very different from Doggy's mother. Doggy was the only one on the block we couldn't call for by yelling up from the street. His mother didn't allow it. When-

ever we tried to, she closed the windows and shut the curtains. Sometimes we would hear her screaming at Doggy when we went upstairs, to his apartment, to call for him, and even after she had come to the door, seen us, and slammed the door in our faces, we could still hear her plaintive voice. But Doggy always came downstairs eventually. Often we had already chosen up for whatever we were playing—stickball, or slapball, or running bases—and it would always take a long time to get him giggling again. That giggle, because we had all become so used to it, was Doggy's only shield of defense and sign of dignity in those aweful moments when Mikey, Fitzy, and Chucky Seltzer all slid into him at the same time in "running bases". Nevertheless, when he came down from those scenes with his mother, he was very slow to giggle, as if he almost realized the power and effect of that high-pitched, senseless sound.

That night, when Doggy finally won a round, Mikey stepped on a card Doggy was trying to pick up from the rug. The card ripped, of course, and when Doggy demanded another card to replace the ripped one, Mikey shook his head in refusal. Doggy was furious. He had been losing steadily all night, and Mikey wouldn't even let him win properly. He began to curse at Mikey, spluttering wetly and forming his large, loose lips into every insult he could remember. Suddenly he stopped. We heard an ominous noise from his mother's bedroom.

"Harold!"

He looked at Mikey with more unsettled fury in his eyes than any insult could contain.

"Yes, mommy . . . .?"

"Come in here."

The sleep-cracked voice from the bedroom reddened Mikey's face under his freckles. We both stared at the bedroom door while Doggy slithered through the small, smoky opening he allowed himself into his mother's room. He immediately closed the door behind him. For a while we heard only one low, sharp, barely controlled voice. And then we also heard Doggy's giggle. The first voice was raised:

"Listen to me! You never listen to me. I don't want you playing with those little bums. Do you understand?"

Again the giggle, neither attentive nor understanding, but humorless, neutral.

"Did you her me? They don't know how to act, and I won't have you growing up like that, like a weed. If you want something to do, there are plently of books here, you don't have to spend your time in the streets . . . ."

But Doggy only giggled again and the other voice rose to a fluttering shout, an embarrassing torment which Mr. Frankfurter, hearing from the kitchen, *didn't want us to hear. The kitchen door swung open and, the blackened wrinkles knotted to the bones of his face, Doggy's father skimmed quickly and quietly in his thin slippers over the deep rug to the bedroom door. But, as he opened the door, his wife, the composure of sleep dissolving on her face, came to the door herself.*

"Why don't you leave Harold alone." She shouted, "Just leave him alone." Her shapeless, wine-colored housecoat trembled. We just stared at her.

"It's not their fault dear, they just like to play with him . . . ." Mr. Frankfurter tried to move his wife back from the door and close it behind them both, but she grabbed the corner of the door and shouted at us over his sloped shoulder.

"We've got enough trouble without you. Do you want me to go crazy?" Finally Mr. Frankfurter succeeded in pushing the door shut. Then we could hear only phrases of their conversation:

"They're only children . . . . he likes them . . . ."

"He doesn't understand . . . . doesn't understand . . . ." A woman's crying twisted out of the end of the phrase and then we heard Doggy's father speaking softly again, but we couldn't hear what he was saying.

After some time, during which Mikey and I forgot our own existences, Doggy and his father, both walking on tiptoes, re-emerged, pushing thin nimbuses of smoke off their heads. Doggy's father took us into the kitchen to talk to us, while Doggy, on the living room rug, re-arranged his card piles.

"Mrs. Frankfurter works very hard at her school," he told us, "And she gets nervous at times, very nervous. Do you see that candle?" We looked up at the wax-filled jar. "Mrs. Frankfurter is burning that candle in memory of her own father who passed away just one year ago today. So she's very upset. And she takes it very seriously when you tease Harold. I know you don't really mean it—it's all a part of growing up—but you must understand that he's our only child and he means a great deal to us. So I'd appreciate it if you could try to make Harold feel that he's really one of the gang."

He patted our shoulders. We nodded seriously. Doggy had told us about the candle before, while we were flipping cards. He had lit the corner of a magazine in its flame to see the smile of the woman on the cover burn, and his mother had caught him. She had ripped the magazine away from him and struck him with its charred corners. He had asked what he did wrong and she had said that he couldn't even understand death; that when people died he should respect their memory and never, ever forget them.

We were all watching Fitzy. Suddenly Mikey challenged Doggy:

"That's not what happens," he looked to Fitzy, explaining, "You don't turn into a candle."

Mikey was as strong as Fitzy, but he was different. Many times he intervened when our baiting of Doggy had passed the boundary of comedy, something we all sensed inwardly, even if we didn't stop laughing at him.

Doggy looked happy. Everybody was watching him. With the back of his wrist he wiped a shiny streak of drool from the crease around the side of his mouth.

"Then what *do* you turn into?" he asked.

"Nothing," Mikey answered, edging his flat, freckly cheeks and crooked yellow teeth right up against Doggy's clean red moon of a face.

"Nothing . . . . ?" Suddenly Doggy sounded as if he were very curious to hear Mikey's opinion.

The two heads moved steadily backward until Doggy was up against the fender again, and then his head rolled back in retreat from the pursuing yellow grimace until Doggy was looking right up into the street light, and only his belly kept Mikey from bending over Doggy's glistening face. Then Mikey withdrew with a satisfied snort.

"Hah. You don't even know what's gonna happen to you after you die."

Doggy squinted at Mikey to see if he could say anything. Then he looked over Mikey's shoulder at Fitzy.

"I'm gonna disappear and nobody's gonna be able to find me in case they wann'a punch me in the arm." Fitzy drew his fist back to punch Doggy's arm but Mikey stood resolutely between them.

"Where you gonna go when you disappear?" Mikey asked.

"Nowheres."

"Whaddaya mean, nowhere?"

"Nowhere."

"Ya can't go nowhere, ya gotta go *somewhere.*"

"Not when I die. Then I won't be nowhere."

Here Mikey lost patience. His lips drew back and, under the street light, his teeth looked even yellower as he bit them together and jabbed at the soft arm muscle near Doggy's shoulder. Doggy swung back half-heartedly, neither hitting Mikey, nor meaning to hit him. As he swung, however, he put himself within range of Fitzy's fist, which, knuckles out, found its way to Doggy's other arm. Now Fitzy was happy.

"Gawhead," he said, "Tell us where you"ll go."

The situation was too familiar to Doggy. They never allowed him to talk the way they talked.

Carefully he looked at Mikey. There was nothing sympathetic about the sneer of Mikey's twisted teeth, nor the dark space between the two front ones.

"I don't *know* where I'll go . . . ."

"There's only two places you can go," Mikey informed him, "Heaven or Hell".

At this point Chucky Seltzer, a small boy with long carefully combed black hair, squealed:

"Doggy's not gonna get into Heaven—he won't fit between the gates."

We all laughed, not because it was funny, but because we wanted to laugh at Doggy.

"In hell they torture you, forever," Mikey told him. "They come in every five minutes and take your clothes off and whip your ass, and when they're not whipping your ass, they make you stand in a big fire."

Doggy giggled, drooling again. There was something about the uncontrollable way the spittle dribbled to his chin that scared us. It was impossible to imagine him not coming around the corner after supper, or not playing stickball, or not going to school. We couldn't. We couldnt think of anything beyond Doggy's large-eyed, drooling giggle.

"Is Fitzy gonna get burned with a fire everyday too? Doggy asked, struck with the sudden possibilities of hell.

"I'm not gonna die. Ever!"

Mikey, confused, turned and looked at Fitzy to find a reason for such a contradiction. Fitzy was smiling—a thin hard smile which taunted Doggy's logic with complete exclusion.

Doggy laughed, spraying an ice cream—and—saliva foam from his mouth. "Everybody dies," he said. Suddenly Fitzy lunged past Mikey and drove his fist into Doggy's stomach. When Doggy staggered, more from surprise than pain, Fitzy put his hand to the side of Doggy's head and pushed, his foot planted behind Doggy's ankles. Doggy fell and seemed to bounce once when he hit the sidewalk.

"I'm never gonna die," Fitzy repeated, kicking at Doggy, who twisted to catch Fitzy's feet in his thigh.

Doggy's giggle shifted to a raucous, loud laugh. "Yes you will, everybody has to die."

"Not me." Fitzy kicked again at Doggy, but the red flannel shirt rolled swiftly away from the moving foot. Doggy was laughing hysterically.

"Bastard!"

Another kick caught Doggy in the shoulder.

"You're all gonna die."

He was laughing, a hollow, reverberating laugh which had for it's source something very far removed from humor, and the more Fitzy kicked

him or slapped him, the more wild and violent Doggy's mirthless convulsions became. Finally something about this unstoppable laughter made Fitzy give the bloated dungarees a chance to roll away, stand up, and run home. But none of us laughed as we usually did when we saw Doggy running.

That night we broke up early.

The next morning was Saturday, and I ate breakfast at the cafeteria with my father, while my mother slept late. My father bought the *Daily News* to look at the Belmont entries and he held the paper to the side of his plate of french toast, reading and hesitantly eating at the same time. I was eating fast because we had a stickball game at ten o'clock. Everything felt cold in my stomach.

By the time my father had finished his french toast, he had worked himself into the middle of the newspaper where the large photographs were. Still chewing, he held the inside of the paper toward me, asking,

"Did you know about this?"

In the center of a large page of black and white pictures I saw, above my father's pointing finger, a blurred photo of a crowd standing in a half circle around a body on a sidewalk. Part of a policeman's uniform was visible within the ring of spectators, and I could barely see two legs limply spread as wide as a ruffled skirt would allow.

I read the caption:

"Patrolmen watch over the mutilated body of Mrs. Getrude Frankfurter of 1779 Grand Concourse, who jumped last night from the roof of her apartment house at 157th street on the Grand Concourse. Mrs. Frankfurter is survived by her husband Mark and her son Harold."

I didn't understand at first. My father took back the paper and we walked home. When we got to our building the other guys, gathered in a quiet group on the sidewalk, were looking up at the steep wall of windows. My father asked me which one was Doggy Frankfurter's. I pointed to it, the closed, curtained window on the fourth floor. My father stared up at Doggy's window for a long time.

"What a terrible thing," he said.

I could tell that he didn't hear anything, but we looked at each other; it seemed to us, standing there, that we could hear Doggy laughing—that crazy, breathy laugh that he brought up from the bottom of his stomach.

HARVARD ADVOCATE

Summer '63
75 cents

DEBUTANTE

david landon

"Elle continuait a offrir le spectacle somptueux et desole d'une existence faite pour l'infine et peu a peu restreinte au presque neant." Marcel Proust, "Les Plaisirs et Les Jours"

As you moved once,
towers dropped to their knees,
the spooks of elegant thieves
sighed in the mirrors for your gold hair,
the glass slid in silvery carpets under your feet,
and out of the gilt-framed emptyness
horses of snow leapt sleepily into the moon.

With a snicker of knives, like ripped silk,
the mirrors fled to infinity,
and a riderless waltz chased after.

You stood bewildered,
and the sea of our voices crashed around you;
trumpets licked you with hot tongues,
young men attended
with the sleek cars of their calculations;

and I was terrified,
hearing you run down the stairway,
as if someone spilled a basket of marbles.

I have read that you married finally;
and I wonder if your days are ripped from you,
as pages from an engagement book;
or if caught in your mother's dull enthusiasms,
restlessness will bring you to adultery.

The thought of you frantic in those endless halls
has brought me to my knees,
and the memory of what has gone
is as if on a day of azur,
the snow got up and left,
and the shadows slid into the sea.

NEW DAY

keith lowe

Sun up, like a man beating a drum or blowing a conchshell, rousing the land from mountain forest to river bed. Laborers from Rose Hall and Greenwich Pen, canecutters from Chagunas Estate, Indians on the Cuyuni savannah and market people from Kwakwani—the whole country rising up from sleep, putting on holiday clothes and coming through their doors to watch the new day dawn on Guiana; coming out in the cool early morning to sing party songs and cry out to grow free like trees under sun. They crying no more blackman sweat to sweeten whiteman tea, no more for coolie to draw water to wash baccra foot. Sun come up to tell woman to tie her head and man to buckle his belt; to get ready to rule; to go out every one to the stations everywhere and pick the party and the man to lead Guiana to her destiny. Now all hear the word and they streaming down the path and overflowing the road. Bright headwraps and sport shirts and faces shining with hope. Suffrage for everybody now. New constitution. New day.

Before daylight, me and Abdulli take up duty in front of this polling station in St. Clare parish. No seat in Guiana—not even the city constituencies—is hotter than this one in St. Clare. For here, Butler, the father of the nation and founder of the Labor Party, is running against Solomon the Lion, second leader of the socialist Independence Party. The rest of Guiana may vote Labor through and through; but in this parish Butler must win the seat to lead them as Prime Minister, or else it will be just a reed-in-the-wind government. I hear that Solomon bringing in a gang from St. Joseph to frighten Laborites from leaving their yards to vote. A truck full of Independence man singing and waving red flowers just passed. They clench their fists and spit and cry "Babylon" at me and Abdulli, but we don't pay them no mind. They fancy we police be the tools of the whiteman government bringing babylon down on Guiana. They too ass-minded to figure out that if it wasn't for us they wouldn't have free election or anything to sing for.

Abdulli start working as a special constable since they killed five people at the riot in Nariva. After that, Government make a law that say no more street meeting. They put all police and soldier on duty, and begin to hire man as special constable. Now, it was me who did get Abdulli the job he had before as a storeman in a Chinaman shop; so yesterday he take me before the police sergeant and tell him I am a good man. The sergeant ask if I can read and write, and I answer that I know how to make a mark when I get pay. But still he ask how I am going to take down statement when I arrest somebody. Then Abdulli tell him that it is all right, for he don't know any man in St. Clare who can give better evidence in court than me. So the sergeant give me a stick and a white band to wear on my arm as a mark that I am a respectable special constable.

And now we two on duty this great morning. We walk up and down under the mango tree by the gate to Mother Burnham house, which Government rent as a polling station. A big dry watercourse runs alongside the yard, and the road passing in front of the gate crosses this gully. The bridge has a wooden railing just whitewashed. The two of us clearing away everybody who make shadow there, and people falling back from us as we wheel the stick over our head.

But while this authority proving sweet, I getting really bitter about Abdulli and the red color of the Independence Party, and they can all see him swaggering up and down in the shirt like a man-o-war flying colors. Now me and Abdulli grow up in the same district and been friends from way back. So that although he is Indian and me a blackman, we used to tell people that we spring from the same mother by different fathers. But politics stronger than blood: my own mother kicked me out of her house when I tell her that I was for Butler, because her Independence party was going to make Guiana suck salt in the end. And no brother man can stop me from backing my party.

"Constable Abdulli," I put it to him, "You think it right and decently proper for a constable to bear colors?"

"You is nothing but a monkey blaming rat for his long tail," he answer.

"What you mean?" I ask him, and I was brushing off my yellow vest.

"The green kerchief round your head, Ezra. Like a beacon for Butler people."

"Look, man. This is just to keep my head cool in the sunhot. And nobody else but you notice the color."

Abdulli stop swaggering after this, and together we watch out for trouble, for every now and then a crowd come marching along the road, singing songs and waving banners. And all morning long it is like drum beating and breeze blowing and people jumping all over Guiana. Nearly everybody come out to vote early in the day.

Around nine o'clock four men stand up talking politics on the bridge. Me and Abdulli move over and order them to break it up, for it against the law to make a crowd thirty yards from a polling station. The tallest one say he not paying no mind to any ignorant special constable, and that if we going to move them we must first read the riot act. What's that, I ask him. He say don't I know that when the white soldiers come to break up the fighting in Nariva, a red-face big-belly captain get up on a barrel and read the riot act before the soldiers fired; and that even though nobody could hear him, and even though they could knock him off the barrel with a rock before he finish reading, he had to read the whole thing. Then they all begin to laugh and jeer panhead constables. But riot act or no riot act, me and Abdulli were moving in to use the stick on them when a jeep drive up with a white police inspector and the same black sergeant who swear me in. The riot-act men scatter like chicken before hawk. Then me and Abdulli stand up straight and salute, and when the inspector ask if everything is all right, we say yes and they drive on to check the other polling stations.

All this time redman Abdulli is working a racket, but not till around half past ten did I catch up with him. For, as much as I know that some rascals go to the doctorshop and buy things to rub the voting ink off their finger so that they can vote again in the name of dead people, I don't expect a constable on election duty to pull anything so shameful. Now plenty people who never did vote before ask us, while they going through the gate, to show them what they should do with the voting paper. I tell them they should mark "X" beside the hand, which is the sign beside Butler name, or beside the head, which is for the Independence Party. Then an old woman, after talking with Abdulli, come and ask me whether the head is a man head or woman head. A little later, a carpenter asked me if the head is bare or with a hat. All the people who talk with him first and then come to ask me what they didn't understand from him always ask something about the head, and never about the hand. So little by little I realize that the man not making the poor people know that is a sign of the hand in heaven or earth.

Man, this vex my spirit like a mad ghost. So without a word more I accost this Abdulli and say to him, "Constable, if you don't look out I going arrest for an election misdemeanor. If you want to pay fifty pounds or spend two years in jail, just keep up what you doing now."

And I really did mean it. No joking this time, man. I really would turn him in, but he say all right, he wouldn't do it no more. Anyway, I chastise him for not understanding the duty, for not realizing that we have power from the sergeant, who get his power from the inspector, he from the commissioner, he from the governor, till we get right back to the Queen, who get power from God. Consider all that, I admonish him. That's how the country have government and how we have free election and how we getting self-rule. Then I warn him that if through mischief he help Solomon and the Independence Party get into power so that later on all Guiana had to squeeze blood out of stone, I was going to squeeze Abdulli before I start on any rock. He laugh for a long time ,but he never did carry on with the racket after that, for I am watching him all the time like a hawk.

After noon, not as many people coming to vote as in the morning. Sun boiling hot now; the shade of the mango tree become smaller, and our beat up and down become just as narrow. About two o'clock Abdulli say he running round the corner to the rumshop, and if the inspector come by I am to tell him that Constable Abdulli gone for a piss and soon will come back. I tell him yes I will do that, and he take off. Now, I like to do this work alone, because Abdulli let down the dignity of the duty with his coolie manners and rough talk to the poor people who ask him about voting. So I am here marching up and down, watching people coming and going in peace through the gate and saying in my mind, "Come down, my country man, come down and put us in power." And they still coming to vote, though less and less now, and I believe we can bury Solomon as of now and begin building Guiana with Butler.

Abdulli come back and go away over and over, and each time I tell him Butler beating hell out of Solomon, but he laugh and go away again just like a fool-fool Independence man. Once the inspector drive up in the jeep and ask me for the other constable. I stand up straight and tell him: "Constable Abdulli gone to make water, sir, and coming back soon on duty." He say all right and drive on. When Abdulli come back and I tell him what happened, he say: "Constable Ezra, you is a rock. I have to make it up to you with a quart. We is just like two brothers, no?" I say yes, nothing can come between us, except the Party. And he take off again round the corner to make more water.

It is about five o'clock now, the country lay quiet and the breeze stop blowing and Mother Burnham cooking dinner. Only one or two people passing through the gate; the crowd gone home and the marchers tired out. The two government clerks and the two party scrutineers inside the polling station getting jolly and call me inside for a rum. I take a quick one and run back out to the road just in time to see Abdulli strolling back from around the corner with a thing holding on to his arm. It is a nice fat Indian girl, wearing a sleeveless red blouse, and all her skin that I can see is as cool as a plaintain leaf. Then the fellows inside call me for another drink, and I shout them to let it be till a little later. At the same time I wonder why they don't call Abdulli too, and if it's me alone they trying to black-up with liquor. Anyway, I put that from my mind because this child swinging down the road with Abdulli. I pull up my armband and call out to him:

"You bringing the young lady to vote, Constable?"

"No, man, she too young for that," he answer, grinning like a monkey.

He left the thing on the other side of the road and come across to the gate. I whisper to him:

"How can a sweet innocent thing like that take up with a drunk ugly bastard like you?"

"She's for you, brother," he answer, looking at me as if I was a prize cow. "Got her for you, man."

Now since I never know Abdulli to be so grateful or generous, I figure the man is really soaked and can't tell what's good for himself. But there is this child across the road, taking a little silk kerchief out of her bosom and putting in back in taking it out over and over, sometimes fanning herself with it; and while I whispering to Abdulli I can see her out of the corner of my eye sizing me up. All around quiet and nobody on the road and shadows on the girls face. I lean against the gate in the tree shade and I tell myself to play cool, Ezra boy, play cool; but all this while I conceiving one hell of a lust for this piece of skin. Then, as sudden as ripe mango fall off tree, she swing across the road and Abdulli clear his throat and she say to me:

"You coming, boy?"

And I so sunstruck that I say, "What you mean? Now? In broad daylight?"

And she say in a voice cool as a palm tree,

"Daylight broad, but grass deep," and start to go down into the gully.

I turn to Abdulli: "What you think, man? What you think, eh?"

"You wasting time," he answer. "You better catch butter while it melt."

It was quiet enough, and not a sign of trouble in the whole Guiana sky. But just to make sure, I say to him:

"Now, Abdulli my boy, if the inspector come around, you tell him Constable Ezra gone for a piss and coming back on duty soon—just like I did tell him for you."

"All right, just like you did for me," he answer, smiling sweet as molasses.

So I go down into that gully to make water, with the smell of cinnamon in the air and red flowers blooming and bursting before my eye. I bore through the gully bush quicker than any mongoose, and creep down it away from the bridge. But little did poor Ezra know what he is jumping into. Oh the girl was there all right, ripe and ready to fall. But all this was a stew the red people been cooking a long time for me. For while I down in the gully bed sporting with this thing, they up in the polling station making merrier sport with the ballot box. Beforehand they did buy out the Labor scrutineer, and now with Abdulli seeing that nobody come in to trouble their pleasure, those fellows inside marking "X" by the dozen for the Independence Party. So while me and this girl racing the sun going down, those boys in the house racing to pack ballots in the box before the government truck come to carry it to the courthouse for counting. Up there and down here, we all having a time.

Oh Ezra! Constable Ezra oh! Ezra who left home for Butler, rise up and save Guiana! Beat the drum, man. Call your people down. O God, they murdering Butler! Bring the gang from Nariva and drive them off the body! O Guiana, Butler was the man to strike the rock and make sweet water flow forth for you, but now you going have to squeeze that rock for blood. My countryman, you going suck rocksalt. Come, Ezra, wake up and make the new day come on the land! But, Lord, Ezra is a deaf man. Ezra is a dead man, going down with the old sun. Guiana is a gully, and I lay down dead in it.

I was to suffer judgment and hell before that sun go down; and at the end of the night, everlasting shame. For just then, the inspector and the sergeant making the last round of the polling stations, and Abdulli know that if they stop to ask for me they will find out the racket going on in the house. So the moment he spy them coming, he shout out:

"Lord, inspector, come quick, sir! A child getting rape down the gully!"

The three of them come tearing through the bush, but I don't hear them soon enough to run. As I pull up my pants I see the inspector point a revolver in my face and he say:

"All right, man, that's enough!"

The sergeant know who I am, and he feeling sorry for me; so he don't say anything but:

"O God, man, what's that you doing?"

The child start crying, but I believe she only making a show for the police. Abdulli move over to help her find her clothes. He whisper to her to tell the police that I didn't force her and that she cry out just for fun. After she did that, the inspector tell the sergeant to take me in for leaving duty, while he go on alone to finish the check of the other polling stations. So he leave us there in the gully and we hear him drive off, and the sergeant still saying, as if he can't believe:

"What's that you doing, man? What I going do with you, eh?"

But I not hearing him, for I bend down and pick up a rock as big as my fist to break Abdulli head. But I couldn't throw it: the man hang down his head so pitiful and sorry. He tell we what was the case, that he couldn't do better than bawl out for rape when he see the inspector, because the whole Independence Party would catch trouble otherwise. The sergeant say he don't give a ha'penny for neither Party, and that everything was all right on his side. The child start laughing and ask Abdulli how the vote marking was going up in the house. Then my vexation mount higher than fire, and I want to drop couple licks in Abdulli skin, bigger than me though he be. I grab him by the collar, but as I draw my hand back to punch him, he break away, grab the girl, and they run away, the two rascals, down the gully. I fling a rock after them.

I waxing so blind vexed, man, that I couldn't help but cry. I didn't know half of what I was doing. I fling away my stick and rip up my armband; but this child's red blouse still hanging from my shirt pocket and with it I wipe my dirty face. The sergeant say he know how I feel, and I must come with him for some liquor to calm my spirits. So we go to the Chinaman shop round the corner and drink a quarter quart together. After he leave, I stay there getting black-up. But soaked as I am, I hear the man on the radio telling the end of the count: the Independence Party win most seats, and Solomon beat Labor leader Butler in St. Clare parish. No man can get soaked enough not to hear the word of doom.

Yes, lord, election day was really judgment day. Now as night heavy on the land, the torches burning all over Guiana, from mountain forest to river bed. Singing break out again like a flood; and red people running wild, so that green people drawing into their yards. In St. Clare they marching with a coffin and having a big burial for Butler. As I stagger out of the shop, I see the fires and the coffin coming and the Independence people jumping around like devils tormenting the poor dead man in hell. I sober up right away, for my skin is in jeopardy. Too late to pull the knot of the green kerchief round my head. So I fling the red blouse over my head and keep it on till I reach home.

A HOT NIGHT

David Landon

In the streets, on a hot night,
they open the doors of the bistros,
and the voices spill out,
as trash from a truck;

The odor of coffee keeps us awake
and we talk till our dry speech scratches,
as fingernails on paper,

and then it rains
and we escape.
How shall we gather so much
silver coin in our small arms?

DISTORTED DIALOGUE

You ask me where I stand
And if I have a voice.
There isn't any answer;
So my answer is, "Of course."

The house that I would build is built,
Lived-in and crumbled; its noble architects
Drowned in a sea of half-forgotten facts.
The white and classic door,
The rich interior
Are shabby, old and ungenteel.
And only I, and sometimes you, are real.

Like a boy carrying a too full glass of milk
Up a flight of uneven, rickety stairs,
I spill emotions that I am aware
Are neater when contained.
Shall I defy my nature with a scowl?
I am too egregious not to complain
And much too much reserved to howl.

David Berman

IN MEMO. C.B.M.

i

Iowa, 1910

Chanticleer has changed his tune
since Eugene would rise from bed, called up
to fetch his satchel in the dark and aid
some ailing patient in the town.

Each night was young and quietly
stood guard over unblinking dreams
till bird had rung him home, and dark
was borne off on a shield of light.

Now they palaver on forever
like old men and bend their knees
limply to light's mastery . . . and toast.
Chanticleer has changed his tune.

It's fifty years since that June night
he rose to fumble for his boots
and ride into the next county:
since that Imperator crowed *Win!*

since Dawn stalked, empty-handed, through the blinds
and led Night off in chains of light.

ii

Minnesota, 1950
The widow speaks:
"The crystal candelabra burn
bright circles in the hall: and I
walk there by flickering wall and turn
slowly in fallen waltz steps by

the Viennese settee all curled
and cushioned there. I may sit
there because my fan is unfurled
there. It's my place. I reserve it.

In the next room I hear Offenbach;
waltz time, and they are playing the last
waltz again. Listen, the clock!
They whirled through midnight hours past.

O now they are playing marches,
my pomp, my circumstance . . . Listen,
in the light under the marble arches
patentleather boots click and glisten;

Blue velvet slippers tap and strum
light song on the blond marble floor.
Jewels toss and flash on the breasts. Rhythm
is all through the room beyond that door.

                    No one can sing
or dance as they! Here, they are dancing!"

four imitations
robert lowell

THE CADET PICTURE OF MY FATHER

(For Viola Bernard)

There's absence in the eyes. The brow's in touch
with something far. Now distant boyishness
and seduction shadow his enormous lips,
the slender aristocratic uniform
with its Franz Josef braid; both the hands bulge
like gloves upon the saber's basket hilt.
The hands are quiet, they reach out toward nothing—
I hardly see them now, as if they were
the first to grasp distance and disappear,
and all the rest lies curtained in itself,
and so withdrawn, I cannot understand
my father as he bleaches on this page—

Oh quickly disappearing photograph
in my more slowly disappearing hand!

Rilke: *Jugend-Bildnis meines Vaters.*

SELF-PORTRAIT

The bone-build of the eyebrows has a mule's
or Pole's noble and narrow steadfastness.
A scared blue child is peering through the eyes,
and there's a kind of weakness, not a fool's,
yet womanish—the gaze of one who serves.
The mouth is just a mouth . . . untidy curves,
quite unpersuasive, yet it says its *yes*,
when forced to act. The forehead cannot frown,
and likes the shade of dumbly looking down.

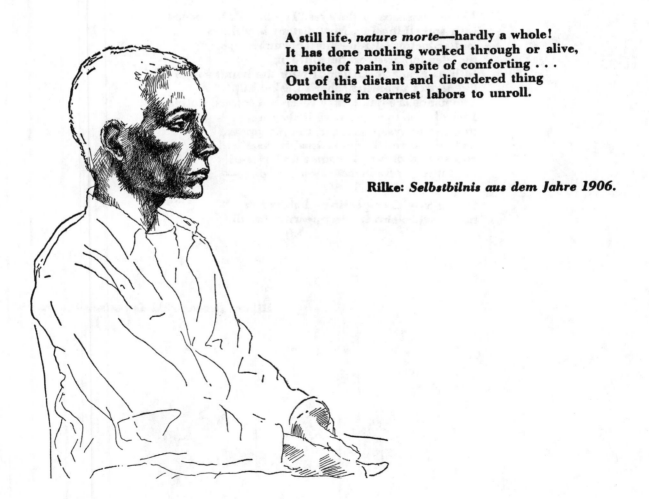

A still life, *nature morte*—hardly a whole!
It has done nothing worked through or alive,
in spite of pain, in spite of comforting . . .
Out of this distant and disordered thing
something in earnest labors to unroll.

Rilke: *Selbstbilnis aus dem Jahre 1906.*

YOU KNOCKED YOURSELF OUT

I

Those unnumbered, ruthless, random stones,
tense, vibrating still, as if slung
by the smothered abysmal fire;
the terror of those Amazon cataracts cascading
down miles to the chaos of implacable embraces;
the rock's lockjaw above the sand's
detonating dazzle—do you remember?

The sky-line, a blinding china saucer?

Do you remember the mountain, that wounded giantess?
The stranded sand-pine
with its nets of roots as mineral as the shards they finger,
as it beetled above the down-slope, only
yawning to engulf the horizon shadows?
Cool that grotto's gullet filled
with salad leaves and butterflies—
do you remember it, dumb, delirious,
there just under the summit's rotunda stone,
three men's length tall?
A king-pin of flint, teetering,
immobile?

Quick wren. Greedy eyes drunk with wonder.
You zig-zagged from fiber to fiber
to conquer the height's speckled crown,
dare-devil, musical child,
and loitered there alone to spy into the lapis lazuli bayou,
where unearthly, moss-browed turtles
were rousing from the ooze.

There the tension of nature at its lowest,
submarine sublimities,
nihilist admonitions!

II

You lifted arms like wings,
and gave the winds back their youth,
as you ran on the inertia of the stock-still air.

No one ever saw
your deft foot rest from the dance.

III

Lucky grace,
how could you help knocking your brains out
on such horny blindness—
you, simple breath, crystal bubble,

a candle, too dazzling
for the shaggy, random, vandalistic
burning of the naked sun!

Ungaretti: Tu ti spezzasti.

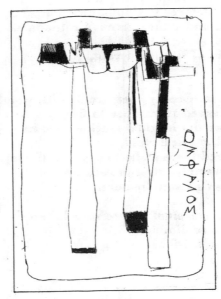

Dimitri Hadzi

RUSSIA 1812

The snow fell, and its power was multiplied.
For the first time the Eagle bowed its head—
dark days! Slowly the Emperor returned—
behind him Moscow! Its onion domes still burned.
The snow rained down in blizzards—rained and froze.
Past each white waste further white waste rose.
None recognized the captains or the flags
Yesterday the Grand Army, today its dregs.
No one could tell the vanguard from the flanks.
The snow! The hurt men struggled from the ranks,
hid in the bellies of dead horse, in stacks
of shattered caissons. By the bivouacs,
one saw the picket dying at his post,
still standing in his saddle, white with frost,
the stone lips frozen to the bugle's mouth!
Bullets and grapeshot mingled with the snow,
that hailed . . . The Guard, surprised at shivering, march
in a dream now; ice rimes the gray mustache.
The snow falls, always snow! The driving mire
submerges; men, trapped in that white empire,
have no more bread and march on barefoot—gaps!
They were no longer living men and troops,
but a dream drifting in a fog, a mystery,
mourners parading under the black sky.
The solitude, vast, terrible to the eye,
was like a mute avenger everywhere,
as snowfall, floating through the quiet air,
buried the huge army in a huge shroud.
Could anyone leave this kingdom? A crowd—
each man, obsessed with dying, was alone.
Men slept—and died! The beaten mob sludged on,
ditching the guns to burn their carriages.
Two foes. The North, the Czar. The North was worse.
In hollows where the snow was piling up,
one saw whole regiments fallen asleep.
Attila's dawn, Cannaes of Hannibal!
The army marching to its funeral!
Litters, wounded, the dead, deserters—swarm,

crushing the bridges down to cross a stream.
They went to sleep ten thousand, woke up four.
Ney, bringing up the former army's rear,
hacked his horse loose from three disputing Cossacks . . .
All night, the *qui vive?* The alert! Attacks;
retreats! White ghosts would wrench away our guns,
or we would see dim, terrible squadrons,
circles of steel, whirlpools of savages,
rush sabering through the camp like dervishes.
And in this way, whole armies died at night.
The Emperor was there, standing—he saw.
This oak already trembling from the axe,
watched his glories drop from him branch by branch:
chiefs, soldiers. Each one had his turn and chance—
they died! Some lived. These still believed his star,
and kept their watch. They loved the man of war,
this small man with his hands behind his back,
whose shadow, moving to and fro, was black
behind the lighted tent. Still believing, they
accused their destiny of *lese-majeste.*
His misfortune had mounted on their back.
The man of glory shook. Cold stupefied
him, then suddenly he felt terrified.
Being without belief, he turned to God:
"God of armies, is this the end?" he cried.
And then at last the expiation came,
as he heard some one call him by his name,
some one half-lost in shadow, who said, "No,
Napoleon." Napoleon understood,
restless, bareheaded, leaden, as he stood
before his butchered legions in the snow.

Victor Hugo: *L'expiation.*

John Lithgow

I am not *an* addict. I am *the* addict. The addict I invented to keep this show on the junk road. I *am* all the addicts and all the junk in the world. I *am* junk and I am hooked forever. Now I am using junk as a basic illustration. Extend it. I am reality and I am hooked on reality. Give me an old wall and a garbage can and I can by God sit there forever. Because I am the wall and I am the garbage can. But I need some one to sit there and look at the wall and the garbage can. That is I need a human host. I can't look at anything. I am blind. I can't sit anywhere. I have nothing to sit on. And let me take this oportunity of replying to my numerous and uh vociferous critics. It is not true that I hate the human species. I just don't like human beings. I don't like animals. What I feel is not hate. In your verbal garbage the closest word is distaste. Still I must live in and on human bodies. An intolerable situation you will agree. To make that situation clearer suppose you were stranded on a planet populated by insects. You are blind. You are a drug addict. But you find a way to make the insects bring you your junk. Even after thousands of years living there you still feel that basic structural distaste for your insect servants. You feel it every time they touch you.

"WHO HIM? DON'T LET HIM OUT HERE."

by William Burroughs

Well that is exactly the way I feel about my human servants. Consequently since my arrival some five hundred thousand years ago I have had one thought in mind. What you call the history of mankind is the history of my escape plan. I don't want 'love'. I don't want 'forgiveness'. All I want is out of here. Question: "Mr. Martin, how did all this start? How did you get here in the first place? If you found conditions so distasteful why didn't you leave at once?"

"God questions I mean good questions, young man. Obviously I am not omnipotent. My arrival here was a wreck. Ship came apart like a rotten undervest. The 'accident' in which I lost my sight. I was the only survivor. The other members of the crew . . . well . . . you understand . . . uh sooner or later . . . So I decided to act sooner. And I have acted sooner ever since. The entire human film was prerecorded. I will explain briefly how this is done. Take a simple virus illness like hepetitis. This illness has an incubation period of two weeks. So if I know when the virus is in—(and I do because I put it there) I know how you will look two weeks from now: yellow. To put it another way. I take a picture or rather a series of pictures of you with hepetitis. Now I put my virus negatives into your liver to develop. (Not far to reach. Remember I live in your body.) The whole hepetitis film is prerecorded two weeks before the opening scene when you notice your eyes are a little yellower than usual. Now this is a simple operation. Not all of my negatives develop by any means. All right now back to basic junk. Some character takes a bang of heroin for the first time. It takes maybe sixty consecutive shots before I can welcome another addict. (Room for one more inside, sir). Having taken one shot it becomes mathematically probable that he will take another given the opportunity and I can always arrange that. Having taken two shots it becomes more probable that he will take a third. One negative developed makes others almost unavoidable. The same procedure can be applied to any human activity. If a man makes a certain amount of money by certain means he will go on making more money by the same means and so forth. Human activites are drearily predictable. It should now be obvious that what you call 'reality' is a function of these precisely predictable because prerecorded human activities. Now what could louse up a prerecorded biologic film? Obviously random factors. That is some one cutting my word and image lines *at random*. In short the cut up method of Brion Gysin which derives from Hassan I Sabbah and the planet Saturn. Well, I've had a spot of trouble before but nothing serious. There was Rimbaud. And a lot of people you never heard of for good reasons. People who got too close one way or another. There was Tristan Tzara and the Surrealist lark. I soon threw a block into that. Broke them all down to window dressers. So why didn't I stop Mr. Gysin in his tracks? I have ways of dealing with wise guys or I wouldn't be here. Early answer to use on anyone considering to interfere. Tricks I learned after the crash. Well perhaps I didn't take it seriously at first. And maybe I wanted to hear what he had to say about getting out. ˙Always keep as many alternative moves open as possible. Next thing the blocade on planet earth is broken. Explorers moving in whole armies. And the usual do good missions talk about educating the natives for self government. And some hick sherrif from the nova heat charging me with 'outrageous colonial mismanagement and attempted nova'. Well they can't hang a nova rap on me. What I planned was simply to move out the biologic film to planet Venus and start over. Take along a few *good* natives to stock the new pitch and for the rest total disposal. That's not nova that's manslaughter. Second degree. And I planned it painless. I dislike screaming. Disturbs my medications."

Question: "Mr. Martin, in the face of the evidence, no one can deny that nova was planned. The reports reek of nova."
"It will be obvious that I myself, as an addict, can only be a determined factor in some one else's equation. It's the old army game. Now you see me now you don't."

Question: "Mr. Martin, you say 'give me a wall and a garbage can and I can sit there forever' almost in the next sentence you say 'All I want is out of here'. Aren't you contradicting yourself?" "You are confused about the word 'self'. I could by God sit there forever if I had a self to sit in that would sit still for it. I don't. As soon as I move in on any self all that self wants is to be somewhere else. Anywhere else. Now there you sit in your so called self. Suppose you could walk out of that self? Some people can incidentally. I don't encourage this but it happens and threatens to become pandemic. So you walk out of your body and stand across the room. Now what form would the being that walks out of your body have? Obviously it would have precisely your form. So all you have done is take the same form from one place to another. You have taken great trouble and pain—(believe me there is no pain like flesh withdrawal consciously experienced) and you have gotten precisely back where you started. To really leave human form you would have to leave human form that is leave the whole concept of word and image. You can not leave the human image in the human image. You cannot leave human form in human form. And you can not think or conceive in non image terms by mathematical definition of a being in my biologic film which *is* a series of images. Does that answer your question? I thought not."

Question: "Mr. Martin tell us something about yourself. Do you have any vices other than uh junk? Any hobbies? Any diversions?" "Your vices other than junk I manipulate but do not share. Sex is profoundly distasteful to a being of my uh mineral origins. Hobbies? Chess. Diversions? I enjoy a good show and a good performer. Just an old showman. Well when you have to kill your audience very few years to keep them in their seats it's about time to pack in."

Question: "Mr. Martin, I gather that your plan to move the show to planet Venus has uh miscarried. Is that correct?"

"Yeah it looks that way."

Question: "In that case, Mr. Martin where will you go when you go if you go?"

"That's quite a problem. You see I'm on the undesireable list with every immigration department in the galaxy.

'Who *him?* Don't let him out here.'

Question: "Mr. Martin don't you have any friends?"

"There are no friends. I found that out after the crash. I found that out before the others. That's why I'm still here. There are no friends. There are allies. There are accomplices. No one wants friends unless he is shit scared or unless he is planning a caper he can't pull off by himself."

Question: "Mr. Martin, what about the others who were involved in this crash? Aren't they still alive some where in some form?"

"You don't have to look far. They are sitting right here."

Question: "Who were these others?"

"There was an army colonel, a technician and a woman."

Question: "Won't you have to come to some sort of terms with your uh former accomplices?"

"To my disgruntled former associates I have this to say. You were all set to cross me up from the count down. You think I can't read your stupid virus mind, lady. And you, you technical bastard, with your mind full of formulae I can't read. And you Colonel Bradly waiting to shoot me in the back. The lot of you. Blind and paralyzed I still beat you to the draw."

Question: "Mr. Martin, what sort of place did you people come from?" "What sort of place did we come from. Well if you want the answer to that question, just look around, buster. Just look around." "Ladies and gentlemen, you have just heard an interview with Mr. Martin, sole survivor of the first attempt to send up a space capsule from planet earth. Mr. Martin has been called The Man of A Thousand Lies. Well he didn't have time for a thousand but I think he did pretty well in the time alloted. And I feel reasonably sure that if the other crew members could be here with us tonight they would also do a pretty good job of lying. But please remember that nothing is true in space, that there is no time in space—that what goes up under such auspices must come down—that the beginning is also the end.

Ladies and gentlemen, these our actors, bid you a long last good night."

POEM | Norman Mailer

The most
  eligible
  bachelor
    in London
  is a category
   conceived
    by presumptive
     witches
     weary
      of doing
       without
    their widow's weeds—

  whispered
    the epigram
   to the boutoniere.

Go fix the flowers, fuck-face
    was the King's reply

306

Donald Bloch

SET THEORY

The discovery of love between parent and child is a terrible thing; yet, it happens all the time. We stand like beasts on opposite walls of a chasm that is too broad to leap across and too deeply cleft to find a path down and up again in time.

Dinner the first night home went quite as Brian had imagined it would; not well. The family sat around the circular kitchen table. A pot of ivy sat in the middle where light from above fell upon its broad leaves and was softened. If father, mother, and son had stretched their arms straight towards one another, they would have formed a triangle, but they didn't. After a few calm moments tranquil enough but for a cough or story that turned out to be not so amusing in the retelling, Martin in need of the salt looked about for it but found there was none.

"Where's the salt, dear?" He managed to suggest in the tone of his question that Lynne had forgotten to set the table altogether. She had summoned them to dine from a bare board and the first thing to ask for was logically enough salt. "Can I have the salt?"

"What do you want the salt for?" Because Martin had come to dinner without his shirt on contradictory to her express wishes, because there were telltale signs about his face that he had brought no appetite with him, and because no matter how attentive she was to the task at hand there was always something she overlooked, Lynne was uncommonly annoyed. "Have you tried the beans without it? Taste them." She scanned the table as if there had been no oversight and the salt were merely in hiding.

"Forgot it?" When she had looked everywhere else, Lynne was obliged to face Martin.

"It's in the cabinet I guess." She longed to add, "where it belongs."

"Do you expect me to get it?" This was discussion not argument. Brian tried the beans for himself and silently agreed with his father that they could use some salt. Head lowered, he listened to his parents while he played with a few vegetables on the end of his fork, pushing them here and there in a pool of their own making.

"No, I don't expect you to get it. Certainly not. I don't *expect* you to do anything." Lynne crossed her knife and fork upon her plate. "Ever." She scraped her chair back and went to the cabinet where she located the salt shaker. "The trouble with you, Martin," Lynne spoke as she shook a few grains of salt onto the palm of one hand, "is that you haven't had to do anything for yourself since you were a child." Satisfied that the salt would flow, she shook the grains from her hand onto the floor, then crossed to the table and reseated herself. "Your mother served your father hand and foot. She waited on him like a slave and I'm not your slave. I mean that." After a rhetorical question—"Or am I supposed to go right on spoiling you?"—Lynne handed Martin the salt and subsided. Brian looked up when Martin replied briefly, "Thanks for the salt."

They ate on in silence for several moments. Brian thought how strange and uncomfortable it was to be back at his permanent address. It was more a place to write letters to than be at, a whistle-stop, a reminder of facts and impressions, a special scent. In the apartment next door a radio played champagne music. Brian with his mouth sucking down whipped potatoes and a weight in his chest bid good journey to the high spirits which had accompanied him home. Reunion just hours ago—the white doorbell, brrrring, first enthusiastic greetings, first embraces, a long hot shower, a miraculously peaceful nap in his own clean bed—and now dinner.

"I'm sorry that the meat isn't better. You can't always tell from just looking at it." Lynne was talking to her plate. "Or from feeling it." Brian was about to explain that after what he had been used to eating recently even the worst piece of beef would seem fit for a king, but Martin spoke first.

"It's lousy. I can't eat it." He pushed his plate an inch back on the table for emphasis. His portion of meat, forlorn, lay there.

"It's not that bad," Lynne said, "or maybe it is." She rose with her plate and her husband's and at the sink scraped their still considerable contents into a paper bag. "Don't *laugh* at me, Martin." The knife in her hand rasped against the china. It wasn't exactly angry she was; her wrath was routinized.

"I like it." Brian's saving comment was late and feeble.

"Good." He wasn't sure who said that.

"Coffee, dear?" Father had lit a cigarette, placed his elbows upon the table, set his head upon his hands.

"For Christ's sake, Martin, give me a chance. I've only got two hands." She held them up, visual proof of what she was saying, and then resumed her methodical scraping. "You'll have your coffee when I can give it to you." Brian anticipated Martin's reaction: retaliation. It was an old record that he could sing along with, a serial he knew the end to, an editorial reprinted in all sizeable dailies on holidays until its original passion had grown limp and predictable.

"Christ's sake, Christ's sake." Martin's voice was for the first time nasty. Grey hairs on his chest supported the claim that he made of growing old waiting for coffee. Voices in opposition until they drowned out the music which came through the wall. Piqued, Lynne put the plate in her hand down too hard on the edge of the sink and it split cleanly in two.

"That's because you're in such a damn big hurry to get away from the table to turn on the God damn television set." Lynne danced with her head to reenforce her words. "Don't bother to deny it, I know you like a book." She threw a finger at Martin. "Can't you for once sit still for more than ten minutes and act like a human being? Your son just got home." Brian disliked the role Lynne's statement cast him in. Martin stood up—"With no choice now," Brian throught, "but to go watch television."—and left the room, but not without a final taunt.

"Nice meal. Skip the coffee."

"Next time you come to the table put a shirt on," Lynne said. "How would he like it if I walked around with no top on? If a button of my blouse is open he screams at me to cover up as if I'd done something immoral and *he* walks around half-naked most of the time. What does he think I am?" She put the halves of the plate, both spotless, deep into the garbage and turned to Brian. The kitchen was small and rectangular. They faced each other from opposite ends of the room, Lynne, sunburnt, freckled, short, broad, and bewildered, framed by a window behind her. Brian couldn't force his eyes past his mother and out that window; his emotions hadn't range enough. He brought his plate to her like an offering.

"It was good, Mom. Really."

Lynne smiled. "I wanted it to be better, Brian, believe me." The saccharine voices of a children's cartoon looped into the room. "I didn't plan it to be so stinking. Tomorrow's will be better." Brian kissed Lynne on the cheek and took her apron off. He made her sit down while he cleared the dishes and then he served coffee.

"Sugar is in the cabinet, Brian."

They had fresh fruit for dessert and talked easily to one another between bites. It was indisputable that once they were alone Lynne asked sensible questions, that she was concerned with Brian and interested in his welfare. "We work better in combinations of two," Brian thought.

Minutes later Martin returned and wordlessly poured himself a cup of coffee from the percolator on the stove. He resumed his place at the table without giving any indication that he realized there were others in the room. The television set was audible inside.

"Do you want some fruit, Martin?" Father looked up like a child forgiven unexpectedly for guilt that he was prepared to acknowledge and to pay for.

"Nuhuh. Just coffee." After stirring his coffee around and around with but the slightest motion of his wrist, Martin withdrew his spoon,

Willard Midgette

mouthed it, and laid it on his saucer. Until the coffee stopped spinning, he looked up dizzily at the light overhead, one hand to his throat where the collar of his shirt lay open. The flesh beneath his eyes hung in purple folds; the eyes themselves were vacant. Brian and Lynne talked as they watched Martin but they were only half-conscious of what they said to each other. The aroma of coffee was strong. Martin drained his cup abruptly in a few noisy swallows.

"If it's an apology you want, I'm sorry. I'm tired." He said this short speech in a decrescendo as he returned to the television. "Your mother, Brian, is a good woman." Most of the words came after he had left the room. His empty cup remained on the table. "Oh boy!" Lynne said. Whether her intent was bitter or sweet Brian couldn't decide. Hardly lifting his cup at all, he sipped his coffee. Lynne could guess at his agitation. He looked bigger bodily than she had ever seen him before, there was a new thickness to his fingers, greater obscurity to his facial expression. She broke from her revery and put a hand in Brian's hair.

"Put the garbage out now like a good fellow, Brian. I don't want it to smell up the kitchen." She rumpled his hair. "Tomorrow you can get a haircut." He was pleased to act. "Hold the bag on the bottom— with both hands." Lynne let him out and stood in the doorway while he walked the length of the corridor to the incinerator. Brian wondered whether if he slid himself down the shoot he could find the furnace door from the inside and escape quickly enough to avoid serious harm. The slight give of the carpet beneath his feet was almost sufficient to trip him.

Mother was not at the door when Brian returned but the apartment was unlocked. She was in the kitchen. The dishwasher was churning and Lynne was seated at the table to all appearances listening to it while she turned a match folder over and over in one hand. Brian sat down too and cut in on her distraction. He asked her about work, the people at her office, the phone calls. She nodded her head and then looked up at him, her eyes lifting a slight bit more slowly than the rest of her head.

"What are you going to do?" The question though fair and inevitable took Brian by surprise. He wanted to respond, "About what?" but said, "We'll see." Lynne nodded again. The match book continuing its somersaults in her palm.

"Do you have any idea?"

"No."

"None at all?"

"Not really. There are things I could say but—" Brian wanted to paint as bleak a picture as possible of his future. Whatever happened would then seem fortunate by comparison to expectations. "Something will turn up. I won't miss out."

"I'd like to know—"

"Brian!" Lynne was interrupted by a shout from Martin. "Lynne!" Hurry up. You've got to see this." They obeyed the summons which grew more urgent. "I'm not kidding. Hurry". On television they saw a jerky newsreel clipping of a hurricane disaster in the Caribbean. A reporter off screen tolled casualties in a fair weather voice while the picture showed people in rags running at random for shelter, branches and furniture blown like bits of paper through the streets, carved shutters ripped from their hinges bouncing on the street pavement, tall trees with lush crowns bent at acute angles with the earth, birds unable to rise into the air but flapping their wings furiously, sheets of rain, smashed glass, a dog whose fur stood on end and whose desperate bark was blown back down his throat by the torrential wind. The succession of shots continued for nearly five minutes. When there was no spoken word, background music of a melancholic sort commented on the action and once in a while the weather was permitted to speak for itself.

"Incredible." Father repeated the word at intervals. "Incredible." A cigarette was burning itself out in his hand. "Incredible. With all we know something like this happens and there's nothing to be done about it." After the newsreel a plea was made for contributions to an emergency relief fund.

"Was that what you called us in here for? Is that what we couldn't miss?" Lynne was angry again. "We had to stop talking and come in here to see that?" Although Father was not answering, Lynne appeared to think herself involved in a dialogue. "I thought you were bleeding to death." The television set answered her every word with an irrelevancy of its own. Brian could not remember the household's being so excitable when he was a child, but then he had gone to bed earlier.

"Anyone for a walk?" Brian hoped that there would be no takers, that Lynne would be intent on destroying the television with her shoe as she threatened and that Martin would be inextricably involved in its defense. He had grown dependent on solitary walks; aimlessness settled him, and privacy. "Wait, I'll be right with you." Lynne had withdrawn from the room and father was lacing his shoes. The cigarette was all ash in the ashtray but smoke still rose in twin streams. "Turn the TV off, Brian. Black knob, to the right." Brian wondered if Father thought keeping his son company obligatory. The TV swallowed its own light, not all at once.

Downstairs, outside they began to walk. It was immediately apparent that Martin had misconstrued the intent of Brian's invitation. He didn't understand what the walk was supposed to be about. He was out for exercise: a brief brisk circuit to work off the dinner he hadn't eaten. Brian was sorry. He walked at his own pace, slowly, and so behind his father by half a step. "We work better in combinations of two," Brian thought. Father talked over his shoulder. When they were alone he chose to talk seriously *in medias res*. "Do you know what it's like for a parent to love a child, Brian, more than himself? more than life itself?"

"No." But at that moment Brian had been considering what amounted to much the same thing.

By herself in the apartment, Lynne returned the dishes to their shelves. Accidently she dropped a glass but it merely chipped and did not break. She rubbed the new rough area of the rim against her lip and then with the suggestion of a shrug replaced the glass in the cabinet. Later she went into the living room and picked up a heavy book. She held it closed on her lap for a while and then put it down. Humming champagne music she went to the kichen for a glass of water and afterwards to the bedroom where, after turning on the television by the blue button to the left, she settled to watch and to knit. Lynne knit well. The evening slipped into night the way a blotter soaks up ink.

The street which Brian and Martin first followed sloped down in a direct perpendicular towards the main street of the town which was a quarter of a mile in the distance. After a few minutes they turned a corner onto a side road where all at once there were no traffic signals, apartments or stores but many small private homes with a front walk of some yards, a bit of land, one or two lamps dully throbbing in an upstairs window. The sidewalk buckled at the base of trees that were soon to lose their leaves again.

"I wish," Father said, "that I could give you the benefit of my years. But that's a silly thing to say, because of course I can't." Martin walked his constant half step ahead of Brian and did most of the talking. Brian responded in monosyllables. He listened to the change re-arrange itself in his father's pocket with every step and listened to his own feet contact the cement. A telephone rang, rang again and was cut short in the middle of a third ring just as the walkers turned another corner. They moved on, staggered, towards the completion of the third side of a square.

"My father was a great man. I didn't realize that until he was dead but in his way he was a *very* great man, among the greatest."

"Mumm."

"We all do the same things. We eat, and, Brian," Father waved his hands in the air not sure on what level of directness to operate, "we defecate. We all sit down to do it. Kings, you, me, my father, holy men, thieves, artists. They're no better or worse than we are, no different from us." Martin paused. "Am I wrong or am I right?"

"Right."

"We all sneeze and we all cough and we all scratch ourselves." If Martin had stopped, Brian would have collided with him. "Don't we all feel happy one minute and sad the very next? The simple truth of it is," he pointed to himself, "we're men. No one deserves to be treated as more or less."

"More or less."

"My father was a great man." They had reached the final corner and turned back onto the hill that sloped towards town. "I couldn't understand that when he was alive." Brian considered bolting home, but rather continued at his steady rate thinking how exquisite a sensation it was to walk more slowly than somebody else. He thought, "If my father is a great man then whose is not? And who is to say that he is not?" and he felt very deferential towards the man just in front of him.

"This is it, Brian. We're back."

When he realized that Martin was ready to go inside, Brian said, "I want to walk some more. I'll be up in a while." Then without a break in his measured stride, he left Martin surprised behind.

"I'm tired, Brian, or I'd come with you. Don't be too long."

Brian walked on in a daze until he turned once more onto the dimly lit street of moderate lives snug in their reasonable comfort. He removed his hands from his pockets and tried to shake them loose. "Like lions," he thought.

Lynne dropped a stitch. "Martin come back. I'm lonely." She resented herself for such honesty. "Martin!" she said aloud. Then she turned the television off (was the movie over?) and undressed. In her nightgown she glided barefoot to the kitchen and after a moment's thought drank most of another glass of tap water. What was left when her thirst died she poured into the base of the ivy on the table. Then she prinked the plant leaves.

Martin was in the elevator. When it stopped he lingered a full minute before realizing there was no motion. Back in the bedroom he kissed Lynne twice and held her hand. He explained to her that Brian was out walking. "He's vague, dear."

Relieved to be by himself, Brian was thinking as he walked, "We work best in combinations of two. One, two, three." He stopped and stood in the shadow of a tree. "Elm, oak, maple?" How in his ignorance was he to know? By their seeds? Perhaps. Perhaps by their leaves?

"What's Brian going to do now, Martin?"

"He'll find something. Whatever it is, don't worry."

And that was precisely what Brian thought below in the shadow as he walked slowly, "Don't worry. Most important of all, don't be sorry."

Robert Dawson

"Why the Americans Raise
Some Insignificant
MONUMENTS
and Others
That Are Very Grand"

To my surprise, several people who have read this poem in manuscript have been unaware of the historical situation out of which it is built. During World War II German prisoners of war were shipped to work-camps in various parts of the United States. Some were held in Minnesota, despite suspicions that Germanic nationalism was strong in that state. My grandfather is of probably Alsatian extraction, by way of several farms in Illinois and Ohio. He told me the story of my poem in 1958. The story is true, but all names, including his, have been changed for purposes of poetry. Why I chose to let him tell his story in my language, you will have to determine yourselves. My title is a chapter title from Tocqueville. — R.D.

Tag, rag, and bobtail carry a high flag.
Insult to injury. "Billy, you circle that fence."
Tough words. My mittens tingle. Hesitance
Climbs no fences. Barb wire. A mad rush might,
Perhaps. But slush to the elbows . . . tear my snowpants . . .
"A sag on the east side," Billy reports. Too grim—
Better watch him. We wind the long way round.
Seven times seventy pounds bear it down.
"Oh no I found the sag, so I get

In the hemp house first." "I knew it —
Knew you'd pull this, Billy, who's idea
Was coming out here anyway?" "So what!
You always think you can boss just cuz you're big,
But my daddy's bigger'n you'll ever be."
"Yeh my dad's bigger'n you an' yours together."
We pummel across the gravel, snap a shutter,
Scrap each other — our friends don't bother,
But enter by the door. When Billy falls,
As in I crawl, I find they've climbed another floor.

High hemp blades, rusty shutes, bales of mould,
Machines for this or that crop, and rows
Of metal moth-balled ghosts smoulder, smoulder
In a concrete canyon. Under the wing-teeth of a combine,
Choked with stale hemp, a meadowlark's nest, see it!
Warped closet doors prepare to creak. We line
Our mouths with whisper.
                              I and another
Grapple a corner, jerk at the hips. Our grips
Spool wet guts out, for the oil cloth rips,
And ventilators spin without a switch. We're
Head over heels but the syphon bursts; green gusts
Of wool plop, plop the wall, and whose the step
That crosses me? I see or fear that I shall see
Grandfather Groskreutz with his troop,
Who once in fields for war manured
Laid strap and heel to these machines.
Oh you who would confuse, belie
The swingle with the swingle tree,
We that were look-alikes, Grampa and I,
Together tell what he told me:

The Germans haunched by a cold concrete wall,
Sucking their paws like bears in winter. "You Adolf
Groskreutz?" bawled the boy sergeant Daniel Riley.
"I'll call you Al. You speak their lingo?" "I think so."
"Well ask the sons o'bitches what they want
To make 'em work. If food is what, you tell 'em
I'll do as best I can. We ain't gittin' much."
"I've heard them talk already. First of all,
The things you call them, they understand,
And, sergeant, it won't serve your business
To be known as a loud swearer among farmers,
Us or them." "For Jesus sake, who
Do you think these are, state visitors!"

"They know who they are. Small soldiers, small farmers,
Low Germans like the most of us who settled this state.
You think because they're prisoners, they've forgotten
Who they are?" "Okay, mister, you wanna help me, you
Know you can. But if folks are sympathizing
With the enemy, why you won't help them
Or yourselves much either." Sergeant Riley
Scratched behind his ear, while I exchanged
Words, words with his prisoners.
                              Some
Were topsoil. Some were ice. A youth
From Pommern was scared of piles . . .
His junge Frau would smile at it. Another
Had a brother on the Lakes, he said,
Who'd sponsor him in Canada, after
The war, and would I take a letter out?
Someone from Bremen had sow eyes. If cut
His look would squeal. A Frieslander,
Wilhelm Groth, spoke only dialect;
The Brementowner spoke for him. The rest
Might have been men of the same village.
They lived at one end of themselves, and we
Lived at the other of ourselves. Blue Earth,
Minnesota! Think of it, you think of it
At Christmas always. Our young wives wear
Maternity before they know for sure,
And little boys are sure to wear our pants
Before they know. In Blue Earth
Cops wear flannels. Ach and ja
Are soda-fountain sentiments. But we
Were bloody for the Jew, our boys bloody
for the State.
                      Long after spring
Had melted even the windward fields,
Bare concrete sucked the cold up
Through deep roots. Daniel Riley
Couldn't mend the flow of temperature,
Though it must be said he tried.
Then joy renewed in planting of the hemp.
To bind the war in Europe, eighteen
Holdings, subsidized, nine hundred
Acres lay in unaccustomed seed.
With farmer after farmer, Riley's krauts
Pledged sweat and separation to our need.
And every farmer, as his field was turned,
Feasted the soldiers in his yard.

But . . .
"Jesus sake, Groskreutz, what 'id
They send us out here for, if not to work!"
"What do your orders say?" "That some pricks 'uve
Beefed about forced labor in the States." "I thought
These men had volunteered . . ." "They had, they did,
And no one's bothered either! It's just I 'spose
The higher ups are 'fraid these krauts 'ud try
Ta weasle into citizens, 'count of workin' here."
"Have you promised them anything?" "Course
I have! I was promised too. You think the guverment
Could build this plant without first knowin'
It had labor for it!"
              After this, Riley and I
Got on less well. Perhaps he thought
I recriminated him. Perhaps I did.
Each day before I woke the hardware store,
I brought a couple dozen day-old doughnuts,
Or a quart of pickled beets, to redeem the
Prisoner's diet. Others did the same, but
Riley saw them all as me, and me as all Germans,
And suspected us, through them, of undermining
His authority.
            He needed me to speak
The northern dialects. The Brementowner
Knew a little English, enough to take commands,
But only Groth of the Germans spoke to him
That only since he needed him to talk.
One morning when they all refused to stir,
They indicated Groth would be their man.

         They wanted to know,
Why couldn't they work, or if the work was done,
Where could they exercise? Riley fumed
As Groth's words passed from Frisian to German,
From German to English. It was as if
Three languages conspired to shame him.
Then Groth asked soap and brushes to clean
The cells. I handed his words to Riley
Good as new, but Riley seemed to think I'd
Damaged them. "Groskreutz, I've had enough
Of yer damn meddling! I'll have these rooms
Scrubbed when I damn well think of it!
He was all knuckles. From his tone
And by the situation, Groth must have known
What was between us. He thrust his face

In Riley's and all the translation was his voice:
"You think that you can control our lives, and that
It makes you worthy of control to have control.
But my heart is bigger than your heart,
And I will outbleed you."
                      Next day,
Riley came down to the hardware store
For brushes and soap. He couldn't resist
The solitude of Groth, nor did he care
To be cruel.
            His commission here
Was like a basement from which
The house had been reaped.
New supplies were a tearful surprise.
Riley went begging.
              While he was gone
The crop came in. Deerfields, Molines
Ganged to the hemphouse, where the house-high
Harvestors glittered like unsmitten shields.
Singly, then by twos and threes deployed,
Stark tractors drew steel cutters through the fields.
What worked for wheat might well have worked
For hemp, if ever works of peace could serve a war,
But none of these whose feet decided gears
Knew how ripe hemp would knot, or how
It caught the blades that cleaved it, twisted them,
Or choked a tractor till it boiled. To whittle
Green confusion from such straps and links,
Scythes, axes, jackknives were no use. We dragged
The mowers to a highway, hitched them to a truck,
Set fire and set them rolling till the flames
Flew from the blades in showers or like seeds.
Riley returned with orders for his men
To process hemp, but he found no hemp.
The cutters, fire-gutted, failed before the crop
Half-filled its crib; and much of what came in,
Came in half-burned. That which was whole,
Beneath the swingle, proved all pulp.
It had no fiber and it left no hope.

Now Riley tried petitions to disperse
The prisoners from Blue Earth. Instead
Their rations were diminished by a fourth.
The farmers who had lost their subsidy
Blamed Riley, or could not afford
To stock the prison larder from their own.

The two from Pommern and from Brementown
Caught virus and were traded. Wilhelm Groth
Congealed by afternoons. Riley turned me out.
One noon late in November he appeared,
Bloodshot and beardy, in the hardware store.
"Groskreutz, I was a prick to you,
When all you wanted was to help my men,
So now I wantcha ta be part of what I planned . . ."
He would provide, he said, Thanksgiving
For the Germans, out of his small sums,
As he put it, wanting not cash, sympathy.
How he'd made up with the Germans, I couldn't see.
I stared at him. He blinked at me.

Snow fell Thanksgiving eve. Cold seeped
Through concrete veins. In Riley's kitchen,
Potatoes, pumpkin pies, fresh ears of corn
Swelled in the oven, simmered in the pot.
He had no turkey, but he thought his corn,
American-style, would do, should do. And now
He melted butter handfulls in a can,
He whistled, scooped an armload and was gone.

The Germans hunched together at the wall,
Licking their claws like crows in winter . . .
Riley strutted in, grinning, with his corn
Steaming and streaming yellow. I was still.
I knew it, knew he hadn't made up!
The Germans rustled when they saw the corn.
Some muttered to each other. Some stood out,
With pig pig on their tongues but knots in their guts.
When Riley gestured broadly, "Dig in! Dig in! ", they
Cackled at him. He picked a cob and bit it
With a show of relish. Now the Germans growled.
"You sons of bitches! you sons of bitches!
What do you want from me!" He went outside
And came back with a swingle. "Now you'll eat,
Or I'll bash it down yer throats!" He picked
Another cob and threw it at Groth. Groth struck
With his bootsole, spilling butter and corn across
The concrete. Riley hit him with the swingle.
With a word in his teeth that no one understood,
He fluttered and was dead.

THROUGH (WHERE) WALLS (WERE)

ROBERT GRENIER

I see
my wife
        in the barn
of a dead New England farmer
        in her old clothes —

        passing the heavy
beams, avoiding the ridge
        pole's shadow on the straw
floor, mount
        a brittle ladder into the loft —

        there
(experimentally)
        seated
in a rotted carriage
        below open sky.

Desmond O'Grady

PROFESSOR KELLEHER

AND THE CHARLES RIVER

The Charles river reaps here like a sickle. April
Light sweeps flat as ice on the inner curve
Of the living water. Overhead, far from the wave, a dove
White gull heads inland. The spring air, still
Lean from winter, thaws. Walking, John
Kelleher and I talk on the civic lawn.

West, to our left, past some trees, over the ivy walls,
The clocktowers, pinnacles, the pillared university yard,
The Protestant past of Cambridge New England selfconsciously dead
In the thawing clay of the Old Burying Ground. Miles
East, over the godless Atlantic, our common brother,
Ploughing his myth-muddy fields, embodies our order.

But here, while the students row by eights and fours on the river—
As my father used row on the Shannon when, still a child,
I'd cross Thomond Bridge every Sunday, my back to the walled
And turreted castle, listening to that uncle Myke deliver
His version of history—I listen now to John Kelleher
Unravel the past a short generation later.

Down at the green bank's nerve ends, its roots half in the river,
A leafing tree gathers refuse. The secret force
Of the water worries away the live earth's under surface.
But his words, for the moment, hold back time's being's destroyer,
While the falling wave on both thighs of the Ocean
Erodes the coasts, at its dying conceptual motion.

Two men, one young, one old, stand stopped acrobats in the blue
Day, their bitch river to heel. Beyond—
Some scraper, tower or ancestral house's gable end.
Then, helplessly, as in some ancient dance, the two
Begin their ageless struggle, while the tree's shadow,
With all its arms, crawls on the offal-strewn meadow.

Locked in their mute struggle there by the blood loosed tide
The two abjure all innocence, tear down past order—
The one calm, dispassionate, clearsighted; the other
Wild with ecstasy, intoxicated, world mad.
Surely some new order is at hand;
Some new form emerging where they stand.

Dusk. The great dim tide of shadows from the past
Gathers for the end—the living and the dead.
All force is fruitful. All opposing powers combine.
Aristocratic privilege, divine sanction, anarchy at last
Yield the new order. The saffron sun sets.
All shadows procession in an acropolis of lights.

A. Peter Fabry

William Ferguson

ANALOGY OF THE BLACK PIANO

First Reader: She wove a marvelous cloth on that dark loom,
colors of crystal, thunderous implication,
and each thread black, and many-colored,
and in the loom the sun-white cloth,
breaking of crystal, wakening waters,
color of wells at midnight, sea at noon;
and in the loom there were two lamps,
one dark, the other fire and light,
and one was of the warmth of the sea,
the other, warmth of diamonds,
and of the darkness and the light was woven
cloth of day and night, or of all time.

Second Reader: This wind, crazy with rain, rattling shingles,
angers the river, charging a dusky bull
through hills heavy with trees, and it is she,
concealing its springs yet guiding the water in full force,
an image of winter come to haunt this season;
but the rain comes with the sound of flowers,
with the sound of trees stretching in clouds
to the low valley. Bells in the town;
I lie on the dry leaves marvelling,
though across the river in the spruces half-moving
the invisible raven waits
predatory in the stillness of the air.

First Reader: Wind cannot touch the whiteness of this cloth
spread out, sun and golden, like the sea
calm at nightfall, or the same raging sea
sacrilege of the moon, and midnight torn from the wall.
this cloth, like the flag of a great ship
now ragged and torn one end to the other.

now coming out glorious pulling at the staff,
and still, it is true, the shining eye
of a bird perhaps, or a quiet god,
looms among cloudbanks, now, and gone,
without message, without a word,
no reassurance, rather a new portent . . .

Second Reader: I am of the land, and of the mountains,
and I have followed this shaggy river
curve after curve, upriver, far from the sea,
and even so, the story is not told,
I cannot understand, even so,
the convolutions of that blessed stream,
the downward coursing, faithful, and
not without colors of lust, the which caught
true in the sun, reflect, yet colored, the whole . . .
the sound of bells, and lamplight tangled in them,
the bones of mountains and the bones of men
approach this chanting, risen from the dead.

First Reader: She weaves a marvelous cloth, an evening
woven in bellnotes, steeple-pierced,
lamps going on, and others dark still,
your village far from the sea, yet with a sign,
an image of water; seabirds circling
as if in search, and a sea-storm welling perhaps
in any lake, no matter how calm,

Second Reader: and in the waving pines
the invisible raven waits
predatory in the stillness of the storm.
O let the spring come, and let no man revile her,
quiet rain, with sun here and there,
and the grass growing greener day by day,
a fine cloth for a child to play upon,

First Reader: and in the loom the sun-white cloth,
green threads for tapestry multicolored,
a miracle half-seen in the doing,

Second Reader: and the river in her soul
flows on in the memory
of storms and seasons, riding the heights of the wind.

Marianne Moore IN LIEU OF THE LYRE

One debarred from enrollment at Harvard,
may have seen towers and been shown the Yard—
animated by Madame de Bouffler's choice rhymes:
Sentir avec ardeur:* with fire; yes, with passion;
rime-prose revived also by word-wizard Achilles (see note)
Chinese Dr. Fang

The Harvard Advocate's formal-informal craftly rare
invitation to Harvard made grateful, Brooklyn's (or Mexico's)
ineditos —
one whose "French aspect" was invented by
Professor Levin,†
a too outspoken outraged refugee from clichés particularly,
who was proffered redress
by the Lowell House Press‡ —
Vermont Stinehour Press, rather. No careless statements
to Kirkland House; least of all inexactness in quoting a fact.

To the Advocate, *gratia sum*§
unavoidably lame as I am, verbal pilgrim
like Thomas Bewick, drinking from his hat-brim,
drops spilled from a waterfall, denominated later by him
a crystalline Fons Bandusian miracle.

It occurs to the guest, — if someone had confessed it in time —
that you might have preferred to the waterfall, pilgrim and hat-brim,
a nutritive axiom such as
"a force at rest is at rest because balanced by some other force (comma):
or "catenary and triangle together hold the span in place,
of a bridge|| (Parenthesis)

or a too often forgotten truly relevant thing, the Roebling cable
was invented by William A. Roebling.

These reflections, Mr. Davis,
in lieu of the lyre.

Sentir avec ardeur. By Madame Boufflers — Marie-Francoise-Catherine de Beauveau, Marquise de Boufflers (1711-1786). See note by Dr. Achilles Fang, annotating Lu Chi's "Wên Fu" (A.D. 261-303) — his "Rhymeprose on Literature" ("rhyme-prose" from "Reimprosa" of German medievalists): 'As far as notes go, I am at one with a contemporary of Rousseau's: Il faut dire en deux mots / Ce qu'on veut dire'; . . . But I cannot claim 'J'ai réussi,' especially because I broke Mme. de Boufflers's injunction ('Il faut éviter l'emploi / Du moi, du moi')" Harvard Journal of Asiatic Studies, Volume 14, Number 3, December, 1951, page 529 (revised, *New Mexico Quarterly*, September, 1952).
†"A Note on her French Aspect", Harry Levin, p.40, *Festschrift for Marianne Moore's Seventy-seventh Birthday* — by Various Hands, Edited by Tambimuttu, $4.95.
‡Referring to Lowell House *separatum: Occassionem Cognose*, (1963) §*Gratia sum* Bewick tailpiece "a trickle of water from a rock, underlined by heart in outline carved on the rock, p. 53, *Memoir of Thomas Bewick Written by Himself*, (Centaur Classics).
||*Brooklyn Bridge, Fact and Symbol* by Alan Trachtenberg (Oxford $5.75).

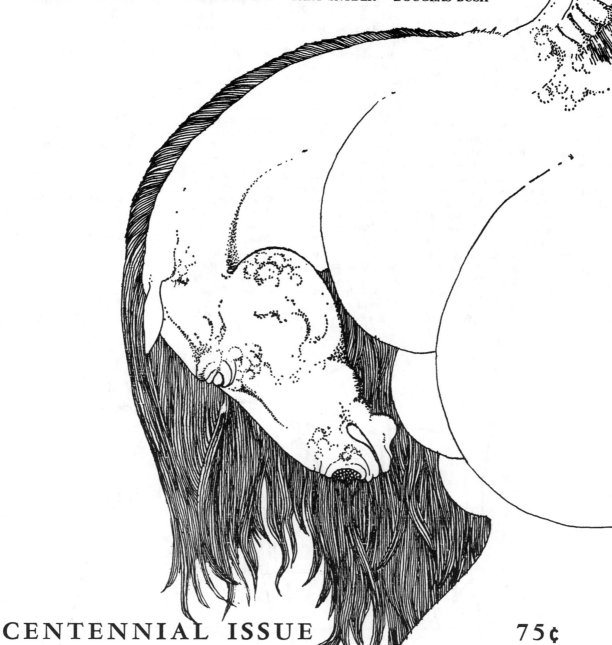

JOHN HAWKES • ADRIENNE RICH • HARRY LEVIN • ROBERT FITZGERALD
DENISE LEVERTOV • CONRAD AIKEN • HOWARD NEMEROV • DONALD HALL

The Harvard Advocate

JONATHAN KOZOL • RICHARD EBERHART • KAY BOYLE • ROBERT BLY
W. H. AUDEN • C. L. BARBER • TIM REYNOLDS • GARY SNYDER • DOUGLAS BUSH

CENTENNIAL ISSUE   75¢

Flake Off, Baby

The Kandy-Kolored Tangerine-Flake Streamling Baby, Tom Wolfe. Farar, Straus; $5.50

You don't have to read the book. Just look at him on the back cover, sitting smiling self-satisfiedly on what looks like a wrought-iron toilet, looking all foppish in buckled shoes, white suit, white tie, long hair and Georgie Porgie cleft-chin, and you know you mustn't like him. As a matter of principle.

Tom Wolfe. Isn't he a regular guy using his nickname like that on a serious book about American art? Did I say American? Old Tom doesn't have readers, he has fans. And a fan-club, too. Only I don't know where to send in for my membership card. They forgot to print the address.

American, yes. But what do they teach there down at Yale, where Tom got his Phd. in American Studies? Is Tom a communist? He believes in a sort of aesthetic class-warfare. Can you beat it? Melville, Faulkner, Charles Ives, Wyeth, Pollock — hell, they're the *elite,* and if you like them you're a petit-bougeois arteriosclerotic nogoodnik. All hope, as Orwell wrote in another connection, lies with the "Proles", whoever they are. Neon signs, Kustom Kars, Murray the K, the Righteous Brothers, "Demo Derbies" — they're *American,* baby, they're Art, like *indigenous.* And don't fight it, D'Artagnan, because IT'S WHAT'S

HAPPENING!

He's a sly one, this Tom; he doesn't come right out and tell you his preposterous thesis. At first it's hard to tell exactly what he's saying; you think you like him, and then it's too late. His style is so distracting. In the book's first paragraph, for example, he repeats the word 'hernia' fifty-seven times. He writes similes like "The music filled the room like a giant egg-slicer." Good God, no one has done anything like this since the days of Christina Rossetti. It sounds so good, so NEW that you nod your head and don't stop to think what he's getting at. At other times he is so boring and repetitious. All old men are "sclerotic", all brassieres "up to the angle of a Nike Missile Launcher." Half asleep, you breathe easily and fall back on the couch, sensing that Tom is a debunker, while all the time he is convinced that Junior Johnson, the champion stock-car racing driver, is in fact "The Last American Hero."

Tom is a man of strong dislikes, though. He really hates those phonies who go in for custom-made suits with tailored buttonholes. (Why custom-suit *afficianados* are despicable and kustomkar 'nuts' are not, he doesn't make clear.) And all those Maecenas-types who showed up for the re-opening of the Museum of Modern Art some months back. Adlai Stevenson. The Rockefellers. Edward Steichen. Phonies. "Sacred egos."

I wonder if Tom believes all this,

or if he just delights in being "outrageous," as the newspaper ads for his book chirp. If *Kandy-Kolored* isn't a hoax, then I suspect it is not Tom, but Doctor Wolfe who is the culprit. For years now the professors of American Studies have been wisely telling us that the nation's distinguishing feature over the past ten decades or so has been its attempt to create a culture of its own from its all but overpowering industrial sterility. No one listens much to what professors say, but Tom graduated and saw all they had told him coming to pass: "The new sensibility . . . the new world, submerged so long, invisible, and now arising, slippy shiny, electric — Super Scuba-man! — out of the vinyl deeps." But does he have to *like* it?

I'm afraid so, for Wolfe is above all a creature of Fashion, and it is fashionable nowadays to find beauty in what is ugly. Mr. David Owen's famous lecture on Queen Victoria's Crystal Palace Exhibition isn't as funny as it used to be because it is "in" again to display *papier-mache* pianos in one's living room. Ah, Tom. When you were at Yale and read Horatio Greenough (only students in the "American Field" read Horatio Greenough) you should have paid heed. He might have been talking about guys like you when he wrote that "Fashion . . . is a uniform with which thinking humanity cripples its gait in the vain hope that the unthinking may keep up with itself."

—Stephen Saltonstall

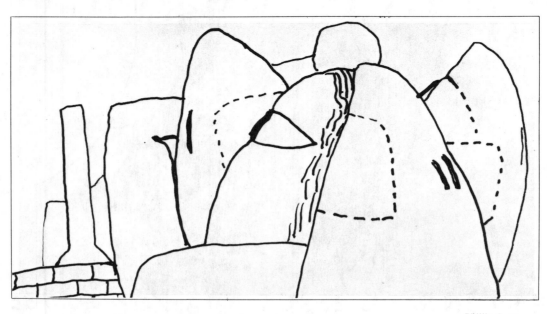

Phillip Guston

Mary Ann Radner

L'ENVOI

You are the long way that I have to go
away from you.

In your face now
comes the reflected strangeness of my face
going from you, a night in a far city.
Your voice moves me away as moving seas
will take me
and you translate me to another tongue.

I who am here within your hand's expanse
will not be here, but far; your holding
is giving me to distances.
My lungs which breathe you, blood which sounds you
will pulse another air
apart from you, my country, my nativity.

These forms of me you name and guess will alter
and be reborn of foreignness; oh you, become
the long way out, away,
how shall I make out of myself
the long way back?

RESURRECTIONS

I: The Sign of Jonas

God called me from the belly of the fish,
Who cleared his throat of me, and I stood of
Unkempt and slimy, weeping, to remember
The captain's wrath at my unholy flight.

How provident the Lord was, to have thought
A refuge for His prophet, in the somber
Waters of death and life a place to sleep
When my soul slept within a tomb of flesh.

I will speak to the men of Nineve —
But wading naked from this circling beach
Let me catch His voice in the squeal of gulls

And read His reprimand in wave-scoffed shells.
Now I relearn the curious hum of speech
And stir to fire again this island's lava.

II: Lazarus: A Testimony

Waking the first time out of death, I shunted
that lurching tenement of earth and oil
which closed me from the looking and enchanged
lantern of spring, and croached above the soil

for the first time amazed, in bone and breath.
I saw how blind I was for centuries
when the trees turned a furious cat ensheathed
in leaves and sun, in flame's perplexities.

Singing with all the tongues of wind, I strolled
forth from the murk and saw my older kin;
"Dark Mary, halted in the listening gold
And Martha, stretching curtains in the sun,

I stand up with the grass; and all my Christ
is what you knew of me who am not lost."

Mao on Style

In the 1940's, when the Chinese Communists were battling Japanese invaders and Kuomintang allies, Mao Tse-tung paused to train his guns on "Party formalism" — that is, jargon in official writing. In line with the Advocate's policy of printing the best critical as well as creative writing available, we have republished the following excerpts from a speech Mao gave at Yenan in 1942, courtesy of Harvard University Press, from Professors Brandt, Schwarz and Fairbank's Documentary History of Chinese Communism. Sad postcript: the sylistic millennium is as fare from Peking as it is from Cambridge. Side by side with Chinese Communst power, a new jargon has taken root.

. . .

"If a man's writing is characterized by Party formalism but he alone reads it, the problem is still unimportant. If he gives it to a second person to read, then its importance has already doubled in comparison, and it is harmful to a significant degree. If in addition he pastes it on the wall, has it mimeographed, publishes it in a newspaper, or prints it as a book, the problem becomes serious and many people can be affected. . . .

. . .

"The task of destroying and sweeping away these conditions is not an easy one. It must be properly done, which means that a reasonable explanation must be given. . . . The first method in reasoning is to give the patients a powerful stimulus, yell at them, 'you're sick!', so that the patients will have a fright and break out in an over-all sweat; then, they can be carefully treated.

"Now I am going to analyse the harmful aspects of Party formalism. . . .

"The first charge against Party formalism is 'Lengthy Empty Phrases, Words Without Substance.' Some of our comrades delight in writing long articles, articles which have not a thing to them and are really like 'the foot-bindings of a lazy old woman, long and foul smelling'. Why do they have to write at such length? And with such emptiness? There is only one explanation: they do not want the articles to be read. . . . . . Since they are bad when long and empty, are they then good if short and empty? No. We should prohibit all writing which contains only empty words. But the first and principal thing to be considered is that the lazy old woman's long, foul-smelling foot-bindings be hurriedly thrown in the privy. Perhaps someone will say, 'But isn't *Das Kapital* also long?' What shall we then do? It's easy; just read it carefully. Two common expressions go, 'Sing the song of the mountain you are on', and 'Look over the dishes before you eat, take the measurements before you cut the garments.' Regardless of what you do, act according to the circumstances; this also applies to writings and speeches. . . .

"The third charge against Party formalism is, 'Shooting Without a Target, Disregarding the Objective.' . . . The point of the proverb, 'To play the lute to the cow', is to ridicule the listener. If we discard this thought and substitute the idea of respecting the audience, what we have left is the idea of ridiculing the one who plays the lute. What is the purpose in playing carelessly without considering the audience? . . .

"The fourth charge against Party formalism is, 'Insipid Language (empty) like a Tramp.' What Shanghai people call a *pi-san* [tramp or vagrant] is very much like a person who practises our Party formalism, dry, shrivelled, extremely unpleasant to see. If in a writing or speech, the same few cliches are repeatedly used, like the 'style of students', without any lively, vigorous expressions, is not this language insipid and repulsive like a *pi-san?* . . . The people's language is very rich in expression; it is lively and vigorous and presents life as it is. Many of us have not mastered it, and as a consequence, in writing articles and giving speeches, we do not use lively, vigorous, really effective language; we only have a few varicose veins. . . . What is a propagandist? Not only are teachers propagandists, journalists propagandists, writers and artists propagandists. All our work cadres are also propagandists. . . . As soon as a man talks with another man he is engaged in propaganda work. . . . If we do not study the language of the masses, we cannot lead the masses.

"The fifth charge against Party formalism is, 'Categorizing (thoughts) Like Drugs in a Chinese Medicine Shop.' If you take a look in a Chinese medicine shop, you see many shelves of drawers in the medicine counter. On each shelf is pasted the name of the drug: *Tang-kuei, Shou-ti, Ta-huang, Mang-hsiao* — everything you need. This method has also been mastered by our comrades. In writing articles, giving speeches, writing books, and writing reports, I, II, III, IV come first; next, 1, 2 3, 4 [both of these series are in Chinese characters]; then *chia, i, ping, ting;* after that, *tzu, ch'ou, mao* [characters in the traditional sexagenary cycle]. Then you still have A, B, C, D, and a, b, c, d. And there are still the arabic numerals, lots of them! Fortunately, the ancients and foreigners have created many symbols for us, so that we can open a Chinese medicine shop without effort. If an article is filled with symbols, but states no problem, analyses no problem, and solves no problem, and neither proposes nor opposes, after much verbiage it is still a Chinese medicine shop — without real content. . . .

"The sixth charge against Party formalism is, 'Irresponsibility Which Does Universal Harm.' What has been discussed above is, on the one hand, caused by infantilism, and on the other by inadequate assumption of responsibility. Take washing the face as an example. We must wash our faces every day; many do not stop at washing their faces once; and after washing their faces they still have to take a look in the mirror and engage in some examination and research (loud laughter), afraid it has not been properly done. You can all see what a sense of responsibility they have! If we will only show the same responsible attitude in writing articles and giving speeches as in washing our faces, it will be all right. . . . In writing articles and giving speeches, many comrades do not want to do research or preparation beforehand. After the articles are written, they are not re-read a few times like looking in the mirror after washing the face, but are released carelessly. The result is 'writing a thousand words in one stroke, but away from the subject by ten thousand miles.' . . .

. . . I hope that our comrades will consider this speech carefully and analyse it. Moreover, each must analyse himself; each must weigh his own self carefully. Consult with your sweethearts, your intimate friends, and the comrades around you on matters which you have thought out clearly, and cure your own disease thoroughly. This is our hope."

Robert Shaw

CASTAWAYS

Caliban, you are all mouth,
gaping with gross howls,
only one tooth
is left and it's half-bad. Prospero scowls,

your voice drops a grudging decibel.
Miranda titters. "Brave monster," she mocks.
You get hell,
hearing her, chopping wood and breaking rocks,

living over the day of what you did —
her flowers that went with her full of music
fell, and skittered and hid.
They tease you now when you trip like a paralytic.

Love for a lady is bad for a brute.
How could she ever know your corded
throat wanted to be a flute
following her? Now all your hoarded

songs wither into spit, and drip. . . .
Once the words she taught you freed your tongue
then you sang to every ship
that wandered by, and waves it wandered among.

You went with her, but her scared shrug
angered her father into taking
away the words. Monster, hug
your warty self all night to a nightmare waking.

Hung in a body of captivity,
fighting for exit, groans escape.
Out of the sea
come the cruisers, crowds gather and gape.

Nothing to learn now from her lips.
No island tunes. Snarl and gulp,
brother. Once I came to grips
with who I wanted and was struck. Does this help?

No. . . . Sore mouth, groan for us both.
Ban, ban, Caliban, cry
past the last tooth
and nail to all newcomers. Let them know why.

W. H. Auden

DEAR DIARY

How odd it now seems
That when he was born there seemed
Nothing odd about writing:
I travelled alone
To Bonn with a boring maid.

* * *

As a child, before
Doctors had thought up the term,
He knew from watching
His maiden-aunts that illness
Could be psycho-somatic.

* * *

Father at the wars.
Mother, tongue-tied with shyness,
Struggling to tell him
The Facts of Life he didn't dare
Tell her he knew already.

* * *

Pleased with a job well done,
He fell asleep drunk,
Set the mattress on fire.

* * *

Once he had shat
In his new apartment,
He began to feel at home.

* * *

Having to cook for himself,
He goes back to dishes
Mother served him.

* * *

Another whole day wasted.
What is called for?
The Whip? Pills? or Patience?

* * *

Thoughts of his own death,
Like the distant roll
Of thunder at a picnic?

* * *

His thoughts pottered
From verses to sex to God
Without punctuation.
Alone on this hot
Saturday afternoon,
He can think of nothing
But lying in certain arms,
As scheduled for Tuesday
At 8. p.m.

* * *

Post coitum homo tristis.
What nonsense! If he could,
He would sing.

* * *

Mulberries dropping,
Twinges of lumbago
As he read *Clarendon*.

* * *

A September night.
Just the two of them, eating
Corn from their garden,
Plucked thirty minutes ago.
Outside: thunder, siling rain.

* * *

October mist.
St. Martin's gossamer.
In the bath-room a stray toad.

* * *

New York. A beautiful hot bath
At any hour,
With cockroaches in it.

* * *

The girl who admired his work
Was astonished to learn
He was not dead.

* * *

He woke in the small hours,
Dismayed by a wilderness
Of hostile thoughts.

* * *

Reflected in the bar-mirror
During their lunch-hour,
A row of faces,
Middle-aged, mute, expecting
No death of their own.

* * *

What was he to say
To the wretched youth? In flight
From a non-father,
An incoherent mother,
In pursuit of—what?

* * *

The class whose vices
He pilloried was his own,
Now extinct except
For lone survivors like him
Who remember its virtues.

THE HARVARD ADVOCATE

SPECIAL ISSUE: BLACK ODYSSEY; A Search for Home

The Undertaker

An old-fashioned lavatory represented on a bare stage by a wooden platform with four downstage steps and containing a large white glistening porcelain tub with heavy claws, a highly polished white toilet with brightly varnished blond wooden seat and lid, and a large marble sink. A pull chain hangs from the darkness overhead, and suspended above the sink and toilet are a marble shelf containing a large black shaving mug with brush and a large rectangle of opaque green glass, representing a window. There is a large Victorian pitcher on a small white table, and to the right of the toilet a white hatrack bearing a long-unused woman's negligee and enormous white garden hat. The pitcher contains several long-stemmed waxen lilies haphazardly arranged.

FATHER. *A small-two undertaker in his mid-forties. He wears a black suit with a flower in his lapel and a stickpin in his somber tie.*

EDWARD. *The undertaker's son, also in his mid-forties. He wears a contemporary light-colored business suit with a white handkerchief protruding from the breast pocket, and a lurid tie.*

Lights up dimly to reveal father seated bolt upright on the toilet lid and holding an old-fashioned silver revolver at right angles to his temple. His face is bright with perspiration and he stares directly and brilliantly at the audience. Suddenly, he is caught in a burst of light suggesting the phosphorescent explosion of a photographer's flash powder, and for a moment smiles. The stage goes dark immediately and from offstage in the darkness come the awkward sounds of a child practicing a cello. The sounds start and stop, a phrase or two is repeated, the music trails into silence. Lights up on the empty lavatory.

EDWARD:
(*Offstage*)
Papa, wait, Papa, please. . . .

FATHER:
(*Offstage*)
Stop it, Edward. Leave me alone.

EDWARD:
(*Offstage*)
Don't, Papa. Wait for me.

FATHER:
(*Offstage*)
Hands off, Edward. Do as I say.
(*sounds of scuffling*)

EDWARD:
(*Offstage*)
Papa, Papa, please. . . .
(*Father enters at a clumsy fast stride from stage right and clutching a small oblong cardboard box. He pauses midstage, wheels, rushes once around the lavatory, again pauses midstage, stares about him in distraction, backs away with as much dignity as possible as Edward enters from stage right at a helpless half-run.*)

EDWARD:
You threw me down!

FATHER:
Stop it, Edward. Keep away.

EDWARD:
You knocked me down, Papa. You pushed me.

FATHER:
Keep off, Edward. Keep your distance.

EDWARD:
How could you do it, Papa?

FATHER:
(*pausing, breathing heavily*)
Are you out of your mind? I've never laid a hand on you, Edward. Not once.

EDWARD:
What about Mama? What would she think?

FATHER:
(*startled, on guard again*)
Keep away from me, Edward. Hands off!

EDWARD:
I won't hurt you, Papa.

FATHER:
Stop it! Keep your hands to yourself.

EDWARD:
(*inching forward*)
It's your work, Papa. It makes you morbid.

FATHER:
Damn it, Edward, what do you know about my work?

EDWARD:
I've tried to please you, Papa. I've done my best.

John Hawkes

FATHER:

Wasted effort. Wasted effort. All of it. But I'll tell you something, Edward. I've been father and mother both to you. Remember that. I'm as good as your own mother was any day. Remember that.

EDWARD:

I love you, Papa. . . .

FATHER:

(*backing abruptly to stage left corner of lavatory*)
Stop it!

EDWARD:

Just let me hold your hand, Papa. Please. . . .

FATHER:

Don't take another step.
(*He breathes heavily, glances sternly about the stage, grows more calm and fondles the box absently.*)
Don't move.
(*He looks at the box then stares at Edward, takes a breath.*)
My work has nothing to do with it. Not a thing. For twenty years—twenty years, Edward—I've embalmed the corpses of penniless Negroes and financed their purchases of suitable caskets at reasonable rates out of my own pocket. And I enjoyed every minute of it, Edward.

EDWARD:

You can't frighten me, Papa, I'm not afraid of dead people.

FATHER:

I'm not trying to frighten you, damn it. Can't you be reasonable, just for once? There's nothing wrong with dead Negroes. Nothing at all.

EDWARD:

But Mama's dead too. That's wrong, isn't it?

FATHER:

You're impossible.

EDWARD:

I know she's dead. You told me yourself.

FATHER:

But I'm your mother now. I've been your mother for years. Remember that.

EDWARD:

I will, Papa. I will.

FATHER:

But you're afraid of the dead Negroes, aren't you, Edward? You're scared to death of them.
(*He chuckles, grows stern again.*)
Why don't you admit it for once in your life?

EDWARD:

You protect me . . . . you take good care of me. . . .

FATHER:

That's enough. . . !

EDWARD:

And I love you, Papa.

FATHER:

Stop. . . !

EDWARD:

I just want to sit on your lap, Papa, I want to feel your beard.

FATHER:

Damnation!
(*He wheels and rushes around the lavatory, appears stage right and backs slowly and suspiciously to a halt.*)
Damnation!
(*Edward faces his father and wrings his hands.*)
I'm going to carry out this business in my own house. Damned if I'm not. And if they rise up out of the cold ground like a mob of raving minstrels and try to stop me, I'll fight them off. Every last one of them. There's gratitude for you. . .

EDWARD:

Papa, Papa, don't forget me, please. . . . I want to be with you, Papa, I want to help. . . .

FATHER:

(*after a moment of shocked silence*)
You? You? I've had enough of you. I will not tolerate you any longer.
(*He raises the box to his ear and shakes it.*)

I will not tolerate this interference any longer.

EDWARD:

What's the matter, Papa? What have I done?

FATHER:

(*laughing, then pulling himself up abruptly*)
There you go again. Worry, worry, worry. Why must you worry all the time?
(*He pulls a handkerchief from his hip pocket and wipes his face.*)
There's nothing the matter. You've done nothing. You're innocent. You're just the innocent son of a middle-aged small-town undertaker.
(*He stuffs the handkerchief into his coat pocket.*)
But I've planted the seeds of death in you, Edward. At least I've done that much anyway.

EDWARD:

Have you, Papa?

FATHER:

Yes, I have, damn it. The seeds of death.

EDWARD:

Poor Papa, you're trembling. . . .

FATHER:

I'm as cool as springwater. I've got a mind of ice. So don't worry about me, Edward. Just look to your own troubles. Just give a little thought to all those dead Negroes coming after you in the night.

EDWARD:

Mama told me never to be afraid.

FATHER:

She did, did she?

EDWARD:

Yes, Papa, that's what she said.

FATHER:

(*pausing deliberately, holding the box to his ear*)
Edward, how old are you?

EDWARD:

I'm twelve years old, Papa. I was twelve last May. Don't you remember? Don't you remember my big layer cake with white frosting and pink flowers? You said it looked like a sarcophagus and sang happy birthday to me while I lit the candles, and. . . .

FATHER:

Then why the devil aren't you in school, Edward? Go to school, for God's sake, and leave me alone.

EDWARD:

It's summer, Papa. It's July.

FATHER:

Go to school anyway, for God's sake. What's the difference? The janitor will let you in. The best concentration is in an empty schoolhouse—any fool knows that. Don't let the summer vacation stop you, Edward. Go sit in that empty schoolhouse and improve your mind while the rest of the fools are off nagging their parents at little stagnant lake resorts around the nation. Go think about the Negroes and the seeds of death. . . . Go do something, Edward—anything—your father's tired now. He's busy.
(*He wipes his face.*)

EDWARD:

I want to whisper something in your ear.

FATHER:

No!

EDWARD:

(*inching forward*)
It's urgent, Papa. Just this once.

FATHER:

By God, Edward. . . .

EDWARD:

I'm desperate, Papa. Don't deny me.
(*He approaches his father as he would a shy horse.*)
Let me whisper in your ear. Just once. I'll die if you don't.

FATHER:

You're making it difficult for me, Edward. You're trying my patience.

EDWARD:

(*approaching closer*)
Just a few soft whispered words, Papa. Please. . . .

FATHER:

Be quick about it, Edward. There isn't much time.
(*Edward speaks awkwardly into his father's ear. Father sighs, puts his hand on Edward's shoulder, then turns downstage abruptly.*)
Now? Now? You want to go walking in the garden with your mother at a time like this? Impossible. . . !

EDWARD:

Now, Papa! Right this minute! For the sake of your son, Papa?

FATHER:

I might have known you'd think of some such nonsense, Edward. You're a persistent child.

EDWARD:

But you'll do it, won't you? Just for me?

FATHER:

The devil take it, Edward—be quick now.
(*From offstage come the labored sounds of the child practicing his cello as Edward embraces his father, turns, climbs the lavatory steps and returns with the woman's hat and negligee, which Father puts on. The cello continues to play while, hand in hand, the two walk up and down as in a garden.*)

EDWARD:

Shall I get the trowel?

FATHER:

Never mind the trowel. We won't need it now.

EDWARD:

You forgot your fan. Shall I get your fan? It's warm.

FATHER:

You're right, Edward. It is warm. It's always warm in July. But never mind the fan.
(*pausing, as if to study the leaves on a low branch*)
My fan wouldn't help the poor leaves, Edward. The leaves are thirsty.

EDWARD:

The worms are thirsty too, Mama. I'll attach the hose.

FATHER:

(*smiling*)

God will send water for the leaves and flowers and worms when the sun goes down, Edward. You'll see. (*They continue to walk.*)

EDWARD:

But don't you even want to prune the roses, Mama?

FATHER:

(*smiling, shaking his head*)
Go thou thy way, and I go mine;
  Apart, yet not afar,
Only a thin veil hangs between
  The pathways where we are. . . .

EDWARD:

(*stopping*)
Mama? I want to tell you my dream. May I tell it, Mama?

FATHER:

Yes, Edward. Tell me the dream.

EDWARD:

Well, it's always the same. I see you in the doorway of a big white house on a hill. There are clouds piled up behind the house and the morning sun is buried inside the clouds. There is no one else in that house, which is covered with white chimneys and shuttered windows. Well, you step down from under the portico, Mama, and raise a gentle hand to your hat. Then you lift your face and turn it left and right as if you're a royal lady trying to greet some prince or maybe an executioner with your lovely smile. Then you are moving, your skin and veins and hat and face all reflecting the peach and rose color of the sun. You descend one lichen-covered step and then another, sway and climb up beside the driver of a small open yellow auto with wooden wheels, white solid tires and brass headlamps. The auto is thumping up and down, Mama, but silently. Behind the single high seat is strapped a little white satin trunk—your trunk, Mama. And the driver, I see, wears a white driving cap and white driving coat, great eyeless goggles and a black muffler wrapped about his throat and hiding his mouth and nose and chin. With one gloved hand he grips a lever as tall and thin as a sword, and there is a sudden flashing when he contracts his arm. With his other hand he is squeezing the black bulb of the horn —though I hear nothing—and is sitting even straighter against the wind. And now he is gripping the steering wheel, holding it at arm's length, and now he turns his head and takes a single long look into your face, Mama, and I see that you are admiring him—or pitying him—and I quiver. And then, Mama, the tires are rolling, the trunk swaying, the muffler beating the air, and suddenly the white coat is brown with the dust of the road and the little auto, severe and shiny like a golden insect, is gaining speed, and I see that you are serene, Mama, serene and unshaken as the downward ride commences, and are merely touching your fingers to the crown of your hat and raising a soft white arm as if to wave to me, and . . . .

FATHER:

(*pulling away*)
Edward! Stop it, Edward!
(*He throws down the hat, struggles out of the negligee and drops it. Sounds of the cello fade.*)
Is this your idea of a joke? Are you trying to trick me, Edward, and desecrate the memory of your mother?

EDWARD:

No, Papa, no. . . .

FATHER:

Well, I'm not going to have it, do you understand?

EDWARD:

Let me finish, Papa. . .

FATHER:

Your mother never pitied me in her life!

EDWARD:

Please, Papa. . . .

FATHER:

And I'll tell you something, Edward. She died in bed, with blood all over the sheets. Blood. Do you hear?

EDWARD:

Don't, Papa, please. . . .

FATHER:

But I'll destroy this nonsense once and for all. Damned if I won't.
(*He runs to the lavatory steps and climbs them.*)

EDWARD:

You were driving the car, Papa, you took her away. And now you're trying to kill me too!

FATHER:

(*turning*)
I'm trying to kill myself, Edward. It has nothing to do with you. Nothing at all.
(*He smiles and raises the box to his ear.*)
(*Sounds of the cello commence as the lights grow dim, revealing merely the silhouette of Father, who sits on the toilet lid and removes the revolver from the box on his knees and holds it at right angles to his temple. The phosphorescent light flashes, as in the beginning, and for a moment the stage goes to full dark. Sounds of the cello cease abruptly. Lights up slowly on Father, who sits with the still unopened box on his knees, and who is now visible to the audience but not to Edward, and on Edward who is now crouching on the lavatory steps.*)

EDWARD:

You didn't mean it, Papa. Tell me you didn't.

FATHER:

(*startled, seizing the box in both hands, then recalling himself and speaking as through a closed door*)
I shall do it, Edward. See if I don't.

EDWARD:

But why? Why?

FATHER:

Some things, Edward, can't be helped.

(*He loosens his tie, opens his collar and coat, wipes his face with the handkerchief which he stuffs again into his coat pocket.*)

Are you there, Edward? I warn you, don't try to go for assistance.

(*He listens.*)

I'm as good as dead already. If you hadn't interfered, Edward, both of us would have been spared the pain of this little discussion. But you're a stubborn child. You know that, don't you?

EDWARD:

(*pausing*)

Yes, Papa.

FATHER:

Good. I'm glad we understand each other.

(*He slips up the lid of the box, peers inside.*)

Another thing, Edward. You weigh too much. A boy of—twelve—shouldn't weigh as much as you do.

EDWARD:

(*pausing*)

That's right, Papa. I'm big for my age.

FATHER:

(*removing the lid of the box entirely and squinting, holding the box to the light*)

You're fat, Edward. You've got too much stomach. You're too big in the arms and thighs. It's unhealthy.

EDWARD:

Yes, Papa.

FATHER:

In my twenty years as an undertaker, most of the Negroes I embalmed were either all fat or all bones. You must try to be somewhere in between, Edward.

(*Pause*)

Are you there?

(*He looks at the door.*)

Answer me, Edward.

EDWARD:

I'm here, Papa.

FATHER:

Good.

(*He again turns his attention to the box, on impulse takes a long sniff of it.*)

Most of my Negroes were preachers. You didn't know that, did you? Preachers or the relatives of preachers. Big fat black men of God or little black shriveled sacks with the calling still in their little protruding bones. The poor devils.

(*He listens suspiciously.*)

I was going to be a preacher myself, once. What do you think of that, Edward?

(*He leans forward, watches the door.*)

EDWARD:

(*pausing*)

That's very interesting, Papa.

FATHER:

I'm glad you think so.

(*He stares into the box.*)

Edward, I'll tell you something—the revolver is silver. You might as well know that much, anyway.

EDWARD:

Put it away, put it away. Papa.

FATHER:

(*smiling*)

I haven't taken it out of the box yet, Edward. Have patience, your father will blow his brains out in a moment. You can't stop me, Edward, even those damn raving minstrels—preachers, all of them—can't stop me.

EDWARD:

(*whispering*)

Papa, Papa, Papa. . . .

FATHER:

What did you say, Edward?

(*He listens.*)

It's not as brutal as you think, my boy. It's just like jumping off a tandem bicycle into a little silvery pool on a hot day in July. Nothing to it. And somebody's always left, Edward. That's what counts.

EDWARD:

(*pausing*)

Papa?

(*Father stands up abruptly, watches the door.*)

Come out of the lavatory. Please.

FATHER:

(*laughing briefly*)

You'd like that, wouldn't you. You'd like me to unlock the door and come out, towel and shaving mug in hand, and tell you the whole thing was a bad dream and that the old black fellow didn't have his claws around my heart after all, and that I'll always be here to embalm the Negroes and listen to your prayers at night. Isn't that so, Edward?

(*He scowls, then smiles.*)

Well, it won't do. You can't trick me, Edward. I've still got a head on my shoulders, thank God for that. The Negroes will have to find somebody else. So will you.

(*He places the box on the toilet lid, moves to the sink, picks up the shaving mug and brush, turns on the tap, then speaks over his shoulder.*)

It's no dream, Edward. It's merely the simple act of a cold mind. I'm going to jump off the tandem bicycle, that's all.

(*He raises the mug and brush and inspects them.*)

EDWARD:

(*listening to the running water*)

Papa? Are you shaving?

FATHER:

(*turning off the water, replacing the mug and brush*)

No, Edward. I have shaved already today, thank you.

EDWARD:

(*pausing*)

I want to smell the toilet water on your cheek, Papa.

FATHER:

(*smiling and seizing the lilies, pulling them from the pitcher and holding them up, inspecting them*)

You've tried that tack already, Edward. It won't do. But sit on my lap, hold my hand, feel my beard, smell the toilet water—you're so physical, Edward. It's the disappointment of my life. I hate to see you depending on such—rubbish. Because that's what it is, all these ear lobes and tender veins and wrinkles that appear in a waxen brow and toenails and cloth and a bit of filling in a tooth—just so much rubbish. After all, I've spent my own life disposing of the remains. I ought to know.

(*He tosses the lilies into the bathtub and smiles.*)

EDWARD:

(*pausing*)

Papa? Is the water warm enough?

FATHER:

(*startled*)

I've turned it off already. I'm not shaving now. I told you that.

(*He peers at the sink, reaches out his hand slowly and tightens the tap.*)

EDWARD:

But it's dripping, Papa.

FATHER:

Nonsense. The tap is not dripping.

(*He leans down slowly and listens.*)

EDWARD:

I hear it, Papa. Don't you? There's a little singing noise in the sink. It must be leaking, Papa.

FATHER:

(*kneeling, inspecting the pipe beneath the sink, then standing, brushing off his knees, seizing the box and facing the door*)

Your little ruses don't fool me, Edward. There's nothing in here but the sound of the breath in my own nose. It's like the sound of butter being spread on toast —one more disturbance, Edward, one more fly on the pile of rubbish. But there's no water in the tap and soon there will be no breath in my nose. We'll turn it off tight—won't we, Edward?—like the tap.

(*He gives the tap a final peremptory twist, again faces the door.*)

But why can't I embalm myself? Why? There might be a certain pleasure if I could embalm myself. To part your your own hair in the middle for the last time, to jerk the fancy tie into place around your own throat, to turn your own body into a rubber effigy and to take care of the eyelids with your own hands—at least there would be a certain satisfaction in disposing of your own rubbish, Edward, don't you agree?

(*He listens.*)

Well, what about it, Edward?

EDWARD:

(*pausing*)

You can't do all that to yourself. You can't.

FATHER:

That's right, Edward. It's impossible. A pathetic impossibility.

(*He sits on the lid of the toilet and partially removes the lid of the box, peers inside.*)

EDWARD:

But you could have been a preacher, Papa. I wish you had been a preacher.

FATHER:

(*smiling*)

Ah yes, I might well have been one of the raving minstrels. I might have been an excellent matchmaker between Christ and the old ladies. But I prefer my way, Edward. I prefer the rubbish reduced to rubbish.

(*He pauses, then raises the box and gives it several vigorous shakes.*)

Do you hear that, Edward? Revolver and bullets. Revolver and bullets, Edward. An old-fashioned toy for a man of strict principles.

(*He laughs.*)

EDWARD:

Let me see them, Papa. Let me have the box. . . .

FATHER:

(*wagging a finger at the door*)

No you don't, Edward. No you don't. The revolver and bullets are mine, my boy. You'll never see them. For the sake of discretion and selfishness, if you like, you'll never see them. You must accept impossibility also, Edward. You must grow as thin as I am and as clearheaded.

(*Slowly he removes the revolver from the box and dangles it before his face.*)

I begged your mother not to die. But there was no stopping your mother. She was a princess.

(*He studies the revolver.*)

And there's no stopping me, I can tell you that. You'll be lucky if you even catch a glimpse of my naked foot inside my black shoe, Edward. You'll never be an undertaker. I prefer that you see nothing when they carry me out of here.

EDWARD:

I won't move, I won't let you go. I'll crouch here forever if I have to, Papa. You'll see.

FATHER:

(*smiling*)

Distance is everywhere, Edward. This is the only way to make it real. And I'll tell you something, Edward —preachers blow their brains out too. Don't think they don't. The best preachers simply turn into undertakers and shoot themselves. Believe me.

(*He smiles.*)

But I've taken the revolver out of the box, Edward.

It's silver.

(*Slowly he shuts one eye, holds the revolver at arm's length and aims it at the door, then lowers it and in both hands, holding the box on his knees, inspects it closely.*)

It's going to make a loud noise. You better plug your ears.

EDWARD:

What's the matter? What's the matter with you, Papa?

FATHER:

(*raising the revolver over his head and again aiming it at the door*)

There's nothing the matter with me, of course. I've always been fond of you — despite your weight. I've always been as fond of you as I once was of a little black dog I discovered in a field of red clay near the Negro church. You know the church, Edward. It's where the chickens always block the road if you're out driving. At any rate, my little black dog approached me on its belly with its fat paws outspread and its grinning snout pushing along in the red clay and its tail thumping and its eyes turned up to mine—its belly was as flat and gray and wide as a distended bladder of some kind, Edward—and that miserable salivating animal seemed to know it was my destiny. A Negro dog, obviously, with my own fate in its belly and in its glistening eyes, because as soon as it reached my feet, with its heart pounding and its stump of a tail beating the damp bloody clay and its little teeth coming loose in its wormy gums, it rolled over. It rolled over, Edward, and dangled its fat a... / paws in the damp air and twisted its little black pear-shaped head so its eyes were fixed on mine and then, wriggling and trembling and groveling at my feet, Edward, it began to cry. I can tell you that that dog's voice was the only human voice I've ever heard—except yours, of course, and your mother's—and there was nothing to do but squat down then and there and rub my own white hand over that dog's flatulent gray belly, which felt more like the warm skin of a gigantic rat than the tender hide of a miserable dog. And do you know what I knew, Edward, squatting there in the dampness and rubbing my poor dog's belly and knotted ears and the slimy pouches in the joints of its legs? I knew that that dog had been born in a dead litter, Edward, and that I was fond of it. I was fond of your mother, Edward—she was a princess—and I have been as fond of you as I was of the dog. That's real devotion, Edward—never let anyone tell you different. That's real innocence, my boy, true purity, true love. But I was separated from that devoted dog even while I was infecting my hand with the touch of its urgent skin—that was part of the beauty of it, Edward—and I've always been separated from you in the same way. So there's nothing the matter with me, Edward. I'm

a man of cold principle and strong compassion. It's just that we've reached the moment when I must make our separation real. The Negroes were singing in the church when I met the dog. And now I am going to fire this gun for the sake of that dog. Do you understand? Do you?

(*He listens.*)

Are you there, Edward? Did you hear me? Speak to me, Edward.

(*He listens.*)

I'm warning you. I'll load the revolver if you don't.

(*He lowers the revolver and stares at it as if he hasn't seen it before.*

EDWARD:

(*pausing, raising his head*)

Don't worry, Papa. I'm going to help you.

FATHER:

What? What's that you say?

EDWARD:

(*rising softly to his feet*)

I'm going to save you, Papa

FATHER:

Nonsense. You haven't been listening to me. You haven't been paying attention.

EDWARD:

Wait, Papa, wait. I'm going to play my cello for you. I will play for you, poor Papa.

FATHER:

No, no, never mind. . . . It will do no good. . . . Do you hear me? No good. . . .

(*Edwards holds out his hand as if to speak, then thinks better of it, smiles, and turns and exits silently stage right. Father scowls, hurriedly wipes his face with the handkerchief.*)

Not the cello, Edward. Please.

(*He listens.*)

I forbid you, Edward. I do not want to hear that cello ever again. Do you understand?

(*He listens.*)

Are you there?

(*He rises silently and steps to the door, for a moment puts his ear to the door and then abruptly faces it.*)

Edward! Answer me!

(*He scowls and listens, unconsciously raises the revolver as if to ward off a blow.*)

This is no time to taunt me, Edward. I will not be an object of mockery.

(*He stares at the door, listens, seems to collapse, lets his arm fall to his side.*)

Edward? Edward?

(*He listens.*)

You won't answer.

(*He grimaces, licks his lips, dabs at his brow with the handkerchief.*)

All right then, I'm going to load the revolver. I'm

going to load the revolver this minute, Edward.

(*He listens, then slowly moves to the sink, stares into it, raises his head and removes the shaving brush from the mug and stands it upright on the shelf, then turns, leans back heavily against the sink and, dangling the revolver in full view, faces the door.*)

I should have done it sooner. I should have done it the day you were born. Then your mother could have held the three-weeks-old baby on her lap in the parlor —in the cool dark funeral parlor, my boy—and the Negroes could have come to pay condolences. They could have put that damn dog beside my body in the casket—that's where he belonged. But it's not too late, Edward. Do you hear?

(*He reaches out casually and places the revolver on the table.*)

It's not too late, my boy. The little shards of bone from your father's temple will be scattered around this lavatory floor like the bloody roots and broken crowns of extracted teeth. Or like bits of broken glass. Or like crushed shells washed up on the tide. Do you hear me, Edward? Scattered like little hard unrecognizable bright particles in the sawdust of an empty butcher's shop.

(*He listens.*)

You can crouch out there if you want to, Edward, and refuse to talk to your father on his dying day. You may deny me your voice if you want to, Edward. But I know what I'm talking about—the sound of this shot will kill everything. Everything. Your dream, your mother, my Negroes, my dog—everything. It will all be gone, Edward, all of it. No cheek, beard, toilet water, no signs of the undertaker. Everything will be gone—except you, of course. Nothing could kill you, Edward. Not even me. Do you hear? Do you comprehend what I'm saying at last?

(*Edward enters awkwardly, quickly, silently, from stage right, holding a bow and carrying an old cello in his arms. He reaches the lavatory steps and, as quietly as possible, stands the cello on the floor, positions it, raises the bow high and readies himself to play.*)

Edward? Is that you?

(*He snatches up the revolver and box, sits belligerently on the toilet lid and holds the box on his lap, aims the revolver unsteadily at the door.*)

You heard it all, Edward, didn't you. Heard it all and refused to talk to your poor father. Left me alone in silence to break the seal by myself. Well, we'll see, Edward. We'll see how you bear this silence in later years.

(*He listens.*)

Edward! Stop scratching at the door of my tomb and speak to me . . . !

(*Lights grow dim in the lavatory while a spotlight slowly fixes Edward in a soft glow.*)

EDWARD:

(*waving the bow above his head*)

Now, Papa. . . . Now I am going to play!

(*Father gasps, jumps, clutches his stomach, drops the box so that the bullets are scattered profusely and hopelessly about the lavatory floor. Still holding the revolver, he stares down at the bullets, slips to his knees on the floor, crouches, but is unable to move and merely turn his bewildered and angry face toward the door. Fervently but clumsily Edward plays a rhapsodic melody on his cello, while Father, after listening for a moment in anger and amazement, slowly climbs to his feet, grips the edge of the sink and suddenly, begins to declaim above the sound of the music.*)

FATHER:

Go thou thy way, and I go mine;
    Apart, yet not afar,
Only a thin veil hangs between
    The pathways where we are. . . .
I know not where thy road may lie,
    Or which way mine will be;
If mine will lead thro' parching sands,
    And thine beside the sea. . . .
I sigh, sometimes, to see thy face
    But since this may not be,
I'll leave thee. . . .

(*He breaks off his recitation.*)

Edward! Edward, stop it!

(*Edward ceases his playing, bow in midair, and Father takes a step from the sink.*)

I've dropped the bullets.

(*He kneels, begins to gather them up, reaching beneath the tub, etc.*)

It's your fault, Edward. I dropped them because of you.

(*Edward remains frozen, holding the cello upright and the bow still in midair. Father rises, holding a handful of bullets in his outstretched cupped palm.*)

EDWARD:

Papa, wait! I'm not finished. . . .

FATHER:

(*dropping the bullets into the tub*)

There you go again. Can't you keep quiet?

(*Slowly Edward lays down cello and bow and kneels on the first lavatory step. Father picks up a single bullet, holds high the revolver and inserts the bullet into the chamber. Then he steps to the door. Lights fade almost to dark on Father and Edward.*)

Edward! I have unlocked the door. There is no point in making someone break down the door to get me. . . .

(*Sounds of the cello are heard offstage. Father, dimly seen, turns and sits on the toilet lid, holds the revolver in his lap.*)

EDWARD:

(*in darkness*)

But may I come in then, Papa? Oh Papa. . . .

(*The stage goes to total darkness.*)

FATHER:

Goodby, Edward. . . .

(*A strong steady light infuses the lavatory, revealing Father with the revolver at right angles to his temple, then slowly fades. The sounds of the cello rise in the darkness, but they cease when a spotlight reveals Edward standing at stage right. He yawns, loosens his tie, pulls a handkerchief from his coat pocket and wipes his brow.*)

EDWARD:

A hot day in summer. A hot day in the middle of July. Hot as the devil. I wish there was a muffler tied around my neck and beating in the wind, old man. And a white driving cap on my head and driving goggles over my eyes, by God.

(*A warm light rises in the empty lavatory as he strolls to the steps and mounts them.*)

Give me a fine old yellow antique automobile and it wouldn't take me a minute to drive off the face of the earth like you, old man.

(*He removes his suitcoat, hangs it on the rack, removes his tie and rolls up his sleeves.*)

But you didn't get so very far after all, my poor old friend. And here I am, still turning on the tap that couldn't save your life . . . .

(*He turns it on.*)

still splashing this water on the skin of my face.

(*He splashes his face, with his fingers wipes the water from his eyes.*)

I've listened to you for thirty years. I still find bits of your angry ending in the linoleum or behind the tub—the Indianheads of my childhood, old man.

(*He picks up the shaving mug and brush, studies them, puts them down.*)

For thirty years I've wanted to shout with pleasure when July rolls around, wanted to shout and rub my own wet tongue and lips against your dog and your Negroes and your silent revolver. For thirty years I've laughed at the sight of you trapped like a black fish between this bathtub and that old white singing toilet. All this time you've lived inside me, with your mockery and jokes. . . . All this time you've been the rusty fishhook lodged inside my brain.

(*He seizes the shaving mug, fills it with water, faces stage right.*)

So come on, old man—I'm waiting.

(*He drinks.*)

Let's get it over with.

(*He listens intently, smiles, and in answer there comes, from offstage, the loud angry sound of a single shot, as the lights fade and sounds of the cello drift faintly across the stage.*)   *CURTAIN*

Abby Porter

Denise
Levertov

THE PULSE

in the dark, I knock my head
on steel petals
curving inward around me.

Somewhere the edict is given:
petals, relax.
Delicately they arch over backward.
All is opened to me —

the air they call *water,*
saline, dawngreen over its sands,
resplendent with fishes.
All day it is morning,

all night the glitter
of all that shines out of itself
crisps the vast swathes of the current.
But my feet are weighted:

only my seafern arms
my human hands
my fingers tipped with fire
sway out into the world.

Fair is the world.
I sing. The ache
up from heel to knee
of the weights

gives to the song its
ground bass.
And before the song
attains even a first refrain

the petals creek and
begin to rise.
They rise and recurl
to a bud's form

and clamp shut.
I wait in the dark.

Jonathan Kozol

THE CONTEST

TEN DAYS AFTER HIS THIRTEENTH BIRTHDAY:

An automobile turns out of the asphalt road, pursues two miles of granite and black hill to the tall walls that hem the sacred grove. His father (Aaron Schreiber, BS Harvard; Harvard MD) discovers the gate to Christ's Chapel, and enters in. As it happens, he has discovered the wrong entrance — not the Main Gate but the Service Gate. And yet: what matter the manner if one arrive in the right place?

The right place is the Headmaster's Study. David will follow his father into the office of Horton Rogers, Latin Master and Headmaster of the school. Aaron is known to Rogers in several ways. One: before David's grandmother could read or speak English, Aaron had been journeying each day from the black tenement into the subway tunnel, within the narrow channel to the last stop, there emerging to do commerce as he might amid the swift aristocrats of Harvard: while Rogers mildly progressed across the court for breakfast among his peers in the College Union. At least one world separated the precise Anglican from the driving insurgent of Judengasse and Judendorf, and yet (specifically) Rogers must accept this fact: they are *classmates*. Thus in insidious ways did Harvard College desecrate the tasteful preference of its scholars, disrupting (but not ovrthrowing) a frail Establishment. Once again, much later, Rogers had reason (which must be need) to traverse a personal path with David's father: Rogers' sister had a dangerous miscarriage. Inquiries were made into the matter of specialists and, with something between fascination and outrage, he discovered that the best man in the field was Dr. Schreiber. So Aaron took the case, handled it well, got the Headmaster's sister past her demon, and earned his reluctant (if not the less fullhearted) admiration.

In later years, when he married and had children, and an obstetrician was demanded

---

in the small hours, Rogers addressed himself as a matter of course to Aaron, became in some qualified sense fond of the man, and finally made the generous mistake of suggesting that he send his son to be groomed at Christ's Chapel.

The difference between David's home in Padan Aram and the Episcopal Gothic halls of Christ's Chapel Meadows was not less great than the sixweek steerage journey that separated the Warsaw ghetto of Hagar's youth from the house in Louisburg Square where Horton Rogers' mother had preened and primped for the December Cotillion of 1880. It took more than one man or one generation to bridge that gap; but two men and two generations could do it. Hagar had made it from Warsaw to Boston Light; Aaron had made it from Boston to Harvard Yard; in more than the journeyman's sense David would be expected to make it to the top of Beacon Hill.

And as he thought back to that morning in the Headmaster's Study, and pictured his father (expendable intermediary) fulfilling the one role sociology alloted, David could not prevent a distressing whimsy from painting the following scene: his father on his knees in the mud beneath the window of an English abbey; a boy of thirteen or fourteen putting one foot on his father's back, then both feet in order to lift himself up to the window-level. Inside the window: a darkpanelled room, a graceful man in a rustcolored jacket and dark trousers, standing before a bookcase. The man turns as David's face appears in the window. He smiles and beckons David to come in. As David climbs down into the room, dusting off his jacket and new trousers, the man sets his pipe in a pewter ashtray and comes forward. He speaks with handsome curiosity: comely restraint. "How'd you manage it, young fellow?"

With proper shyness, David points out the window: "My father — he's down there in the mud; I climbed in on his back."

The man in the rustcolored jacket breaks into appreciative laughter: "Good show, young fellow! Good show!"

"Is it all right for him to stay out there?" David says. "Will anyone mind?"

The schoolmaster chuckles a bit, then says in a generous manner: "No, no, let him stay. Nobody will see him." After a moment's pause, he adds: "Of course you won't be using that entrance any longer; from now on you can come in the regular way."

"Oh thank you sir," says David.

Then, thinking again of the clever fellow's ingenuity, the master comes forward and pats David twice on the shoulder. He repeats, in a genial and approving manner: "Darn good show, David Schreiber! We can use you, David Schreiber!"

Borden Rogers was the Headmaster's son; he was not blond-haired and blue-eyed but he carried off his brown hair and brown eyes more successfully than David Schreiber did. Peter Stanton's father was also a master at Christ's Chapel. Barker and Barnett were children of Harvard deans. Henry Cutter's father was a professor at the Medical School. Bucky Clapp's father was headmaster of a girl's school called Miss Brattle's Country Day. All in all, David could see that the boys in his class at Christ's Chapel belonged to a closely wrought unity of blood, money, and values, although (even at that age) he could see that the latter two were already on the wane; and the first and vital element would be prey within a decade's time to the impure adulteration of such alien fluid as his own.

About one thing there was no debate in David's heart: moral qualms did not enter the field. He felt himself a wholly free agent within the reasonable bounds of Christ Chapel Meadows. His father had made the mistake or generous sacrifice of placing him in a world of rarified air where he himself was unable to survive; his penalty would be that of all self-effacing parents: David's inward (later, outward) self would acclimate its basic characteristics to function on a new and different level. And if he should never come back, in any genuine sense, to the world his mother and father still inhabited, it would not be wholly a matter of choice with him, not just the snobbish volition of a thankless child but rather perhaps a process of natural law:

the working-out of an easy postulate: that the son could no longer breathe the old kind of air, any more than his father would be able to breathe the new.

Crandall Brooks goes around the class. He is stern, one-browed, glass-jawed; his eyes are the clear blue heirlooms of a handsome Aryan line.

"Barker?"

"Here, sir: High Church."

"Barnett?"

"Here, sir: High Church."

"Clapp?"

"Yes, sir: High Church."

"Cutter?"

"Sir, Presbyterian!"

Loud guffaws and cheekpops; Fat Jellicoe, sitting behind Cutter, kicks mercilessly at his deskchair: bam! bam! bam! while sundry soprano boyvoices cry out: "He's a nigger! Cutter's black! Poor Cutter! Cutter's blackassed!"

Crandall Brooks blinks his blue heirlooms, slowly sensing (albeit in an unselfreproaching fashion) that he might have made a mistake. But Cutter's holding up all right. A good fellow. Lots of pluck. On with the game. If you're in the club you've got to obey the rules. If you don't like the rules, you didn't have to join.

"Duncan?"

"Endicott?"

"Frost?"

"High Church."

"Sir: High Church!"

"Sir: Lutheran."

"Grantley?"

"Harkness?"

"Henley?"

"Hodges?"

"High Church!"

"High Church!"

"High Church!"

"High Church!"

The four voices come from the same back row. Crandell smiles at something as he jots down his figures on the back of an envelope.

"Ireland?"

"Jaspers?"

"Jellicoe?"

Fat Jellicoe prepares for the big joke; he looks around at Barker and Stanton and nods; they poke each other in the ribs and catch Bucky Clapp's attention; the class pokes and jabs; the signal ripples about the room.

Timmy Ireland answers his name: "Sir: I'm a Lutheran."

Skeleton-tall Jaspers answers his name: "Sir: Anglican!"

The class titters with laughter; everyone is ready for the joke.

Fat Jellicoe sits forward in his chair. He cocks his pink face innocently up at the master: "Sir: I'm a little Jewish boy."

The class explodes into anticipated laughter, even though the reason for it does not seem so great now as before; it was not such a good joke after all.

Crandall Brooks is not completely stupid He realizes at last the error he has made; he is ready to concede his carelessness. Next year, he will not make the same mistake. How then to get through the game without causing any more unneeded pity upon a brow in the second row. Cleverness serves the crisis. The master knows what to do.

"Johnson?"

"High Church!"

"Lawrence?"

"High Church!"

"Lowell?"

"Sir: High Church!"

"Morley?"

"Newbegin?"

"Parker?"

"Strethers?"

"Truslow?"

Lobotomy of the mind: a term recurrent in David's thoughts. The cold steel blade of the knife. . . .

The night at Black Quarry grew chill with the imminence of autumn's first dawn. In uneven sleep before the morning David sweated rapidly a sick chill sweat. His elbows were pressed to his sides, his hands drawn up beneath his chest. He dreamed a rapacious series of meaningless ordeals: the chewing, biting, sucking of a hard rubbery substance: the passage in blanched moonglare over an etherous terrain: the formulation of phrases, their rearrangement. . . .

The stench in the room was an old thing: the reek of many muscular young men exuding perspiration as the afternoon died its winter death. He could see the room clearly: the large rubberized mat, the stuffed weights and pulleys against the far wall, the exercising tables on the side, the benches for the parents and the teams, the woodn stools for the referee and timer; beyond it all, the frosted windows, the darkness of the encroaching night, and the distant stone tower of Christ's Chapel Hall.

But now there was no time for thought. It was too late for that. David was on the verge of being pinned. If he lost this round, he lost the match; if he lost the match, he lost all. He sensed the peculiar importance of the match — something greater than anyone else in the room could have guessed. The boys on the bench and the visitors

began to cheer for David:
Give him a Ra!
Ra! Ra! Ra!
Give him a Ra!
Ra! Ra! Ra!
Give him a Ra!

It was good to know that they were with him. But it would not help much so long as his man held him in that Nelson. All at once, the blind fellow switched his body position and altered his hold: he reached down between David's legs to get him in a Full-Body-Press. The hand that caught him between the legs was frenetic and rapacious; it clutched at his groin. It was only at that moment that David realized his mistake: he no longer had on his supporter! He tried to think where he could have lost it; it must have fallen off while he was limbering up. But then he noticed an odd coincidence: his opponent was not wearing one either. Perhaps the Hebrew coach, seeing the plight of the Christ's Chapel boy, decided it would only be fair sport to even the scales, and ordered his own man to go naked onto the mat. (That would be good show, David thought.)

At about the same moment, the girls on the bench noticed the same thing: *that the two wrestlers were naked!* They had nothing on their bodies! no wrestling-tights, no jerseys, no supporters! David did not like the feeling of the blind man's body crawling and stretching all over his own with that greasy oil-slick. Now at least he knew what the smell had been: it was Oil of Pomegranite. The Hebrew wrestlers always rubbed it over their bodies. Christ's Chapel used Wintergreen ointment, which was traditional in the league.

When he realized that his man was ready to burst his testicles within his fist, David became doubly frightened. Moreover, something about the finger-action on his penis had caused a considerable erection. It was impossible to conceal, even though the man was lying on top of it. David shuddered to imagine the girls in the audience. He could just bet this was the last match Bucky's father would let the Brattle girls attend! At that moment, while their two bodies were almost entirely contiguous on the mat, David heard his opponent making strange spluttering sounds through his nose; then he realized the poor fellow was trying to talk:

"Shhh! Pssssssst! Da-da-da. . . ."

He felt awfully sorry for the fellow. It was surely a pitiful business. But what was his horror when he opened his eyes at last! (How long had he kept them closed? Had anyone seen?) What was his horror when he looked at last upon that apelike face and saw those bulging eyeballs rolling in enormous sockets beneath the receding forehead. There was an anthropoid face if he ever saw one! And where else had he seen it — but . . .

He shuddered with recognition! He trembled and felt an enormous desire to be sick. That face! That face! That hateful face! That detestable semitic face! Those yellowed teeth! That unmistakable nose! That dark and sallow skin! Where could there be two like that in the world? He felt a sudden pressing and squeezing at his testicles, as though to get his attention. Then these words finally spluttered forth, very jerkily, and directly into his ear (along with a great deal of saliva):

"They wouldn't let me in unless I did it. I'm sorry, son, if I've embarrassed you; I don't want to retard your career; but I had to see you, and they only let blind men on the team. So I did it. I did it with a fire-poker. But, don't worry! I can still see. See!" (He blinked one whiteclouded eye feverishly.) "They don't know it but I have a cataract — I can still see through that. I can see you beautifully and you look good to me. It's a fine sight for an old father's eyes to know his boy is still in there pitching."

David felt an irresistible wave of repulsion surge through him. Scrutinizing the hideous face in front of him, he wanted to vomit. "But — you're so ugly!" he said. And then he asked: "Do you realize how you have humiliated me? what this means in terms of years wasted, progress retarded?"

"I'm sorry, son." And tears of a thick whitish substance oozed from the corners of the old man's eyes. "You are the dearest thing there is to me in the world, and I only wanted to have a little look at you. Just to see your face: your fine clean face. You are incorruptible, my son. Incorruptible. You are clean inside and out: a gentleman through and through. I'm proud of you, my boy. I don't even need your love as a reward. Hate me if you wish. Any emotion will do as well: just to know you are thinking of me."

David looked into his father's oozing cataract: "This is the worst moment of my life. I have always hated you, but never so much as at this instant."

"That's all right, boy. That's all right!" (squeezing at the testicles.) "Is there anything I can do to make it up to you? Just name it and I'll do it."

Fury burned in David's eyes. "Yes," he said at last, "you can let me loose so I won't be beaten. That's what you can do, if you're father at all."

He was trying to decide the year. It must have been his last winter. He was wrestling one-thirty-two; he was limbering up his muscles. He was doing exercises. One! and two and one! and two. The coach (a little stunted man: Ben Baker, the Bio Master) came up to him and asked how the ankle felt. "The ankle is good, sir." "She's okay, is she?" "Yes, sir." The coach scrutinized him carefully, then patted him on the back: "Good stuff, Schreiber! Good stuff! You're a good man!" "Thank you, sir." "Schreiber, I want you to suck a lemon: when the acid gets on your tongue it turns to sugar: $H_2O + CO_2$ yields H_2CO_3." "Yes, sir! Thank you, sir!" "Good going, boy!" David sucked at the lemon-rind and began hopping from foot to foot. One! and two and one! and two. He had not noticed the large audience before; all the parents were coming for the match; all the girls from Miss Brattle's Country Day; some girls came all the way from Virginia. Everyone came. David limbered up: he loosened his muscles: he sucked his lemon. The Headmaster came across the mat: "How are we going to do, boy?" "We're going to win, sir." Horton smiled proudly: "Good show, Schreiber. You're a good man." Then, putting his arm over David's shoulder, he whispered, "You know, just between you and me Schreiber, I've never regretted letting you in."

David sat on the bench in his black tights. He watched the Hebrew boys practising on the other side of the mat. The School for the Hebrew Blind produced the best wrestlers in the League — something about not being able to see improved muscle-tone: tensile strength and visceral acuity correlated: he didn't entirely understand it. Ben Baker had explained it once.

David bit his lower lip as he tried to determine which of the blind wrestlers was his man. They all looked awfully big. He didn't see a single one that could have made one-thirty-two. They always went easy on the weights of the blind; it didn't seem fair to David. A game was a game. If you joined the team you had to obey the rules. If you didn't like the rules you didn't have to join. Like putting out your hand first so the blind man could find you. Was that sort of thing really necessary?

Suddenly the referee got up in the middl of the mat, holding his stool. He announced the next match but he did not give th names. David was bothered by this. Whe you are in the running, you want all you names down on the board. Otherwise yo don't know where you are. But then Davi realized they were waiting for *him;* the were calling out *his* name. His presenc was desired at the center of the mat.

The whistle was blown three times. Th referee ran to the side of the mat and sa on his little stool. David moved forwar stealthily, his head and shoulders lov knees bent, weight forward. He move carefully, swinging his arms cleverly, turr ing his head from side to side. He imagine the muscularity of his calves.

As the fellow approached him, Davi noticed that his arms and shoulders wer thickly knotted with muscles; there was dark growth of hair upon his chest; his hea was heavy and stumplike at the end of short solid neck. He began dangling hi arms in David's direction. David reache out one hand and offered it to the blin man; he felt a desperate fist clutch hi wrist.

The first informal give and take wa over. Now they were in it for good. Th strong hand of his opponent clamped ir exorably on the back of David's neck. On of his own hands pressed on the back of th blind man's neck. Their shoulders an heads remained low as they sprang an lunged with a bouncing rhythm back an forth across the mat. The point at this stag was to conserve your strength. "Conserv your strength, Schreiber," the coach woul say, the same way he siad, "Suck a lemor Schreiber," or "Keep you eyes on your ma Schreiber." But David could not keep hi eyes on his man; his head was being presse down. The hand of the blind man was to strong to resist. David wondered why hi opponent would not let him see his face as if he were ashamed of something, as he were embarrassed of being blind.

Then David began to notice somethin extremely unpleasant. The Hebrew ma was sweating profusely; and his swea exuded the foulest odor that David ha ever smelled. "Why don't they ever wash? he wondered. And the more he though about it the more furious he became. seemd unbelievable that any man coul smell so foul; even in the crowded swea bathed wrestling-room the odor of David opponent stood out unmistakably from a the other smells. The girls from Miss Brattle's School drew scented handkerchiefs up to their noses. And their eyes spoke words of unimaginable distress. Their boyfriends on the team caught the silent message and glared back at them with brave offers in the set of their jaws.

At that moment his opponent made a wild lunge for David's knees, wrapped his arms about them, and threw him over. The next thing David knew, he was being strangled and pressed down upon the mat by a Three-Quarter-Nelson. He struggled to keep his shoulders from meeting the mat. Meanwhile a startling thought occurred to him, something for which he suffered untold regrets: he had wrestled this man before! He knew it as certainly as he knew he was about to be pinned. That smell, those heavy shoulders, that hairy chest, the dark hue of the skin — all these things struck home with David: they were all somehow familiar to his inmost memory. He was certain that he had wrestled with this man before, and not just once, but many times. There had been a whole history of matches. Where was it? And when?

Sam Homans

The Harvard Advocate

"Am I a father or aren't I?" said his opponent. "Just watch this!" And suddenly the old man wrenched his arm out from between David's thighs, and seemed to have injured his wrist. He examined it for a moment, and in that split second David was up and on him. He wasted no time. To the redoubled cheers of his team-mates and their girls, David grabbed the blind man's weak arm and twisted it behind his back, pulling it out on the other side of his shoulder. Then he dug his knees into the trapped man's stomach, and locked his legs down on the mat by manipulating the arches and insteps of his own feet. Now he had him where he wanted him. He smiled hideously and triumphantly; this was one chance of revenge in a million: he would be a fool to pass it by! Gouging his victim's intestines with his bony knee, David leaned forward over the face whose every detail he so unflinchingly despised. He knew what had to be done. First giving a sharp crack to the wounded arm to make sure the ligaments were split, David splayed out his own two longest fingers (on his left hand; he was the only lefty in his family) and gloated over the nasty sties that the poor fellow thought to pass off for eyeballs.

"What are you going to do, my boy?" said the old man in a gentle loving voice that quivered with only the slightest crackle of fear.

"I am going to dig out the last streams of light in your eyes," David said. "That's what I'm going to do."

"Oh please, son! Please don't do that. Then I shan't be able to see you even a bit. And all my life's work shall have been in vain. I shan't even have the blessed joy of seeing you triumph over all the world."

"That's the whole idea, old man. Take a good look if you want. It's the last look you'll ever have."

"It's a beautiful face, son. A fine courageous countenance. Handsome through and through. You will do great things, boy. I will not be here to see them, but you will do great things."

"You'll be here," said David. "You just won't see them." And he laughed malignantly. He splayed out his two nail-sharp fingers, and tested their length. Catching the spirit of the thing, the bench and the visitors began to cheer!

Pluck out his eyes!
Ra Ra Ra!
Pluck out his eyes!
Ra Ra Ra!

Meanwhile the other bench, realizing their man needed support, began to chant a Hebrew cheer:

Yisgaddal, Yisgaddash!

Yisborach, V'yishtabbach!
V'yispoar, V'yisromam!
V'yisnasseh, V'yishaddor!
V'yishalleh, V'yishallol!
O-men! O-men! O-men!

"Prayers won't help you now, poor fellow," thought David with a wince of pity. (Supposing he were down there and somebody were about to pluck out his eyes?) But he quickly banished such reservations from his mind. There was no time for pity now. That should have been thought of long ago. He could have kicked himself for forgetting, but now it was too late. *I am about my father's work,* he thought. If anyone asked about it, that is what he would say: *his father's work!* (He laughed at the very thought of it!) Now the cheering reached a deafening peak; the voices of all the Brattle girls were with him:

Dimitri Hadzi

Ra Ra Ra!
Pluck out his eyes!
Ra Ra Ra!

He heard the coach saying, "Keep your eyes on your man, Schreiber! Muscle tone correlated with visceral acuity. Go to it, Schreiber!" He waited no longer but bore down now upon his object: his nails pierced the first glassy level of the cornea, digging into the gelatinous area where the pigments and optic nerves were twisted about. As he scraped at the bottoms of the eyeballs, he could feel, specifically, the pupils, the irises, the tear-ducts, the tear-glands. The cataract itself was neither more nor less than an obnoxious white creamlike substance with brown tinges as when curd begins to oxidize. He scraped it all up in the ends of his nails. Meanwhile the Hebrew boys kept cheering their man:

Yisgaddal! Yisgaddash!
O-men! O-men!

They certainly do have pluck, thought David. He could tell that the audience thought so too. As when in the ballpark a fellow misses a catch but leaps several feet in the air in the effort, wrenching his knee, a murmur of assent and approval begins to rise in the stands — so now the visitors' and home-benches alike began to ripple with the natural sympathy and pity which are aroused in all human hearts at the sight of human pain. Soon the entire room was bursting with applause and rocking to the chant that came from all sides of the mat:

Good for the Jew!
He's not dead!
Good for the Jew!
He's not dead!

David found himself forgotten in the surge of applause for the beaten man. He heard Horton Rogers saying to one of the masters: "I'm sure I've seen that man before. I wonder if he's the fellow who begs in the Boston Gardens during the Ice Capades?" David was jealous of the beaten man. He felt it was a hollow victory. But wasn't it always like that? Hadn't he always been cheated? And, in that instant, a tremendous fury began to surge in David's heart. He knew what he would have to do. All at once, amidst startled cries from both sides of the mat, David began to vomit unrelentingly upon the bleeding face of his victim; the vomit dripped and spewed also on his own chest and stomach and testicles. He vomited convulsively for several seconds; then, when the solid substance was exhausted, he continued an erratic and uncontrollable retching for several minutes more. The voices of the people in the room became less and less important: they ceased to qualify. And, as they lost significance, they also lost volume: they became dimmer and dimmer, more and more blurred. Waves of nauseous fatigue heaved David to and fro on the mat. He felt hot and cold chills burning and numbing his skin; his shoulders and back seemed very cold. He tried to pull the cover up over his waist, but it would not come; something was holding it back: a weight of some sort. It was caught. He trembled frantically and began to shiver. His forehead was hot with fever; his eyes felt heavy. He was afraid he would vomit again but he had not had anything more to eat. All he could do was retch. He felt the tearing start in again on his stomach. Suddenly, in infantile panic, he sat up in bed and gasped for breath. He did not begin to retch a second time but instead felt hot tears moving over his cheeks, and his chest was heaving with sobs.

Robert Bly   DEATH

1.
Faces appear and vanish.
The eyes real, staring at us out of portholes
(like owls out of holes in oaks)

2.
We go sailing on the black road toward death,
Slipping over the ice!
The dark days end, clumps of darkness
                hanging in the trees,
And we notice nothing!

3.
The hours after supper, precious hours, hours full of sweetness,
When our bones
Give off fragrance . . .

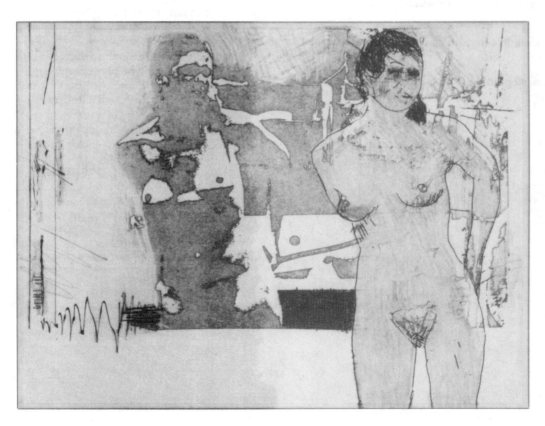

Peik Larsen

Donald Hall

THE WIT AND WISDOM OF
DONALD HALL

1.
A man who touches a cabbage is seldom sorry.

2.
The feeling is mutual.

3.
The same goat has three blind eyes.

4.
Cecilia! You are wearing an American flag!

5.
Witches ride when brooms go empty.

6.
It is better to bend a strawberry.

7.
Never tie a left-handed horse to a wet rubberplant.

8.
You are stepping on my garterbelt.

Richard Eberhart

LOOKING HEAD ON

I sit looking at my features.
They are hard as rock, they are, in fact,
Fired in clay by Winslow Eaves.
I look at the features.

No man has seen his own face,
Except by mirror or photography.
We, who live so much within, look out
From ourselves, through the fires,

But cannot see ourselves as others see us.
I look out. I have been looking in
Through decades of the world's history.
How dramatic to look at your own face

Hard as rock, fired in clay, as the sculptor
Sees it. Which, then, is reality?
Is it the flesh that pulses, fails?
Is it the rock-like likeness, clay-lasting?

Bold is the opposition,
Hard to define in a day.
We leap in virility, but
There is the slower finality of clay.

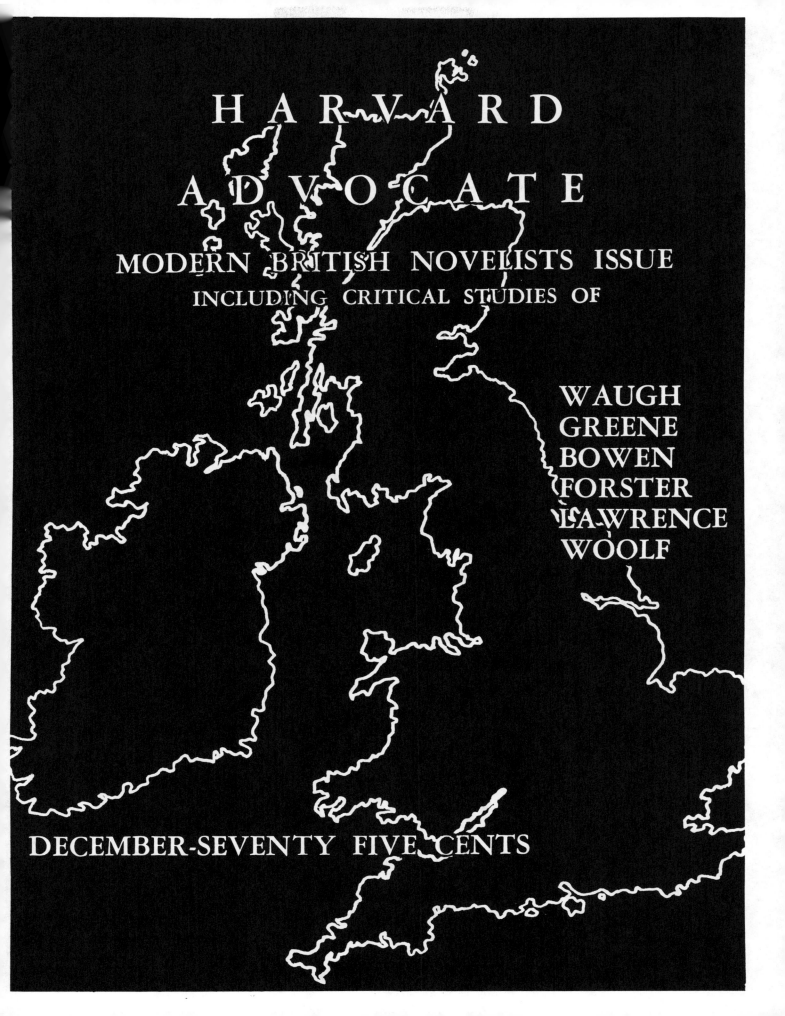

Early Poems by SYLVIA PLATH

DANSE MACABRE

Down among strict roots and rocks,
    eclipsed beneath blind lid of land
goes the grass-embroidered box.

Arranged in sheets of ice, the fond
    skeleton still craves to have
fever from the world behind.

Hands reach back to relics of
    nippled moons, extinct and cold,
frozen in designs of love.

At twelve, each skull in aureoled
    with recollection's ticking thorns
winding up the raveled mold.

Needles nag like unicorns,
    assault a sleeping virgin's shroud
till her stubborn body burns.

Lured by brigands in the blood,
    shanks of bone now resurrect,
inveigled to forsake the sod.

Eloping from their slabs, abstract
    couples court by milk of moon:
sheer silver blurs their phantom act.

Luminous, the town of stone
    anticipates the warning sound
of cockcrow crying up the dawn.

With kiss of cinders, ghosts descend,
    compelled to deadlock underground.

These poems first appeared in The Smith Review *from 1953 to 1955, and are made available through the courtesy of Mrs. Marcia Bradley and the Smith College Archives.*

ADMONITION

If you dissect a bird
    To diagram the tongue,
You'll cut the chord
    Articulating song.

If you flay a beast
    To marvel at the mane,
You'll wreck the rest
    From which the fur began.

If you assault a fish
    To analyze the fin,
Your hands will crush
    The generating bone.

If you pluck out the heart
    To find what makes it move,
You'll halt the clock
    That syncopates our love.

CIRCUS IN THREE RINGS

In the circus tent of a hurricane
    designed by a drunken god
my extravagant heart blows up again
    in a rampage of champagne-colored rain,
        and the fragments whir like a weather vane
while the angels all applaud.

Daring as death and debonair
    I invade my lion's den;
a rose of jeopardy flames in my hair
    yet I flourish my whip with a fatal flair,
        defending my perilous wounds with a chair
while the gnawings of love begin.

Mocking as Mephistopheles,
    eclipsed by magician's disguise,
my demon of doom tilts on a trapeze,
    winged rabbits revolving about his knees,
        only to vanish with devilish ease
in a smoke that sears my eyes.

MAD GIRL'S LOVE SONG

I shut my eyes and all the world drops dead;
I lift my lids and all is born again.
(I think I made you up inside my head.)

The stars go waltzing out in blue and red,
And arbitrary blackness gallops in:
I shut my eyes and all the world drops dead.

I dreamed that you bewitched me into bed
And sung me moonstruck, kissed me quite insane.
(I think I made you up inside my head.)

God topples from the sky, hell's fires fade;
Exit seraphim and Satan's men:
I shut my eyes and all the world drops dead.

I fancied you'd return the way you said,
But I grow old and I forget your name.
(I think I made you up inside my head.)

I should have loved a thunder-bird instead;
At least when spring comes they roar back again.
I shut my eyes and all the world drops dead.
(I think I made you up inside my head.)

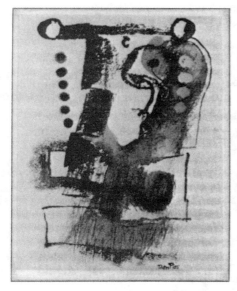

DAN PLAS

DIALOGUE EN ROUTE

"If only something exciting would happen!"
Said Eve the elevator-girl ace
To Adam the arrogant matador
As they shot past the forty-ninth floor
In a rocketing vertical clockcase
Fast as a fallible falcon.

"I wish millionaire uncles and aunts
Would umbrella like liberal toadstools
In a deluge of nickels and dimes,
Filet mignon and walloping wines:
A flock of philanthropical fools
To indulge my extravagant wants!"

Erect in his folderol cloak
Sham Adam the matador cried:
"Oh for G-man to die of the choler
And for my every chimerical dollar
To breed innumerable bills bona fide:
A hot hyperbolical joke!"
Sighed Eve: "I wish venomous nematodes
Were bewitched to assiduous lovers
Each one an inverterate gallant
With Valentino's crack technical talent
For recreation down under the covers:
Erotic and elegant episodes!"

Added Adam that simian swell
With his modish opposable thumb:
"Oh, for ubiquitous free aphrodisiacs
And for pumpkins to purr into Cadillacs
And Voluptuous Venus to come
Waltzing up to me out of her cockleshell!"

"If only something exciting would happen!"
Yawned Eve the elevator-girl ace
To Adam the Arrogant matador
As they shot past the ninety-fourth floor
To corral the conundrum of space,
That cryptic celestial phenomenon.

They both watched the barometer sink
As the world swiveled round in its orbit
And thousands were born and dropped dead.
When from the enormous, inane overhead
Came, too quick for the pair to absorb it,
A Gargantuan galactical wink.

353

John Berryman

THREE NEW DREAM SONGS

HENRY'S UNDER-STANDING

He was reading late, at Richard's, down in Maine,
aged 32? Richard & Helen long in bed,
my good wife long in bed.
All I had to do was strip & get into my bed,
putting the marker in the book, & sleep,
& wake to a hot breakfast.

Off the coast was an island, P'tit Manaan,
the bluff from Richard's lawn was almost sheer.
A chill at four o'clock.
It only takes a few minutes to make a man.
A concentration upon now & here.
Suddenly, unlike Bach,

& horribly, unlike Bach, it occurred to me
that *one* night, instead of warm pajamas,
I'd take off all my clothes
& cross the damp cold lawn & down the bluff
into the terrible water & walk forever
under it out toward the island.

Henry's nocturnal habits were the terror of his women.
First it appears he snored, lying on his back.
Then he thrashed & tossed,
changing position like a task fleet. Then, inhuman,
he woke every hour or so — they couldn't keep track
of mobile Henry, lost

at 3 a.m., off for more drugs or a cigarette,
reading old mail, writing new letters, scribbling
excessive Songs;
back then to bed, to the old tune or get set
for a stercoraceous cough, without quibbling
death-like. His women's wrongs

they hoarded & forgave, mysterious, sweet;
but you'll admit it was no way to live
or even keep alive.
I won't mention the dreams I won't repeat
sweating & shaking: something's gotta give:
up for good at five.

HENRY BY NIGHT

☞

Bizarre Apollo, half what Henry dreamed,
half real, wandered back on stage from the other wing
with its incredible circuitry.
All went well. The moon? What the moon seemed
to Henry in his basement: shadows gathering
around an archaic sea

with craters grand on the television screen,
as dead as Delphi treeless, tourist gone
& the god decidedly gone.
Selene slid by the Far-Shooter, mean
of plagues & arrows, whom the doom clampt on,
both embarrassed in the Christian dawn.

(That roar you hear as the rocket lifts is money, hurt.)

Which dawn has ended, and it is full day.
And the mountain of Mao flesh, did it once respond
'Let all moons bloom'? O no,
these events are for kids & selenographers, say,
a deep breath, creating no permanent bond
between the passive watchers & moonglow.

APOLLO 8

☞

THANKSGIVING

JAMES ATLAS

"O body swayed to music, O brightening glance,
How can we know the dancer from the dance?"

W. B. Yeats

1

I stand in the lobby of Grant Central Station,
clutching a Harvard bookbag and *The Collected*
Yeats. This cavernous waiting room, the arching dome:
I long to drift through some Byzantine cathedral,
lingering by pale mosaics or gliding on
a tapestry.

       Here the close benches beneath the
balcony kneel like pews. Through wide glass doors across
the marble floor, trains idle on the dripping tracks;
I decide on a seat between a nun reading
Valley of the Dolls and a rabbi, gingerly
hiding my bookbag under a trenchcoat. O Rome!
pensioners pray in Nedicks, we rise like a choir
from our worship of the *Times*. My train is late.

2

Uptown. Lovers breathe promises in vestibules.
I come out of a movie on West 76th
Street, looking like Joyce in my overcoat. Pale light
from Buddha lamps in a pawnshop window settles
in the hollows of my eyes. The wind billows my
sleeves out like long balloons, snow is disappearing
in the darkness.

       Suddenly I want to be told
that the subways rushing beneath these streets would be
unknown to Pius, or to gleaners in the Pyrenees.

3

In my room at the Earle Hotel, I wake to a
rattle of milk-trucks edging cautiously through the
alley. Dawn, and below my window West Eighth Street
recedes into the distances of Manhattan.

Dreams vanish like stars above Long Island Sound. If
only I yearned for less than this, to disappear
in the wash of Sunday morning's brilliance, floating
out to sea in the dawn's sad tide, lost in shallows

somewhere beyond the Brooklyn Bridge. Brightening sky!
the sun settles like dust on these etiolated
walls. Hearing voices murmur across the hall, or
the woman who walks her goat in Washington Square

bleating for home: I tell you, there is nothing else!
Wagner on Sunday, branches pointing like wands toward
the clouds, and the heavy stillness of this hour:
I am Daedelus, this hotel my swaying tower.

I.A. Richards

Alaskan Meander

Flying this low, below that river bed
There shows another, another under that . . .
Palimpsest meanderings outspread.

Horizon-wide, the piedmont falls so flat
The streams can wander — freely, we might say,
Cut where they will, spill over, twine and plait,

Explore, essay, renegue, revert or play
What ox-bow game they please; lick at a bank,
Silt up a channel; anyway, have their way.

Not so at all. We've something else to thank!
All streams in sight in parallel have told
A common story: it was the West that sank

Tilting all beds together; each stream rolled
The way it had to. East and West in turn
Sway—see-saw—up and down. All flow's controlled.

The whole world wiggles; wriggle we must and learn
How the earthwave within us bulges by,
Troughs us and hoists, whichever way we yearn.

Not harsh or crabbed, as dull schools imply,
But queer beyond all that we may discern,
Beyond our like or loathing, grin or sigh,

How daunting is divine autonomy.

Past Perfect

In the deep woods we have walked so sure;
In their thick snows we have slept secure,
Travelling light.
Night after night
By our camp fires we have lain so sure.

Through the steep seas we have steered so sure;
By their white teeth we have swept secure,
Near but clear.
Year by year
On their cresting waves we have swayed so sure.

On the high cliffs we have moved so sure;
On their tilting slabs we have stepped secure
By the piton's ring,
Sling by sling,
Within their verge we have crept so sure.

Across the void have we swung so sure,
On a spun thread we have leapt secure
Jocund and sublime.
On our thread of time
Over the abyss we have hung so sure.

NON-FICTION
Whitt Collins

I started working in the mines in 19 and 11. I was 12 years old, barefoot as a yard dog. Me and my older brother Harrison rode the coal together. Then I went to trapping. That's when they had mules going back and forth hauling the cars through and I'd open and shut the trap door so the air would keep going all around. We got but a dollar a day then working for 10 or 12 hours. You see, my Dad was blind for twenty years and my maw had to work to take care of us. That's why I went to work. I kept my maw until she died and then I got married. By the time I was 18 I was getting two dollars and ten cents a day driving a mule. Me and my wife and kids were living in a tent.

I've worked in the mines all my life. Sometimes jobs were hard to find. They'd lay off, you understand, and the only thing I had to do was to pack my suitcase and hunt another job somewhere else. I always did manage to feed my family — yea — I always did manage somehow. Never did starve. Oh, I might get in debt sometimes, you know, but then I'd get a job and pay it back. I could always get anything I wanted, anywhere, because I was always honest and paid my debts. My word, money or no money, was enough.

I've done everything in the mine. I've run a motor, run a machine, run a joy. I've laid track, set timber, built braddishes, hung wire — that's trolley wire for the motors to run on, to get juice to them. I've worked on the tippel. Yea, and I was mine boss too. It started from a dollar and kept raising until now. Now it's thirty a day for eight hours. Most I ever made was $18 a shift.

It's the dangerousest thing I know of — to work in a mine. I can look back through my life and I can't imagine or study just how I'm living. I escaped death so many times. I saw so many killed. And I hauled so many out in cars. I've hauled as high as two out in one car that's been killed by slate fall. Their heads was as big as a waterbucket where the slate had mashed them. Terrible to look at. Why it made you to dread to go in the mines when when you saw all this, you understand. It made you have a dread on your mind. I was just lucky that I come through. Just lucky that I come through. I've seen time after time in a mine when I thought that would be all of me.

What's always been the trouble of mine safety is that the operators never give the men time to make it safe. They always want another car of coal. Back when there's mules in the mines. you know what they'd tell us drivers? "Now bring the harness or bring the coal. If we kill a mule we'll buy another and if we kills a man we'll hire a new one. I want the coal." So they didn't care nothin about man or beast nor nothin else, only another car of coal. That's how people get killed in the mines. It's the company rushing them and not giving them time to make theirselves safe. I've come up through it. I know.

I was working in one mine when a colored fellow got killed and the mine boss brought him outside and kept him in the supply house until the next morning. He wouldn't tell the men because he knew they'd quit work. That was the ruling — a man gets killed in the mines and the men generally lay off for a day. That day shift comes out and the night shift won't go in. So that mine boss just brought that dead man out and hid him until the following day.

Naturally I didn't mind it to work in a mine. That's what I took up and that's what I wanted to do. Loading coal is the hardest but that's what I always liked to do the best. But they always grabbed me off that and put me on the motor. I was a good motor man. There wasn't nothin I couldn't do. I quit a million jobs but I was never fired off one.

NOTES TOWARDS A RADICAL LITERATURE
in the form of a simple lesson to
be read aloud

James Atlas

Bourgeois society broke up human relationships into atoms, and gave them unprecedented flexibility and mobility. Primitive unity of consciousness which was the foundation of a monumental religious art disappeared, and with it went primitive economic relationships. As a result of the Reformation, religion became individualistic. The religious symbols of art having had their cord cut from the heavens, fell on their heads and sought support in the uncertain mysticism of individual consciousness.
— Leon Trotsky, *Literature and Revolution*

1.

What has happened to us in our time? Literature has survived through the act of becoming a witness to its own decline. What we are experiencing is not a period of decadence or ennui that presages resurgence, not a transition between antithetical modes; rather, it is the experience of surprise we should be astonished at the existence of literature, at its presence in our lives.

2.

The tradition of European literature until the beginning of this century emerges from a rigid dialectic of events; there is a logic of recurrence to its history. Notions about the Elizabethan cosmos mirrored the social structure of England in order to justify the chosen forms of metaphysical poetry. Shakespeare, suspended between the nascent energy of a mercantile economy and the subtle atrophy of feudalism, had drawn on these two complex sources and accumulated an entire world from the surplus of their contradictions. Literary form was rooted in the circumstances of economic life. The universe materialized as a truth. Whatever social class provoked revolt, it was that class which provided the literature to accomplish and define revolt. So that what followed from Milton's Puritan heresies, from Bunyan's natural piety, was no less than an enormous metamorphosis: radical belief took on other properties, anchored in reality. Prosperity, not salvation, could be gained through works. Where art had signified both product and collective enterprise to the medieval artisan, the rise of capitalism in England during the 17th century required the banishment of those pursuits that failed to promulgate its ends. Trotsky writes: "Man placed himself in the center of the universe, and therefore in the center of art also." Literature became an illustration of the individual's conflicts with history. This is essentially where we find ourselves now.

3.

The order characteristic of English neo-classicism gave way to an apocalyptic Romanticism in a moment of revolution. Schiller learned that "Just as nature began gradually to disappear from human life as *experience* and as the (active and perceiving) *subject,* so we see her arise in the world of poetry as *idea* and *object.*" A radical dialectic appears in the form of a struggle between opposing literary styles; with Wordsworth, nature is objectified. The virtues of transcendence are no longer imbued with a religious motive, but with an ethical one. The English Romantics, like the later Victorians, shared in the nervous reaction against industrialism, but their aesthetics are inseparable from this larger transformation. Nature mediates between the tensions of experience and idea. "Romanticism becomes simply one of the forms of Naturalism," according to Brandes, when it embraces the 'realistic element' of life, the object. The words of Wilhelm Dilthey are useful here: "When we have grasper the sum of all the achievements of understanding the objectification of life, in contrast to the subjectivity of experience, opens up within it." Coleridge, borrowing the term from Kant, referred to understanding in this way. Later we will look at the objectification of material conditions in light of Marxist theory.

4.

Like the sun, Wordsworth stood at a fixed point in his universe, instilled with the properties of motion; events circled him like planets, observable yet remote from his own sphere. Cardinal Newman, author of the *Apologia Pro Vita Sua,* shared half a century with Wordsworth, and resembled the poet in choosing a vantage at some distance from this world; what excited him were the shadowy arguments between Anglicanism and Catholicism during a period of English history when the outward struggles of the Church were being determined by other crises: Evangelicalism, a secular Utilitarianism, even a dangerous alliance between morality and science. More and more, in view of the turmoil that relentlessly disrupted England throughout the 19th century, Newman strikes us as a brooding, mystic figure, as irate as Hildebrand had been, as fervent as Peter Damian. Still, orthodox belief, while submitting to an arduous process of demystification, echoed conflicts that could not have been classified as belonging to its realm. The vestiges of this nostalgic prayer betrayed themselves in defense of individual consciousness.

5.

The contradiction between what Engels and Lenin believed literature to represent has yet to be reconciled. For Lenin, the purpose of writing was didactic ("Literature must become Party literature"), while Engels insisted that its only obligation was to reveal economic conflicts and their eventual resolution within the text. He appreciated Balzac more than Zola. Criticism in Communist countries since the Revolution has largely abided by Lenin's demands; Georg Lukács, the leading figure in this program, has wavered in his ideology during those times when it verged on becoming archaic or exclusive. The German Marxist critics associated with the Frankfurt School have remained closer to Engels in this respect. As a result, essayists like Walter Benjamin and T. W. Adorno have written out of a reverence for literature, occasionally condoned its bourgeois style, and so have been able to produce the most exciting work. The problem at hand is how to learn from a given literary style the conditions that gave rise to it. Henri Lefebvre has pointed out that "Human relations seem to be nothing more than relations between things." The structure of the novel reflects this change in the Naturalistic intentions of Zola, "to reconstruct the societies in their real life." The object occupies the stage.

6.

Kafka once remarked that "Capitalism is a condition both of the world and of the soul." If this is true, then any attack must be launched on two fronts. To begin with, what Marx spoke of as reification has come to pass on a grand scale; the abstract relations of production have become realities: "A commodity is therefore a mysterious thing, simply because in it the social character of men's labour appears to them as an objective character stamped upon the product of that labor." Just so, the novel *objectifies* conditions; the protagonist is usually observed in relation to the things of this world. Much of contemporary literature is obsessed with the sorrows of alienation, disturbed by our estrangement from what used to be the truth about our lives: essentially, that we deserved them. Have we become objects as well?

7.

There has been a great deal of talk about a "language revolution"; whatever this revolution may have been to Kafka, to the Prague Circle, or to the Geneva School, it is we, the writers of the present generation, who represent its legacy. Options are no longer open to us, for this reason: the literary traditions usually belonged to the most radical or reactionary classes of a given period; literature became a possession of the vanguard or the polemical right. But, as George Steiner has been among the first to recognize, linguistic theory, "Like most true revolutions, has behind it a distinctive failure of nerve.' What has happened, then? The implications of this crises were warded off, and now have been forgotten.

8.

The great American writers of the 19th century suffered from the irony of being compelled to live out the destiny that belonged to them, and then finding themselves alone. Theirs was not a shared dream, even though they claimed it as their own historical legacy. And because literature is not really *useful,* they struggled to become theologians of the spirit. That tradition has receded infinitely from our grasp, leaving the writers of our time with a dream, and nothing more. Literature has been appropriated by the bourgeoisie, the single class in America divested of possibility. As such, the literature it produces has no radical intentions. Its uses must be transferred to where they will do the most good. As it is now, writers are no more than articulate victims. This is why poetry has become so spare, the novel so laconic. Literature is not *active,* as it was before.

9.

Ponge, the French poet, writes about soap, about clocks, about fish; he instructs us in the proximity of the object to our consciousness, reducing the distance between ourselves and things. In this way, alienation is overcome, the object is celebrated as what it is: an object. Modern American poets, lost in Baudelaire's forest of symbols, transpose their alienation onto the landscape; barns become mountains, the snow becomes a crowd of small heads. Surrealism is the culmination of lyric poetry, in that it calls for an identification with the innate. The pathology of German Romanticism, with all its longing for an ideal world, assumes a new form in poets like Mark Strand, Donald Justice, and Robert Bly. The weather comes alive and batters them, the seasons leap forward like a team of horses. Metaphors are mistaken for associations, the revelation of resemblances. Nature reverts to its pre-Romantic definition: as expressed by Schiller in Lesson 3, it is both *experience* and "the (active and perceiving) *subject.*" The object is subverted, the world appears as a phenomenon, rather than as a system of relations. This confuses us no end.

10.

Richard Gilman has argued that "Art is a new action for which life has no precedents."

We must find precedents for our actions, for our work.

We must locate preconditions, rooted in what we know of history.

Because there are no precedents for what we are doing, we must invent them. Unfortunately, this is impossible.

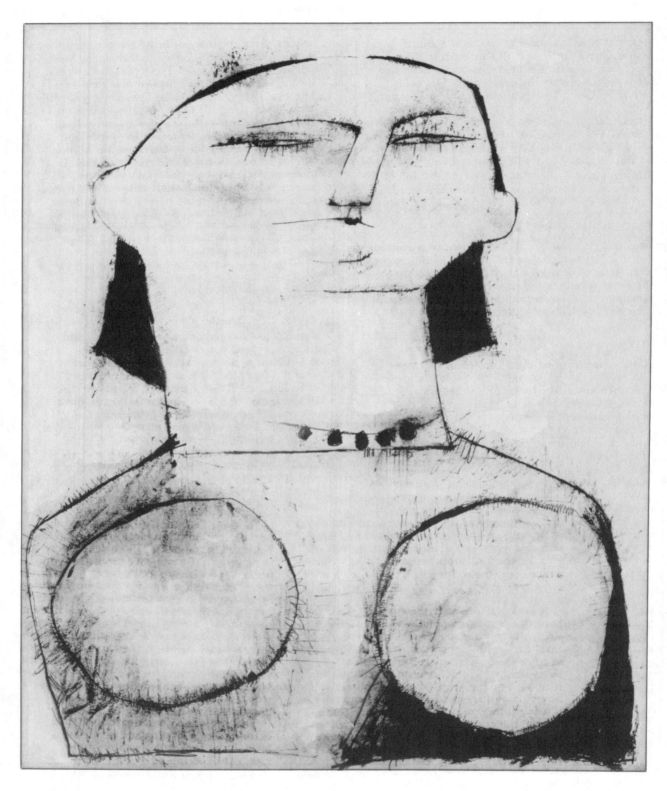

Chesley McClaren

LOUIS REED

© 1971 Louis Reed

Sweet Jane

Standing on the corner
suitcase in my hand
Jack is in his corset
Jane is in her vest
and me I'm in a rock 'n' roll band

riding in a Stutz Bear Cat, Jim
you know those were different times
all the poets studied rules of verse
and those ladies rolled their eyes

Sweet Jane
oh Sweet Jane
oh whoa, Sweet Jane

I'll tell you something
Jack he is a banker
and Jane she is a clerk
and both of them save their monies
and when they come home from work
ooohhh sittin' down by the fire
the radio does play
the classical music there, Jim
the *March of the Wooden Soldiers*
all you protest kids
you can hear Jack say

Sweet Jane
oh Sweet Jane
oh whoa, Sweet Jane

Some people they like to go out dancing
and other peoples they have to work
just watch me now
and there are even some evil mothers
they're going to tell you that everything is just dirt
you know that women never really faint
and that villains always blink their eyes
and that you know children are the only ones who blush
and that life is just to die
but anyone who had a heart
they wouldn't turn around and break it
and anyone who played a part
they wouldn't turn around and hate it

heavenly wine and roses
seemed to whisper to him
when she smiled

heavenly wine and roses
seemed to whisper to her
when he smiled

Sweet Jane
oh whoa, Sweet Jane
Sweet Jane Sweet Jane Sweet Jane
Sweet Jane Sweet Jane Sweet Jane

Pain

"I adore," she said, wicked as a whipperwill.
"Me too," me, rolling her over to approach her other side.
"I only enjoy it if it causes pain," I said. "It's nothing sexual."
"I never would have guessed," she said as it tightened,
loving the fright and fear of it, the it of it.
"I adore pain," she said in gulps biting her own hand,
and then they were off, two spacelike butterflies
split down the middle, reflecting the city in twos
the fact that he adored it too,
the fact that they both hated women.

Toshi Katayama

THE BAD GOOD WRITER
AND THE GOOD BAD WRITER

James Park Sloan

THE BAD GOOD WRITER

Rabbit Redux (re dux: the definition from Webster's reproduced for your convenience on the inside flap), Updike's latest, is also the latest of a triad including *Mr. Sammler's Planet* by Saul Bellow and *The Tenants* by Bernard Malamud. Each attempts to explain our times for our times. Each is a sort of manual of, by and for us WASP cum Jewish squares, coming to terms on our behalf with moon landings, drug culture and Negro genitals. Estimable subjects, all.

Updike, Bellow and Malamud: each is a certified "good writer." What do we mean by that? To keep one's membership in this fraternity, one must first of all avoid journalism. If facts appear in one's books, they must be disguised, renamed or tangential. Mailer transgressed this rule early on in his career, with the effect that he need no longer be pantingly evaluated in *The New York Review of Books*. Capote came perilously close, after all the dust had settled, with *In Cold Blood*.

There is more, however, to qualification as a "good writer" than mere renunciation of journalism. The "bad writer" may also avoid the gross reportage of facts, yet avoid it in the wrong way. Leon Uris, for instance, who researches international crises, then changes names, motives and meanings. Rule One for card-carrying literary artists: changing Charles de Gaulle to Pierre la Croix is not enough. One must do more than change the names.

A novel by a "good writer" must "really be written." Facts must be not so much avoided as teased, encircled, obscured, distorted and, occasionally, trampled by words. Stradlater, the prep-school jock in *The Catcher in the Rye*, articulated this second rule, perhaps a little bluntly, when he told Holden it didn't matter what his essay was about as long as it was "descriptive as hell."

Great writing and bad writing often have in common a great wholeness of idea — political, metaphysical or existential. Thus both Dostoyevsky and Irving Wallace have coherent and sweeping positions on politics. "Good writers" never take massive positions; it is the sort of thing that can get a man laughed out of his expository writing section, or off the front page of the *New York Times Book Review*. Instead of ideas, the good writer has *ambience*.

John Updike is the current American high priest of ambience. At one point (the stage of *Augie March* and *Seize the Day*) Saul Bellow seemed to have the inside track. Since *Herzog*, however, Bellow has been almost too good to remain a mere good writer.

Joyce Carol Oates has launched a vigorous challenge to Updike over the past five years. Her *Esquire* story of the catatonic little girl eating uncooked spaghetti is second to none in the ambience race. Yet as a whole, her work still trails off dangerously — on the one hand toward the macabre, the Gothic; on the other hand toward whimsy. Ambience must never degenerate into whimsy.

Ambience is made of sensory observations which all add up to something less than an idea. A character whose monologue reveals ambience seems always on the brink — the brink of remembering, or learning, or figuring out. A pure work of ambience gives itself away from the title on (*Rabbit Redux;* L. Woiwode's *What I'm Going to Do, I Think).* The character must never tip over this brink. Moon shots provide great opportunity for such brinksmanship as do drug freaks, Negroes and fat wives, but one is required to look at each of these phenomena from the posture of a muddled and wistful aesthete.

Since he began writing about intellectuals, who are capable of having ideas, Bellow has constantly overshot ambience. A man like Sammler, who knew H.G. Wells and is capable of reading a technical treatise about the moon, is too clear-headed for his internal monologue to constitute much of a mood piece.

Rabbit Redux is a supreme work of ambience. There is not an idea in it of more than .22 caliber. The hero is not a wistful aesthete, but a middle-American linotypist. All the better: Updike is free to lead toward the Nirvana of muddled, wistful aestheticism through a protagonist in whom the absence of any idea is not unnatural.

Who reads this kind of writing, and why? The people who read Updike are people who like to believe they are thinking when their minds are not producing any concrete output. In this respect, they are the aesthetic equivalent of the Marxist sloganeer. They are horrified by the suggestion that human cerebration is an algorithm, like a computer. Chomsky the linguist turns them off; Chomsky the humanitarian turns them on. They are people who believe that taking long drives in the country while the leaves are turning is a sign of great sensitivity.

The insinuation that "there is more here than meets the eye" gives justification to the housewife/reader as she turns from removal of brassiere to removal of brassiere. Updike's novels are anti-intellectual pastiches written to make anti-intellectual readers feel more cerebral.

The language of *Rabbit Redux* is metaphoric. It is the sort of poetry which results when a man in a bar begins to wax eloquent about the rays of light splashing in through the window. In other words, it demeans both the descriptive power of poetry and the poor goddamn photons.

Rabbit Redux is particularly crammed with a drunk's poetry of the human body. The description, for instance, of Rabbit drying his wife after a bath: "The backs of her thighs, the stray black hairs, the moss moist between. 'OK,' she says, and steps off. He stands to pat dry the down beneath the sweep of her upheld hair: Nature is full of nests." (p. 33) Or the description of his wife in bed: "Her waist where no bones are nips like a bird dipping." (p. 27)

At one point Rabbit watches a white girl perform fellatio with a black man. By switching on a light in mid-scene, he is able to describe skin coloration with a rhapsodic intensity which would do credit to a beery sophomore describing the pennants on the wall at Cronin's.

Ambience is something that *is,* or *happens,* or *has happened.* It is totally passive, and has nothing to do with people doing things. In fact, people doing things are likely to break the mood — and thus are to be avoided. The heroes of Updike novels are prone to masturbation and vulnerable to castration; nor are they on much of a quest to understand themselves. For the most part, they just want to be sure they don't miss out on the way it looks, feels, tastes, sounds and smells.

We cannot fairly call Updike a bad writer. Bad writers are writers who are at a loss when they don't have something specific to say. Updike (as John Aldridge has already noted) has produced an entire oeuvre with nothing to say. This capacity for pure verbiage has often been a mark of the great and near-great in our time. Updike, however, does not belong in the company of Celine, Beckett and Joyce. He belongs in an equally select company, who are published in the *New Yorker,* reviewed in the Sunday *Times* and honored by our scattershot domestic literary awards: the bad good writer.

The bad good writer is essentially a non-novelist, a person who writes imitations of the form and is clever enough to sell them as the genuine article.

The great novelist has a shattering effect on human perspective. The passage of time, the focus of telescope or microscope and the extension or enclosure of space are the tools by which the major novelist calls a universe into being. In this respect, greatness in fiction is not too different from greatness in scientific inquiry. Levi-Strauss is great because he presents man at such an enormous remove; Freud because he presents man at hyper-proximity. The visions coming from these two scientists are no more different than Joycean man from the man of Robbe-Grillet.

The bad good novelist does little to human perspective. *Rabbit Redux* is made up of footage shot from eyeball level. Ambience, or the enjoyment of the light playing through the beer glass, requires a consistent level. To study man as though he were an insect or a cosmos would almost certainly spoil the mood.

H.G. Wells used the moon to extend man's scope a quarter of a million miles. Updike in *Rabbit Redux* uses the same object to keep man anchored in Brewer, Pennsylvania.

Greatness also requires an act of faith. The great novelist is like the true religious believer. Either he narrates from fervid certainty or he refuses to narrate at all. Either God *is,* to be spoken for, or He *is not,* to be spoken against.

Rabbit Redux is to the novel as the sermons of Bishop Sheen are to God. Updike, in short, does not really believe in the novel. Or, at best, his belief in it is minimal, functional and mercenary. Novels sell better than poetry, just like Catholicism sells better than advising people to be squares for no reason at all. The Updike novel is a painted harlot: an essentially ugly woman (so he thinks of it) who tries to improve matters with lots of makeup and promiscuous behavior. No man who finds a woman beautiful wants to dress her like a whore. No writer who believes in the form of the novel will burden it with all that poetry.

THE GOOD BAD WRITER

If the bad good writer is obsessed by ambience — by the light refracted through the beer glass — then he has a perfect anti-self on the other side of the profession: the writer who is contemptuous of words and moods and gratuitous description. Everything described in an Updike novel is sublimely purposeless; nothing is described in a true "pop" novel unless the description is purposeful. It sets the scene. It sells you the trip you can't afford: Copenhagen, Italy, Israel, New York, Detroit. The men in an Updike novel are props for the smoke, the light and the beer glass. In a pop novel, the beer glass — or, more commonly, the martini — is a prop for the men. It is as if Updike and Leon Uris each possessed one dimension of Dostoyevsky.

Some bad writers, however, are not so easily categorized. Let us look back over the snobbery of sophistication and age to first encounters. Can others, like myself, remember the shattering revelation of their first reading of *The Fountainhead*? I have a confession to make, I read it three times.

What is one to make of a writer like Ayn Rand? When one is over the first flirtation with individualism/objectivism (Did she really use all that jargon?), it can easily become one of those adolescent episodes one would rather forget. Ayn Rand is an easy person to make fun of: *She thought she was writing against the tyranny of Russian collectivism, when actually her appeal was against the tyranny of the American high school.*

How bad can Ayn Rand be? *The Fountainhead* has been in continuous print for twenty-nine years. Generation after generation it is read by the same adolescent constituency, not the class president/jock, but the nonconformist, the embryo intellectual. I sometimes wonder how many of us there are, provincials, who read *The Fountainhead*, told off our middle class parents and ended up voting for Eugene McCarthy and writing novels ourselves.

Just as the surface of an Updike novel bears nothing but literary virtues, the surface of an Ayn Rand novel bears nothing but literary vices. The *New York Times Book Review*, which does a knee jerk of sympathy at the first description of sunlight in a smoky haze, does a knee jerk of antipathy at the first paragraph (they are all alike) of what the author has dubbed "romantic realism." Ayn Rand is not a stylist. She does not intersperse four-letter-words with paragraphs made of participial phrases. The waists of her heroines do not "nip like birds dipping."

She is, admittedly, illiberal. In American literary circles, illiberals are weighed on a special scale. She lacks the clarity, the depth and the ideological wholeness of a Nietzsche, a Dostoyevsky — even a Chesterton. Why not, we hear, read Nietzsche and have the genuine article, illiberalism in a setting of philosophical rigor. Yet no one suggests chucking Updike in favor of Bentham and Mill. Although Bentham and Mill saw the world from the same fundamental perspective of vague good will, we still have a motive for reading Updike: the smell of leaves, the light through the beer glass.

The claims against Ayn Rand are legion. Unlike the great novelists, she has done nothing to expand the form of the novel. She doesn't even bother to sprinkle her prose with poetry. To her mind, the form of the novel is purely a vehicle — a vehicle in which she places conviction, but a vehicle. Its sole function is to output ideas for young minds (even she can no longer believe she is read by grownups), ideas presented not with alliteration, metaphor and rhyme, but with the literal sound of dynamite.

A great novelist, a Camus or Mauriac or Dostoyevsky, is allowed some measure for what he teaches. A bad novelist like Ayn Rand, we are carefully taught, cannot be credited for didacticism even when she is manifestly on target. In American literary circles, the bad novelist is shunted off into a limbo where his works need not even be reviewed with put-downs; this limbo the bad novelist shares with yesterday's heroes, like James T. Farrell (he is still alive and publishes a book every year or two), and today's forlorn esoterica, such as John Hawkes (he, too, is alive).

Does this dismissal stand? In practical terms, it does. Just as Richard Daley reigns as mayor regardless of how many votes he stole in the last election, so do the editors of the *Times Book Review* and novelists like John Updike preside over American letters. Literary history is unlikely to decide that a total unknown was the true literary force of midcentury America. It is a nice dream for undiscovered masters like John Hawkes, but such literary rediscovery is about as likely as political historians deciding that the Reverend Jesse Jackson was the real power of midcentury Chicago. An audience, whatever one says, is essential to art. The exceptions spring most quickly to mind — Kafka, Van Gogh — but the simple fact is that most great artists have had a solid constituency throughout most of their careers.

Perhaps that is why it is so pleasing that good bad writers like Ayn Rand exist. She is living proof that the genuine eccentric, the alien, can occasionally make it. By virtue of her enduring constituency, she is impossible to dismiss. We all grow up, and most of us grow out of our participation in Ayn Rand Circles. But quite a few of us, I suspect, are quirkier liberals and richer, stronger human beings for having read her. Wasn't that the criterion of F.R. Leavis — that a good book should be life-giving? If so, let us be thankful for some of our bad novelists.

OCTAVIO PAZ

translations by Elizabeth Bishop with the author

La llave de agua

Adelante de Rishikesh
el Granges es todavía verde.
El horizonte de vidrio
se rompe entre los picos.
Caminamos sobre cristales.
Arriba y abajo
grandes golfos de calma.
En los espacios azules
rocas blancas, nubes negras.
Dijiste:
   Le pays est plein de scources.
Esa noche mojé mis manos en tus pechos.

The key of water

After Rishikesh
the Ganges is still green.
The glass horizon
breaks among the peaks.
We walk upon crystals.
Above and below
great gulfs of calm.
In the blue spaces
white rocks, black clouds.
You said:
   Le pays est plein de sources.
That night I layed my hands in your breasts.

Por la calle de Galeana

Golpean martillos allá arriba
   voces pulverizadas
Desde la punta de la tarde bajan.
   verticalmente los albañiles

Estamos entre azul y buenas noches
   aquí comienzan los baldíos
Un charco anémico de pronto llamea
   la sombra del colibrí lo incendia

Al llegar a las primeras casas
   el verano se oxida
Alguien ha cerrado la puerta alguien
   habla con su sombra

Pardea ya no hay nadie en la calle
   ni siquiera este perro
asustado de andar solo por ella
   Da miedo cerrar los ojos

Mexico, a 18 de junio de 1971

Along Galeana Street

Hammers pound there above
   pulverized voices
From the top of the afternoon
   the builders come straight down

We're between blue and good evening
   here begin vacant lots
A pale puddle suddenly blazes
   the shade of the hummingbird ignites it

Reaching the first houses
   the summer oxidizes
Someone has closed the door someone
   speaks with his shadow

It darkens   There's no one in the street now
   not even this dog
scared to walk through it alone
   One's afraid to close one's eyes

Mexico, 18 June 1971

An Article of Faith

by Father James H. Flye

In 1905, on the Cumberland plateau in Middle Tennessee, two miles from Sewanee, some members of the Order of the Holy Cross, a monastic order of the Episcopal Church, started a little mission center, and for some young boys who were put under their care and a few others from the neighborhood, they provided teaching in school subjects and religion. From this developed Saint Andrew's School, which in a dozen years had come to have some seventy-five boarding boys and a few day students, with grades of instruction from primary up through High School.

It was a rural setting, a property of perhaps 200 acres, some wooded, some under cultivation as a farm; a few dwellings, the school buildings, and the small monastery or priory where members of the Order lived.

My connection with the place began in September, 1918, when I went there to teach in the school and be of assistance in some religious services and ministrations. My wife and I lived in a cottage on the school grounds. After the end of the school year, I stayed on there through the summer, as did some other persons of the staff and a few of the boys.

Mrs. Agee, whose home was in Knoxville, had friends at Saint Andrew's and in 1918, two years after the death of her husband, she with her two children had spent the summer there, living in one of the cottages. In 1919 they came

FATHER JAMES HAROLD FLYE met James Agee when Agee's family first arrived at St. Andrew's School. Their friendship flourished through four decades and is acknowledged, in part, with the publication of the *Letters of James Agee to Father Flye*. This article represents his first attempt to record for a periodical the remembrances he touched on in the editions of the letters. He is 86 years old and lives in New York City.

again, and it was thus that I came to know them. James (or Rufus, as he was then called, using his middle name which he came to dislike and later dropped entirely) was then in his tenth year, and Emma two years younger. And so began one of the most cherished and rewarding relationships of my life.

Many factors act as deterrents to rapport between individuals, but a difference of chronological age is not necessarily such, as Rufus and I soon discovered. Here was a friendly, intelligent boy, of active mind, fond of reading, with a good store of knowledge and eager for more. There was no lack of things for us to talk about. He was interested in fossils and shells, knowing many by their scientific names which he used fluently and naturally. Then there was the subject of possible pets, and we discussed monkeys, ponies, elephants, rabbits, pigeons, and kangaroos, with citations from pet books and books of Natural History. Then foreign countries, and Indian life, and Scout lore and woodscraft. He wanted a bow and arrows and we made a bow which he used some. Later he wanted a 22 rifle. It wasn't considered advisable to buy him one, but we borrowed one and did some target shooting. He wouldn't have thought of shooting at birds or rabbits or other living things.

But besides talk and doings such as just mentioned, there were real bonds between us in spirit, feelings and instincts. He was very tender-hearted, touched to quick sympathy and pity at the sight or thought of suffering, human or other, and incapable of willingly causing it. He had a keen sense of humor and comedy, but was never comfortable with teasing or banter. He was by nature affectionate and trustful, with many endearing traits, and I felt deep tenderness and affection for him at this lovely age.

It may not be out of place here to include something told me years later by his mother of an incident in his childhood in Knoxville. "A friend of mine," she said, "was interested in a Settlement School out at the woolen mills. The women brought their children and they had to have people there in the nursery with them all day long while they worked in the mills. And she was taking Rufus in a little pony-cart or something. She had him with her to ride around to some of those places and she was telling him about those children. And Rufus said, 'Well, why do they have to stay in such a place? What are they there for?' She explained that they were very, very poor, which they were. And she said, 'You know, some of them don't even have shoes and stockings to wear.' And Rufus's eyes commenced to fill up and he was taking his shoes and stockings off then and there to give to whoever would need them. And that was like him, too. That continued to be like him, you know."

Some have felt James Agee saw in me something of a surrogate for his father, but I do not think this was the case. Our friendship and association and feeling toward each other were such, it seems to me, as we might equally well have had if his father had been living. As to the word "Father", by the way, used by James Agee, that was simply standard usage at Saint Andrew's in addressing or speaking of any priest.

With the passing of summer, I had assumed that Mrs. Agee would be returning to Knoxville, but she decided that as the cottage where they were living would still be had, she would stay on through the winter and have the children attend Saint Andrew's School*

I was glad that our association was not to be broken off, but could not help wondering how things would be with a boy like that in the regimen and surroundings to which he would have to adjust, with few of the boys of anything like his type or background. And he would undoubtedly be in trouble in the matter of some school rules and requirements; not by his intentionally breaking them, for he was not of defiant or uncooperative spirit, but because, though he meant well, he was absent-minded, forgetful of details, absorbed in what he was doing and not sufficiently conscious of time.

Life at Saint Andrew's School at that time was of rather plain and simple type. Most of the boys had very little money, and some really none. The charge for tuition and board was extremely low, and the school could not have carried on without the contributions sent in for its support. It was quite different from places modeled after the pattern of English schools. There was no system of rank and status within the student body, or between "old" and "new" boys, but general free choice of association and personal relations. Most of the boys were from rural or small-town background. The range in age was from a few very young boys to those in their upper 'teens, and three or four who after service in the first World War had come back to school for more education. The boys for the most part got on with

---

*This arrangement was made and continued for the next four years, with visits in vacations at the home of Mrs. Agee's parents. In late February, 1924, when her father was not well, she left Saint Andrew's and in 1924–25 Rufus attended High School in Knoxville.

each other very well, and the general spirit was friendly and pleasant. The boys took care of their own living quarters (with regular inspections) and each had some assigned job (changed every two weeks)—cleaning, waiting on table, pantry duty or other inside or outside work about the place. As to scholastic aptitude and ability, the range was from boys who would never make any progress with "book learning" to those who would go to college and do well.

The religious commitment of Saint Andrew's was definite and strong. The head person there was the Prior, appointed by and responsible to the Father Superior of the Order of the Holy Cross at West Park, New York, who would from time to time come for a visit. At the time of which we are writing, the Prior was also Headmaster of the School, and he taught one or two classes. The members of the Order were not aloof but friendly men and held in warm regard.

The aim and hope of the Holy Cross Fathers at Saint Andrew's was to be of service in promoting Christian faith and practice in the form called Anglo-Catholic; a term designating the religious position of those in the Episcopal Church (or the Anglican Communion) who emphasize the organic historic continuity of the Church and the teachings, rites and practice which bear witness to this. Some other places then or later with that same religious alignment would be the Church of the Advent and the Church of St. John the Evangelist in Boston and the monastery of the Cowley Fathers in Cambridge.

In the School, attendance was required at daily chapel service and on Sundays at the Sung Mass and at Evensong; Grace was said at meals in the School Dining Room; and religious instruction was a required course in the curriculum. There was due observance of Lent, Holy Week, and other special seasons and days of the Christian Year, and Church boys

were encouraged to go to Confession and Holy Communion. Many of the boys were acolytes, and liked to take part thus in the Church services. And each year would see a number of boys from other backgrounds coming into the Church. It should be said here that what was emphasized in the religious teaching given at Saint Andrew's, whether in sermons or group instruction or personally, was not mere externals, though these had their place, but real Christian faith and devotion.

In this setting, then, James Agee spent the years of his school life from the age of ten to fourteen. For most of that time he had quarters in a dormitory, it being felt that this was better for him than living at home. Our friendship continued and developed, but not in any exclusive way. I was on very good terms with all the boys and we had many very pleasant associations; but with him there was a special fulness of understanding and communication. When he was eleven, just for fun, outside of school hours, I started him with French, in which he did well; and somewhat later, with another boy four years older who had had some French, we continued and read *Tartarin de Tarascon* which they greatly enjoyed. When he reached the Ninth Grade (High School) he was for the first time in one of my classes (English History), in which he was an excellent student.

After his return with his mother to Knoxville in the spring of 1923 I saw him occasionally; and in the summer of 1925 we spent two months in France and England, travelling mostly by bicycle. That Fall he entered Phillips Exeter Academy, and during the next several years we met very seldom, but kept such contact as we might by writing. From 1941 to 1954 I took parish duty each summer in New York and we would see each other often.

When he first began to think of creative writing, or make any attempts at it in prose or verse, is not certain, but this does not seem to

THE HARVARD ADVOCATE
COMMEMORATIVE TO

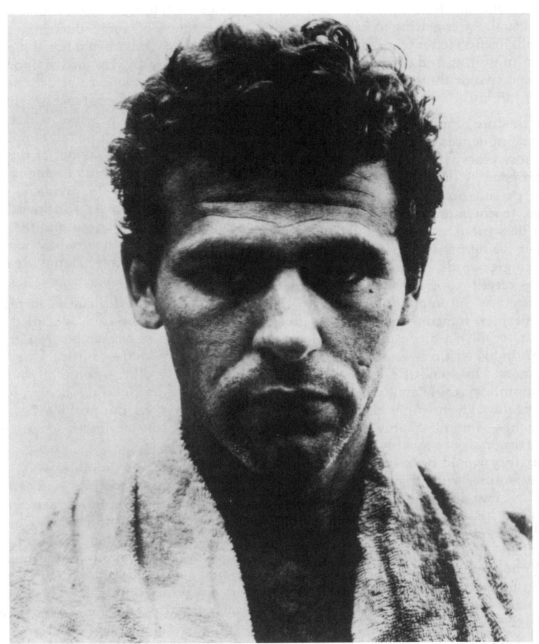

Walker Evans

James Agee

have been while he was at Saint Andrew's. On our trip abroad he spoke sometimes of wishing he could write something about things we had seen, but such feeling and such writing are not unusual. After getting to Exeter, however, that Fall, his first letter to me spoke of his keen interest in writing and of his having written a story and two or three poems for publication in the *Monthly*.

A rich store of memories, impressions, and no doubt influences remained with James Agee from those years at Saint Andrew's: that Cumberland country of Middle Tennessee and its people; persons of all ages whom he had known —boys, teachers and others; and that school life in its various aspects and relations. I remember seeing pages of pencilled jottings by him—single words, phrases, idioms, proper names—recalling persons, places, incidents, or experiences, unintelligible except to himself or perhaps someone in whom these might also stir recall. He made use of memories of this sort in his writings, and would have liked to use more. The scene of *The Morning Watch* —the dormitory, the Maundy Thursday Watch in relays through the night before the Blessed Sacrament—is unmistakably Saint Andrew's, and the originals of probably all the characters in that story would be easily recognizable by anyone familiar with that place in the early 1920's. He had deeply perceptive understanding toward his fellow human beings in their individual lives and would have liked to write more about them, and also to write some form of autobiography. *A Death in the Family* (which though called fiction is largely factual) shows what could be done with one episode in a life narrative.

Mrs. Agee was a devout and faithful Church member of Anglo-Catholic convictions to whom the religious faith and practice at Saint Andrew's meant a great deal, and Rufus grew up well grounded in this teaching and practice

and familiar with the language of the Bible and Book of Common Prayer. He was an acolyte and used to serve often at the altar. In later years he felt unable to commit himself to full acceptance of some doctrinal statements of the Church, but he had not abjured religion or Christian faith. He had a humble sense of wonder and reverence before the mysteries of the universe, of existence, of life, of human lives—a religious sense. There were many things about which he felt simply that he did not know, but he was not of those who sit in the seat of the scornful. I remember his declaring his belief in "a divine or supernatural consciousness, power and love." As between the essentially religious and the non- or antireligious, there is no doubt whatever in which category James Agee belongs. Read *Dedication* in the book of his poems.

He often had difficulties in regard to commitments, for he could not pledge himself to full support of or membership in an organization of any kind—political, social, economic, religious or other—some of whose principles or policies he could not accept. He knew very well, however, the problems and difficulties of anyone considering this matter and what he should do.

He was truly humble, very conscious of weakness, shortcomings and failures; a kind and loving person with great capacity for understanding and compassion. He will continue to speak through his writings, and to many there will be communicated thus the realization that here was one who had similar desires, hopes, uncertainties, moods and emotions to theirs, and would understand how they feel. For he did understand, and perhaps with the thought that through something he had been able to put into writing some might come to feel more deeply the bond of our common humanity.

"FRIENDSHIP ROSE"
THE GRENADINES

Richard Dey

In any week she makes the same run twice:
Kingstown, Bequia, Union, Carriacou,
St. George's. And then she makes the inter-island
run back through this island paradise.
She swarms with gulls, freight, banana bunches
hung from her booms, people and a cargo
of sunlight. She's a schooner built by eye.
a sturdy workboat, gaff-rigged, grey, about
90 feet, wooden, reliable. Everybody's been aboard her.
          As familiar
as small terns and Mount Gay rum, she's almost
a navigational aid among the islands
which to those sailing through them give
the illusion of moving. Should trade winds tire,
she's got a diesel to drive her windlessly
along, among the islands and illusions
of islands which the hazed shadows of clouds
in the distance give a sailor. Most days
there's nothing more disturbing than the "Rose's"
wide wake among the islands which
from certain perspectives appear to grow,
one out ot the other.
          Out of the seafields
and into the cloudwinds rise these volcanic peaks,
each perhaps another Pelee which razed
St. Pierre, the Paris of the West Indies:
where prayer in a town of prayer found no air
or wings unweighted with sulphur, and vessels burned
like tar to charred barges:
                         vessels more noble
than the "Rose" grey, built by eye, reliable
who moves among the islands and illusions
of islands like a man through memory.

"Auguries of Innocence"

ANTHONY HECHT

A small, unsmiling child,
Held upon her shoulder,
Stares from a photograph
Slightly out of kilter.
It slipped from a loaded folder
Where the income tax was filed.
The light seems cut in half
By a glum, October filter.

Of course, the child is right.
The unleafed branches knot
Into hopeless riddles behind him,
And the air is clearly cold.
Given the stinted light
To which fate and film consigned him,
Who'd smile at his own lot,
Even at one year old?

And yet his mother smiles.
Is it a grown-up make-believe,
As when anyone takes your picture,
Or some nobler, Roman virtue?
Vanity? Folly? The wiles
That some have up their sleeve?
A proud and flinty stricture
Against showing that things can hurt you,

Or a dark, Medean smile?
I'd be the last to know.
A speechless child of one
Could better construe the omens,
Unriddle our gifts for guile.
There's no sign from my son.
But it needs no Greeks or Romans
to foresee the ice and snow.

Hooks and Eyes for a Bibliophile's Breeches
An Essay on Book-Collecting
Peter Theroux

On what was surely an occasion of note, three hundred years ago in Salonika, Sabbatai Zevi (1626-1676), religious zealot and messianic pretender, actually married a book. Though I myself have kept shy of matrimony with even the most beloved of my books, I will confess, here, a perhaps unnaturally deep love for them—and go on to hope that there is enough bell-metal in my pen to convey the vehemence of a bibliomaniacal passion, to which such extravagances are not altogether alien. The book-collector, you see, is as much voluptuary as scholar, and sees a book's value in terms of both the excellence of the writing, and that second story which every volume has to tell: where and how it was made, of what, by whom—this together with particular details pertaining to its rarity and its physical make-up, which signify in importance second only to the intellectual joys the book conveys.

I am a book-collector, a proud avocationist in what Eric Quayle (wrongly) asserts to be the "least vicious" of hobbies (we are quite savage). We collectors are puzzled and often piqued unpleasantly by the common, absurd notion whereby we are only a pack of myopic, semi-crazed old pedants fretting over a book's colophon, dull dogs full of humorless zeal and no conversation, who suck our fingers free of pounce. I can speak only for myself, I realize, since the diversity of bibliophiles is matched only by the wide multiplicity of the things they love and collect. The collection's the thing, though: the collector is merely the pale Usher, dusting his lexicons, and imports, for the nonce, little: let's to books. What defines an item for my shelves?

Neither age only, nor even beauty, nor a work's merit by itself make a "find". All together, they do. Beauty, frankly, means the least: strictly applied, the aesthetic standards set for books by de Worde or Grolier, Viscount d'Aguisy, would wipe out whole shelves in even the finest of libraries. The aesthete in one must make room for the scholar: gilt spines, silk endpapers, elaborate watermarks and painted fore-edges are all very well, but the collector's eye, schooled in rarities, skims past imposing calfskin encyclopediae, to settle on, say, a plain first-edition of *Some People* (witty and rare), which might be autographed—such is the collector's fund of hope—or a rare illustrated copy of *Foutue a l'Hollandaise* by Mme. Sokolova Kneginja (Zagreb, 1899). No nook is too dark, no aisle too strait, no shelf too high, no crouch too painful to prevent the devoted bibliophile from prevailing at last, triumphantly clasping a dusty *Anatomy of Melancholy* (water-stained, crudely rejointed, but—ah!—complete), which would have gone undiscovered had he been a whit less conscientious or a shade less passionate than he was.

Tell the book-collector of some uncharted bookshop off in a distant borough—hint that you saw heavy old cartons in the basement—and watch him bolt his breakfast, take up his bookbag, and go spatterdashing out into the rain to begin his search. For what? For books! For the rare old riches nestling alongside the lowest tripe, concealed, captive, misshelved and mispriced by the clumsy, thankfully illiterate old panders who usually run book-shops, whose crude, mercantile dealings with great books make their trade little more than some species of white slavery. Understand his excitement; after all, this could be the day he finally comes upon the rare *Whimzies* (1631). Or *Venus in the Cloyster*, or Solyman Brown's *Dentologia: A Poem on the Diseases of the Teeth, in five Cantos*. Who knows?

My own collection reflects my tastes well since I do not extend the "investment" aspect of collecting to the point where I would clutter my shelves with valuable but unwanted purchases; more on that later. One's focus reveals; my weaknesses are immediately apparent: two full shelves of Vladimir Nabokov (his complete works in English, all first editions, including *Lolita* in the very rare two-volume Olympia Press edition, 1955); most of the thirty-seven books of Edward Gorey, all of them autographed; four volumes of Baron Corvo which cost me in eyestrain and inconvenience what I luckily saved in dollars; Byron's works in the first 1826 edition (eight little duodecimo volumes); *Joyce and Aquinas* by W. Noone S.J., signed by the Jesuit himself; a first edition of Trollope's *Autobiography* (for which a Charing Cross Rd. bookseller charged me "arf a craown"); and—here—let me show you an early copy, in red half-morocco, with marbled boards and endpapers, of Huysman's *l'Oblat*.

And then there are my treasures, most of them gifts; the Limited Editions Club *Ulysses* (#883 of 1500 copies, illustrated and signed by Henri Matisse); Homer's *Odyssey* done into English by Butcher and Lang (first edition, 1879); an elegant brown-and-gilt copy of the first translation of *Anna Karenina* (in which the "foreign term" *vodka* is glossed as "brandy"). Here is a two-volume Rabelais, Paris, 1659, pridefully placed beside the three-volume boxed Urquhart and Motteux translation (London, 1926). Permit me to add, here, that a good collection (*vide* mine) is a monument not only to good taste and sound intellect, but to acute financial sense. There are prizes to be had outside of Sotheby's, certainly, and "finds" that are not Caxtons are tucked away in dim corners of nearly every bookstore you see; what's wanting is the eye of a gyrfalcon, the purse of a Shylock, the thoroughness of Pliny, the patience of St. Monica, and a nose as formidable and aristocratic as Cyrano de Bergerac's, for booksmelling is, of course, a form of drug addiction; and if this amalgam seems improbable, I call my collection to witness that it is not. I invite you to my study. I own an eighteenth-centure miscellany full of such bawdiness as *The Gardenhouse Intrigue, Cupid's Bee Hive*, and *Pancharis, Quean of Love, or Woman Unveil'd*; had I passed it by as a mere curiosity and poked it back into its place, I would have missed Pope's *Essay on Criticism* (Sixth Edition, 1719) and his *Ode on St. Cecilia's Day* (Third

Edition, 1719), and Joseph Addison's poem of the same title (First Edition, 1699), all of which were bound into the same volume. The same volume! I delight in the arduous chase and the easy kill. I love to scour the terrain. My eye condescends to every low crooked shelf, to every listing stack tied with twine, to every dented box, for what might be concealed there. You've read about the violet by the mossy stone? As have I, as have I. Each bookstore has its dungeon, each dungeon its fettered princes awaiting liberation.

I must check my rhapsody, I know, but let me show you a few more. Here is a first edition of *Tess of the d'Urbervilles*, there *Hadrian the Seventh*. Here are Fitzgerald's translations of the *Iliad* and the *Odyssey*, sought out and kindly autographed. Come closer. This copy of *Go Down, Moses*, has the signature "Wm. Faulkner" on the half-title page, and has a long history as a gift: recipient to spouse, spouse to friend, friend to brother—me. (I ignore the "Idaho U. Library Discard" stamp in the back.) Lastly, here is a huge and indestructible leather volume of Shakespeare's *Works*, fast by the Yale facsimile of the first Folio. No, wait, let me show you this little copy of Scott's *Lady of the Lake*, bound in actual Birnam wood, and I have done.

I do not subscribe to that ruinous dictum whereby only first-editions, incunabula, and signed copies are worth having; in fact, new books are often welcome into my little bibliocracy. The Heritage Press, the Folio Society, the Libited Editions Club, Godine Inc., and the Fantod Press all produce books worth collecting. But I am sparfling my lore with dubious wisdom; my chatter might undo me. I cannot help but see each reader as a rival, each peruser of this very essay as a dangerous enemy who, now entrusted with some bibliophile secrets, might shamble in a bookstore three steps ahead of me and pick up a "find" before I can get to it—look over its valuable points with a look of cretinous stupefaction—pay up and carry it off, leaving me paper-pale, twitching with horror, my week ruined.

Yet I bibliobsessively seek quarities. The clack of a bell announces my entry into a small bookstore; the old proprietor and I exchange polite smiles, and I stroll down a snuff-colored aisle, sampling to my right and to my left. My heart quops: is that a Confederate book, printed on wallpaper? I sigh: it is not. Ever hunting bargains, you see, I yet always cherish hopes of finding a treasure. What will this heap reveal—Mathelia's rare *Nothing*, perhaps, or the yet rarer *! ! !* by George Heyworth? Will this be the day, I ask myself, that I find a book printed on *pâpier de guimauve* (edible paper) or bound in shahtoosh, the finest of all cloths? I hear the bookseller several feet away, coughing and rattling his newspaper (booksellers never read books, you'll note) and cannot help but wonder, will he be the man to sell me a book bound in human skin (technically, "cutis bound"—an oyster-gray binding, this, with the nap of chicken derma)? My foot is asleep. Perhaps that book, over behind *this* book, is that wonderful edition of Homer I once heard about, printed on rubber to read in the bath. I disregard the cramps in my legs to reach up for that book, there— could this be, finally, Francis Glass's *Washington Vita*, a Latin biography of our first president? No, sadly. The thought of finding a book with Mary Wordsworth's bookplate and bound, for such was

her custom, in the fabric of an old dress, is never completely out of my head. Are there any zipper bibles left? They were an American invention (1933). When will I stumble on a book written in Wolof, Micmac, Zmudz, or R'lyeh? When indeed? I leave the store with a complete edition of Florio's Montaigne: good. There have been richer days and poorer. I have more anecdotes.

Once in West Barnstable, Massachusetts, an unprosperous *bouquiniste* sold me a first edition of Borges' *Labyrinths* (a minor rarity and first-rate book) for $1.50—then gracefully reduced the price to a dollar, since I was buying three books. The good angel Common Decency hissed in my ear. I ignored her. The least vicious of hobbies?? Similarly, I once bought a book illustrated and signed by Fritz Eichenberg, paying only half-price for it because of what the cashier mistakenly thought was the previous owner's indelible signature. Not a word of correction parted my lips: the least vicious of hobbies, indeed. Inside every book-collector beats the heart of a Guiccardini.

A frequent fly in the ointment: that much-desired book in the window, set at a slightly inflated price, and the ensuing pain of indecision, whereby hangs many a tale. It can be difficult. It can be dicey. I am a veteran of the dead-end search, of the empty bookbag, of the primrose path that proved to be a cul-de-sac; but it is the odd failure, the tragic overspending, and the buy, mediocre in retrospect, that give my rare bargins their true bouquet. Shall I tell you about the time I *didn't* buy Tolstoy's scarce pamphlet *Tolstoy on Shakespeare*, and nearly died from depression that night? Luckily it was still there the next day, and now it is on my shelf. We persevere mightily; every book-collector, whatever the enormity of his setbacks, belongs to the pick-up-and-bloody-well-carry-on school of thought.

Let me now treat of my small crucifixions: those damaged, stained, torn or wormed-through books. I am no mean hand at restoring them if need be. I have spent patient hours de-foxing pages (cleansing them of those freckley brown spots that disfigure their pages), repairing leather (common vaseline is the best thing for this), toiling over soiled prelims and embrowned endpapers with infinite care, with an eye toward the worth and the readability of the finished book. I do not, as some do, regard restoration as the chiefest joy of bibliophilia, but I often get deeply involved in surgery on the day's purchase and hunch over amongst gluepots, tissue strips, erasewheels, and plates of water, painstakingly doctoring the boards of an old leather tome and perhaps guiltily thinking of the next day's French exam or a paper due in three days—resolving, more than likely, to keep working and to leave the conjugations until breakfast, and to sacrifice a movie in the interests of the paper—but specifically in the interests of the bookish labor in front of me just then. A restoring job within the scope of my powers never fails to produce a rapturous warmth as I place it in my one-book-richer library, but of course there are quite hopeless cases: shaved catchwords (a page's first word printed at the bottom right of the preceding page), crooked joints, scars, haphazard backing and those criminal cases of mere idiot abuse—in any of which cases there is no alternative to packing it off, in a jiffy-bag, to a relatively inexpensive restorer in Portugal. It is clear, I think, that the purchase of a book is no affair of the moment.

To what end all this fuss? The creation of a body of great books, garnered enthusiastically from all over by a relentless sophiophile, and united by his love and concern. A perfect library is a democracy, providing equal room for Boswell and for *Flushed With Pride* (the definitive biography of T. Crapper, inventor of the chain-pull); the gorbellied brainchildren of Henry James and Charles Dickens are neighbors with Twain's *1601*, Strachey's facetiae, and Gorey's *Limerick*; the *Arabian Nights* is on excellent terms with Aquinas—in short, fully as democratic as the alphabet which sets Richardson and Rochester a scant four books apart, and from which only Shakespeare, Milton, and the two-volume Oxford English Dictionary—all on my desk—are exempt.

I take pleasure in shifting them about. I rearrange them, set them to rights, gladly find excuses to hold and compare them; for I am no packrat. I do not scamper off with armloads of precious books, only to latch them up in hair-trunks, there to molder and warp. My books are accessible, readable, and—every one of them—read. They render service. My Chaucer-lover's Chaucer is no bibliothecal dream, it is the well-built Robinson edition. My Huysmans set, once softbounds on fine paper, is now bound in red and stamped gold, each book, forever. In short, I pamper what is pamperable and expect the rest of my collection to bear with my reading.

What better place than here to set off myself and my fellow bibliophiles from the company of our would-be brother "collectors", e.g., the funless oil-magnate with his long gallery of Renoirs, the teenager with his bins of saved-up bottlecaps, and spinsters whose parlors are mere Disneylands of Wedgewood—idlers, these. Book-collecting is not an outlet for frustration, ennui, impotence, or random energies; it is not a bogus religion, it is not a desparate alternative to knitting socks or watching television. The bibliophile—antiquary, voluptuary, priest—has a calling; he is no soulmate of

the matchbox-saver, the tycoon, the clutterphile, or the shrewd crunchfist who buys books with the cold eye of an auctioneer, whose books are merely a burden to him until they treble in value.

Choice means selection. Exclusion, then, is a condition of bibliophilia, for we true collectors distinguish ourselves as much by what we leave behind as by what we acquire. My private *index librorum prohibitorum* includes comic books, cookbooks, sexual banalia, uninteresting psalmodies, anatomical studies of animals, histories of costume, horticultural texts, and *any* books on mathematics, ever were they printed in the year ought. That shelf of old phrenologies? Keep it. These quaint volumes on naval customs? They're yours.

Books precede and outlast us. They are cemeteries of the living. The solemn buckram sepulchers contain the wildest of life, and the carousing corpses within—begot by an author, realized by a printer, first freed by a paperknife—now wait only for sight to fall on their pages for them to rise up and live—little resurrections performed for every new reader. *Every* book has its Finnegans. Every collector who has stood gazing paternally on his silent brood of old books before going to bed, is conscious of this cheery fact, that a book is, paradoxically, our ancestor and our child—and sometimes our wife.

The nuptials of Zevi grow less and less foreign to my comprehension. While I was not there, regrettably, to give him my joyous congratulations on his splendid match, the day he took the Torah, the Scroll of Laro to himself, for better, for worse, for richer, for poorer, in sickness and in health, to be sundered by death alone, I yet, today, gratefully pen an appreciation of an obsession, his and mine, to shred up and sprinkle down the temporal and spatial void that separates us, confetti to grace the wedding whose heartiest well-wisher lived three centuries too late. ❧

Jenny Amadeo-Holl

377

Lorcan O'Neill

The Director's Slide Show
Charles Glazier

This box is all from Mexico, our trip down last summer. I just got them back, I've never seen them before. Major asked me not to show them to anyone, but I can show them to you. Off with the lights and now I find the switch and on slides. How do you focus this thing? There. This one was in Mexico. This is the airport we landed at. We came in on a little turboprop, two motors, and I was scared, I had my seatbelt on tight. It was a tiny airport. Major took this one from the top of the stairs, that's my head sticking up in the bottom of the picture there. When I first looked out at that little airport building I thought it was a public bathroom with tinted glass windows instead of walls. It made me laugh, and I almost tripped coming down the aluminum steps, not like an actress. Audrey came down nice and fast, heels and all. That's what she gets paid for.

Focus. Oh, here we are, standing with the crowd in front of the airport, waving at the camera. Major took this one too, he took all of them. I've got to focus this better. Damn. Reason I want it focused . . . there, now look, see me squinting? That's not just because the sun was bright. Major never let me wear my glasses when we were coming in at an airport in case there were photographers from *People* magazine around. I couldn't have cared less. I'm no actress, I don't have to worry about my looks. But he made me. I got lost in more airports than you would believe, always ended up in the ladies room feeling the faucets and not even recognizing myself in the mirror. Next.

This is the truck, the equipment truck. You can see my trailer too, that thing on wheels sticking out behind the truck. Anyway, one of the reasons I wanted to see these slides is I broke my glasses in half while we drove out of the motel, I sat on my purse or something because they were broken when I got to my room. I couldn't see anything without them, I had to hold one half up to my eye like some old lady in the parlor, and most of the time I just didn't bother. I walked around blind the whole time, I never really knew what was going on.

This is Mario. The slide doesn't show it, he had skin the color of a ripe cantelope. See how good he looks on the slide? He's got perfect skin for movie work, the orange comes out tan on color film. But he looked horrible in person, an orange blur like a balloon. Now I see, it looks like he had a pretty good face. Downtown they call that classic Spanish features. That's where I found him listed in the files, under classic Spanish features. I thought his name was perfect, that's why I took him. But he was a horrible actor. The first day we ran through the script. He'd already had it for two weeks but he still didn't know a line. We sat out on the pooldeck and I read the lines out loud to him and had him repeat. He was very slow. I was wearing a new two-piece suit and the sun was shining off my stomach. I greased myself and put the script on the deck between my legs, staring down so I wouldn't have to look at Mario, I was so angry. My belly seemed huge and white like I was pregnant, so I kept smearing more coconut oil on it. Of course, I got a great burn, coconut oil just makes your skin fry.

Christ, Major got me. He always did that, took a picture without telling me. I look awful, don't I? Got my legs stuck out like an old lady. Look at that belly. Just like I said, I was a mess down there.

Here's the beach. This was the location for the second half of the ad, we tried shooting that scene the first night. Right now, in the slide, it's twilight. This film doesn't come close, the sky was almost green, incredible sunsets down there, very mysterious. You see all those shapes down by the water? Those are rusty old landing boats, they made a war movie about Guadalcanal there the year before and left all sorts of war junk lying around. We had a hard time finding a spot with no tanks in the picture, kind of tricky. The advance man blew it. But we went there because they like movie people. Nichols made *Catch-22* there a few years before, I think we even took the time to drive out to the airfield he made for a movie set. So we went down where people would at least smile while they took our money. I actually felt a little honored when they sent that crowd out to meet us at the airport, it was like making a real movie. Next.

That's funny. This one's out of order. We're back on the pooldeck. This is a picture of the General, but you can't really see him. He's in that shadow over there under the bougainvillia. He was a retired air force general, he always sat there in the shade because of a skin disease he got in Thailand. He reminded me of the man who lived across the street from us at home. He used to sit in his garage in a lawn chair all weekend watching cars driving by. You couldn't really see him but you knew he was there. You could see the General's gold shining in the dark sometimes. He had a gold-headed cane, gold stars on his jacket shoulders, gold bracelets and a gold watch, gold rings. It was spooky talking to him. The maitre d' introduced us and I had a zombie with him. Those zombies are wicked. Major was sitting in the sun talking to Audrey in her bikini, I couldn't concentrate on what the General was saying because I was trying to see what Major and Audrey were doing over there. The General kept asking me about Major, how we got along, how he stayed busy while I was making all the money. The General was a trouble maker, actually he was the one who got me started about Major and Audrey. He had these long white fingers and he kept clicking his gold rings on the glass table top.

Back on the beach again, the first night still. You can see we've got the lights all set up. It's supposed to be nighttime but the cameras need light. So you shoot at night for the actors, turn on the lights for the cameras, and then you use lens filters for the film to make it look dark again. I'm the one who has to think of things like that, make sure everyone's happy. Reminds me of raising the kids sometimes.

A picture of Major smiling. I wonder who took it. He looks nice here, doesn't he? He had the kind of skin that looked good in real life too, and he had a nice smile. He didn't smile much that trip. It was hot. That was mainly what bothered me too. You were hot all day, all night, no one could sleep except the

Mexicans. We brought our own water down but everyone drank beer all day and wine for sleeping. I had to go to the bathroom all day long, it was embarrassing. Drunk all day and blind too, I got confused by the heat. I had to keep sending Major back to the room for the right section of the script and he kept bitching about it. I couldn't read my margin notes, I couldn't see anything. I just remember how awful Mario was. He was awful.

Back at the beach during the first night's shooting. That's Mario trying to act. Look at the funny way he looks in the lights, green. I guess Major didn't have a filter on his camera, we all look sort of sick. Mario was so bad we had to make huge cue cards with a magic marker, and he kept squinting at them instead of saying his lines. Nearsighted too, I guess. I felt sorry for him that first night, he was so bad. Only three days of shooting and the first wasted, gone. I felt like time was running out already. Everyone was mad, Audrey because she didn't even get in front of the camera that night. She just stood around talking to Major behind my back, I watched Mario and drank zombies out of a thermos.

Here's Audrey on the beach, showing off her figure. Next. Audrey again, in town somewhere. Next. Audrey on the pooldeck. Major took a lot of pictures of her. Very pretty, a good actress too. I had to admire that, she knew her lines. She couldn't do anything with them, but all I wanted was the lines. It's the lines that count, people aren't looking for entertainment in these things. They just want information.

This is a bar in town. Everyone, cast and crew, had to drink together because I didn't want anyone getting into trouble. I didn't have time to go bail out some cameraman. I drank a lot of beer and some stuff like the ouzo we used to get in college. It was clear and looked like it had oil swirled in it, like the mineral water and glycerine I had to drink for my stomach when I got back home. Major got completely drunk and passed out, I had Mario carry him out to the car. Mario was very nice about it. The next day Major said that Mario took some money out of his wallet while he was pretending to be asleep. I said, Why were you pretending to be asleep? I don't think he did anything about the money after that. Next.

Someone must have hung onto Major's camera, Mario I guess. This is the inside of another bar. We lost almost everyone after this, they drove back to the hotel. Mario said he would stay and take me back when I was ready. I wasn't sleepy at all, he suggested a walk along the waterfront.

This is the dock. I didn't think Mario took a picture here. The moon shows how flat the water was, its light looked like a needle on a table. Mario and I sat in front of that big statue there, it's dedicated to some fisherman who saved some guy from drowning. Mario translated the bronze letters for me. Look at that dock. It's really a wharf, I guess. It was made out of rocks, but they fitted together like bricks, the sides down to the water were perfectly smooth, just tiny cracks between the stones. I asked Mario how it had been built, he said that it was old. All these Mexican mysteries.

Next. The dock again. How could he take a picture of it? I don't even remember the camera around his neck, I would have known. All these mysteries. Next.

The fish market the second day. This was horrible too, this huge room all white like a hospital with these big white-washed sinks full of dead fish. It really smelled, but Mario wanted fish for lunch and I was going into town anyway to get film and smokes. I don't know why I took this picture, I probably thought it was picturesque. Over there, that last sink, that's turtle heads. You can't see because it's out of focus. They were all piled up, made me think of those wrecking yards you drive by with all the cars piled up staring at the highway with their headlights. Except that there were real eyes and they were open, sort of sleepy. Some of them had part of the shoulders hanging onto the neck like they just got torn off. I got a lot of nice fish for two pesos. Two pesos, that's almost nothing. You can get almost anything for almost nothing down there. The fisherman was very polite, smiled when I gave him the money. He had an eye all white with glaucoma like my father.

Drug store, Mexican style. Don't know why half these pictures were taken. It looks just like Rexall, doesn't it? Racks of books and sunglasses. I got Major some sunglasses.

Major on the pooldeck in his new sunglasses. At least some of these slides are in order. He said the glasses didn't fit right but he wore them anyway. He was just being bitchy because I got back so late the night before.

Here's Major talking with the General. This is the only time I saw them talk, though later it turned out they talked a lot. You can see Major's feet sticking out of that shadow. Mario must have taken this one, I was swimming the whole time and anyway it's in focus. I guess Mario had the camera for awhile, kept it overnight. Or maybe he went into town with me that morning and took those slides too. I'm a little confused, all the heat and hangover and more beer.

There's the General going back to his room, just blurry in the corner there. Mario had a good photo eye, he got a nice action shot here with the General walking out of the frame and Major's feet sticking into the sun still. Major never told me what the General said, he just looked at me weird when I asked.

These are all while we were shooting the bedroom scene that afternoon. I'll run through them fast. Mario was supposed to be tempting Audrey with the coffee, he couldn't remember to pick up the can with the label showing. Audrey just sat on the edge of the bed watching him blow ten takes in a row. I thought about dubbing a track back in the studio, but no money in the budget for that. We sweated it out and when I couldn't take any more I kicked everyone out and lay down. I didn't even have them take the lights out, just the cameras. We were using my room for the set to save money, but I couldn't sleep under cameras even if I knew they were empty and no one was behind them. Major came in and said the General had insulted us, but he wouldn't tell me what the General said. I'll bet it was something about me and Mario. I didn't have the strength to tell him about the botch we'd made of the afternoon's shooting. One day and two nights left and we had to do both the beach and bedroom scenes over again. I'd lost the left half of my glasses somewhere, dropped them off the dock when I got frightened or something, and Major tied the right half to a loop of string to hang around my neck. He told me I should cool off in the pool before dinner, I said I didn't feel like it. He got out a cigarette and lit it for me, but it wasn't a cigarette. I was surprised, he said we were in Mexico and everyone else was smoking it. I shared it with him, sitting on the edge of the bed with an ashtray between us. It felt nice, I felt cooler and I made a note to take some home. I was just beginning to relax and Major starts bugging me about Mario,

Why does Mario have the camera, Mario took my money, all that, and when I said, Why don't you do something about it? he just walked out on me.

More bedroom scenes. I guess I decided we'd try to finish the bedroom scene that night instead of moving out to the beach. It went well, I began to think we'd be alright. Mario was very apologetic about the afternoon, he flirted with me to make up for it. He took some uppers, they helped him remember his lines and we were done by ten. We left all the equipment in my room and went into town to get drunker. Major passed out again, here he is lying across the table. Don't I look disgusted? I was tired from the pot, but I felt like I had to be the life of the party with the crew. I had Mario take Major out to the car again.

The dock again. We didn't go there the second night. Maybe we did. The first and second nights. Or the second and third nights. Anyway, one night we were there and we saw some boys in a motorboat. No, this was all the third night. The moon was up, the boat's motor was whining and you could see the boat's wake crossing the moonlight. They came in next to the dock for awhile, four boys in Sears sportshirts. They had fishscales all over their arms reflecting green and red when they moved below us. Mario asked them something and then told me they were sons of fishermen, they were hunting for watersnakes to sell to the hotel restaurant. Expensive delicacy that I should try, he said. He was always telling me all the stuff I should try down there.

The pooldeck just after dawn. Major saw me crossing the pooldeck from Mario's room, followed me into my room wanting to know where I'd been all night. I told him Mario had drowned, I had pushed him off the dock.

Here's Mario and me on the pooldeck, must be the first day. No, with that sunburn I have, it's at least the second day. Rehearsing the script again. Audrey sitting in a bikini at the table behind us, talking with Major. So who took this picture?

And who took this one? I don't recognize anything, it looks like some airport, LAX and I'm lost in the bathroom again. Next.

Mario must have taken this one, me rehearsing Audrey on the pooldeck before dinner. Third day? We were about to go and finish the bedroom scene before dinner. She wanted to get fancy, her last chance at stardom, and I reminded her to be dumb. She was very upset the last day, she told me she was overdue and she wasn't sure who to blame. She started forgetting her lines, it took an hour to get a perfect take. Mario was suddenly a tower of strength, no need for cue cards. He kept smiling at me and I kept smiling back even though I didn't want to and then we'd both look at Major and stop smiling. I wanted some uppers for myself, I was tired from staying up all night.

Dinner at the hotel. I don't know which night, it doesn't matter. I didn't order the snake. Mario's skin was so orange by candlelight I thought of asking the cameraman for a filter to tape over the right half of my glasses so he wouldn't look so gross. He laughed and said he couldn't spare one. Major looks very angry here. There's the General in the background at that corner table. I can't see his rings but I know they're there. Major kept looking over his shoulder at him. He told me the General had retired because he made millions of dollars while he was stationed in Thailand. He wouldn't tell me doing what

exactly, something about drugs, and I got mad because he was acting so mysterious. He only did that when he was jealous.

The dock, out of place as usual. I don't know who took some of these pictures, they just keep popping up like a bad dream. Next.

We went out to the beach for the last night's shooting. Mario had to carry Audrey down to a boat and row off under the moonlight. It was lucky we had good weather. I timed our trip so we'd have nearly a full moon for all three nights, that's part of the job. Mario was coming down now, he was weak, kept asking for more speed. No lines to remember, he still managed to drop Audrey in the sand and blow his jump into the boat each time. We had to wait while he changed to dry pants after every take. I let him use my trailer because he was embarrassed. Wet pants piled up on the sand next to the trailer door. Major kept looking at them and laughing. I ate some uppers and someone gave me a zombie in thermos. I drank it down like medicine.

Here's Audrey waiting. She was afraid of getting her only dress wet, she was stiff in Mario's arms when I wanted her to be like a bag of groceries, and Mario finally slipped and dropped her in the water. She cried for nearly an hour while I held the dress next to a spotlamp to get it dry. It was past ten, we were running out of time.

Here's Major back on the pool deck. Nothing to say, next. Nothing to say. Town shots, dirty Mexicans. They were all dirty, they smelled. Good servants at the hotel. The toilets didn't work.

Audrey tearing her wet dress off. A good action shot, I bet Mario did it.

The dock, the snake. Mario has his arms around me, so who took this picture? Was Major following us around? Maybe it was the General. The boys in the boat went out and came back again yelling in Spanish. Mario and I ignored them. Then they threw something, I looked up, there's the pink watersnake in the air. It turns end over end like a stick, lands on Mario's head and I scream into his ear. Its head swings over, brushes my forehead with its lips, Mario throws it off. It curls up on the dock between us flicking its tongue at my ankles, and Mario stepped on its head then. The houses all were dark on the shore, the boys were laughing, the snake twisted around looking for its head until it slid off into the water. Mario drove me back to the room. That was the last night. It had to be the last night, after we finished at the beach. He drove, I knew where we were going. I couldn't sit still in the seat, I kept looking for two round tooth-holes on his arm. He drove very smooth, staring at the road, and we got to his room without saying a word.

Who took this picture?

Who took this picture?

Major's feet sticking out of the shadow again. The General walking out of the picture again. Major went back down there after the judge said yes, said he had enlisted and laughed when I said he could keep the house if he'd take the kids. What did I say to him? Something about Mario. I made up a story that he drowned after he ran away from me, or I drowned him, or something. All he wanted was a free ride back to the border, I guess. Next.

Who took these pictures? Mario couldn't have done it. ✤

THE HARVARD ADVOCATE

COMMEMORATIVE TO

circa 1950, courtesy of William Alfred

Robert Lowell

Three Following Han-Shan

April Bernard

1. Apology

I too am climbing Cold Mountain
But the Way is choked by brambles:
Ah, my rebellious youth, my fears
That what is greater than me will swallow me.
Can I learn to kiss the big mouth that breathes
A new life into my soul?
A woman prone to drowning should not scorn
The beautiful arms that would sway her to shore.

2. Advice

Every dawn I climb, and startle the birds
Like black questions into a pale yellow sky.
Once I left a sprig of partridge berry there
And next day it was gone.
If you go, wear thick-soled boots.
The gods on Cold Mountain are deaf;
They do not trust love, but something older,
For which I have not yet learned the name.

3. Meditation

I'm tired of taking and giving advice.
Lips caked with wine and sea sediment.
Him I love as a stubborn child loves
And am careful though unkind.
Tonight Han-shan is neither province nor poet,
It is the bed where I sleep alone.
Stars and nighthawks keep to themselves,
And sleep is short because the mountain is cold.

Letter
Judith Baumel

He writes: This note is only to relate
I think I'm calm though isolated now.
My world is flat and dulled in winter greys.
The beach I'm staying on unfolds for miles
On either side of Richard's summer home
So I can take long walks, alone, of course.
My tracks in snow remain distinct for days
Frozen in the clear unflurried air.
I'd be surprised to see, oh, anything
That is alive, a squirrel, or a gull.
But just this morning saw, in the front yard,
The prints of civilized existence turned
Wild and frenzied — anxious footsteps paced
In back and forth direction, shoeprints from
Familiar boots both obvious and strange.
Uncomfortable signs, a record there
Of just the man I wanted least to know
But knew then anyway. And also knew:
Those things I've left behind might calm or hide
The restless pain. Though still, realizing this,
All I hoped for was a heavy snow.

Cocytus Riposte
Richard Nalley

Here sound climbs the plain state of sound
and my whispers flex in the heart like blood.

My wash descends the abrupt wave
of your breath
from that world which accepts repose
in the literal kingdom
of your eyes and fingertips.

Immutable and pure,
captive in the muscular world, your sigh.

Adam Simon

MAILER'S VISIT

On March 6, Norman Mailer, novelist and *Advocate* alumnus, spoke at Sanders Theatre to benefit this magazine. He read from his then forthcoming novel, *Ancient Evenings*, and answered questions on a variety of topics. It was an exciting night for us at the *Advocate*; we felt alive and significant as a literary organization in a way we hadn't felt in a while. About three hundred people paid to hear Mr. Mailer speak, and most of them were not disappointed.

Mailer commented on the beauty of Sanders Theatre—the history it represented—which led him to urge us to stage the event there rather than at the Science Center. He sneered at the plastic he would have found on its walls. He sneered also at plastic glasses at modern garden parties. Near the end of the reading, Mailer suggested that some people might want to leave because the passage he was about to read would take approximately half an hour and was, as he put it, "boring." Some took him up on this. More, I guess, than he expected because moments later, as he watched about thirty or forty file out, he quipped, "Harvard isn't what it used to be."

Mailer had some comparisons on his mind—old and new; young and old; early sixties and early eighties; the earthy, sensually religious culture of Ancient Egypt and the synthetic, unholistic culture of our world. This turned out to be a good theme for the evening. The reading ended at tenfifteen, exactly two hours after it had begun. After sorting out the autograph seekers, we marched Mailer off through the Yard to a party for our membership and its guests in his honor.

We were all tired and we all needed a drink. We all had several. Most of us who remained at the party for a long time left drunk. As the evening progressed, the conversation grew more heady and less intelligible. The adults present gave way to the students, who were eager to converse with Mailer. A sort of antagonistic strain, however, developed almost automatically between Mailer and some of the students. It is difficult to figure out where it came from. It was not simply drunken belligerence—though that was surely there. I suspect it had much to do with Mailer's success as a writer, and especially the nature of that success. It's a rare thing, success both financial and critical—as burdensome to Mailer himself, perhaps, as it is suspicious to his readers and enviable to his peers.

Some of those present were frustrated by his refusal to talk literature. Others developed the courage to open their mouths only after several drinks and then found themselves verbally and mentally helpless. Still, the evening left us feeling as if something important had happened, though we weren't quite sure what.

The next day, the gossip came in like a flood. Snippets of the night's events, blurred and aggrandized by the alcohol, circulated. Everybody seemed to have something to regret or complain about.

Then, a day or two passed, and the excitement faded. It's difficult now to even recall the details.

"Harvard isn't what it used to be," said Mailer.

Who knows?

The best image I have of the evening is of all us young people sitting around Mailer—he in a chair, most of us on the floor—arguing and babbling and drinking and drinking. We sat around this mock heroic figure, not so much worshipping as trying to get a handle on his significance. Especially as people who would aspire to his success—critical and financial.

The other strong memory I have is of his departure and what seemed to be the real pleasure he expressed to have shared our company. There was a kind tolerance about him. I think he realized we were just feeling him out. And he even threw in a few tokens of himself—or his alleged self—the drinking, the flirtation, the rhetoric of the barroom brawler. Each of these came out as if in sample, as if to show the duality of his success—and maybe the duality of the American Dream.

Mailer is definitely at his best off-the-cuff. Impromptu, tough, hit-and-run, straightforward, refusing to let the oil of his personality mix with the water of his world. The sincerity with which he answered a question about Jack Abbott was impressive. Such quick, emotional self-consciousness has been one of the outstanding features of his writing.

I don't know if Harvard is what it used to be. Probably, it isn't. Nonetheless, we had no qualms about biting the hand that fed us that night, if only gently. We are, after all, democrats, and Mailer was pleased ultimately by our liberality. But we were pretty shame-faced the next day . . . .

DAVID LONGOBARDI

THREE POVERTIES

Fred Moten

I

No wind
has soothed this stance
posture beneath
a row of stems of star

by cubicles reduced in
simplicity of black to
the simplest line in
the barest meadow of

leaf and still slant
above a weaving path
with spaces that
reveal an intricacy of

nothing in a calm at
Jackson—hard
as bronze a
starved Rubens

paused at
a clearing of glass to
turn back
free strands

softly "not duchess/a
hundred yards from
a carriage"—
the chill is her perfect poetry.

II

Quickened, apace with kids,
she ain't as old until
remembering her age, the purse
holds less and less and
she leans, reaching for

no cigarette,
no light from scratching
walls, and hears hard
wind break windows and
cold snow

burn no hat of
Dora Jones, 57,
delivered a time ago from
involuntary servitude
to this.

III

At the ICU a look of intensest poverty,
unpeaceful, like in a 'hood or a homeland,
tense and tremoring, not from reasoned
energy but vague reaction, boxes and cords
breathing an effigy of whom we could've
kept alive that night or many nights before
if we'd have kicked his ass or thrown his
keys in the ditch or kept him from the
punchbowl but we were in it too tough ourselves—

Two Pirate Stories

Debra S. Rosenblum

One story begins with the sister and the summer. If it were not for the summer, the sister would not be coming to this house, the white one. She would stay as she was, where she was, with her typewriter and a boyfriend. But it is summertime and she is due to arrive any minute now: it is for her that the boy has hidden himself in the front hall closet. Their front hall closet is mirrored on the outside and it represents the smallest portion of a home that could be flawless: the ceilings high, the hallways wide and gleaming, a seashell cleaned through and through. A mother and a father lie upstairs somewhere: right now is their nap time for the day is too bright hot and everyone has just had lunch. It is afternoon, the boy thinks as he crouches. Afternoon, afternoon, afternoon. He can say it in Spanish as well but he chooses not to for it would not serve any purpose. There is a purpose to this boy as he crouches in the darkness for he is a boy of great definition. There he is and there is chewing gum, still unchewed, in the pocket of his shorts. There he is behind the mirror: he must not make a sound, stay perfectly still because he does not want to ruin this day's plans. Many things can happen. Many things can go wrong.

Here are some of the things that can go wrong. As planned, the sister will walk through the front door of the house and a long, black shadow will flow from her feet down the length of the hall, her darkness running parallel to the mirrored door of the front hall closet and, so triggered, the brother will jump out to surprise and greet his sister. He might even cry Boo. If his timing is right, his sister will scream and then hide her face, red, for now she has seen the joke and after a while of blushing and laughing she will hand him the case and say Here, here is my typeweriter that I have brought here just for you and will let you use until the end of the summer. But things may not work out. The boy may jump out too early, or too late or will stumble over his shoelaces, his zipper unzipped, and thereby become the object of his sister's jokes for the rest of the summer. Or, his timing my be right, absolutely so, and he will scare his sister, but scare her so thoroughly that she loses control and lets go of the typewriter. And the hallway will echo with the bitter jangle of an expensive machine as it breaks into too many pieces. There they will stand, boy and girl, blank and dumbfounded by the apparent ease with which tragedy can work its way into their young lives.

In the movie, there is silence and the same holds true for music, but how can silence show itself in a story between two people? Will lots of white space—lines unfilled, contacts not made—do the trick? And, then, how does one silence distinguish itself from another?

Pirate silence hangs sweet and more wondrous than any other silence in the world. To the observer, it is no more than the small sand space that lies between two boys as they play on the deserted beach. But to those within the pirate kingdom, it becomes a giant curtain swinging back and forth, throwing its shadow to one side, then the other, to create the black/white differential between the One Who Has Dreams and the One Who Has Nightmares.

The Boy Who Has Nightmares has come to this beach every summer since he was born. When he digs, he digs for pirate treasure and he knows that the deeper he digs, the darker and wetter the sand becomes. The darkness of the hole that he makes does not equal the darkness of the sand that he finds but one darkness is the greater reflection of the other.

This is the first summer here for the Boy Who Has Dreams. The Mother of this boy carries a sickness in her leg and so the family has purchased the white house by the sea for her to keep her leg in. It is not enough, the Dreaming Pirate thinks, for the leg has swollen so that it already fills an entire wing of the house. Soon, it will grow too large and they will have to move the mother to another house altogether.

They were pirates in their way, but they kept this from all others. They found each other on the beach. That day was the first for the One Who Has Dreams, his first day on a beach, and the day was a grey one, not a beach day at all but a movie day. Or a sleeping day. Only the other one, the One Who Has Nightmares was out and he was digging.

Digging for what? the new boy wanted to know.

On any given beach, a Pirate Who Has Nightmares can provide two reasons for digging a hole. The hole can be for treasure. Or the hole can be a trap.

A trap? the new boy asked. A trap for what?

The other boy brushed his hands on his shorts and stood up to survey his progress. He pointed up the beach. See, he said, there's that Magician there. Every day he comes closer and closer. Once we finish this hole, we'll put leaves over it and he'll fall in and be trapped.

The Boy Who Has Dreams could not see the magician. The other boy shaded his eye with his hands. He squinted. Yeah, he agreed, he's pretty far right now but if you can't see him today, you'll see him tomorrow. Believe me.

Again, the Boy Who Has Dreams looked up the beach: he did not see a beach the same as the one that he was standing on but, rather, the picture on the cover of a care. It is for this reason that the beach can go on forever and if the boy runs fast and far enough he will find himself small and compressed into a musical note for that is what becomes of people in an inverse world. If there is a magician, he is still inside the car and the Boy Who Has Dreams will never see him until he steps out of the paper. And, if he is not inside, he must be behind the things somehow.

So, his new friend asked, you want to help?

Catch the magician?

And find the treasure.

Treasure? the new boy was not sure.

Pirate treasure. The other one took his arm. My name is Drew. I am a pirate.

My name is Andy, said the one Boy Who Has Dreams. I am pleased to meet you.

And he became a pirate too.

Question: For what reason is there chewing gum?

Answer: Chewing gum functions best when wet and therefore malleable and tacky. In this state it can be spread quite easily over the metal keys of a typewriter.

Q: And then?

A: And then it will harden. Try removing it now.

Q: And now what happens?

A: You brat! You filthy little brat! How could you do such a thing? What is the matter with you? You must be sick, You hear what I'm saying? I hate you! God, do I hate you!

Q: Is that all?

A: IhateyouIhateyouIhateyou...

Q: Is that all?

A: Hello, hello is Jordy there? Oh Tom, it's Laurel. Could you please put on Jordy please? (pause) Jordy, is that *you*? O Jordy, I miss you so much I can't belive it. Do you know what my brother did to me? He smeared his gum all over my typewriter. I can't believe how sick he is, he's sick. (pause) I don't care if he's a kid, I never did that when I was a kid, *did you*? He's just impossible: I don't know how I'm going to survive the summer with him and without you (pause) What's that? What's that? O Jordy I swear to you, he's listening on the extension, I wouldn't put it past him. (pause). No, I haven't heard from her, have you? Well, how do you like that, my own roommate. You have? (pause) and *her*? You've heard from her too? What does she want? (pause). Oh yeah? Well good luck...Listen Jordy, can you hear that.

Can you hear me? Can't you hear, my brother is listening to us! I can't believe it! He's such a shit! Brat!

Q: Is that all?

A: And that's all folks.

Q: And what are the parents doing?

A: The parents are napping upstairs.

Q: Together?

A: They nap in separate parts of the house. One likes to receive the afternoon sun. The other one suffers from heat rash.

Q: Which one suffers from heat rash?

A: It depends on the afternoon. But it's never more or less than one.

The boys are digging on the empty beach. Every day has been like this, cold and on the verge of rain. Andy, the One Who Has Dreams, is beginning to wonder where other people have ever appeared on this beach. Even the magician has not arrived.

The One Who Has Nighmares: But can't you feel him coming closer?

Andy, the Dream Boy, does not know. Why do they want to catch the magician anyway?

Nightmare Boy: The Magician is bad.

Why is he bad? the other wants to know.

Nightmare Boy: He wears all black.

You know, Andy said tracing his toe across the sand, there must be more to it than that.

Nightmare Boy: He's after the treasure too.

Andy can bury his foot. There must be more to it than that, he says.

Nightmare Boy: He's a magician. He could make us disappear.

Andy turns his head from side to side. Faster, faster, if he does this long enough, he can make himself dizzy, he can make himself sick. If he invests enough of his energy, all of his energy into this head-shaking motion he can make himself another boy. He can make himself fly and it is then, when he leaves the ground that he will find the treasure and the sun and the people that should be on this beach. He is sure that he can never find anything right here because he does not know how. His friend, the Boy Who Has Nightmares, knows where to dig and how to dig. He knows all the stories to tell. Here is the story of his nightmare:

The One Who Has Nightmares: My mother, my father and I are one the beach. My baby brother is napping back at the beach house. I am a little boy and playing at the shore. I pick up shells, I throw rocks so smooth that I keeps the smaller ones in my mouth. Then I see the man who is younger than my father and younger than my uncle, my uncle also lives at the beach. My uncle and my father are identical twins: so are my aunt and my mother. The man on the beach wears a long-sleeved shirt, a jacket and slacks. He must be very hot for this is the hottest day of the summer. It is a record-breaking day and the man picks me up and twirls me around singing helicopter, helicopter and then he teaches me how to skip stones in the ocean. Soon, my parents wander over to talk to the man and soon it is the three of them talking and I am left alone. I build a house in the sand but they do not see. I stand on my head and walk on my hands. I run into the ocean: Help me, help me, I'm drowning but nobody comes for me and when I come out of the water nobody is there until my uncle arrives and tells me that I'll have to stay at his house tonight because my parents are having a guest over for dinner: they're letting him stay in my room I begin to cry: O no Uncle Bob, that man has a gun. We can't let him stay with Mom and Dad. He'll hurt them and Baby Brother too. Uncle Bob laughs and musses my hair. O Sport, he chuckles, what a fine imagination you have.

That night, after dinner, I watch my family on television. The camera has been placed in the living room of our summer house: a black man is holding a microphone. An automobile, our automobile, is parked in the middle of our living room. My father has opened the back door of the car: he is going to inspect the back seat and the floor. The man from the beach stands behind him. My father climbs in and the camera follows him. The man from the beach remains outside. My father addresses the camera. My son, he says, this is for my son who is staying up the street with my brother. I want him to see that we're okay so that he doesn't worry. We'll see him tomorrow. You see, my uncle says switching off the set, your folks are fine. Now go to bed.

The next morning I wake to find that my whole family has been killed. My father's body was discovered in the back seat of the car in our living room. All of the victims, my mother, my father, my baby brother, were beaten and then shot. The murders were committed by a stranger: the police have no idea. My uncle becomes my father, my aunt becomes my mother. I have a sister now, and not a baby brother.

The One Who Has Dreams touches the other. Was that your nightmare? he asks. Or did that really happen?

But the other does not answer he has run to stand at the edge of the water where he skips a few stones. But his friend cannot tell how well he does because it is hard to see skips when there are waves. The One Who Has Nightmares returns to his hole and resumes his digging.

The Boy Who Has Nightmares: when we have the magician in our trap he will do anything to escape. He will find that treasure for us. He will let us use his magic. Look at this.

The boy lowers himself into the hole and, for a moment, his friend Andy fears that he has vanished and become space. But it is not this way: the boy climbs

out, covered with sand and the day is over.

It is time for dinner.

And what happens then?

The sweater was white when the room-mate gave it to the sister as a gift. Now someone has taken a lipstick and scrawled "Jordy does not love Laurel" on the back.

"Ruined!" she screams. "I can't believe you! First the typewriter and now this! You are a sick, sick little boy!"

"Sure blame me."

"Who am I supposed to blame? The cat?"

"We don't have a cat."

"What a wit you are. I'll have you know that the typewriter is permanently damaged. I removed all the gum, with peanut butter I did, and it still doesn't work. You must have done something else to it. Why are you so sick?"

"Why do you always blame me?"

And then what happens?

A glass when it is thrown is nearly invisible: it is the merest whirr and becomes real only upon contact. That contact is noise and sharpness and blood.

"You!" she cries. "I'm going to get you!"

But the boy is gone.

"Brat!"

But the boy has disappeared.

Why did I come here? the sister asks herself.

And then: How come even my brother does not love me?

She picks the larger shards of glass from the floor. She will not concern herself with the smaller fragments, the ones that exist only to stick and cut, and, most unseen, enter the bloodstream. Some other time.

She disposes of the glass and, wiping away the tears, she leaves the kitchen. She wants to go to her brother's bedroom.

And then she remembers.

And then what happens?

And what do you think?

A hole is the same as a depression in the sand. When two pirates finish digging a hole and cover it with leaves, they expect that the depression will soon be filled: it will not be a depression anymore.

Any minute now, Drew who has Nightmares tells Andy who has Dreams, he'll be ours forever.

And has stopped saying that he cannot see the magician. He is prepared to wait. He will not test the trap as Drew has done, and he will not venture into the ocean that is cold: he fears becoming cold and sick. He fears becoming lost in this world.

What do other boys do on other beaches? Andy has a vision of sunshine and flying frisbees and pretty-girl laughter. But he has never seen such a beach. For him the beach contains silence and holes. His mother is ill.

How are you doing? his friend wants to know.

Fine, he replies. Absolutely fine.

That's good, Drew pats his back. What did you dream last night?

But Andy cannot tell him.

Can't remember, huh?

Something like that.

They are prepared to wait. Wait and wait and waves move in and waves go away for it is tide time and the waves crawl closer, closer, and then recede, unreachable, black the whole time for the ocean is such melted holes that appear, sometimes, as the holes beneath the sand. And now one boy whistles. There he is, he whispers to the other. I told you.

And, sure enough, a black dot is moving towards them. At first Andy believes that it is the hole that has escaped them somehow and is now seeking its revenge. But this is not the way. As it moves, the black dot turns into a human figure carrying a large case.

Be careful, Drew warns Andy. You never know when they have a gun.

What can one girl find in a drawer when it's her brother's drawer? What does one girl find in the room of her brother when it is his summer room and not a real room at all?

Packs and packs of chewing gum?

Tubes and tubes of lipstick?

No. What she finds is a small notebook, buff-colored and covered with swastikas. The front of it reads:"This is the Journal of Andrew J. Murrary and is not meant for the eyes of anyone particularly my sister the unloved, unwashed and ugly Laurel P. Murray." The sentence ends itself with three swastikas. The sister opens the notebook. What can one little boy, one sick little boy, write? How much pain can paper bring? But her hands are shaking as she reads the first line.

Life, it says, *is going by much too fast.*

Hasn't she heard something like this before? It must be from some movie. She flips through.

Thanksgiving is the dumbest holiday: just a chance for supermarket owners to get rich.

Wasn't I home for Thanksgiving? Laurel asks herself. Of course I was. What did I wrong?

She reads on: *people you think are your friends turn out not to be your friends: they only want you for something.*

Laurel does not keep a journal. One of her roommates, the only one she thinks about, the one she calls "my room-mate" does not keep a journal either but she does like to write. When Laurel is bored at school and Jordy has forgotten to call and Laurel has nothing to do, she reads what's in her room-mate's waste-paper basket.

There are certain people who I don't want to mention but they have it in for you from the start.

The rainiest day of the semester and Laurel is inside. Where is Jordy? Where is her room-mate? She has not seen her room-mate for three days because this roommate has acquired a new boyfriend. Laurel begins to go through her waste-basket.

There are some people you can't even hate.

Laurel is going through her room-mate's wastebasket. There she finds memos and math notes and gum. She is about to give up when she hears the tiny little cry, a a microscopic wail. At the bottom of the basket there is a tiny, little thing. Uggh, Laurel thinks, we have bugs. But it is not a bug at all. It is a living baby fetus.

The worst are the ones that you thought that you loved and it turns out that you hate them the most.

All of the room-mates took part in caring for the fetus. They kept it in a shoebox. Laurel thought of it as hers more than theirs for she had found it. Her roommate could not expain how it had turned up in her waste-basket but she was the one who offered to take care of it over spring vacation. She was the only one staying in the room over break: she and her boyfriend would be there while the other three went home.

These are the people that should go straight to Hell.

She stands there in her brother's room. Her brother's room is white, not unlike her room at school. Most rooms that she can think of have been white. Her typewiter sits in the corner of this room. Usually she leaves her typewriter at school or with her room-mate for the summer. This summer, however, her brother asked her to bring home the typewriter for him to use. So she did.

Once upon a time there was a boy who had a sister who went away to college and, so, she wasn't his sister anymore. This is how one story begins.

They had kept the fetus in a shoebox full of tissue paper and fed it cider and granola. In less than nine months, they told themselves, they would have a baby. Then they all went away.

One story begins with the boy who wants to kill the girl.

Look. There is more to a wet face than meets the eyes. Where is Laurel now? She is in her brother's room, the white one. Where is her brother? Out on the beach where she can get him. How much pain can paper bring? The parents are taking their naps upstairs. It is afternoon.

And then what happens?

The girl is going to get her brother. He is a sick little boy, not to mention a brat and a pain. She was never like this. Jordy was never like this. O no. The girl is going to the beach, is heading towards the door to leave his room, to leave the house, to get her brother from the beach. But then she stops. She turns, returns to the typewriter and puts it into the case. This is where it belongs she thinks. I will bury it in its case. I will give it a decent burial.

Again she heads for the door, this time lugging the typewriter in its big black case. And slowly she moves and how slow she has been for it has taken her this long to see how the typewriter, like everything else, has grown into a dead thing. ●

Collette Creppel

RONDEAU: WHY PHILLIP LASCELLE'S FATHER SET SAIL FOR FRANCE ON AUGUST 24, 1922

Peter Gadol

A swan on the Seine, Cocteau thought
he saw, when in truth he had caught
sight of one Phillip Lascelle,
white-clothed and punting. While
the young American cafe-sat and dreamt

of expatriating into autumn, Cocteau bought
a croissant across the street. Then they met,
(was it at the Folies-Bergeres?), and well,
Cocteau convinced the swan of the Seine

to forget college, the family business. Quite
a time, Lascelle spent...The opium salons taught
him the special diction of the surreal.
But Cocteau grew bored of Phillip Lascelle:
one night, from a third floor window, out
flew Lascelle, a white flutter, a swan on the Seine.

A Conversation with Sam Shepard

Amy Lippman

THE ADVOCATE: As you are writing a play, do you have a certain idea of what the play's ending will be?
SHEPARD: No. I think for me, every play has its own force, its own momentum, its own rhythm and tempo. That's the fascination of it. It's like people who hear music in their heads, or in the air, or wherever. They attract it in a certain way and it begins to speak to them. It has its own peculiar set of rules, and circumstances, and complicated structures that you can't necessarily dictate. I think a play is like that. What you're trying to do, in a way, is have a meeting. You're trying to have a meeting with this thing that's already taking place. So, I can't really say that I have a beginning, middle, and end every time I sit down to write a play. *Every moment* of the play is a beginning, a middle, and an end.

THE ADVOCATE: So, it's a very ephemeral process?
SHEPARD: Yeah, it is. A play's like music. It's ephemeral. It's always elusive. It's appearing and disappearing all the time. You never reach a final point with it.

THE ADVOCATE: Do you see productions of your own work?
SHEPARD: No. For the most part, it doesn't interest me, no. The initial production is very exciting because you're involved, you're engaged in it. After that point, though, I'd just as soon let it go and go on to the next play, because the next one's going to be even that much more exciting than the one before it. It's only that original thing, seeing it come into being. Then, I'm willing to let it go.

THE ADVOCATE: Critics of your plays such as *Curse of the Starving Class*, *Buried Child*, and *True West* have often referred to them as chronicling the break-up of the American family. To what extent is that a legitimate reading of those plays?
SHEPARD: I'm not interested in the American social scene at all. It totally bores me. I'm not interested in the social predicament. It's stupid. And the thing you bring up about the break-up of the family isn't particularly American; it's all over the world. Because I was born in America, it comes out as the American family. But I'm not interested in writing a treatise on the American

family. That's ridiculous. I mean, that's not fair or unfair to read that into my plays. It just seems an incomplete, a partial way of looking at the play. People get off on tripping out on these social implications of the play and how that matches up to contemporary America. And that's okay. But that's not why I'm writing plays.

THE ADVOCATE: So, why are you writing plays?
SHEPARD: I have to. I have a mission (laughs). No, I don't know why I do it. Why not?

THE ADVOCATE: You collaborated on the writing of two of your collected plays, *Tongues* and *Savage/Love*.
SHEPARD: Yeah, the one's with Joe (Joseph Chaikin). Well, that was a very unique circumstance, working with someone that I'd known as a friend for a long time and never really had a chance to work intimately with, one on one. I was hanging around the Open Theatre and I knew Joe. We had a lot of things in common. So we just sat down and collaborated on this thing, just cooked it up. The thing that was unique about them, I think, is that they were designed for one performer, for him in particular. That was the impulse behind the whole thing. It's very different than writing by yourself.

THE ADVOCATE: Do you consider your work to revolve around myths?
SHEPARD: Well, so many people have different ideas of what the word means.
THE ADVOCATE: What does it mean to you?

SHEPARD: It means a lot of things to me. One thing it means is a lie. Another thing it means is an ancient formula that is expressed as a means of handing down a very specific knowledge. That's a true myth—an ancient myth like Osiris, an old Egyptian myth that comes down from antiquity. The thing that's powerful about a myth is that it's the communication of emotions, at the same time ancient and for all time. If, for instance, you look at *Romeo and Juliet* as a myth, the feelings that you are confronted with in a play like that are true for all time. They'll always be true.
THE ADVOCATE: What relationship does that have to your plays?

SHEPARD: Well, hopefully in writing a play, you can snare emotions that aren't just personal emotions, not just catharsis, not just psychological emotions that you're getting off your chest, but emotions and feelings that are connected with everybody. Hopefully. It's not true all the time; sometimes it's nothing but self-indulgence. But if you work hard enough toward being true to what you intuitively feel is going down in the play, you might be able to catch that kind of thing. So that you suddenly hook up with feelings that are on a very broad scale. But you start with something personal and see how it follows out and opens to something that's much bigger. That's what I'm interested in.

THE ADVOCATE: Should one then be able to project his own experience onto what has occurred on stage?

SHEPARD: Yeah, you can do that if you want to. But it doesn't have any real value. The only time it has value is when you hook up with something that you *don't* know. Something that you can't pin down. Something where you say, "I feel something here that's going on that's deeply mysterious. I know that it's true, but I can't put my finger on it." I'm not interested if it reminds you of your mother, or your sister, or your cousin, or anything like that. So what? Everybody has something like that. That's what I mean about this social thing, that similarities between social neuroses in American society really don't mean much in the long run because they're always going to change. But if emotions that come up during a play call up questions, or seem to remind you of something that you can't quite put your finger on, then it starts to get interesting. Then it starts to move in a direction we all know, regardless of where we come from or who we are. It starts to hook up in a certain way. Those, to me, are mythic emotions.

THE ADVOCATE: What ties do you feel to the American West?

SHEPARD: Well, it's all subjective. I just feel like the West is much more ancient than the East. Much more. It is. It was even founded before the East. I don't know if you've travelled out here at all but there are areas like Wyoming, Texas, Montana, and places like that, where you really feel this ancient thing about the land. Ancient. That it's primordial; that it goes way, way back. Of course, you can say that about New England. But it doesn't have the same power to me, because it's this thing about space. No wonder these mysterious cults in Indian religions sprung up, you know? It wasn't as though these people were just...just fell down from the sky. It has to do with the relationship between the land and the people. No wonder there were these religions that were so powerful, so awesome, and

persisted for hundreds and hundreds of years. It's because of the land—the relationship between the human being and the ground. And I think that's typically Western and, I think, much more attractive than this tight, little, forest civilization that happened back East, on the East Coast. It's much more physical and emotional to me. New England and the East Coast have always been an intellectual community. Also, I was raised out here, so I guess it's just an outcome of my background. I just feel like I'll never get over the fact of being from here.

THE ADVOCATE: There's a very disorienting element in some of your plays. In certain places the dialogue is very realistic but the situation seems very surrealistic, and this dichotomy is never resolved.

SHEPARD: I think it's a cheap trick to resolve things. It's totally a complete lie to make resolutions. I've always felt that, particularly in theater when everything's tied up at the end with a neat little ribbon and you're delivered this package. You walk out of the theater feeling that everything's resolved and you know what the play's about. So what? It's almost as though why go through all that if you're just going to tie it all up at the end? It seems like a lie to me—the resolutions, the denouement, and all the rest of it. And it's been handed down as if that is the way to write plays.

THE ADVOCATE: What's the alternative?

SHEPARD: Well, there are many, many alternatives. But I think it's all dependent again on the elements that you start with and what your interest is in those elements. If you're only interested in taking a couple of characters, however many, and having them clash for a while, and then resolve their problems, then why not go to group therapy, or something?

THE ADVOCATE: What do *you* do?

SHEPARD: I think of it more like music. If you play an instrument and you meet somebody else who plays an instrument, and the two of you sit down and start to play music, it's really interesting to see where that music goes between two musicians. It might not go anywhere you thought it would go; it might go in directions that you never even thought of before. You see what I mean? So you take two characters and you set them in motion. It's very interesting to follow this thing that they're on. It's a great adventure—it's like getting on a wild horse.

THE ADVOCATE: But aren't you, the playwright, controlling everything? You're *creating* it, aren't you?

SHEPARD: I'm not creating that.

THE ADVOCATE: It doesn't happen by itself, does it?

SHEPARD: No, but in a way, it's already in the air. I really believe that's true. These things are in the air, all around us. And all I'm trying to do is latch onto them. I don't feel like it's a big creative act, like I'm inventing all of this. I mean, I'm not putting myself in the same category as Mozart at all, don't get me wrong, but the story with him was that he heard this music. It was going on, and he was just open to it somehow, latched onto it, and wrote it down. *True West* is like that. *True West* is following these two guys, blow by blow, just following them, trying to stick with them, and stick with the actual moment by moment thing of it. I mean, I wrote that thing... it took me a long time to write that play.

THE ADVOCATE: Why?

SHEPARD: Because I went down a lot of blind alleys. I tried to make them go in one direction, and they didn't want to go that way.

THE ADVOCATE: How did you know when it was right, then?

SHEPARD: I just *knew*. Just like you know it's right when you're with somebody. When you're with the wrong person, or when you're with the right person. You know it like that. You don't know it through the head—you have a feeling.

THE ADVOCATE: How did you know when to end it?

SHEPARD: Well, I've always had a problem with endings. I never know when to end a play. I'd just as soon not end anything. But you have to stop at some point, just to let people out of the theater. I don't like endings and I have a hard time with them. So *True West* doesn't really have an ending; it has a confrontation. A resolution isn't an ending; it's a strangulation.

THE ADVOCATE: Is the point then to leave the audience hanging?

SHEPARD: No, no. I'm not intentionally trying to leave people up in the air. But I also don't want to give people the impression that it's over (*laughs*).

THE ADVOCATE: Do you write for an audience?

SHEPARD: Well, you know, that's an interesting question because, here again, the question comes up, what is the audience? Who is the audience? In a way, you write for yourself as a certain kind of audience. In the midst of writing, it always feels as though I'm writing for the thing itself. I'm writing to have the thing itself be true. And then I feel like an audience would be able to relate to it. The theater's about a relationship.

THE ADVOCATE: Between the actors and the audience?

SHEPARD: If there's no relationship on stage, there's not going to be any in the theater. But that has to be answered first in the writing. If you and I sit down on stage as two actors, and we don't have a relationship, what's the point? ... A relationship's both invisible and

SHEPARD: Yeah, I think so. And through the actors. The actors have to open to it. The director's responsible for opening the actors to that meeting, and every time they shy away from it, to open them more and more to it, to a point where it's always present. Like in that scene you saw today. You have two characters on the stage that don't want anything to do with each other. Superficially, they hate each other. They turn their backs to each other and there's *still* a relationship in that. They're related by turning away from each other. You see what I mean? So they don't need to be in communion with each other. They don't have to be in sympathy with each other—they're just flat-out related. Like a blind person and his dog, there's a relationship there.

THE ADVOCATE: How are you affected by criticism, both favorable and unfavorable, of your work?

SHEPARD: Well, I'm not immune to it. But you've got to follow this thing that you're on, no matter what. You've got to follow this thing that keeps telling you blow by blow what to do. It's very apparent (to you) what the next thing is. But critics can't tell you that. How could a critic know what your inner condition is as a writer? ... I'm not saying (criticism) doesn't have a pull on me. It has a definite pull on me. But whether you believe it or not is what counts. It's like, I don't know, I've been in a few rodeos, and the first team roping that I won had more of a feeling of accomplishment and pride of achievement than I ever did getting the Pulitzer Prize.... At the same time, I'm not trying to throw anything up in anybody's face. I'm glad that the plays are successful and that they do something to people. But I'm not trying to win another Pulitzer Prize or anything.

THE ADVOCATE: Do you feel as if the media has certain expectations of you?

SHEPARD: Sure. It's hard to know what they're expecting. If they're expecting me to be myself, I can guarantee that will happen all the way down the line. If they're expecting me to be Eugene O'Neill, they may be disappointed. (*laughs*)

THE ADVOCATE: What writers have influenced you? What playwrights?

SHEPARD: I don't know. What's the point?

THE ADVOCATE: Do you go to see plays?

SHEPARD: I don't go to the theater at all. I hate the theater. I really do, I can't stand it. I think it's totally disappointing for the most part. It's just always embarrassing, I find. But every once in a while, something real is taking place.

THE ADVOCATE: So, as for contemporary influences on your work—

SHEPARD: Have you ever been to a rodeo?

THE ADVOCATE: No.

SHEPARD: Well, there's more drama that goes down in a rodeo than one hundred plays you can go to see. It's a real confrontation, a real thing going on. With a real audience, an actively involved audience. You should go to a couple of rodeos after you go to the theater.

THE ADVOCATE: Do you consider your plays "experimental"?

SHEPARD: I guess they are. I mean, it's all experimental. Experiment, by its very nature, has to do with risk. If there's no risk, there's no experiment. And every play's a risk. You take a huge risk with something like that.

THE ADVOCATE: In its appeal? Its success?

SHEPARD: No, a big risk in going into unknown territory. You don't know where you're going.

THE ADVOCATE: Are the risks in creating unusual situations, or a totally new way of presenting something? What risks do you mean?

SHEPARD: Well, I don't know if you feel this or not, but I feel like there are territories within us that are totally unknown. Huge territories. We think we know ourselves, when we really know only this little bitty part. We have this social person that we present to each other. We have all these galaxies inside of us. Huge, unknown territories. And if we don't enter those in art of one kind or another, whether it's playwriting, or painting, or music, or whatever, then I don't understand the point in doing anything. If you don't enter into these areas that are deeply mysterious and dangerous, then you're not doing anything as far as I can tell. You're just trying to make something so that people will like it.

THE ADVOCATE: How does that relate to your own work?

SHEPARD: It's the reason I write. I try to go into parts of myself that are unknown. And I think that those parts are related to everybody. They're not unique to me. They're not my personal domain.

THE ADVOCATE: Is there then something cathartic about the whole process of writing?

SHEPARD: No. Catharsis is getting rid of something. I'm not looking to get rid of it; I'm looking to find it. I'm not doing this in order to vent demons. I want to shake hands with them.

THE ADVOCATE: How long have you been writing plays?

SHEPARD: Seventeen, eighteen years.

THE ADVOCATE: How have your plays changed?

SHEPARD: Well, actually, they're the same. They're just closer to a verification of what these emotions are. In a way, that old cliche about somebody doing the same thing over, and over, and over again their whole lives is true. I feel like that's true. I'm doing the same thing over each time. I'm trying to get closer to the source.

THE ADVOCATE: Are you more adept at doing that now than you were eighteen years ago?

SHEPARD: I'm more . . . not adept, I'm more *determined* to do it. I'm less afraid. Because there's something absolutely terrifying about going into yourself. . . . It's something that I don't understand. If I understood it, I probably wouldn't write. That's why it's very difficult to talk about, and why a lot of this sounds like it's evasive.

THE ADVOCATE: Do you feel that you have discovered certain things, dealt with them in your plays, and then moved onto something else?

SHEPARD: Well, I haven't left anything behind . . . That's not true. I've gotten rid of a lot of useless stuff. A lot of tricks.

THE ADVOCATE: Dramatic tricks?

SHEPARD: Yeah. Like allowing things to unravel in a direction that you know they're not going to go by themselves. Like this play (*Fool for Love*), for instance. I wrote about sixteen versions of it, and every time I came back to the first five pages. I'd write like seventy, eighty pages and then bring it all the way back to the first five pages and start again—throw out sixty, seventy pages. So, I've got literally at least a dozen different versions of the play, but the first five pages are the same in every one.

THE ADVOCATE: Is that because what you felt initially about it was the truest?

SHEPARD: Yes. The very first meeting there was something there. I knew there was something there, and I just had to keep trying. They weren't just drafts. Every time I think *this is the play*. I'm not writing a draft—I wrote twelve *plays*.

THE ADVOCATE: As an actor, how do you approach a role?

SHEPARD: I don't really consider myself an actor. In film you can get away with a whole lot that you can't on stage. I think almost anyone can get away with being in a film.

THE ADVOCATE: Is that just the nature of the medium?

SHEPARD: Yeah. Because if you're in a tight close-up, you don't have to do much. You don't have to do anything; you just say the lines. You don't have to act. So, I mean, with film acting, for me, it's just a matter of corresponding certain parts of myself to the character, finding corresponding parts and just becoming those parts all the time. I'm not a method actor or anything. I don't have any complicated scheme behind it.

THE ADVOCATE: Could you act in your own plays?

SHEPARD: I could, but I don't want to.

THE ADVOCATE: Why?

SHEPARD: Well, because part of the reason for writing them is to see them. You can't see them if you're in them at the same time. I like having that distance.

THE ADVOCATE: Music plays a more significant role in some of your plays than in others.

SHEPARD: I think they're all musical. I like to look at the language and the inner rhythms of the play, and all that to me is related to music directly. In *True West* there are coyote sounds and crickets and things like that. And the dialogue is musical. It's a musical, *True West*. I think it's very related to music, the whole rhythmic structure of it. Rhythm is the delineation of time in space, but it only makes sense with silences on either side of it. You can't have a rhythm that doesn't have silence in it. I studied for a long time with a drummer from Ghana. He was totally amazing. And I found out that, particularly in African music, every rhythm is related. You can play 4/4, 5/8 and 6/8 all together at the same time and there's a convergence. At some point there's a convergence. Even though it sounds like these things are going off in totally crazy directions that are beating up against each other, they'll always come back. That was a big revelation to me, that rhythm on top of rhythm on top of rhythm always has a meaning. So the same is true on the stage. There are many possible rhythmic structures that an actor can hit, but there's only one true one. There's one moment that he has to meet.

THE ADVOCATE: How do you find that moment?

But that little simple scene at the beginning of that act, it's great. It's perfect. I could watch that all day. It's just got a musical thing to it, you know? That kind of thing happened.

SHEPARD: Well, that's very complex. It has to do with an emotional relaxation, where suddenly the tension goes and it's just *there*. I was a drummer for a long time and I realized that a lot of the time you're straining to keep the time. And then there are times when all that drops away and everything just . . . it just all rides together. And those are the times it became simple. Absolutely simple.

THE ADVOCATE: Do you feel closer to certain plays because they contain more of a sense of that?

SHEPARD: Oh, yeah. Some of them have real dumb rhythms. It depends on each piece, though; every piece is different. Like there's only one little part of *Buried Child* that I like, that I could watch over and over and over again. One little tiny section. It's at the beginning of Act Two, I think. Just the little dialogue between the children and the old man on the couch by the television. That's the only part that interests me anymore.

THE ADVOCATE: Why?

SHEPARD: Because the rest of it just seems verbose and overblown. It seems unnecessarily complicated.

THE ADVOCATE: Do you see your work as evolving to a certain point?

SHEPARD: No, I don't see it like that at all. Maybe it's just going in a circle. I don't know; I really can't tell you whether it's evolving or not. I mean, it's definitely different than it was. There's more at stake now; there's a bigger risk. ●

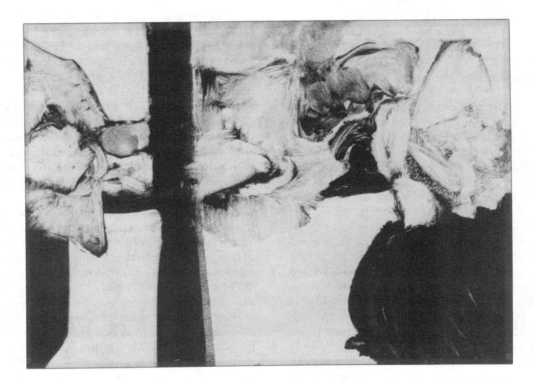

Jennifer Tate

The Shot

Austin Wilkie

Strackler wanted to shoot again and told Hal get off those clothes, that shirt and shoes I mean you can keep your slacks on and into that bed, quick this light's too good. What should I do said Hal, my subtext you know. Doesn't matter said Strackler. He was right then Hal's roommate and they had lived together before. Just under those covers said Strackler, now you're waking up. Now open your eyes. Now blink. Now turn on that lamp, it's middle of the night. Hal heard camera whirring all this time. Yawn said Strackler. Pretend you're on an airplane and there's no gum. We'll do it again.

Maddie came to the door of that room and said I think I'm going to scream. She had on red long underwear and her head wrapped by a blue towel around her hair also red which couldn't be seen just then. What's the matter now said Strackler still with the camera covering up one eye. That jerk said Maddie. I called she's still not home. Maddie leaned on the wall. Strackler said don't worry you can try later on. Hal looking out the window and then at her said can you get me a cigarette Maddie. Good, that'll be very good for the shot said Strackler. Bring me two in.

All Hal knew was this was Strackler's movie where Hal was the star and did what Strackler told him to even if that was not always clear. Let's get back to it said Strackler. What am I supposed to be doing said Hal. It's like this said Strackler. Let me think. He stood there and his hand went to play with his ear and putting his lips together for a moment like he was about to speak said it's as if you were very tired and came home wanting to go to bed, and you did. And you woke up and felt like, not like you had been asleep for long but only for a split second except you weren't tired anymore. D'you see. Maddie gave Strackler and Hal each one lit cigarette. You don't mind if I smoke here in your bed said Hal to Strackler. No no, it's good said Strackler and puffed on his own. Can we try it again Hal with the cigarette too said Strackler.

This time Maddie stayed up leaning by the wall watching Strackler. She was a tall girl who made Hal happy to see her standing and manicuring those nails on one hand with the other. Back behind the camera Strackler pressed its button in front to start it whirring again. Hal's head went down back by the pillow and

opening his eyes he blinked but Strackler stopped him. No said Strackler, wrinkle your nose up first before the eyes. Do I have an itch said Hal. Strackler said if you want it that way that's fine. Good so I know I have an itch said Hal but the phone rang and Strackler said let's take a break.

Thick smoke was in the room from those two cigarettes they were smoking. It's Jane said Maddie, who should talk to her. You said Strackler. I will if you want said Hal. No it's better if she does it said Strackler, besides we should talk about his shot which is an important one. So how does this fit in said Hal, with the rest. The rest said Strackler. The part we shot yesterday said Hal. This is the beginning said Strackler, you're waking up in the middle of the night. What we shot yesterday we won't use if this shot's better. She won't do it said Maddie coming into that room again, she says she's busy. It was worth a try said Strackler, don't worry we'll just try someone else. All this had to do with finding a date for Hal. I'm cold said Hal. Pull those covers up around your neck then said Strackler which Hal did. No I think I've changed my mind said Strackler, it's better for this if you're cold and he opened a window. OK now said Strackler. Do you want me to call again said Maddie. No one said anything then Strackler said let's get this done first.

Now Maddie was crouching down the wall her knees pushing out in front of her. Hold this said Stackler over his shoulder handing another lamp to her. Don't shine it right on his face but that way so there's shadow Strackler said. Now move your nose he said and Hal heard camera whirring. Don't smile Strackler said, why would you smile at night where you wake up from a nightmare. About what said Hal, I'm sorry it makes it easier if I know. OK said Strackler letting the camera down, let me see. How about if you just imagine you killed a child a little child by hitting it on the head with a brick but you can't remember why or where only you know you've done it. What kind of child said Hal. That doesn't matter only you know you've done it and hid its body so no one will ever find out but you're afraid you can't. So every where you go it's on your mind the dead child but you can't tell anyone. That's awful said Maddie and she bounced once on her knees. Is that good said Strackler. I can do that I think said Hal. So let's give it a try said Strackler.

Beautiful baby beautiful said Strackler and he bent down closer the camera close to his eye and pressing its button made it whir. Now yawn said Strackler. The phone rang and Strackler said don't get it Maddie I need you for the light they'll call back whoever it is. Hal did another yawn. OK now think about that child and you've got that brick in your left hand said Strackler. On the sheet next to Hal's shoulder were strands of Maddie's hair which were the same as what he saw now that the blue towel was off her head and on the doorknob. Hal thought about that child it would be a boy. But maybe Strackler meant a girl. He would ask but to Strackler it would not matter which although this did to Hal.

Why have I killed it Hal said. No one knows said Strackler, not even you. It teased you said Maddie. We'll have to do this again said Strackler, the light went bad last time. Get another two cigarettes he said to Maddie who went to get them. Strackler looked at the wall thinking about the shot until Maddie came back to that room with cigarettes and also a lighter. During this time Hal rubbing his toes for them to keep warm watched out the window as it went darker quickly the way it does when the day is almost over. How does it look said Hal, just before it happens. What said Strackler. That child said Hal. Strackler said I don't know it doesn't really matter pretend you've already

hit and hid it and thrown away the brick. Its eyes are frightened said Maddie. Its eyes are frightening and round and its mouth is open a tiny bit but looks very small. Its nose is a button and the cheeks are round but white and its neck is soft. It looks at you and its face is scared and wants to run away but also curious and wants to stay until the last moment when something terrible happens. And you can stand there and look at it with that brick in your hand which it sees and it won't run away from you until you hit it in the face because you see it's frozen there like a bunny.

Hal only looked at her as she said all this and didn't move only listened trying to see it all. Strackler listened and nodded his head yes with his teeth together and a serious look. Maddie finished and leaned back by that wall from where she had bent forward with her hands together almost touching but not. It was darker now. You look hungry said Strackler, maybe you want dinner. Hal said I almost forgot about it. You can get dressed maybe we'll finish all this later said Strackler. All done then said Hal. Nearly said Strackler, at least with this shot but I need to do it again. Hal got up and Strackler smoothed the covers straight on the bed where Hal had been and plumped the pillow. Then all three stood for one moment in that room with its white walls and lamps all on bright and white carpet before Hal turned quickly now to go with Maddie moving behind and after shutting the door where he left. ●

Toshihiko Takemoto·

First I Heard A Low Quiet, Voice

Kate Lewis

At last our pieces rest in place:
the short curtains seem content
to rest in their hasty brackets,

the couch is not as large as first seemed.
Hardly enough to fill a bit of the room
and insufficient in banishing outdoor noise.

From the third floor, above us,
the wife speaks in a low voice;
I hear a sudden crack at their window,

a glass set to rest on the ledge.
His tones are deeper rooted
and comprise most of the argument

which courses down and across the courtyard.
The anger seems anxious to reach us
though they may be no less in love than we.

Moving has harshened my own voice too;
at month's end I'll be a squat grackle
noising away at the day.

The tremors cease upstairs leaving me
midsentence, blustering.
I would have said how dark it looks

how much painting left to do,
but I left those young sounds
perched and raised for later.

Still Life

Rachel Klayman

She is a red dress walking down the street. She is a red dress, red stiletto heels, and a red scarf. Walking quickly, with an air of purpose. Up and down the street.

She imagines that the air stops, shocked, when it reaches an edge of the dress, the hem or the sleeve. People, too, stop, shocked, perhaps out of habit. Red is for stopping, after all, red is for danger, for loose morals; even in black and white on TV's late-night movie, red brings ruin on Jezebel. The roses no lover has ever sent her are a deep, exclamatory red. It is a color that catches the attention.

The dress flutters lightly against her, conspiratorial, sulky, familiar as skin. She bought it only yesterday: on sale, marked down. Finding it was a stroke of luck since she is thin, so thin her wrist and ankle bones poke almost through the skin and skirts slip off her narrow hips or gasp open at the waist. This dress fits her to a tee. *Very snazzy*, the salesgirl said. *Looks like it's made for you honey.* Other salesgirls gathered around, tilting their heads this way and that as though to get a better vantage point. They straightened the elastic, buttoned the cuffs, removed a stray thread so that she could get a final look, weighed the full effect of its brightness against her skin. They were very judicious. *Won't find another one at this price. It's not only her color, it's terribly chic. Looks like her lucky day.* They praised the sheen of the fabric, they spoke of camisoles and ankle bracelets, they milled around her absently. She felt numbed by the flamboyance of the dress.

This is exactly what I want, Gloria said at last, and they looked at each other, startled at the sound of her voice.

Now, walking up and down the street, testing the limits of her invisibility, she is approached by a pale blue jacket wielding an umbrella with a spiked tip. It is an acquaintance. He compliments the dress and jabs the ground with his umbrella in absent-minded emphasis. "Thank you," she says on behalf of it. She feels almost flammable against the clear sky. Three staccato steps and a fourth for the curb, a step over a muddy section of the morning paper. She averts her eyes, afraid to glimpse the day's hazards: dated, paged, disassembled. She knows how news can hurry time and has been ducking the thought.

Better not to think about it, but lately she has even been afraid to go to sleep. It is too disappointing to enter that zone of perfect anonymity only to be reclaimed in the morning. Mornings tremble on the verge of disaster. These past weeks she has been too aware of her body. At night she lies awake (it takes her thirty some minutes to fall asleep on the average, Danner claimed to have kept track) and her eyes look out from behind the sockets. Sometimes, just for a moment, she suspects that the eyes have a life of their own. Furled snails peering out from their shells, for instance, their color wave-washed to the white of an eye. She tries to trick her body into making an admission by turning suddenly on mirrors, but nothing comes of it. It's ridiculous, she knows, Jack even told her so, but her heart seems to follow a rhythm of its own, a waltz step, sometimes the beat of Latin music. Being able to identify the rhythm is no comfort at all.

In a few days maybe she will have it aborted. Nine weeks old, it hardly looks human. Judging from what she has read, it looks more like a fish. Her friend DeDe showed her how to take the core of an avocado and grow a plant over a jar of water, using toothpicks. Somehow, out of the hard brown core of the avocado a slim leafy thing, an ache of green, emerged. The core cracked and the plant grew from within. She couldn't throw the plant out because it fascinated her, but just the same its timid strivings made her sick. Slowly the shoots deepened in color. Slender fronds crept from the husk and pushed blindly toward the striped tattoo of sun on the windowsill. Finally she put the plant on the hall table, where it didn't get any light at all and died of neglect. Since then she has avoided keeping plants and crosses streets to pass up florists' shops. DeDe knows a doctor who will perform the abortion for $285 in cash.

Then again, she could wait just a bit longer, she does not like to tamper with existing conditions. She does not like the plastic gloves that they peel on and off, the white smocks that bell out complacently, the metal stirrups, the instruments that pinch and scrape, stirring delicately like tiny blades of grass. And there is the money. She hasn't saved the money, though Jack has said more than once that he will lend her what she needs as soon as she decides. Sometimes she thinks she can feel it taking shape, silently dividing and massing, its heart ticking drunkenly. *Eavesdropper, interloper,* she whispers when they are alone. *That* is neurotic, she reminds herself, and she buys a very expensive red dress of imitation silk. Also heels and a scarf. The dress wasn't on sale, but she will tell people that it was in order to justify to herself the fact that she spent the money she was saving for the abortion.

Yesterday she went to the bank to withdraw the money to buy the dress. As she was filling out a yellow slip at the counter she noticed that the security guard was staring at her. He was wiry-looking, as lean and honed-down as a sprinter. He was standing in a semblance of ease with his hands joined behind his back. But there could be no mistake, he was eyeing her closely. She became nervous and filled out the slip incorrectly. She took another, looking at the guard out of the corner of her eye. Did she look so bizarre, did she look like someone worth zeroing in on? Perhaps he was trying to signal her that something was wrong, that the heel of her shoe was coming unstuck, or that she had left her purse unattended. She glanced surreptitiously at herself. No crooked seams. The surveillance made her angry. She marched up to the guard, clutching the trigger of her leather purse, and said, *Why may I ask are you staring at me? I think it is a form of harassment.* The guard apologized and she felt vindicated. A clerk even came over and asked her if anything was wrong, and wouldn't she perhaps like to take a seat somewhere and sort things out. She said no thank you. Then she noticed that the guard and the clerk were both staring at her. She would like now to go back and say a few things to their employers about how they invest their efforts. But she cannot

take responsibility for improving everyone she meets.

Now her bank account is almost overdrawn and the truth of it is that the abortion available to her is unusually expensive. Avoiding the area hospital and clinic where Danner is a nurse will cost her. Danner told her in a voice made colorless by the phone, *Stay away, I don't want you taking up room in my life anymore.* That's not what he really meant. She translates, filtering out the anger, for anger is always transient, and it is the skeleton of what he says that interests her: *Go away for a bit, I am depressed and need time to myself.* She has a job translating technical documents from the German, so she is in the habit of recasting phrases. She feels lucky to have this talent. For instance, when he says, *I don't believe in love,* this means, *I am afraid that you will leave me.* Insecure people often pretend to be cold and haughty, she knows that much.

She is sure he will invite her back in a week or two. It has only been thirty-eight days since they separated. She is ready to take things up where they left off. Dessert chilling in the refrigerator, a tulip skirt, the sun a crimson bloom on the sky. She has had the skirt dry-cleaned. It hangs in the closet, tilted slightly to one side with a rakish look. It hangs, sheathed in plastic, protected from dust-motes, ready to be zipped up, danced in, undone. He doesn't know about the pregnancy, though. Danner wouldn't like that. They both hate children.

Danner has sporty glasses and special chemicals to clean the lenses with. He has a way of doing things. It is important not to disrupt this way of doing things. The comb must lie diagonally on the edge of the sink, the flawless white tongues of his hospital shoes must never be tucked under but straight, the toaster must run parallel to the electric can opener. Danner doesn't like plants either. Little crusty brown leaves might litter the floor.

Lately Gloria has felt so much pain that she knows Danner will ask her back. It is a dull thick pain that falls around her like a heavy shawl, a pain of such import it ought to guarantee his return. The sheer force of her grief must eventually, by some law of gravity or the heart, effect some change. Once, a few months back, she told him she didn't like his shoes, they were too much like mice. The noise they made on an uncarpeted floor. He frowned when she said that. *Irrational.* That did not translate to anything but itself. Yesterday, on the off chance that he is harboring a grudge, she sent him a note at the clinic.

I do like the shoes.
love always,
Gloria

* * *

"That you, Gloree?" her brother Jack asks when she comes in the door. That means hello. He is in the bedroom but he already knows it's her because of the hollow tympanic sound her heels make on the wooden floor.

She says hello back in a fierce, happy way. In the red dress, she feels especially friendly. Tonight it doesn't even bother her that the Chinese newspapers which entirely cover three of the living room walls are falling down. She can ignore or accept the yellowing, seedy look it gives the room. She scotch-tapes a section or two back up, squinting at the incomprehensible groupings of lines. Jack knows thousands of characters, he is gifted at languages. As she moves closer, trying to intuit the meaning of some ripply lines within an open square, something crunches underfoot. She has trampled the kite—a Chinese dragon—that has lain all week on the living room floor.

"Wait till you see what I did, Jack," she says, sighing. "Damn. These shoes of mine really did a job on your dragon." She is not used to living with a man who doesn't pick up after himself. The dragon leers up at her. It has sharp painted teeth that curve in a neat arc. She smiles back at it. It is Jack's and she has broken it, so she should admire it at least.

"That's okay," he says, emerging. "It was cheap anyway." It is obvious that he doesn't care. What interests Jack most about China is the philosophy. He wants to be at one with the world. He is perfectly willing to put Gloria up temporarily, until Danner invites her back to his apartment. Gloria has explained to Jack that she is expecting a call from that man Danner any day now. She says it like this: *enn-nee day now*, to emphasize the immediacy of it.

"No sweat off my back," he says. She doesn't have the faintest idea of how to translate that into German.

Having talked as much as she has to, she moves into the kitchen, where she can sit at the table with her legal pad and a sheaf of notes and work phrase by phrase on a German text about auto mechanics. Carburetor, axle, windshield. *Der Vergaser, die Antriebsachse, die Windschutzscheibe.* Connect A to B, dispose of C. *Das Getriebe.* Transmission. Carburetor, heartbeat. Transmission, spinal cord. Only Danner

had the gift of seeing correspondences in everything. The unswerving line of the bedsheet was a horizon and her heartbeat was steady, singular, and correct to the minute as though he wound and set her daily with the clock.

The sense of the passage escapes her like sand between her fingers. She sits quite still. Somewhere inside her the words huddle, scarcely breathing, shy and budded, and it is impossible to write a thing.

* * *

The clock reads ten past ten. Twenty more minutes to wait. She leans against a pillar, watching the folds of her dress fan out against it, the material sparkling here and there. *Cerise*, the tag had said. *Dry clean only.* She has worn it eight days now. She has no intention of having it cleaned or even of washing it herself. Jack doesn't seem to notice or is perhaps too polite to mention it. DeDe and she haven't seen each other all week.

But this morning, a Saturday, DeDe called, 9:00 a.m., her voice ecstatic. "Oh Gloria, it's a gorgeous day!" The words sang through the wires. "Feels like spring beginning. God, I'm glad we've put last month's cold weather behind us." DeDe said she felt an expectation of happiness, a longing for the fabulous which she had to share. So Gloria is waiting in the subway station, is on her way to meet DeDe and go walking.

Should she tell DeDe that lately she feels like Danner? Unless things are done a certain way, exact to each serif of every letter, the day will topple in on her, flimsy with bad luck. If her sash isn't straight, if her egg is overcooked, she may miss the train to work. If the train is late then he doesn't love her, if it's on time she still has a chance. But she is wrong to doubt him. She settles back, letting the cloth slide whispering through her fingers. He is sure to call any day. *I am going to have a baby with a moustache*, she will say. *Just like you.* That will surprise him so much that he will have to talk to her, convince her to get rid of it in a hospital room, amidst a harmony of whites and antiseptic smells.

Ten weeks old, she muses. Still frail and unformed. It is not too late to do something. On her way here she saw a man with wire-rimmed glasses, frames that glinted, thin as violin notes. She always loved the way the rims of Danner's glasses had colors in them, how the plastic caught the light and refracted it.

She looks at the clock, gauging the odds. And she rocks forward, then back, heel to toe, sighing and humming, counting each heartbeat.●

The Dancing Time

Michael Lance Ross

The mongoose sleeps with his red eyes closed
and the whipping tail curled round his head.
His small paws twitch in dark repose
and he is mad in sleep, is desperate
in his long dream's hunt.

He hunts the slow, loose rinkhals curled
in coolness in the black-rock shade.
The snake has eyes that never close
but watch the changes of the ageless veld
as the seasons flow.

The dancing time has come when the grass
is sun-scorched, lying low and brittled black
and crickets scream but dare not move
under the eyes of the desert birds.
Then the old snake stirs

and slides slowly out, uncoiling
fold after dusty fold, his black neck-ring
a string of dark and precious pearls.
The ancient rhythm of the far rain thrums
and the mongoose comes.

On many ribs and silent feet,
the snake and mongoose do their dance;
the rinkhals splendid, smooth and strict,
rising straight as a river plant. The mongoose jerks
and his dream is real.

Now he has mission and machinery;
a jabbing, hungry mammal heart, strange
to any ritual for the rains.
He loves these dying thumps, blood reflecting
to the furious eye.

THE WEST RAIL

DAN VILMURE

The West Rail was an all-night filling station owned by a young guy named Wilson. He always dressed like an ice cream man, in white cotton trousers and a white Oxford shirt, but that's not to say he didn't look good. He was sharp all-around, Wilson was, and folks often wondered what a guy like that was doing working at a dirty old gas station. He had a winning way about him — didn't smoke or cuss but didn't mind folks who did — and whatever time of the day you saw him, whether early in the morning or late at night, he'd be sitting in a lawn chair outside the station office with a book the size of a cinder block sitting in his lap. He was awful smart, and made good conversation, and he kept his blond hair greased and parted down the middle so it fell in two long V-shaped flaps over the sockets of his eyes. His only trouble was he didn't pay enough attention to what was going on around him, and a lot of times when you talked to him you had to repeat yourself till you were blue in the face. But that didn't matter none to me. Even though Wilson was a lot different than other folks, there wasn't nobody I'd rather get bluegilled talking to.

From the corner of the station I could see him sitting in his old familiar spot, dressed in his new shirt and pants in his old familiar fashion. A can of Off sat propped atop a six-pack beside his chair, and I couldn't see the title of the book in his lap, though I squinted. Wilson himself was busy poring through it, his round reading glasses on the crooked tip of his nose, and all around his head moths and nightflies formed a sort of buzzing halo. A gray stream of hosewater ran below Wilson's chair and over Wilson's naked feet, and I could see his tan deckshoes on a nearby vending machine. From somewhere in the background a radio played, and though I noticed Wilson's lips were moving I didn't know if they were moving with what he happened to be reading, or singing along to the radio station. Knowing Wilson it was probably something altogether different. He was the kind of fella who thought better three ways than most did one.

I was tempted to stay and shoot the breeze with him, but I didn't want him to see me looking so punk. He might get worried and try to take me to the hospital or something; he was that type. So I stood behind the edge of the shop and watched him read awhile, waiting for

him to maybe doze off a little, but he didn't show any signs. Now and then he'd rub his eyes slow and hard with his hands all balled up into fists, close his book, and stare off into the distance with a heartbreak look that could drown an orphan in her own tears. I wondered if he was the type of person who didn't need sleep, or maybe the type of person who needed it but couldn't get it.

While I was watching him a woman in a beat up Chevy pulled in and filled up her tank. She walked over to Wilson smiling and wiping her forehead with a handkerchief. Wilson grinned at her and took her money and said wasn't it a hot night for the rain and everything. She said yes sir, it sure was, but didn't he look like he had it beat? She pointed to the six-pack of beer by his side and he laughed and picked one up and handed the sweating bottle to her. She took it and said thank you and now she knew where to come to at three-thirty in the morning when she wanted a cheap tank of gas and a cold bottle of beer. Wilson said maybe the gas wasn't so cheap and the beer not so cold but she could come back any time as far as he was concerned. She blushed a little at that and said thank you and good night, and she drove off in her Chevy that looked like it might not make it around the next street corner. As soon as the lady'd pulled away a trucker in a big diesel came in behind her. He was a big strapping guy with wild red hair and he swung his rig to the side of the pump, put it in park, slammed the cardoor with a bang, and skipped half-walking half-running on over to Wilson. How-do, Wilson told him, and took his credit card. Just sweet, the trucker said, couldn't be better. He was on an eighteen hour run to the capital and back, and if he made it in fifteen, he said, bouncing up and down on his heels like it was cold out, he'd get a two hundred dollar bonus. Wilson said that sounded like a tough run but he wished him all the luck in the world. When he'd finished with the trucker's credit card, Wilson bent over to offer the man a bottle of beer, but the trucker held up his hand. Union rules, he said, then he folded his arms against the side of his head to show Wilson how drinking beer put him to sleep. Wilson laughed and told him alright, alright, he wasn't the type to put a beer between a trucker and two hundred dollars. The trucker smiled, took back his credit card, said thanks for everything, and pumped Wilson's hand like a maniac. Then he half-walked half-ran back to his rig and filled her with gas. I wondered why Wilson hadn't made the trucker pump before he'd paid like he had the lady, but I supposed Wilson was the type to trust everybody for any reason, to let them pump gas and pay for it in whatever order suited them best.

As soon as the trucker had filled his tank and pulled away, Wilson stood and stretched and waved away the bugs and moths around his head and went into his office to turn up the radio. Springsteen was on and I would've turned it up too. While he was in there I proceeded to head off across the station lot as calm as I could so's to keep from attracting Wilson's attention, but it was awfully dark at the West Rail. The big neon WR sign had burnt out about a week ago, and as I walked across the lot my foot tread across the rubber tube that rung the bell that told Wilson he had a customer. Sure enough, he saw me, and when he called out my name, what else could I do?

"Hello you!" Wilson shouted, flailing his arms.

I went over to him.

"Hey there, Wilson. How's it going? Me, I was just out walking around. Fell down and scraped myself up nasty there a while back. What do you think of this rain? Gee, she's funny, ain't she?"

Wilson stood cockeyed, staring at my cuts and bruises.

"You must a fell down pretty good there."

"Oh, I did! Boy, you should've seen me. Fell right down. Was a regular move-on!" He scratched his jaw and ran his fingers around beneath his collar, sizing me up. At last he shook his head and laughed and flopped back down in his lawn chair, satisfied that whatever fist I fell down on or into was my affair and mine alone.

"Yeah, well. Haw haw haw. I've fallen down a few times in my day too. Yes sir!" He bent over and picked up a beer. "You want one of these here — Oh now hold it. I forgot. You're a little too young now, ain't you? Almost did something I shouldn't've," he said. "Haw haw haw!" He put the beer back down with the rest of the six-pack, straightened the book on his lap and cleared his throat. "Oh, this weather shore is something. Can you believe her? I ain't never seen nothing like her. Hey? You know what?"

"What?"

"You're just in time." He stood up and went to his office and came back with two pairs of sunglasses. He gave me one. "Put them on."

"Why?"

"Now now. You just do like I tell you and put them on. There's gonna be an eclipse." He got up again and went around to the side of the building and came back with another lawn chair. "Take a load off," he said. I did.

When I was comfortable he sat down in his chair and put on his shades. "I look like a real dude," he grinned. "Don't I?" I laughed a little and told him he did. He nodded and swallowed and slumped down with his arms stretched out behind him. Half-sitting, half-laying there, he rested in the chair, star-gazing. "I remember my first eclipse," he said. "I was about your age then. Nineteen something or other, it isn't important. The week before it came people couldn't stop talking about it. Total solar eclipse. It was in the papers and on television. Don't look directly at it, folks said. It'll blind you for life. I remember there were barkers on streetcorners selling special solar eclipse sunglasses for ten dollars a shot. Who had that kind of money? Most everybody was asleep when the eclipse came anyway. But my sister and me, I remember, we sat on the roof of our house until four o'clock in the morning, just waiting for the fool thing to show."

I straightened my sunglasses. "Did it?"

Wilson looked at me.

"Did it what?"

I looked at him.

"Did it show?"

"Oh!" Wilson said. He laughed and picked up a bottle of beer. He looked at it for awhile then put it back down. "Yeah, it showed. Sure it did. You can't hide an eclipse."

Wilson was very quiet then. The whole world was.

"Wilson?"

"What's that? What'd you say?"

I sat up in my seat.

"I can't be staying long. What time does the thing show?"

He stared at me, confused. He took off his sunglasses and fiddled with the pagemarker in his book.

"What thing? What do you mean, thing?"

I shook my head.

"Your eclipse."

"Oh!" Wilson said, chuckling. "That's right. Er, well—" He cleared his throat and counted on his fingers. "I'd say, about, uh, two hours and a half. That ain't long, but of course if you've got to go." He bent over to pick up a bottle of beer, then stared at his hand and laughed. "There I go again! Haw haw haw!" He put the beer back down and cleared his throat. "You're in for a real treat, you are. It's not every day that you get to see a meteor shower."

I stared at him.

"Meteor shower?"

"How's that?"

"You just said meteor shower. I thought there was going to be an eclipse?"

"What's that, meteor shower? Who said that? I didn't say anything about no eclipse. Hey! — What happened to your face there, buddy? You're all beat up."

Wilson sweated heavily through his clothes, and his

Kenton Jakub

eyes were ticking nervously. I wanted to tell him that I'd fallen down, but I remembered how I'd told him that already. It wasn't important, I supposed. Wilson was Wilson. You could take him or leave him. When a man in a station wagon pulled up at the full-service island Wilson told me to help myself to whatever beer I wanted and he hurried off to help the customer. The customer looked Wilson up and down when he arrived to pump gas, and you could tell Wilson had made some kind of an impression. He sure was respectable looking in his white ice cream suit. The customer didn't even notice his bare feet and wriggling toes. He just stood there looking him over and grinning from ear to ear. It's not every day that a sharp guy like Wilson pumps your gas.

The customer paid and left and Wilson came back over and sat down. I got up.

"What's this? Are you leaving? Hey now — You just got here."

"I know," I told him. "But I've got to go."

He ran his fingers back under his collar, looking me over with that helpless way of his. "You don't have to go. Or do you? Well, well, well. Want a beer?"

He picked one up and held it out to me. I took it and said goodbye. As I was walking away he called out to me.

"Hey! Ain't you gonna wait and see the comet?"

I told him no, I was gonna go home and sit on my roof and watch it. And sure enough, when I got home, who did I see sitting there on my roof but my brother. I climbed up and said hello.

"Quiet," he told me. "Comet's coming."●

the quiet man

Emily Greenley

he admires in a painting negative
space, in a song the "particular

blue lines"   . silence
he holds like several white eggs (in the attitude

of a loss).   of form and flesh
he is not insensible; his hand rounded

still with the presumed egg: stirrings
of denial— much like those, I imagine, of

⟨entire hollows of time⟩a life suspended.

WHEN *THE ADVOCATE* WAS BANNED

JAMES LAUGHLIN

In 1986, *The Harvard Advocate* celebrates its 120th anniversary. This year also marks the fiftieth anniversary of New Directions publishing house, founded in 1936 during the Depression by Harvard undergraduate and *Advocate* member, James Laughlin. Laughlin spent his sophomore year in Europe, meeting and working with many of the writers he would later publish, including Dylan Thomas, Rainer Maria Rilke, and Ezra Pound. It was Pound that introduced him to the work of Henry Miller by giving him a copy of *Tropic of Cancer.*

Eventually Laughlin's New Directions would publish twenty of Henry Miller's books, but Laughlin first secured a Henry Miller story for *The Harvard Advocate.* When "Glittering Pie" appeared in the September, 1935 *Advocate* the issue was confiscated. The following speech given at a 1984 Signet dinner in honor of Laughlin describes the incident. We are pleased to print it as the first in our series of anniversary reminiscences.

As we get on in years, and especially when we return to Harvard on an occasion such as this, it's only natural to want to recapture the past. *Recherchez le temps perdu*, as Proust put it. But even in these surroundings, where there are so many memories, the recapture isn't too easy for me, because my earliest memory of the Signet, which goes back to the night of my initiation, is of a quite remarkable scandal and disaster. It was a traumatic event which has never left my consciousness and which I still recall with horror. But I must obliterate it, and that, I think, I can only do by a process of cauterization, by creating, if you will indulge me, an even more flagrant scandal.

This renouvellement requires a text, and since it is obviously a psychological process, I shall take it from Freud, the wise magician of our century. Let me recall to you Freud's essay, *Die Enhauptung der Doppelgaenger* that is, *The Decapitation of the Other Self.* Now some of you may have skipped this extraordinary work because of the challenges to its authenticity. Ernest Jones, Freud's biographer, has told us that the *Enhauptung* is a forgery. Jones believes that it was forged, in a good copy of Freud's hand, by a Viennese bookseller named Goldwasser who sold it for a very large sum to Princess Marie Bonaparte. But I prefer the testimony of Freud's old friend, Wilhelm Fliess, the surgeon who did intricate operations on people's noses to cure them of sexual hysteria. In a letter to Dr. Hans Sachs, which appears to be authentic, Fliess wrote that Freud had shown him the *Enhauptung* and that they had discussed it. Freud told him, Fliess declares, that the *Decapitation*

referred to Freud's rejection of the Seduction Theory, and that in abandoning the Seduction Theory Freud felt that he was cutting off his own head, or should we more symbolically say, a very important member.

Whatever the facts, or the interpretation, the concept is valuable to me because tonight I must exorcize my *doppelgaenger*, I must lay my "other self" to rest. Now who is my *doppelgaenger*? Who is the figure who has followed me, has shadowed me, who has inspired my emulation and my jealousy for so many years? I can now reveal that it is none other than my oldest friend, our fellow Signetarian, John Slocum.

Slocum and I first met when we were 10-year-olds at Adirondack Camp. I shall pass over certain incidents of that camp summer which are not, perhaps, greatly to the credit of either of us. We did not meet again for many years, but what was my delight, on taking my first meal at the Harvard Union, to discover Slocum, a manly chap, whose disposition had greatly improved. But I let myself be taken in by his winning smile and only now understand that he was intending my ruin. We both joined the *Advocate*, and, thanks to our native literary talents, rose rapidly in the hierarchy of that maternal institution. I shall pass over the affair of the *Advocate's* new roof, and of the evening when my punch was spiked and, in a poetic frenzy, I hurled a dozen ink bottles at Professor Cross, causing great disfigurement to the walls, which I had to pay to have repainted.

The first really sinister intrigue of my *doppelgaenger* was when he persuaded me to obtain for the pages of the *Advocate* a story from my friend Henry Miller. This was a charming piece called *Glittering Pie*, which was full of high spirits and good humor, a characteristic Miller effusion. It is in the form of a letter from Henry to his friend Alfie Perles in Paris, in which Henry satirizes the culture of California, where he was then living. Permit me to read you a paragraph from Miller's *Glittering Pie* so that you will get the sense of it and understand what follows.

At the burlesk Sunday afternoon I heard Gypsy Rose Lee sing "Give Me a Lei!" She had a Hawaiian lei in her hand and she was telling how it felt to get a good lei, how even her mother would be grateful for a lei once in a while. She said she'd take a lei on the piano, or on the floor. An old-fashioned lei, too, if needs be. The funny part of it is the house was almost empty. After the first half-hour every one gets up

Gordon Green

nonchalantly and moves down front to the good seats. The strippers talk to their customers as they do their stunt. The *coup de grace* comes when, after having divested themselves of every stitch of clothing, there is left only a spangled girdle with a fig leaf dangling in front—sometimes a little monkey beard which is quite ravishing. As they draw towards the wings they stick their bottoms out and slip the girdle off. Sometimes they darken the stage and give a belly dance in radium paint. It's good to see the belly button glowing like a glow worm, or like a bright half-dollar. It's better still to see them — —, — — — — — — — —. Then there is the loud speaker through which some idiotic jake roars: "Give the little ladies a hand please!" Or else—"Now ladies and gentleman, we are going to present you that most charming personality fresh from Hollywood—Miss Chlorine Duval of the Casino de Paris." Said Chlorine Duval is generally streamlined, with the face of an angel and a thin squeaky voice that barely carries across the footlights. When she opens her trap you see that she is a half-wit; when she dances you see that she is a nymphomaniac; when you go to bed with her you see that she is syphilitic.

Henry's little masterpiece was immediately popular with the undergraduate body and the *Advocate* was selling as it never had sold before because of it. Then, to our chagrin, the Advocate House was raided by the Cambridge constabulary, who cared off all unsold copies. Next day a young district attorney, who was running for re-election, went on the air to denounce sex and sin at Harvard. And the next day there were such headlines in the Boston papers as DECADENCE AT HARVARD and SEX IN MT. AUBURN STREET. The University Hall was blessedly tranquil, but we were besieged with visitors from Scollay Square who wanted to buy copies—and we had none to sell. In the end, the District Attorney was pacified with two tickets on the 50-yard line for the Yale Game, and the matter was dropped. Only much later did I ask myself: how did the Keystone Cops find out about *Glittering Pie*? They certainly were not regular readers of the magazine. But now I know. My *doppelgaenger* tipped them off. He was plotting my disgrace. He reasoned that after such publicity I would be invited to no more debutante parties at the Somerset Club, and that all of the little lovelies would be his. How wrong he was. I became more popular than ever.

My *doppelgaenger* was not so easily daunted. His next move was extremely subtle. He played on my vanity and social ambition in a way I could not suspect. He lobbied for my election to the Signet, and when that happened he coached me for my initiation "part." He told me that the Signetarians were a raucous and randy bunch, and that I could win their instant approval by preparing a paper as much in the tone of Miller's *Glittering Pie* as possible. I put my pornographic gifts to the test and produced a little story called *A Natural History*, which recounted events of a moonlight evening on a Florida beach when the giant sea turtles were coming up onto the beach to lay their eggs in holes in the sand. The heroine of this tale was the ornament of the local police department, an extremely well-put-together female motorcycle cop aged 18 who was a veritable firecracker. I will not sully your chaste ears with a quotation, but can say that never were turtle eggs put to more bizarre purpose.

I was hardly five minutes into my narration when I realized that I had been misinformed about the Signetarians. After a couple of titters, a deadly and prolonged hush fell over the room. As the tale became more perfervid, members began to arise from their seats and leave the room. When Professor Ballantyne of the Music Department left, he paused to ask me: "Is that the way they talk in the better homes of Pittsburgh?" It was a traumatic experience. I trembled in shame and broke out in perspiration. And there, somewhere in the dark in the back of the room, my *Doppelgaenger*, was smiling and licking his lips.

Well, I have made my horrid confession. I have recaptured the past. I have performed the rites of exorcism prescribed in *Die Enhauptung der Doppelgaenger*. I feel better already. *Una vita nuova.*

And I hope that I have learned my lesson. To prove that my evil mind is purged, and that I have finally set my feet on the *bon chemin*, may I conclude with two recent compositions? ●